SURVEY
OF
SOCIAL
SCIENCE

SURVEY
OF
SOCIAL
SCIENCE

GOVERNMENT AND POLITICS
SERIES

Volume 1
1-444

A—Constitutional Law in the United States

Edited by
FRANK N. MAGILL

Consulting Editor
JOSEPH M. BESSETTE
CLAREMONT MCKENNA COLLEGE

SALEM PRESS

Pasadena, California   Englewood Cliffs, New Jersey

Library of Congress Cataloging-in-Publication Data
Survey of social science: government and politics series /
edited by Frank N. Magill; consulting editor Joseph M.
Bessette.
     p.   cm.
Includes bibliographical references and index.
     1. Political science—Encyclopedias. 2. United States—
Politics and government—Encyclopedias. I. Magill,
Frank Northen, 1907-   . II. Bessette, Joseph M.
JA61.S88   1995
320'.03—dc20
ISBN 0-89356-745-0 (set)   95-30408
ISBN 0-89356-746-9 (volume 1)   CIP

PRINTED IN THE UNITED STATES OF AMERICA

PUBLISHER'S NOTE

The *Government and Politics Series* is the fourth in the *Survey of Social Science*. Its five volumes follow sets on *Economics* (1991, five volumes), *Psychology* (1993, six volumes), and *Sociology* (1994, five volumes). Each set is designed to provide general readers with insights into a major field of the social sciences whose topics are typically accessible only to academicians and experts in the field. By presenting clearly and simply written information in a quickly retrievable format, *Survey of Social Science* volumes provide nonspecialists with views of essential areas that are increasingly important to laypersons, as well as specialists. While the scope of the *Government and Politics Series* has no geographical or chronological boundaries, the bulk of its articles naturally emphasize North American institutions, politics, and governments, with particular attention to the United States.

Averaging six pages in length, the set's 342 articles follow a familiar Magill ready-reference format. Beginning with a straightforward topical title, each article immediately identifies its "field of study," briefly explains the topic's meaning and significance, and defines the "principal terms" that it uses. Its main text is then divided into three sections: "Overview" introduces and explains the topic. "Applications" discusses case studies that demonstrate how the topic works in actual practice, how it has been explored in scholarly studies, or how its principles apply to everyday politics. "Context" places the subject within its broadest historical, geographical, and philosophical framework, noting its significance in the modern world.

The annotated "bibliography" that follows directs readers to other published sources, which are chosen both for their relevance and for their accessibility to nonspecialists. Finally, a list of "cross-references" identifies other articles in the set that are most closely related to its own subject.

Several other tools are also provided to help readers find information in the set as a whole—which is arranged alphabetically by article titles. Readers looking for information on political parties, for example, will find an article titled "Political Parties" in its expected alphabetical position. Cross-references at the end of that article direct readers to such related articles as "The Democratic Party," "Multiparty Systems," "One-Party Systems," "Political Party Conventions," "Political Party Roles," "The Republican Party," "Two-Party Systems," and other topics.

Each of the five volumes in the set opens with a table of its contents and ends with an alphabetical list of the articles contained in the entire set, as well as a list of the entire contents grouped by categories. In addition, volume 5 contains a glossary that defines important terms, and a comprehensive, cross-referenced index that directs readers to specific events, government institutions, laws, places, personages, and political concepts.

The *Government and Politics Series* is as broad in scope as the vast discipline of government and politics itself is. While recognizing that the subject matter of this complex discipline overlaps considerably, the set divides its articles into thirteen fields of study: civil rights and liberties; comparative government; economic issues; functions of government; history of government and politics; international government and politics; law and jurisprudence; local and regional government; military; political philosophy; politics (general); religion and government; and types of government.

Government and politics may well be the oldest social science. Its study goes back at least as far as the ancient Greek philosophers such as Aristotle and Plato—whose writings remain central in modern studies of political philosophy. The *Government and Politics Series* examines the philosophical bases of government and politics in more than eighty-five articles. These include examinations of the ideas of more than twenty seminal figures—including Aristotle, Plato, Thomas Burke, Immanuel Kant, John Locke, John Stuart Mill, Jean-Jacques Rousseau, and others. The set also contains articles discussing such broad currents of political thought as anarchism, conservatism, liberalism, Marxism-Leninism, postmodernism, and utilitarianism. Other articles consider the philosophical bases beneath such concepts as citizenship, equality and egalitarianism, federalism, political ethics, political party roles, self-determination, succession, and others.

Closely related to the field of political philosophy is the civil rights and liberties field. This field's articles examine the most basic issues of civil rights and liberties. More narrowly focused articles include discussions of such subjects as feminist politics, gay and lesbian politics, and the right to bear arms.

The full richness of modern politics throughout the world is explained in more than sixty articles on aspects of "politics" itself. These include discussions of activism and protest movements; political campaigning and election processes; various dimensions of party politics and organization; the media; and political leadership. This category also includes essays examining such specific topics as filibustering, lobbying, and term limits, as well as broad discussions of political issues relating to African Americans, American Indians, Asian Americans, Latinos, and women.

The subject of international government and politics itself is treated in thirty-four articles. Given the complex dynamics of international relations, it is entirely appropriate that the *Government and Politics Series* approaches this subject from a variety of perspectives. Hence, readers will find articles presenting discussions of such broad subjects as international relations, international law, foreign policy, treaties, and world political organization, as well as narrower topics, such as the North Atlantic Treaty Organization, the United Nations, and the World Bank.

Forty-five articles explore the specialized functions of government. These articles range from examinations of such broad topics as legislative and executive functions to narrower discussions of commerce regulation; disaster relief; postal service; and management of agriculture, education, energy, health care, land, resources, and transportation. This field also encompasses articles on the arts, entitlements, public utilities, public works, the Social Security system, and much more.

The full breadth of the series most clearly emerges in the dozens of articles falling under the headings of comparative government, history, religion, and types of government. Under the comparative government heading, for example, readers will find articles on Great Britain, Canada, China, Mexico, and Russia, as well as surveys of

Africa, Asia, and the Pacific Islands. Readers will also find governments from all parts of the world and all epochs discussed in more than twenty-five articles on types of government. These cover such topics as democracies and social democracies; colonial governments and empires; commonwealths, confederations, federations, and leagues; dictatorships, police states, and totalitarian governments; and feudalism, monarchies, and oligarchies. The international scope of the series also emerges in the religion category, which includes articles on Buddhism, Confucianism, Hinduism, Islam, the Vatican, and Zionism.

Additional issues in comparative studies are discussed under the headings of economic issues, local and regional government, and law and jurisprudence. The ten articles in the economics field range from a broad discussion of business and national economies to examinations of government funding, taxation, and budgets, as well as considerations of the economic and political impact of industrialization and urbanization. Many readers will find the eleven articles on local and regional government to be of special interest because they address the political issues closest to average citizens. Likewise, the ten articles under the law and jurisprudence heading touch on many issues that directly affect citizens, such as the day-to-day operation of local court systems. These articles also include discussions of the U.S. Constitution and the Supreme Court, as well as constitutionalism and legal systems generally.

Finally, there are eight articles dealing with military topics. These include discussions of military organization, military and revolutionary governments, and war.

Salem Press gratefully acknowledges the many academicians and professionals who contributed their time, talents, and expertise to *Survey of Social Science: Government and Politics Series*. A full list of these individuals and their affiliations appears on the following pages. We extend our special thanks to Consulting Editor Joseph M. Bessette of California's Claremont McKenna College for his valuable contributions.

CONTRIBUTORS

Steven C. Abell
University of Detroit Mercy

Joseph K. Adjaye
University of Pittsburgh

Richard Adler
University of Michigan, Dearborn

Olusoji A. Akomolafe
Le Moyne-Owen College

Stanley Archer
Texas A&M University

James A. Baer
Northern Virginia Community College

Charles F. Bahmueller
Center for Civic Education

Timothy Bakken
Trenton State College

Danny L. Balfour
University of Akron

Jonathan J. Bean
Ohio State University

Patricia A. Behlar
Pittsburgh State University

Richard P. Benton
Trinity College, Hartford

Charles Merrell Berg
University of Kansas

Joseph M. Bessette
Claremont McKenna College

George P. Blum
University of the Pacific

Warren J. Blumenfeld
Northhampton, Massachusetts

Steve D. Boilard
Western Kentucky University

John A. Britton
Francis Marion University

Anthony R. Brunello
Eckerd College

Robert D. Bryant
Georgetown College

Harry Caltagirone
Liberty University

David E. Camacho
Northern Arizona University

Edmund J. Campion
University of Tennessee

Michael R. Candelaria
St. John's College

Byron D. Cannon
University of Utah

Richard K. Caputo
Barry University

David Carleton
Middle Tennessee State University

Brenda Carlyle
St. Mary-of-the-Woods College

Brian J. Carroll
California Baptist College

Thomas W. Casstevens
Oakland University

John W. Cavanaugh
University of South Carolina

James B. Christoph
Indiana University

Lawrence J. Connin
Pennsylvania State University

Michael Kurt Corbello
Southeastern Louisiana University

Frank L. Davis
Lehigh University

Richard Davis
Brigham Young University

Loring D. Emery
Hamburg, Pennsylvania

Santa Falcone
University of New Mexico

John L. Farbo
University of Idaho

David John Farmer
Virginia Commonwealth University

GOVERNMENT AND POLITICS

James Feast
Baruch College of the City University
of New York

Alan M. Fisher
California State University,
Dominguez Hills

John C. Foltz
University of Idaho

Michael J. Fontenot
Southern University at Baton Rouge

C. George Fry
Lutheran College of Health Professions

Roger G. Gaddis
Gardner-Webb University

Michael J. Garcia
Metropolitan State College of Denver

Karen Garner
University of Texas at Austin

Nancy M. Gordon
Amherst, Massachusetts

Robert F. Gorman
Southwest Texas State University

Robert Charles Graham
Hanover College

Johnpeter Horst Grill
Mississippi State University

Nancy N. Haanstad
Weber State University

Michael Haas
University of Hawaii, Manoa

Deborah Moore Haddad
Ohio State University

Frank E. Hagan
Mercyhurst College

Mark David Hall
East Central University

Michael S. Hamilton
University of Southern Maine

Roger D. Haney
Murray State University

Mary T. Hanna
Whitman College

Jan Carol Hardt
Gettysburg College

Kevin R. Hardwick
Canisius College

F. Frederick Hawley
Western Carolina University

Allison L. Hayes
Western Carolina University

Peter B. Heller
Manhattan College

Arthur W. Helweg
Western Michigan University

Carl W. Hoagstrom
Ohio Northern University

Charles C. Jackson
Northern Kentucky University

Jeffery L. Jackson
State University of New York at Buffalo

Robert Jacobs
Central Washington University

Robert L. Jenkins
Mississippi State University

Ronald C. Kahn
Oberlin College

Charles Louis Kammer III
The College of Wooster

Carolyn Ann Kawecki
Hood College

W. D. Kay
Northeastern University

Gregory C. Kozlowski
DePaul University

Judy Bell Krutky
Baldwin-Wallace College

Melvin A. Kulbicki
York College

John C. Kuzenski
Vanderbilt University

Josephine M. LaPlante
University of Southern Maine

Eugene Larson
Los Angeles Pierce College

CONTRIBUTORS

Thomas A. Lewis
Mount Senario College

Jiu-Hwa Lo Upshur
Eastern Michigan University

Ronald W. Long
West Virginia Institute of Technology

R. M. Longyear
University of Kentucky

David C. Lukowitz
Hamline University

Erin McKenna
Pacific Lutheran University

Paul Madden
Hardin Simmons University

Eduardo Magalhães III
Simpson College

Philip Magnier
Fairfield, Iowa

Yale R. Magrass
University of Massachusetts, Dartmouth

Edward S. Malecki
California State University, Los Angeles

Cecilia G. Manrique
University of Wisconsin—La Crosse

Richard W. Mansbach
Iowa State University

Robert Maranto
Lafayette College

Joseph R. Marbach
Seton Hall University

Michael Margolis
University of Cincinatti

William J. Mark
Lassen College

Thomas D. Matijasic
Prestonsburg Community College

Steve J. Mazurana
University of Northern Colorado

Jonathan Mendilow
Rider University

Michael W. Messmer
Virginia Commonwealth University

Joan E. Meznar
University of South Carolina

Laurence Miller
Western Washington University

William V. Moore
College of Charleston

Thomas J. Mortillaro
Nicholls State University

Turhon A. Murad
California State University, Chico

Paul T. Neal
Temple University

Joseph L. Nogee
University of Houston

James H. Nolt
Vanderbilt University

Norma Corigliano Noonan
Augsburg College

John F. O'Connell
College of the Holy Cross

Patrick M. O'Neil
Broome Community College

David L. Paletz
Duke University

Keeok Park
University of Virginia

W. David Patterson
Southern Methodist University

W. David Patton
Boise State University

Darryl Paulson
University of South Florida

Leslie Pendleton
Austin, Texas

Nis Petersen
Jersey City State College

Steven L. Piott
Clarion University

John Patrick Piskulich
Oakland University

Elizabeth Rholetter Purdy
University of South Carolina, Aiken

Gregory P. Rabb
Jamestown Community College

John F. Racine
University of Hawaii, West Oahu

Andrew Raposa
Westfield State College

Samory Rashid
Indiana State University

Sudha Ratan
Georgia Southern University

Margaret A. Ray
Mary Washington College

Paul Bradford Raymond
University of Southern Indiana

Paul L. Redditt
Georgetown College

Gregory P. Rich
Fayetteville State University

James W. Riddlesperger, Jr.
Texas Christian University

Carl Rollyson
*Baruch College of the City University
of New York*

Joseph R. Rudolph, Jr.
Towson State University

Jack M. Ruhl
Western Michigan University

Sunil K. Sahu
DePauw University

Jerry Purvis Sanson
Louisiana State University, Alexandria

John E. Santosuosso
Florida Southern College

Sean J. Savage
St. Mary's College, Notre Dame

Debbie Schiedel
Portland, Oregon

John H. Serembus
Widener University

Daniel M. Shea
University of Akron

R. Baird Shuman
University of Illinois at Urbana-Champaign

Michael J. Siler
California State University, Los Angeles

Donald C. Simmons, Jr.
Troy State University

Sanford S. Singer
University of Dayton

Christopher E. Smith
Michigan State University

Matthew Westcott Smith
State University of New York at Buffalo

William L. Smith
Georgia Southern University

Ira Smolensky
Monmouth College, Illinois

John A. Sondey
South Dakota State University

J. Christopher Soper
Pepperdine University

Vincent James Strickler
Brigham Young University

Irene Struthers
Morro Bay, California

Timothy E. Sullivan
Towson State University

William A. Taggart
New Mexico State University

Robert D. Talbott
University of Northern Iowa

Harold D. Tallant
Georgetown College

Donald G. Tannenbaum
Gettysburg College

Andrew J. Taylor
University of Connecticut

G. Thomas Taylor
University of Maine

Stephen C. Taylor
Delaware State University

Susan M. Taylor
Indiana University, South Bend

Carl A. Thames
Columbia, Missouri

CONTRIBUTORS

Jack Ray Thomas
Bowling Green State University

Leslie V. Tischauser
Prairie State College

Paul B. Trescott
Southern Illinois University

Robert D. Ubriaco, Jr.
Webster University

Stephen D. Van Beek
San Jose State University

Fred R. van Hartesveldt
Fort Valley State College

C. Danielle Vinson
Duke University

Harvey Wallace
California State University, Fresno

Enbao Wang
Lewis-Clark State College

Dana Ward
Pitzer College

Christopher L. Warren
Florida International University

A. J. L. Waskey, Jr.
Dalton College

Robert P. Watson
Northern Arizona University

Samuel E. Watson III
Midwestern State University

Donald A. Watt
Southern Arkansas University

Priscilla A. Watt
Magnolia, Arkansas

William L. Waugh, Jr.
Georgia State University

Donald V. Weatherman
Lyon College

Shanda D. Wedlock
Fresno, California

Marcia J. Weiss
Point Park College

Donald M. Whaley
Salisbury State University

Richard Whitworth
Ball State University

Miles W. Williams
Central Missouri State University

John F. Wilson
University of Hawaii, Manoa

Richard L. Wilson
University of Tennessee, Chattanooga

Michael Witkoski
Columbia, South Carolina

Richard A. Yanikoski
DePaul University

Clifton K. Yearley
State University of New York at Buffalo

Philip R. Zampini
Westfield State College

CONTENTS

GOVERNMENT AND POLITICS

SURVEY
OF
SOCIAL
SCIENCE

ACCOUNTABILITY IN U.S. GOVERNMENT

Field of study: Functions of government

Accountability in government means holding public officials and agencies responsible for their actions.

Principal terms
> FREEDOM OF INFORMATION ACT (1966): U.S. federal law granting
> public access to most government information
> LEGISLATIVE OVERSIGHT: monitoring by legislative bodies of the rules
> and regulations formulated by administrative agencies
> NATIONAL PERFORMANCE REVIEW: U.S. federal government
> commission established to examine the operations of federal
> agencies and make recommendations on how to improve them
> PERFORMANCE APPRAISAL: system of assessing and providing
> accountability for individual job performance
> PRIVACY ACT OF 1974: U.S. federal law limiting the kinds of
> information on individuals and groups that government agencies
> may collect and disseminate
> PROGRAM EVALUATION: process of measuring the efficiency and
> effectiveness of government programs against available resources
> and performance goals
> SUNSET LAW: requirement that a specified government program
> periodically demonstrate its effectiveness or be dissolved
> SUNSHINE LAW: requirement that elected officials engaged in official
> government business do so in public meetings to facilitate public and
> media oversight
> WHISTLE-BLOWER: person who brings public attention to instances of
> corruption and maladministration in government

Overview
Unless people are held accountable for their actions, it is widely believed, they may possibly lie, cheat, steal, loaf, or abuse their power. It is further believed that those in government are no different, and that their actions need to be examined publicly. The principal means of assuring accountability in government at the policy-making level is through the election of government officials. In theory, officials responsive to constituent needs will be reelected, and those who are not responsive will be forced out of office. For politically appointed officials, direct accountability is to the elected officials who appoint them, as well as to the public they serve. In practice, it is uncertain that the public in fact holds elected officials accountable for their actions or the actions of their appointees. In some cases, it is difficult to determine responsibility for the actions of elected officials, and, in other cases, individual responsibility is unclear because of the number of actors in the political process. Nevertheless, there

are clear mechanisms for holding elected officials accountable.

Holding nonelected public employees accountable for their actions is more difficult. Career public employees are generally protected by civil service laws from politically motivated interference. However, they are accountable to senior officials for their job performance. Performance appraisals provide mechanisms for measuring job performance, merit-pay systems provide rewards for good performance, and disciplinary systems provide punishments for poor performance. In short, there are mechanisms of accountability for personal job performance, although research suggests that merit pay has little effect on productivity among public or private sector employees.

Public employees are also held accountable, to some extent, for the performance of their agencies. In the 1960's, people examining the federal budget began to focus on the relationships between the resources allocated to programs and the goods produced or services delivered. By the 1970's, they began to examine service levels more closely, and concerns about agency and program effectiveness and efficiency were often addressed through mandatory program evaluations. The performances of agencies were measured in terms of program goals and objectives; however, it is easier to measure economic performance or cost efficiency than it is to measure abstract program effectiveness. As a consequence, public agencies have increasingly been held accountable for their efficiency, rather than for their effectiveness in meeting program goals. Increasingly, legislation creating programs includes "sunset laws" that require the responsible agencies periodically to demonstrate the effectiveness of their programs or have their programs eliminated.

As programs have expanded, concerns have also increased about the amount of power exercised by career public employees and the responsiveness of those employees to elected public officials and to the public at large. Public employees exercise professional discretion in the application of laws and regulations, make decisions about who will receive goods and services, translate general legislation into specific programs, make administrative rules and regulations, and recommend new laws. Although there is a popular perception that elected officials make laws and bureaucrats simply implement them, bureaucratic discretion is an unavoidable and necessary part of the political process.

From the public's perspective, the issue is how to hold public employees accountable for their decisions and actions. Since the 1960's, public oversight of government operations has been enhanced through requirements for direct public participation in decision making. Citizens are involved through participation in public hearings, advisory committees, interest groups, and other means. Requirements for "maximum feasible participation" of the public in program decision making has reinforced the principle that public administration should be open to public scrutiny. Similarly, "sunshine laws" in many states require public officials to hold meetings in which policy is made in public so that media representatives, as well as other citizens, can attend and participate. Only meetings that deal with very sensitive issues, such as law enforcement and personnel actions, are closed to the public, and then only when public safety or individual rights would be jeopardized if made public.

At the federal level, the 1966 Freedom of Information Act allows private individuals access to agency information and the 1974 Privacy Act gives private citizens access to records that an agency may have collected on them. Individuals can learn how the information is being used, correct errors in the records, and act to prevent unauthorized disclosures of the information.

From a public employee's perspective, the problem is how to act ethically and legally when there are conflicts among the desires of elected officials, the needs of the public at large, the demands of managers, and the employee's own standards of conduct. The issue of accountability may be very difficult to sort out at that level, and the professional ethics of the employee may be the only guarantee that the dilemma will be recognized and addressed. The encouragement of public employees to "blow the whistle" on waste, fraud, and abuse reinforces the ethic of public service, although federal laws passed in the 1970's to encourage and protect whistle-blowers found little support in the 1980's. Whistle-blowers may still lose their jobs and, in some cases, face criminal prosecution for releasing certain information to the public.

Professionalization of the public sector also means increased pressures to recognize and adhere to standards of conduct and performance. Public employees are increasingly being held accountable to their various professional organizations. For example, government accountants have standards of conduct and performance, as well as well-defined accounting principles to follow. Professional guidance is provided to city managers through the International City Management Association, to city and regional planners through the American Planning Association, to government financial managers through the Government Finance Officers Association, and so on. Professional organizations may also regulate the minimum qualifications necessary to work in professional positions as well as encourage ethical conduct and standards of performance. The American Society for Public Administration provides a professional code of conduct and an increasingly broad range of training programs to a broad range of public employees. The expanding opportunities for professional development are changing career development patterns in many agencies. However, professionalization has been an uneven process. There are agencies staffed with well-educated, highly trained personnel using state-of-the-art technologies, and there are agencies, largely at the local level, that operate out of private garages with little expertise and little motivation to improve. Even within governments, some agencies are very professionally run and others are not. Accountability has a different meaning in a poorly run agency—it is a threat.

Public employees are also held accountable to the law. Recent judicial decisions have found that local government officials are frequently personally liable for their actions. When implementing or enforcing laws, local officials are protected from liability. When exercising their own discretion, they may be held legally liable.

Applications

The federal Inspector General Act of 1978 created offices of inspector general (IG) in twelve federal departments and agencies. By 1989, there were inspectors general in almost all federal agencies. The act's initial intent was to consolidate investigative functions under the direction of presidentially appointed IGs, to provide a more focused attack on waste, fraud, and abuse. The IGs are responsible to both the president and the Congress, although the president can remove an IG without congressional approval and IGs were frequently removed during the 1980's.

The inspectors general are given great latitude in the organization of their offices and in setting their priorities. Their purpose is to increase government accountability. The specific goals are: "compliance accountability," that is, investigating compliance with federal regulations by agency officials, contractors, clients, and others; "performance accountability," that is, requiring appropriate attention of individuals to performance goals; and "capacity-based accountability," that is, requiring attention to the investment of adequate resources to permit effective performance.

The offices of inspectors general have generally been credited with reducing waste, fraud, and abuse, although there were no firm estimates of such problems against which effectiveness can be measured. While the overall impact of the IGs is difficult to measure, the cumulative effect in terms of cost savings, prosecutions for wrongdoing, and improvements in agency operations has been positive. The "politicization" of IG offices during the 1980's, including the tendency of IGs to focus on programs that did not enjoy the support of the Reagan Administration, created some distrust within the federal bureaucracy. However, to the extent that the offices did focus attention on and attract resources to areas needing administrative attention, the IGs were appreciated.

Context

Pressure for greater government accountability is largely a result of growth in government programs, limited fiscal resources to support programs, increasing professionalization of the public sector, and a general societal interest in management reform, as well as partisan political opposition to large government programs. Large, complex programs are difficult to manage, and senior officials, both elected and nonelected, are seeking more information on the performance of programs. Much the same has occurred in the private sector as boards of directors and shareholders have demanded more and better information concerning corporate performance.

Shrinking public budgets are also requiring greater attention to cost-saving measures. Political speeches of the early 1980's frequently referred to the need to eliminate waste, fraud, and abuse. In some measure the rhetoric reflected a general public perception that the government at all levels was not working as effectively and efficiently as it should. However, the rhetoric also reflected growing political opposition to a broad range of social programs. The rhetoric also included references to "getting a bigger bang for the buck." Program evaluations and policy analyses increasingly relied on cost-benefit analysis, usually in terms of dollars rather than measures of program effectiveness, to measure performance. Senior public officials more often talked in terms of reducing service levels and eliminating programs, rather than increasing productivity.

Another historic trend has been a growing interest in management reform. Strategies for reform include increasing accountability for public agencies, but also providing greater flexibility in program management so that public officials can assume greater responsibility for the operations and the outcomes of programs. Similarly, recommendations to increase administrative flexibility and responsibility for federal programs were made in the report by the National Performance Review, chaired by Vice President Al Gore, in 1993. The recommendations were for smaller, more narrowly focused, and more directly accountable programs.[i]

On the whole, the accountability movement has met with acceptance in some areas of government and has encountered obstacles in other areas. While accountability is a central value in agencies that have historically been open to public participation, it is still a difficult value to implement in agencies that have historically been closed, such as national security and law enforcement agencies. Increased professionalization and more experience with public, media, judicial, legislative, and executive oversight should encourage agencies to accept accountability as an important value in public administration.

Bibliography

Bowers, James R. *Regulating the Regulators: An Introduction to the Legislative Oversight of Administrative Rulemaking.* New York: Praeger, 1990. A thorough study of the problems of legislative oversight in state government, drawing upon the experience in Illinois.

Frederickson, George H., ed. *Ethics and Public Administration.* Armonk, N.Y.: M. E. Sharpe, 1993. A collection of scholarly studies of the state of ethics in the public sector in the early 1990's. The focus is on what seems to work and what does not.

Glazer, Myron Peretz, and Penina Migdal Glazer. *The Whistleblowers: Exposing Corruption in Government and Industry.* New York: Basic Books, 1989. Examines the ethics of whistle-blowing in the public and private sectors, drawing upon examples from the Department of Defense, the New York Police Department, the Environmental Protection Agency, and other agencies.

Kerwin, Cornelius M. *Rulemaking: How Government Agencies Write Law and Make Policy.* Washington, D.C.: Congressional Quarterly Press, 1994. Chapter 6 examines the process of overseeing agency rule making and holding officials accountable for their decisions.

Light, Paul C. *Monitoring Government: Inspectors General and the Search for Accountability.* Washington, D.C.: Brookings Institution: Governance Institute, 1993. Examines the legislation establishing federal offices of inspectors general and assesses their effectiveness.

National Performance Review (U.S.). *From Red Tape to Results: Creating a Government That Works Better and Costs Less, Accompanying Report of the National Performance Review.* Washington, D.C.: Office of the Vice President, 1993. Public document that spells out the Clinton Administration agenda for improving government management.

Osborne, David, and Ted Gaebler. *Reinventing Government: How the Entrepreneurial Spirit Is Transforming the Public Sector*. Reading, Mass.: Addison-Wesley, 1992. One of the most influential books in public management, this work focuses attention on the obstacles to managerial flexibility and recommends fundamental reform of government processes.

Pressman, Jeffrey L., and Aaron Wildavsky. *Implementation: How Great Expectations in Washington Are Dashed in Oakland: Or, Why It's Amazing That Federal Programs Work at All, This Being a Saga of the Economic Development Administration as Told by Two Sympathetic Observers Who Seek to Build Morals on a Foundation of Ruined Hopes*. 3d ed. Berkeley: University of California Press, 1984. Classic study of the politics of program implementation and the roles of public and private actors in the evolution of a program designed in Washington, D.C., and implemented in California.

Richter, William L., Frances Burke, and Jameson W. Doig, eds. *Combating Corruption/ Encouraging Ethics: A Sourcebook for Public Service Ethics*. Washington, D.C.: American Society for Public Administration, 1990. Deals broadly with the dimensions of public sector ethics and the issues of corruption, abuse of authority, whistle-blowing, professional standards, and "open" government.

Rosen, Bernard. *Holding Government Bureaucracies Accountable*. 2d ed. New York: Praeger, 1989. Deals broadly with the issue of bureaucratic accountability to the executive and legislative branches, the public, and the courts and instruments to increase accountability.

William L. Waugh, Jr.

Cross-References

Administrative Procedures in U.S. Government, p. 14; The Civil Service in the United States, p. 310; Clientelism, p. 337; Confucianism and Government, p. 405; Elected Versus Appointed Offices in the United States, p. 572; Executive Functions in U.S. Government, p. 636; Filibuster, p. 694; Government Agencies, p. 765; Invisible Government, p. 975; Legislative Body Types, p. 1091; Legitimacy, p. 1105; Policy Development and Implementation, p. 1414; Political Action Committees, p. 1420; Political Ethics, p. 1461; Public Policy, p. 1633; Regulatory Agencies in the United States, p. 1678; Resource Management, p. 1718; Voting Behavior in the United States, p. 2109.

ACTIVIST POLITICS

Field of study: Politics

Political activism comprises all the conventional and unconventional ways in which the public participates in political systems. Activist politics is a narrower concept describing a style of political advocacy that became an important part of American political processes during the late twentieth century; it emphasizes broad public involvement, public-awareness campaigns, and confrontational tactics.

Principal terms

ADVOCACY: act or process of promoting a cause

CIVIL DISOBEDIENCE: refusal to obey a law that one considers morally unjust or unconstitutional

COALITION: temporary alliance or association of groups to advance a common cause

CONFRONTATION: bold, defiant, or antagonistic encounter between individuals or groups

ELITIST: representative of a select few

GRASSROOTS ACTION: political activity initiated at the lowest level of political systems

SOCIAL CLASS OR STATUS: an individual's place in the social structure, usually based on income, education, and occupational prestige

Overview

The term "activism" pertains to the overall level of public political activity in a society. Historically, American activism has taken many forms. Most activists rely on conventional, or commonly accepted, methods of influence: voting, campaigning for candidates, contributing money to elections or causes, direct communication with public officials, and participation in political parties or interest groups. Less conventional activities include protest, civil disobedience, boycotts, hunger strikes, and even violence.

Most Americans have historically engaged in limited political activities: voting, discussions with family and friends, and occasional letter writing. The overall amount of political activity in the United States has varied greatly over time. For example, the early 1960's marked one of the highest rates of electoral participation during the twentieth century, while the 1970's marked one of the lowest. Mass demonstrations, on the other hand, increased dramatically in the 1960's and early 1970's, but declined by the late 1970's.

The label "activist politics" emerged to characterize a style of political advocacy increasingly common after the 1960's, as activist groups began promoting issues that were new to the political agenda—such as nonsmokers' rights—or that were overlooked by more established interest groups or political parties, such as term limits. The goal of such activism was as much to increase public awareness as to enact specific laws or policies. Activist politics rely heavily on confrontation and less conventional forms of participation, such as protest marches, demonstrations, teach-ins, boycotts, and civil disobedience—all mechanisms that attract media attention and build support. As groups achieve success, their political momentum builds, and they tend to turn to more conventional political techniques, such as lobbying, lawsuits, and participation in the regulatory process.

Activist politics and activism are not synonymous. Most American citizens are not activists. In *Participation in America: Political Democracy and Social Equality* (1972), Sidney Verba and Norman Nie documented how often the public participated in local, state, and national politics. Fewer than 12 percent of the people in their study had high levels of activity, and others specialized either in election campaigns or community-based projects. Other researchers found that most activists were more likely to engage in conventional activities than in protests or civil disobedience. Regardless of their styles, politically active persons differed from the average citizen in having higher levels of income and education, more politically relevant skills and resources—such as literacy, time, expertise, money—and stronger belief in their ability to have their views considered by government.

Activist political groups grew in number and influence after World War II, due, in part, to the growing role of the mass media in American politics. By the 1970's, most Americans received the bulk of their political information from television. A medium attuned to the dramatic qualities of events, television is more national in focus than other news media, such as newspapers. These two qualities helped popularize activist politics. The tactics and successes of the 1950's and 1960's civil rights activists were captured live on television and conveyed to all parts of the country, inspiring other political movements. Television's preference for the dramatic also encouraged activists to find new ways to appeal to potential supporters.

Activist politics is a political style, not a specific agenda or political philosophy. The New Left orientation characteristic of the 1960's Vietnam antiwar protests was replaced by more interests. Some 1990's activist groups advocated broad social changes, such as the homosexual rights movement on the political left and the "prolife" movement on the right. Other movements sought to change political processes rather than address specific political issues; the term-limit movement is one example. Some movements represented single issues or localized concerns. For example, "NIMBY" (not in my back yard) organizations often emerge in communities where landfills, highways, prisons, or other facilities are to be located. Most such movements disappear after the facilities are constructed.

Three characteristics set activist groups apart from more traditional interest groups, such as professional associations and unions: their broad base of membership, emphasis on direct member involvement, and wide range of political targets.

In contrast to many interest groups that are organized around specific economic interests or defined social groups, activist groups tend to cut across social class or region. Advocates for medically assisted suicide for the terminally ill, for example, come from many walks of life, religions, and ethnic groups. Neighborhood associations may represent both business and residential interests within their communities. One type of activist group, known as public-interest groups, became especially important in the 1960's and 1970's. Such groups advocate causes that benefit the wider community, such as consumer and environmental protection; members do not expect to benefit directly from their groups' achievements.

A second characteristic of activist groups is the use of tactics that rely heavily on confrontation and grassroots action. Resource needs, political philosophy, and group dynamics influence these tactics. "People power" often serves as a means to attract other political resources, and demonstrations or actions involving large numbers capture mass media attention. Media coverage in turn increases interest in causes, enhancing the credibility of activists' demands, while encouraging other groups with more political resources to become involved.

Philosophical beliefs also contribute to the grassroots approach. Many people drawn to activist politics find the goals, structure, and leadership of traditional interest groups too inflexible or the interests they represent too narrow. The 1960's marked renewed interest in "participatory democracy" and populism: the belief that "the little guy" needed to take a stand against a government and economic system that had grown distant and unrepresentative of his interests. Proponents of participatory democracy have led many activist groups. For example, Tom Hayden, who helped author the 1962 *Port Huron Statement* calling for participatory democracy, became an activist against the Vietnam War, a consumer advocate, and eventually a California state legislator.

A confrontational style helps build cohesion and motivation among group members. Although sociological researchers have found that people with higher incomes and education participate more, strong identification with a group can compensate for the lower involvement associated with social class. This tends to occur when a group's ties are strong, the group believes it receives unfavorable treatment, and it attributes this treatment to the attitudes of the wider society rather than to its own behavior. Activist rhetoric and confrontational tactics accentuate each of these compensating factors.

A final characteristic of activist politics is its broad range of targets: Activists seek to influence the public debate as well as government action. Some public awareness activities have no specific target. For example, the AIDS quilt project displayed commemorative panels about individual victims of acquired immune deficiency syndrome; the size and diversity of the panels were themselves a political statement. Other activities target nonpolitical as well as political actors. For example, ACT UP, a militant AIDS activist group, staged demonstrations near political conventions, pharmaceutical firms, scientific conferences, and federal agencies.

Activist groups may also alternate between tactics intended to confront authorities and those that advance a specific political solution; they are adept at forming coalitions with more established groups. For example, the spotted owl controversy pitted environmental activists against Northwestern logging interests. Some groups, notably Earth First!, engaged in sit-ins at logging sites and blocked movement of logging equipment. Others, such as the Sierra Club, obtained court injunctions to stop logging activity until the federal government implemented timber management plans consistent with its Endangered Species Act.

Activist groups' loose structure, style, and broad range of targets create political assets and liabilities. While their ability to dramatize issues and capture public attention can attract many supporters and quickly elevate issues to a governmental agenda, the slow, resource-intensive effort to draft legislation or engage in protracted lawsuits may frustrate supporters and require a more formal structure. Many activist groups experience a crisis when their political aims receive serious attention in the governmental system. How they weather a crisis depends on their leadership, resources, ability to sustain member involvement, and willingness to adapt.

Applications

Two cases illustrate the variety of issues and tactics associated with activist politics. The animal-rights movement holds that all living creatures should be treated with respect and that humans are not superior to animals. People for the Ethical Treatment of Animals (PETA) first came to national prominence in 1981, when Maryland authorities arrested the director of a private research laboratory on charges of cruelty to animal subjects; the charges were based on data a PETA cofounder collected while working undercover at the lab. This groundbreaking action—the first time that a scientific research laboratory was raided for animal cruelty—served as a catalyst for nationwide confrontations over animal rights. Other groups inspired by the Silver Spring Monkey case raided laboratories and released animal subjects. Antifur activists protested in front of fur salons; some even slashed coats or splashed them with paint. Opponents of hunting disrupted the opening days of the season and even followed hunters into the woods to scare off prey. As the animal-rights movement grew in prominence, PETA also changed. In 1991 it had more than one hundred paid staff members, an annual budget of more than $5 million, a successful magazine, and thousands of dues-paying members. Though in the forefront of legislative and legal efforts to secure animal rights, it still engaged in direct action. Its boycott of fur products typifies the mix of strategies: celebrities appeared in its "I'd rather go naked than wear fur" advertisements, but the target of the boycott was the individual consumer.

In contrast to animal-rights activists, advocates for the rights of the disabled have employed more conventional tactics. Americans with disabilities represent one of the largest minority groups in the country. The 1990 Americans with Disabilities Act, which extended civil rights protections to people with physical and mental impairments, represented the culmination of years of local and national lobbying and lawsuits. The 1990 legislation was built on a series of laws: the 1968 Architectural Barriers Act, the Rehabilitation Act of 1973, and the Education for All Handicapped Children Act of 1975. Each law experienced delays and problems in implementation; by the 1980's, outrage over the failure to achieve progress fueled a growth in class consciousness among the disabled. Cutbacks in regulatory action under the Republican administrations of the 1980's led advocates to seek broad action. Scattered protests against inaccessible buildings and buses raised the visibility of the issue, but for the most part, advocates worked within the political system. A coalition of disability rights, civil rights, and AIDS-policy groups worked directly with members of Congress—many of whom had personal experiences with disabilities—to craft the bill. President George Bush also gave support. The strategy led business concerns to be cautious; none wanted to appear prejudiced against a civil rights bill on a "fast track" in Congress.

Despite the diversity of their interests, both movements have common elements: successful dramatization of their cases in the media, mobilization of broad-based or previously unorganized interests, a mix of tactics, and eventual integration into the political mainstream.

Context

The question of who would be active in American politics has plagued the United States since its inception. James Madison, the fourth president and primary author of the Federalist Papers, warned that organized pressure groups—which he called "factions"—were inevitable. The most permanent ones, and therefore the most divisive, were based on the distribution of property. To prevent factional conflict from engulfing the new nation, Madison argued that power should be dispersed across many branches of government, and many points of view should be incorporated so that no one perspective could dominate governmental decisions. Madison's view is at the heart of the theory known as American pluralism.

The question of "who governs" has been the subject of much twentieth century debate. Those who reply that it is the political and social elite who rule point to the fact that those who participate the most come from the most powerful social classes and that they raise issues likely to benefit their own circumstances. In *The Semi-Sovereign People* (1960), E. E. Schattschneider sums this up by stating that "the flaw in the pluralist heaven is that the heavenly chorus sings with a strong upper-class accent. Probably about 90 percent of the people cannot get into the pressure system." Activist politics is a response to this sense of exclusion. The growth of the mass media after World War II enabled people to learn more about social divisions in society. The successes of the Civil Rights movement gave hope to other interests. Civil rights activists, drawing on the nonviolent protest and civil disobedience techniques of Indian independence leader Mohandas Gandhi and the confrontational tactics of America's own abolition, suffrage, and labor movements, demonstrated how powerful the politics of activism could become.

Growth of new activist groups quickly followed. Community organizers, such as Saul Alinsky, offered practical models to action. Alinsky argued that lack of participation in many communities was a logical response to successive failures, leaving communities "organized for apathy." In his view, community activism required the reactivation of a sense of political identity. By targeting specific issues and confronting persons in power, communities heightened their awareness of their own power.

Alinsky cautioned that such issues needed to be vitally important to a community, unlikely to antagonize possible supporters, and easy to win. With a proven political success, a group would grow strong enough to tackle the more complex issues on its agenda. The schools of community organization that Alinsky and others founded went on to train hundreds of community activists.

As the activist style grew in frequency and success, new interests entered the political process. The 1960's saw the emergence of protests against the Vietnam War, women's and gay liberation movements, and consumer and environmental movements. The 1970's saw the beginning of a backlash in which opponents of liberal reform used activist tactics to counter New Left gains. The New Right, prolife movement, Moral Majority, and taxpayer revolts of the late 1970's and early 1980's are notable examples. The 1980's and 1990's saw still further growth in activism, with the emergence of the nuclear freeze campaign, AIDS activism, and human rights protests against apartheid in South Africa.

Each instance of activist politics has drawn into the political process people who were previously disillusioned with or excluded from government. While the tactics and confrontational style of activist politics may raise social tensions, they also help to bridge the gap in influence between the "haves" and the "have nots." In this, they help to reaffirm the pluralist tradition.

Bibliography

Alinsky, Saul D. *Rules for Radicals: A Practical Primer for Realistic Radicals*. New York: Random House, 1971. A history of twentieth century political activism with a detailed guide to organizing community action and using confrontational tactics.

Conway, M. Margaret. *Political Participation in the United States*. 2d ed. Washington, D.C.: Congressional Quarterly Press, 1991. Documents the styles and social characteristics of political participants and the causes and effects of participation.

Dahl, Robert A. *Who Governs? Democracy and Power in an American City*. New Haven, Conn.: Yale University Press, 1966. Groundbreaking analysis of the elitist-pluralist debate suited to students of history and politics.

Gamson, William A. *The Strategy of Social Protest*. Homewood, Ill.: Dorsey Press, 1975. Detailed statistical analysis of nineteenth and twentieth century social reform movements, with attention to issues of leadership, member characteristics, tactics, and group success. A classic in political sociology.

Hamilton, Alexander, John Jay, and James Madison. *The Federalist Papers*, edited by Clinton Rossiter. New York: New American Library, 1961. A series of classic political essays that explain the founding premises of the Constitution of the United States. Madison's Federalist No. 10 is one of the most frequently cited documents in American politics.

Miller, James. *Democracy Is in the Streets: From Port Huron to the Siege of Chicago*. New York: Simon and Schuster, 1987. Illustrated history of the 1960's New Left movement. Includes the *Port Huron Statement*.

Williams, Juan. *Eyes on the Prize: America's Civil Rights Years, 1954-1965*. New

York: Penguin, 1988. One of the best descriptions of the events, leaders, organizations, and strategies of the Civil Rights movement, this book is a companion to a public television documentary.

Carolyn Ann Kawecki

Cross-References

Aging and Politics in the United States, p. 35; Citizen Movements, p. 248; Citizenship Rights and Responsibilities, p. 260; Civic Education, p. 278; Civil Disobedience, p. 285; Civil Unrest and Rioting, p. 317; Consumer Politics, p. 445; Democracy, p. 513; Gay and Lesbian Politics, p. 732; Grassroots Politics, p. 797; Interest Groups, p. 936; The Left and the Right, p. 1079; The New Right, p. 1293; Political Correctness, p. 1441; Political Participation, p. 1479; Protest Movements, p. 1621; Radicalism, p. 1661; Technology and Citizen-Government Relations, p. 1949.

ADMINISTRATIVE PROCEDURES IN U.S. GOVERNMENT

Field of study: Functions of government

Administrative agencies have burgeoned as government has become increasingly complex. Agencies have derivative authority, drawn from the three branches of government, and function in a quasi-legislative, quasi-executive, or quasi-judicial capacity.

Principal terms

ADJUDICATION: acting as a court, in a quasi-judicial capacity

ADMINISTRATIVE LAW: area of law dealing with government agencies

ADMINISTRATIVE PROCEDURE ACT (APA): 1946 act of Congress to bring regularity and predictability to agency process

DELEGATION OF AUTHORITY: giving government agencies the power to perform legislative, executive, and judicial functions

INFORMAL DECISIONS: decisions based on something other than formal hearings, such as calling for an inspection or issuing orders to prevent imminent harm

JUDICIAL REVIEW: check on administrative power through legal interpretation

RULE MAKING: legislative authority granted by Congress; formalization of regulations and rules which define issues and limit power

Overview

Administrative law seeks to reduce arbitrariness and unfairness in bureaucracy. By regulation and by defining procedures, the law seeks to control administrative power and keep a check on abuse and excesses. The growth of administrative law has been pragmatic, designed to meet specific needs. As modern American government has become increasingly complex and specialized, the need for expertise has also increased. As vast new governmental programs have been created, so too has the need for providing specific, authoritative statements of the obligations of government and the benefits it is to provide. Profoundly influencing life in the United States, the administrative branch of government is often referred to as the fourth branch of government.

Although the decades of the 1970's and 1980's saw an explosive growth in government programs with ambitious objectives, American administrative law is often said to date from creation of the Interstate Commerce Commission in 1887. The era of the New Deal was also important in the growth of administrative law; many new and innovative programs and agencies emerged, causing President Franklin Delano Roosevelt to call for the creation of a committee to study administrative procedures. The committee's report, *Administrative Procedures in Government Agencies* (1941), made recommendations that led to the Administrative Procedure Act (APA) in 1946.

The APA was designed to produce uniformity and regularity among administrative agencies.

The APA divides all administrative procedure into three categories: rule making, adjudication, and other functions such as informing, inspecting, licensing, and so on. Rule making, a major administrative procedure, has as its core elements: information, participation, and accountability (judicial review). An administrative rule is the whole or a part of an agency statement of general or particular applicability and future effect designed to implement, interpret, or prescribe law or policy. Rules generally fill a vacuum left by the three major branches of government in the formulation of public policy and legal goals and objectives. They generally apply to and affect groups rather than individuals and are said to be the administrative equivalent of statutes.

Section 553 of the APA contains provisions for "notice and comment" rule making, also known as informal rule making. Kenneth Culp Davis, influential legal commentator on administrative law, has called notice and comment rule making one of the greatest inventions of American government. A simple and flexible procedure, informal rule making contains three procedural requirements: prior notice, generally by publication of items in the *Federal Register*, which contains either the terms or substance of the proposed rule or a description of the subjects and issues involved, as well as a reference to the legal authority for issuing the rule and information about opportunities for public participation; an opportunity for interested persons to participate through submission of written comments; and the requirement that final rules must be issued with a general statement of basis and purpose after consideration of public comments.

Oral hearings are not required, but interested persons may be allowed to submit written or oral testimony at the discretion of the agency. Notices of proposed rules are codified in the *Code of Federal Regulations* and organized into fifty categories, called "titles" and "chapters," which correspond to public programs, policies, or agencies. An unpublished regulation may be determined by a court to have no legal effect. Supplementing the record in the above documents with an informal proceeding with decision makers and staff members but without documentation leads to difficulties in judicial review. The inadequacy or absence of a record in informal rule-making proceedings, therefore, has been one of the stimuli for requiring more formal procedures than those set out in section 553.

Formal rule making, or "rule making on the record," involves a hearing in which interested persons are given an opportunity to testify and cross-examine adverse witnesses before a rule is issued. Whether informal or formal rule making is required will depend on the relevant statute and the nature of the interest involved. A middle ground between informal and formal rule making, referred to as hybrid rule making, emerged in the late 1960's as a result of the dissatisfaction with rule-making procedures set out in the APA. A general grant of rule-making authority and a requirement that the rules be subject to substantial evidence review was interpreted as necessitating hybrid procedures, including evidentiary hearings on certain contested issues.

Rules issued after a formal rule-making proceeding are subjected to closer judicial review than those of informal rule making. Rules issued after informal proceedings fall within the least formal "arbitrary and capricious" standard of review. The reviewing court applying that standard will consider the available data and reasoning processes by which the administrator made a decision and determine whether the agency's factual analysis is reasonable. Regulations issued after formal rule making are measured by the "substantial evidence" test: whether the agency has produced credible evidence on the record to support its factual findings. Thus the scope of judicial review of rules and rule making is very limited. The reviewing court checks, but does not supplant, agency action. While the court is the final interpreter of the law and statutory guidelines, it will not substitute its own judgment for that of the administrator on factual issues.

Rule-making proceedings have become a popular method of formulating policy as a result of their efficiency and speed. The proceedings place all affected parties on notice of impending changes in regulatory policy and provide them with an opportunity to voice comments and objections prior to the finalization of an agency's position on a given subject. Rule making has grown out of a necessity to discharge the numerous mandates from Congress that could not be executed through case-by-case adjudication.

Adjudication, the second major administrative function, may be divided into two types: informal and formal. Informal decision making has already been discussed with reference to rule making. Formal adjudications, called "evidentiary hearings," "full hearings," or "trial-type hearings," differ significantly from court trials. Comprising a relatively small proportion of the total number of decisions made by administrative agencies, nevertheless, the volume of administrative trial-type hearings is substantial. For example, it has been reported that in fiscal year 1978 the majority of formal administrative proceedings involved welfare and disability benefits conducted by the Social Security Administration, and approximately another 20,000 formal adjudications were held in other agencies.

Agency adjudications, which are required by statute to be determined on the record after opportunity for an agency hearing under APA sections 554-557, require adequate notice to the opposing party of the time and place of the hearing and the matters to be asserted. That requirement exists to satisfy the constitutional mandate of procedural due process of law. The complaint and other documents involved in administrative adjudication are less formal than those in civil litigation. Interested persons or organizations not named as parties in the case may also participate in the hearing by testifying at the request of one of the named parties, requesting permission to file a brief, or otherwise taking legal action known as intervention. Most formal agency adjudications are preceded by staff investigation, which parallels civil and criminal law's discovery, in which all relevant information useful to the decision makers is collected.

Significant differences in scope of judicial review exist. The initial decision of the administrative law judge is tentative, reviewable by the agency heads. While an appellate court normally has only limited power of judicial review of facts found by the trial court, and no additional information may be presented initially at the appellate level, the reviewing body in the agency has all the powers which it would have in making the initial decision, except as it may limit the issues on notice or by rule. Therefore, a party may present additional data or arguments to the reviewing body, which may consider them and revise its findings and conclusions accordingly. The party in civil litigation may not do so.

At an administrative hearing the parties are represented by legal counsel, witnesses may be cross-examined, and objections may be raised. While these aspects of the hearing are similar to those of a trial, certain important distinctions also exist. Rules for introduction and presentation of evidence are more liberal and less formal than in a court trial, and written evidence may be substituted for direct oral testimony, especially in claims for money or benefits or license applications. Throughout the administrative hearing, there is a strong tendency favoring the admission of questioned or challenged evidence. Even hearsay evidence, commonly excluded at trial, may be admitted at the administrative hearing and weighed accordingly. The written decision issued at the conclusion of the hearing details the agency's conclusions and findings of fact and enables a reviewing court to evaluate the propriety of the agency's action. It should be noted that the agency's internal grievance procedure must be followed and all administrative remedies exhausted before a court of law will review agency action.

Another administrative function is licensing: to ensure conformity with certain established standards, determine violations, and impose penalties. Still another is investigation, comprising the examination of papers, records, and other data, such as those required by government agencies (for example, tax records), as well as inspection of premises, generally necessitating a warrant except in exigent circumstances or regulated businesses such as those dealing in alcohol or firearms. If an agency's demand for information is resisted, it may subpoena the information, provided that the agency states its purpose so that a court may determine whether it is engaged in a lawful inquiry not designed to harass or intimidate. Reasonableness, constituting specificity and relevancy of purpose, is the standard which the agency subpoena must meet.

Access to complete and accurate information is important to ensure the fairness of the administrative process and to permit interested persons an opportunity to discover, present, or challenge information. Collection and disclosure also serve the public by making administrators accountable and revealing ineffectiveness and areas where reform should be considered. Clashes have arisen between statutes that authorize investigation and the constitutional guarantees and safeguards of the Fourth Amendment protecting private parties against unreasonable searches and seizures and the Fifth Amendment's guarantee against compulsory self-incrimination. Computerization of records and files containing sensitive information has caused increased fears on the part of citizens that personal data may be misused. Criminal law enforcement personnel often perform functions analogous to those of administrators in the investigative area.

Applications

Beginning with the Carter Administration in 1977 and continuing with the Reagan Administration in 1981, the political climate favored reducing the role of government in American life. Deregulation became the order of the day. In the rush to "get government off the backs" of business and citizens, entire industries were deregulated, such as airlines, railroads, trucking, natural gas, crude oil, and banking. In short, administrative control of these areas has been relaxed and price controls abolished, making possible increased competition.

The latter decades of the twentieth century have seen increased efforts on the part of the presidents to influence agency regulatory activities. Presidents Gerald Ford, Jimmy Carter, and Ronald Reagan issued executive orders affecting rule making that placed it under closer scrutiny by the president and his advisers, theoretically aiming to achieve consistency in a wide range of regulatory programs. Critics of this approach argue, however, that changes in rules brought about by presidential representatives violate the spirit of the initial legislation through which Congress delegated rule making to certain agencies. Additionally, in an effort to facilitate public comment on proposed rules, President Carter issued an executive order requiring that regulations were to be written in plain English.

The general trend, in which courts have tended to defer to an agency's interpretation of its own rules, changed. In addition to supplementary executive branch review, after 1978, as part of a broader initiative to supplement regulatory reform (known as regulatory analysis), all existing and proposed regulations were to be subjected to detailed cost-benefit analysis. The Office of Management and Budget (OMB) is the body charged with reviewing the adequacy and accuracy of proposed regulation. It has also been suggested that intervention from OMB violates the spirit and intent of the APA.

Context

Administrative agencies are usually created in response to a public demand or a need to redress serious social problems. Near the end of the nineteenth century, the Interstate Commerce Commission and the Federal Trade Commission were created in an attempt to control monopolies and powerful corporations. Administrative agencies proliferated during the era of the New Deal in order to provide stabilization and regulation in the economy. Agencies also established and administered price controls and rationing during wartime. As new technologies developed in communications, broadcasting, and energy, the government created bureaus to supervise and control those fledgling industries. During the era of the 1960's, when poverty and racial discrimination became issues of public concern, programs designed to redress injustices were introduced. Later, as risks to health and safety and environmental threats emerged as newsworthy subjects and public awareness increased, new agencies and programs emerged to address those matters.

Administrative agencies deal with diverse social problems. As a result of the limited scope of their responsibilities, agencies can develop expertise in a given area. Their standards of decision making are discretionary and can be tailored to fit a given situation. The inherent flexibility of agencies, however, has been criticized as permitting unchecked power and unrestrained government, leading to bureaucratic excesses. In an effort to prevent that from occurring and yet to permit agencies the flexibility necessary for their operation, the body of administrative law has developed to check overreaching and arbitrariness in government.

Arguably, the administrative process may be said to have developed in the 1790's, when the First U.S. Congress enacted legislation authorizing administrative officers to estimate duties payable on imports and adjudicate claims to military pensions for war veterans. Some legal historians, however, have traced the origins of administrative law from the latter part of the twelfth century in England, when the first book on the common law was published. By the eighteenth and early nineteenth centuries the justices of the peace had become chief administrators. The Industrial Revolution in Great Britain brought about greater centralization of administration and diminished powers of the justices of the peace.

In colonial America the justices of the peace and magistrates were also the most important officers, responsible for numerous local ordinances and laws. Eventually the power structure shifted from local government units to those at the state or federal level. The Industrial Revolution also required intervention by the national government in many formerly unregulated areas.

Bibliography

Barry, Donald D., and Howard R. Whitcomb. *The Legal Foundations of Public Administration.* 2d ed. St. Paul, Minn.: West, 1987. A college textbook on public administration containing edited cases and explanatory narrative.

Committee on Administrative Procedure appointed by the Attorney General. *Administrative Procedure in Government Agencies.* Charlottesville: University Press of Virginia, 1968. Reprint of the Attorney General's Committee on Administrative Procedure, published in 1941. A starting point for serious examination of the administrative process.

Davis, Kenneth Culp. *Discretionary Justice: A Preliminary Inquiry.* Westport, Conn.: Greenwood Press, 1980. Examination of the exercise and abuse of discretion in administrative law.

Gellhorn, Ernest, and Barry B. Boyer. *Administrative Law and Process in a Nutshell.* 2d ed. St. Paul, Minn.: West, 1981. Excellent and concise overview of administrative law written for lawyers and law students.

Kerwin, Cornelius M. *Rulemaking: How Government Agencies Write Law and Make Policy.* Washington, D.C.: Congressional Quarterly Press, 1994. General text for students and practitioners of public administration and public policy. Timely, readable, and clear.

Schwartz, Bernard. *Administrative Law.* 2d ed. Boston: Little, Brown, 1984. Lengthy legal treatise detailing administrative law and procedure. Copious references.

Tolchin, Susan J., and Martin Tolchin. *Dismantling America: The Rush to Deregulate.*

Boston: Houghton Mifflin, 1983. Factual study of deregulation and its effect on numerous industries and businesses, emphasizing the years of the Reagan Administration.

Marcia J. Weiss

Cross-References

Congress, p. 412; Courts: U.S. Federal, p. 471; Federal Mandates, p. 662; Government Agencies, p. 765; Intergovernmental Relations, p. 942; Judicial Review, p. 1012; Law Enforcement, p. 1059; Legislative Functions of Government, p. 1098; The Presidency in the United States, p. 1590; Public Policy, p. 1633; Social Services, p. 1858.

AFRICA: POLITICS AND GOVERNMENTS

Field of study: Comparative government

The aftermath of decolonialization in Africa saw the emergence of autocracies imposed on heterogeneous populations whose loyalty was to ethnic and religious subcultures. The prolonged economic crisis of the 1980's further eroded the legitimacy of such regimes.

Principal terms
AUTOCRACY: absolute authority vested in a single nonelected individual or small group
DECOLONIALIZATION: freedom from European control gained by indigenous populations
DEMOCRATIZATION: replacing nonelected absolute governments by elected, responsible, and limited ones
LEGITIMATION CRISIS: growing inability of government to justify its authority on any basis other than coercion
MAGREB: North African coastal states bordering on the Mediterranean
WEAK-STRONG-STATE SYNDROME: situation of a government with strong coercive capacity but weak popular support

Overview

The landmass of Africa is second in area only to the continent of Asia. It features the fastest demographic growth rate, from less than 100 million at the beginning of the twentieth century to a projected 1 billion by the beginning of the twenty-first. Despite this large population, it contains huge, sparsely inhabited areas. Politically, the continent and its surrounding islands contain more than fifty independent states, ranging from relative giants such as the Sudan and Algeria to dwarfs such as Djibouti, São Tomé, and Príncipe. Nigeria has a population of more than 110 million and the Seychelles about 100,000. Any discussion of Africa must therefore be contingent on its enormous diversity.

One may nevertheless identify significant similarities among the majority of its states. Foremost is their colonial past. This is shared by most of the Third World, but Africa is marked by certain distinguishing features. The conquest of Latin America came after swift and violent campaigns by Spanish and Portuguese adventurers, who settled in large numbers in the richest parts, from which they controlled the peripheries. In Asia, colonialism followed the West's economic infiltration of existing native entities, developing into a direct takeover or indirect control in which traditional native elites were responsible for little more than maintaining law and order. In Africa, however, contact with the Europeans was limited primarily to coastal areas from which, at the close of the nineteenth century, the Europeans expanded into the interior in a competitive land grab reflecting Western rivalry for power. The artificial units thus carved out were subjected to legal systems based on European codes and to white bureaucratic control staffed by Africans only at the lower levels.

From such differences among continents varying postcolonial patterns developed. The colonial territories of Latin America evolved into independent states with predominantly Spanish or Portuguese cultures. In Asia, withdrawal of colonial rule freed local elites to govern independently. In Africa, the modern machinery of control was handed over to African leaders. The new African states retained, however, their artificial borders; the population, in turn, retained traditional cultural and tribal loyalties. These loyalties did not necessarily correspond to the arbitrary boundaries, both cultural and political, fixed by the former authorities.

This explains another distinctive feature common in varying degrees to most African states, the importance of tribe or race. More than two thousand such groups have been identified, and in many states one may still find Europeans occupying key positions and enjoying special status. A glaring example of the social and political consequences of these divisions is South Africa, where up to the 1990's segregation and separation of the races were officially adopted to ensure a hierarchy of power dominated by whites, with Africans granted political rights only in the tribal homelands to which they had been assigned.

Egypt and the Magreb, or northern states bordering on the Mediterranean, form a distinct group owing to their relative cohesiveness. Egypt has retained its cultural identity as heir to a five-thousand-year-old civilization, despite its people's conversion to Islam following the Arabian conquest in the seventh century C.E., its inclusion in the Ottoman Empire as a province from the sixteenth century, and its falling under British control in 1882 to the end of World War II. The Magreb states are more fragmented, and loyalty to clan and tribe is especially noticeable in the interior, where the Berbers have not abandoned their heritage. The Atlas Mountains in Morocco have favored the perpetuation of a dual population structure, with Berber tribes periodically in conflict among themselves and against the central government. The seventh century Arab conquest and settlement and, except for Morocco, the shared history of inclusion within the Ottoman Empire provide the populations with a common religion and language. Some Magreb states have a long continuous history, which contributes to a sense of political identity. Tunisia was a self-governing Ottoman province from the late 1500's to its conquest by France in 1881, and Morocco has been ruled for the last 1,200 years by a dynasty descending from a relative of Muhammad. Libya, however, was carved out of several provinces early in the twentieth century, but intermarriage between Arabs and Berbers has made it the most Arabized society in the Magreb.

Sudan holds an intermediate position between this relative homogeneity of the North African coastal countries and the conditions typical of the states between them and South Africa. Divided by mountains and the swamps of the White Nile, Sudan has two distinct regions. The north was closely associated with Egypt, from which the Arabs spread to form, in time, a homogeneous society. The south remained relatively unaffected and is still populated by tribes retaining their ethnic identities and adhering to animistic and Christian faiths. In the 1880's both parts were united under British rule as an extension of Great Britain's protectorate over Egypt. Since independence in 1956, the country has been divided by civil war, which was intensified in 1983 by the imposition of Islamic religious law and by attempts to enforce greater administrative consolidation.

This division between north and south Sudan illustrates the weak-strong-state syndrome that, while not unknown elsewhere, has manifested itself most strongly in sub-Saharan Africa. The state's weakness lies in the lack of legitimacy inherent in what, without common culture and history, are mere flags, national anthems, and paraphernalia identifying the state with its people. What was really involved in these Western trappings was only the ceding of the right to use the instruments of power. The ability of the colonial governments to rule had not emanated from a general acceptance of their right to rule but rather from their superior power. The African successors inherited the bureaucratic frameworks together with police and armed forces equipped with modern weapons, but they lacked the capacity to call on forces from without. They typically were associated with specific segments of the population and so were subject to threats by the rest. The weakness of the lack of tradition, legitimacy, and general concord was also a source of strength, allowing the state, unhampered by any mediating forces, to play a despotic role unmatched by any of the authoritarian states of the First and Second worlds. What is more, the governmental structures bequeathed to the newly independent states tended to reflect the colonial imperative of ensuring the mother country's control over the Africans. Power flowed from the center in the capital to local subdivisions that rarely achieved any significant degree of autonomy. The most developed bureaucracies were those enforcing law and order and administering the economy, especially the extraction of resources.

The weak-strong-state syndrome presented newly independent countries with the need for changes both on the objective, social-economic plane and on the subjective plane of culture, values, and attitudes. Most immediate was the problem of nation building. This demanded a shift of loyalty away from local frameworks to the state. It also necessitated bridging the gaps between the relatively modern city and the rural areas that were largely unaffected by the changes introduced by the colonial powers. This task was made more complicated because independence movements were usually based on urban populations who often were unified only in their differentiation from the Europeans. The urban African populations did not necessarily share language or religious beliefs. What was required for national unification, therefore, was an educational and economic infrastructure, which needed not only large-scale investment but also an administration capable of organizing such enterprises and qualified personnel to carry them out. Over and above the shortage of such resources, any attempt to attain social, economic, and political realignment was bound to rouse the resistance of groups with other interests.

Such challenges led to the emergence of nondemocratic governments. The parting gifts of the colonial powers were democratic constitutions and institutions modeled on the mother countries. The two dominant patterns were instituted by Britain and France. The former developed a system of indirect rule through local elites, resulting in the preservation of communal divisions. This, coupled with relatively long processes of preparation for independence, facilitated the introduction of electoral politics. The French tended to centralize governance, reducing the power of local chiefs, and this fostered elite cohesion and the introduction of presidential arrangements in emulation of the French Fifth Republic. At the close of the 1980's, however, among all sub-Saharan states only Botswana, Senegal, and Gambia still had multiparty systems. Other multiparty—though hardly democratic—systems operated in Morocco, Tunisia, and Egypt. Sudan abolished its political parties in 1989, and in South Africa meaningful democratic participation was still restricted to the white minority. All the other African governments had been transformed through violent coups or constitutional manipulations into personal dictatorships, military regimes, or single-party systems often only months after achieving independence. Some states suffered the rise of individuals who exploited the colonial machinery to plunder the nation for the benefit of themselves and their cronies. Others were subjected to the tribe-based dictatorships.

Africa also had regimes inspired by loftier ideals. Marxism offered a vision of future-oriented unity based on economic development and the transcendence of all divisions, reached through the operation of a centralized state. The most original and uniquely African attempt at single-party government was expounded by Julius K. Nyerere of Tanzania and adopted with modifications by leaders such as Félix Houphouët-Boigny of the Ivory Coast and Robert Mugabe of Zimbabwe. The legitimacy of single-party government was based on two broad conceptions: one, that competitive democracy is a Western luxury import that Africa cannot afford because it perpetuates and politicizes ethnic, religious, and regional differences, threatening state unity; two, that a resolution of the discords hindering material progress, unity, and democracy lay in a return to the precolonial system in which all matters were discussed by all and decisions were taken by consensus.

Whether clothed in ideological terms or proclaimed cynically, justifications of autocratic rule exposed the causes of the legitimacy crisis that led to democratic reforms in Morocco, Tunisia, Algeria, and Egypt in the 1980's and to a wave of democratization that swept the sub-Saharan states beginning in 1990. The discrediting of authoritarian models of government, following the end of the Cold War and the fall of communism in Eastern Europe and the Soviet Union, was not lost on Africa. In 1990, the first dictatorial regime to fall was the seventeen-year Marxist rule of Mathieu Kerekou of Benin. In a short time, all the other Marxist regimes also fell. The authoritarian regimes had staked their legitimacy on the attainment of social and economic development and the melding of heterogeneous populations. The early postcolonization era had seen an appreciable degree of success in these areas. Industrialism and improved transportation opened new opportunities and led to remarkable urban growth. The expansion of educational networks had spread literacy, and advances in medicine had lowered infant mortality and increased longevity. The unrivaled economic slump that began in the early 1980's, however—exacerbated by the falling prices of commodities, corruption, mismanagement, and drought—frustrated many hopes. Africa became the only continent to experience economic retrogression, in some instances back to preindependence levels, recording an average annual decline of some 2 percent in per capita income. As trade imbalances grew and repressive regimes scared away potential investors, African states applied to the International Monetary Fund and the World Bank. These agencies, however, conditioned loans on austerity programs that added to public misery and on antistatist reforms that further discredited the governments. Donor countries, such as England and France, demanded a relaxation of dictatorial methods in return for further assistance. Small wonder, therefore, that public expressions of protest spread like wildfire from country to country and that the regimes found it increasingly difficult to resist the demand for responsive government and multiparty democracy. South Africa, with the highest gross national product in the continent, ample natural resources, and a modern infrastructure, was not subject to the degree of economic depression that afflicted most other states. It was nevertheless also affected by the general atmosphere of change. The process of reform upon which South Africa embarked in the mid-1980's culminated in the end of apartheid and the formation of a government of unity headed by Nelson Mandela.

By the mid-1990's, Africa's break with the past was still far from complete. Some autocratic regimes had succeeded in defeating or postponing the new democratic trends. The syndrome of the weak-strong-state persisted, threatening to give rise to parties based on ethnic groups, with the attendant dangers to democracy and to the existence of the states themselves. Democracy does not necessarily bring wealth, as Africa is learning. Despite this fact, for many of the African states a major shift is taking place, and nearly any change from their current situation holds a hope for a better future.

Applications

Democratization in Africa has yielded uneven results. The problems of the process vary from state to state. In Madagascar and Benin, there has been successful systematic change. In 1991, Didier Ratsiraka, Madagascar's president since 1975, faced widespread opposition that organized almost daily demonstrations of up to a half-million participants. The opposition demanded the replacement of single-party rule through elections. Ratsiraka gave way, and a transitional government was formed to organize an election. In 1993, the main leader of the prodemocracy campaign, Albert Zafy, won the presidential ballot, leading the eight contestants with 45 percent of the vote. A stable government was set up, replacing precolonial white rule and postcolonial rule by an elite.

Benin illustrates the role of government bankruptcy and foreign involvement in democratization. Benin's military-run Marxist regime was forced to surrender to striking civil servants owed a year's salary and to French demands for opening up the system in return for aid. Benin also illustrates the dangers attendant on sudden transition to a multiparty system in Africa. In a population of four million, no fewer than eighteen hundred candidates representing twenty-six ethnically based parties competed for the sixty-four seats of the National Assembly, while fourteen candidates vied for the office of president. The political intimidation, corruption, and intrigue which accompanied the elections augur ill for the capability of the new government to assert its legitimacy and act decisively.

Kenya, on the other hand, illustrates the ability of some African autocrats to survive the multiparty test. Inheriting the single-party system of the charismatic Jomo Kenyatta, Daniel arap Moi buttressed his regime by upgrading the power of his tribe. After 1978 the country experienced a gradual economic decline as population growth outstripped economic growth. The regime's insistence on continued single-party rule led to increasingly repressive tactics which in turn provoked the United States to cut its aid and the World Bank to cancel all new commitments. Bowing to these pressures, Moi agreed to a multiparty contest. Owing to the failure of the opposition parties to unify, he narrowly won with 36 percent of the vote. He was widely accused of exploiting his incumbency to rig the elections, and allegations of government complicity in instances of "ethnic cleansing" surfaced.

In Angola, a former Marxist ruler, José Eduardo dos Santos, was unchallenged in his electoral victory after multiparty elections supervised by the United Nations. Jonas Savimbi, however, head of the opposition, which is based in the Ovimbudu tribe, renewed Angola's protracted civil war rather than accede victory to the northern tribes.

Context

The integration into the world economic system of the Third World began centuries ago and gathered speed during the late nineteenth and early twentieth centuries. With the breakup of the European empires in Africa and Asia following World War II, the growing political significance of the Third World has led to increased attention to its problems. This is in part a demographic question. The combined populations of the United States, Russia, and Europe account for less than one-fifth of the world population. Increased attention to the Third World is also a product of the linking of the globe by modern communication systems and the flow of goods and populations across borders.

With the breakup of the Soviet Union, the focus of world politics shifted from the East-West dimension to what is sometimes called the North-South dimension. There are two schools of study of the Third World. One school assumes a slow and steady convergence of the Third World with the First. This is the development theory. The other school foresees the Third World's continued dependence on the First World. This is the dependency theory. In both schools the assumption is of the paramount importance of economic factors and the relative stability of political institutions. The evolution of African governments casts doubts on such assumptions. The numerous outbreaks of civil strife along ethnic lines point out an essential factor. Neither the nature of African governments nor their changes can be appreciated without due consideration of the ethnic histories of their diverse populations. The weakness of development theory has been shown by the preponderance of nondemocratic regimes up until the 1990's, while the weakness of dependence theory has been highlighted by the independent direction of the changes of African governments. In the 1950's, one could reasonably have expected the African independence movements to lead their countries along democratic lines, since so many of the independence movement leaders were intellectuals who had been exposed to Western education and culture. What was not sufficiently realized was that even in Europe democracy is a tender plant of recent growth that could not be simply and easily transplanted. On the other hand, the democratization that has recently taken place in so many African states proves that a public insistent on changes of direction can enforce its will on its leaders. Public opinion cannot be ignored, especially in light of the rapid development of national and international communication.

Bibliography

Cammack, Paul, David Pool, and William Tordoff. *Third World Politics: A Comparative Introduction.* Baltimore: The Johns Hopkins University Press, 1988. Excellent introduction to Third World politics.

Davidson, Basil. *The Black Man's Burden: Africa and the Curse of the Nation-State.* New York: Time Books, 1992. Analysis of the scourge of tribalism in the context of the African strong states, focusing on Zaïre as the most horrendous example (written before the Somali and Rwanda atrocities). Of striking interest are the parallels drawn with the independent states emerging after the fall of the Austria-Hungarian, Nazi, and Soviet empires.

Decalo, Samuel. "The Process, Prospects, and Constraints of Democratization in Africa." *African Affairs* 91 (January, 1992): 7-36. Succinct analysis of the major causes of democratization in Africa and the obstacles in its way.

Healey, John, and Mark Robinson. *Democracy, Governance, and Economic Policy: Sub-Saharan Africa in Comparative Perspective.* London: Overseas Development Institute, 1992. Description of the political culture of the African states during the economically successful 1960's and 1970's, the weaknesses that worsened the subsequent decline, and the problems impeding revival.

Leslie, Winsom. *Zaire: Continuity and Political Change in an Oppressive State.* Boulder, Colo.: Westview Press, 1993. Overview of Zaïre as one of the most terrible examples of the weak-strong-state syndrome.

Jonathan Mendilow

Cross-References

AFRICAN AMERICAN POLITICS

Field of study: Politics

Long excluded from mainstream electoral politics and subjected to discriminatory treatment in the United States—particularly in the South—African Americans have a tradition of using alternative means of achieving their political goals. Such techniques as direct action, lobbying, and litigation have historically played important roles in African American politics.

Principal terms

CROSSOVER APPEAL: ability of a political candidate to attract voters of another race or party

DERACIALIZATION: placing issues in race-neutral rather than race-specific terms

DIRECT ACTION: boycotts, marches, and demonstrations undertaken to help force political or legal change

LITIGATION: using the courts and the judicial system to protect one's interests and constitutional rights

LOBBYING: attempting to influence government policy, particularly in legislatures, by applying public pressure or employing professional lobbyists

UNJUST LAW: law that is out of harmony with natural law, or that applies only to certain groups or individuals

VOTE DILUTION: reduction of a minority group's ability to vote as a bloc through such means as substituting at-large elections for district elections

Overview

In 1960, James Q. Wilson wrote that "any book on Negroes, particularly on their politics, ought to be published in a loose-leaf binder so that it can be corrected and updated on a monthly basis." Wilson's words were as accurate more than three decades later as when they were first spoken. By the mid-1990's, the American political scene had been transformed as thousands of African Americans occupied positions of political power. These ranged from cabinet positions in presidential administrations and positions on the U.S. Supreme Court to elective offices in city councils and state governors' offices.

Too often, political power is thought of as simply electoral politics. While electoral politics is a key component of political power, it is only one of the ways in which African Americans have exerted political influence. In fact, prior to the 1960's, most black Americans were routinely denied access to the ballot box and had to rely on other means to advance their political agenda. Litigation, lobbying, and direct action were essential tools in the struggle of African Americans to secure their political rights, including the right to vote.

At the time of the founding of the United States, most African Americans were slaves who were considered to be property and not persons. As such, they were given no special political rights under the Constitution. The original Constitution tacitly preserved the institution of slavery and counted slaves as three-fifths of a person for purposes of determining congressional representation in Southern states. It was not until after the Civil War that the Reconstruction Congress abolished slavery and attempted to extend political rights to blacks.

The passage of the thirteenth, fourteenth, and fifteenth amendments to the Constitution are particularly important. The Thirteenth Amendment, passed in 1865, formally abolished slavery. The Fourteenth Amendment, passed in 1868, was designed to provide African Americans with "the equal protection of the laws." In other words, there would not be one set of laws for white Americans and another set of laws for everyone else. Finally, the Fifteenth Amendment, passed in 1870, said that the right to vote could not be "denied or abridged . . . on account of race, color or previous condition of servitude."

It is important to note that the Fifteenth Amendment did not explicitly give African Americans the vote. It said only that one could not be denied the right to vote because of race. The distinction is important because it allowed Southern states—in which 90 percent of the black population then lived—to eliminate black voters by the adoption of other nonracial devices.

Fearing black political domination, white Southerners pushed their state legislatures to adopt a variety of laws to disfranchise black voters. Residency requirements as long as two years in some states were adopted. Poll taxes, requiring payment of one or two dollars a year in order to vote, were instituted. The most significant barrier to black voting was the literacy test. In order to vote, the voters had to demonstrate their knowledge about the state and national political systems. The problem for blacks was that white officials had the sole discretion of deciding who had passed the literacy test and few blacks were given passing marks as late as the 1960's. Residency requirements, poll taxes, and literacy tests appear to be race-neutral because they ostensibly applied equally to both blacks and whites. In reality, all three devices were designed to discriminate against potential black voters. Lacking property, blacks tended to move about more frequently than whites and were thus less likely to meet the residency requirements. Black incomes lagged far behind those of whites, so they were much less likely to be able to afford the poll tax. The fact that most blacks were denied education combined with discriminatory administration made literacy tests a potent tool for the elimination of the black voter. In many Southern states one final voting requirement virtually guaranteed that African Americans could not vote—the notorious "grandfather clauses," which required aspiring voters to show that their grandfathers had voted. It was a requirement that virtually no former slave could satisfy.

Shut out of the electoral process, African Americans had to turn to other ways to exercise political influence. Several black organizations, especially the National Association for the Advancement of Colored People (NAACP), turned to the courts for political protection. As the U.S. Supreme Court stated in *NAACP v. Button* (1964),

"Groups which find themselves unable to achieve their objectives through the ballot frequently turn to the courts." The advantage of litigation as a political approach is that it allowed an organization such as the NAACP to capitalize on its large pool of talented lawyers. Perhaps none was so talented as Thurgood Marshall, who headed the NAACP Legal Defense and Education Fund. As an NAACP attorney, Marshall argued thirty-two cases before the Supreme Court and was victorious twenty-nine times. His greatest victory came in *Brown v. Board of Education* (1954), the landmark decision that declared segregation in public schools to be unconstitutional. In 1967 President Lyndon B. Johnson appointed Marshall to the Supreme Court, where Marshall served for more than two decades as an associate justice.

The disadvantages of litigation are time, money, and "paper victories." It can take years for a case to work its way through the court system. Of the small number of cases that reach the Supreme Court, an even smaller percentage are actually heard. Utilizing the courts is expensive and this limits its usefulness. Finally, even if the courts rule favorably, they cannot implement their decisions. African Americans frequently found themselves victorious before the courts, only to see nothing really changed, leaving them with only a paper victory. In 1963 Martin Luther King, Jr., the nation's leading civil rights advocate, wrote that "the failure of the nation, over a decade, to implement the majestic implications of these decisions led to the slow ebb of the Negro's faith in litigation as the dominant method to achieve his freedom."

A second political approach that blacks utilized was lobbying. Once again, the NAACP excelled in this approach, particularly when it lobbied against the nomination of certain individuals to government positions. It was, for example, instrumental in persuading the U.S. Senate to reject the nominations of John Parker (1930), Clement Haynesworth (1969), and G. Harrold Carswell (1970) to the Supreme Court. The NAACP also lobbied vigorously for the passage of various civil rights and voting rights laws. A clear advantage of lobbying is that it is a constitutionally protected right. The First Amendment protects the right of Americans "to petition the Government for a redress of grievances." In addition, lobbying does not require large expenditures in order to be effective. The problem with this approach was that there were few blacks in Congress until the 1970's, so there were not many sympathetic ears. In addition, the rules of Congress, particularly the filibuster, often stymied attempts to pass civil rights legislation.

A third political approach used by African Americans to advance their political agenda has been nonviolent direct action. Martin Luther King, Jr., head of the Southern Christian Leadership Conference, is best identified with this approach. King combined his religious views with the techniques of Mohandas Gandhi, the leader of the national independence movement in India, to arrive at his nonviolent direct action approach. King believed that unjust laws, such as those supporting segregation, must be directly challenged. According to King, unjust laws were out of harmony with either moral law or the laws of God; were binding on only certain groups in society, such as African Americans; or were laws that people had no part in making because they were denied the right to vote.

The advantage of nonviolent direct action was that it allowed individuals such as King to transform a local issue, such as segregation, into a national issue of human and civil rights. In addition, it provided the opportunity for African Americans of all social classes to take to the streets to pressure political leaders to change the status quo. A weakness of the direct action approach was that it was difficult to sustain over long periods of time, during which participants frequently found themselves out of jobs or subject to violence.

With the passage of the 1964 federal Civil Rights Act, fundamental political rights were finally restored to African Americans, particularly the right to vote. After the passage of this legislation, the number of black elected officials began rising by almost 20 percent a year. Black mayors have been elected in major American cities including New York, Chicago, Los Angeles, Detroit, Atlanta, Cleveland, Seattle, New Orleans, and Philadelphia.

The passage of voting rights legislation shifted African Americans from "protests to politics." Electoral politics, however, is not without its limitations. Various methods of vote dilution have prevented minorities from casting an effective vote. Vote dilution schemes include at-large elections, run-off elections, and racial gerrymandering. Also, it is often difficult to translate votes into public policy. Laws can be passed, but unless there is the financial and political commitment to implement those laws, nothing may actually change.

Applications

On May 17, 1954, the United States Supreme Court handed down its decision in the landmark *Brown v. Board of Education* case. The Court unanimously ruled that racial separation in public schools deprives minorities of equal educational opportunities and concluded that separate educational facilities are "inherently unequal." Arguing this case on behalf of all African Americans was Thurgood Marshall, head of the NAACP Legal Defense and Education Fund. Marshall, like many black attorneys, earned his law degree at Howard University in Washington, D.C. The goal of Marshall and the NAACP was to overturn the infamous "separate but equal" decision handed down by the Supreme Court in *Plessy v. Ferguson* (1896). The "separate but equal" doctrine allowed states and local governments to maintain segregated facilities so long as they were "equal" in quality.

From its founding in 1909, the NAACP concentrated much of its activity on combating the *Plessy* decision. Instead of directly attacking *Plessy*, the NAACP initially sought to ensure that blacks received "equal" facilities. In a series of Supreme Court cases in the 1930's and 1940's, the NAACP repeatedly demonstrated that schools for blacks were not equal in quality and resources to white schools. After numerous victories in getting the Court to enforce the "equal" portion of the "separate but equal" decision, the NAACP decided to challenge the "separate but equal" policy directly. Five different challenges to segregated schools emerged in 1949. These five cases were eventually consolidated into the *Brown* case, and the Supreme Court handed down its historic decision five years later. "Separate but equal" schools were out and unitary schools became the law of the land.

The *Brown* decision clearly indicates many of the problems with the litigation approach. To begin with, the law was not on the side of African Americans. In fact, the law reflected in *Plessy* stated that segregation was legal. The NAACP faced the difficult task of convincing the court to overturn established policy. Second, it took decades for the NAACP to persuade the courts to change its decisions. Finally, once the Court agreed to end segregated schools, no immediate change occurred. Ten years after the *Brown* decision, less than 3 percent of blacks in the South were attending integrated schools.

Beginning in 1957, the U.S. Congress passed civil rights laws designed to provide political equality for black Americans. Civil rights laws were passed in 1957, 1960, and 1964. Although these laws provided some improvements, they did little to extend voting rights to African Americans. In 1964, only one-third of black Southerners were registered to vote. In the state of Mississippi, less than 10 percent were registered. African Americans focused their attention on securing voting rights. They believed that if voting rights were obtained, other rights would follow. If African Americans had voting rights, they could force segregationist politicians to moderate their views. In addition, the vote could be used to elect blacks to political office.

While the NAACP used its Washington lobbyists to seek passage of a voting rights bill, Martin Luther King, Jr., and the Southern Christian Leadership Conference (SCLC) instituted nonviolent direct action. The SCLC selected Selma, Alabama, as the community to launch a protest for two reasons. First, almost no blacks were allowed to vote in Selma; second, the SCLC believed that the local sheriff, Jim Clark, could be easily provoked. The SCLC believed that Clark and his deputies would use violence against the protestors, that this violence would anger the public, and that would result in pressure on Congress to pass a voting rights bill.

The SCLC was correct concerning Clark and the use of violence. On March 7, 1965, Clark and his deputies viciously attacked demonstrators who were planning to march from Selma to Montgomery, Alabama. In what became known as "bloody Sunday," Sheriff Clark and his deputies brutalized the marchers. Shown live on national television, the public outcry was so great that Congress was indeed pressured to pass the 1965 Voting Rights Act.

The Voting Rights Act, more than any other single piece of legislation, changed the political landscape of the South. Blacks registered in massive numbers, and there was an explosion in the number of black elected officials. The price of this political victory, however, was high. Hundreds of demonstrators were injured during the protests, and three civil rights workers were killed during the Selma protests.

Context

Although African Americans were shut out of electoral politics until the late twentieth century, they have always found ways to participate in the political system. Denied the vote, black Americans used litigation, lobbying, and nonviolent direct action to further their political agenda. All these techniques continued to be used to improve the lives of African Americans.

Fortunately for the American political system, African Americans have been included rather than excluded from the system. The politics of exclusion forces African Americans to consider revolutionary approaches to secure their political rights. In the 1960's, Stokely Carmichael, a leader of the "Black Power" movement, and political scientist Charles Hamilton wrote *Black Power*. The authors called for black Americans to create their own political organizations rather than rely on the existing institutions, which they considered to be racist and irrelevant. In other words, Carmichael and Hamilton argued that American political institutions had failed and blacks needed to look elsewhere for their liberation.

The politics of inclusion argues for African American participation in all aspects of the political system. The participation must be more than mere "tokenism"; it must be a genuine influence in the political dialogue. African Americans, like all other groups in the American population, want a fair share of the political pie. Because African Americans constitute only about 12 percent of the United States population, they must often form coalitions with other groups in order to obtain their goals. Crossover appeal and deracialization are two strategies that have been used by the black community. Crossover appeal is the ability of black candidates to attract white voters. For example, former Los Angeles mayor Thomas Bradley and former Virginia governor Douglas Wilder were elected because of their crossover appeal. Crossover appeal also applies to the ability of white candidates to attract black voters.

Deracialization is the process of putting issues in race-neutral terms and appealing to universal values. Instead of pushing for expanded health care to benefit those unable to provide adequate protection for themselves and their families—a group that might disproportionately include African Americans—organizations push for universal health care. Selling the program as race-neutral rather than race-specific might enhance the prospects of victory. The danger of race-neutral politics is that it overlooks a multitude of problems where race should be discussed rather than ignored.

Bibliography

Barker, Lucius J., and Mack Jones. *African Americans and the Political System.* Englewood Cliffs, N.J.: Prentice-Hall, 1994. Excellent overview of the different ways blacks have influenced the political system.

Carmichael, Stokely, and Charles Hamilton. *Black Power: The Politics of Liberation in America.* New York: Vintage Books, 1967. Classic study that argues for a revolutionary approach with blacks organizing and controlling their own political destiny.

Franklin, John Hope, and Alfred A. Moss, Jr. *From Slavery to Freedom.* 6th ed. New York: Alfred A. Knopf, 1988. Perhaps the best history of African Americans throughout American history.

Keech, William. *The Impact of Negro Voting: The Role of the Vote in the Quest for Equality.* Chicago: Rand McNally, 1968. Analyzes the areas where the vote has resulted in significant changes, and those areas where it has had limited impact.

Swain, Carol M. *Black Faces, Black Interests: The Representation of African Americans in Politics.* Cambridge, Mass.: Harvard University Press, 1993. Argues that the creation of black-majority districts may not be the best way to guarantee black representation.

Wilson, James Q. *Negro Politics.* Glencoe, Ill.: Free Press, 1960. Examines why African Americans in the North exerted so little political leadership prior to the Civil Rights movement.

Darryl Paulson

Cross-References

Civil Disobedience, p. 285; Civil Rights and Liberties, p. 298; Civil Rights Protection, p. 304; The Democratic Party, p. 520; Interest Groups, p. 936; Latino Politics, p. 1052; Lobbying and Lobbyists, p. 1130; Pan-Africanism, p. 1369; Protest Movements, p. 1621; Race and Ethnicity, p. 1654; Slavery and U.S. Political History, p. 1821; The Supreme Court: Role in Government and Law, p. 1935; Voting Behavior in the United States, p. 2109.

AGING AND POLITICS IN THE UNITED STATES

Field of study: Civil rights and liberties

Elderly American citizens, who have become increasingly politically conscious, focus much of their political interest on issues related to health care and social security benefits. The American Association of Retired Persons is a very influential political entity.

Principal terms
COLA: acronym for cost-of-living adjustment to social security that is indexed to inflation
DEMOGRAPHICS: characteristics of populations
DOUBLE DIPPING: retiring from one job and taking another job, thus simultaneously receiving both retirement benefits and a salary
ELDER ISSUES: issues particularly related to the elderly, such as health care and social security benefits
GRAY LOBBY: term used to denote politically active groups of older citizens
LOBBY: group seeking to influence legislators so that legislation desired by the group will be passed

Overview

The growing political activity of older citizens in the United States and elsewhere is the result of increased longevity and to improved health. Increased longevity is shown by the changed number of older Americans. There were three million Americans age sixty-five or over at the start of the twentieth century; there were close to forty million toward the century's close. The number of the elderly exceeds the number of teenagers. The shift in American social composition reflects the fact that most of today's American citizens will live well past age sixty-five, something previously possible for only about 10 percent of the U.S. population.

These changes are due to modern medicine and to the much greater affluence of many older people. The latter economic condition derives from better retirement plans, the existence of social security payments, and enhanced opportunities to save money earned in the workplace. The result has been that many more older people have become politically active. This trend is shown by the demographics of voting in the late 1980's and early 1990's. Nearly 70 percent of Americans aged fifty-five to seventy-five have voted in most elections, compared to about half that percentage of those eighteen to twenty-four years old exercising their right to vote.

As of the mid-1990's, there were about thirty major politically involved organizations for older people in the United States. Examples include the National Council for Senior Citizens and the National Alliance of Senior Citizens. A "gray lobby" that aggressively seeks the advancement of elder issues has developed. The main focus for the gray lobby is considered to be the American Association of Retired Persons (AARP). This organization, which was founded in 1958, first served mostly to provide greatly needed insurance for retirees. By the early 1990's the AARP had grown to about 30 million members, or nearly half of all Americans above the age of fifty. This giant, often quite conscientious AARP membership, which rivals in its population many of the world's nations, has developed great political clout.

According to those who control the AARP, the organization must seek to bring to the service of the nation the many lifetimes of leadership experience which it comprises. As a consequence of this leadership experience, AARP leaders have stated, the AARP has a mandate to assume increasing leadership roles at the community, state, and national levels. It has been proposed that such roles for the AARP will diminish pollution, illiteracy, violence, poverty, and a great many other problems that currently plague society.

AARP leaders are accused of an agenda of almost total self-interest because of the organization's efforts to increase health and social security benefits for the elder citizen. The AARP's leaders maintain that rather than dealing solely with elder issues, the organization is really attempting to attack a major overall societal ill—poverty. They also note—and correctly—that millions of American elders, especially single women and minorities, are living in abject poverty. Consequently, the AARP argues, the problem of poverty needs to be addressed and poor elders must be enabled to achieve financial security.

Other issues that the AARP deems worthy of its attention are age discrimination in the workplace, home security for elders, and the development of special modes of transportation for the physically disabled. Again accused of being self-serving, the AARP states that the solution of such social issues will provide political landmarks that will aid people of all ages. The AARP argues that as it succeeds on discrimination issues of particular interest to elders, other types of discrimination will become easier to fight, that home security is needed by other groups as well, and that many young people are also physically disadvantaged. The organization is correct in these arguments, whether or not any altruism motivates its stance on issues.

Many critics accuse the AARP of ignoring the will of the majority of its members. Horace Deets and the other AARP leaders point out AARP unity, a huge amount of organizational volunteerism at all levels, and the great significance to the AARP of every individual member. In contrast, the AARP's many critics point out that a great many AARP leaders seem to feel free to ignore most average members' thoughts.

AARP leader John Rother has made comments that may imply that AARP does not report members' opinions but acts after developing, among its leadership, a more educated and better informed judgment. Furthermore, several polls show that less than 20 percent of AARP members join it to support the political agenda of elder issues for which it lobbies. Moreover, presuming 30 million AARP members, the self-proclaimed presence of only about 400,000 active AARP members means that about 1 percent of these members controls the organization. Members of AARP councils are not elected by a general vote of the membership; instead they are chosen by incumbent leaders, further diminishing any general control of the organization by its overall membership.

Applications

The top priorities of most politically active older Americans, especially those in the AARP, are the protection and expansion of Social Security, Medicare, and Medicaid. This is not surprising because of the exceptional needs for these benefits of the elderly, especially a great many impoverished Hispanics, blacks, Native Americans, and single women. Social Security payments are essential because too often it was impossible for people to maintain useful amounts of savings prior to retirement. Similarly, even presuming existing and expanding social security benefits, soaring health care costs make it impossible to obtain indispensable health care without Medicare and Medicaid dollars.

The activities of the AARP in the gray lobby are all quite well thought out. This is not surprising because most of the members of its national leadership cadre are ex-teachers and intellectuals. The AARP publishes *Modern Maturity*, which has become the magazine with the third-highest circulation numbers in the United States (about 20 million subscribers in the early 1990's). This attractive, trendy magazine is replete with tips on entitlements, retirement communities, travel, and many other aspects of life that are deemed particularly of interest to senior citizens. Unsurprisingly, it is also an excellent AARP propaganda tool. The magazine contains information and AARP political doctrine on virtually every issue that is associated with the agenda of the gray lobby. Other aspects of the AARP's media efforts include a wire service that provides the media with information on virtually every elder issue, and weekly television shows.

In addition, in numerous cases AARP activists confront specific politicians, engaging in public debate on issues associated with the special needs of the elderly. This technique is particularly useful because a large percentage of older citizens are retired and have much more time to pursue a political agenda than members of the current work force. AARP members are as likely to be available for political confrontations as to stuff envelopes. Furthermore, the elderly are often perceived by politicians at all levels as voting in a bloc. Such availability and potential bloc voting has often resulted in rapid political retreats from stands on elder issues that are undesired by the gray lobby.

One example often cited is part of the aftermath of the 1987 Wall Street crash. Many national legislators then strongly considered putting into effect a proposal to cut down social security cost-of-living adjustments (COLAs) to the elderly. Mobilization of the gray lobby quickly put an end to that planned endeavor. The AARP, however, does not obtain its goals all the time. A case in point is the repeal by Congress, in 1989, of the AARP-backed Medicare Catastrophic Coverage plan, passed in 1988. The AARP is viewed as being quite successful generally. Successes include landmarks such as the passage of the Older Americans Act in 1965, the establishment of the Federal Council on Aging in 1973, the changing of most mandatory retirements from age sixty-five to age seventy in 1978, and the total elimination of mandatory retirement in almost every type of American job in 1986.

As a consequence of the political successes of the AARP and other members of the gray lobby, more than 30 percent of the annual federal budget was expended on elder citizens by the early 1990's. It is deemed probable that these benefits, if maintained at the same level, would constitute almost two-thirds of the federal budget within forty years, due to projected increases in the number of elderly people. This might prove fiscally problematic because in many cases the standard of living of the elderly has improved much faster than that of younger people, disadvantaging the people who will feed money into the tax system. Moreover, special tax privileges protect the assets of the elderly and they receive special discounts on many services and activities (for example, banking and travel).

Another result of the political actions of the gray lobby is development of retirement communities that geographically separate many of today's elderly people from the mainstream of society. This separation has as one of its results the somewhat better focus of elderly people's political feelings and actions. It also, however, leads to an unfortunate presumption by other segments of the population that a great many senior citizens are withdrawing from society at large to sit back and enjoy their preferments. This has, in many cases, led to resentment of older Americans and to many vigorous allegations of senior citizen greed.

Context

The society of the United States is changing constantly and must continue to change because of the increased life spans and political agendas of the elderly. This is producing the seeds of future contention. The major inflammatory issue is the changed scope and prospects of the social security program, which began in 1935, and is associated with Medicare and Medicaid. In 1935, U.S. demographics favored the concept of social security as an old-age insurance. America's population was then made up mostly of young workers and the relatively small group of people who were over sixty-five were poor and had a short life expectancy. Thus, the demands of the system matched well with the nominal contributions made by workers and their employers. It also satisfied some aspects of the political desires of many Americans for social justice.

Subsequent, rapidly increasing numbers of people covered, inclusion of Medicare and Medicaid, lobbying by interest groups, and inflation have led to large increases of payments required of workers. The huge expense to the nation is exemplified by annual costs exceeding three hundred billion dollars in the late 1980's and a service group of nearly forty million.

The politics of the gray lobby has been seen by many as being associated with some potentially unfair activities. These include rising social security and health costs, aspects of COLAs, and efforts to fight legislation aimed at addressing the economic differences between people needing benefits given to the aged and those who receive them atop large retirement incomes. Taxation of Social Security benefits—the only effort toward the goal of economic fairness in social security—returns only 10 percent of the total funds defrayed. A different course of action may be needed, especially presuming expected cost increases.

Exactly what course of action might be taken is unclear. A great many older individuals argue that their overall benefits are a just return on an investment—their payments. When health benefits are added to the picture this position may be indefensible. In addition, regardless of feelings, the projected decline of the percentage of workers in the population who remain available to make Social Security payments may require development of alternatives.

Possible political consequences of these problems include the polarization of the nation according to age groups. Some experts visualize "age wars" that will occur when an overburdened younger generation rebels and refuses to pay the taxes needed to maintain social security and health programs. Others pose solutions associated with the phasing out of Social Security and its replacement with self-insurance. It would seem most sensible for the gray lobby, the younger Americans, and their elected representatives to cooperate in devising workable solutions to these problems based upon sound thinking and on sensible politics.

The population at large, as well as the aged, will undoubtedly have to address some political issues related to aging. These issues include redefining old age entitlements and how revenues are allocated, deciding which medical techniques should and should not be provided to the elderly at public cost, discouraging early retirement from work, discouraging double dipping, and encouraging the elderly to interact with younger people in ways that aid society as a whole.

Bibliography

Deets, Horace B. "The State of the AARP." *Vital Speeches of the Day* 56 (1990): 715-718. Text of a speech by the executive director of the AARP, laying out some of the problems of modern society and their solutions, according to AARP leadership.

Dychtwald, Ken, and Joe Flower. *Age Wave: The Challenges and Opportunities of an Aging America.* New York: Bantam Books, 1990. Covers many issues of importance at a time when the number of older Americans is increasing greatly.

Fairlie, Henry. "Talkin' 'bout My Generation." *The New Republic* 198 (March 28, 1988): 19-22. Discusses problems associated with the gray lobby. Fairlie proposes that the elderly should be more altruistic and less materialistic.

Novack, Janet. "Strength from Its Gray Roots." *Forbes* 148 (November 25, 1991): 89-94. Contends that the staff of the AARP ignores the views of its own membership in important issues. Much useful information on the AARP is included.

Pifer, Alan, and Lydia Bronte. *Our Aging Society: Paradox and Promise.* New York: W. W. Norton, 1986. Covers issues of importance to the understanding of aspects of aging. Describes the demography of aging, alteration of the demographics of family and childbearing, the special problems of minorities, and aspects of medicine and health care.

U.S. Department of Health and Human Services. *Aging America: Trends and Projections.* Washington, D.C.: 1991. This fact book provides a large amount of background information on the status of the aging in America.

Sanford S. Singer

Cross-References
Budgets of National Governments, p. 158; Consumer Politics, p. 445; Government Agencies, p. 765; Health Care Management, p. 810; Nonpartisan Political Organizations, p. 1326; The Social Security System, p. 1852.

AGRICULTURAL MANAGEMENT

Field of study: Functions of government

The production of food is such an important key to human survival that governments find many reasons for involving themselves in agriculture in order to ensure the adequate nutrition and health of their citizens. Most governments have programs to increase agricultural production, to protect farmers from foreign competition, and to assist farmers when natural disasters occur.

Principal terms

COMPARATIVE ADVANTAGE: situation that exists when one country is able to provide a good or service at a lower cost than another

GATT (GENERAL AGREEMENT ON TARIFFS AND TRADE): 1947 agreement among twenty-three nations (including the United States) that reduced tariffs and other trade barriers in order to facilitate global economic growth and development

GRADES AND STANDARDS: system of classifying commodities by their quality

PRICE SUPPORTS, TARGET PRICES, AND DEFICIENCY PAYMENTS: federal government programs instituted to keep commodity prices above designated levels

PROGRAM CROP: agricultural crop protected by federal government programs

USDA (U.S. DEPARTMENT OF AGRICULTURE): cabinet-level department of the federal government created to protect and foster U.S. agriculture

Overview

Many introductory economics courses cite agriculture as one of the best examples of a free competitive market. Such a market is characterized by a large number of firms (farms) producing an identical product (a commodity such as corn, soybeans, or wheat), where no firm has control over a substantial amount of production such that it could influence the price received. In many countries around the world, however, agriculture is an industry which has significant governmental involvement.

Ensuring adequate food supplies is commonly called "food security." Typically, a country wants to ensure the production of important foodstuffs. As an example, Japan's populace was cut off from imports of a variety of foods during World War II. In order to guarantee domestic rice production, the Japanese government supports this industry through subsidies to farmers and by placing a nearly complete ban on imported rice.

Closely associated with food security is a nation's desire to protect or support a particular domestic industry. Frequently, this desire manifests itself in efforts toward saving small farms, preserving rural communities, or supporting farmers' incomes.

Reasons for doing these things typically tend to be political—such as not wanting to put farmers out of work, support for tradition, or concern about the effect of a declining farm population on rural communities. Government protection may be needed because foreign farmers can provide the product more cheaply or efficiently, and export it. When this occurs, the country which could export its commodity most cheaply is said to have a comparative advantage. The U.S. sugar industry is an example of a protected industry. The world market price for cane sugar grown in the tropics is cheaper than the price for which domestic producers can sell it. Nevertheless, the U.S. industry has sought and received the protection of import quotas and tariffs on imported sugar. Other U.S. commodities receive direct government payments for raising program crops.

Governments also intervene in agriculture to protect the health of their citizens, and to protect domestic crops and livestock from harmful pathogens. Laws regarding agricultural production and food processing spell out what products can and cannot be used on food. Inspection services are often a governmental function that ensures adherence to grade and quality standards. These services allow for an efficient operation of the market for these commodities and permit buyers to determine what they are buying. Import restrictions sometimes center on concerns about quality of food.

Food assistance programs are in place in many countries. These programs allow for qualifying participants to receive free food or foodstuffs at substantially reduced cost. Typically, such programs are open to those living below some established poverty level. Providing nutrition and food education is another role that many governments assume regarding food products. This role may take the form of setting standards and requirements for food labeling, whereby food ingredients and nutritional content are included on labels. Such rules allow consumers to make informed decisions regarding both the value and nutritional quality of the food they purchase.

Agricultural production is subject to the vagaries of weather, pests, and disease. Many governments provide disaster relief to farmers who have suffered serious loss resulting from natural calamities such as floods, droughts, pests, or blight.

Growing awareness of the environmental impact of farming has led to increased government regulation of agricultural practices. More stringent requirements have been placed on the research, testing, and marketing of herbicides, insecticides, and animal health products. In some countries, incentives have also been put in place to encourage tillage methods, crop rotations, and other techniques that conserve soil and reduce fuel use.

Governments involve themselves in agriculture in order to promote political agendas. The phrase "food as a weapon" was coined to describe the use of agricultural production to achieve foreign policy objectives. Food and technical agricultural assistance are given as a reward for favors and withheld as a retaliatory action. In the United States, Public Law 480 (administered by the USDA), more commonly known as the "Food for Peace" program, has been the source of millions of tons of commodities given to foreign nations. On the retaliation side, politicians have used export embargoes to punish countries for certain behaviors. The Soviet grain embargo of 1980, in which the United States placed an embargo on shipments of wheat, feed grains, soybeans, and other selected products to the USSR after its invasion of Afghanistan, is an example of this type of policy.

Applications

There are numerous methods that governments have at their disposal to intervene in agriculture, depending upon the goals that are to be achieved. Tariffs are sometimes used by an importing country to protect domestic industries. A tariff is a tax on imports. It may be specific, in which case it is levied as a fixed sum per unit of an imported commodity, or it may be "value added," in which case it is applied at a percentage rate with reference to the value of the import. The effect of such an action is to raise the price of a commodity relative to domestically produced goods—with the goal of increasing consumption of the domestic commodities. Another term for a tariff is "import duty."

Nontariff barriers to trade cover all restrictions on imports and exports other than tariffs. Import quotas are the most widely used nontariff barrier. Quotas simply set an absolute limit on the quantity of a product that may be imported into a country. Quotas limit the supply of a commodity shipped to the importing country, and will tend to have the effect of raising the price of the commodity in the importing country.

An export quota is the opposite of an import quota. It imposes a limit on the quantity of a good that can be exported. The purpose of this may be to stabilize the export earnings of the exporting country by restricting the supply of the commodity, thereby sustaining the price. This approach will work only if the commodity in question has no substitutes and the exporting country has few competitors in the export market. Otherwise, importing countries will buy the commodity from competing nations, and there will be little impact on the world market price.

Embargoes are a strategy often employed to accomplish a political objective, to hold down the domestic price of the commodity, or to accomplish a disease prevention objective. An embargo is a complete stoppage of either the import or export of a commodity. One of the problems with implementing embargoes is that they are effective only if the exporting country has limited or no competitors in the international market. If this is not the case, then the importing country can buy the commodity in question from other sources and the embargo ends up hurting producers in the exporting country rather than having the intended effect on the target country.

Export subsidies are a fixed government payment per unit of product exported. They may be used to help reduce burdensome supplies of surplus commodities. The United States has sometimes sold manufactured dairy products in the export market at a price lower than the domestic price support level, in order to move surplus product (the surplus having arisen as a result of dairy support programs). Export subsidies may also be put into place for humanitarian reasons. An example of an export subsidy is low-interest loans on the export of commodities.

Sanitary regulations are another nontariff method to limit imports. Such regulations are put into place with the supposed intent of having imported commodities meet certain health, appearance, or quality standards. In many cases these regulations are in place for legitimate reasons. However, these rules are sometimes implemented to limit imports and protect domestic industries.

Governments also intervene in agriculture through domestic programs. In the United States, major program products include wheat, corn, rice, cotton, and dairy foods. For crops, typical support has been through a target price and deficiency payment program, which works in the following way: A target price is established for the program crop. If the market price drops below the target price, an amount equal to the difference, known as the deficiency payment, is paid in cash or in kind (an in-kind payment is an amount of the commodity equal in value to the deficiency payment). For dairy farmers, a mandated milk price, set by the government, is what milk processors must pay. If such a price results in a surplus of processed products on the market, the government purchases this surplus in the form of cheese and butter.

Grading and inspection services are often a government function. In the United States, the Federal Grain Inspection Service (a branch of the USDA), sets standards for and inspects and grades all grain shipped for export. For domestic consumption, the USDA inspects and grades meat, milk, eggs, and some fruits.

Context

The scope of government intervention varies greatly among countries and within countries. Almost every nation supports agricultural research, and many provide indirect assistance to farmers in the form of special credit institutions and support for farm supply and marketing cooperatives. The principal differences among nations are found in the degree to which they intervene in supporting farm product prices and in subsidizing food consumption and exports. Japan is at one end of the spectrum among industrial nations—nearly all farm and food prices in Japan are strongly influenced by government decisions. Japanese farmers are almost completely insulated from world market forces. New Zealand lies close to the other extreme. Farm prices there are influenced little by government intervention; they are dictated mainly by world supply-and-demand conditions. The United States falls somewhere between these extremes. In the United States, government action strongly influences the prices of some commodities but not others.

There are numerous reasons why governments choose to become involved in agriculture. Among the reasons most frequently cited are to ensure adequate food supplies, to protect and preserve small-scale farms, to reduce price instability, and to minimize dependence on imports. One can view government intervention as a response to either a food problem or a farm problem. A food problem arises whenever output fails to match demand, thus exerting upward pressure on food prices. A farm problem is the opposite; it arises whenever output exceeds demand, thus depressing farm prices. In practice, it has proved to be extremely difficult to match agricultural output with demand. Consequently, most countries have to contend with either a food problem or a farm problem.

Policy choices are continually being made regarding government involvement in agriculture. These choices center on issues such as the extent to which free trade is to prevail, the role of government in international markets, and the nature and extent of assistance programs provided to other nations. From an international standpoint, policies allowing free trade will foster production in those countries whose comparative advantages are the greatest. At the other extreme, policies allowing protectionism will foster conditions under which each country produces to meet its own need. Considerable progress has been made toward freer trade through organizations such as GATT.

From a world perspective, the arguments for free trade are strong. Among the strongest arguments is that increased production and reduced prices result from freer trade. As the economies of the world become more intertwined, trade liberalization will likely increase.

Bibliography

Hallberg, Milton C. *Policy for American Agriculture: Choices and Consequences.* Ames: Iowa State University Press, 1992. Provides the basic information needed for future policy analysis and development. Contains an extensive glossary and a chronology of legislation and executive orders affecting U.S. agriculture since 1862.

Hill, Lowell D., ed. *Role of Government in a Market Economy.* Ames: Iowa State University Press, 1982. Provides different points of view on the role of governments in agricultural markets. Shows that there is no consensus on the proper role of government in agricultural markets but should help readers evaluate their own beliefs.

Knutson, Ronald, J. B. Penn, and William T. Boehm. *Agricultural and Food Policy.* Englewood Cliffs, N.J.: Prentice-Hall, 1983. Covers all areas of agricultural policy, including the role of trade, international trade and development policy, U.S. farm policy, consumer food concerns, and land and water resource issues.

Robinson, Kenneth L. *Farm and Food Policies and Their Consequences.* Englewood Cliffs, N.J.: Prentice-Hall, 1989. A guide for policy analysis, rather than for prescription. Addresses issues that have dominated farm and food policy debates over the past fifty years.

Sanderson, Fred H., ed. *Agricultural Protectionism in the Industrialized World.* Washington, D.C.: Resources for the Future, 1990. Describes domestic agricultural policies of six major industrialized nations or groups of nations that are the most important traders of agricultural products (the United States, the European Community, Canada, Japan, Australia, and New Zealand).

Thompson, Paul B. *The Ethics of Aid and Trade.* New York: Cambridge University Press, 1992. Covers the principles of U.S. agricultural policy and foreign aid. Describes the traditional military-territorial model of the nation-state, which defines international duties in terms of protecting citizens' property. Replaces this model with the notion of the trading state, whose role is the establishment of international institutions that stabilize and facilitate cultural, intellectual, and commercial exchange.

Tweeten, Luther. *Farm Policy Analysis*. Boulder, Colo.: Westview Press, 1989. Gives the foundations needed to understand, interpret, and analyze farm policy. Makes extensive use of classic welfare analysis to show the impact of farm policies on producers, consumers, taxpayers, and the economy as a whole.

John C. Foltz

Cross-References

Business and Government, p. 177; Commerce Regulation, p. 357; Disaster Relief in the United States, p. 558; Environmental Protection, p. 617; Food Politics, p. 706; International Agreements, p. 949; Land Management in the United States, p. 1045; Research, Development, and Planning, p. 1711; Sanctions, p. 1777; Underdeveloped Nations, p. 2039; The World Bank, p. 2153.

ALLIANCES

Field of study: International government and politics

Alliances are temporary joinings of sovereign states for specific purposes. States may join together in a military alliance, uniting to repel an attack or to pursue more aggressive objectives. States also may join together to achieve economic objectives, such as increasing trade. In all cases, an alliance presumes common interests among its members.

Principal terms

ALLY: state that coordinates its defense policy with that of one or more other states, frequently on the basis of a formal treaty

BALANCE OF POWER: the objective of alliance building in eighteenth and nineteenth century Europe, whereby states joined to counter the power of other states or alliances

BANDWAGONING: forming an alliance with another state to lessen its potential as an enemy; contrasts with "balance of power" behavior

BLOC: alliance characterized by comparative homogeneity and ideological commonalities among allies

COALITION: usually short-lived alliance formed to address an immediate threat or specific issue

NON-ALIGNED MOVEMENT: movement begun in the 1950's by little-developed states in the tropics and the Southern Hemisphere seeking to avoid political alliance with either of the Cold War's ideological camps

PACT: agreement, often written, between states to coordinate or unify their policies

TREATY: instrument of international law between states; usually a more formal and longer-lived type of pact

TREATY ORGANIZATION: institutionalized association of states which, on the basis of a formal treaty, pledge assistance or policy coordination for an indefinite period; the North Atlantic Treaty Organization (NATO) and Warsaw Pact were important treaty organizations during the Cold War

Overview

Countries form alliances to advance or protect their shared interests. Because the international system encompasses scores of states that by definition are sovereign, each state is alone responsible for protecting and advancing its own interests. Yet where common interests are recognized, two or more states may voluntarily enter into association to pursue their objectives jointly. If the association is not meant to be permanent and is directed at some generally defined purpose, it is considered an alliance.

Many alliances are founded on some type of formal agreement, such as a treaty, wherein members pledge specific obligations for fixed periods of time. As instruments of international law, treaties impose certain obligations upon their parties. Less formal arrangements also may serve as the bases of alliances, including pacts, protocols, and charters. In all cases, the alliance partners agree to unite in addressing a common concern. Yet this unity does not come at the cost of the sovereignty, which is a defining characteristic of each member state. The agreements that serve as the basis for an alliance are thus limited by the fact that their individual signatories retain their sovereignty. There is therefore always some question as to how reliable an alliance partner might be, since no coercive international sovereign exists to enforce international agreements and laws—a fact that prompts the formation of alliances in the first place. Historically, there are many instances of states abandoning, or even turning against, their alliance partners.

The notion of an "alliance" presumes that the member states are united "against" some other state or alliance. Potential foes or competitors need not be concretely identified; members of a mutual security pact, for example, might pledge to defend one another against an attack from any outside force. In a looser definition of alliance, states might agree only that they will not assist an outside power which attacks one of their allies. More frequently, however, alliances are temporary cooperative arrangements, meant to achieve specific military (or other) objectives by working in concert. Sometimes those objectives may be proactive, such as uniting for the purpose of seizing a third party's territory. An alliance also may be formed for objectives which are preventative, such as uniting to deter a potential attack from a third party.

Alliances can be classified by the nature of the motives that spur their creation. Some are founded upon primarily economic motives, such as mutual exchanges of most favored nation trade status, or agreements to divide, share, or conquer markets. Typically, however, alliances are viewed as associations designed to achieve military or security objectives. For example, states might combine their military resources to control a strategic waterway. Yet many alliances use a variety of resources that include not only military force but also economic sanctions and diplomatic bargaining to achieve their objectives. Further, there is considerable overlap between "military" and "economic" interests. Access to oil, for example, might be either a strategic military necessity or a lucrative economic asset. Possession of a seaport might be crucial for either military or commercial interests. In short, an alliance can employ numerous methods to achieve its members' common interests, which can be of many types.

In addition to common economic and security interests, ideological or cultural affinity might play a role in alliance formation. Indeed, alliances between like-minded states are sometimes presumed, even in the absence of formal agreements. This fact has given rise to the notion of "natural allies"—countries whose peoples are culturally, linguistically, politically, or ideologically so similar that they should be allied. Many Americans attach such a strong sense of morality to their views about their country's foreign relations that they are in many ways sympathetic to the concept of natural allies. Particularly wide acceptance has been given to the notion of a "special relationship" between the United States and Great Britain. On the other hand, the post-World War II reversals that the United States has suffered in its relations with Germany and Japan, as well as its shifting alliances with Iran and Iraq in the 1970's and 1980's, speak against the concept of natural allies. Instead, one is reminded of President George Washington's 1796 farewell address, in which he said that "it is our true policy to steer clear of permanent alliances with any portion of the foreign world."

Beyond the question of natural allies, some have questioned the very logic of alliances. Following Washington, President Thomas Jefferson admonished his country to avoid "entangling alliances." Although the United States has been actively involved in numerous alliances, particularly in the twentieth century, Jefferson's sentiment was given lip service by later presidents as well. The appeal of international independence, if not outright isolationism, has resonated within many countries around the globe. In the decades after World War II, a number of states, primarily in the southern parts of the world, sought to avoid partisan association with either of the two northern superpowers, the United States and the Soviet Union. This "nonaligned movement" nevertheless gave rise to an alliance of its own. The countries that participated in the nonaligned movement formed the "Group of 77," which voted as a bloc in the United Nations and otherwise sought to coordinate policies and pursue joint objectives in international trade and other affairs. Whatever their particular values, alliances appear to be an integral part of international relations.

Applications

Shifting, fluid alliances characterized international relations within Europe between the sixteenth and early twentieth centuries. Warfare was viewed as a legitimate tool for the achievement of political objectives, and a set of rules and conventions for the conduct of war was generally accepted and (usually) observed by the major powers. Throughout these years, shifting groupings of countries allied for the purposes of joint military invasions and collective defense. These groupings constantly formed and re-formed to meet the particular threats and opportunities posed at the time. European politics thus was characterized as a "balance-of-power" system, for alliances were formed with the intention of countering (or "balancing") the collective power of potential and actual foes. Because the logic of balance of power required flexibility in the creation of alliances, warring powers generally sought to ensure that the defeat of a major adversary, or "great power," did not entirely eliminate that country as a significant military player in future European politics. One's enemy of today might become one's ally of tomorrow.

The demise of the balance-of-power system, and subsequent advent of a bipolar European order premised on two more or less "permanent" alliances, was set in motion by World War I. Two primary alliances fought in that war: the Triple Entente (France, Russia, and Great Britain) and the Triple Alliance (Germany, Austria-Hungary, and Italy). The war represented a departure from classic balance-of-power warfare of earlier years in several ways, including the introduction of more deadly and less discriminating weapons, such as aerial bombing and mustard gas. Popular acceptance of warfare as a political tool was diminishing. The defeat of the Triple Alliance in 1918 was especially important for the demise of the balance-of-power system, in that the victors sought to eliminate the military capabilities of the defeated. The war was thus viewed not as "a continuation of political relations . . . by other means," but as a "war to end all wars." Notwithstanding those intentions, within two decades Germany and Italy rose again as military powers and, with Japan, allied to become chief protagonists in another world war.

Unlike many of the European wars of the earlier balance-of-power period, World War II was understood by many as an ideological contest between fascism and liberal democracy. Yet there are problems with this view, largely illustrated by the actions of the Soviet Union. In the early stages of the war, the Soviet Union—whose ideological dogma placed Germany among capitalist enemies of socialism—signed a nonaggression pact with the Nazi regime, which itself was stridently anticommunist. After the two countries carried out a secret protocol to conquer and divide Poland, Germany abrogated the nonaggression pact and attacked the Soviet Union. The Soviet Union then joined the capitalist countries Britain and France (and later the United States) against Germany. The case of the Soviet Union therefore suggests that even during World War II, national self-interest was more important than ideological affinity as the cohesive force of an alliance.

For more than four decades after World War II, the countries of Europe split into two enduring and ideologically defined "treaty organizations." The Soviet Union and most of Eastern Europe formed the Warsaw Pact, while Western Europe allied with the United States and Canada to form the North Atlantic Treaty Organization (NATO). The longevity, rigidity, and ideological cohesion of the two organizations, as well as the lack of direct military engagement between them, suggested that Europe's balance-of-power system was dead.

The bipolar nature of the ensuing Cold War did not mean an end to the existence of temporary, ad hoc alliances on a lower level, however. In particular, France, West Germany, Britain, and the United States informally grouped their collective power in various ways to influence the policies and strategic goals of the Western bloc. Notable was France's attempt to create an economic "alliance" with other European states that would redeem their U.S. dollars for gold in an effort to end the privileged position of the United States in the international monetary system. France's efforts were unsuccessful, largely because Germany allied with the United States on this issue, deliberately holding a large quantity of U.S. dollars. The Cold War also witnessed alliances of sorts that spanned the East-West divide. For example, although the United States did not establish a formal alliance with China, by the 1970's the two countries were working together to pursue their shared economic and military interests, at the expense of the Soviet Union.

Even more remarkable alliances developed after the end of the Cold War. In 1990, shortly after the bipolar system ended with the collapse of communism in the Soviet Union and Eastern Europe, twenty-nine countries contributed military forces to counter Iraq's invasion of Kuwait. Since about two-thirds of the troops were American, it is unclear whether the United States truly needed the military support of other states to achieve its military objective of forcing Iraq from Kuwait. It is clear, however, that the range of nations represented in the coalition was important for political reasons. It symbolized a "world alliance," sanctioned by the United Nations, responding to a violation of international law. The participation of the Persian Gulf states of Egypt, Saudi Arabia, and Syria was especially important in this regard. Whether or not the Persian Gulf War really ushered in a "New World Order," as U.S. president George Bush claimed, it did illustrate that larger and ideologically disparate alliances could reach across the old East-West divide of the Cold War.

Context

The role of alliances in international politics in many ways resembles the role of interest groups within pluralistic democracies. Just as interest groups—or "factions," as constitutional framer James Madison called them—are formed by individuals pooling their votes and resources, alliances are formed by states combining their military, economic, and political resources. Both factions and alliances are created in order to promote the common interests of their members. Both are formed voluntarily, without direction or sanction from a higher power.

The analogy between factions and alliances is not complete. Interest groups exist within domestic political systems and are thus subject to the laws and constitutional provisions of their governments. National governments monopolize legitimate force to enforce their laws. There is no counterpart for this system-dominating sovereign in the international environment. Differences among states, and between alliances, thus can give rise to military attacks which can be addressed only with countervailing force. Warfare, as such, is unique to the international system. Nevertheless, the comparison with factions is useful for understanding the theoretical value and behavior of alliances.

Madison assumed that factions would pursue their own interests, even when those interests were in conflict with the interests of the polity as a whole. Yet he believed that those persons who felt threatened by a faction acting against their interests would form their own faction to balance the potential threat. This logic is parallel to the balance-of-power politics of pre-World War II Europe. Like factions in a domestic political system, alliances can be formed among like-interested states desiring to pool their power in response to a potential threat. Presumably, these groupings—alliances or factions—will be formed and adjusted until an "equilibrium" of power is reached. At that point, the system is considered stable and the various parties are relatively secure from an overwhelming attack on their crucial interests.

The adequacy of Madison's pluralism model has been challenged by various thinkers who often question the ability of certain "disfranchised" or "underendowed" groups to have their voices heard. Madisonian pluralism is sometimes seen to be inadequate for protecting the interests of minorities, however defined. Similarly, the cold, power-focused logic of alliance politics sometimes is criticized as unjust, allowing the strong to maintain enormous influence in the international system, and affording the weak with the Hobson's choice of "bandwagoning" or suffering the consequences. These critics sometimes advocate a greater respect for international law, and a few even advocate a world government. Yet one must ask whether balance-of-power politics causes undue power to accrue to the strong or merely reflects the natural logic of an international system whose power already is unequally distributed. Either way, the role of alliances and alliance building in international affairs remains central.

Bibliography

Hamilton, Alexander, James Madison, and John Jay. *The Federalist Papers*, edited by Clinton Rossiter. New York: New American Library, 1961. When ratification of the newly drafted U.S. Constitution was being debated, three of the document's most articulate Framers published these essays in New York newspapers to explain it. Much of the reasoning that Madison uses in Federalist No. 10 and No. 51 to defend pluralism might be transferred to alliance behavior in a balance-of-power system.

Liska, George. *Alliances and the Third World*. Baltimore: The Johns Hopkins University Press, 1968. Brief examination of the role of alliances in the politics of less-developed countries. Although dated, it is useful for its insights about alliance politics in the nonindustrialized world.

_____. *Nations in Alliance: The Limits of Interdependence*. Baltimore: The Johns Hopkins University Press, 1962. Scholarly look at the enduring characteristics of alliances and how alliance politics work in international affairs. Examines how and why alliances are formed and dissolved, as well as the concepts of nonalignment and neutralism.

Rothstein, Robert L. *Alliances and Small Powers*. New York: Columbia University Press, 1968. Study of the role of small and weak states in international alliances the central thesis of which is "that Small Powers are something more than or different from Great Powers writ small." Includes case studies from the period between the two world wars and concludes with analysis of small powers in alliances in the post-World War II period.

Walt, Stephen M. *The Origins of Alliances*. Ithaca, N.Y.: Cornell University Press, 1987. Scholarly examination of the forces that shape alliances in a competitive international system. Analyzes theories that political scientists have developed about alliances and offers a historical review of alliances since World War II.

Steve D. Boilard

Cross-References

Commonwealths, p. 364; Confederations, p. 391; Federations, p. 675; Foreign Relations, p. 718; International Agreements, p. 949; International Relations, p. 969; Isolationism and Protectionism, p. 1000; Leagues, p. 1072; National Security, p. 1261; North Atlantic Treaty Organization, p. 1332; Supranational Government Institutions, p. 1922; Trade with Foreign Nations, p. 2000; Treaties, p. 2020.

AMBASSADORS AND EMBASSIES

Field of study: International government and politics

Ambassadors are the representatives of their home states in foreign lands whose task is to further the interests of their governments and fellow citizens abroad. The official headquarters of ambassadors and their staffs are embassies.

Principal terms
AGREEMENT: official response by a potential host state indicating the acceptability (*persona grata*) of an individual under consideration for diplomatic service
AMBASSADOR: senior diplomatic officer stationed at an embassy
CONSUL: representative of a state who lives abroad to promote the business interests of and provide selected services to citizens living or traveling abroad
CONSULATE: extension of an embassy serving to protect its citizens abroad and to perform administrative tasks
DIPLOMACY: methods used by states to pursue objectives related to their international interests
DIPLOMAT: official deputy, appointed by a head of state, who represents his or her country under the direction of that head of state
EMBASSY: group of diplomats headed by an ambassador, or their official headquarters
FOREIGN POLICY: state's goals and objectives and the strategy by which those goals are realized
FOREIGN SERVICE: division of the government that maintains embassies, missions, and consulates in other states
STATE DEPARTMENT: department within the executive branch of the U.S. government that is responsible for diplomatic relations

Overview

No matter how large a country is or what its natural and economic resources are, it cannot easily isolate itself from the global community. In order to survive and prosper, a state must remain an active participant in world events. Active involvement in the world cannot be accomplished without diplomacy. Even procedures that one takes for granted, such as mailing a letter to another country, require the cooperation of two or more governments.

One of the basic tenets of diplomacy is that it cannot begin unless two parties agree to discuss their mutual concerns and goals. Before an ambassador or other representative of a state is sent to a foreign land in an effort to begin dialogue, the host state needs to agree to recognize that person as the legitimate delegate. The host state indicates the *persona grata* status, or acceptability, of individuals under consideration for service as a diplomatic officer. While this act is normally a formality, if for some reason the host state feels that the ambassador or other accompanying personnel are unacceptable, it may sever communications. Even after both parties agree on an ambassador, that person may at any time be declared *persona non grata* (unacceptable). The presence of an unwelcome diplomat may create a hostile environment and thus hinder negotiations.

Upon arrival in the host state, an ambassador and all accompanying staff are considered representatives of their head of state. For example, a United States ambassador is part of the executive branch of government. As the U.S. president's deputy abroad, the ambassador represents that office and the U.S. government. Ironically, although ambassadorships are one of the most important and influential positions in government, they remain one of the few positions in government still subject to the old patronage system. Major contributors to presidential campaigns are often appointed to such positions despite a notable lack of qualifications. This has often led to animosity between career and noncareer foreign service officers. Many argue that short-term political appointees are nothing more than figureheads and do little, as a result, to further the overall welfare of their native country.

The role of the ambassador in more recent times has become more ceremonial and less critical to the decision-making process. Today the post of the ambassador is primarily a symbolic one. Decisions about United States foreign policy are now made in Washington, D.C., by the Department of State or some other agency. The effect of technological change on embassies and their functions has been tremendous. Prior to the advent of modern communications, a country's ambassador and staff were a critical part of the decision-making process. Treaties and agreements were often negotiated and agreed upon by ambassadors without prior approval of their superiors. Live news coverage of political turmoil, war, and negotiations has greatly complicated the ambassador's job. Public scrutiny, once almost nonexistent, now forces the ambassador to keep public opinion in mind at all times.

An ambassador would be completely ineffective without a capable staff. As former U.S. ambassador Willard L. Beaulac once stated, an ambassador without a staff is like a "general without an army." Second to the ambassador, the most important member of an embassy team is the deputy chief of mission (DCM). Historically, the function of the DCM has varied depending on the demands of the ambassador. Ideally, the DCM is informed of all activity conducted by the embassy. If for some reason the ambassador is unable to fulfill his or her duties, the DCM assumes the responsibilities of the ambassador.

The subordinates of the ambassador and the DCM perform a variety of functions, all of which are necessary for the smooth operation of an embassy. The real work in any embassy is carried out by foreign service officers. Foreign service officers are often required to deal with a variety of issues that demand an expertise or knowledge of a variety of fields, including history, international law, politics, economics, diplomacy, and military science. Occasionally, the avoidance of war depends on the capabilities of these individuals. Increased demand for specialized expertise has forced embassies to augment their staffs. Many embassies now have several hundred full-time personnel. As a result of technologies such as the telephone, fax machines, and computers, some junior foreign service officers abroad now do little more than gather information. Such new developments, however, do not mean that the ambassador's subordinates are not a vital part of the diplomatic process. No government wants to make an important foreign policy decision without appropriate information.

The emergence of a global economic system has placed greater demands on embassies. Countries may wish to establish diplomatic posts in more than one city in a foreign country. For example, an Asian country may wish to establish a consulate in Los Angeles, as well as an embassy in Washington, D.C., in order to facilitate trade. Consulates are considered extensions of the embassy. The primary function of a consulate is the protection of citizens abroad. Consulates also promote trade and issue visas to foreigners.

The activities of diplomats and embassies require that they receive special considerations and privileges not normally given to visitors in foreign lands. An embassy is considered an extension of the ambassador's native soil. It cannot be entered by the host country without permission. Any effort to enter embassy grounds without permission may be considered a violation of sovereignty. The laws enforced in an embassy are not those of the host country but rather the foreign nation's domestic laws. The existence of these rules has often resulted in the use of embassies as havens for those who seek political asylum. Occasionally, asylum seekers remain in embassies for years.

Diplomats and their families are also given diplomatic immunity. Like sovereignty, immunity is a basic principle of diplomatic practice. Immunity means that diplomats and their families are not subject to the host state's civil or criminal laws. Immunity from harm is a necessity for government representatives; otherwise negotiations could not be freely conducted. Although officially protected by the traditions of diplomatic practice, ambassadors and their personnel are not always guaranteed safety. As a country's official representative in a foreign land, the embassy is particularly susceptible to attacks by those displeased with the policies of the country that embassy represents. Some see attacks on ambassadors and embassies as a way of attracting international attention to their cause or as a means of accomplishing their ends. The picketing of foreign embassies is, as a result, common in many countries. The United States government, in an effort to protect visiting diplomats, has made it a crime to picket within five hundred feet of an embassy.

The United States government maintains a network of embassies and consulates in more than 150 countries. Each embassy and consulate reports to the State Department and carries out instructions and policies of the president and of the United States. The United States also has established special missions to the North Atlantic Treaty Organization, the European Community, the United Nations, the European office of the United Nations, the Organization for Economic Cooperation and Development, and the Organization of American States.

Applications

The level of cooperation and trust between any two countries varies over time. Events unfolding in either country or elsewhere in the world may alter the course of diplomatic relations between states. Diplomatic relations between the United States and Nicaragua during the early twentieth century provide an excellent example. The role of foreign service personnel in charting the course of a country's foreign policy can be easily identified by a review of the events as they unfolded in Nicaragua.

From 1893 to 1909, Nicaragua was ruled by a dictator, General José Santos Zelaya. The United States, through formal diplomatic channels, initially tried to establish amiable ties with Zelaya. Relations between the two parties soured, however, after the United States announced that Panama was to be the site of the new canal to be built in Central America. (The canal is known today as the Panama Canal.) After 1902, foreign service officers in the region began to report that information collected suggested that Zelaya was no longer a friend of the United States government and no longer supported its interests in the region. It appeared to many foreign observers that U.S. investments in Nicaragua were being threatened by his increasingly hostile government.

As the reports of hostility increased, President William Taft's secretary of state, Philander C. Knox, and other foreign service personnel began encouraging conservative rebels in Nicaragua who were already considering a coup to oust the dictator. Initially U.S. representatives in Nicaragua were given strict orders to maintain neutrality during the coup. A few days after the coup began, however, the United States abandoned its policy of neutrality. The abrupt change in policy occurred as a result of the death of two Americans who were charged with subversive activities and ordered executed by Zelaya. The American mission in Nicaragua and the Department of State, following standard procedure under such circumstances, collected information and began to formulate an updated policy toward the Zelaya government, taking into consideration the recent chain of events. The decision was then made by the State Department to sever all formal diplomatic ties with the Zelaya government of Nicaragua. The United States mission in Nicaragua was officially withdrawn.

Once the coup was complete and a new provisional government was established by General Juan J. Estrada, the U.S. government began informal negotiations for the reestablishment of formalized relations between the two countries. During those negotiations, the Estrada government agreed to hold elections in Nicaragua and to other specific terms in exchange for official recognition by the United States. Estrada realized that without help from the United States in the form of loans, investments, and trade, his economy would have difficulty surviving. In exchange for meeting United States demands, the newly formed Nicaraguan government received the official recognition it needed. Elliot Northcott, with *persona grata* status from the Nicaraguan government, was named minister (one rank below ambassador) to that country in January of 1911. Normal diplomatic relations between the two countries were resumed.

After a brief shake-up in the Nicaraguan government, Adolfo Díaz, Estrada's former vice president, who followed him as president, began to request assistance through the revived diplomatic channels. His goal was to secure loans from the United States that would ease the financial burden on his country. Diplomatic representatives from both countries eventually agreed upon and signed a loan treaty. President William Howard Taft encouraged the United States Senate to ratify the treaty, but it was not passed by that body. It is important to note that the membership of the legislative branch is under no obligation to follow the lead of the Department of State as part of the executive branch. The failure of the United States government to approve the loan ultimately undermined the credibility of the Díaz government. By 1912, the political situation in Nicaragua was so unstable that President Taft sent in United States Marines in an effort to maintain political stability and protect American investments.

The aforementioned events, taking place in Nicaragua between 1893 and 1911, are indicative of the role typically played by the Department of State, as a representative of the United States government, in world affairs. Through the use of official and unofficial diplomatic channels, foreign service officers, ambassadors, spies, and the State Department, the government gathers information, negotiates agreements and treaties, and reevaluates on a daily basis the course of American foreign policy within the context of a rapidly changing world. Almost all governments have some agency similar to the Department of State that serves a similar function. As the aforementioned events suggest, countries often use a variety of political means in order to achieve desired ends. The use of political pressure, the granting of special trade status, nonrecognition, loans, aid programs, weapons sales, and the use of force are all options available to governments. The decision to follow a particular course of action in an effort to achieve a desired result is ultimately determined by a country's foreign service officers and its department of state (or equivalent).

Context

People have always had a need to communicate with their neighbors and to establish the terms of their relationship. Diplomacy, as a result, existed long before the advent of civilization. Perhaps the establishment of territorial limits was the first order of diplomatic negotiations. The messengers and negotiators of prehistory were not part of an institutionalized system. Yet, in many ways, the methods of diplomacy currently in use differ little from those of past generations.

The current ambassadorial system was first established during the fourteenth century by the Italian city-states of that day. These first permanent embassies were so successful that others were soon established throughout Europe. During that time, there were no formalized rules regarding the classification of diplomatic agents or the treatment of diplomats. Diplomatic titles and rankings varied from state to state. It was not until the late Middle Ages that some diplomats came to be called "ambaxator."

By the early nineteenth century, efforts were under way to classify diplomatic agents according to office and to formalize their functions. Although there have been minor adjustments in ranking since the modern art of diplomacy began, the top-ranking diplomatic officials exchanged by states remain as follows: ambassadors, ministers, minister residents, chargés d'affaires, and consuls. The current general guidelines of diplomatic practice were not officially agreed upon by most states, however, until the mid-twentieth century.

Bibliography

Beaulac, Willard L. *Career Diplomat: A Career in the Foreign Service of the United States*. New York: Macmillan, 1964. A former U.S. ambassador to Argentina, the author gives great insight into the life of a career diplomat.

Clarfield, Gerard H., and Walter V. Scholes, eds. *United States Diplomatic History*. 2 vols. Boston: Houghton Mifflin, 1973. Diplomatic history of the United States, covering the period from 1900 to the beginning of the Cold War in the late 1940's. A timeless collection of essays related to United States foreign policy.

Jackson, Henry M., ed. *The Secretary of State and the Ambassador: Jackson Subcommittee Papers on the Conduct of American Foreign Policy*. New York: Praeger, 1964. Containing the proceedings of the U.S. Senate's subcommittee on National Security Staffing and Operations, this volume discusses many issues related to foreign service.

Miller, Robert Hopkins, ed. *Inside an Embassy: The Political Role of Diplomats Abroad*. Washington, D.C.: Congressional Quarterly, 1992. Multiauthor work on the political role of diplomats, with relevant case studies included in each chapter.

Nicolson, Harold. *The Evolution of Diplomatic Method*. London: Constable, 1954. Exploration of the historical evolution of diplomatic methods by a leading British diplomat.

Queller, Donald E. *The Office of Ambassador in the Middle Ages*. Princeton, N.J.: Princeton University Press, 1967. Describes the beginnings of the modern system of diplomacy.

Steiner, Zara, ed. *The Times Survey of Foreign Ministries of the World*. London: Times Books, 1982. Addresses the distinctions between how various states conduct foreign affairs. Each chapter traces the evolutionary development of foreign policy administration in a different country.

Thayer, Charles Wheeler. *Diplomat*. London: Michael Joseph, 1960. History of the British diplomatic service.

Donald C. Simmons, Jr.

Cross-References

Alliances, p. 47; Bureaucracy, p. 164; Civil Rights Protection, p. 304; Conflict Resolution, p. 397; Foreign Relations, p. 718; Geopolitics, p. 759; Immigration and Emigration, p. 868; International Agreements, p. 949; International Law, p. 956; International Relations, p. 969; Peace, p. 1390; The Presidency in the United States, p. 1590; Terrorism, p. 1962; Treaties, p. 2020; United Nations, p. 2045.

AMERICAN INDIAN GOVERNMENTS

Field of study: Comparative government

American Indians developed many different types of government based on consensus and local rule, and based on persuasion rather than vested power. Many traditional systems survived the onslaught of white civilization, existing side-by-side with governments imposed from outside; the late twentieth century saw a reawakening of interest in traditional tribal governments.

Principal terms
BUREAU OF INDIAN AFFAIRS (BIA): branch of the U.S. federal government organized in 1824 to conduct relations with Indians; it later assumed control over reservations
CLAN: tribal subgroup in which members are related by family ties
INDIAN REORGANIZATION ACT: legislation enacted in 1934 that was intended to restore a measure of tribal authority and self-determination
SACHEM: term used by the Indians of the Northeast that essentially means chief or leader
SOVEREIGNTY: freedom from outside political control

Overview

American Indian peoples developed a wide variety of governmental forms after coming to the New World more than twenty thousand years ago. There were hundreds, perhaps thousands, of different American Indian cultures or "tribes" (a European superimposition) in North America before the coming of Europeans. The types of American Indian societies that existed before contact with Europeans ranged from the simple hunting-and-gathering societies typical of the Great Basin and California culture areas to such highly stratified and complex societies as the Nootka of the Northwest Coast and the hierarchical Natchez tribe in the Southeast. The Natchez were an atypical Southeast culture ruled by a powerful leader with the inherited title "Great Sun." While this great variety of political systems makes generalizations difficult, several clear patterns can be noted.

Native American groups seldom had individual leaders who wielded considerable political power as it is conceived today. Individual chiefs seldom led more than a single village or tribal subgroup. There were some exceptions—Powhatan, for example, led a confederacy of some thirty tribes in the Virginia area at the time English colonists arrived. Nevertheless, the concept of the powerful chief who governed an entire tribe was largely a white invention. The concept fit naturally with the European tradition of kings and queens with a "divine right" to rule. In addition, Europeans found it more expedient to negotiate with a single tribal leader when making treaties. The practice often caused considerable difficulties, however, as tribal members who did not agree with the terms of a treaty did not feel compelled to obey them—in keeping with their traditional practices. By contrast, European colonists and their American descendants—in keeping with their own quite different tradition—believed that a treaty should bind all tribal members.

Decisions were typically made by village or tribal councils. Rather than accepting rule by the majority, Native Americans preferred to make decisions by consensus—discussing and arguing in councils until either everyone agreed with a policy or those who disagreed left. Tribal members who disagreed with a policy were not bound to obey it. If the disagreement concerned a crucial issue, those opposed to a decision might even leave the community and start a new group of their own.

All tribes had to develop ways to deal with people who violated acceptable norms of behavior. Strictly speaking, there was no "crime" in the modern sense, because tribal societies had no written sets of laws (American Indian societies did not have written languages until after contact with Europeans). There were, of course, acts that were considered disruptive or harmful to others and were therefore disapproved of, such as theft, murder, and disputes between individuals and families. Tribes varied in how they handled such problems. In some cases it was up to individual families to settle disputes; in others a tribal council dealt with the problem. In cases of murder, revenge was widely accepted and a murderer could be killed by a member of the victim's family with no censure. In some societies, murder could be atoned for by the paying of a fine to the victim's family. People who were habitually disruptive became social outcasts who faced isolation or expulsion from their communities.

From the beginnings of contact with Europeans, the experience was a catastrophe for Native Americans. Many thousands of people died from diseases brought from Europe such as whooping cough, smallpox, and influenza. Indians who survived could maintain their traditional governments and cultures so long as they could move away from whites and could find sufficient land on which to hunt or to grow food. Space soon became a problem, however, as Indians were frequently forced by whites to move to lands that were too different from their homelands, too poor in resources, or simply too confining to allow traditional lifeways to continue. Nevertheless, through the mid-nineteenth century, many tribes continued their traditional consensus-style governments and left enforcement of law and order in the hands of families or victims.

During the late eighteenth and most of the nineteenth centuries, the U.S. federal government treated each Indian tribe as it did any sovereign state, in a manner that implied equality between the two governments. The government officially recognized Indians as residents of foreign nations that happened to be located within the United States and its territories. Some 371 treaties were signed between Native Americans and representatives of the United States between 1778 and 1871. Treaty making stopped in 1871, however, and the U.S. government thereafter considered tribes to be wards of the state. By the 1870's and 1880's, most tribes in the United States had been assigned reservation lands and confined to them. In many cases, the reservation system led to the disappearance of traditional forms of government; in others, traditional governments found ways to change and adapt to the new situation. In either case, confinement to reservations and the concomitant reliance on the U.S. government to meet basic needs meant that Indian life, even if isolated on a rural reservation, was bound by the dictates of white society and its federal and state governments.

Historically, U.S. government policy has alternated between respecting the integrity of Indian societies and trying to force Indians to assimilate into American society and give up their "primitive" traditional ways. In general, since the 1870's, government policy favored assimilation; this policy in turn implied that Indians did not need to control their own societies, since the societies would gradually disappear as Indians became "Americans."

The general push for assimilation lasted until 1934, when reformers got Congress to pass the Indian Reorganization Act. This law reversed federal policy and called for a measure of tribal self-government. Tribes could now create new governments—but only if they were based on Bureau of Indian Affairs models, rather than on traditional forms. Tribes were given a year within which to vote on new constitutions. One hundred eighty-one tribes voted for "reorganization," while seventy-seven voted against it. Many Indians objected that they had had little influence in creating these new governments and that the new forms went against ancient customs. For example, the BIA model stressed majority rule rather than the traditional consensus. Tribes voting against reorganization resented having whites dictate their choices yet another time.

Under the new law, the standard constitution established a council containing five to eleven members, elected by tribal members for four-year terms, with a chairperson and a vice chair. The council had power "to act in all matters that concern the welfare of the tribe." It was responsible for creating a reservation court system and appointing judges and police officers. The courts could follow tribal customs in handing out verdicts and punishments, but they could hear only cases involving misdemeanors and minor crimes. Major crimes—such as murder, assault, and other felonies—still went to non-Indian courts. Further, Indian courts had no jurisdiction over non-Indians in any matter.

Applications

Further insight into traditional American Indian governments can best be gained by looking at a few tribal governments in greater detail; the Narragansett, Iroquois Confederacy, and Cherokee can serve as examples. The Narragansett Indians, who lived in the area of modern Rhode Island, had a system of government similar to other woodland peoples of the Northeast. Tribespeople lived in small, independent villages, each of which had two hereditary leaders; they seldom met in larger gatherings. One ruler, called the sachem, made decisions on such questions as when to go to war, when to accept peace terms, and how to settle disputes over property, land, or hunting rights. The other leader, who was usually younger and a close relative of the sachem, acted as a diplomat or ambassador, meeting with leaders from other villages to negotiate trading rights or to form alliances in case of attack. The sachem received advice from a council of elders and warriors who had proved their bravery in battle. Sachems could not make rulings unless they had achieved consensus in the council. Council members were expected to do what was best for the group. People who disagreed with any decision were free to move to another village or region. Sachems frequently consulted pawpaws, or spiritual advisers, who were believed to commune with the gods and who could predict the future.

In the area of present New York state, five warring tribes came together around 1500 to make a permanent peace. These members of the Iroquois League pledged themselves to freedom, tolerance, consensus, and brotherhood. The Iroquois lived in large villages, some having populations of more than three thousand. Their homes were "longhouses" inhabited by fifty or more members of extended families. The oldest woman in each house was in charge and acted as judge by settling disputes between family members and village residents. Elderly women played an important role in politics by appointing the warriors who represented the village in tribal councils.

Before the Great Peace, the Iroquois shared a common language but lived in isolated communities and frequently made war on one another. A holy man named Deganawida convinced the five tribes—the Mohawks, Oneidas, Onondagas, Cayugas, and Senecas—that peaceful relations would improve the lives of everyone. Furthermore, neighboring Huron and Chippewa hunters were threatening to move into Iroquois hunting lands. The confederacy established a permanent council of fifty sachems, ten from each tribe, that would meet annually in the summer in Onondaga territory. At first village councils chose sachems, but the position soon became hereditary. Other warriors, the so-called Pine Tree Sachems, could attend council meetings and speak freely, but could not vote in final decisions. Council decisions did not have to be accepted by every tribe. Individual tribes could do what they wanted, so long as they acted peacefully. Iroquois society was matrilineal (descent was traced through the mother's family), and the Iroquois were unusual in that women held village and family positions of power. Membership on the tribal council was, however, reserved for men. The Iroquois Confederacy's form of government was commented on and admired by statesmen of the English colonies and other European societies. Benjamin Franklin was among those impressed by the Iroquois Confederacy, and its style of government almost certainly had some influence on the Founders of the United States.

The Cherokee of northern Georgia had a traditional political system based on a "town" government. The tribe contained dozens of independent towns, held together by language and culture. Towns consisted of all the people who worshipped and prayed together to a particular god. No formal organization existed beyond this local government until the 1760's. Each town had a council that made decisions concerning relations with other towns and tribes. Council members decided such questions as where to plant crops and when to repair religious buildings. In cases involving disputes between individuals over property or personal injury, families and clans settled matters themselves. Even in cases of murder, families, rather than town officials, administered justice. Murder usually led to "blood revenge" and the murderer could be killed by the victim's family.

The entire population of each town—perhaps several hundred people—attended the council meetings, but two groups dominated the proceedings. Much power and prestige went to the religious leader and to the "beloved men," elderly persons renowned for their wisdom. Deliberation was calm and orderly, proceeding until the council reached a unanimous decision. Debates often lasted for several days as leaders tried to persuade others of the correctness of their opinions. If consensus proved impossible, any group leading the opposition was expected to withdraw; it was then not bound by the council's decision.

The Cherokee also provide a poignant example of how contact with whites affected Indian systems of government. By the 1760's, a tribal council had been organized to unify the Cherokee people in their struggle against white expansion. Each village sent a delegation of "headmen" to its meetings. A town could withdraw from the council if it disagreed with its decision, a tradition that made unified resistance impossible. The Cherokee intellectual Sequoia recognized the problem. To help mold tribal unity he invented a Cherokee syllabary in the 1820's so the Cherokee language could be written, and he published a newspaper advocating unity. He also helped draft a constitution.

In 1828 the Cherokee became the first Indian tribe to adopt a written constitution. It created a general council that controlled lands and public property and it negotiated with the United States. It divided Cherokee territory into eight districts, with elected representatives from each on the council. A principal chief, chosen by the council, acted as the executive and could veto council actions. The council passed laws covering road building, budgets, and tax laws, and it acted as a court handing out punishment for horse stealing, murder, theft, and other crimes. It appointed judges to hear minor disputes and outlawed "blood revenge." The traditional framework of village government was replaced by a more centralized administration.

Context

Sovereignty—or rather, a lack of it—has been a primary issue in Indian government since the mid-nineteenth century, and particularly since the reservation system was established. The erosion of Indian sovereignty was a gradual process that occurred because European Americans overwhelmed the Indians in terms of numbers and firepower and because they simply wanted the Indians out of their way.

The placement of Indians on reservations was the most crucial event in the loss of Indian sovereignty, and most American tribes were relocated to reservations by the 1870's. The U.S. government was involved in reservation affairs in numerous ways, including assigning (white) Indian agents to oversee reservations. In 1878, Congress voted to create the Indian Police: Indians themselves would be responsible for maintaining order on reservations. This plan was motivated less by the desire to allow Indians some self-government than by the need to lessen the policing responsibilities of the U.S. Army. In 1883, the Department of the Interior established what were called Courts of Indian Offenses, in which Indian judges had jurisdiction over Indian crime on reservations. By 1900, Courts of Indian Offenses were established on about two-thirds of reservations. In some cases they existed side-by-side with the traditional systems for handling legal issues. (Eventually they fell out of favor, however, and by the 1990's, only a few remained.) In 1885, the Major Crimes Act took away Indian jurisdiction over felonies, turning it over to federal judges.

Passage of the Indian Reorganization Act in 1934 gave a measure of self-government to the tribes that voted to accept the BIA model for a new tribal government. Not even twenty years passed, however, before a new push for assimilation occurred—the "termination" program of the 1950's, under which tribes were urged to terminate their official relationships with the U.S. government. The termination and relocation programs (the relocation program attempted to relocate rural reservation Indians to urban areas) tried to destroy what remained of Indian sovereignty. More than a hundred tribes were dissolved by Congress, and control over their reservations was given to state governments. Termination of reservations was supposed to help achieve the long-term goal of assimilation. Under the relocation program, more than thirty-five thousand Native Americans were relocated to cities, where they were expected to find jobs. By the end of the decade, however, more than 80 percent of these relocated Indians had returned to their old homes and the program was ended. Eventually, many terminated tribes managed to regain their federally recognized tribal status.

The 1960's and 1970's saw renewed demands for sovereignty by American Indian activists. Indians regained some sovereignty under the Indian Civil Rights Act of 1968. Activists in the American Indian Movement (AIM) criticized this bill, however, because it fell far short of restoring full sovereignty. The 1975 Indian Self-Determination and Education Assistance Act granted Indians a greater ability to determine their political, economic, and social development. Traditional forms of government could be re-created, but they were still subject to BIA interference. In 1988, Congress allowed ten indigenous nations to try true self-governance, including economic planning, without BIA controls. The Indian Gaming Regulatory Act of the same year gave Native Americans the right to promote gambling on their lands, subject to state government approval. Revenue from this source has provided the capital to improve the quality of life for many reservation residents, but it has also provoked conflict, sometimes deadly, between tribal supporters and opponents of gambling.

Bibliography

King, Duane H., ed. *The Cherokee Indian Nation: A Troubled History*. Knoxville: University of Tennessee Press, 1979. Essays on the history and culture of the Cherokees, with a detailed examination of their government and its system of law and order.

O'Brien, Sharon. *American Indian Tribal Governments*. Norman: University of Oklahoma Press, 1989. Useful description of the variety of governments found among North American natives. Contains an extensive bibliography and a helpful index.

Olson, James S., and Raymond Wilson. *Native Americans in the Twentieth Century*. Provo, Utah: Brigham Young University Press, 1984. Well-written and interesting survey of government policies affecting reservation and nonreservation Indians. Extensive bibliography.

Simmons, William S. *The Narragansett*. New York: Chelsea House, 1989. Part of the Chelsea House series on the Indians of North America. Each volume contains a history of tribal customs and social structure. The books are well illustrated, have short bibliographies, and are written by experts on each tribe.

Taylor, Graham D. *The New Deal and American Indian Tribalism: The Administration of the Indian Reorganization Act, 1934-35*. Lincoln: University of Nebraska Press, 1980. Discusses the issues involved in the debate over new constitutions. Raises significant questions about the intentions and goals of the reorganizers and presents various sides in the debate.

Wallace, Anthony F. C. *The Death and Rebirth of the Seneca*. New York: Alfred A. Knopf, 1970. Written by an anthropologist who is also a psychiatrist, this is still one of the best accounts of the Seneca. Includes a detailed examination of political, social, and religious traditions and discusses changes in customs brought about by contact with Europeans.

Leslie V. Tischauser

Cross-References

Confederations, p. 391; Federations, p. 675; Indigenous Peoples' Governments, p. 903; Leagues, p. 1072; Nomadic Peoples' Governments, p. 1306; Race and Ethnicity, p. 1654; Tribal Government, p. 2027.

ANARCHISM

Field of study: Political philosophy

Anarchism is a political philosophy that rejects all forms of coercive authority. Anarchists believe that since every form of government is oppressive, the state should be abolished. Anarchists have played leading roles in the movement to abolish slavery and in the pacifist, women's rights, labor, and environmental movements.

Principal terms

ANARCHO-SYNDICALISTS: anarchists who believe that the anarchist society should be organized around trade unions

CHRISTIAN ANARCHISTS: anarchists who reject all governments as sinful and believe the rules of anarchist society should be based on the Bible

COERCIVE AUTHORITY: power to compel obedience through the use of pressure, threat, or force

COMMUNIST ANARCHISTS: anarchists who believe property should be held in common, that individuals should produce what they can and take from a common storehouse what they need

DIRECT ACTION: putting anarchist principles into action immediately in one's own life through such means as defying coercive restrictions or joining with others to form anarchist communities

INDIVIDUALIST ANARCHISTS: anarchists who stress that the individual should be autonomous and that individuals are entitled to own the product of their labor

MORAL SUASION: attempt to use reason to persuade people to accept a particular point of view

Overview

A political philosophy that rejects all forms of coercive authority, anarchism envisions a society without a state. This anarchist society would be a collection of free individuals, each having sovereignty over his or her own life, exercising his or her own judgment to decide what is best to do.

Modern anarchistic philosophy originated in William Godwin's analysis of authority. Godwin, an eighteenth century English philosopher, distinguished between authority based on coercion and authority based on superior knowledge or wisdom (the kind of authority people have in mind when they refer to someone who has great knowledge of a subject as an "authority"). In Godwin's view the second kind of authority is legitimate: individuals should study an issue for themselves and reach an independent judgment or, in areas where individuals lack knowledge, voluntarily defer to leadership of people who know more. The authority of the state, Godwin argued, was authority of the first kind: The state does not possess greater knowledge or wisdom, but greater force. The state does not get people to comply with laws by persuading people that it knows best, but uses violence or the threat of violence. Godwin viewed authority based on coercion as illegitimate. Therefore, he reasoned, the state is illegitimate and should be abolished.

Critics have argued that anarchism would result in chaos, that the state is necessary to maintain order. Anarchists have replied that the state, far from maintaining order, is the greatest producer of social discord. The state, anarchists argue, is a criminal: it steals, through taxes, and it murders, through capital punishment and war. Powerful religious groups use the state to force their moral code on everyone, anarchists contend, and the wealthy use the state to oppress the poor. The "order" created by the state is artificial, repressive, and unjust. Remove the state, anarchists argue, and the result will be a natural social order, which, while not necessarily perfect, will be more harmonious, more just, and more free.

For anarchists, lack of a state does not mean lack of social organization. In anarchist society, individuals might hold themselves aloof or might join with others either on the basis of affinity (as groups of friends or lovers who provide one another mutual aid) or on the basis of economic interest (to produce or exchange goods and services). The nineteenth-century French anarchist Pierre-Joseph Proudhon, for example, envisioned an anarchist society organized around a federation of workers' cooperatives and communes.

As American anarchist Edward Abbey has said, in anarchist society there would be no rulers, but there would be rules. An anarchist society, in order to work, would require self-government. For anarchists, the freedom of the individual to do what he or she thinks best is of fundamental importance. In an anarchist society, then, people must be tolerant and must restrain themselves from interfering with the freedom of others: individuals would be free, in other words, to do what they wanted as long as they did not interfere with the ability of others to do the same.

Christian anarchists, such as author Leo Tolstoy, go further. They see violence as a sin. Because all governments rest on violence, Christian anarchists argue, all governments are sinful and should be abolished. Christian anarchists recognize no laws but God's and believe the rules of anarchist society should be based on the Bible.

As historian George Woodcock has pointed out, asceticism pervades anarchist thinking. In the anarchist vision of society, people would not have wealth and luxury. They would work only enough to fulfill simple, basic needs and would spend the rest of their time in leisure, contemplation, and spiritual pursuits.

In part, anarchists have been suspicious of wealth because they have viewed it as distracting from intellectual and spiritual concerns, but anarchists also have mistrusted wealth because they believe great wealth concentrated in the hands of the few gives the wealthy minority the power to oppress the majority. Anarchists have been especially critical of capitalism and the disparity in wealth that that system produces. Anarchists disagree, however, on how the economy should be organized.

Communist anarchists such as Pyotr Kropotkin have argued that property should be held in common: Individuals would have access to communally owned machinery, tools, and resources; they would produce according to their abilities; and they would take what they need from a common storehouse. Individualist anarchists would abolish rent, profit, interest, and dividends, but would recognize the right of the individual to own the product of his or her own labor.

Because anarchists view government as illegitimate, they have rejected political means—voting or legislation—to achieve the anarchist ideal. Instead anarchists have relied on moral suasion or direct action. Moral suasion is the attempt to reason with people, to persuade them to accept the anarchist point of view. Direct action is the defiance of law, the putting of anarchist principles immediately into practice, without waiting for the laws to be changed or for everyone to be persuaded to accept anarchism. Direct action may include a general strike, for example, or refusal to be drafted into the military. For some anarchists direct action includes violent revolution. Anarchists reject the idea of an organized revolution commanded by heroic leaders. Instead anarchists envision a spontaneous revolution in which each individual makes his or her own decision to revolt. Some anarchists have advocated terrorist acts such as the assassination of government officials to inspire a revolution by showing people how to liberate themselves. Anarchists who have advocated violence have been in the minority. The majority of anarchists have argued that the creation of a nonviolent society—the goal of anarchism—requires nonviolent means.

Applications

Two examples illustrate direct action. In his essay "Civil Disobedience" (1849), Henry David Thoreau shows how an individual might put anarchism into practice in his or her own life. Thoreau's analysis of authority is like Godwin's. Majority rule in America, Thoreau argues, is not based on the fact that the majority knows more or is a better judge of right or wrong than the individual, but on the fact that the majority is physically stronger. Thoreau argues that people are not obligated to obey the majority when it is wrong: One is obligated to do only what one thinks is right.

Thoreau urged individuals to refuse allegiance to the state. Thoreau did not call for people to challenge the state on every issue: He paid his highway tax, he said, because he wanted to be a good neighbor, and he was willing to accept the authority of the state on issues where he thought the state knew best. But in cases in which the state required people to violate their own sense of right conduct, in which the state required people to be part of an injustice to others, Thoreau urged people to break the law, as he violated it when he refused to pay his poll tax because the government supported slavery. Thoreau called on the government to tolerate those who had withdrawn their allegiance, and he foresaw a day when every individual would have declared independence and a peaceful revolution would be complete.

Modern Times, a community founded by anarchists Josiah Warren and Stephen Pearl Andrews on Long Island, New York, in 1851, shows how a group of people might institute anarchism among themselves. Warren had seen the failure of New Harmony, a community established in Indiana by Scottish philanthropist Robert Owen, a disciple of Godwin. Warren attributed the failure to New Harmony's communism. Some members, while sharing equally in the community's property, failed to do their share of work, and their failure caused New Harmony's economic collapse.

Warren reasoned that in a communist community, people had a duty to work hard since their actions affected the welfare of everyone. But that duty, he argued, encroached upon individual freedom. Only by separating everyone's economic interest from everyone else's could individuals be free. People, Warren concluded, should hold private property and support themselves through their own labor so that how much they might choose to work would affect no one but themselves.

At Modern Times people owned small cottages and individual lots and supported themselves by farming or working at a trade. Individuals were entitled to own the product of their own labor. To exchange goods and services, the community instituted "labor notes," issued by individuals promising to pay the bearer so many hours of labor. One member, for example, promised to pay in sign painting, another in shoemaking. Each person became his or her own banker issuing currency backed by the reputation of that person in the community. Residents would accept the currency if the person could be trusted to do the work. Residents at Modern Times eliminated profit. The time it took to produce an item determined the item's price. To purchase an item, a resident would pay the producer the number of hours of labor the item took to make.

People at Modern Times held a variety of beliefs. Some residents were free thinkers, others belonged to various religious groups. There were antislavery reformers, women's rights advocates, vegetarians, and antialcohol and antitobacco people. What allowed people with differing views to live in harmony was agreement to obey the rule of individual sovereignty: Individuals were free to do as they pleased as long as they did not interfere with the right of others to do the same. In short, the only rule of the community was "mind your own business." If a person refused to obey the rule of individual sovereignty and encroached on the freedom of others, members of the community dealt with the problem by shunning the person—members refused to buy from, sell to, or speak to the offender (in the decade-long history of Modern Times only one such incident took place). Despite lack of government, courts, or police, Modern Times had no theft and no violence.

Residents of Modern Times also practiced free love. Since anarchists reject the state and its laws, anarchists also reject the idea of legal marriage. Residents of Modern Times were free to do whatever they wished sexually as long as they did not interfere with the freedom of others. Some residents had a variety of lovers; others practiced monogamy. One man lived in a polygamous arrangement with three women. It became the custom at Modern Times, if one considered oneself married, to wear a red thread on one's finger; to end the marriage one untied the thread.

Context

Since the nineteenth century, anarchists in Europe and the United States have been active on behalf of many social causes. In America in the early nineteenth century, the Christian anarchist William Lloyd Garrison founded the movement to abolish slavery, and he and other Christian anarchists were leaders in the pacifist and women's rights movements. Individualist anarchists in nineteenth century America campaigned for sexual freedom and defended free speech against government attempts to censor material that had sexual content.

In Europe in the nineteenth century, anarchists were concerned mainly about the poverty of the working class. The dominant forms of anarchism in Europe were anarcho-syndicalism—which wanted anarchist society to be organized around trade unions—and communist anarchism. In 1864 anarchists joined with Marxist socialists and with trade unionists to form the International Workingmen's Association (First International). European workers who immigrated into the United States in the late nineteenth century brought the ideas of communist anarchism with them, and anarchists became prominent in the American labor movement.

Some anarchists in the labor movement advocated "propaganda of the deed," terrorist acts meant to inspire a workers' revolution. In the United States, anarchist Alexander Berkman made an unsuccessful attempt to assassinate Henry Clay Frick, manager of one of Andrew Carnegie's steel mills. In Europe, anarchists assassinated the king of Italy, the empress of Austria-Hungary, the president of France, and the prime minister of Spain. This violence created in the public mind an image of anarchists as being bloodthirsty and evil, though only a minority of anarchists advocated violence. These acts of violence also brought government repression of anarchists in Europe and America. (Hundreds of American anarchists were deported in 1919, including the leading American anarchist, Emma Goldman.) By the early twentieth century, the anarchist movement was in decline.

Anarchism emerged again in the youth rebellion of the 1960's. The writings of American anarchist Paul Goodman were influential among young radicals. Anarchist communes appeared in the United States. The civil rights and antiwar movements drew on direct-action tactics associated with anarchism: street demonstrations and civil disobedience. Such radicals as Abbie Hoffman in America and Daniel Cohn-Bendit, leader of the student uprising in France in 1968, found in anarchist ideas a powerful instrument for attacking racism, poverty, war, and government bureaucracies. Anarcho-feminist groups began to attack the oppression of women.

In the United States in the 1980's, anarchism was connected with the environmental movement. American writer Edward Abbey denounced capitalism for wasting resources and destroying the environment, suggested that the ascetic anarchist life is more in harmony with nature, and urged environmentalists to commit acts of sabotage against developers and timber companies. Abbey's ideas inspired the radical environmentalist group Earth First!

Throughout its history, what has distinguished anarchism from other political philosophies has been anarchism's uncompromising demand for individual freedom and uncompromising hostility to oppression in all forms—whether oppression of the individual by the state, the poor by the rich, women by men, or one race by another.

Bibliography

Abbey, Edward. *One Life at a Time, Please.* New York: Henry Holt, 1988. Essays that introduce Abbey's anarchist politics and his environmental concerns.

Ditzion, Sidney. *Marriage, Morals, and Sex in America: A History of Ideas.* Expanded edition. New York: Octagon Books, 1969. Study of American sexual attitudes with information about anarchists' ideas regarding sex, including a discussion of William Godwin's sexual theories and an account of the role American anarchists played in campaigns for sexual freedom and free speech.

Goldman, Emma. *Anarchism, and Other Essays.* Reprint. New York: Dover, 1969. Goldman defines anarchism and deals with the questions of political violence and the relationship between anarchism and feminism.

Hoffman, Abbie. *Soon to Be a Major Motion Picture.* New York: Putnam, 1980. Autobiography of the leading American anarchist of the 1960's.

Kedward, Harry Roderick. *The Anarchists: The Men Who Shocked an Era.* New York: American Heritage Press, 1971. Brief history of anarchism, concentrating on the years from 1880 to 1914. Useful for its illustrations.

Krimerman, Leonard I., and Lewis Perry, eds. *Patterns of Anarchy: A Collection of Writings on the Anarchist Tradition.* Garden City, N.Y.: Anchor Books, 1966. Best anthology of anarchists' writings. Contains not only selections from famous anarchists like William Godwin, Leo Tolstoy, and Pyotr Kropotkin, but also from more obscure anarchists such as Benjamin Tucker and Adin Ballou. Bibliography.

Le Guin, Ursula K. *The Dispossessed.* New York: Harper & Row, 1974. Excellent novel by a noted science fiction writer. Speculates what life in an anarchist society would be like.

Shatz, Marshall S., ed. *The Essential Works of Anarchism.* New York: Quadrangle Books, 1972. An anthology with both classic anarchist writings by such people as Godwin and Proudhon and anarchist writings from the twentieth century by such people as Paul Goodman and Daniel Cohn-Bendit.

Stern, Madeleine B. *The Pantarch: A Biography of Stephen Pearl Andrews.* Austin: University of Texas Press, 1968. Biography of one of the most important individualist anarchists in nineteenth century America. Contains an account of the Modern Times community.

Woodcock, George. *Anarchism: A History of Libertarian Ideas and Movements.* Cleveland: Meridian Books, 1962. A history of anarchism, contains an excellent discussion of anarchist ideas and chapters on each of the major anarchist thinkers. Weak on American anarchism. Bibliography.

Donald M. Whaley

Cross-References

Activist Politics, p. 7; Anarchism in Marxist Thought, p. 72; Burke's Political Philosophy, p. 171; Civil Disobedience, p. 285; Civil Unrest and Rioting, p. 317; Force, p. 712; Military Conscription and Conscientious Objection, p. 1185; Political Philosophy, p. 1505; Political Violence, p. 1539; Protest Movements, p. 1621; Radicalism, p. 1661; Revolutions, p. 1738; The State, p. 1878; Terrorism, p. 1962; Utopianism, p. 2084.

ANARCHISM IN MARXIST THOUGHT

Field of study: Political philosophy

Marxist anarchism is one part of the philosophy of Karl Marx. Marxist thought is the foundation for socialism and communism. It is so open to interpretation that many different forms of socialism have emerged over the last 150 years, including democratic socialism, communism, theological socialism, and anarchism.

Principal terms

ANARCHISM: concept of a world with little or no government

BOURGEOISIE: business interests that employ workers and, in Marx's philosophy, exploit them

CLASS STRUGGLE: Marxist idea that classes clash as the workers (proletariat) seek to improve their lot at the expense of the middle class (bourgeoisie) and upper-class capitalists

DICTATORSHIP OF THE PROLETARIAT: concept that once the labor revolution was successful a period of worker dictatorship would ensue until the final establishment of socialism

NATIONALISM: people's support of their nation and their opposition to internationalism

PROLETARIAT: the working classes, especially urban workers. Marx paid little attention to the peasants

SOCIALISM: term applied to the political philosophy of Karl Marx

Overview

Marxist anarchism is one aspect, or perhaps area of interpretation, of the philosophy of Karl Marx (1818-1883). It has proven to be open to interpretation and misinterpretation by his followers and opponents in the nineteenth and twentieth centuries. There is evidence that Marx was not the founder of anarchism at all and in fact opposed it. Michael Bakunin (1814-1876), a Russian socialist, believed that government was the problem that humanity had to eradicate. This is the central tenet of anarchism.

Marx rejected this assault on the state, insisting that the capitalist economic system was the enemy and that it had to be destroyed. Marx and Bakunin clashed in 1872 and Bakunin was forced out of the First Communist International. Later anarchists believed that anarchism would come after socialism had been adopted in the world, and that therefore anarchism was the inevitable conclusion of socialism. When anarchism was established, the world would be a peaceful place where people would guide their own lives and would get along together. Governments, if they existed at all, would serve to carry out the wishes of the world's population. Opponents of anarchism, however, could point to the many violent acts of anarchists in Europe and the United States and to Bakunin's support for violent revolution. This led them to claim that anarchists were destroyers of society, bomb throwers, assassins, robbers, and murderers. The supporters of anarchism maintained that the people who carried out these acts were not true anarchists but merely took the name and believed that anarchism meant complete freedom with no restrictions upon the individual. In the public mind, Marxist anarchism came to be associated with violence and with the idea that there should be no governments, concepts that frightened most people.

Among the many interpreters of Marxist anarchism three may be examined as the most prominent. Herbert Marcuse (1898-1979) came to the conclusion that Marxism could not be adopted in the Western world through a workers' rebellion because the lot of the workers had improved, particularly during and following World War II. Therefore, other means to enlist the workers had to be found. Such means included ecological crises or the oppression of races and women. In other words, the old, traditional Marxist concept of the workers' revolution based on economic need and miserable working conditions needed to be shifted to workers' revolution resulting from the mishandling of nature and the oppression of women and minorities. Marcuse believed that the result of revolution had to be anarchism.

György Lukács (1885-1971), a Hungarian, emphasized the traditional Marxist view that radical class consciousness was the base for a socialist revolution. He believed that even though the economic lives of the workers were improving in the twentieth century there was still much unhappiness among the working classes, especially when they viewed the great wealth of the capitalists, which contrasted so sharply with the workers' economic conditions. He had already witnessed Marxist revolution in Russia and was convinced that ultimately the rest of the world would experience a similar revolution. He also noted that the middle and upper levels of the peasantry in Russia supported the anarchist idea of a stateless society.

Antonio Gramsci (1891-1937), an Italian Marxist, eventually came to conclude that class power would ultimately overturn the capitalist world but that violence would not be required to bring about the revolution. He was a member of the Italian Socialist Party and then participated in establishing the Italian Communist Party. He believed that socialism could be adopted through the ballot box. As proof of this idea he managed to gain election to the legislature and served in the Italian parliament in 1924; however, when the Fascists came to power he was arrested, sentenced to twenty years in prison, and died there. He wrote that the submerged class would be led to insurrection peacefully rather than violently. It was perhaps his prison experience which convinced him to implore his followers to shun violence and rely on peaceful means to gain their objectives. His conclusion, however, was that once the revolution occurred, whether peaceful or violent, the end result would be anarchism. Marcuse, Lukács, and Gramsci differed on the means to the ultimate objective—social revolution and anarchism—but all forecast anarchism as the future of humanity.

As the Marxists of the twentieth century wrote on what Marx meant, the variety of ideas that emerged was enormous. This was possible because the world had changed so greatly from the period in which Marx wrote. Marx lived in an age when monarchies dominated, when workers were exploited mercilessly, and when upper- and middle-class capitalists dominated the economy. In his era there was no computer network, no aviation industry, and no telecommunications, all of which have made the world smaller. These developments have not borne out the Marxist idea of internationalism, as might be expected. Instead, nationalism has grown.

Additionally, when Marx claimed that a proletarian revolution would destroy capitalism he did not foresee the fact that labor unions would challenge the established order and that government and business would take steps to halt the injustices that were commonplace in his world and thereby head off the threat of working-class revolution. For example, inheritance and income taxes reduced the wealth of the capitalist class and brought it closer to the working classes. At the same time, free public schools were created that enabled at least a portion of the proletariat to gain an education. World War I created a labor shortage, which enabled the proletariat to press for reforms and force the capitalist class to grant those reforms.

Still, according to theory, when economic problems became great enough, the proletariat would put aside its internecine hostility and direct its anger toward the capitalists. At that time revolution would break out and the result would be communism and the dictatorship of the proletariat. After a period of dictatorship the workers would gain their rights and improve their economic status. When the masses lived in liberty, and when everyone worked and everyone was cared for, the state would no longer have any function. The state, based on force, would not be necessary because there would be no one to coerce. Therefore, the state would whither away and die, and anarchism would finally come to pass. Some anarchists, however, Alexander Berkman (1870-1936) among them, did not trust the Marxist dictatorship of the proletariat as a stage toward anarchism. They believed that the revolution, when it came, should pass immediately to anarchism, to freedom and liberty with no government. Berkman even quoted Thomas Jefferson: "That government that governs least, governs best." For Berkman this was the essence of anarchism. Therefore, the ultimate objective of all Marxists, anarchists included, was little or no government. The difference, however, is that communists envision a series of stages to reach the point of no government while anarchists are convinced that society can move directly from capitalism to anarchy (a stateless, classless, and propertyless society), without intervening stages, particularly without the dictatorship of the proletariat. Anarchists, socialists, and communists all accept some of Marx's philosophy but interpret it differently.

Anarchists differ from other socialists in the presentation of their ideas. The concepts of Marx, Friedrich Engels (1820-1895), and Georg Wilhelm Friedrich Hegel (1770-1831) can be very difficult to understand. Their presentation is frequently verbose, with large numbers of complex sentences. Anarchists, on the other hand, tend to make a conscious effort to keep their writing simple so that all may understand it. Their view was that they were writing for those who had little education, and if they did not write in simple language, they could not get their ideas across to the people they were trying to enlist in their movement.

Applications

Anarchists for the most part have been associated with violence. On May 3, 1886, a small group of anarchists protested police action in breaking up a strike. The next day, as the protesters made antigovernment speeches in the Haymarket Square in Chicago, the police attempted to disband their meeting. Someone threw a bomb at the police. Seven anarchists were arrested although no one knew who actually threw the bomb. The seven were convicted and sentenced to death. Two were pardoned, one committed suicide while in prison, and the remaining four were executed. The general public supported the executions because people feared anarchists' supposedly violent program. To Marxist anarchists these supposed bomb throwers were not true anarchists but merely violent individuals who did not understand Marxist anarchism.

   In Europe the major achievement of the socialists, communists, and to a lesser degree anarchists came in Russia during World War I, when a workers' rebellion overthrew the monarchy and established a republican government. Many different philosophies were represented among the revolutionaries; a civil war was fought until one group, the Bolsheviks, emerged successful in 1920. While anarchists had been hopeful that this successful revolution would bring socialism and eventually anarchism to Russia, they were disappointed by what the Bolsheviks did once in power. Marxist anarchists generally came to oppose the Marxist Bolshevik government. This was a clear distinction between Marxist communists and Marxist anarchists. Bolsheviks wanted to force people to live in communism while Marxist anarchists wanted people to choose anarchism voluntarily. Consequently, the Bolsheviks carried out widespread arrests of anarchists, and those who survived decided that the Russian Revolution was not for them. Pyotr Kropotkin (1824-1921), one of the leading advocates of Marxist anarchism, was among those who became disenchanted with the Bolsheviks. He spent the last years of his life writing critical articles about the Russian Revolution. Other anarchists went underground, and many emigrated to other countries. They continued to work for anarchism, but their great hope in the Russian Revolution died. They concentrated on bringing their message to other European countries and to the United States.

   In the United States, the majority of the population came to fear the violence of anarchism. Two anarchists, Nicola Sacco and Bartolomeo Vanzetti, were arrested in 1920 for robbery and murder in Massachusetts. The evidence against them was flimsy, but they were convicted and the antianarchist mood of the nation helped the jury convict them. Their appeals lasted for seven years, but when all efforts were finally exhausted they were electrocuted in 1927. This famous case was a major theme for reform among liberals and radicals in the decade of the 1920's, but hysterical fear of anarchism overshadowed the efforts of socialists, communists, and anarchists to exploit the case for their benefit.

   Later, in Spain, a so-called Popular Front composed of republicans, socialists, labor unions, anarchists, and communists won the elections in 1936. One estimate numbered the anarchists, unionists, and other left-wing groups at a million-and-a-half men and women. Of these, probably thirty thousand were hardcore anarchists, with the remainder being union members, communists, and socialists. The country's right-wing forces were not willing to accept the electoral result, and soon a civil war ensued. Eventually, Germany and Italy entered the struggle on the side of the right-wing army, while the

Soviet Union came to the assistance of the Popular Front government. The United States, England, and France, while opposing Germany and Italy and their intervention in the war, refused to assist the Popular Front government because of the participation of communists and anarchists in the Popular Front and because of the entry of the Soviet Union on the side of the Popular Front. Public sentiment in the Western democracies helped contribute to their governments' inaction. Ultimately, the right wing was successful, the Popular Front was crushed, and the hopes of anarchists for a free society came to an end.

For Marxist anarchists, the brief life of the Popular Front was a clear indication that anarchism could work, in contrast to the Russian Revolution, which destroyed anarchism. In Spain, anarchism succeeded for only a brief time and did not reach the final stage of a classless, governmentless society, not because of any flaws in the system but because fascism was able to defeat anarchism on the battlefield.

In both Europe and the United States, the press played a prominent role in building public opinion against Marxist anarchists. The anarchists' reputation for violence was important to the newspapers in their quest to sell their product. Few journalists or editorialists tried to examine anarchism seriously. Instead, by focusing on the violence associated with the movement, they stirred up the public. Unfortunately, anarchism came in for a significant amount of mindless criticism. Those who studied it carefully and dispassionately were often college professors, whose books and articles did not gain much attention from the general public.

Context

Marxist anarchism emerged as a political philosophy in the late nineteenth century. It grew out of a stew of ideas among the leading communists, who were struggling to put together a philosophy that all could accept. Marx himself did not agree that the state was the major obstacle to the development of communism but that capitalism, and the economic system the capitalists controlled, was. The anarchists who based their concepts on Marx were a small part of the communist movement. Some of their members, and others who simply took the name anarchist, tried to overthrow governments by resorting to violence. All anarchists unfairly became the objects of fear and hatred on the part of politicians and the general public. By the early twentieth century, anarchists were notorious in Europe and the United States. They came to be associated with immigrants in the United States and contributed to the hostility directed at those who spoke little or no English. When strikes or any act of civil disobedience occurred, or when any clash between police and strikers or protestors took place, the public immediately assumed European immigrants were the leaders and that those leaders were Marxist anarchists.

Anarchists gathered a large number of headlines in both Europe and the United States in the late nineteenth and early twentieth centuries but their number was small. When the Russian Revolution came in 1917, communists replaced anarchists as the villains in the minds of people in the West. The last great surge of anarchism was in Spain's Popular Front government in 1936. Following World War II, the communists overshadowed the anarchists. In that period some anarchists continued to preach their philosophy, but their numbers were so few that they no longer commanded much attention in the world. Ultimately, even communism has been in decline. Marxism, then, has steadily declined as a challenger to capitalism, and it appears that instead of capitalism being destroyed as Marx prophesied, it is Marxist communism and anarchism that is on the way to extinction.

Bibliography

Berkman, Alexander. *What Is Communist Anarchism?* New York: Dover, 1972. Examination of anarchism—what it is and what it is not—in an easy-to-read format.

Goodway, David, ed. *For Anarchism: History, Theory and Practice.* London: Routledge & Keegan Paul, 1989. Articles on anarchism in different countries and anarchism as it relates to Marxism.

Gottlieb, Roger S., ed. *An Anthology of Western Marxism: From Lukács and Gramsci to Socialist-Feminism.* New York: Oxford University Press, 1989. Three of this volume's articles are taken from the works of Marcuse, Gramsci, and Lukács.

Gramsci, Antonio. *Antonio Gramsci: Pre-Prison Writings.* Edited by Richard Bellamy. Translated by Virginia Cox. Cambridge, England: Cambridge University Press, 1994. Compilation of Gramsci's ideas on a wide range of subjects from Marx to soccer.

Lukács, György. *Conversations with Lukács: Hans Heinz Holz, Leo Kofler, Wolfgang Abendroth.* Edited by Theo Pinkus. Cambridge, Mass.: MIT Press, 1975. Examines the role of class in society and in politics.

Marcuse, Herbert. *Counter Revolution and Revolt.* Boston: Beacon Press, 1972. Discusses the integration of the working class into the capitalist class, altering the Marxist concept of revolution. A readable volume.

Marx, Karl, and Friedrich Engels. *The Communist Manifesto.* Edited by Joseph Katz. Translated by Samuel Moore. New York: Washington Square Press, 1964. Pamphlet written for workers, today read largely by college students. It sets forth the ideas of class struggle and internationalism.

Novack, George. *Polemics in Marxist Philosophy.* New York: Monad Press, 1978. Sections deal with György Lukács and the American labor movement.

Pennock, J. Roland, and John W. Chapman, eds. *Anarchism.* New York: New York University Press, 1978. A series of articles on various aspects of anarchism.

Jack Ray Thomas

Cross-References

ARISTOCRACY, OLIGARCHY, AND PLUTOCRACY

Field of study: Political philosophy

Aristocracy, oligarchy, and plutocracy are systems of rule by the hereditary elite, the select, and the wealthy, respectively. All three are forms of government wherein ruling groups are small in numbers.

Principal terms
ARISTOCRACY: rule by a portion of the population that is selected by heredity and marriage
DEMOCRACY: rule by the people or by representatives selected by popular vote
ELITE: the few people at the top of a system of social stratification
MONARCHY: rule by a single person often selected by heredity or arranged marriage
OCHLOCRACY: rule by the whole—mob rule
OLIGARCHY: rule by a few
PLUTOCRACY: rule by a portion of the population selected on the basis of wealth
SELF-DETERMINATION: assumption of independent government
TIMOCRACY: rule by those who own property, also rule by military leaders
TYRANNY: rule by single person maintained in office by force and given to arbitrary conduct

Overview

A system of government with a long and successful history is aristocracy. The term, coined by Aristotle, comes from the Greek *aristos*, meaning "best," and *archia*, meaning "rule." It is a government composed of a hereditary elite. Aristotle's meaning, however, was simply "rule by the best." Aristotle believed that the best would be few, rather than many. In the Greek city-states of his time, the number of men directly involved in the diverse governmental bodies was a sizeable proportion of the entire male population. Plato and Aristotle knew from experience that this was unworkable for very large populations. In fact, Plato argued that the population of each city should be limited to 5,040 citizens.

In early Greece the population of states such as Athens was divided into three nearly equal portions: native-born citizens, resident foreigners, and slaves. Since women, foreigners, and slaves had no part in the government, the body of government was taken from a fraction of the population. From this fraction a best part was desired. Curiously, a common attribute of early political philosophies is that the selected best would be those with the most education. Plato even proposes in his *Republic* that those selected to rule be taken aside in their youth and educated in isolation. Other selections of those who would best rule were proposed as well: the trades, the teaching class, and those whose military experience had given them leadership qualities.

Another group suggested was the farmers, whose dependence on the soil, the only true wealth in ancient times, made them the most sensitive to the state's interests. This reasoning is allied to the justification for timocracy, or rule by those who own things of value, specifically real property. In theory, people who own land or houses have the skills for managing property and the desire to see it protected. Under such a plan the rulers, whether farmers or landowners, are the haves rather than the have-nots.

Aristocrats tend to be owners of property, but that is not their distinguishing characteristic. Unlike timocracy, in which the qualification for rule is ownership, aristocracy perpetuates itself by hereditary succession. The ruling class evolves a culture distinct from that of the lower classes. It becomes a model of style, patterns of speech, educational curricula, and even forms of amusement. For those in the class, it is safest to allow only those who are born into that culture to continue its traditions.

A result of the hereditary system of choosing those who have power is the evolution of the aristocracy into a plutocracy. A strictly hereditary system of succession fails when family fortunes change, since it has no economic base except family property, which may diminish in value with each generation. Eventually, the newly rich emerge as a new, or merge into the old, aristocracy by virtue of their ability to buy land, marriages, and titles. Membership in the ruling group belongs to the highest bidder.

As entry into the aristocracy becomes a matter of sheer economics, the culture of the nation changes. Accumulation of wealth is seen as the primary aspiration. From the lowest member in government to the highest, rule is by those who can afford it.

Aristocracies have maintained themselves for centuries, however, as a result of certain conditions. One condition is that wealth may not be diminished from generation to generation if only one child (typically the oldest male) inherits all the family's wealth, and if that one child marries another aristocrat. Another condition is that the aristocracy, being wealthy, tends to stay that way, leaving scant opportunity for others to become rich and buy their way into power. In this way aristocracies have achieved their long and successful hold on power.

In most nations the total amount of wealth is fixed. Except for nations that have an exportable source of income such as rare metals, crops, or petroleum, growth of wealth among the few comes at the expense of the many. While the wealthy have reserves to sustain them in the face of minor losses, the poor, already at the subsistence level, do not. Reverses in the fortunes of the entire nation may burden the poor to the extent that their only recourse is confiscation of the property of the wealthy by revolution.

This leads one to conclude that there is a fundamental flaw in plutocracies. What is more, upon further consideration, it becomes clear that every form of government is unstable. In illustration, Herodotus mentions this curious circular reasoning: A monarchy is the best aristocracy, concentrating the best in one person. Unfortunately, the monarch, being human, is tempted to tyranny. Democracy is the best medicine to combat tyranny until it becomes so universal that it degenerates into mob rule and anarchy. The people then need aristocracy to restore order and function. In an aristocracy, the logical form is monarchy, and so on.

Despite this inherent tendency in all governments to become unstable, some governments have endured for many years. The usual explanation for long-lasting governments is that they result from a balance in the various forces that tend toward instability, from an organic flexibility in the face of change, and from a broad acceptance of the social structure on the part of its members.

Oligarchy in its many forms is the most common form of government. Only the smallest government entity can afford the cumbersome processes of true democracy or ochlocracy. The so-called democracy of many modern states is not a government by popular rule. It is a republic in which the ruling oligarchy is selected by a democratic process, but the actual rule is by a very small fraction of the whole people.

Similarly, constitutional monarchies have a small ruling group as advisers and limiters of the monarch's power. As in the true oligarchy, the monarch rules at the indulgence of the nobility or legislature. The monarch must look to them for personal protection, raising of taxes from the people, maintenance of public works, and provision for defense of the state. Even this logical and effective system must evolve. Services provided to the monarch by the nobility are more effectively managed by central authorities of specialists. Eventually the monarch's protectors become the nucleus of a true aristocracy and the monarch becomes a figurehead of the government, having only an advisory capacity.

Plutocracy is a form of aristocracy that is also characteristic of many republics. To succeed in democratic elections, candidates must advertise to the voters, and advertising is so expensive that in effect only the wealthy may run for office. They must also build a base of support among those who aspire to lesser offices, sometimes by buying appointments. While this practice seems not entirely honorable, it is the system of selection extant in many modern democracies. This system, too, is mutable; in poor economic times, popular feeling rises against the government and those in office are replaced with newcomers.

Applications

The oligarchic form of government is nearly universal. The few rule the many in nearly all countries; what varies is the matter of who the few are.

In the United States and other nations oligarchy takes the form of the democratic republic, wherein a group selected by popular vote is empowered to rule. As originally conceived by the Founders, the government of the United States was to be composed of those most able, the supposition being that public service would be an onerous but necessary duty of those best suited to serve. The system evolved so that gradually the government consisted of those most willing to serve in order to reap the benefits of the power and the wealth that power creates. Instead of a burden to be borne by worthy men taking time from their own affairs, government in the United States has become a boon to those willing to live off the efforts of the people.

Another example of evolution of oligarchic government is that of England, where there are two legislative chambers, the House of Lords and the House of Commons.

Both bodies were once empowered to rule, but now the aristocratic portion, the House of Lords, has been stripped of most of its power, including action on financial bills, a pivotal function. This is just one recent step along the road to democracy in that country. Once a monarchy, England's government evolved into an assisted monarchy. Then, as more power was taken from the crown, England slowly became a constitutional monarchy and now, curiously, it is ruled by a single-chamber "bicameral" legislature.

In modern republics considerable power is concentrated in another elite, the "cabinet." Nominally a part of the executive branch of government and therefore without a law-making function, the cabinet is often composed of experts of narrow experience. Legislators often defer to the cabinet members in their special areas of judgment. In critical issues, such as commerce, defense, and public health, the cabinet members offer expert advice, however one-sided politically. The less-informed legislators may defer to the content, if not the political intent, of these experts.

Finally, an elite that exerts a large influence on the modern state is the judicial branch. Laws are enacted by the legislature and carried out by the presiding executive officer. They are only effective, however, so long as they can be defended. If there is popular feeling that they are not in keeping with the general framework of the state's laws, the laws may be challenged.

Context

As industrial nations of the West strive to assist emergent countries to develop representative governments, thought must be given to the inherent instability of these systems. The emergent countries for the most part are not rich enough in resources to delay the inevitable; given power in the government, the poor among their populations will exert pressures to improve their condition. Many of these regions are recently defined, either as a conglomeration of traditional small chiefdoms or as newly separated portions of larger entities previously forced together by the Western nations after World War II. In either situation the emergent countries have no political traditions resembling those that their mentors intend them to form. Most of these entities were previously monarchies.

The idea of self-determination, which ended the Spanish, French, and British empires was a European invention hard for the peoples who had lived under these empires to understand. Understanding self-determination at the individual level was even harder. Freed of the British rule, Kenya experimented disastrously with ochlocracy before a republican government was created. Every difficulty in forming and maintaining stable governments in politically mature nations is exacerbated in newly formed states. There is the pressure of poverty; there is a tradition of plutocracy or tyrannical monarchy; there is in even the poorest new nation a core of wealthy to whom the citizens are inured to defer; and there is a paucity of educated persons from which to recruit a group of qualified administrators.

More tragically, the ruling government of many emergent nations is of different cultural background, nationality, or race from the general population. When there arises any question of establishing a representative government, the wall between the traditional ruling ethnic group and the rest of the population must be made invisible. Suddenly, after perhaps centuries of an "us-versus-them" culture, the two groups must work together so that a new selection of leaders may be made.

It is likely that experience with self-determination among the more affluent members of the old regimes will serve as an example to the elite in newer nations, but the newer nations' instabilities will have to be controlled. The poor must be succored by donations from outside or forced redistribution of the wealth that is in the hands of the traditional plutocracy. A profile of representation must be made so that no one of the traditionally inimical groups can preponderate.

Bibliography

Aristotle. *Aristotle's Politics*. Translated by Benjamin Jowett. New York: Modern Library, 1943. Important in this translation is an expanded table of contents using the philosopher's own organization.

Durant, Will. *The Story of Philosophy*. Garden City, N.Y.: Garden City Publishing, 1927. Historical account of philosophical thought from Plato to John Dewey.

Ebenstein, William. *Great Political Thinkers*. New York: Holt, Rinehart and Winston, 1960. Readings of the philosophers and religious leaders from Plato to Freud.

Melden, A. I., ed. *Ethical Theories*. Englewood Cliffs, N.J.: Prentice-Hall, 1950. Readings of seventeen major classical and modern philosophers on the question of ethics.

Sabine, George. *A History of Political Theory*. New York: Holt, Rinehart and Winston, 1961. History of political thought as it was expressed in lay and church governments from before Plato to World War II.

Schmandt, Henry, and Paul Steinbicker. *Fundamentals of Government*. Milwaukee, Wis.: Bruce, 1963. Treatise on the elements of government, types of government, and their relationship to the current governments of modern states.

Strauss, Leo, and Joseph Cropsey. *History of Political Philosophy*. Chicago: Rand McNally, 1963. Discussion of the political thought of philosophers from Plato to Dewey, including John Calvin and Martin Luther. It has a historical rather than theoretical focus.

Loring D. Emery

Cross-References

Aristotle's Political Philosophy, p. 83; The City-State, p. 272; Class Conflict, p. 331; Dante's Political Philosophy, p. 483; Equality and Egalitarianism, p. 630; Government Types, p. 785; Ochlocracy, p. 1338; Oligarchy, p. 1344; Plato's Political Philosophy, p. 1396; Pluralism, p. 1402; Political Myths and the Philosophies of Mosca and Pareto, p. 1474; Political Participation, p. 1479; Polity, p. 1545; Populism, p. 1551; Spinoza's Political Philosophy, p. 1872; The State, p. 1878; Superpowers and World Politics, p. 1916; Underdeveloped Nations, p. 2039.

ARISTOTLE'S POLITICAL PHILOSOPHY

Field of study: Political philosophy

Aristotle's political philosophy integrates the belief in the possibility of developing an optimum government, one which provides its citizens with the political participation needed for a good life, with a pragmatic, systematic analysis of the less-than-ideal states that exist in the world.

Principal terms
CITIZEN: member of a state
CONSTITUTION: basic laws of a state, concerning control of the government and how members of the government are selected
DESPOTIC RULE: governing in which rulers consult only their own desires in making decisions
FREE RULE: governing in which the governor takes into account the concerns of the ruled in making decisions
MIXED CONSTITUTION: government charter that combines features of different political types, such as a democracy and aristocracy
POLIS: political community of the city-state, made up of citizens and noncitizens, which aims at assuring its citizens a good life

Overview

The classical philosopher and natural scientist Aristotle, who lived in the fourth century B.C.E., viewed his treatise *The Politics* as a companion volume to his *Nicomachean Ethics*, since the latter book lays down the principles of living the good life, while the former sets up as a model of the ideal state the one that best provides all of its citizens with a good life. Unlike most Greek political thinkers of his time, who draw up elaborate plans for perfect governments, Aristotle accepts that there is little possibility that a perfect state will come to be and so devotes most of *The Politics* to providing a taxonomy of the various types of state then in existence.

The good life, which the state should make possible, is not one of enjoyment and pleasures, rather it combines the exercise of virtues, such as temperance and prudence, with participation in politics and time given to intellectual pursuits. Although this might seem a strenuous existence, Aristotle claims that it is the one that all free men (he excludes women and slaves from full humanity) naturally desire, although they can be turned away from this desire by passions. Further, since the components of the good life all entail group effort, in collegial intellectual pursuits and legislating, for example, then one can conclude, as Aristotle puts it in one of the most celebrated pronouncements in *The Politics*: "Man is by nature a political animal." This does not mean that man instinctively strives for political office, but that, like a bee, he can only function as part of a society.

From this consideration arises Aristotle's claim that government, which might be thought of as man-made, is, in fact, primarily natural. The acorn of the state is the household, in the sense that the household contains the elementary types of rule. Any government will rule either despotically, in which case only the desires of the rulers are taken account of, or freely, in which case the good of the whole society is considered by decision makers. These types of rule correspond to the varieties of paternal governance in a household. The male head of the house will rule slaves despotically, believing they are innately incapable of rationality and, hence, must always be controlled. Free rule, by contrast, is exercised over women and children, who have some but not full rationality. Such free rule is as concerned with benefiting the governed as aiding the governor.

Beginning with these two ways of ruling, Aristotle constructs, in the middle section of *The Politics*, a typology of governments. It is worth noting that *The Politics* was written during Aristotle's second residence in Athens. After his first stay, ending in 346 B.C.E., he had lived at the Macedonian imperial court as tutor to the youth who would later be called Alexander the Great, and had also lived in other, smaller kingdoms. This had given him the chance to see the inner workings of various forms of government, imparting the authority of experience to his survey of the possible types of government.

Two factors are used to construct his classification: size of the governing group and type of governance. Combinations of these factors lead to six generic types of rule: monarchy, free rule by one; tyranny, despotic rule by one; aristocracy, free rule by a select group; oligarchy, despotic rule by a select group; polity, free rule by the majority of the citizens; and democracy (or ochlocracy), despotic rule by the majority.

Aristotle makes his prejudices known. He forthrightly says what the aim of the best state should be. Once he enters into the study of the various types of constitution, however, he shows himself to be quite objective both in exploring the workings of each type of state and even in making recommendations to rulers about how to maintain their governments, no matter how despotic, once they are in place. This manifest objectivity sets Aristotle apart from other ancient authors, who tended more toward moralizing, and it makes his *The Politics* the founding document of objective political science.

Aristotle is also quite matter-of-fact in his use of his categories. When he turns to the examination of actual constitutions, he admits that most do not fit neatly into one of his six groupings, but bundle together features from different groupings.

After he outlines the varieties of constitutions, the Greek notes what types of institutions best fit each political architecture and what causes instability among them. He then devises remedies for political crises, usually insisting on moderation as a key strategy for retaining power. The value of the golden mean is a favorite point of Aristotle's, and it appears also in his appreciation of mixed constitutions. Such a constitution, for example, one that allows some offices to be voted for by the whole citizenry (as in a polity), while others are voted for by a select group (as in an aristocracy), makes use of elements from more than one of the basic government forms. Aristotle feels that this sort of amalgamation makes for the most stable and just state.

The importance of moderation also appears in the value he grants citizens from the middle strata, those who are well off but not rich. Aristotle feels that a city-state tends to acquire a governmental structure according to what classes predominate in its population. If, for example, the population contains a number of rich, powerful, unscrupulous citizens, then an oligarchy will most likely be the chosen form of government. If there are two or more equally strong population strata, a mixed constitution will result. A middle group standing between the rich and the poor generally acts to broker between the two extreme groups, and it will rule most judiciously if it holds the reins of the state.

In making these last two points about the value of the middle strata and mixed constitutions, Aristotle draws up a prescription for the relatively best state, which needs to be distinguished from the ideally best state, which he describes at the end of the book. The latter is the state which is dependent on the premise that a state might possess a large number of virtuous men who could form a ruling aristocracy. The relatively best state, by contrast, which mixes polity and aristocracy, is one that almost any community could develop and support.

Since communities often seem incapable of producing enough virtuous citizens to create the ideally best community, it is appropriate that Aristotle should close his discussion of the ideal polis by describing the type of education that could be used to mold superior men, ones who would not be blinded by passion in their search for the good life. It is suggested that, if this education were instituted, at least the coming generation would live in the ideal state.

Applications

There are two ways in which a work of political philosophy can affect the world. It may be read by leaders and guide or influence their political activities. The writings of British philosopher John Locke, for example, were important to the United States' Founders, who incorporated some of his ideas into the country's original structure. Alternatively, even if the work is ignored by practical men, it may have intellectual repercussions in academic circles. Plato's work, though not ignored by politicians, has ultimately had far greater influence on writers than on doers.

As a result of the accidents of history, Aristotle's *The Politics* has had little impact on leaders; in addition, because of the vagaries of textual transmission, its effect on Western political writing, though substantial, was long delayed. Aristotle intended that his book be consulted by leaders. In it, he offers advice on how to retain and consolidate power. The trouble is that Aristotle tailors his advice to city-states, small units that were politically and economically limited to controlling one city and its environs. The city-state had dominated Greek political structure from the time of the poet Hesiod (around 700 B.C.E.) until Aristotle's youth (around 370 B.C.E.), but during the thinker's lifetime, these city-states became vassals under the military rule of Macedon, which was first led by Philip and then Alexander, whom Aristotle had tutored. The city-states' constitutions became subject to approval and revision by the subjugating power. For example, Athens' constitution was rewritten to the Macedonians' liking. Although

Alexander's empire collapsed after his death, the land's city-states never regained their independence, becoming pawns of various empires until the region was swallowed up in the Roman empire in the third century B.C.E. Whether Aristotle was writing hopefully or nostalgically is unknown, but Aristotle was addressing issues that were no longer pertinent, since they had to do with political units whose independence had been lost.

These historical events also affected the transmission of *The Politics* to the scholarly community. When Alexander the Great died in 323 B.C.E. and his kingdom was in turmoil, feelings ran high in Athens against anyone associated with the tyrant, such as his former teacher. Aristotle hastened out of the city, remarking that he did not want a second crime against philosophy on the city's conscience. (The first crime was the unjust execution of the philosopher Socrates some years before.)

Though Aristotle's work continued to be taught at the school that he had founded, he died outside of the center of intellectual life at the time. It is said that his works were not collected until more than two hundred years after his death, and, whether this story is true or not, the Romans, who were deeply attracted to Greek thought, admired the political writings of Aristotle's teacher Plato, while *The Politics* was seldom looked into.

Things changed in the medieval period with the thirteenth century translation of *The Politics*. Thomas Aquinas, who was the age's major Christian theologian, borrowed from Aristotle's social and scientific writings when forging a new Christian world view. To fit *The Politics* into the contemporary situation, though, called for some adjustments. Monarchy was the reigning political form in the Middle Ages, so close attention was paid to the Greek's thoughts on good and bad kingship, while his ideas on aristocracy and democracy were neglected. Moreover, Aristotle's conception of the good life had to be expanded so that it could accommodate Christian virtues.

Although such manhandling of Aristotle's ideas may seem unfortunate, it is testimony to the importance of his work and its role in ongoing political discourse. Since the thirteenth century it has become part of the tradition, a constant challenge and inspiration for later political thinkers of all stripes.

Context

The book from classical Greece that outshone *The Politics* for the Romans and for many peoples thereafter was Plato's *The Republic*. Aristotle's and Plato's works share fundamental concerns but differ on procedures, conceptual foundations, and style. Aristotle was Plato's student for twenty years, but in *The Politics* he does not remark the underlying continuity of his work with his teacher's. Both *The Politics* and *The Republic* envision what the ideal state would be like. Both writers busy themselves with classifying various constitutions and, finally, both argue that education is of cardinal importance in creating a stable state.

Yet the differences between the two texts are great. Plato devotes considerable space to describing an ideal state, which he does not pretend could ever be realized. According to his philosophical premises, heaven contains ideal prototypes of objects and virtues, impossible standards that earthly replicas imitate but can never faithfully reproduce. His *The Republic* is an attempt to sketch what such a heavenly model of government would be like. Aristotle's premises are quite different. He believes that everyone, according to nature, has a desire for a good life. Since this positive tendency can be found everywhere, in all types of states are found traces of good features to be remarked and possible improvements to be suggested.

The methodology of each thinker follows from his underlying premises. Plato rejects some of his fellow citizens' most cherished practices in devising an optimal state. In his state, for example, the leaders are not able to possess private property or get married. Not worrying whether humans would be capable of such sacrifice, Plato argues that only under such conditions would the leaders be completely devoted to the state. Aristotle, by contrast, who believed that relative good is as worthy of consideration as absolute good and who further believed that empirical analysis of existing data should guide research, measures contemporary states as much against one another as against an ideal yardstick. He molds his advice to current prejudice and is scandalized by Plato's high-handed dismissal of marriage and private property.

Of special importance in studying these works is their status as texts. Plato's book is eloquently composed. Pretending to be the record of a discussion of leisured aristocrats with Socrates, it is by turns witty, allegorical, and pithy: a work not only of intelligent, consistent, passionate philosophizing, but also of beautiful prose. On the other hand, gauging by internal indications such as repetitions and abrupt transitions, *The Politics* is not a finished work. While Aristotle did write polished works for public perusal, this book seems to be incomplete lecture notes. The rough writing style has been said to match the work's realistic content. This lack of grace made Aristotle's work much less attractive to early readers, such as the Romans, in comparison to Plato's book.

By now, however, it is recognized that *The Politics* and *The Republic* are of equal stature, measuring the height and breadth of ancient political thought.

Bibliography

Barker, Ernest. *The Political Thought of Plato and Aristotle*. New York: Dover, 1959. A thorough analysis and comparison of the political ideas of the two major Greek thinkers. Much of the book merely repeats in a readable fashion what Aristotle has said.

Johnson, Curtis N. *Aristotle's Theory of the State*. New York: St. Martin's Press, 1990. Defends the thesis that the main point of *The Politics* is to answer the question: What is a state? Explains how secondary themes are related to this primary enquiry and indicates how these less-important themes have misled readers.

Mulgan, R. G. *Aristotle's Political Theory: An Introduction for Students of Political Theory*. Oxford, England: Clarendon Press, 1977. Treats Aristotle as a contemporary, showing his continuing relevance to political science. Disagrees with those who say *The Politics* is not unified, saying that Aristotle offers alternative theories but not ones that contradict one another.

Nichols, Mary P. *Citizens and Statesmen: A Study of Aristotle's Politics.* Savage, Md.: Rowman & Littlefield, 1992. Divides the interpreters of Aristotle into those who find inequality at the center of the Greek's thoughts and those who highlight his belief in participatory government. Agrees with the latter viewpoint and tries to show how Aristotle offers a richer perspective on citizenship than that given by today's liberalism.

Sinclair, T. A. *A History of Greek Political Thought.* Cleveland: World, 1968. Examines Greek political thinking from Homer to the country's first years under the Roman yoke. Provides historical detail, telling, for example, that prominent teachers were sometimes called upon to draw up constitutions for city-states in newly established colonies.

James Feast

Cross-References

Aristocracy, Oligarchy, and Plutocracy, p. 78; The City-State, p. 272; Civic Education, p. 278; Conservatism, p. 419; Democracy, p. 513; Despotism and Tyranny, p. 527; The Family and Politics in the United States, p. 649; History of Government, p. 829; Hooker's Political Philosophy, p. 842; Monarchy in History, p. 1221; Ochlocracy, p. 1338; Oligarchy, p. 1344; Plato's Political Philosophy, p. 1396; Political Philosophy, p. 1505; Statesmanship, p. 1898; Thomas Aquinas' Political Philosophy, p. 1974; Urban Governments, p. 2052.

ARMED FORCES

Field of study: Military

As extensions of their national governments, armed forces act as deterrents against foreign attack, as tools for national expansion, and as arbiters of foreign policy.

Principal terms
ARMED FORCES: personnel who are trained and equipped to conduct armed conflict
DEMILITARIZED ZONE: geographical area within which hostile combatants agree that no military action may take place
GUNBOAT DIPLOMACY: attempt to achieve diplomatic goals by threatening military action
NATO (NORTH ATLANTIC TREATY ORGANIZATION): mutual defense alliance among North American and Western European nations
WARSAW PACT (WARSAW TREATY ORGANIZATION): mutual defense alliance among Eastern European nations formed by the Soviet Union in 1955

Overview

A nation's armed forces function in different ways, depending on the type of government in place in that nation. In most nations, the military is directly under a civilian leadership and answers directly to the head of state. Since the armed forces in most countries form an adjunct to the civilian government, they have no inherent powers of their own.

The lack of autonomous power by the military is usually by design. Since the basic function of any military is to plan, prepare for, and conduct war, the existence of a military branch of a government is a threat to the sovereignty of that government. Because of this, even the world's most despotic governments have subordinated the military to a civilian leadership.

In the Soviet Union, during the height of the tyranny of Joseph Stalin, the military was a separate organization from the government. Internal policies were carried out by the Ministry of State Security, or KGB, rather than by the defense ministry. This pattern has been true for most totalitarian regimes throughout history.

In the United States, the military is subordinate to the secretary of defense, a civilian office. The secretary of defense is a cabinet member and answers directly to the president, who is the commander in chief of the armed forces. At the state level, the National Guard in each state responds directly to the governor of the state. The National Guard is strictly limited concerning the type of actions it can become involved in and normally functions as a reserve force for the national military.

As an extension of the civilian government, the military normally takes on the attitudes of the government. If the government is aggressive, the military will take on more strident tones. If the government is more benevolent, the military remains in a more preparatory state.

Regardless of the type of government, a military force requires a large outlay of money. This is due to the need to recruit members, pay them, feed and house them, provide for their health needs, and supply them with weapons and the training to use them effectively. The military does not actually add to the economy unless it is used to acquire more land that can be used to produce an income. The armed forces themselves use funds rather than creating them. Many argue, however, that preventing war is a worthwhile investment. When a nation maintains a large standing military force, aggressive nations may be deterred from attacking it. Maintaining the peace allows the country to conduct business as usual without outside interference. On the other hand, maintaining a large standing military force is very draining on the country's economy. Many have speculated that the breakup of the Soviet Union was caused by excessive military spending.

Some countries join multinational alliances, such as the North Atlantic Treaty Organization (NATO) or the Warsaw Pact, to avoid maintaining a large military. Such alliances allow member nations to focus more on economic development by combining their military force with the armed forces of the other member countries if one of the countries is attacked. The level of involvement by each country and the specific military objectives are determined by the treaty organization's charter.

The differences between NATO and the Warsaw Pact help illustrate the differences in the function of the armed forces in relation to the government. NATO members have chosen to join and take an active part in determining the objectives of the organization, whereas the former Warsaw Pact members had only nominal voices in the employment of their forces. NATO forces are committed to the mutual benefit of all; Warsaw Pact forces were there by direction of the central committee of the Soviet Union and had little voice in the use of their own forces.

Membership in a treaty organization can have disadvantages. For example, a specific country can become involved in a war that is not necessarily in its best interest. Situations can arise that put the member at an unacceptable risk, such as the deployment of intermediate-range nuclear weapons in Western Europe under NATO. European member states believed that the United States was putting them at risk for a first-strike offensive from the Soviet Union.

Using the armed forces as an extension of foreign policy traditionally has been accepted, although it has been called the final step in diplomacy. Maintaining a large, well-equipped military enables a government to negotiate with other countries from a position of strength as well as to impose its will on small nations. Used effectively, it can drastically shorten the process of negotiation. Used badly, it can foster long-lasting ill will toward a country. In the 1980's, under President Ronald Reagan, the United States was accused of using gunboat diplomacy, achieving its political goals under the threat of military intervention.

Because of the destructive power of the military, it is essential to have a national leadership that approaches problems from a diplomatic perspective rather than one of force. Many critics argue against the need for a large military, contending that use of the armed forces is an inappropriate way to achieve national goals. Achieving objectives by force rather than negotiating a mutually beneficial agreement invariably leaves the receiving party with bad feelings toward the aggressor and can cause future problems with any negotiation.

Applications

The military often has been used as an extension of diplomacy throughout history. A recent example of this is the situation that existed between the United States and Haiti from 1991 to 1994. During that time, the elected president of Haiti was forced out of office and the national leadership was assumed by a military general. Once that happened, there were widespread abuses of power by the police and the military, resulting in civil rights abuses and the general subduing of the people.

Unfortunately, the qualities that propel a leader to the head of a military organization are often the same qualities that prevent him from being an effective politician. The lack of political ability generally results in an abuse of power, usually with disastrous results. This was the situation in Haiti. To counteract this, U.S. president Bill Clinton informed the military leadership of Haiti that its civil rights violations were unacceptable and that it was incumbent upon the military leader to reinstate Haiti's ousted president.

Negotiations went on for more than three years, when President Clinton finally realized that diplomatic negotiations weren't going to work. He then informed the military leadership of Haiti that time had run out and that if they continued to commit civil rights abuses, the United States would remove them by force. The military leadership continued.

Two days before the deadline for action on the part of the military leadership, Clinton sent a team of negotiators to try to persuade the military leaders to step down. The negotiations ended after two days when the Haitian government learned that U.S. military forces were en route to Haiti. The military government agreed to step down, avoiding a potentially bloody confrontation.

In this instance, the existence of a large military force was the key ingredient in a diplomatic endeavor. The existence of the military, and the obvious willingness to use it, forced the illegal government in Haiti into accepting the terms outlined in the negotiations. There was no military action other than a peacekeeping mission outlined by the United Nations. Lives were saved, the objectives were reached, and the people of Haiti had a new chance to return to their normal lives.

In most countries, the military exists to provide a sense of security so that business within the country can function unimpeded and the people can conduct their lives without fear. Where adversaries share a border, the existence of a standing military is often the difference between continuing to exist as a sovereign nation and being subjected to overthrow by the adversary.

An example of this is the situation in North Korea and South Korea. During the Korean War (1951-1954), the two sides fought bitterly. Finally, an armistice was negotiated by the United Nations, and a demilitarized zone was established. North Korea remained allied with China and the Soviet Union, and South Korea retained alliances with the United States and several other countries. Actual hostilities were ended, but the governments of North Korea and South Korea never signed the armistice, so they technically remained at war. Because of the ongoing tensions and the constant threat of invasion, both countries continued to maintain large standing military forces and large reserve forces.

South Korea, with its ties to the United States and its position as an economic power on the Pacific Rim, suffered much less from the economic burden of maintaining a military force than did North Korea. After the breakup of the former Soviet Union, North Korea faced numerous problems, mainly in the economic area. Without its markets in the Soviet Union, North Korea's economy declined, and many feared that to avoid going bankrupt, it would attack South Korea.

The Korean situation is an excellent example of the mixed blessing of maintaining a large military force. Because of the stagnant economy and shrinking marketplace, North Korea's leadership would like to use its large military to "annex" South Korea and take over its economic position in the world. In part, the large military has contributed to the problems of the country because of the great cost of maintaining it. South Korea, however, has had an equally large military, augmented by the United States, that has prevented North Korea from invading. In North Korea, the military has disrupted the economy, whereas in South Korea, the military has enabled the economy to continue to grow, and the cost of maintaining it has been offset by the economic benefits.

An example of another situation is Japan since World War II. Under the terms of its surrender, the Japanese government was forbidden to maintain a military force for other than limited self-defense purposes. The United States agreed to provide for the defense of Japan and has maintained a relatively large military force in that country since the war. Relieved of the necessity of maintaining a large standing military, the Japanese government concentrated on promoting economic development, and its national economy now ranks among the world leaders.

Originally, the United Nations was established for a similar purpose. With the Security Council acting as the world police force, it was believed that an organization of nations would protect the interests of both weak and strong countries without the need for any of the member nations to maintain a large military force. Unfortunately, the goals of the United Nations have been rendered ineffective by internal political maneuvering.

Context

Armed forces exist as extensions of national will. Depending on that will, the armed forces can be the savior of a country or the cause of its destruction. For example, if Germany had not developed such a large armed force in the late 1930's, it probably would not have become involved in a war that resulted in the country's being politically divided for forty years. On the other hand, if Joseph Stalin had not developed a large armed force, the Soviet Union probably would not have controlled a large segment of Eastern Europe for more than seventy years.

The success or failure of a country depends more on a competent government than on a large military force. The biggest gun does not make the best leader, as many countries have learned throughout history. Badly used, the military can become an aggressive, destructive force that drains the national economy and stifles growth. Used properly, the armed forces can be an effective extension of the national will, helping the country to achieve many goals that would otherwise be out of its reach and enabling the country to continue its economic growth and maintain its stability and security.

Progress in making the United Nations a more effective force in the world community in the late twentieth century brings hope that the need for a large standing military within any one country will diminish. Many believe that strengthening the enforcement powers of the United Nations' joint resolutions could force countries to maintain peaceful relations with other countries and eventually eliminate the practice of wide-scale warfare.

Until that happens, many countries will be reluctant to give up the security of maintaining their own war-making capability. There will likely continue to be instances where a country believes it needs a military force, if only for defensive purposes. As history has shown, situations constantly change, and the process of change is often a threat to another nation's sovereignty. The ability to respond effectively to that threat is the primary function of the armed forces, making its relationship to government one of national security.

Bibliography

Ferrara, Peter L. *NATO: An Entangled Alliance*. New York: Franklin Watts, 1984. Informative book on the formation of the North Atlantic Treaty Organization. Describes in readable terms the benefits and liabilities of belonging to the organization.

McNamara, Robert S. *The Essence of Security*. New York: Harper & Row, 1968. Describes the policy decisions made by McNamara while he was secretary of defense and provides considerable insight into the process of forming a defense policy.

Mahon, John K. *History of the Militia and the National Guard*. New York: Macmillan, 1983. Historical examination of the existence of the militia and its relationship to the regular armed forces. Also discusses the debates between the need for a standing military and the reliance on militia units and describes the successes and failures of the national guard.

Pruitt, Dean G., and Richard C. Snyder, eds. *Theory and Research on the Causes of War*. Englewood Cliffs, N.J.: Prentice-Hall, 1969. Twenty-two readings and seven essays concerning the rationales used in preparing for and making war. Examines the historical perspectives and contrasts them with the world situation in the 1960's.

U.S. Department of Defense. *Soviet Military Power*. 7th ed. Washington, D.C.: Government Printing Office, 1988. Assessment of the Soviet military threat to the interests of the United States. Contains specific military capabilities and a description of the perceived intent of the Soviet government.

Carl A. Thames

Cross-References

Arms Control, p. 95; Conflict Resolution, p. 397; Despotism and Tyranny, p. 527; Dictatorships, p. 546; International Relations, p. 969; Military Governments, p. 1192; Military Structure, p. 1198; North Atlantic Treaty Organization, p. 1332; Superpowers and World Politics, p. 1916; Totalitarianism, p. 1987; War, p. 2129.

ARMS CONTROL

Field of study: International government and politics

Arms control seeks to reduce the risk of war, especially nuclear war, by regulating arms competition and reducing incentives for war. The end of the Cold War in the late 1980's and early 1990's was accompanied by several arms-control agreements between the United States and the Soviet Union.

Principal terms

ARMS RACE: rivalry among countries to outdo one another in level or quality of armaments

BALLISTIC MISSILE: missile that follows a high-arch trajectory, often outside the earth's atmosphere, after thrust has ended

DETERRENCE: strategy that seeks to prevent an adversary from attacking by threatening to retaliate with equal or greater force

DISARMAMENT: policies designed to reduce existing armaments

NONPROLIFERATION: preventing the transfer of nuclear weapons or technology to countries that do not have nuclear weapons

STABILITY: condition in which countries have little incentive to use nuclear weapons first

THROW WEIGHT: combined weight of a ballistic missile's reentry vehicle(s)

Overview

Prior to the nuclear age, there were a number of important efforts to limit or reduce armaments. For example, the Rush-Bagot Convention (1817) between the United States and Great Britain for naval disarmament in the Great Lakes was an important step in reducing tension between the two countries. Another successful initiative was the Washington Naval Treaty (1922), in which five major powers—the United States, Britain, Japan, France, and Italy—agreed to reduce the number of battleships and aircraft carriers while maintaining existing ratios of vessels. A third agreement was the 1924 Geneva Protocol, eventually signed by over 110 states, which prohibited the use of chemical and bacteriological weapons.

Most efforts to limit or eliminate armaments had little success, however, especially in the presence of political tension. Two international peace conferences were held in The Hague in 1899 and 1907 to foster the peaceful settlement of disputes and disarmament. Although the conferences led to agreements about the rules of war and methods of peaceful settlement, little was accomplished in promoting arms limitation. Article 8 of the Covenant of the League of Nations called for the reduction of armaments to the lowest point "consistent with national safety," and the League's council sponsored a World Disarmament Conference in 1932. The conference accomplished little and broke up after Adolf Hitler came to power in Germany the following year.

Like the League, the United Nations was also given the responsibility to promote disarmament. A United Nations Disarmament Commission was established in 1952 by the General Assembly and came to include all members. In time, the primary responsibility for limiting armaments shifted away from the unwieldy commission to a smaller committee, known as the Conference on Disarmament, composed of forty states meeting regularly in Geneva. In addition, the General Assembly has held three special sessions (1978, 1982, and 1988) to heighten awareness about the need for disarmament. For the most part, arms control agreements between the United States and the Soviet Union were negotiated outside the U.N. framework.

Advocates of disarmament call for the abolition of nuclear weapons. Until the October, 1986, summit meeting of U.S. president Ronald Reagan and Soviet leader Mikhail Gorbachev in Reykjavik, Iceland, however, no serious consideration was given to abolishing nuclear weapons. At that meeting, Gorbachev proposed halving nuclear arsenals, and President Reagan responded by proposing their complete elimination over a period of ten years. Unfortunately, Reagan's refusal to halt the Strategic Defense Initiative ("Star Wars") brought an end to negotiations on these two proposals.

The idea of arms control, as distinct from disarmament, took root during the Cold War when the Soviet-American arms race appeared to be leading to nuclear holocaust. Arms control is not the same as disarmament. Disarmament aims to reduce, and ultimately eliminate, armaments. It is premised on the belief that arms cause war. Arms control, by contrast, is premised on the belief that certain types of weapons create incentives for countries to act in haste and attack first. Advocates of arms control seek to limit or eliminate certain classes of arms in order to reduce incentives to start a war. In addition, they seek to reduce the consequences of war if it takes place.

During the Cold War—especially after the 1962 Cuban Missile Crisis, during which the United States and Soviet Union approached the brink of nuclear war—leaders became concerned that a crisis might arise between the superpowers that could lead one of them to initiate nuclear war. In such an event nuclear deterrence—the strategy by which the superpowers sought to prevent each other from attacking by threatening devastating retaliation—would have failed. As long as the superpowers retained a capacity to inflict unacceptable amounts of damage on each other after a nuclear attack, there was little incentive to strike first. This condition, known as "mutual assured destruction," means that a country that starts a nuclear war would be committing suicide because its adversary would be able to retaliate with nuclear weapons. If nuclear retaliatory forces became vulnerable to a first strike, however, both sides might have an incentive during periods of tension to use their weapons before they are destroyed in a strike by the other side.

By this logic, certain weapons are regarded as more dangerous than others and that therefore they should be targeted for reduction or elimination. For example, fast, highly accurate ballistic missiles are dangerous because they can be used to destroy an enemy's missiles and bombers, thereby reducing its capacity to retaliate. Weapons systems that are vulnerable to an enemy attack—bombers or large missiles, for example—are dangerous because an enemy might be tempted to destroy them in a sudden attack.

The logic of arms control also leads to unexpected and nonobvious conclusions. For example, arms specialists might advocate more rather than fewer weapons because, if one side has only a few weapons, its enemies might be tempted to launch a surprise attack in the belief that they can destroy its ability to retaliate. Increasing the number of weapons on both sides reduces the prospects for a successful first strike. Arms specialists might also recommend improving weapons systems by making them mobile or by placing them in underground silos or by putting them in submarines, with an eye to making them less vulnerable to an enemy attack. Finally, by the logic of arms control, certain actions that appear to be defensive in nature—for example, constructing air raid shelters or deploying an anti-missile system—may be seen as very dangerous because they reduce adversaries' ability to retaliate after being attacked.

Applications

From the late 1950's through the early 1990's, four types of arms-control agreements have been concluded: agreements to limit nuclear testing, agreements to reduce the risk of American-Soviet misunderstandings and thus nuclear war, agreements to prevent the proliferation of nuclear weapons to other countries, and agreements limiting the nuclear arsenals of the superpowers.

An important first step toward limiting nuclear testing was taken in 1963 when the United States and the Soviet Union agreed to ban the testing of nuclear weapons in the atmosphere, in space, or under water. The Threshold Test Ban (1974) limited underground testing to nuclear devices of less than 150 kilotons. These agreements virtually eliminated what had become a serious environmental hazard and illustrated that the Soviet Union and the United States could achieve meaningful arms control.

Concern that a nuclear accident or inadvertent war might erupt between the superpowers in a period of political tension led to the conclusion of a series of measures designed to build confidence and trust. In 1963, a direct Soviet-American teletype link for use in crises (the original "hot line") was established and was modernized in 1984. An agreement designed to reduce the possibility of accidental or unintended use of nuclear weapons was concluded in 1971 and was supplemented by additional measures in 1973. Finally, in 1987, crisis communication centers were established in Moscow and Washington to facilitate communication during moments of acute tension.

Although the United States and the Soviet Union long had an overwhelming nuclear dominance, additional states have developed nuclear weapons. Great Britain, France, China, India, and almost certainly Israel and Pakistan have nuclear weapons. A number of treaties were concluded to prevent the spread of nuclear weapons to, or the militarization of, particular regions. The Antarctic Treaty (1959) banned military activity in that region, the Outer Space Treaty (1966) prohibited the use of outer space for military purposes, and the Seabed Treaty (1971) prohibited placing nuclear weapons on the ocean seabed beyond territorial waters. The most important agreement to limit the spread of nuclear weapons was the Nuclear Nonproliferation Treaty (1968), by which nuclear states agreed not to transfer nuclear arms to nonnuclear states or to assist them to build their own. Nonnuclear states agreed not to accept nuclear weapons or to seek to acquire them. In addition, nonnuclear states agreed to inspection of nuclear facilities by the International Atomic Energy Agency to assure that there was no diversion of fissionable material that could be used for military purposes.

Without question the most significant arms-control measures placed limits on, or, in a few cases, actually reduced superpower arsenals. Complicating American-Soviet negotiations was the fact that the composition of the two sides' arsenals were very different. The United States relied heavily on manned bombers and nuclear-armed submarines, while the Soviet Union relied especially on large land-based missiles. Soviet missiles' payloads (measured by their throw weight) were generally heavier than those of the United States, but U.S. missiles were more accurate. Short-range U.S. nuclear weapons based in Western Europe could reach Soviet soil, while similar Soviet weapons threatened America's European allies but not the United States itself. In addition, short-range American aircraft with nuclear weapons could reach Soviet territory from aircraft carriers. Finally, the United States insisted that French and British nuclear forces should not be counted as part of its arsenal, while Soviet negotiators argued that they should be taken into account in any arms-control agreement.

In 1972, following three years of intense negotiations, the United States and the Soviet Union concluded the first set of Strategic Arms Limitation Talks (SALT I). SALT I consisted of two accords. One, the Interim Agreement on Strategic Offensive Arms, provided for a five-year freeze on the number of U.S. and Soviet fixed intercontinental land-based (ICBM) and sea-based (SLBM) ballistic missiles. Each side could increase its number of SLBMs but only if it reduced by equal numbers its force of ICBMs. The accord, however, only modestly slowed the arms race because it ignored the deployment of highly destabilizing multiple independently targetable reentry vehicles (MIRVs). MIRV technology allowed the superpowers to place ten or more nuclear warheads on a single missile.

The second component of SALT I was the Anti-Ballistic Missile Treaty. Anti-ballistic missiles would be destabilizing because, if placed around cities, they reduced the damage that retaliatory forces could do to an attacker's cities and population, thereby lessening deterrence. The treaty initially limited both sides to two ABM sites, then reduced to one in 1974. The agreement proved to be highly durable.

In 1979, U.S. president Jimmy Carter and Soviet president Leonid Brezhnev signed SALT II, which provided for equal limits on offensive weapons—2,400 missiles and bombers and 1,320 MIRV launchers—with reductions in ensuing years. In reaction to the 1979 Soviet intervention in Afghanistan, however, Carter withdrew the treaty from Senate consideration, and it was never ratified. In fact, both sides did adhere to the terms of the treaty in the years that followed.

An arms-control breakthrough came after Mikhail Gorbachev became Soviet president. In 1987, the superpowers signed the Intermediate-Range Nuclear Forces

Treaty, which dealt with production or deployment of missiles with a range of 300 to 3,400 miles. This treaty was a first in that it reduced nuclear weapons significantly and provided for on-site inspections to verify that both sides were carrying out the agreement.

Four years later, in the Strategic Arms Reduction Talks (START I) Treaty, the superpowers agreed to major cuts in nuclear warheads—from 11,600 to 8,600 for the United States, and from 10,222 to 6,500 for Russia by the year 2000. In the same year, the superpowers agreed to reduce short-range land, air, and sea-based nuclear weapons and to take nuclear forces off alert status. START II, signed in 1992, provided for still more dramatic cuts to be carried out in two stages, so that by the year 2003 each side would have no more than 3,000 to 3,500 nuclear warheads. Other superpower accords were reached to reduce chemical weapons (1990) and drastically cut conventional forces in Central Europe (1990).

Context

The end of the Cold War shifted the focus of arms-control efforts to some extent. Although United States-Russian arms-control negotiations continue, the two issues of the disposal of existing stockpiles of nuclear weapons and the proliferation of nuclear weapons to other countries have become prominent. The fear that, given Russia's economic and political woes, Russian nuclear materials or weapons may fall into the wrong hands illustrates that the two issues are related. In addition, the breakup of the Soviet Union created three newly independent nuclear powers—Ukraine, Belarus, and Kazakhstan. Although the three have publicly affirmed that they will abide by the terms of START I, the question of whether to give up nuclear weapons is hotly debated in Ukraine, and the United States and Russia have sought to use the prospect of economic and technical assistance to persuade Ukraine to carry out disarmament.

Nuclear proliferation puts more fingers on the nuclear trigger and complicates the mechanics of deterrence for everyone. In addition, nuclear forces developed and deployed by developing countries such as Pakistan are likely to be unsophisticated and highly vulnerable to attack. As a result, the relationship between adversaries such as Pakistan and India or Israel and Iraq will be unstable, and may lead to nuclear war.

Numerous states have the scientific capability or the financial resources to build or acquire nuclear weapons, and some are tempted to do so. Brazil and South Africa were well on their way to achieving nuclear capability when they decided not to do so. Pakistan, though refusing to admit it, already has or is close to acquiring nuclear weapons in order to deter India, which also has such weapons. Iraq, too, aided by American and European (especially German) companies, was well on its way to building nuclear weapons when the Persian Gulf War erupted in 1991. Ten years before, Israel had bombed a nuclear facility in Iraq because of concern that Iraqi leader Saddam Hussein was on the verge of building nuclear weapons.

One signatory of the Nonproliferation Treaty, North Korea, has consistently refused to let inspectors investigate its nuclear facilities as it is obliged to do under the treaty, and it has threatened from time to time to abrogate the treaty. In the early 1990's it appeared that, in violation of the treaty, North Korea had diverted nuclear fuel to develop nuclear weapons.

Bibliography

Clausen, Peter A. *Nonproliferation and the National Interest: America's Response to the Spread of Nuclear Weapons.* New York: Harper Collins, 1993. Coherent, thoughtful, and well-organized analysis of nuclear proliferation and its consequences for the United States.

Freedman, Lawrence. *The Evolution of Nuclear Strategy.* 2d ed. New York: St. Martin's Press, 1989. Comprehensive historical evaluation of changes in technology, policy, and the strategy of deterrence from World War II to the end of the Reagan Administration.

Goldblat, Jozef. *Arms Control: A Guide to Negotiations and Agreements.* London: Sage, 1994. The most comprehensive overview of arms control efforts and agreements.

Lebow, Richard Ned. *Nuclear Crisis Management: A Dangerous Illusion.* Ithaca, N.Y.: Cornell University Press, 1987. Analysis of the different ways in which crises in the nuclear age threaten to erupt into war.

Newhouse, John. *Cold Dawn: The Story of SALT.* New York: Holt, Rinehart and Winston, 1973. Analysis of tortuous U.S.-Soviet negotiations to achieve SALT I. Illustrates the complexity of arms-control issues.

Nye, Joseph S., Jr. *Nuclear Ethics.* New York: Free Press, 1986. Analysis of the moral implications of nuclear arms and the degree to which they accord with ethical principles.

Perkins, Ray, Jr. *The ABCs of the Soviet-American Nuclear Arms Race.* Pacific Grove, Calif.: Brooks/Cole, 1991. Coherent and accessible analysis of the technology and politics of the superpower arms race and the effort to negotiate arms-control agreements.

World Armaments and Disarmament: SIPRI Yearbooks, 1968/69-1993. New York: Oxford University Press. Annual publication by the Stockholm International Peace Research Institute that provides the best available summary of developments in arms control and arms proliferation.

Richard W. Mansbach

Cross-References

Alliances, p. 47; Armed Forces, p. 89; Conflict Resolution, p. 397; Diplomacy and International Negotiation, p. 552; International Agreements, p. 949; International Law, p. 956; International Relations, p. 969; North Atlantic Treaty Organization, p. 1332; Superpowers and World Politics, p. 1916; Treaties, p. 2020; War, p. 2129.

THE ARTS AND GOVERNMENT

Field of study: Functions of government

Governments, whether democratic or totalitarian, have vested interests in influencing artistic activity. On the one hand, they encourage those artistic endeavors thought to be in the state's best interests; on the other hand, they regulate or suppress artistic activities deemed inimical to the power, influence, or general welfare of the state.

Principal terms
ARTS: forms of human expression subject to aesthetic criteria capable of ennobling or illuminating the human experience
FOLK ARTS: artistic expressions and crafts intended primarily for utilitarian or religious use that are not generally subject to aesthetic criteria
HIGH ARTS: fine arts—such as opera, painting, and sculpture—that are commissioned and enjoyed primarily by the aristocratic or upper classes and the highly educated
PATRONAGE: system of financial support of artists and artistic activity by governmental or religious institutions and private benefactors
POPULAR ARTS: widely distributed art forms that are reproduced and disseminated by mechanical or electronic means—such as magazines, film, and television—that are designed for mass consumption
REGULATION OF THE ARTS: constraints imposed—or threatened—by government in response to political, economic, or cultural pressures

Overview

From the dawn of recorded civilization to the present day, the arts have played a central role in both supporting and critiquing the aims of government. It is thus hardly surprising that governments have taken a direct interest in the activities of artists and their audiences, directly sponsoring artistic activities thought useful to the goals of the state, while regulating and even suppressing those activities deemed inimical. In totalitarian regimes such as Joseph Stalin's Soviet Union or Adolf Hitler's Nazi Germany, the arts (whether popular arts such as film or high arts such as music, painting, and theater) have been harnessed in direct support of explicit governmental policies. In modern capitalistic democracies, government arts policies have ranged from a "hands off" approach, as in the United States, to a more activist stance, as in Canada where the threat of U.S. "cultural imperialism" to a sense of Canadian national identity has spurred the creation of such state-supported arts-oriented agencies as the Canadian Broadcasting Corporation (1932) and the National Film Board of Canada (1939).

The issue of government regulation of the arts, whether exported or imported or consumed within the bounds of the state, rests on the assumption that the arts have unique powers capable of affecting human behavior and influencing attitudes about the nature of the human enterprise, including the role of the state. Among the first pronouncements attesting such powers were those regarding the influence of music by Plato in *The Republic* and Aristotle in *The Politics*. While encouraging the acquisition of "correct" musical taste and judgment for ethical development, both of these ancient political philosophers warned against the debilitating effects of "low" or "popular" music. Similarly, Plato urged the ostracism of poets from his ideal state because, he believed, they cater to the emotions, the antirational part of human nature. Taking exception to Plato's recommendation for suppressing poetry, Aristotle argues in *The Poetics* that the tragic mode of poetry in drama benefits the state by helping citizens purge themselves of debilitating emotions such as pity and fear through the psychological process of catharsis.

Plato and Aristotle based their commentaries on music and poetry largely on their observations of the roles played by the arts in religious ritual and celebration. As Western civilization evolved after the coming of Christianity, the arts—especially music, painting, and architecture—played increasingly integral roles in the Roman Catholic church and its various offshoots following the Protestant Reformation. Many of the masterworks of such artists as the sculptor Michelangelo and the composer Johann Sebastian Bach were commissioned by religious institutions. By adding weight to the belief in art's power to move the human spirit, this system of artistic patronage began a powerful model that was emulated on a progressively grander scale by civic and private patrons throughout Europe. Indeed, during the Age of Exploration, the establishment of colonial empires and global trade helped create an increasingly wealthy and worldly European aristocracy and mercantile class. In the process, the acquisition and display of art took on new values. While still appreciated for its capacity to provoke aesthetic experience, art gradually became a means for the rich and powerful publicly to display their refinement and sophistication. This added social-cultural value was significant in raising the status of both artists and their patrons. During this dynamic period artistic patronage expanded from the churches to include the courts of Europe's major nation-states and commercial centers. The lines separating church, state, and commerce often overlapped; in cities such as Paris or Venice, patronage for large-scale projects (such as Florence's Church of San Lorenz) came from civic as well as church and private resources.

In the nineteenth century, the trend toward secularization of the arts accelerated. Inspired by the masterworks of composers such as Wolfgang Amadeus Mozart and Ludwig van Beethoven, the social role of the artist shifted from one of anonymity to celebrity. With a rapidly growing base of wealth fueled by expanding colonial empires and the new wonders of the Industrial Revolution, as well as the egalitarian ideals promulgated by the French Revolution, the cult of individual artistic genius flourished. In music, for example, the aptly named Age of Romanticism gave rise to Richard Wagner, Hector Berlioz, Frédéric Chopin, Robert Schumann, and Peter Ilich Tchaikovsky—whose works were often performed for a paying public in state and municipal opera houses and concert halls. Indeed, the arts had become a matter of civic pride that deserved government support. At another level, the rise of the novel, a literary form encouraged by the development of the printing press, made possible the wide dissemination of the works of such writers as Charles Dickens, whose exposé on the slums of London in *Oliver Twist* (1837) inspired reform legislation improving the lot of the working poor, and Harriet Beecher Stowe, whose *Uncle Tom's Cabin* (1851) may have helped to bring on the U.S. Civil War.

As a new century approached, ever newer and more miraculous technological innovations continued to transform the artistic landscape. Such marvels as the phonograph, motion pictures, radio, photography, the penny novel, and cheap daily newspapers produced seismic shifts in the means of producing, distributing, consuming, and valuing art. In their wake, as the high arts of the elite gave way to the popular arts of the masses, there were new concerns over content, copyright, and access—concerns that could be systematically addressed only by governmental intervention.

Applications

As the film age dawned at the turn of the twentieth century, the first cries for film censorship were heard in response to such short, single-reel films as *The Execution of Mary Queen of Scots* (1894) and *The Kiss* (1896). While establishing sex and violence as staples of screen entertainment, such films also provoked the institution of municipal and state censorship boards. In 1915, as the American film industry's more ambitious producers sought to establish the new medium as a genuine art form on a par with the fine arts of music and theater, the industry was dealt a blow by the U.S. Supreme Court in a decision that declared the movies "a business pure and simple." By depriving film of First Amendment protections, the Supreme Court opened the door to additional forms of city and state censorship. The case also encouraged efforts to establish a federal censorship board, thus spurring the film industry to regulate its product through the Motion Picture Producers and Distributors of America (MPPDA) in 1922. Acting as a buffer between the film industry and public groups pressing for more stringent governmental control, the MPPDA became a model for mass-media trade associations, such as those representing the television, recording, and video game industries seeking protection from regulatory pressures. In 1952, the Supreme Court reversed itself in a case that finally granted to film the First Amendment protection of free speech. Nevertheless, the seesaw battle over regulation, especially as it relates to admitting children and teenagers to movies containing explicit sex or violence or "adult language," continues to manifest itself in the film industry's constant revamping of its own rating system.

Although the mass-media popular arts have usually sought to ward off regulatory controls, there have been instances in which an industry has appealed to government for help. Such was the case with radio in the 1920's. As more and more broadcasters hit the air, signals collided in cacophonous disarray. Under the aegis of U.S. secretary of commerce Herbert Hoover, the Radio Act of 1927 set up a licensing system with specific frequency assignments that alleviated many of these problems, while paving the way for the Federal Communications Act of 1934—the bedrock of U.S. broadcasting law. When television began its massive expansion following World War II, broadcasters appealed to the Federal Communications Commission to establish the technical standards for color television. Once again, government acted at the behest of industry.

While employing thousands of writers, directors, actors, and countless other artisans and craftspeople to produce its middle-brow entertainments, commercial broadcasters prior to the late 1960's were encouraged to support occasional high-art projects such as the National Broadcasting Company's commissioning of Gian Carlo Menotti's Christmas opera, *Amahl and the Night Visitors* (1951). This and similar "high-brow" programs were part of a "public service" strategy designed to assist network affiliates in their applications for license renewals from the Federal Communication Commission. With the establishment in 1967 of the federally supported Corporation for Public Broadcasting (which regularly aired high-arts fare such as "Masterpiece Theater") and such cable television services as the Arts and Entertainment Network, commercial broadcasters reduced their own high-arts programming because of its limited mass appeal. Nevertheless, when the televisual world is configured to include broadcast television as well as its electronic extensions through cassettes and cable, it is clear that American audiences have access to an unprecedented array of programming designed for and catering to a wide range of cultural tastes.

Following precedents of government supported art in Europe and Japan, the U.S. Congress passed a bill in 1964 authorizing the establishment of the National Endowment for the Arts (NEA) and the National Endowment for the Humanities (NEH). The NEA became particularly helpful in providing support for performing artists at the national level and, through its subsidization of state-supported arts agencies, performing artists at the regional and local levels as well. The NEH, for its part, made possible a large number of grants to university professors for conducting research on various aspects of the arts as they pertain to a broad range of social and cultural issues. The establishment of the American Film Institute (AFI) in 1967, through a private nonprofit organization, has derived much of its funding from the NEA and from contributions by the film and television industries. Dedicated to "preserving the heritage and advancing the art of film in America," the AFI has helped to preserve thousands of films and to train future filmmakers at its Center for Advanced Film Studies in Los Angeles. The AFI has also drawn attention to such noted screen artists as director Orson Welles and actress Katharine Hepburn through its annual television tributes. In similar fashion, the NEA has focused public attention on the arts through such awards programs as its American Jazz Masters Fellowships, which include among their honorees such jazz stalwarts as pianist Billy Taylor and bassist Ray Brown. Another form of official governmental recognition has come from the U.S. Postal Service, which has celebrated artists ranging from Duke Ellington to Elvis Presley on commemorative postage stamps.

In times of political or economic stress, governments often utilize the arts to underscore and build support for policy. During the Great Depression of the 1930's, for example, thousands of U.S. artists were paid to paint murals in post offices, act in plays, write books about the country, and document the era photographically in programs set up under the federal government's Works Project Administration. At the same time, film critic-turned-documentarian Pare Lorentz produced two critically acclaimed films for the U.S. Resettlement Administration, *The Plow That Broke the Plains* (1936) and *The River* (1937). Because they supported relief programs sponsored by President Franklin D. Roosevelt's New Deal, Lorentz's films were criticized by congressional Republicans as partisan political propaganda. As a result, Depression-era governmental filmmaking came to a halt.

With America's entry into World War II in 1941, the federal government went back into the film business. The Pentagon's Office of War Information had two objectives. One was to create a series of indoctrination and training films for men and women in uniform. Under the aegis of "Why We Fight," Academy Award-winning director Frank Capra supervised seven highly effective films that helped galvanize GIs' commitment to battle. For the home front, the government instigated feature films portraying the country's allies as brave, trustworthy, and resourceful. Suddenly, even Soviet communists were glamorized in films such as *Mission to Moscow* (1943) and *The North Star* (1943). The propagandistic fingerprints of the government were everywhere, even in musicals, westerns, and romantic comedies. Ironically, filmmakers such as scriptwriter Lillian Hellman, who were praised for their favorable wartime portrayals of America's Soviet allies, found themselves after the war accused of being communist fellow-travelers by bodies such as the House Committee on Un-American Activities for having helped just a few years earlier to make the very films that had been lauded for their patriotic contributions to the war effort.

In the midst of the Civil Rights and women's liberation movements of the 1960's, the federal government enacted legislation requiring affirmative action protocols for workplace hires and promotions. Though responding slowly, the motion picture and television industries gradually increased opportunities for women, African Americans, and other minorities in positions both in front of and behind the camera, an opening-up process that in large part can be attributed to such affirmative action mandates.

The U.S. government has also played a large role in protecting the "intellectual property" of its creative artists through its copyright laws. As technology continues to grow in sophistication and portability, however, the pirating of licensed films and recordings remains a problem. Other related technologically derived problems concern such new artistic practices as "sampling," in which an element of a record (such as a drum riff) can be appropriated for an entirely new recording—a process made possible by electronic digital technology. Like the colorization of films originally made in black and white, the legal, as well as ethical, dimensions of such practices are shadowy. Because of America's global domination of the popular arts, the U.S. government has played an increasingly large role in protecting these important and growing American exports through such trade pacts as the North American Free Trade Agreement (NAFTA) and the General Agreement on Tariffs and Trade (GATT). In attempts to resist American hegemony in the international film, television, and music markets, the governments of countries such as Canada and France continue to devise programs to counter the deluge of American popular art products by supporting their own indigenous arts industries.

Context

The fault line separating the twentieth and twenty-first centuries stands at the epicenter of what many cultural commentators describe as the postmodern condition, a moment in history when basic assumptions about the role and, indeed, the very nature of the arts and government are being questioned. Already, we have witnessed the virtual collapse of any useful distinctions that previously demarcated folk, popular, mass, and high arts. Indeed, in this era of transnational conglomerates, art is entertainment. Packaged and therefore "commodified," the arts can perhaps most clearly be understood as commerce. While the arts still possess the capacity to delight as well as to inform, their ubiquitous presence and corporate resonance make their future prospects as vehicles for promoting significant social or cultural change problematic. For governments seeking political and economic stability, the neoconservative nature of contemporary arts, where even "radical" expressions such as rap music are almost immediately defused by the process by commodification, this is a desirable state of affairs. From this perspective, the basic function of government is to protect and promote the arts as commerce.

Nevertheless, other paradigms have developed at the edges of the mainstream in response to the multiple needs of marginalized groups identified primarily by race, gender, class, political ideology, and geography. Will governments encourage the kinds of alternative discourses sought by such groups? Will governments encourage the kind of activist art that promotes the redistribution of explanatory power among society's silenced minorities? These are among the issues whose resolution will largely determine, along with technologic advances, the nature of future relationships between the arts and government.

Bibliography

Benjamin, Walter. "The Work of Art in the Age of Mechanical Reproduction." In *Film Theory and Criticism: Introductory Readings*. 4th ed. Edited by Gerald Mast et al. New York: Oxford University Press, 1992. Classic essay from 1935 that remains a touchstone of contemporary discourse on the unique status of mass-produced art such as film.

Gans, Herbert J. *Popular Culture and High Culture: An Analysis and Evaluation of Taste*. New York: Basic Books, 1974. Brilliantly argued sociological brief for cultural pluralism that makes a case for taking mass mediated popular arts seriously and argues against government support of the arts.

Jowett, Garth. *Film: The Democratic Art*. Boston: Little, Brown, 1976. Masterfully written social history of film, with detailed treatment of the dynamic matrix relating censorship to various political, economic, and societal pressures.

Koppes, Clayton R., and Gregory D. Black. *Hollywood Goes to War: How Politics,*

Profits, and Propaganda Shaped World War II Movies. Berkeley: University of California Press, 1990. Fascinating account of how the U.S. War Department ensured that propaganda favorable to U.S. foreign policy was included in Hollywood entertainment films during World War II.

Randall, Richard S. *Censorship of the Movies: The Social and Political Control of a Mass Medium*. Madison: University of Wisconsin Press, 1968. Excellent case study of the ways in which a modern mass art form has responded to censorship pressures.

Taylor, Fannie, and Anthony L. Barresi. *The Arts at a New Frontier: The National Endowment for the Arts*. New York: Plenum Press, 1984. Fascinating account of the National Endowment for the Arts, the first federal support program for artists, which tracks the agency's first ten years under the directorships of Roger Stevens and Nancy Hanks.

Charles Merrell Berg

Cross-References

Business and Government, p. 177; Commerce Regulation, p. 357; Communications Management, p. 370; Education Management, p. 565; Industrialization, p. 916; Public Policy, p. 1633; Regulatory Agencies in the United States, p. 1678; Trade with Foreign Nations, p. 2000.

ASIA: POLITICS AND GOVERNMENTS

Field of study: Comparative government

Asian nations experienced two thousand years of feudal dynasties and hundreds of years of European domination. Democracy, communist rule, and authoritarian regimes were major forms of government in Asia after World War II. Economically, Asia has been the most dynamic region in the world since the 1970's.

Principal terms
> AUTHORITARIAN RULE: government under which political activity and liberty are restricted and in which great power is exercised by a small group
> COLONIAL RULE: regime established by a foreign power under which sovereignty of the host nation is lost
> COMMUNIST RULE: regime that maintains a Marxist ideology, a dictatorship of one political party, and a centrally planned economy with public ownership
> CONFUCIANISM: philosophy that guides interpersonal relationships and relationships with rulers
> FEUDAL DYNASTY: family that maintains over generations its ruling power, characterized by the dominance of aristocracy and landowners over peasants
> HINDUISM: Indian religion and philosophy that prescribe a caste system; its broadest divisions are: priests (the highest class), rulers, farmers, and workers

Overview

Asia accounts for 30 percent of the earth's landmass and 60 percent of the world's population. Geographically, it may be divided into East Asia (China, Mongolia, the Korean Peninsula, Japan and the Russian Far East), Southeast Asia (Vietnam, Laos, Cambodia, Thailand, Burma, Malaysia, Singapore, Indonesia, and the Philippines), and South Asia (India, Pakistan, Afghanistan, Bangladesh, and Sri Lanka). In addition, Asia may be said to include most of the Middle East nations, such as Iran and Saudi Arabia, as well as Central Asia, which includes some republics of the former Soviet Union, such as Kazakhstan and Uzbekistan.

The history of the forms of government in Asia can be divided into three periods: feudal dynasties, European colonial rule, and post-World War II development. Asia is so diverse that discussion of the politics and governments of Asia will be limited, for reasons of space, to three important nations—China, Japan, and India.

The major form of early political system was the feudal dynasty. China has the longest history of feudal dynastic society, which lasted for over two thousand years. In feudal China, the emperor had unlimited power over his subjects. He directly appointed central and local officials. The Chinese feudal system was also characterized by the influence of Confucianism and the merit system. The Confucian code regulates proper relationships among various people: subjects to emperor, son to father, and wife to husband. Confucianism also emphasizes the importance of family and collective responsibility for social harmony. The merit system was unique—the government recruited officials through competitive examinations to test mastery of Confucian classics. Capable intellectuals were chosen to serve in the government. The Chinese feudal system and Confucianism had great influence on Japan, Korea, and Vietnam.

The Japanese have been ruled by one royal family since the first century B.C.E. In the fifth century, the Japanese started to borrow aspects of Chinese culture and copied China's governing system. They did not adopt the Chinese merit system, however, but instead passed down power on the basis of heredity. Isolated from mainland Asia by the sea, Japan developed a strong military tradition because of hundreds of years of civil war.

The European powers began colonizing Asia in the seventeenth century. By the end of the nineteenth century, most Asian nations had been colonized. The British ruled India, Pakistan, Burma, Malaya, and most of the Middle East. The French colonized Indochina, including Vietnam, Laos, and Cambodia. The Spanish (later the Americans) controlled the Philippines. The Dutch occupied Indonesia. In the Opium Wars of the 1830's to 1840's, Britain defeated China and occupied Hong Kong. By the 1890's, China was divided into several spheres of influence by the European powers and had been semicolonized. Japan was the exception. In the last decades of the nineteenth century, Japan was rapidly modernized and became a military power. In 1894, Japan defeated China in a war and seized Taiwan. Later, Japan ruled Korea and China's Manchuria. During World War II, the Japanese occupied China and most Southeast Asian nations.

India is a nation with great cultural, religious, and ethnic diversity. Although India is the birthplace of Buddhism, more than 80 percent of the population is Hindu and more than 10 percent is Muslim. The people of the country speak 211 different languages. To exploit India, the British colonialists established effective centralized administration and achieved territorial integration through its networks of highways and railroads and its telecommunications and mail systems. In the nineteenth century, nationalism grew among the educated Indians, who demanded national independence from colonial rule. The leading organization for the nationalist movement was the Indian National Congress, which was founded in 1885. One of the leaders of the Congress was Mohandas K. Gandhi. India finally won its independence in 1947.

World War II weakened Western colonial rule over Asia. After the war, Asian nations gained their independence from colonial powers. In the following decades, three types of government emerged: constitutional democracy, communist regime, and authoritarian rule.

Japan, India, and Sri Lanka became democratic countries. Japan was defeated in World War II and occupied by American forces under General Douglas MacArthur. At MacArthur's request, the Japanese drafted a new constitution in 1947, and the country has been a democracy since that time. This imposed democratic system stabilized over the following decades. India's independence leaders fully understood the dangers inherent in the diversity of culture and religion in their nation. They designed a highly centralized democratic government under a federal system. Although Indian society is extremely diverse, the Indian democratic system is stable. In fact, India is the most populous democracy in the world.

Communist governments emerged in several Asian countries after World War II: the People's Republic of China, Mongolia, North Korea, Vietnam, Laos, and Cambodia. These countries were characterized by their Marxist ideology, one-party dictatorship, and a centrally planned economy. Most of these countries continue with this political system in the post-Cold War era. Ruled by Mao Tse-tung from 1949 to 1976, China established its political and economic systems based on the Soviet model. Since 1978, under the direction of Deng Xiaoping, China began a market-oriented economic reform and an open-door policy, under which Western technology, capital, and management skills were introduced into China.

The third type of government is authoritarian rule. From the 1950's to the 1990's, authoritarian government has existed in several countries, such as South Korea, Taiwan, the Philippines, Burma, Malaysia, and Singapore. Authoritarian rulers may declare martial law, ban opposition political parties, arrest political dissidents and maintain absolute authority for decades in their countries. Unlike communist rule, however, private ownership and a market economy were allowed in these countries, though the government played a strong role in them. Some of the authoritarian countries have developed toward democracy in the 1990's.

Applications

China is ruled by one political party. The guiding principle of the political system is Marxism-Leninism and Mao Tse-tung's thought. Under the 1982 constitution, the National People's Congress (NPC), China's legislature, is the highest body of the country. The president of the country is elected by the NPC. The president has the power to appoint the premier of the state council, the executive body of the state. In reality, however, the power of the government is retained by the party's political bureau and its standing committee. Major government leaders, such as the president of the state, the premier, and vice premiers, are also members of the political bureau or of its standing committee. The political bureau usually consists of about twenty members while the standing committee consists of about six. The highest position in the party is general secretary. The general secretary is also chairman of the military affairs council and is the commander in chief of the military. In 1989, Jiang Zemin became the general secretary of the party. Jiang has also been the president of the state since 1992. In fact, China has a dual rule by the party and the state administration at each level of government: central, provincial, and county. State bodies must be responsible both to the next-higher level of state administration and to the corresponding level of the party organization. Since the 1980's, the Chinese government has tried to reform its dual rule system by separating the government from the party, but the two systems remain intertwined, and the party is still the real source of decision making.

A unique characteristic of China's political system is the function of the Chinese People's Political Consultative Council (CPPCC), a multiparty organization controlled by elites who support policies of the Communist Party. The CPPCC was established in 1949 and played an active role in the 1950's and in Deng Xiaoping's era. The CPPCC members have the right to make proposals for government policy making and to question the implementation of policies. For Chinese leaders, the CPPCC serves to demonstrate the broad base of the communist rule. In the 1990's noncommunist elites have also held leading positions in the government. For example, Rong Yiren, a former capitalist who supports communist rule, was elected as vice president of the state in 1992.

As Marxist ideology declined, Confucianism revived in China in the 1990's. This phenomenon has three sources: First, the communist government is using traditional culture to strengthen its rule because Confucianism stresses social order and obligation to superiors. Second, Confucianism is employed to resist Western cultural influences, such as individualism, in a modernizing China. Finally, many Chinese believe there is a connection between Confucianism and the economic success of Japan, South Korea, Taiwan, Hong Kong, and Singapore. Therefore, it is hoped that Confucianism will also serve China's modernization.

The key change in Japanese history was the end of unchallenged imperial power. The principle of democracy was introduced in the 1947 constitution. As stipulated in the constitution, Japan has a parliamentary form of government that is similar to the British system. The emperor is only the symbolic head of state. The head of the government is the prime minister, who is chosen by the majority party in the Diet (parliament), which is the highest political body of the state. The Diet is divided into the House of Representatives (the lower house, with 511 members serving four-year terms) and the House of Councillors (the upper house, with 252 members serving six-year terms). The lower house has more power than the upper house. Since the 1950's the Liberal Democratic Party (LDP) had always won the elections of the Diet and dominated Japanese politics. As a result of the end of the Cold War and of scandals, internal splits, and opposition coalition, the LDP finally fell in 1993 after thirty-eight years in power. From August, 1993, when the first coalition government was established, to 1994, several cabinets emerged and subsequently fell. Japan entered into a transition period from the LDP's dominance to a competitive multiparty system. Under a new election law, the election system under which one district could send several representatives to the Diet, was to be replaced by a new system with "one district, one representative." Major opposition parties declared that they would reorganize as one party. It was expected that opposition parties would play an even stronger role in the future.

Another important element in Japanese politics is that the constitution renounces war and pledges that military forces will be kept small. Until recently, Japan spent less than 1 percent of the nation's GNP on defense. This low amount of defense spending has given the Japanese a competitive advantage in international trade. In the 1990's, at America's request, Japan increased its defense spending and sent its troops overseas as part of the United Nations peacekeeping forces.

Under India's federal and democratic system, based on the constitution adopted in 1950, the country is divided into twenty-three states and eight union territories. At the national level, the legislature, known as the federal parliament, consists of two houses. The lower house, the House of the People, is more powerful than the upper house, the Council of States. The head of the state is the president, who is elected by an electoral college made up of members from the federal parliament and state assemblies. The head of the government is the prime minister, who appoints the cabinet, directs policy making, and represents the nation abroad. The prime minister is elected by the majority party or a coalition in the House of the People. Since independence, the prime minister has always been, except for two brief periods, the leader of the Congress Party. As a result of a party split in 1967, the National Congress lost its dominant position in the parliament. The stability and integrity of democratic India are due to strong central government and charismatic leaders, including Jawaharlal Nehru and Indira Gandhi. The assassination of Rajiv Gandhi in 1991 left India with no strong leader for the immediate future.

Context

Asian nations experienced a long history of feudalism. Their cultural heritage was made up of elements which contributed to continuous dynastic authoritarianism. Western colonization of Asia and the introduction of capitalism, the theory of democracy, and modern science and technology finally disintegrated Asian feudal society. The end of World War II ushered in democracy, communism, and authoritarian rule. In the 1990's, Asia began another dramatic change. In democratic nations, the phenomenon of one majority party organizing the government seemed to end. In Japan, the Liberal Democratic Party ceased to be the ruling party. Though Asian communist countries survived the end of the Cold War, governments such as China's and Vietnam's are changing greatly because of their adoption of a market economy. Communist rule was challenged by prodemocratic forces in these countries. In China, the communist regime was weakened when the Chinese government cracked down on the 1989 student demonstrations in Beijing's central square. These communist countries may evolve into a new type of authoritarian government, with market economies and with their societies much more liberalized. Those countries with an authoritarian type of government were largely on the road to democracy during the 1990's. In South Korea, Taiwan, the Philippines, and Thailand, multiparty systems and free elections were introduced.

Two factors explain these changes in Asia: the Cold War and the nationalist movement. During the Cold War, Asian anticommunist countries were allies of the United States. Strong and stable governments in these countries were considered necessary for containment of communist expansion in the region and they were supported by the United States. This support explains the continuation of Japan's one-party rule for four decades and of authoritarian rule in South Korea, Taiwan, the

Philippines, and Indonesia. Beginning in the 1990's, this international political climate changed.

As for Asian communist countries, their adoption of a market economy is indicative of the failure of their former centrally planned economies. Why did Asian communist governments not collapse at the end of the Cold War? On the one hand, the standards of living of people in these countries have been improved under a market system. This occurred in both China and Vietnam. On the other hand, Asian communist revolutions resulted from nationalist movements of anticolonialism and for national independence. They were revolutions which erupted within their societies. In China, Mao Tse-tung proclaimed that the Chinese people had stood up to foreign power when the Chinese revolution achieved victory in 1949. Vietnam was colonized by the French in the nineteenth century. In 1954, the Vietnamese defeated the French colonialists. Unfortunately, the United States replaced France and got involved in Vietnam at this time. The communists finally reunified Vietnam in 1975 after American withdrawal in 1973. The Vietnamese government followed the Chinese model and adopted a market economy in 1986.

One last significant aspect of Asian governments is the strong role that the government has played in economy. The Asian economy has been dynamic since the 1970's. The first successful economy in the region was that of Japan. Japan became the world's second largest economy in the 1980's. The Japanese model, including a strong government role in the economy and an export-oriented strategy, was followed by the "four little dragons" (South Korea, Taiwan, Hong Kong, and Singapore), China, Vietnam, and other Southeast Asian nations.

In conclusion, democracy and modernization will be the main themes of the Asian region. During this process, governments will continue to play a strong role. It is clear that while the Asian countries are modernizing their political and economic systems, they still favor maintaining their cultural traditions, such as Confucianism and Hinduism.

Bibliography

Baxter, Craig, et al. *Government and Politics in South Asia*. 3d ed. Boulder, Colo.: Westview Press, 1993. Detailed study of the history and politics of South Asian nations, including India, Pakistan, Bangladesh, and Sri Lanka. Many tables and illustrations.

Chan, Steve. *East Asian Dynamism: Growth, Order, and Security in the Pacific Region*. 2d ed. Boulder, Colo.: Westview Press, 1993. Examines the history of Asia, the policy dilemmas posed by the pursuit of economic growth, political order, and military security, and issues such as democracy and free trade.

Collinwood, Dean W., ed. *Global Studies. Japan and the Pacific Rim*. 2d ed. Guilford, Conn.: Dushkin, 1993. Includes recent publications about Japanese dominance in the Asia-Pacific region and the development of interregion relationships in the 1990's.

Magstadt, Thomas M. "Asia" and "The Middle East." In *Nations and Governments:*

Comparative Politics in Regional Perspective. 2d ed. New York: St. Martin's Press, 1994. College textbook comparing the politics of all regions of the world, including Asia and the Middle East.

Norton, James K., ed. *Global Studies: India and South Asia.* Guilford, Conn.: Dushkin, 1993. Surveys the politics and economy of South Asian nations and includes essays and reports about the development of the region in the 1990's.

Wang, James C. F. *Contemporary Chinese Politics: An Introduction.* 4th ed. Englewood Cliffs, N.J.: Prentice Hall, 1992. Includes governmental institutions, administrative structure, the Communist Party and its ideology, the military, economy, and foreign affairs.

Enbao Wang

Cross-References

Buddhism and Government, p. 152; Chinese Communism, p. 223; Comparative Government, p. 384; Confucianism and Government, p. 405; Democracy, p. 513; Empires and Empire Building, p. 597; Feudalism, p. 688; Hinduism and Government, p. 823; Independence Movements and Transitions, p. 896; Indigenous Peoples' Governments, p. 903; Islam and Government, p. 994; Nomadic Peoples' Governments, p. 1306; Pacific Islander Governments, p. 1362; Self-Determination, p. 1796.

ASIAN AMERICAN POLITICS

Field of study: Politics

Asian Americans are the fastest-growing component of the United States population. People of Asian ancestry are mainly concentrated in five metropolitan areas— Honolulu, San Francisco, Los Angeles, Chicago, and New York. Since the 1960's this group has engaged in political action of two kinds—electoral politics and mass protest politics.

Principal terms
EMIGRATION: process of leaving one country to settle in another
ENFRANCHISEMENT: granting of rights of electoral participation
IMMIGRATION: process of arriving in a country for resettlement from another country
NATURALIZATION: conferring of citizenship on immigrants
PREJUDICE: preconceived opinion that emphasizes negative perceptions of people or situations

Overview
Asian Americans are a rapidly expanding minority group in the United States. In 1970, there were 1.5 million Asian Americans, almost all of them in Hawaii and California. By 1990, there were almost 7.9 million and the census projects that there will be 20 million by the year 2020. The initial wave of Asian immigration to the United States took place between the 1850's and the 1930's. During this period, almost a million people from China, Japan, Korea, the Philippines, and India immigrated to the United States and to Hawaii. By comparison, almost 35 million European immigrants arrived in the country during those same years. A second wave of Asian emigration from Southeast Asia took place in the 1970's as a consequence of American involvement in Vietnam. In this period, almost a half-million Indochinese were resettled in the United States at a time when the national economy was experiencing difficulties, leading to much discussion about the costs and the long-range benefits of such immigration. The two waves of immigrants arrived in the United States under very different conditions, and their experiences provide an understanding of some of the important issues guiding Asian American political activism.

The first wave of Asian American immigration in the nineteenth century was a response to socio-political forces in the home country that encouraged outward emigration (push factors) and changing economic conditions in the United States which attracted immigrants from Asia and elsewhere (pull factors). Chinese immigrants who were the first to arrive were driven out of their home country by political and social instability in the same years that the discovery of gold in the western part of the United States led to new economic opportunities. In contrast, early immigrants from Japan, Korea, and the Philippines were recruited by agents for work in the sugar plantations of Hawaii, while immigrants from India, who were mainly of the Sikh faith, were attracted by job opportunities in North America. The opening up of the western United States generated new demands for cheap labor to build the railroads and to cultivate land. The result was that American recruiters found it profitable to turn to Asian countries for an abundant supply of cheap labor.

The arrival of Asian immigrants caused some concern about their growing numbers and led to systematic attempts to exclude them. Based on prejudice, these exclusionary acts included economic discrimination, political disfranchisement, physical violence, immigration exclusion, social segregation, and incarceration. All groups encountered these types of actions. The Chinese, being the first immigrants, faced tremendous prejudice that was actively propagated by three groups of people: diplomats, who resented the elaborate ceremonies and protocols at the Chinese court, where they were treated as inferior, and who reacted by treating the Chinese in a similarly prejudiced fashion; merchants who resented restrictions on trade; and missionaries who were unhappy over the slow rate of Chinese conversions to Christianity. All helped create a negative image of the Chinese in the United States. The result was that in many states, laws were passed to prevent aliens from leasing land, and Asian immigrants were also denied the right of naturalization, which meant that they had no political power, since they could not vote. Deprived of political rights, Asians were also subjected to much violence, both organized and spontaneous, leading to the death and maiming of a number of immigrants. The dislike of Asian immigrants finally led the United States Congress to enact the 1882 Chinese Exclusion Law, which suspended the entry of Chinese labor for ten years but exempted merchants, students, teachers, diplomats, and travelers from its provisions. The Immigration Acts of 1917 and 1924 were used to ban other Asian groups, such as Indians and Japanese, from the country. Efforts were also made to segregate Asian Americans in the public schools while antimiscegenation laws prevented social interaction and intermarriage between whites and Asians in many states.

Efforts to segregate and exclude Asian Americans from all spheres of American life led to the first attempts toward political organization among Asians. The earliest such attempts organization took place at the turn of the century among the Chinese and the Japanese. Asian Americans tended to form associations based on shared dialect, residence, and occupation, among other criteria. In the case of the Chinese, a group of six such associations became known as the Chinese Six Companies and they were the first to challenge anti-Chinese legislation using European American lawyers. The Japanese Association of America was similarly formed in 1908 to counter anti-Japanese sentiment in California. In both the Chinese and the Japanese cases, the consuls general of these countries played an important role in sponsoring and aiding the activities of these groups. The Asian American associations thus maintained close connections with their home countries. In fact, in the case of Koreans and Indians, the earliest political organizations in the United States were a response to political problems in the countries of origin. The Koreans were probably the most political of all Asian communities, their chief organization being the church. Their initial concerns were focused on the Japanese occupation of Korea, and their political efforts were geared toward publicizing the plight of, and helping to liberate, their homeland. In a similar vein, Asian Indians of the Sikh faith organized to fight for Indian independence by setting up the Ghadar (Independence) Party. Filipinos, too, had their own organization geared toward fighting for independence.

The political activism that originated in concerns for Asian American homelands became the vehicle later for protesting the weak position of Asian Americans in the U.S. economy. For example, Chinese garment and laundry workers organized strikes and engaged in litigation to improve their economic and social status. Litigation in particular proved a successful strategy for more well-to-do Asian Americans. Between 1883 and 1943, 1,100 cases brought by Asian Americans in the lower courts were published in the *Federal Reporter*. The U.S. Supreme Court issued written opinions in 170 cases dealing with Asian Americans. These cases challenged laws and regulations aimed at excluding Asian Americans from the economic and political mainstream in the United States.

Political activism in the Asian American community in the 1950's and 1960's took a number of different forms. Young activists, inspired by Chinese communist methods, attempted to organize garment and restaurant workers, set up social service agencies, and protest against a variety of social ills. Other less radical individuals aimed at setting up legal aid organizations, health care clinics, and language instruction programs. The results of these efforts still provide crucial assistance to new immigrants arriving in the United States. At the same time, Asian community groups across the United States have begun to join forces on issues that concern all Asian Americans. For example, in recent years, the work of such groups at the local, state, and national levels led the U.S. Civil Rights Commission to recognize in 1986 that violence against Asian Americans, and specifically Southeast Asian refugees, immigrant entrepreneurs, and Koreans, was a problem that was national in scope.

Asian Americans participated in electoral politics as early as the 1920's and 1930's. Japanese American participation in Hawaiian politics increased dramatically in the period after World War II, when veterans of that war used the G.I. Bill to go to law school and later entered politics. Between the 1950's and 1980's about 55 percent of the leadership positions in the Hawaiian state legislature were held by Japanese Americans. The most famous of these has been Senator Daniel K. Inouye, who entered Congress when Hawaii became a state in 1959.

Chinese and Indian immigrants were also successful in U.S. electoral politics. Wing F. Ong, a Chinese who came to the United States in 1918 at the age of fourteen, went on to receive a law degree and ran several successful campaigns for seats in the Arizona state House of Representatives. An Indian immigrant, Dilip Singh Saund, came to the United States to obtain a Ph.D. in mathematics but became a farmer in California and went on to run successfully for Congress in 1956 and 1958. In the inland United States, however, Asian Americans have had a harder time gaining visibility since they are a small fraction of the population there. Those who have made it into political office have been instrumental in increasing national awareness regarding discrimination and prejudice against Asian Americans.

The wave of Asian immigrants in the 1970's consisted mostly of refugees representing five groups—Vietnamese, Chinese Vietnamese, Cambodians, Hmong, and
Laotians. In general, this group has had a difficult resettlement experience. Many
members of this group were former soldiers, officers of regular armies, or white-collar
workers and as such possess occupational skills that were not easily transferable to
the United States economy. Most important, many of them had little or no knowledge
of English. The result is that in a state such as California, which has attracted large
numbers of these immigrants, there has been growing public resentment of immigration as a drain on the economy in general and on public assistance programs in
particular. Asian American activism in these states has been geared toward providing
resources and assistance to these recently arrived immigrants. Studies have shown that
the longer the duration of residence in the United States, the higher the level of
educational attainment and language proficiency in this group.

Applications

The growing involvement of Asian Americans in politics is visible in the success
with which they have influenced public opinion about two related issues—the recognition of the wrong done to Japanese Americans who were interned during World
War II and the problems posed by violence against Asian Americans.

The first issue grew out of the U.S. government's internment of 40,000 Japanese
along with 70,000 of their American-born children in "relocation camps" after the
Japanese attack on Pearl Harbor in December, 1941. Given only a week to dispose of
their property, many of these people sold their possessions at a great loss. The
internment camps, by forbidding Japanese language schools and the practice of
Shintoism, and by encouraging cultural assimilation with white society, helped to
weaken the traditional authority of community elders. The internment of Japanese in
hastily constructed camps continued until the end of the war in August, 1945, and left
the community shaken and unsure of its status in American society. In fact, most
Japanese who had been interred were unwilling to talk about it until the 1970's, when
community activists began seeking reparations. A National Committee for Redress
was formed within the Japanese American Citizens League (JACL), and at its 1978
convention, the JACL adopted a resolution calling for $25,000 in reparations for each
individual interned during the war. There were protests from both European Americans
and Japanese Americans who were unhappy with this attempt to reopen old wounds.
As a result, the JACL called on Congress to set up a commission to determine if in
fact an injustice had been done to those who had been interred. The Commission on
Wartime Relocation and Internment of Civilians, which was created by Congress in
response to this request, held hearings and heard testimony from 750 people, at the
end of which it concluded that a "grave injustice" had in fact been done. Once the
commission reported its findings, the JACL mobilized its resources to get a redress
bill passed in Congress. Japanese Americans in both houses were responsible for
shepherding the bill through Congress. In 1987, the House voted 243 to 141 and the

Senate 69 to 27 to ask the nation to issue an official apology to Japanese Americans and to compensate each living internee with $20,000.

Incidents of violence against people of Asian descent since the 1980's has also led the Asian American community to mobilize in recent years. In June, 1982, a twenty-seven-year-old Chinese American man, Vincent Chin, was beaten to death in Detroit by Ronald Ebens, a European American man. In a plea bargain, Ebens pleaded guilty to the lesser charge of manslaughter and was sentenced to three years' probation and a fine of $3,000 plus $780 in court fees. The Asian American community across the United States, horrified at the light sentence handed out to Ebens, mobilized. A group called the American Citizens for Justice was formed and got the U.S. Justice Department to commence an investigation on the grounds that the victim's civil rights had been violated. The investigation led to Ebens' conviction by a jury in federal district court. Even though the conviction was later overturned on a technicality by a federal appeals court, it helped the Asian American community discover the power of community activism and organization. Seven years later, when a Chinese American was killed in Raleigh, North Carolina, by a European American man, Asian Americans were quick to get involved. They organized the American Justice Coalition to represent the parents of the murdered man and to prevent the kind of plea bargain that had taken place in the Ebens case years earlier. In March, 1990, the jury found the man, Robert Piche, guilty, and the judge sentenced him to thirty-seven years in prison. As a spokesperson for the American Justice Coalition declared, "I think this case shows that justice can be won if we as Asian Americans are willing to stand up and make clear in public that we will fight for justice."

Context

Political activism by Asian Americans has led to increased awareness regarding their problems. Violence directed against Asian Americans may have helped to mobilize Asian Americans, but there are many other issues being addressed by individuals and organizations that make up the community. For example, in recent years, concern has been voiced about access to higher education. In the 1960's and 1970's, increased immigration from Asian countries and the rise in numbers of well educated Asian parents seeking the best education for their children led to an influx of Asian students into elite colleges and universities on the east and west coasts. Administrators at these schools began to think that Asians were "overrepresented." At some schools, such as the University of California at Berkeley, administrative changes might have helped discourage Asian American students from applying for admission. The result has been that more and more Asian American parents, regardless of ideological differences, are joining hands to guarantee better educational opportunities for their children. Asian American students are also becoming politically active on various campuses; one of their efforts has been to change the curricula to reflect more upon their own history and experiences. As a result, many universities, especially on the West Coast, have introduced Asian American studies courses and programs.

There has also been activism on behalf of recent immigrants from Vietnam,

Cambodia, and Laos, many of whom do not speak English and who are confined to urban ghettos where the opportunity for regular employment is limited. The result of this poverty and lack of opportunity has been an outbreak of Asian gangs and drug-related violence, which is of serious concern to the leadership of the Asian American communities. The growing discrepancy in education, wealth, and opportunities between descendants of earlier immigrants and recent immigrants is especially worrisome to groups that traditionally focus less on individual accomplishment and more on group success. There is only a limited sense of Asian American identity, however; Asian Americans have tended to see themselves as Korean Americans, Japanese Americans, Asian Indians, and so on. Leadership is correspondingly fragmented, and until this changes the political successes are likely to be limited to those areas where self-interest urges cooperation.

Bibliography

Aguilar-San Juan, Karin, ed. *The State of Asian America: Activism and Resistance in the 1990's*. Boston, Mass.: South End Press, 1994. Writings by people actively involved in Asian American politics provide cases for classroom discussion.

Chan, Sucheng. *Asian Americans: An Interpretive History*. Boston: Twayne, 1991. History of the Asian American experience in the United States.

Fawcett, James T., and Benjamin V. Carino, eds. *Pacific Bridges: The New Immigration from Asia and the Pacific Islands*. New York: Center for Migration Studies, 1987. Study of recent trends in Asian American immigration.

Reimers, David. *Still the Golden Door: The Third World Comes to America*. New York: Columbia University Press, 1985. Examines the impact of the 1965 immigration reforms, and later attempts to restrict such immigration, on recent Asian American immigration.

Tachiki, Amy, et al., eds. *Roots: An Asian American Reader*. Los Angeles: Continental Graphics, 1971. Writings by Asian Americans that trace the diverse heritage of the group.

Sudha Ratan

Cross-References

Activist Politics, p. 7; Elected Versus Appointed Offices in the United States, p. 572; Grassroots Politics, p. 797; Immigrants and Politics, p. 861; Interest Groups, p. 936; Latino Politics, p. 1052; Political Participation, p. 1479; Protest Movements, p. 1621; Race and Ethnicity, p. 1654; Voting Behavior in the United States, p. 2109.

AUGUSTINE'S POLITICAL PHILOSOPHY

Field of study: Political philosophy

In The City of God *Saint Augustine contrasts the eternal "City of God" with the ephemeral nature of human government. This highly influential work argues that Christians should accept established governments to the degree that the actions of such governments are not in contradiction with the essential beliefs of Christianity.*

Principal terms
CITY OF GOD: what Christians consider to be their true homeland, where they will go in the next life
CITY OF MAN: governments that function solely according to human standards
CYCLICAL IDEA OF HISTORY: pagan belief that people and not God determine the history of events in this world
DEATH: sole way for people to pass from the City of Man to the City of God
EVIL: inevitable result of any decision to reject God's teaching
NATURAL THEOLOGY: theological reflections based on human reason alone and not on Christian revelation
ROMAN EMPIRE: political system that dominated most of Europe and North Africa until the fifth century
SUPREME GOOD: represents for Augustine the beatific vision which awaits those who spend eternity in heaven

Overview

Born Aurelius Augustinus, Saint Augustine was born on November 13, 354 C.E., in Tagaste, which is now the Algerian city of Souk Ahras. His father was a pagan and his mother was the Christian saint Monica, who prayed for years that her son would convert to Christianity and end his profligate lifestyle. Her wish was granted on Easter Day, 387, when Augustine and his adolescent son Adeodatus converted to Christianity. Just four years after his ordination in 391, Augustine became the bishop of Hippo, a post that he occupied for the rest of his life. He died on August 28, 430, in Hippo, now the Algerian city of Annaba. Just one year after his death, Vandals sacked Hippo.

During his thirty-five years as the bishop of Hippo, there was major political and social disorder throughout the Roman Empire, and many bitter controversies and heresies created serious divisions among Christians. Although Augustine wrote extensively and eloquently on numerous theological topics, he has remained famous above all for his masterful autobiography, *Confessions* (397-401), and for his theoretical work *The City of God*, which he began writing in 413 and completed in 426.

Just three years before he began work on *The City of God*, the Visigoths, led by Alario, sacked Rome, and numerous Italians fled to the more distant regions of the

Roman Empire, including Hippo. Augustine encouraged members of his diocese to treat these refugees well. The chaos created by the crumbling of the once powerful Roman Empire served to convince Augustine that it would be unwise for Christians to place excessive trust in any political system. The only political system that Augustine knew was the Roman Empire, and he perceptively recognized that the basic flaw that caused its collapse was its desire to enslave and dominate other nations. Those who lived in the distant corners of this empire were profoundly alienated from Rome, and they felt no loyalty to the empire that had exploited them. When the Goths, Visigoths, and Vandals invaded various regions of the empire, few people outside Rome believed that these invaders would be any worse than those who had imposed their exploitative "Roman peace" on their subjects.

In his prefatory letter to his disciple Marcellinus, Augustine explains that his purpose in writing *The City of God* is not to propose a new form of government to replace the Roman Empire, but to explain that Christians can endure political and social instability because of their conviction that God will bring them eternal joy in the next life. Augustine did not, however, believe that Christians should be indifferent to politics. He argues that it would be unconscionable for Christians to fight in "unjust wars" of exploitation and domination or to participate in pagan religious services. In their personal lives, Christians must remain faithful to the Ten Commandments and to the teachings of Jesus Christ. No compromise with evil can be tolerated. This does not mean, however, that Christians should be so rash as to create political instability or to seek the overthrow of established governments. Augustine seems to suggest that Christians should be ever vigilant lest their ethical purity be corrupted by political temptation. Augustine was perhaps somewhat pessimistic because he did not believe any new government would necessarily represent an improvement over the discredited Roman Empire.

In book nineteen of *The City of God*, Augustine argues that the Christian view of the "supreme good" refers to the beatific vision, whereas for pagans the "supreme good" refers solely to the quality of life on this earth. This belief does not exempt Christians from their moral responsibilities toward others. Temporal matters are extremely important, because it is only through patience, acts of kindness, and generosity that Christians can hope to persuade pagans to accept Christianity. Augustine himself resisted for many years his mother's arguments, and he did not convert to Christianity until the age of thirty-three. He later appreciated the patience which his mother had shown him while he was still a pagan. Augustine repeatedly told the priests and lay members of his diocese in Hippo that it was their religious duty to receive with open arms both pagan and Christian refugees who had fled from the chaos in Italy. Augustine's concern for the welfare of others was real, but he believed that religion and not governments should teach people how to act honorably and ethically.

Compromises are unavoidable in the realm of politics, but Augustine argues that it is exceedingly unwise for Christians to place themselves in positions in which they might have to compromise their religious beliefs. He states that Christians need to maintain a healthy suspicion of all governments. Augustine recognizes that in the best of all possible worlds, governments are created in order to improve the quality of life for people, but all the political systems of which Augustine knew served the interests of only small ruling classes and not the general citizens, who felt profoundly alienated from their own governments. The disintegration of the once seemingly invincible Roman Empire reminded Augustine that Julius Caesar and his fellow rebels had destroyed the Roman Republic, which no foreign power could have ever conquered. The Roman Republic and Empire were both destroyed from within. Augustine argues that men and women who believe that they can attain true and meaningful happiness in the service of their country are deluding themselves.

Like many other church fathers, Augustine praises the courage and high ethical standards of virtuous pagans such as Cicero. Cicero accomplished much good as an effective lawyer and as an honest Roman consul, but when the Roman Civil War ended with the destruction of the Roman Republic and the establishment of a military dictatorship which came to be known as the Roman Empire, Cicero was quickly killed because of his refusal to compromise his ethical and political beliefs. Cicero led an exemplary life, but his involvement in politics brought about his death. Augustine believed that it was very dangerous for Christians to place any true hope in political systems created by men and women. Augustine, comfortable living in his distant corner of the crumbling Roman Empire, was not tempted by the corrupting influence of politics. In Hippo, he strove to improve the quality of the spiritual and temporal life of those in his diocese, and through his writings he hoped to lead his fellow Christians to an acceptance of their own responsibilities toward others and to a deeper under-standing of the essential mysteries of Christianity. Augustine wrote extensively on the horrors of war and the beauty of peace in this life, but he believed that perfect tranquillity cannot be experienced in this life. Christians must be very active in helping others, but they should never believe that governments are there to serve all people equally. Governments strive to dominate and exploit people, whereas Christianity respects the dignity of each individual and seeks to save everyone. In the history of political theory and ethics, *The City of God* remains a significant work because in it Augustine argues quite eloquently that the rights of individual men and women are more important than the success or failure of any specific form of government.

Applications

A convert from paganism to Christianity, Augustine knew that generations of Christians had been persecuted for their religious beliefs. Roman emperors understood that Christians did not accept the idea that Roman citizens were required to obey Roman emperors because they were gods. Christians willingly obeyed many, but not all, Roman laws. Although tolerance of Christianity became widespread during the third century, Augustine realized that Christianity would not spread throughout the world if people believed that general acceptance of Christianity would contribute to social disorder. Augustine strove to separate the growth of Christianity from the success of any specific government. Augustine understood that no political system created by people could endure for more than a few centuries. Christianity, unlike governments, is concerned not with worldly success but with eternal salvation.

A first reading of *The City of God* might lead readers to conclude that Augustine believed that Christians should accept whichever government they happened to live under. Such an interpretation distorts Augustine's understanding of the constantly evolving relationship between political systems created by people and the divinely created city of God. If a proposed new form of government does not greatly improve the quality of life for each individual, Augustine argues that there is no rational basis for Christians to oppose an existing government. All things being equal, Augustine preferred established governments, whose strengths and weaknesses were known to all people, to the possibility of disorder and chaos, which could result from an unproven political system.

Like many later conservative political thinkers such as Edmund Burke and Alexis de Tocqueville, Augustine did not believe that changing political systems of government necessarily improved the general quality of life for citizens. Burke and Tocqueville, for example, argued that the overthrow of the French monarchy during the French Revolution resulted in fewer and not more political rights for the French. Like Burke and Tocqueville, Augustine recognized that there are definite limits to the general obligations for people to obey laws promulgated by human governments. Augustine argued that when a serious conflict exists between one's ethical and religious beliefs and human laws, a Christian is morally required to disobey the human laws. Civil disobedience is required of Christians in extreme cases, lest their cooperation with evil be perceived as the approval of immoral actions. A Christian must, however, be willing to accept the consequences of such disobedience to unjust laws.

Although Augustine wrote *The City of God* more than fifteen hundred years ago, his cogent arguments in favor of civil disobedience remain as powerful today as they were during the last years of the Roman Empire. Two twentieth century examples illustrate the continuing validity of Augustine's insights into the moral need for civil disobedience. The eminent German theologian Dietrich Bonhoeffer concluded that it was a Christian's religious obligation to resist the Nazis. Bonhoeffer left the safety of his position as a professor of theology in Union Theological Seminary in New York in order to join the German Resistance. He understood that this act would probably result in his death, but he willingly accepted his moral responsibility to play an active role in resisting the evil of the Nazi regime. He was eventually arrested by the Gestapo, but as his prison letters demonstrate, he accepted the inevitability of his execution with tranquillity. He believed that he had made the correct moral and religious decision when he chose to fight the Nazis.

Another well-known example of the religious motivation for civil disobedience can be found in the famous letter which Martin Luther King, Jr., wrote from his cell in a Birmingham, Alabama, jail to fellow clergymen. King had been arrested because of his participation in nonviolent protests against racial discrimination in Alabama. From his cell, King asked his fellow clergymen why they had not denounced laws that were clearly incompatible with Christ's teaching on the dignity and equality of all people. He wondered why so many clergymen had chosen to denounce his nonviolent actions of civil disobedience instead of joining him in protesting against unjust laws. Like Bonhoeffer, King willingly accepted the consequences of his decision to obey the higher law of God and to disobey unjust laws promulgated by people who did not respect the dignity and basic rights of each individual.

Context

Augustine wrote *The City of God* at a turning point in the history of Christianity. After having been persecuted for several generations, Christians saw the disintegration of the Roman Empire. Augustine sensed that Christians might obtain a degree of political power in whichever government eventually replaced the Roman Empire. He wanted his readers to understand that they should always avoid politically expedient but immoral actions that were incompatible with the teachings of Christianity. Augustine believed firmly that even a praiseworthy end can never justify the recourse to immoral means. Augustine wanted Christians who become involved in the political arena to realize that they must never separate their religious beliefs from their political actions.

Such a rigorous ethical position does create problems for Christians who are more interested in achieving political victories than in remaining faithful to their religious beliefs. During the U.S. presidential campaign of 1860, Abraham Lincoln made it quite clear that slavery was a moral evil which should no longer be permitted in any American state. Abraham Lincoln knew quite well that taking such a position might well result in his defeat in November, 1860, but he would not compromise his religious belief in order to win an election. Readers of *The City of God* can still be moved by its idealistic attitude toward politics. Augustine believed that Christians who are not afraid of losing political power can make a positive contribution to the lives of their fellow citizens. Augustine would have been appalled by Machiavelli's argument in *The Prince* that it is sometimes necessary for a Christian prince to undertake amoral actions in order to achieve a desirable political goal. *The City of God* continues to remind readers that every political decision that one makes constitutes an ethical choice which must be compatible with one's moral and religious beliefs.

Bibliography

Brown, Peter. *Augustine of Hippo*. Berkeley: University of California Press, 1967. Most reliable and complete biography of Augustine. Bibliography.

Deane, Herbert A. *The Political and Social Ideas of St. Augustine*. New York: Columbia University Press, 1963. Thoughtful analysis of Augustine's political ideas in the context of the historical events of his life.

Gilson, Etienne. *The Christian Philosophy of Saint Augustine*. Translated by L. E. M. Lynch. New York: Random House, 1960. Describes Augustine's true importance in the development of early Christian thought.

Markus, Robert A. *"Saeculum": History and Society in the Theology of St. Augustine*. Cambridge, England: Cambridge University Press, 1970. Describes the theological foundation for Augustine's political views. Bibliography.

Meer, Frederik van der. *Augustine the Bishop.* Translated by Brian Battershaw and G. R. Lamb. New York: Harper & Row, 1965. Describes Augustine's activities as a bishop from 395 to 430. Very helpful, this book has to a large degree been superseded by Peter Brown's more complete biography.

O'Donnell, James J. *Augustine.* Boston: Twayne, 1985. Introduction to Augustine's writings. Intended for general readers. Bibliography.

Edmund J. Campion

Cross-References

Burke's Political Philosophy, p. 171; Church and Government in History, p. 230; Civil Disobedience, p. 285; Colonialism and Anticolonialism, p. 351; Conservatism, p. 419; Empires and Empire Building, p. 597; John of Salisbury's Political Philosophy, p. 1006; Machiavelli's Political Philosophy, p. 1148; Plato's Political Philosophy, p. 1396; Political Philosophy, p. 1505; Religion and Politics, p. 1685; Thomas Aquinas' Political Philosophy, p. 1974; Tocqueville's Political Philosophy, p. 1981.

AUTOCRACY AND ABSOLUTISM

Field of study: Political philosophy

One of the most common forms of government in history, autocracy is the rule of a single person who holds absolute power. Absolute power is that which is not constrained by opposing forces, interests, or institutions.

Principal terms

ABSOLUTISM: government system of total and unqualified power

AUTHORITARIANISM: system of rule by the one or the few over the many

COMMUNIST REGIME: government of a dictatorship of a communist party, often featuring autocratic rule

DICTATORSHIP: government by a single ruler or oligarchy

FASCIST REGIME: government based on racist and radically nationalist ideals

MONARCHY: rule of a king or queen

TOTALITARIANISM: government in which the state exerts total control over the lives of the people

Overview

Autocracy and systems of government that attempt to exercise absolute power over their people are more common in human history than democratic systems of government. Autocracy is the rule of one person over the many, and absolutism is the concentration of all political power in the hands of the ruler. In contrast, democracy is the rule of the people, and most democratic systems place limitations on those to whom the people grant power. Democracies employ laws and government institutions to control leaders and take measures to ensure that people elected to political office are not able to rule above the law. Democracies have rules by which leaders may be peaceably removed from office, and the citizens have freedom of speech, press, and association. Autocratic systems do not typically share such features of democracy and generally avoid sharing power with the citizens.

Modern political observers are more likely to use the terms "authoritarianism" or "totalitarianism" to describe systems of government that tend toward autocracy and absolute power. Autocracy and absolutism typically describe governments in the past in which a single person ruled in the name of the few. Modern authoritarianism is, in contrast, the rule of a single person or group in the name of the many. This is an important distinction when looking at autocratic regimes in historical context, because modern governments have developed new ways to make it appear that the ruler, no matter how tyrannical, is governing in the name of the people and for the good of the state and society. Ancient civilizations typically were governed by kings or emperors who ruled in their own name.

Philosophers have long debated the relative merits of autocratic and absolutist governments. For example, the ancient Greek philosopher Aristotle studied many different constitutions to discover what type of regime was most stable and likely to succeed. He concluded that pure autocracy was bound to fail because of the concentration of wealth and power in the hands of a few. Aristotle believed that a mixed system of monarchy, oligarchy, and democracy was best because wealth and power may be balanced. Centuries later, Italian philosopher Niccolò Machiavelli wrote a powerful little book entitled *The Prince* (1513). Machiavelli believed that when a society is unstable or corrupt, the only kind of ruler who might succeed is ruthless. This prince must have the cunning of a fox and the ferocity of a lion in political affairs. Machiavelli wrote *The Prince* to advise such a prince on how to gain and maintain power.

Another philosopher who concerned himself with absolute governments was Thomas Hobbes, whose most famous book on the subject is entitled *Leviathan* (1651). Noted for an analytical approach that emphasizes human nature and political psychology, *Leviathan* argues in favor of an absolutist monarchy as the most suitable form of government. Hobbes believed that human beings are so selfish and aggressive that absolute government is required to control them. Government is based on a contract between subjects and rulers, according to Hobbes, but by this contract the people must place all of their rights and powers into the hands of the sovereign. It is the duty of the sovereign to rule and guide the state to secure the property and lives of the people. Hobbes believed this was necessary for people to live together in peace, and thus he defended the idea of absolutism.

History has witnessed a variety of autocratic systems. Every society has developed some form of government or system of authority. Governments are organized for the protection and good of the people, for the distribution of goods and resources, for the coordination of productive work, and for the resolution of conflicts. Traditional and ancient societies, often organized as tribes or extended families, sought the leadership of a strong or wise person. This practice naturally resulted in the appointment of kings, chiefs, or religious leaders as the ultimate authorities. Such systems were frequently autocratic, although internal social relationships could develop informal methods of sharing power. Legitimacy attributed to a ruler as God's chosen one has been prevalent for ages. A government based on religious authority or governed by a religious institution is called a theocracy. Pure theocracies have been less common than governments by those who sought the help of divine ordination. Absolutist monarchs supported by divine authority have been among the most powerful in history.

Traditional autocrats and monarchs endeavored to keep power within their family. Dynastic families have ruled states in many forms, but the most familiar is the pattern where the king or queen passes the throne on to someone born in the line of succession. Thus, ruling families attempt, for as long as their power and line holds, to possess absolute power and hand it to a leading heir. When successful, the family and its line maintains an identity which is indistinguishable from that of the nation and the land itself. For example, the Russian czar claimed to be the embodiment of the Russian people and the Orthodox faith. King Louis XIV of France proclaimed: "I am the state."

Modern states, except in a few rare examples, no longer reflect the same sense of personal identification of the autocratic ruler with the nation. Monarchy, dynastic families, and the idea of the divine right of kings lost much legitimacy with the emergence of large complex nation-states and mass societies. Modern nation-states are founded in some form on the consent of the people, and this has much to do with their size and populations, the need for standing professional armies, and the institutional complexity of their governments. The character of the modern state requires the active participation of large numbers of people. As a result of this requirement, autocracies in the name of the autocrat have been superseded by autocracies in the name of the people.

The most visible examples of modern autocratic regimes founded on ideas and organizations that mobilize masses of people are the socialist regimes of the twentieth century. Regimes that have approximated a state with total control in one person's hands were the fascist regimes of Germany and Italy and the communist political systems established on the model of the Soviet Union. Typically, with these governments, the autocrats, whether called führer, comrade, chairman, caudillo, or captain, professed to be leaders in service of the people. They did not claim to have the divinely ordained right to rule or to embody the state. Rather than receive power as their due, they "accepted" what was called a popular mandate. The church was either suppressed or played a supporting role under the rule of these autocrats. It did not play the symbolic role of conferring power to the autocrat.

In modern times, however, religious institutions have played a significant role in the formation of an autocracy. In Iran in 1979, Ruhollah Khomeini, an ayatollah (leader) of the Shiite Islamic sect, assumed control of the country. It may be argued that his rule, which lasted until his death in 1989, was not an autocracy. He received overwhelming popular approval, and he established an Islamic republic with a president and prime minister. On the other hand, many modern autocrats have also established the trappings of democracy, and in similar ways—with councils or parliaments that approve the autocrat's measures, with government agencies that in name represent various democratic interests, and, often, with referendums and elections. History offers many examples of autocrats who obtained power with popular approval. One measure of whether a ruler is an autocrat may be the fortunes of those who, during the autocrat's rule, oppose the autocrat's will. Exile, prison, and execution have often been the fate of people who threaten or who are perceived to threaten an autocrat's power.

Another feature of modern autocracy is advanced use of technology and development in the techniques of the promotion of ideology. These developments have been identified as tools in the creation of totalitarianism. Totalitarianism is government control of not only political and economic power, but also of the personal and social relationships of the people. The governments that seek such power have often been autocratic. Obviously, such an ambition requires enormous power and resources. In fact, few systems have come close to realizing totalitarianism because of the great costs and difficulty. Many have tried. The modern era has also seen a large number of personal and military dictatorships, which do not have a totalitarian ideology but seek only to oppress and control society on behalf of a tiny elite. Even so, such authoritarian regimes typically claim to rule in the name of the people.

Applications

Modern autocracy and absolutism exist within a framework of the political organizations (courts, ministries, bureaus) of the nation-state. Modern autocratic regimes have a variety of forms but tend to fall into three general categories: the one-party state, corporatist dictatorship, and military regime. The one-party state is typified by those states in which only one political party exists by law. Examples include Nazi Germany and the states of the Soviet Union. Corporatist dictatorships have autocratic heads of government who work to ensure that corporate interests are protected. Examples include countries in Africa and Central America. Dictatorships, autocracies, and other authoritarian governments often are also military regimes since they rely on military force to maintain power. Military regimes, however, may be considered a distinct category of autocratic government if they retain military organization when in power. What follows are brief descriptions of modern autocracies that serve as examples of each category.

In 1917, Vladimir Lenin led a revolutionary party called the Bolsheviks to power in Russia. The Russian czar had abdicated the throne in the wake of the nation's failure in World War I, and the country was in a shambles. A follower of the ideas of Karl Marx, Lenin built a political party organized for a revolutionary struggle. Lenin believed that the only kind of communist party that could obtain power in Russia would need to be led by trained, professional revolutionaries. Lenin's Bolsheviks would be an elite vanguard who could seize control in Russia in the name of all the workers, to create conditions for a new kind of utopian socialist society. The party represented an elite, but Lenin argued that, guided by Marxist principles, it could create a society that was modern, free from competition and want, and ultimately democratic. In October, 1917, the Bolsheviks (later called the Communist Party) established the first revolutionary communist regime.

What followed was the evolution of a society that was completely dominated by the single party. Lenin died in 1922 and was succeeded by Joseph Stalin. Stalin became the first of the modern totalitarian autocrats, leading the Communist Party as its general secretary. Under Stalin, the party destroyed all political opposition. Stalin was a deeply suspicious man who used his power to destroy his competitors within the communist party. He erected a powerful secret police, which used terror to extinguish opponents and to repress the whole Soviet society. A system of internal concentration camps was created to imprison political prisoners and use them for forced labor. Entire populations were obliterated and removed to far-flung territories of Russia, and every aspect of the economy came under state control and planning. The whole society was subjected to the fulfillment of plans that sought to make the Soviet Union an industrial and military power.

Stalin governed as the absolute dictator of the Soviet Union from 1924 to 1953. At the time of his death, the bureaucracy of the Soviet Communist Party controlled the hierarchies of the military, police, and judiciary. Communist Party control extended to all forms of social activities: education, art, literature, athletics, and youth organizations. Stalin's single-party autocracy exercised near absolute control over the lives of the people who lived under its power.

Although Stalin's successors never had the massive personal power that he held, the pattern was set for the Secretary of the party to become head of a dictatorial bureaucracy which had no opposition until the time of Mikhail Gorbachev in 1985. More importantly, despite the variations in style of the twentieth century communist regimes, the basic model that all adhered to was the Soviet one-party state.

In another example of one-party autocracy, Adolf Hitler, as head of a fascist movement known as the Nazi Party, came to power in Germany in 1933. Nazi fascists believed that white, Germanic peoples were a superior race, and that the German people had been betrayed after their defeat in World War I. As the Bolshevik Party in Russia had, the Nazis (short for National Socialists) overthrew the existing government and created a one-party state. The Nazis were different, however, in that they believed in the power of the total state from the beginning. Hitler was seen to embody the soul, blood, and soil of the German people. The Nazis blamed Jewish people for weakening the German race, and selling Germany out to the allies in World War I. Hitler hoped to destroy the Jews and rode a tide of popular nationalist sentiment in an economically depressed Germany.

The Nazis used innovative techniques of mobilization, organizing political thugs and paramilitary guards to terrorize people and stage massive marches. By 1933, Hitler had made political bargains with conservative German elites, and utilizing the electoral process, Hitler became chancellor of Germany. The Nazis were poised to establish a one-party dictatorship.

Hitler became the purest of autocrats. In the years leading up to World War II, the Nazi Party diminished in importance. Consumed by military affairs and thirsty for total and personal power, Hitler surrounded himself with an elite guard. This elite guard replaced the party organization in power and importance, and along with the secret police—known as the Gestapo—ruled Nazi Germany through police terror and propaganda. The Nazis controlled the press, arts, architecture, education, and family life. They also carried out the infamous "final solution," the Nazi plan to exterminate the Jewish communities of Europe.

Two of the most prevalent forms of modern autocratic dictatorships are corporatist and military regimes. A corporatist regime is a system in which dictatorial power is held on behalf of the most powerful, largest, and wealthiest corporate elites within a society. The dictatorship rules to secure the interests of elites, while excluding and repressing the general population and any dissenters. A military regime is one in which the locus of power is held by the military and is usually led by an autocratic supreme commander. Military regimes may rule on behalf of wealthy elite classes, or strictly on the narrow interests of leading military elites, and they tend to be the most brutal and corrupt of authoritarian systems.

An example of a regime that was both corporatist and military was the dictatorship of General Augusto Pinochet in Chile. General Pinochet led a military overthrow of the democratic government of Chile in 1973. Although a military dictatorship, the Pinochet government pursued policies which eliminated socialist opposition parties, and emphasized free-market capitalism that served the interests of powerful corporate elites. Thus, the Chilean military came to power to strengthen the capitalist market, but terrorized opposition parties and dissenters.

Context

For people who live in democracies it may be difficult to accept the recurrent theme of authoritarianism and autocracy in history. The term "dictator" derives from the Roman Empire, in which a single person would rule by decree in time of emergency. The word "tyrant" comes from the ancient Greeks to describe despotic rulers who governed above the law. Monarchy and absolutism dominated civilizations for centuries. The notion that people should govern themselves has not changed the predominance of authoritarian forms of government in the modern era. In times of stress, war, and economic depression, people may become vulnerable to leaders who offer simple answers to complex questions. People may accept authoritarian prescriptions to solve social ills, thus choosing force, cruelty, and repression, rather than the more difficult process of negotiation, participation, and compromise.

With the fall of many communist regimes in the late twentieth century, many people believed that the world was ready for a global expansion of democracy. In reality, such times of great transformations can also create conflict, disorientation, and war. Economic and social instability is fertile ground for authoritarians who appeal to powerful elites who wish to hold their wealth and power and to unhappy people who seek an identity and sense of purpose. Environmental problems and competition for scarce global resources can also foment authoritarian movements.

Any state whose political institutions are weak and unable to solve conflicts effectively can give way to dictatorship. Military and corporatist regimes have prospered in developing countries, particularly in Latin America and the African continent. Often, the only people with the skill, organization, and tools to obtain power in unstable and developing nations are the military corps. This means that in a world of scarce resources, instability, and change, authoritarian temptations will persist.

Bibliography

Arendt, Hannah. *The Origins of Totalitarianism*. 2d ed. New York: Meridian Books, 1958. Theoretical and historical analysis of the social basis for totalitarian movements and systems in modern society.

Bracher, Karl Dietrich. *The German Dictatorship: The Origins, Structure, and Effects of National Socialism*. New York: Holt, Rinehart and Winston, 1970. Account of the rise and organization of the Nazi regime, with insight into the driving forces of its success.

Hobbes, Thomas. *Leviathan*. Edited by Michael Oakeshott. New York: Macmillan,

1962. Classic political treatise of the seventeenth century arguing in favor of absolutist monarchy.

Lee, Stephen J. *The European Dictatorships, 1918-1945*. London: Methuen, 1987. History of the rise of dictatorships in Russia, Germany, Italy, Spain, and elsewhere in twentieth century Europe.

Nordlinger, Eric A. *Soldiers in Politics: Military Coups and Governments*. Englewood Cliffs, N.J.: Prentice-Hall, 1977. Excellent treatment of the subject of the organization and rise of military governments. Provides a typology of military coups.

Perlmutter, Amos. *Modern Authoritarianism: A Comparative Institutional Analysis*. New Haven, Conn.: Yale University Press, 1981. Technical and schematic theory of the institutional innovations of modern authoritarian regimes.

Anthony R. Brunello

Cross-References

Aristocracy, Oligarchy, and Plutocracy, p. 78; Bonapartism, p. 140; Communist Parties, p. 377; Conservatism, p. 419; Corporatism, p. 452; Dictatorships, p. 546; Force, p. 712; History of Government, p. 829; Islam and Government, p. 994; Military Governments, p. 1192; Monarchy in History, p. 1221; Nationalism, p. 1268; Nietzsche's Political Philosophy, p. 1300; Plato's Political Philosophy, p. 1396; Political Philosophy, p. 1505.

THE BILL OF RIGHTS

Field of study: Civil rights and liberties

The U.S. Bill of Rights provides protection of civil and legal rights against encroachment by the federal or state governments and is a fundamental guarantee of rights enjoyed by citizens throughout the United States.

Principal terms
> DUE PROCESS: guarantees that legal process shall conform to standards necessary to achieve justice and fairness
> FUNDAMENTAL RIGHTS: rights implicit in the concept of ordered liberty and in those principles of justice rooted in tradition and conscience
> INCORPORATION OF BILL OF RIGHTS: process by which the Supreme Court made the provisions of the Bill of Rights applicable to the states, also called absorption
> PRIVILEGES AND IMMUNITIES: rights that belong to citizens of the United Kingdom and other countries, more extensive than fundamental rights
> PROCEDURAL RIGHTS: rights of legal procedures necessary for due process and fair trial, for example, trial by jury and indictment by grand jury

Overview
The first ten amendments to the Constitution of the United States form the federal Bill of Rights. A bill of rights was not included in the Constitution when it was framed in 1789 because the Framers did not believe that it was necessary. Since the federal government was a limited government, there was no need to protect the rights of the citizens. The Framers also believed that the greatest danger to the rights of the citizens came from the states, not the federal government, and most of the states had a bill of rights in their constitutions. When the Constitution was submitted to the states for ratification, the greatest objection to it was its lack of a bill of rights. Supporters of the Constitution, led by James Madison, agreed to submit to the states such a bill after the Constitution was adopted. Twelve proposed amendments passed the House of Representatives and the Senate and were sent to the states. Ten of them were accepted and became the Bill of Rights in December, 1791.

The First Amendment contains the fundamental freedoms of speech, press, petition, and religion. The right to keep and bear arms is expressed in the Second Amendment. The Third Amendment prohibits quartering of troops in private homes. The Fourth Amendment provides for people to be secure in their person, homes, and papers against unreasonable search and seizure, and sets limits for search warrants. Procedural rights are guaranteed in the Fifth, Sixth, Seventh, and Eighth amendments. Indictment by a grand jury in criminal cases, protection against double jeopardy or self-incrimination, and prohibitions against depriving persons of life, liberty, or property except by due process and against taking private property without just compensation are examples of rights guaranteed by the Fifth Amendment. The Sixth Amendment includes the right to a speedy and public trial by an impartial jury in a court previously established by law in the state and district where the crime occurred. The Sixth Amendment guarantees that the accused shall be informed of the charges, be confronted with the witnesses, have subpoena power, and shall be allowed counsel. The right of trial by jury in civil cases is included in the Seventh Amendment. The Eighth Amendment prohibits excessive bail and cruel and unusual punishment.

The Ninth and Tenth amendments ensure that the Bill of Rights is not used to deprive the people or the states of their implied rights or reserved powers. The Ninth Amendment states that the enumeration of rights does not mean that others, not included in the document, are denied. Powers not delegated to the federal government nor denied to the states are reserved to the states or to the people by the Tenth Amendment.

From the adoption of the Bill of Rights until the 1830's, cases involving Bill of Rights guarantees were not taken to the Supreme Court because it was believed that the judges on the Court would not rule favorably. Even the Alien and Sedition Acts, which were a clear violation of citizen rights, were not tested.

Beginning in the 1830's, the Supreme Court accepted cases involving the Bill of Rights. John Marshall's decision in *Barron v. Baltimore* in 1833 established the principle that the Bill of Rights did not apply to the states. This view was universally accepted until 1868 when the Fourteenth Amendment was ratified. The Fourteenth Amendment states:

All persons born or naturalized in the United States, and subject to the jurisdiction thereof, are citizens of the United States and of the State wherein they reside. No State shall make or enforce any law which shall abridge the privileges or immunities of citizens of the United States; nor shall any State deprive any person of life, liberty, or property, without due process of law; nor deny to any person within its jurisdiction the equal protection of the laws.

It is possible to read this amendment and conclude that the states could no longer violate the rights included in the federal Bill of Rights. This interpretation is controversial and has never been accepted by the Supreme Court. Later the Court gradually incorporated most of the guarantees of the Bill of Rights under the due process clause.

The first time that the Supreme Court considered the definition of the privileges and immunities clause of the Fourteenth Amendment was the *Slaughterhouse* cases of 1873. Although the cases did not directly address the question of incorporation of the Bill of Rights, the majority of the Court declared that the Thirteenth, Fourteenth, and Fifteenth amendments were intended to protect the rights of the new freedmen and were not intended to protect the fundamental rights of the citizens against state actions. The decision mentioned travel to and from the capital and on the high seas and protection of the citizen on the high seas and in foreign countries as fundamental rights protected by the amendment. Other fundamental rights included in the Bill of Rights remained subject to the police powers of the states.

In 1897 in *Chicago, Burlington & Quincy Railroad Co. v. Chicago* the due process clause of the Fourteenth Amendment was used to apply Fifth Amendment property rights to the states, and in 1925 in *Gitlow v. New York* the Supreme Court said:

> For present purposes we may and do assume that freedom of speech and of the press—which are protected by the First Amendment from abridgement by Congress—are among the fundamental personal rights and "liberties" protected by the due process clause of the Fourteenth Amendment from impairment by the States.

During the 1930's the Court began the "modernization" of the Bill of Rights by incorporating most of the Bill of Rights in the Fourteenth Amendment. By this process the Court applied the federal guarantees to the states. In 1931 two cases, *Near v. Minnesota* and *Stromberg v. California*, applied the First Amendment rights of freedom of speech and press to the states. Additional Bill of Rights guarantees were applied to the states in succeeding cases. In 1932 in *Powell v. Alabama* the Supreme Court declared that the right to counsel granted in the Sixth Amendment was a right the states must grant in state courts, and in 1937 in *DeJonge v. Oregon* the Court gave federal protection to freedom of assembly.

When the Court decided *Palko v. Connecticut* in 1937, the rights protected by the due process clause of the Fourteenth Amendment had been expanded without reference to the privileges and immunities clause. But with *Palko* the Court addressed the relationship between the privileges and immunities clause and the due process clause. Even though the prohibition against double jeopardy in the Fifth Amendment was extended to the state courts, the Supreme Court stated in its decision that all the guarantees in the Bill of Rights apply to the federal government but not to the states. Many of the procedural guarantees in the Bill of Rights did not limit state courts, but such fundamental rights as freedom of speech and press, the free exercise of religion, peaceable assembly, and benefit of counsel were protected from state encroachment by the due process clause of the Fourteenth Amendment. The Court ruled that the rights in the Bill of Rights are privileges and immunities, only some of which are so important they cannot be violated by either the federal government or the states. The importance of each right must be decided by the Court on a case-by-case basis.

President Franklin D. Roosevelt appointed more liberal justices to the Court, and the new justices argued that all the Fourteenth Amendment privileges and immunities limited the states. Even though this principle was a minority opinion of the Court and not accepted as the basis for decisions, the Court did include more and more of the Bill of Rights guarantees in the protection of the due process clause, except during World War II when some restrictions upon these rights were permitted in the interest of security.

Beginning in the 1950's incorporation of the Bill of Rights made great strides. Federalism was given less consideration, and the rights of individuals, especially minorities, became more important. By the end of the decade of the 1960's, most of the Bill of Rights had been applied to the states. The Court continued to use the due process clause, rather than the privileges and immunities clause, to justify the application.

By 1991 all the rights included in the first eight amendments were protected from state encroachment, except the Second Amendment right to keep and bear arms, the Third Amendment right that prohibits quartering of troops in private homes, the Fifth Amendment right to a grand jury indictment, the Sixth Amendment right of twelve jurors in a criminal trial, and the Seventh Amendment right of a civil jury. The Supreme Court has held that state procedures are adequate to protect the values inherent in those Bill of Rights guarantees.

Applications

The Bill of Rights is more important in protecting individual liberties than the Constitution itself. Amendments Four through Eight provide procedural guidelines for federal criminal trials. Since most suspects are charged in state courts, the protection of the rights of the accused in state courts is more important for the majority of citizens. The Supreme Court was slow in incorporating procedural rights in Amendments Four through Eight, taking until 1961. During the 1960's, under the leadership of Chief Justice Earl Warren, the Supreme Court, in a series of cases, incorporated most of the procedural rights contained in the Bill of Rights, including protection from self-incrimination, double jeopardy, and cruel and unusual punishment, as well as the guarantee of right to counsel, a speedy and public trial, and a jury trial.

Public opinion became increasingly critical of the Supreme Court for "coddling criminals" and tying the hands of the police. With the resignation of Earl Warren and the appointment of Warren Burger as chief justice in 1969, the court began to expand the powers of government and to lessen the protection of individuals. Although guarantees were not eliminated, the Court accepted limitations on the Bill of Rights that permitted the states greater freedom in exercising police powers and allowed for fewer procedural restraints.

In *Williams v. Florida*, in 1970, the Court ruled that state juries need not contain twelve members, as required in federal trials. In 1972, in *Apodaca v. Oregon* and *Johnson v. Louisiana*, the Court ruled that juries in state cases do not have to decide by a unanimous verdict. Those defending the rights of minorities expressed concern because juries of less than twelve people are less apt to protect minority rights and a nonunanimous verdict can provide even less protection to minorities.

The scope and meaning of the right limiting search and seizure has also been subject to controversy and to case-by-case variation in interpretation. The basic requirement for obtaining a search warrant has always been reasonable grounds for the belief that criminal activity is taking place. The Court has allowed exceptions to this basic requirement. Searches incidental to a lawful arrest, searches of premises where suspects have fled, searches of vehicles, and seizure of evidence discovered in plain view are all allowed without a warrant.

Cases granting greater search and seizure powers are *Adams v. Florida* (1972),

United States v. Robinson (1974), and *Gustafson v. Florida* (1974). All were decided by a Court that was less willing to incorporate procedural rights. In the first case greater flexibility was permitted in stop-and-frisk standards. Only reasonable suspicion was required. Search and seizure incidental to a lawful arrest was approved in the other two cases. These two cases permitted the use of any evidence obtained in such a search and seizure even if it had no relationship to the crime for which the arrest was made.

The Supreme Court has given the states greater flexibility in the exercise of those powers in order to facilitate law enforcement or to achieve moral goals deemed desirable for the community, but the guarantees of the Bill of Rights continue to apply to the states and are a protection from the arbitrary exercise of power by the federal and state governments.

Context

The Bill of Rights was adopted to protect the rights and liberties of the citizens against actions by the federal government. The adoption of the Fourteenth Amendment in 1868 provided a basis for incorporation, that is, the application of the guarantees of the Bill of Rights to the states. The due process clause of the Fourteenth Amendment was interpreted by the Supreme Court to require the incorporation of fundamental rights, but few rights were incorporated until the 1920's and 1930's when the fundamental freedoms were defined as freedom of speech, press, religion, and assembly.

During the 1960's, incorporation of the procedural rights in amendments Four through Eight took place. The Supreme Court reflected the citizens' concerns with civil rights and with discrimination against minorities and women. Later, the public became concerned with law and order and morality. The more conservative justices appointed after 1968 began to increase the police powers of the states and to limit Bill of Rights guarantees both at the federal and state levels.

The Court is not directly influenced by public opinion in making its decisions, but the climate of the times is often reflected in Court opinions. The Court is influenced by the country's political and social thinking in several ways. Various interest groups participate in cases before the justices as friends of the court. Presidents use new appointments to attempt to get their political point of view represented on the Court. Although the president can never be sure how an independent justice will decide an issue, the Court is influenced by new justices and especially by chief justices with leadership ability. Consequently, the opinions of the Court do follow public opinion and concerns.

Bibliography

Berger, Raoul. *Government by Judiciary: The Transformation of the Fourteenth Amendment.* Cambridge, Mass.: Harvard University Press, 1977. Asserts that through interpretation of the Fourteenth Amendment the Supreme Court amends the Constitution. Reviews the background of the amendment to determine original intent and calls for a "rollback" of decisions incorporating the Bill of Rights.

Black, Hugo L. "Minority Opinion" in *Adamson v. California.* 332 United States 46

(1947). Famous and cogent argument for incorporation of the Bill of Rights through the use of the privileges and immunities clause.

Curtis, Michael Kent. *No State Shall Abridge: The Fourteenth Amendment and the Bill of Rights.* Durham, N.C.: Duke University Press, 1986. States that the Bill of Rights and the Fourteenth Amendment can be interpreted only by reviewing the writings and arguments at the time of their passage. Favors incorporation.

Konvitz, Milton R. *Bill of Rights Reader: Leading Constitutional Cases.* 3d ed. Ithaca, N.Y.: Cornell University Press, 1965. Includes important Bill of Rights cases and includes the legal basis for majority and minority opinions.

Rhodehamel, John H., Stephen F. Rohde, and Paul Von Blum. *Foundations of Freedom.* Los Angeles: Constitutional Rights Foundation, 1991. A brief and readable history of the Bill of Rights, the English background, colonial experience, and adoption. Discusses the changes that occurred with the Civil War, industrialization, World War I, and incorporation.

St. John, Jeffrey. *Forge of Union, Anvil of Liberty: A Correspondent's Report on the First Federal Elections, the First Federal Congress, and the Bill of Rights.* Ottawa, Ill.: Jameson Books, 1992. Describes the formation of the U.S. government, putting the adoption of the Bill of Rights into historical context. Uses the narrative technique of a newspaper.

Schwartz, Bernard. *The Great Rights of Mankind: A History of the American Bill of Rights.* New York: Oxford University Press, 1977. Presents the background of the Bill of Rights starting with the great English charters, colonial and revolutionary precedents. Concludes with a legislative history of the amendments.

Robert D. Talbott

Cross-References

Civil Liberties Protection, p. 291; Civil Rights Protection, p. 304; The Constitution of the United States, p. 425; Constitutional Law in the United States, p. 439; Courts: U.S. Federal, p. 471; Judicial Review, p. 1012; Locke's Political Philosophy, p. 1142; Right to Bear Arms and the Second Amendment, p. 1750; The Supreme Court: Organization and Purpose, p. 1929; The Supreme Court: Role in Government and Law, p. 1935.

BONAPARTISM

Field of study: Political philosophy

Often characterized as a form of government run by a benevolent dictator, Bonapartism had its origins in France during the reigns of two famous members of the Bonaparte family: Napoleon I (r. 1804-1814) and Louis Napoleon, or Napoleon III (r. 1852-1870).

Principal terms

BOURBON RESTORATION: period of restored French monarchy that followed Napoleon I's First Empire

CONCERT OF EUROPE: system of international consultation established at the Congress of Vienna in 1815 initially designed to keep post-Napoleonic France subordinate to the other countries of Europe

NAPOLEONIC CODE: civil laws established by Napoleon I that were eventually adopted in many European and Latin American countries

SENATUS CONSULTUM: legislative acts issued by the upper house, usually after "preparatory direction" from above

Overview

Bonapartism involves more than the fact that two members of the Bonaparte family—Napoleon Bonaparte and his nephew Louis Bonaparte, also known as Napoleon III—ruled France as emperors of the First and Second empires (1804-1814 and 1852-1870). To be sure, Bonapartism would seem to be inseparable from the fact of empire imposed by military strength. The historical phenomenon of Bonapartism, however, implies much more than imperial grandeur and military power, although the military was critical in both emperors' regimes.

The first characteristic of Bonapartism that gives the term a wider application involves its promise of stability in a time of difficult transition between two radically different systems of government, society, and economics. Such was the promise when Napoleon I guaranteed that France would not face chaos if enemies of the First Republic (1792-1804) tried to turn back the clock to appease reactionary political and economic interests. Similarly, Louis Napoleon's actions in the wake of the 1848 revolution and declaration of the Second Republic (1848-1852) prevented total and precipitous reversals that could have led to civil war. Both Bonapartes achieved a measure of stability by combining bids for popular support with compromises for conservative interests.

A second feature of Bonapartism that survived the specific historical context of nineteenth century France was the view that the state's executive leadership should always appear to be above party politics. The purpose of such appearance is that the executive may, by observing it, better represent general interests within the polity. Primary among these interests is public security, but other needs, such as general administration, law, and economic order, fell under the executive purview of the two historical Bonapartes.

Although the politics of Bonapartism obviously involved factors of personal leadership and intrigues, much of its success had to do with institutional compromises. These compromises took the interests of different groups in French society into account. Most groups feared the consequences of not accepting compromise. The long-overdue compromises mitigated the disadvantages of the high concentrations of political power that both imperial regimes brought. Areas of institutional compromise included legislation on Church-state relations, development of universal standards for civil law, and the extension under state sponsorship of major commercial, banking, and public works concerns.

The political legacy of Bonapartism includes two basic concepts. One is "benevolent dictatorship," or strong leadership that serves the interests of the state. The second is the presumed ability of such strong leadership to overcome parliamentary paralysis or parliamentary irresponsibility. In both historical cases in which Bonapartes rose to control France, this second factor can be seen to have been paramount. Significantly, when Bonapartist chiefs of state assumed control, support for their actions came—not simultaneously, nor for the same reasons—from left-of-center republicans as well as from monarchist conservatives.

Napoleon Bonaparte's foundation of the First Empire illustrates this point. When the authority of the first consul (Napoleon's title as head of the Consulate between 1799 and 1804) was threatened by a royalist plot, his action was quick and ruthless. Several high military figures who had served under him were arrested—most notably, Jean Victor Moreau, who had defeated the Prussians at Hohenlinden. The first consul also implicated the Bourbon Duke Louis-Antoine Henri d'Enghien in the plot by employing what many considered to be fabricated evidence. In March, 1804, the Duke was tried by a military court and executed.

What Napoleon did next not only secured his position, but also enhanced it dramatically. He called upon the upper legislative house, the senate, to proclaim that "heredity in the supreme magistracy is an essential." As the senators had been led to hope that their own legislative offices would be made hereditary, they cooperated fully, declaring Napoleon to be emperor, with a number of exceptional powers. Some of these powers would be used to concentrate more authority under the emperor's office, at the expense of the same legislative elites who had named him. To further legitimize his new supreme authority, Napoleon resorted to a device that became typical of Bonapartism: a national plebiscite to approve or disapprove the senate's declaration. More than four and a half million voters approved, while no more than a few thousand dared cast negative votes. In stages, Napoleon I—as his nephew would do some decades later—courted a small coterie of influential supporters, who took the place, in terms of real power, of what became a largely symbolic legislative body. Bonapartist leadership used the military elite and multiple bids for recognition of France's glory abroad to attract influential members to the governing coterie, while at the same time helping the people forget that they were being governed by firm imperial hands.

Applications

Legal issues that were of concern to the Bonapartes and to those who believed in the "guiding hand" precedents established by them tended to address major questions of the nature of government itself, not everyday matters of administration or law-making.

For Napoleon I, a number of questions left over from the time of the First Republic called for a strong hand to assure some change without the risk of conservative reactions or radical rejections. His power to pass laws that no group of the representative political system could have sponsored on its own was exemplified in at least two major areas: in church-state relations and in the establishment of a single balanced code of civil law. The Concordat of 1801 signed with Pope Pius VII defined the limits of ecclesiastical autonomy in France and succeeded in bringing a very large number of conservative priests and bishops (called "legitimate" clergy) back in support of a regime that they had denounced since the revolution had established the strongly secular civil constitution of the clergy. The Concordat managed to keep a degree of state influence over the church in France. This influence extended to matters that the liberals (as opposed to radical revolutionaries) had deemed "beyond negotiation," such as editing the catechism, subjecting papal bulls or legates to "national" church interpretation, and regulation of seminaries.

The second major area in which Napoleon I demonstrated expertise in leadership was his balancing the political extremes set loose by the Revolution. This balance took the form of what came to be called the *Code Napoléon*, or French Civil Code. Promulgated before Napoleon became emperor, its provisions became the basis for civil jurisdictions in the empire until 1815, with periodic readjustments in France thereafter. It continues to be applied in countries that were under Napoleon's rule.

Like the 1801 Concordat, the Code was intended to strike a balance between what the Revolution had destroyed (feudal and canon law) and the needs of a society increasingly based on ideas of private property and contract rights. While it retained some features of the First Republic's emphasis on protection of the individual (such as family inheritances to be shared equitably, bankruptcy, and protection against indigency), the Code assured that those who had acquired interest in economic institutions (private property and banking) would be secure against radical social reform. The Code was one element of internal institutional stabilization that helped gain support for Bonaparte's later insistence that full governing control should be passed to him as emperor.

Napoleon I knew that symbolic concessions to his more conservative backers would enhance the loyalty of influential supporters who did not want a return to the old regime. One way this was done after declaration of the First Empire in 1804 was by recognizing a new nobility, complete with titles but without the privileges held by the prerevolutionary estate. Many new nobles came from wealthy families who were anxious not to be labeled mere bourgeoisie in a time of such obvious splendor.

Another Napoleonic institution of compromise that easily translated into support for Bonapartism was introduction of the Legion of Honor, which has survived for nearly two centuries. Awarding state honors to individuals whose exemplary private careers merited public attention proved to be a means of spreading recognition of influence—without granting independent political privilege—to different sectors of French society. Pride in recognition of individual accomplishment in the military, scientific, commercial, and public service arenas tended to cut across class lines, creating a sense of loyalty to the higher authority of the state that bestowed such recognition.

Proof of the intelligence of the legislative and political practices that Napoleon instituted lies in the fact that many of his legislative principles survived, mainly intact, even during the Bourbon and Orleanist monarchical restoration (1815-1848). As republicanism again pushed the pendulum of political unrest toward the breaking point in 1848, the stage was set for Napoleon's nephew to demonstrate that, even in a very different socio-economic environment, there was a need for guidance from above to prompt French legislators who could not, or would not, recognize the objective need for change in certain domains. Bonapartism again maintained that only a higher authority could do so. Those fearful that the Second Republic would go to extremes agreed, first by electing Louis Bonaparte as president, and then acquiescing in 1852, when the president carried off a coup, making him emperor.

Whatever Louis Napoleon's understanding was of his higher calling to transform France once again into an empire, the role he fulfilled in domestic politics bore a remarkable resemblance to that of his uncle. The nature of the problems confronting the Second Republic, however, tended to reflect the economic realities of the second half of the nineteenth century more than they did the increasingly scant remnants of the late eighteenth century. One issue that republican legislators tried unsuccessfully to address during the tumultuous months after the 1848 revolution was how to alleviate some of the hardships of the industrial working class without upsetting bourgeois interests that had come to constitute the base of French society.

During the period of his political exile and opposition to the restoration monarchy, Louis Bonaparte went on record as a champion of workers' movements. His early efforts to gain support from the poorer classes did not always conform to the more conservative views of people who had backed Napoleon I. Indeed it was not totally clear how he would reconcile differences between his right- and left-wing supporters. Upon the declaration of the Second Empire in 1852, his actions began to reveal a pattern that answered this question.

Laws granting the right to strike did not come until the second half of Bonaparte's rule, but he began his reign with basic legislation supporting worker cooperative support societies (*mutuels*). Other examples of Bonapartist stewardship for institutions answering the needs of the working classes included a greatly expanded role for the Polytech Association (originally founded in the 1830's) to offer courses on economics and technology—as well as French grammar and mathematics—to workers who might otherwise have had no other access to education.

Concessions to the needs of the less privileged classes, however, certainly did not lead to openings either in the legislature (the Corps Législatif remained largely symbolic) or in broader areas of political expression such as the press. A strictly controlled press was part of the government apparatus. Its function was not only to provide public information concerning activities within the generally closed circle of ministerial business, but also to limit coverage of government inadequacies.

There are many examples of a main tactic of mid-nineteenth century Bonapartism, executive initiative involving legislation that would have stood little chance of passing if it had been left to the opposing liberal and conservative blocs. By the mid-1860's, when he had done much of what he believed needed to be done, the emperor claimed to be anxious to prepare the way for liberalization of many institutions that, before the Bonapartist period of executive sponsorship, had been tied to specific interests. Reform of some of these institutions, such as the press, banking, and legislative representation, was deemed essential for the continuing expansion of France's potential as a modern nation. Although the work was never concluded to the satisfaction of its liberal supporters, some sectors began to obtain some vital concessions that joined their interests more closely to those of a Bonapartist government.

Toward the end of the Second Empire, Louis Napoleon resorted to the Bonapartist device of a yes-or-no plebiscite to try to block Corps Législatif efforts to use a serious labor crisis as an excuse to alter France's constitution, ostensibly to increase democratic representation. For Bonpartists, the move may have been a cover for expanding the influence of a discontented bourgeoisie. The outbreak of the Franco-Prussian war in 1870 and defeat of the Second Empire, however, left the resolution of this internal struggle to the successor Third Republic, which lasted until the end of World War II.

Context

The spirit of directed compromise in Bonapartism has never disappeared completely. Executive authoritarianism can be easily identified and defended or denounced, depending on presumed degrees of benevolence that may be attached to particular regimes. If one separates out the obvious stigmas associated with fascist experiments that limited democracy—but claimed to represent the "higher interests" of all classes within the Italian, Spanish, and German polities—some definite characteristics of Bonapartism can be seen in each. Superficially, Mussolini's declaration that strict state direction had finally made "the trains run on time" in Italy covered a number of other more profound issues that had direct importance to commercial, banking, and industrial, as well as working-class interests.

Extensive studies of the internal workings of Hitler's Third Reich also emphasize that—behind the ominous shadow of Nazi dictatorship—there was an underlying desire to demonstrate that all classes of German society would benefit from legislation dealing with workers' security and public education.

Two other examples of executive "benevolence" in the post-World War II period did not (as did the two Bonapartes and the German and Italian fascist states) fall precipitously. One was the Franco regime in Spain, and another is France's Fifth Republic, founded by Charles de Gaulle in 1958. In the case of de Gaulle, a very Bonapartist move was made to introduce a new constitution that, by giving impressive powers of authority to the presidents of the Fifth Republic (beginning with de Gaulle himself), would make it difficult for competing political parties to paralyze the government by blocking either key legislation or cabinet appointments.

After considering such examples of how the principles of Bonapartism could reappear in quite different historical and geographical contexts, one main point may be recalled to distinguish between dictatorship and Bonapartist authoritarianism. Dictatorship eventually erases any need to justify executive control in the name of the polity as a whole (the case of all twentieth century fascist regimes), but Bonapartism retains the caveat that, in the end, the people should decide a country's destiny. The device of plebiscites, characteristic of both Bonapartes, was repeated by de Gaulle in the Fifth Republic and eventually paved the way for his own withdrawal from the presidency in 1968.

Bibliography

Bruun, Geoffrey. *Europe and the French Imperium, 1799-1814.* New York: Harper & Brothers, 1938. Contains detailed, readable coverage of both internal and international developments during the Consulate and First Empire.

Gooch, Brison D., ed. *Napoleon III, Man of Destiny; Enlightened Statesman or Proto-Fascist?* New York: Holt, Rinehart and Winston, 1963. Part of a series on key themes of European history. Compares Napoleon III's accomplishments with those of Napoleon I, Mussolini, and Hitler.

_____. *The Reign of Napoleon III.* Chicago: Rand McNally, 1969. Includes detailed biographical information on Louis Napoleon and analysis of his foreign and domestic policies.

Guérard, Albert. *Reflections on the Napoleonic Legend.* London: T. Fisher Unwin, 1924. Bonapartism within a context of political ideologies rather than historical events.

Kulstein, David I. *Napoleon III and the Working Class: A Study of Government Propaganda Under the Second Empire.* Sacramento: California State Colleges, 1969. Traces Bonapartist propaganda in its attempts to influence the working class, which was feared to be ready to join the Communist cause.

Byron D. Cannon

Cross-References

Autocracy and Absolutism, p. 127; Charismatic Leadership, p. 209; Cult of Personality, p. 477; Executive Functions in U.S. Government, p. 636; Heads of State, p. 804; History of Government, p. 829; Liberalism, p. 1118; Oligarchy, p. 1344; Parliamentary Government, p. 1377.

THE BRITISH PARLIAMENTARY SYSTEM

Field of study: Comparative government

Parliament is the legislative branch of the British government. Through its House of Commons and House of Lords, Parliament passes laws, scrutinizes the operations of government, and represents the interests of parties, pressure groups, and citizens.

Principal terms

BICAMERAL LEGISLATURE: lawmaking body with two separate and distinct chambers

CABINET: committee of senior politicians selected by the prime minister to run the government

COLLECTIVE RESPONSIBILITY: members of the cabinet and government present a united front to Parliament in defense of their actions and decisions

HOUSE OF COMMONS: one body of Parliament, consisting of 651 members who serve terms of up to five years and represent single-member constituencies

HOUSE OF LORDS: one body of Parliament, consisting of more than twelve hundred members who serve by virtue of birthright, appointment, or position held

LOYAL OPPOSITION: members of nongoverning parties in Parliament whose political task is to oppose government's policy and suggest alternative programs

PARLIAMENTARY SUPREMACY: Parliament has the right to make and change any law, and its decisions are not open to challenge by British courts

Overview

Regarded by many as the mother of democratic legislatures, the British Parliament consists of two separate bodies, the House of Commons and the House of Lords. The House of Commons had 651 members as of 1985, elected from single-member constituencies. Their normal term of office is five years but can be less if early elections are called. The House of Commons increased in size during the late twentieth century. From 1974 to 1983, there were 635 members. Population shifts required boundary commissions to add new districts and redraw district boundary lines to make districts roughly equal in population size. The House of Lords is composed of more than twelve hundred members, none of whom are elected. Peers, as members of the House of Lords are called, represent no one but themselves. They are there by reason of birthright (hereditary peers), appointment by the Crown at the direction of the prime minister (lifetime peers), or by virtue of holding a position (peers who sit on the high appeals court in Britain or bishops and archbishops of the Church of England). The chief executive—who is the prime minister—and the cabinet remain in office only as long as they maintain the political support of a majority in the House of Commons.

The modern British Parliament carries out several key functions in the governmental system: lawmaking; representation of the interests of political parties, political interest groups, and vocal constituents; monitoring ministries, agencies, and civil servants to ensure that programs are properly administered; informing the public, through floor debates and questions addressed to cabinet ministers about important national problems; and providing support or opposition to the government's legislative bills and policies. Parliamentary sovereignty means that Parliament may make or unmake any law. No person or judicial body can declare an act of Parliament "unconstitutional" or unlawful. A serious challenge to the principle of parliamentary sovereignty concerns British integration into the European Union. In 1993, the European Court of Justice ruled in two cases of individuals challenging decisions of their governments. The rulings in these cases clearly support the right of individuals to bring national governments to court and the prevalence of European Union law over a member state's law.

The monarch is the official head of state, but the active head of government is the prime minister. Although appointments (such as those of cabinet ministers and junior ministers) are made, acts of Parliament are passed, and other functions of government are carried out in the name of the monarch, the real political decisions are made by the prime minister and the cabinet. For example, Queen Elizabeth II opened each session of Parliament for several decades with a "speech from the throne" in the House of Lords, but that speech typically was written by the prime minister and members of the cabinet, then dutifully read by the queen.

The prime minister is selected from the party (or coalition of parties) holding a majority in the House of Commons. The government, in the British meaning of the word, comprises the country's political leaders and key policymakers. The large majority of them are members of Parliament, (M.P.s), primarily from the House of Commons. In the late twentieth century, the prime minister had the power to appoint twenty-one M.P.s to cabinet posts, an additional sixty to sixty-five M.P.s to subcabinet offices, and about thirty to forty M.P.s to positions of parliamentary secretary. This means that one-third or more of the majority party's parliamentary delegation is also part of the executive policy-making elite. In accordance with the principle of collective responsibility, members of the cabinet and government present a united front to Parliament in defense of their bills, actions, and decisions.

The "loyal opposition" consists of members of parties in the minority in Parliament. Their political task is to oppose the government's policy direction and suggest alternative programs in Parliament. Parliament may force the resignation of the prime minister and cabinet through a defeat on the floor of the House of Commons of a major bill, through a confidence vote, or through a successful motion of censure brought by the opposition. A government with a secure party majority in the House of Commons is unlikely to be forced out of office through losing a vote of confidence or through a censure motion. If forced to resign, the prime minister and cabinet may be replaced by other leaders of the majority party or by the opposition. The prime minister more likely will request the monarch to dissolve Parliament and call for new elections.

Voters then choose the party they wish to see direct the government.

Parliamentary committees hold considerably fewer political powers than do their American congressional counterparts. An individual standing committee might consider a variety of bills, but its membership changes for each bill. Once the House of Commons or House of Lords has approved the main principle of a bill, a committee cannot make amendments or revisions that change that principle unless such changes are introduced or accepted by the government. Sixteen select committees monitor particular departments or responsibilities of government; committee jurisdictions include agriculture, education, and foreign affairs.

The House of Lords plays a smaller role in Parliament than does the House of Commons. The House of Lords examines and recommends revisions to bills passed by the House of Commons, initiates noncontroversial public bills, delays some bills, and seriously scrutinizes a few issues of national significance. Certain members of the House of Lords also act as judges. Specifically appointed for life, a small number of peers sit as the supreme judicial tribunal in Britain. A lower court of appeals might recommend that some point of law involved in a case is of considerable public importance and ask that this legal point be decided by the highest court of appeals, the Law Lords. Usually five or seven peers chosen from a larger appellate committee will hand down a decision in such cases.

Applications

A crucial factor in the early historical development of Parliament was the struggle between the monarch and members of Parliament for control over taxes and spending. That balance of power over budgetary policy came to lie primarily with civil servants, the treasury, and the cabinet rather than with Parliament. Parliament must adopt any budget submitted by the government.

In cabinet meetings, the treasury makes the first recommendations on expenditure amounts or revisions in tax sources. Treasury ministers, especially the chancellor of the exchequer and the chief secretary of the treasury, act as guardians of the public purse. Ministers fight for their preferred programs and the funding for them, using political bargaining and tools of persuasion.

The cabinet presents its expenditure plan to Parliament for adoption or possible revision. The major debates on public spending occur during the twenty-six "supply days" in each parliamentary session. During these debates, leaders of the opposition use individual budgetary proposals as a background for more specific or general assaults on the shortcomings of government policies. Majority party leaders defend the government's budget. Parliament cannot increase expenditures for a department beyond those recommended by a minister, nor may Parliament initiate revenue decreases. Only a minister can introduce a proposal for taxation.

Parliament as a whole is too large a body to scrutinize budgetary proposals beyond the debates on a measure's principles. The House of Commons created two committees to more closely examine the details of government budget estimates. The Treasury and Civil Service Select Committee is composed of a small number of well-informed members of Parliament. The committee focuses on important spending issues, in detail. The Public Accounts Committee, headed by a member of the opposition, conducts program evaluation and monitors expenditures after they have been made. The committee spotlights mismanagement and unintended practices but has few parliamentary powers to change practices beyond calling attention to problems.

The balance of power on the revenue or taxing side of the budget is weighed in favor of the executive branch headed by the prime minister. Parliament has not introduced a committee structure for as careful a review of revenue proposals as for expenditure measures. A subcommittee of the Treasury and Civil Service Select Committee conducts some investigations of revenue issues, but debates on finance bills are limited. The government makes the budget an important measure of confidence in the majority party leadership. The Parliament Act of 1911 limits the power of the House of Lords. Passage of budget bills can be delayed for one month after passage in the House of Commons. After one month, a budget becomes law even without formal approval by the House of Lords.

The surprising and sudden removal from office of Prime Minister Margaret Thatcher in 1990 and her replacement by Conservative Party member John Major shocked Great Britain. The manner of her departure was unprecedented in the parliamentary politics of the post-World War II era. Thatcher had no wish to resign and had not been defeated in an election. She had won three consecutive parliamentary elections as leader of the Conservative Party and had served longer as prime minister than anyone else in the twentieth century. Thatcher was removed neither through a cabinet-sponsored revolt nor by a vote of no confidence on the floor of the House of Commons. Instead, a secret ballot among Conservative Party members dismissed the Conservative prime minister.

No prime minister and cabinet with a workable party majority had been overthrown in the twentieth century by an adverse vote in the House of Commons. Labour prime ministers in 1924 and 1979 headed minority governments dependent on the support of minor parties. In 1979, for example, Welsh Nationalists voted with the Labour Government but Ulster Unionists, Scottish Nationalists, Liberals, and Conservative M.P.s joined to defeat the government by one vote. Parliament was dissolved, and in the subsequent general election voters returned a Conservative government to power.

In 1940, the government fell after a censure debate in the House of Commons on the handling of the war. The government was not defeated by a division of votes, but its majority was significantly smaller than its normal parliamentary majority. Prime Minister Neville Chamberlain felt obliged to resign as a result of the harsh criticism directed at him during the debate, the pressure of public opinion, and the readiness of the Conservative Party to appoint another prime minister from its ranks.

A faltering economy and disaffection within the cabinet contributed to Thatcher's downfall in November, 1990. An unpopular poll tax pushed through Parliament by Thatcher's government, splits in the Conservative Party over Britain's further integration into the European Community, and forced cabinet resignations tarnished her management image. A serious backbench challenger, former cabinet member Michael

Heseltine, attacked Thatcher's authority and forced a vote among the parliamentary party members. The first ballot revealed that Thatcher obtained 204 votes to Heseltine's 152, with 16 Conservatives abstaining. Thatcher thus fell 4 votes short of the number required by party rules for outright victory, so a second ballot was necessary. Thatcher, advised by cabinet colleagues that she would not prevail on the second ballot, resigned as prime minister. John Major, favored by Thatcher, was declared the winner on the second ballot when the other two contenders (one of whom was Heseltine) conceded defeat. Major took office as prime minister on November 28, 1990.

Context

The concept of representation has not always been a popular political ideal even within Western political systems, much less worldwide. Gradually, the notion of a spokesperson for a community came to be accepted, and monarchs came to be viewed as representing their entire realms. By 1200, the British king was expected to consult with advisers in order to discover and declare the law. In 1215, the nobility pressured King John to sign the Magna Carta and to recognize as a right of his subjects "to have the Common Council of the Kingdom" for purposes of advising on raising new taxes. Church officials, earls, and barons were included among the king's advisers.

The advisory and representative roles of different political interests as undertaken by the Common Council evolved into Parlement (parliament) and the forerunner of the House of Lords. The House of Commons developed from the summoning of the first commoners (knights, merchants, guildsmen, and burgesses) to Parliament. These commoners were required to bring forth the record of local cases to the king's high court, ratify the imposition of special taxes by the king, carry the king's proclamations, and report the monarch's decisions to local communities.

Conflict between supporters of Parliament and of royalty led to civil war as some kings sought to reverse the powers and privileges asserted by Parliament. King Charles I was beheaded in 1649. Although the monarchy was reestablished in 1660, political struggles persisted between the king and Parliament. From 1714 to 1727, George I allowed his cabinet to meet in his absence. A role developed for a "prime" minister to coordinate policies, relieving the king of this responsibility.

Acts of 1832 and 1867 expanded the electorate and brought about the loss of political influence of the aristocracy, gentry, and House of Lords. Power passed to the middle classes and the House of Commons, with the cabinet and prime minister dominating parliamentary politics. The history of Parliament thus shows a passage of power from the elite to the masses, or at least to their representatives.

Bibliography

Bagehot, Walter. *The English Constitution, and Other Political Essays.* Rev. ed. New York: D. Appleton, 1908. Offers important guidance in understanding Parliament's development and is an authoritative work on different aspects of the British constitution. Reviews defects and advantages of parliamentary practices. Argues that the act of 1832 made the two houses of Parliament distinct.

Birch, Anthony H. *The British System of Government*. 7th ed. Boston: Allen & Unwin, 1986. Places Parliament within the political environment of medieval and modern British institutions, parties, pressure groups, and active citizens furthering their own interests. Analyzes many changes the British government has undergone, especially in the workings of Parliament.

Butt, Ronald. *The Power of Parliament*. New York: Walker, 1967. Assesses the place of Parliament in both historical context and the practice of contemporary British politics. Not merely a descriptive account of how Parliament functions or a study of political procedures; evaluates allegations that Parliament has declined and the advisability of specific reforms of Parliament.

Christie, Kenneth. *Problems in European Politics*. Chicago: Nelson-Hall, 1995. A final chapter focuses on the European Community and the challenges it presents to the British Parliament. Chapter 6 discusses the important issue of whether the European Community will be rooted in active cooperation between independent sovereign states, as outlined by British prime minister Margaret Thatcher, or will be some version of a federal system.

Hollis, Christopher. *Parliament and Its Sovereignty*. London: Hollis & Carter, 1973. A former member of Parliament scrutinizes the concept of parliamentary sovereignty, contending that parliamentary sovereignty was absolute prior to British entry into the European Community in 1972.

Leonard, Dick, and Valentine Herman, eds. *The Backbencher and Parliament: A Reader*. London: Macmillan, 1972. Differing from other books on Parliament, this work focuses on the tasks and responsibilities of ordinary individual members of Parliament, called backbenchers. Both officeholders in the House of Commons and backbenchers offer insiders' views of political activities. Scholars from outside Parliament contribute to a balanced understanding of the House of Commons.

Norton, Philip. *The British Polity*. 3d ed. New York: Longman, 1994. Useful and informative account of British politics. Explains contemporary parliamentary politics in the context of a continuity of British values and institutions. Weighs changes in parliamentary practices. Contains maps and results of recent opinion polls.

Steve J. Mazurana

Cross-References

Cabinet Government, p. 184; The Canadian Parliamentary System, p. 190; Conservatism, p. 419; Elections, p. 578; Executive Functions in U.S. Government, p. 636; Government Types, p. 785; Heads of State, p. 804; History of Government, p. 829; Legal Systems in Anglo-American Governments, p. 1085; Legislative Body Types, p. 1091; Legislative Functions of Government, p. 1098; Monarchy in Constitutional Governments, p. 1215; Parliamentary Government, p. 1377; Political Party Roles, p. 1499; Power Divisions in Governments, p. 1578; Public Policy, p. 1633; Scientific Humanism, p. 1784; Taxation and Appropriation, p. 1941; Voting in History, p. 2116.

BUDDHISM AND GOVERNMENT

Field of study: Religion and government

Like all religions, Buddhism contains codes of conduct for its adherents. These ethical guidelines are not only for interactions between individuals, but also between groups. Thus Buddhism and politics meet in determining what the social goals should be and how they should be structured.

Principal terms
BUDDHA: literally, "the enlightened one," the designation for the founder of Buddhism, Gautama Siddhartha of the Shakya tribe
DHARMA: teachings of Buddhism, often represented by a wheel
MAHAYANA BUDDHISM: "the great vehicle," the form of Buddhism found in Central and East Asia, which emphasizes sharing spiritual merit, and claims to best convey Buddha's insights
SANGHA: community of monks that carries on the central task of teaching and, especially in Theravada Buddhism, is the principal religious structure
SUTRA: book, or collection of teachings relating to the Buddha
THERAVADA BUDDHISM: "the way of the elders," the form of Buddhism found most often in Sri Lanka and Southeast Asia, which emphasizes monasticism and claims to be structured like early Buddhism

Overview

Buddhism is a religion based upon the teachings of Gautama Siddhartha, "the Buddha," who lived in the sixth century B.C.E. While the main focus of his teachings was directed toward the liberation of sentient beings from the cycle of rebirth, not all his teachings ignored social issues. The dharma, the doctrines of Buddha, includes statements that deal with social and political issues. In addition, the process of people living their lives guided by the religion in a historical context has forced Buddhists to come to an understanding of the relationship between Buddhism and government.

According to Buddhist traditions, Gautama, the son of the ruler of a small kingdom, was dissatisfied with the world and vowed to seek a solution for the problems that all people face. He left home, seeking a teacher who could give him the proper guidance. When he did not find one, he set out on his own to find the solution. After six years of strict self-mortifications and meditation, he decided that a middle road between extreme asceticism and indulgent worldly life would be more favorable to finding the solution. The solution was found as he meditated in Banaras when he was about thirty-five years of age. He taught for forty-five years, and upon his death is said to have fully entered Nirvana and ended his cycle of rebirth.

Among the extensive Buddhist scriptures, a few deal directly with political and social issues. Among the scriptures accepted by all Buddhists is the *Digha Nikaya* (the

Long Discourses), in which Gautama taught about the origin of society and the state. He believed the state was the result of a social contract. With the appearance of evil, the people chose the person best able to combat the social effects of evil to be the king. This text emphasizes that the king is not different from the others, just better prepared for the responsibilities. This is in accordance with Gautama's teachings on the emerging caste system, which he totally rejected. Gautama believed in the essential equality of all people. He taught that people from all levels of society are capable of enlightenment, just as all face the potential of unpleasant births. It is the person's character that should determine his or her status. In the later developments of Mahayana Buddhism, the role of the king was elevated. Few of the newer sutras deal with the issue of government, but the *Sutra of the Excellent Golden Light* proclaims a doctrine similar to the European doctrine of the "Divine Right of Kings," or the Chinese "Mandate of Heaven." Perhaps coming from the example of Asoka, a monarch of the Magadha Empire in the third century B.C.E., this book of scripture states that the righteous king is responsible for the ordering of society based upon morality, which then confers the continued blessings of the gods. As he is able to fulfill his responsibilities, then he is worthy to be considered among the sons of the gods.

Asoka is seen as the ideal Buddhist ruler and credited with transforming its teachings into a political system. Early in his reign, Asoka followed the traditional political path of seeking greater political and military power, expanding his empire by military conquest. After he was exposed to Buddhist teachings, he renounced his militaristic policy. His priority changed to expanding the influence of the dharma inside and outside his territory. Since his lavish support of the Sangha attracted many opportunists, he sponsored the Third Great Council to purify it. He enacted laws that made it impossible for those who had been dismissed from the Sangha to continue to represent themselves as monks. This illustrates the traditional relationship between the Sangha and the ruler. The ruler is responsible for ensuring that the society is prosperous, that the members of the Sangha are adequately cared for, and that the Sangha does not depart from the ideals and discipline upon which it is based. At the same time, the Sangha teaches, shapes the culture of the society for the accumulation of merit for all of its members, and generally is supportive of the monarch.

In the modern era, while Buddhist leaders have sought to have a supportive government and what might be considered a Buddhist society, there is no specifically Buddhist form of government. Although monarchy has been the traditional style of government in Buddhist areas, the religious teachings are not inconsistent with democracy. Within the Sangha, all monks are supposed to be equal and certain decisions require a vote of the monks. Thus while Buddhism did not inspire the development of democracy in Asian countries, it is not in opposition to it. In the twentieth century, some Buddhist leaders have sought to have Buddhism declared the state religion. Others have been content to have a secular state whose laws reflect a way of life in harmony with the dharma. In either case, freedom of religion usually has not been a major issue in modern Buddhist states.

The traditional role of the Sangha passively serving the government is being challenged in many areas. Some within the Sangha believe that monks should participate directly in politics to counteract anything that is anti-Buddhist. They have a limited political agenda, pushing for Buddhism as a state religion, opposing communism or other political philosophies that try to negate religion, and seeking to ensure that the legal system is in accordance with Buddhist teachings. Those seeking social changes claim that Buddha not only meditated, but also tried to work for the welfare of people. These monks point out that Buddha did not turn his back on those in distress, therefore neither should his monks. They believe monks are in a special position to help through politics, because their relative detachment and monastic rules make them less susceptible to greed and delusion, and monks generally can not hold political office.

An additional change in the political activity of Buddhism has resulted from the increased number of Buddhist organizations led by persons who are not monks and thus are not bound by the laws that regulate the monastic lifestyle. While there is often debate about how some of these groups fit into Buddhism, there is little doubt that the lay-led organizations have felt fewer qualms about entering the political system. Thus in Japan, the Soka Gakkai sect, founded in 1930 as a lay support group for monks in the Nichiren monastic tradition, has not only stressed zealous missionary activities but also founded a political party, Komeito. Its objective is to establish a Buddhist democracy through a union of Buddhism and politics. While there technically has been a division between the two organizations, the number of individuals who belong to both groups shows that strong ties between the two continue.

The initial relationship between Buddhism and government was not strong. No religion works in a vacuum, however; therefore, social forces affect the religion just as the goals of the religion affect society. As people understood that certain conditions were more conducive to obtaining salvation, it became imperative to try to set up those conditions, for example, through cooperation between political and religious leaders. This led to the view that the government was responsible for providing a religious foundation so that citizens could live more in accordance with the dharma. Normally this has been the result of the monks instructing the rulers in the dharma and allowing the rulers to implement the teachings. As systems of government throughout Asia change, it is unclear whether this will remain the pattern in the future or if some other method of including the dharma in the political system will develop.

Applications

During the twentieth century, modern Asian states have emerged in which there is a new relationship between Buddhism and the government. Whereas in precolonial times Buddhism was often the religion of the monarch, and therefore the state religion, the democratic institutions put in place by Europeans often included a stronger separation between the religious hierarchy and the political leadership. At the same time separation of religion and the state was being put in place by the departing Europeans, Buddhism was being called upon to play a unifying role within some states. In reaction to the European Christian rulers of the colonial era, the people looked to their own religions, such as Buddhism, for political guidance and leadership. For politicians, the indigenous religion was seen as a source of social unity; for many citizens, it was seen as a force that could be used to cleanse the country of European influences.

In Sri Lanka, the Sinhalese, the largest and dominant ethnic group, have been Buddhists for more than twenty-three hundred years. In most precolonial kingdoms, Buddhist monks and rulers had the traditional symbiotic relationship. When the Portuguese took control of part of Sri Lanka (then known as Ceylon) in the early sixteenth century, they encouraged Christian missionaries to destroy temples and be ruthless in their conversion practices. When the Dutch took control from the Portuguese, missionary activity continued but on a milder scale. When the British dislodged the Dutch in 1815, freedom of religion was allowed, but the British gave preference to those who had become Christians and did not allow any strong Buddhist organizations to form. Under the pressure of European rule, Buddhism underwent a revival, and its leaders supported movements for independence. In the first general election, politically active monks emerged, which was a total change from the precolonial pattern. While their efforts were unsuccessful, a precedent had been set. In the 1956 election, the Sri Lanka Freedom Party (SLFP), which was supported by many Buddhist leaders, won the election on a pro-Buddhist, pro-Sinhalese platform. Some monks even went so far as to create the United Monks' Front, which aggressively campaigned for the SLFP. The reforms promised by the SLFP were carried through unevenly. The overall effect was to give the Sinhalese a major advantage over the Hindu Tamils and other minorities in higher education and employment. By 1965, both of the major Sinhalese political parties supported a move to make Sri Lanka more Buddhist, and various monks actively supported both parties.

In 1972, a new constitution was written for Sri Lanka giving Buddhism the foremost place in the country since it is the religion of the majority. Throughout the country's history, the political leaders have listened to the leaders of the Sangha or of the various monastic political movements. While the violence between the Tamils and the Sinhalese on the island does not reflect Buddhist teachings, the monks do not want to give up the special status Buddhism has today. For the politician, Buddhism has become a source of political strength, a common bond among the Sinhalese versus other ethnic or religious groups. Even in this case, the monks active in politics are not seeking election to leadership positions in the government, but identify and campaign for candidates who share their political and religious ideology.

Unlike Sri Lanka, Thailand has continued a more traditional relationship between the Sangha and the state. Even though the form of government changed from an absolute to a constitutional monarchy in 1932, the state, especially the king, and the Sangha are seen as interrelated. There is freedom of religion in Thailand, but for most people, to be Thai is to be Buddhist and to acknowledge the sovereignty of the king. The king is understood to be the protector of Buddhism, which means that the king must have gained much good karma in former lives. In turn, the Sangha gives legitimacy to the king and his government. The Council of Elders, which oversees the

Sangha at the national level, has formal consultations with the Department of Religious Affairs in the Ministry of Education. From the regional to the district levels, the leaders of the Sangha have official consultations with the state leaders. Thus there is structural interdependence, just as there is an ideology of interdependence. Although much of the system is based on the historic relationship between the king and the Sangha, the leaders of the government seek the blessings of the Sangha to legitimize their role in the government. In return for supporting the government, the Sangha expects the government not only to give material support to the Sangha, but also to enact laws that will be beneficial to Buddhists, or to the continuation of Buddhism. Although religious movements developed in the 1970's and 1980's that challenged the traditional view of the state, the traditional relationships continued into the 1990's.

In Buddhist countries, there have been rare exceptions to the noninvolvement of religious leaders in politics. The Dalai Lama in Tibet combined the role of spiritual and political leader of the nation. Tibetan Buddhism is much different, however, from that practiced in most countries. In virtually all other situations, direct involvement in anything as worldly as a governmental office is seen as a violation of monastic rules. Thus the influence that Buddhism has on the state generally is through the guidance given to the lay rulers, and much less often through clergy-directed political demonstrations or activities.

Context

Any attempt to understand a political system must take into consideration the social framework within which the political system is to operate. Religion is one aspect of society that helps establish the world view of those who are its adherents. The moral precepts and social vision of a dominant religion in a country will affect the political system. Thus in countries where Buddhism is the religion of a substantial portion of the population, the government cannot help but be affected by it. In some locations, this means a formal relationship between the Sangha, representing Buddhism, and the state. Even within secular states, Buddhism is a factor that must be considered as the government develops its policies.

Although the central focus of Buddhism is not directed toward worldly things, certain conditions are more conducive to obtaining salvation than others might be. Usually social and political stability are seen to be an essential part of this. Buddhism generally has not been a revolutionary religion. It has tended to support the status quo, and given justification for revolutions only after the fact. The basic relationship between the religion and the state usually has followed the pattern established during the life of the Buddha. As monks, Gautama and his followers depended on pious lay followers to provide food and support to the members of the Sangha. Wealthy or powerful individuals not only gave them what was needed on a daily basis, but also provided monasteries in which they could reside during the rainy season when travel was impossible. As later exemplified by Asoka, the political and economic leaders of the society became the benefactors of the Sangha, and in turn, the Sangha provided religious instruction, educational opportunities, and legitimacy for the benefactor's status. Some twentieth century Buddhist leaders have been interested in developing basic Buddhist principles of equality through socialist philosophies, but they have remained in the minority. Buddhist ideals can be used to support monarchies or democracies. As long as the government does not undertake policies that are overtly anti-Buddhist, it can generally assume there will be good relations with the Buddhist hierarchy.

Bibliography

Little, David. *Sri Lanka: The Invention of Enmity*. Washington, D.C.: United States Institute of Peace Press, 1994. Examines the strife within Sri Lanka since independence, with special attention to the role that religion played in the conflict.

Marty, Martin E., and R. Scott Appleby. *Fundamentalisms and the State*. Chicago: University of Chicago Press, 1993. Studies the impact of conservative religious groups. Chapters 16 and 24 focus on Buddhist political movements in South and Southeast Asia.

_____, eds. *Fundamentalisms Observed*. Chicago: University of Chicago Press, 1991. First volume of a five-volume series, this book examines the impact that a variety of fundamentalist groups have had on their societies. Chapters 11 and 14 deal with religious-based political movements in Theravada nations and Japan.

Spiro, Melford E. *Buddhism and Society: A Great Tradition and Its Burmese Vicissitudes*. New York: Harper & Row, 1970. Complete description and analysis of the role Buddhism plays in Burmese society.

Tambiah, Stanley J. *Buddhism Betrayed? Religion, Politics and Violence in Sri Lanka*. Chicago: University of Chicago Press, 1992. Outlines the changing relationships between Buddhist leaders and political leaders, and how each relates to the various ethnic groups in Sri Lanka.

Donald A. Watt

Cross-References

Asia: Politics and Governments, p. 108; Caste Systems, p. 203; Confucianism and Government, p. 405; Hinduism and Government, p. 823; Independence Movements and Transitions, p. 896; Ochlocracy, p. 1338; Race and Ethnicity, p. 1654; Religion and Politics, p. 1685; The Social Contract, p. 1827; Theocracy, p. 1968.

BUDGETS OF NATIONAL GOVERNMENTS

Field of study: Economic issues

A nation's budget is a primary operational document. It is through its budget and budget-making process that a political system acts, deciding who shall wield influence, who shall assume costs, who shall receive benefits, what concerns will be addressed, and how government shall proceed.

Principal terms

BUDGET DEFICIT: amount by which expenditures exceed receipts within a fiscal year, an amount the government must borrow

EXECUTIVE BRANCH OF GOVERNMENT: administrative agencies of government, under the direction of a chief executive

FISCAL POLICY: tax, spending, and debt policies of the government, intended to improve the performance of the economy with respect to employment, inflation, and economic growth

FISCAL YEAR: twelve-month period covered by a single budget; the fiscal year of the U.S. government runs from October 1 to September 30

LEGISLATIVE BRANCH OF GOVERNMENT: elected or appointed deliberative body with authority to enact, amend, and repeal laws, such as a congress, parliament, kenneset, or diet

NATIONAL BUDGET: accounting document of the national government, authorizing all taxes, fees, borrowing, and spending to operate the government for a single fiscal year

NATIONAL PUBLIC DEBT: total fiscal obligations of the national government

Overview

Government administrators, just like their counterparts in private organizations, require a plan for their actions. Budgets are administrative plans outlining all anticipated government receipts, or money to be collected, in the form of taxes, fees, and tariffs, and all government expenditures, or spending, for salaries, equipment, construction, programs, and so on. Technically, budgets are only plans for government receipts and expenditures. National budgets are, in practice, much more. Appearing to be merely administrative documents, they are also profoundly political documents.

The political process of creating a national budget varies among countries and political systems. In a parliamentary form of government, in which a prime minister is usually assured a loyal majority in the legislature, responsibility for developing a budget rests almost exclusively with the executive branch. In the United States, by contrast, with separately elected legislative and executive branches of government, the creation of a national budget involves extensive negotiation between the two.

The budget-making process may also vary over time within a single political system. In the United States, the Congress dominated the budget process from the adoption of the Constitution in 1789 until 1921. The enactment of the Budget and Accounting Act of 1921 significantly shifted the responsibility and power for creating budgets to the president. The balance of budget-making power was then changed again with the adoption of the Congressional Budget Act of 1974, which provided for a more equal distribution of power between the two branches.

There is no uniform pattern with respect to the mechanisms of creating budgets in different political systems. The issues of who has the authority to propose, review, authorize, and implement budgets changes from one country to another and within a country over time. There are, however, political aspects that characterize nearly all national budgetary processes.

First, the national budget is a primary tool for action and accountability. In the course of seeking office, politicians in all countries make promises and commitments, and have policy goals they would like to accomplish. The most common yardstick for evaluating the accomplishment of these goals is budget outlays. If a prime minister in Great Britain, for example, campaigns successfully on a pledge to increase health care for disadvantaged citizens, the perception of his or her success in meeting that pledge will depend largely on whether or not health care expenditures increase during his or her term in office. The national budget is a tool by which politicians act, and a gauge by which politicians are judged.

Second, national budgets are necessarily a focal point of competition among politicians. Governments operate with finite financial resources that are never adequate to meet all the needs and goals of all politicians, administrators, interest groups, and citizens. All political systems are characterized by competition for budget resources. Much political conflict and intrigue, on a day-to-day basis, has to do with the maneuvering involved as politicians jockey to avoid budget cuts or to secure budget increases for favored programs.

Further, competition for budget resources is a primary basis for activism by both individual citizens and interest groups. This participation usually takes the form of lobbying, but can involve other kinds of political action as well. For several weeks during the spring of 1994, for example, French students demonstrated and rioted to protest proposed budget cuts for student-related programs. Budgets, in short, are nearly always at the center of a nation's political attention.

Third, national budgets are the way governments allocate social costs and benefits. In choosing how much to tax and what taxes to use, governments determine who will bear the burden of supporting public programs and institutions. In the United States, there is a heavy reliance on a progressive income tax, so that those who earn more income are assigned a larger burden than those who earn less. In much of Europe, by contrast, there is a much heavier reliance on taxes tied to the consumption of goods and services. Those who spend more of their income are assigned a heavier burden than those who save their money.

Similarly, governments choose to distribute social benefits to some, and to withhold from or limit them to others. As decisions are made to spend more on agricultural subsidies and less on highways, on health care instead of education, or on social welfare rather than military programs, social benefits come to some and elude others. All budget decisions involve such social and political considerations. Political competition over budgets, not surprisingly, can be intense.

Finally, national budgets are the mechanism by which governments make fiscal policy. By manipulating taxes, spending, and debt, governments attempt to manage the nation's economy. By increasing government spending, economic growth and employment can be increased, and by limiting spending, inflation can be dampened. By reducing public debt, interest rates can be lowered and investment rates increased. Governments can manipulate the budget in an effort to address broader economic problems.

Politics is thus an integral part of a nation's budget-making process. Politics shapes budgets as politicians use them to meet commitments. People and groups both in and out of government compete for limited financial resources, efforts are made to shift social costs and benefits, and fiscal policy is developed. The politics of budgeting are further complicated by the fact that these various considerations work at cross-purposes. A sound fiscal policy, for example, may involve an unacceptable redistribution of social costs, or the competition for resources may undercut a politician's sincere effort to meet campaign commitments. As a result, the creation and implementation of a national budget often consumes much of a nation's political attention, effort, and capital. In many political systems, the national budget is often the single most important political issue.

Applications

Analysts evaluating George Bush's lost bid for a second term as president in November, 1992, rank his 1990 budget deal with Congress as a leading reason. The negotiations for the 1990 budget, and the final shape of the deal, demonstrate the politics that permeate national budgeting. One sees the defense and abandonment of political promises, intense competition within and between political parties, fights over the distribution of social costs and benefits, concern for fiscal policy, and, for President Bush and his administration at least, profound political costs.

In February, 1990, the Bush Administration projected a $64 billion budget deficit for fiscal year 1991. As the economy worsened dramatically, however, the deficit projection soared until, by September, it reached $294 billion. The deteriorating situation, and the likely fiscal impact, worried private economists and financiers, and moved the administration and Congress to a commitment that something needed to be done. The intensely political process of deciding what that something would be began in May, 1990, and ended five months later with the adoption of a budget in late October.

Along the way, much of President Bush's political future was determined. Both the administration and the Congress were determined to avoid political liabilities. Bush had campaigned in 1988 on a "no new taxes" pledge that he did not wish to abandon.

Democrats had repeatedly lost presidential elections as a "tax and spend" party, and did not want to add to this perception. The two agreed to enter into a budget "summit," as a way of negotiating a deal in a manner that ensured any political costs would be shared by the opposing parties.

Despite insisting at the outset that there were no preconditions on the negotiations, the administration quickly insisted it would veto any tax increases. Democrats saw this as a ploy to saddle them with the political responsibility for any tax increases, and stalled the negotiations. Faced with the prospect of no deal, and politically outmaneuvered, the administration capitulated. At the end of June, a brief statement was posted on the bulletin board in the White House press room, recognizing the need for "tax revenue increases." The president's pledge was abandoned.

Negotiations resumed, only to stall again, this time over the issue of the proper distribution of social costs. Having already conceded to higher taxes of some kind, the administration adopted a position of opposing any increases in income tax rates. In addition, however, the administration wanted to cut the capital gains tax, which would disproportionately favor wealthy investors. Democrats would only agree to a capital gains cut if income tax rates were raised on the wealthy. With this, negotiations collapsed, only to be restarted with a smaller group of congressional leaders.

With the 1991 fiscal year beginning on October 1, a deal was finally reached on September 30. The new budget made large increases in gasoline and alcohol taxes and significant cuts in Medicare, the health program for senior citizens. The administration had thus held to its position against increased income tax rates. The deal was so unpopular, however, that 60 percent of the Republicans in the House of Representatives abandoned the president, and the plan was defeated in Congress on October 5. With this, the government found itself already in the 1991 fiscal year, but without a budget, and the government was shut down and employees sent home until temporary funding was agreed to on October 7.

New negotiations were begun once again, but with the administration very much on the political defensive. Congressional Democrats framed the debate as a choice between millionaires and Medicare—the "M and M" strategy. They pushed to limit cuts in Medicare by increased taxes on the rich, including a special new tax on millionaires. With little room to maneuver, the administration ultimately agreed to a deal that dropped the millionaire tax and provided a small cut in the capital gains tax, but that did agree to higher tax rates on the wealthy.

On October 27, a 1991 budget was adopted. President Bush had abandoned his campaign pledge against new taxes, and then abandoned his second pledge against higher income tax rates. He was perceived as caring more about the wealthy, because of his support for capital gains tax cuts and opposition to the millionaire tax, than he did about middle-income senior citizens, because of his support of Medicare cuts. Further, many perceived him as politically unreliable and inept. From mid-August until the adoption of the budget, Bush's popularity rating dropped by more than twenty points. The politics of the budgetary process dominated the national agenda for much of the year, and significantly undermined Bush's reelection effort.

Context

California politician Jesse Unruh once said that money is "the mother's milk of politics." The comment captures the importance of money—taxation, public debt, and spending. The budget is the embodiment of these money issues, and, as such, is a central operational political document in a political system. Governments do not act but through their budgets. National budgets represent what a given government is, does, and stands for.

Budget processes always vary; executives, legislatures, or bureaucrats may dominate a budget system at any given time. What does not vary is the political centrality of the budget. Political activity is organized around budgets. Politicians campaign on proposals for favored budget increases and decreases; presidents, prime ministers, and legislators seek to manipulate the budget to meet their own political agendas; bureaucrats fight to protect their own programs and agencies; pressure groups fight and campaign for favorable budget considerations; the media focus public attention on budget battles; citizens vote on the basis of budget promises and outcomes. Much of "the politics of a nation," is, in fact, the politics of the budget.

The budgetary process in most countries, as these many political interests are played out, is often chaotic, ugly, and, at times anyway, seemingly irrational. It has been likened to the production of sausage—not to be viewed or appreciated by the squeamish. It is important to appreciate, however, that this chaos is in fact politics at the highest level, and that a good measure of chaos is essential to the workings of a political system, particularly a democratic system. Much of the arguing and bickering, the campaigning, the pressure and lobbying, the political threats and deal making, is democratic politics and pluralism at work. It demonstrates the existence of a forum within which competing interests can seek influence, in which compromises are demanded, and in which results can be legitimized and accepted. Budgeting issues are important to a nation, and the strength and heat of the political debate is a reflection of this fact.

A national budget is a window through which observers can view the workings of a political system and see the priorities of a nation. As circumstances and priorities change, as new social problems emerge, as new political groups organize and grow in strength, these developments can be tracked through the budget. It is a gauge of which individuals and groups wield significant influence, and which do not. A budget is an operational and administrative document, and it is at the same time a fundamental piece of the political system.

Bibliography

Birnbaum, Jeffrey H., and Alan S. Murray. *Showdown at Gucci Gulch: Lawmakers, Lobbyists, and the Unlikely Triumph of Tax Reform.* New York: Random House, 1987. Discussion of politics, budgeting, and taxation, charting the lobbying and deal making involved with the passage of the 1986 U.S. tax reform bill.

Cranford, John. *Budgeting for America.* 2d ed. Washington, D.C.: Congressional Quarterly, 1989. Treatment of budget issues, with a review of economic and fiscal policies, the process of budgeting in the United States, and deficit politics.

Kettl, Donald F. *Deficit Politics: Public Budgeting in Its Institutional and Historical Context.* New York: Macmillan, 1992. Discussion of the history of chronic budget deficits in the United States, focusing on why the system seems unable to address the problem.

Rubin, Irene S. *The Politics of Public Budgeting: Getting and Spending, Borrowing, and Balancing.* Chatham, N.J.: Chatham House, 1990. Discussion of budgeting issues, with an emphasis on the politics involved.

Shuman, Howard E. *Politics and the Budget: The Struggle Between the President and the Congress.* 3d ed. Englewood Cliffs, N.J.: Prentice-Hall, 1992. Thorough review of the politics of the 1990 budget deal.

Stockman, David A. *The Triumph of Politics: How the Reagan Revolution Failed.* New York: Harper & Row, 1986. Devastating look at budget politics, examining the effect of elections, lobbyists, and interest groups on efforts to cut spending in the 1980's.

United States. Office of Management and Budget. *Budget of the United States Government, Fiscal Year 1994.* Washington, D.C.: Executive Office of the President, Office of Management and Budget, 1993. Budget proposal of the president for fiscal year 1994.

Wildavsky, Aaron. *The Politics of the Budgetary Process.* 4th ed. Boston: Little, Brown, 1984. Classic, dense, and preeminent work on budget politics.

David Carleton

Cross-References

Debts and Deficits in the U.S. Federal Budget, p. 489; Federal Mandates, p. 662; Funding of Government, p. 724; Grants-in-Aid, p. 791; Interest Groups, p. 936; Iron Triangles, p. 981; Keynesianism, Monetarism, and Supply-Side Economics, p. 1032; Lobbying and Lobbyists, p. 1130; National Economies, p. 1248; Policy Development and Implementation, p. 1414; Research, Development, and Planning, p. 1711; Taxation and Appropriation, p. 1941; Treasury Systems in the United States, p. 2013.

BUREAUCRACY

Field of study: Types of government

Bureaucracies are complex, generally large, organizations staffed by career employees. As a virtually universal feature of all levels of governments everywhere, they are charged with administering the policies and programs created by political officers.

Principal terms
BUREAUCRAT: employee of the executive branch of a government or one who administers public programs and services
CIVIL SERVICE: personnel system in the United States created by the 1883 Pendleton Act, which mandated that staffing be based on competitive exams and competence
NEUTRAL COMPETENCE: notion that a bureaucracy implements the functions of its government competently and impartially, without regard to purely political concerns
POLITICS-ADMINISTRATION DICHOTOMY: traditional view holding that because a bureaucracy's administrative functions are distinct from the political activities of elected officials, bureaucrats should not participate in political or policy-making activities
PUBLIC ADMINISTRATION: processes and organizations that carry out the laws and policies of government; also a field of academic study and an area of professional training
PUBLIC SECTOR: that part of society which is within the governmental or public realm, in contrast to the private businesses and corporations in the private sector

Overview

Both the term "bureaucracy" and the systematic study of the subject can be traced to Max Weber (1864-1920), the German sociologist and organization theorist. Drawing on organization studies of ancient Egypt, Rome, and China, Weber sought to identify characteristics that are common to all bureaucracies, from the church to the military to governments. He found these structural components: fixed and official jurisdictional areas of responsibility for employees and departments; hierarchies firmly established with line workers subordinate to managers; communications and operating procedures that are formalized in written documents; many employees who perform specialized tasks; employees who are trained to know their job tasks and responsibilities; employees are expected to work to their full capacities; and established rules and regulations forming standard operating procedures governing all aspects of the organization. Later organization theorists and reformers expanded Weber's work in an attempt to build control into organizations, a process that would eventually lead to popular perceptions of bureaucracies as inflexible, inhuman, and inefficient.

Although Weber is considered the father of modern bureaucracies, bureaucratic-authoritarian regimes have a long history and might be regarded as the dominant governmental system for most of the last three millennia. The ancient Chinese system of political leadership, which remained comparatively stable for roughly two thousand years, utilized a bureaucracy. Their imperial bureaucracy was centralized with a rudimentary civil service that administered an educational system, mining operations, and vast public works projects such as building the Great Wall and developing agricultural irrigation.

Modern bureaucracy in world government grew out of such developments as industrialization and urbanization, which increased the need for large-scale social organization. Short-term crises often have also stimulated growth in the size and scope of bureaucracies as governments have assumed wider responsibilities. During the Great Depression, for example, the U.S. federal government created a vast range of relief programs that required bureaucratic management. Throughout the world, government bureaucracies have expanded in response to disorder—both within countries and as a result of foreign wars. More recently, modernization and the drive for greater quality of life in the industrialized world have occasioned an expansion of the bureaucracy into functions such as stimulating economies, promoting social equity, and fighting poverty.

Most of the basic elements of bureaucracy are now common throughout the world. Virtually everywhere they function as the executive branches of their governments, in which their responsibilities are divided among departments defined by public functional areas. Most modern bureaucracies share an interest in greater efficiency and effectiveness in services delivery. A distinction between line and staff components is found in nearly every bureaucratic system. The goals of bureaucracies everywhere emphasize simplicity, minimizing levels of supervision and lines of communication, and focusing on how to deliver public services, rather than why or what they should deliver.

Although the bureaucracies are far from monolithic, there are basic units or bureaucratic types which comprise, for example, the executive branch of the U.S. federal government. The federal bureaucracy is organized in large functional departments, corresponding to the primary activities of government, such as justice and agriculture. Most departments are headed by political appointees who are typically political allies of the president. Most of these department heads hold the title of cabinet secretary. Under the secretaries are deputies, under and assistant secretaries who head the various smaller functional units within each large agency. Within the federal executive branch there were fourteen executive departments employing roughly 65 percent of all federal employees during the mid-1990's. From the largest to the smallest employers, these agencies included the departments of Defense, Veterans Affairs, Treasury, Health and Human Services, Agriculture, Justice, Interior, Transportation, Commerce, State, Labor, Energy, Housing and Urban Development (HUD), and Education. In terms of budgets, Health and Human Services was the largest, followed by Defense and Treasury. The Department of Commerce had the smallest budget. Most of these departments were created well after the Constitution was adopted in 1789. The departments of State, Treasury, and War (now Defense), however, were original departments, although Treasury was originally conceived as a congressional department, rather than an executive one.

Several federal departments are known as "clientele" departments, in that they are not designed to serve the broad needs of government or the general public, but were created in response to serve special interest groups. The three oldest such departments are Agriculture (created in 1862), Commerce (1903), and Labor (1913). The departments of Education and Veteran's Affairs were created in 1979 and 1989, respectively.

The federal bureaucracy has also contained as many as sixty independent agencies that report directly to the president or to Congress. Most of these agencies are smaller than the departments. During the early 1990's, for example, the Federal Maritime Commission had fewer than four hundred employees. The National Aeronautics and Space Administration (NASA), however, had more employees than the departments of Education, Energy, Housing and Urban Development, and Labor combined. There were several reasons for positioning such agencies apart from larger departments. By maintaining greater autonomy from cabinet-level departments, they could avoid presidential control; this was particularly important for certain regulatory commissions. Likewise, autonomous agencies might be less likely to be influenced by clientele. Several presidents made agencies independent from larger departments in order to insulate them from partisan politics. Finally, some agencies were made independent because the unique functions that they provided did not match those of any of the larger departments. NASA is a good example.

Another component of the federal bureaucracy is the government corporation, such as the Tennessee Valley Authority (TVA). These bodies function in a gray area; they are quasi-public entities, but they perform government or public tasks. They typically operate like businesses; while some are nonprofit, others make money. As nonpolitical bodies, government corporations are headed by commissions or boards, whose memberships are either apolitical or bipartisan in composition. Prominent examples of government corporations include the Federal Reserve System, Federal Deposit Insurance Corporation (FDIC), and the U.S. Postal Service. The Resolution Trust Corporation was established in 1989 to sell assets recovered from failed savings and loans institutions. The fourth type of federal bureaucracy components includes advisory committees and minor boards or commissions. These organizations are usually small and are staffed by temporary personnel who simply recommend or review proposals. Although these four examples of bureaucracy make up the executive branch of the federal government—the branch most often associated with bureaucracy—bureaucracy is also present in other branches of the government. For example, a growing bureaucracy has arisen to serve Congress. It comprises large congressional staffs, the General Accounting Office (GAO), the Congressional Research Service, the Office of Science and Technology, and the Congressional Budget Office. So too has bureaucracy appeared in the judicial branch. The Executive Office of the President alone has also grown to considerable size; its bureaucratic structures have included such offices as the Council of Economic Advisors, Office of Management and Budget, National Security Council, Office of National Drug Control Policy, and the Office of the U.S. Trade Representative. There even emerged a political bureaucracy resulting from extensive use of pollsters, media specialists, policy advisers, speech writers, and fund-raisers.

By the mid-1990's there were roughly 3 million federal civilian employees, nearly 2.5 million military personnel, and another 11 million government workers at the state and local levels. Together, they constituted the public bureaucracy, an institution much maligned by American society for its supposed largess, waste, and unresponsiveness. But there are always going to be popular misconceptions about the bureaucracy. Bureaucracies are composed of individuals from nearly all professions and fields. Approximately one-fourth of federal bureaucrats have been classified as profession-als—the same number who have been administrators—and another one-fourth have been technical employees. As professionals bureaucrats are highly trained; a larger percentage of them complete higher education than their counterparts in the private sector. After the end of World War II the scope and function of government grew considerably, along with the budgets necessary to support this growth. The same, however, cannot be said of the federal workforce.

Popular perceptions to the contrary, although the size of the federal bureaucracy increased dramatically during Franklin D. Roosevelt's presidency, it remained com-paratively stable after 1945. Significant growth has occurred, however, in local and state bureaucracies. Nevertheless, as a percentage of the total workforce, public sector employment in the United States has remained relatively stable. Another popular misconception is that most federal bureaucrats work in Washington, D.C.; generally, however, only about 11 percent work in that area. The federal bureaucracy generally accounts for only about one-quarter of all U.S. public sector employees. In fact, the total federal civilian workforce has been smaller than that of the combined totals of the government bureaucracies in California, New York, and Texas. The size of the federal bureaucracy should also be seen in an international perspective. Government in the United States has been much less bureaucratic than that of many nations of the Western world. As a percentage of total national workforce, government employees in countries such as the United Kingdom, France, and Sweden usually comprise well over 30 percent of their national workforces, compared to only about 18 percent in the United States. In less developed nations the government is often the largest employer, next to agriculture. In many communities worldwide government is the largest local employer.

Applications

Despite the ideal of limited government in the United States, many critics contend that the bureaucracy has become too powerful and is playing a role far beyond the neutral one intended for it. The same might be said of the bureaucracy worldwide. Others, noting the role the bureaucracy plays in policy-making, have referred to it as the "fourth branch" of government. Indeed, severe criticism has marked most discussions of the bureaucracy in recent years. Not surprisingly, "bureaucracy bashing" has become a cornerstone of modern political campaigns, especially among conservatives who often run "against" the bureaucracy.

The bureaucracy is often perceived by the public and described by critics as power-hungry, inflexible, laden with excessive rules and regulations ("red tape") to the point of being inefficient, ineffective, and indifferent to the needs of the public.

Many citizens of governments around the world have lost confidence in the bureaucracy. Scholars, politicians, and muckraking reporters routinely uncover incidents of waste, fraud, and abuse in the bureaucracy. The degree of hostility and criticism leveled at the bureaucracy has exacted a terrible toll in another way. Today, the term "bureaucracy" has such a negative connotation that the description "bureaucratic" is equated with mediocrity, lethargy, and even incompetence. Bureaucracy has become such a negative symbol or image in American society that its very reputation may impede its work or deter qualified people from seeking positions in it.

The foundations of bureaucracy advocated and envisioned a system in which bureaucrats would be responsive to their elected masters, would remain neutral in their political views, would implement policies to the letter of the law irrespective of personal political beliefs, and would be competent in their jobs. If criticisms of the bureaucracy are to be believed, each of these tenets has been breached and the crisis of modern government may be a crisis of a lack of competence and responsiveness on the part of the bureaucracy.

Passionate and convincing arguments have been made for and against bureaucracy. A source of contention underlying the debate, however, has to do with the difficulty in measuring bureaucratic performance. The tasks of natural resource conservation, housing the homeless, combatting illegal drug use, eradicating poverty and crime, and maintaining national security all provide cases in point. How does one determine bureaucratic efficiency or effectiveness in such complex matters? Critics often compare government bureaucracy to the private sector to support allegations of inefficiency and ineffectiveness. Such comparisons may be invalid. Unlike businesses in the private sector, government departments rarely operate for profits, nor do they have the incentive of commercial competition driving them. By contrast, government bureaucracy often operates according to equity and the "public good"—entirely different concepts than efficiency and profitability. Moreover, the bureaucracy is usually charged with delivering programs that private businesses cannot or will not deliver and with performing tasks that are inherently difficult to carry out profitably.

During the 1980's one of the most criticized and debated federal government operations was the U.S. Postal Service. Some critics charged the postal service with inefficiency and advocated "privatizing" the service—an idea that raised the question of whether its tasks could be performed profitably by private businesses. No definitive answers were found, so the debate continued. Meanwhile, many other public sector services were contracted out to private businesses.

Numerous commissions have been convened, volumes written, and research conducted by leading scholars and think tanks calling for reform, if not the complete reinvention, of the bureaucracy. Indeed, the evidence against the bureaucracy seems staggering. Nevertheless, an argument can be made that many bureaucratic endeavors are reasonably efficient and effective. Consider the improved quality of life that most Americans enjoy thanks to federal food inspection and nutrition programs, product labeling and safety laws, disaster and emergency relief operations, and the social security system.

Whether or not bureaucracy deserves the widespread criticism it receives, debate on the issue remains unresolved. Despite criticism, bureaucracy has emerged as a dominant institution worldwide and has become a political force in and of itself.

Context

Although the United States was founded on the concept of limited government, in practice this does not appear to be the case today. Indeed, limited government has been replaced by "positive government." As the nation's population grew and the fabric of the nation became increasingly industrialized, urbanized, and modernized, the scope, function, and size of government expanded accordingly. As the late nineteenth century Industrial Revolution prompted the governmental response that was the progressive movement, the Great Depression led to the unprecedented economic regulations and social experiments of the New Deal, social consciousness of the 1960's paved the way for the liberal Great Society programs of President Lyndon B. Johnson and the consumer, environmental, and workplace initiatives of the late 1960's and 1970's.

Bureaucratic reform has been attempted with mixed results. Initiatives have been aimed at making the bureaucracy function more like a business, reducing red tape and eliminating personnel, offering more incentives for bureaucrats to improve their performance, and even "privatizing" public operations by contracting them out to private businesses. As a result of increased involvement in society by the public sector, large and complex bureaucracies have emerged to meet new challenges and deliver the vast array of public programs and policies that touch nearly every facet of ordinary citizens' lives. Bureaucratic bodies manage the public lands, buildings, and parks that people frequent. Food is inspected and certified by bureaucratic departments. Other bureaucratic agencies grant driver's licenses, monitor broadcasting stations, plan and build the roads, and mandate safety features for automobiles. The bureaucracy that emerged between the World Wars is now a dominant feature of the modern world and is present in large businesses, hospitals, the military, and government. Indeed, it can be said that modern society has been built by, and depends on, bureaucracies.

Bibliography

Goodsell, Charles T. *The Case for Bureaucracy: A Public Administration Polemic.* 3d ed. Chatham, N.J.: Chatham House, 1994. Provides indepth examination of both the perceptions and performance of the bureaucracy. It is also perhaps the most powerful case against conventional wisdom that sees the bureaucracy as inefficient and unresponsive.

Hummel, Ralph P. *The Bureaucratic Experience: A Critique of Life in the Modern*

Organization. 4th ed. New York: St. Martin's Press, 1994. Comprehensive analysis of the role of bureaucracies in society, the functions of bureaucrats, and how public organizations work.

Lane, Frederick S. *Current Issues in Public Administration.* 5th ed. New York: St. Martin's Press, 1994. Invaluable collection of essays by leading voices in the field, covering a broad spectrum of issues pertaining to public organizations and the challenge of government administration.

Levine, Herbert M. *Public Administration Debated.* Englewood Cliffs, N.J.: Prentice-Hall, 1988. Compilation of arguments concerning vital practical issues facing modern bureaucracy.

Meier, Kenneth J. *Politics and the Bureaucracy: Policymaking in the Fourth Branch of Government.* 3d ed. Pacific Grove, Calif.: Brooks/Cole, 1993. Blend of theory and practice that examines bureaucratic power and the political and policy-making activities of the federal bureaucracy, with useful examples.

Robert P. Watson

Cross-References

Accountability in U.S. Government, p. 1; Administrative Procedures in U.S. Government, p. 14; City Government in the United States, p. 266; The Civil Service in the United States, p. 310; County Government, p. 458; Executive Functions in U.S. Government, p. 636; Government Agencies, p. 765; Intergovernmental Relations, p. 942; Political Ethics, p. 1461; Regulatory Agencies in the United States, p. 1678; State and Local Government, p. 1885; State Government, p. 1891.

BURKE'S POLITICAL PHILOSOPHY

Field of study: Political philosophy

Edmund Burke, a practicing politician, wrote voluminously and articulated the British reaction against the French Revolution of 1789. His writings provide the theoretical framework for much of modern conservatism.

Principal terms
CONSERVATISM: preference for maintaining the status quo and accepting only slow, evolutionary change
JACOBIN: member of the most radical faction in the French Revolution, used more generally to denote a left extremist
RATIONALISM: practice of explaining the supernatural in ways that do not conflict with reason, or of treating reason as the ultimate authority
SENSATIONALISM: philosophical conception that ideas are derived solely from human sensation
TORY: one inclined to support royal authority, landowners, and the Church of England
WHIG: one inclined to control royal authority and support the development of commerce

Overview

The thinker who provided the foundation for modern conservatism, Edmund Burke was always a politician. His ideas and writings are best understood within the context of the political interests that he represented. He wrote in reaction to historical events, and hence never produced a systematic statement of principles such as might be expected of a philosopher. The result of this case-by-case approach is, not surprisingly, inconsistency, and students must piece together Burke's ideas for themselves.

Born in Dublin in 1729, Burke originally intended to make a career in the law, but after matriculating at Dublin's Trinity College and going to London for legal studies, he turned permanently to literary work and politics. His first publication, *Vindication of Natural Society* (1756), lampooned the political ideas of Lord Bolingbroke (1678-1751) and established him as a commentator to be reckoned with. By 1765 he was personal secretary to the Marquis of Rockingham (1730-1782), a leader of the Whig Party and member of Parliament. Although Burke's social position worked against his admission to the aristocratic Whig leadership, his eloquence led to his becoming the most important party spokesman. Rockingham's faction remained in office only about a year during the decade before the American Revolution, but Burke was never out of politics from 1765 until his death in 1797. His political philosophy grew out of his writings as party spokesman.

Burke drew ideas from the sensationalist school of John Locke. Burke agreed with

Locke that government was based on a social contract (an agreement between governor and governed) but disagreed with Locke's development of the rule of law from natural law, instead grounding the rule of law in divine order. For Burke, human law is a flawed and more specific statement of God's law. Burke also rejected Locke's argument that the social contract was subject to renewal, insisting that a person's attitudes about duty and morality were created by his or her interactions within society. To reject one's role in society would be to reject all moral law and duty. This view does not leave much room for change and none for dramatic change. Burke seemed quite inconsistent, therefore, when he approved of the Revolution of 1688 in England and the American Revolution a century later but denounced the revolt that began in France in 1789. The inconsistency was, however, minimal if one accepts the ramifications of his theory.

Burke also rejected the ideas of religious relativism that developed during the Enlightenment, insisting that humans were a mix of good and evil, with good predominant as a result of family influence, education, and religion. Traditional institutions such as the church and government provided societal structure and support for the positive elements in human nature.

Burke's tying of human to divine law and social order to tradition and self-discipline indicates his respect for the existing social structure and government and underlies his resistance to change. He did, however, insist on impartiality in the application of law. Tyranny was as unacceptable to him as revolution, and in his eyes the interests and class structure of society were as much barriers to the one as to the other. However, any democratic system that asserted that citizens had the right to rule also had to allow them the right to change the government. Burke rejected such a right. Freedom, then, for Burke was the liberty to act within the constraints of the laws and rights that had evolved in one's society and not license to do as one pleased.

When writing about the Glorious Revolution of 1688 from which his own Whig Party had emerged as the dominant political force in Britain, Burke defended the constitutional arrangements that emerged. The supposed revolutionaries were in fact defending their traditional rights, and the true revolution would have consisted of the monarchy's continuing to enlarge its powers and prerogatives. Although this interpretation of the events of 1688 is open to many questions, Burke's position did provide the Whig Party with a justification for its stand on monarchial power and the liberties of Englishmen. By Burke's reasoning, the constitution was properly balanced between the king and the Whig magnates, and when King George III attacked the idea of party government, he attacked the constitution. Burke ably defended the party system in his *Thoughts on the Cause of the Present Discontents* (1770).

The American Revolution caused a bitter split in British politics. Whigs, taking a Burkean view, insisted that the colonists were defending their traditional rights and so should be conciliated. King George and his supporters organized around the resurgent Tory Party rejected any negotiations with rebels in arms. With the government (1770-1782) of Lord North, the king and his allies got their way. Burke's constituents in Bristol, a major port, were profiting handsomely from the war and did not care for his opposition to it. In his *Letter to the Sheriffs of Bristol* (1777), Burke laid out his view of representative government. The representative was not merely the creature of the voters sent to give voice to their prejudices, but must answer to his own conscience and to God in seeking what was best for the nation as a whole. This was, ironically, the sort of representation that the American colonists had rejected, as did the voters of Bristol, who did not reelect Edmund Burke. He endorsed the American effort to defend traditional rights concerning trade and taxes, but, by logical extension of his reasoned arguments, he had to denounce their calls for changes in the constitution. Burke did not make friends on either side of the Atlantic.

In 1782, North fell and was replaced by Rockingham, Burke's old patron. After a brief honeymoon of popularity, the new government was increasingly accused of radicalism, and turned to Burke to make the case that its program was actually one of return to tradition. In return for his pen, Burke was made paymaster of the forces and a number of his relatives got civil service posts, but the fact that he got no seat in the cabinet was notice that the aristocratic Whig leaders had not forgotten his origins. Although the Rockingham government lasted less than a year and Burke never held office again, he remained the champion of Whig ideals. He influenced many of the policies of the late eighteenth century.

The Whigs made economic reforms that reduced the power of the Crown to influence politics through patronage, but they did so without attacking the patronage structure that had long been traditional in English government. In May, 1782, the English government gave up control of legislation by the Irish Parliament, thereby respecting the traditional rights and customs of Ireland. The American war was settled by making peace with the rebels, although the party split over the issue. All of these policies, intended to support or restore traditional political and property rights of the king's subjects, reflect Burke's influence. To regard these policies as consistent does require that one accept the Burkean interpretation of the constitution.

Despite his influence over Whig Party philosophy, Burke would probably have been remembered more as a spokesman than as a philosopher had it not been for his next confrontation with revolution. When the French Revolution erupted in 1789, many Englishmen, led by prominent Whigs such as Charles James Fox (1749-1806), regarded it as similar to English struggles to assert the traditional rights of the people and praised it accordingly. Burke, on the other hand, quickly predicted the increasing violence and the overturning of traditional institutions that in fact marked the Revolution's course. His *Reflections on the French Revolution* (1790), which was read all over the Continent, is an eloquent appeal for resistance to the efforts of the revolutionaries to uproot the existing political structure and eliminate the social and economic power of the aristocracy. The balance of the French constitution would be destroyed, Burke argued, and tyranny would follow. The Jacobin determination that any means were justified to establish liberty and equality would mean anarchy and the end of order, justice, and security. The confusion of anarchy would make the people welcome a despot who would destroy all the ideas of the revolutionaries. Burke was so passionate in his opposition to the French Revolution that in his *Appeal from the New to the Old Whigs* (1791), in which he defends himself against a charge of inconsistency made by Fox, he even advocates suppression of free speech (that supported the revolution) in England.

Ultimately, the balance of the constitution and the evolution of rights and liberties are the central points of Burke's political philosophy. Those who fight to ensure the continuation, or even the growth and development of traditional institutions—Whigs in 1688 and Americans in 1776—he supported, but those who would destroy what is proven and workable, however flawed, in favor of some abstract and supposedly preferable principle, he condemned. Although sometimes inconsistent on details, Burke is consistent in his overall support for balance, tradition, and slow change only if needed to maintain an institution.

Applications

In France in 1789, the revolutionaries' cries of "Liberty, Fraternity, and Equality" were certainly too abstract to fit with Burkean philosophy, which emphasizes concrete, existing institutions, but their plan for constitutional monarchy could be seen as a return to the traditional liberties lost in the reigns of Louis XIV and his descendants. Many of Burke's colleagues in England supported the revolt. Fox, one of the most important Whig politicians, broke with Burke when he spoke out against it.

Although a few, including Fox, continued their support for the Revolution, the increasing level of violence in France quickly drew English opinion largely to Burke's side. Events moved quickly from the storming of the Bastille on July 14, 1789, to a mob's forcing the royal family to move from Versailles to Paris in October, to the declaration of constitutional monarchy in July of 1790. Perhaps Burke might have accepted this much, but the radical Jacobin faction was gaining power. The flight of King Louis XVI destroyed the hope of stable monarchy and war with Europe followed. The result in France was the Reign of Terror, dominated by the Committee of Public Safety, headed by the Jacobin leader Maximilien Robespierre. During the Reign of Terror, the king was executed.

Burke's predictions were proving true, and the English began to give his views more weight. The pro-revolution Whigs lost almost all of their political power. Reforms such as the effort to redistribute Parliamentary seats and to free Catholics from restrictions on their civil liberties came to be regarded as dangerous radicalism. Joseph Priestley (1733-1804), a Unitarian minister and scientist who openly praised the ideals of the revolutionaries, was attacked and his home in Birmingham burned. He immigrated to America for safety. King George III suggested that Priestley had gotten what he had asked for. England became the most determined foe of revolutionary and Napoleonic France. The two nations were at peace for less than eighteen months between 1792 and 1814.

Burke, who died in 1797, would not necessarily have agreed with all the extreme measures taken as a result of opposition to the French Revolution. He did, however, use all of his great persuasive power to urge English resistance to it. What is more, he produced during a parliamentary speech a dagger which he incorrectly claimed was an example of weapons being produced for an uprising in England. It seems he knew that the charge was untrue when he made it. In the *Appeal from the Old Whigs to the New*, he suggested the suppression of free expression in England. His horror at the efforts of extremists such as the Jacobins to destroy institutions in the name of abstract ideals was enormous. The result of such destruction was certainly chaos and despotism, the latter representing complete constitutional imbalance. Rarely has a philosopher had both the opportunity and skill to help put his ideas into practice, but Burke did.

Context

Burke's political philosophy became the foundation for much of modern conservative thought. In nineteenth century England it was the Tory (later Conservative) Party that embraced his ideas while the Whig (later Liberal) Party became more reform-minded. Benjamin Disraeli, one of the most important Conservative leaders of the nineteenth century, built his political thought on a Burkean foundation. Disraeli led the Conservative Party to seek some constitutional change both to avoid more radical reform and to win more electoral support. Thus, Burke's idea of slow changes, made to preserve as much of the traditional structure as possible, was very much a pattern of English constitutional change. Suffrage expanded in a series of Reform Bills in 1832, 1867, and 1884. Not until 1911 was the House of Lords, made up exclusively of members of the English peerage, deprived of full power as a branch of the legislature. The argument that this was a pattern of development to democracy is sometimes called the Whig interpretation of history. Burke, convinced that society is not rational and that therefore society cannot be organized after rational, ideal concepts, would have been pleased to see the evolution of political structure, rather than revolution, in nineteenth century Great Britain.

To twentieth century conservatives, Burke offers the idea of natural law based on divine statute, which may be used as an alternative to the relativism of modern liberalism. Burke insisted on the importance of universal standards of morality. This gives modern conservatives a basis for opposition to the liberal desires to overturn social barriers in areas such as women's rights and sexual freedom. Such changes, conservatives believe, threaten to undermine traditional institutions such as the family, and they are probably right in believing that Burke would have resisted such change.

Bibliography

Canavan, Francis P. *The Political Reason of Edmund Burke*. Durham, N.C.: Duke University Press, 1960. Argues that Burke was quite consistent in his political thought.

Chapman, Gerald W. *Edmund Burke: The Practical Imagination*. Cambridge, Mass.: Harvard University Press, 1967. Defends the traditional view that Burke's ideas reflected circumstances rather than being systematic.

Cobban, Alfred. *Edmund Burke and the Revolt Against the Eighteenth Century*. Winchester, Mass.: Allen & Unwin, 1929. Sets Burke's ideas in context of the

Enlightenment and the early Romantic era, vital for a clear understanding of Burkean thought.

Cone, Carl B. *Burke and the Nature of Politics*. Lexington: University of Kentucky Press, 1957. Biographical study of Burke with little emphasis on his political philosophy.

Mansfield, Harvey, Jr. "Edmund Burke." In *History of Political Philosophy*, edited by Leo Strauss and Joseph Cropsey. 3d ed. Chicago: University of Chicago Press, 1987. Prepared as a textbook, its information is accessible. An excellent starting point.

Parkin, Charles W. *The Moral Basis of Burke's Political Thought*. Cambridge, England: Cambridge University Press, 1956. Argues that a consistent moral basis underlies Burke's thought.

Stanlis, Peter J. *Edmund Burke and the Natural Law*. Ann Arbor: University of Michigan Press, 1958. Insists that Burke held a consistent and correct position on natural law.

Fred R. van Hartesveldt

Cross-References

Anarchism, p. 66; Capitalism, p. 197; Citizenship Rights and Responsibilities, p. 260; Conservatism, p. 419; Elitism, p. 591; Hobbes's Political Philosophy, p. 836; Hooker's Political Philosophy, p. 842; Individual Versus State Rights, p. 910; The Left and the Right, p. 1079; Locke's Political Philosophy, p. 1142; Neo-Conservatism, p. 1281; Political Economy, p. 1455; Political Party Roles, p. 1499; Political Philosophy, p. 1505; Right of Revolution, p. 1744; Rousseau's Political Philosophy, p. 1756; The Social Contract, p. 1827.

BUSINESS AND GOVERNMENT

Field of study: Economic issues

Business and government are two institutions. Governments promote and regulate business activity. The relationship between business and government is affected by a variety of factors, including cultural attitudes, the state of the economy, and the existence of competing interest groups.

Principal terms

DEREGULATION: removal of government regulation

INDUSTRIAL POLICY: government policies aimed at improving the performance of industry

IRON TRIANGLE: close relationship formed among business, regulators, and legislators

PRIVATIZATION: sale of government-owned business or enterprise to private investors

REGULATION: government-imposed restriction on business activity

Overview

Business and government are two important institutions operating within all but the most primitive societies. A business is an economic enterprise seeking to profit from the sale of goods or services. Businesses range in size from a firm owned and operated by a single person to a large corporation run by professional managers and owned by many shareholders. Governments are rule-making bodies that enact laws and regulations affecting business and the rest of society. Governments operate on regional, national, and international levels.

Government policies toward business fall into two categories: promotion and regulation. The promotion of business can involve indirect and direct aid. Governments promote business indirectly by creating a political and legal environment conducive to risk-taking. Bankruptcy laws, for example, may encourage risk-taking by entrepreneurs because failure will not reduce them to lifelong poverty. Similarly, government charters of incorporation may serve to encourage investors to risk capital in a new enterprise by limiting their debt liability if the company fails. Governments protect the property rights of business owners by giving them legal sanction; under patent law this protection extends to intellectual property. Governments can also shield business from a hostile public by passing symbolic legislation which gives vent to public anger about business practices. For example, the passage of antitrust legislation in the United States defused popular discontent with big business while posing no real threat to the continued growth of large corporations. The mere passage of such legislation served to legitimize big business in the eyes of many citizens.

Direct government promotion of business can take many forms: subsidies (cash payments), tariff protection, government-approved monopolies, tax reductions, and financing (through direct and guaranteed loans). In addition, governments purchase many of the goods and services produced by business. In 1987, for example, U.S. government purchases amounted to 20 percent of gross national product (the total output of goods and services). Defense firms, in particular, depend upon government orders for their existence.

For a variety of reasons, governments also regulate business activity. In those industries considered vital to the public interest (such as electric utilities, postal service, and transportation), governments may regulate the price of goods produced by business, or establish state-owned monopolies to produce that good for public consumption. Governments sometimes impose restrictions on businesses when they commit acts, such as price fixing, that threaten the general welfare. Government regulation of business also stems from concerns with reducing pollution, protecting the consumer, preserving opportunity for small businesses, or guarding national security. Indeed, in most industrialized nations there are few limits on government regulation of business. Government regulation affects hiring (equal opportunity laws), employee relations (hour and wage legislation), occupational safety, product design, and pricing. Governments can impose other responsibilities on businesses, such as requiring them to provide health insurance to their employees.

Governments in developing nations have placed additional regulations on multinational corporations. Critics of the multinationals believe that the sheer size of these corporations threatens the national sovereignty of small, underdeveloped nations. They also maintain that multinationals keep developing economies dependent upon foreign business. Domestic entrepreneurs, these critics argue, simply cannot compete with established firms from abroad. Supporters of the multinational corporations argue that these companies bring much-needed capital investment and technology to developing countries. Many critics have succeeded, however, in convincing governments to regulate multinational corporations by restricting their market share, placing limits on the earnings that they can take overseas, and by requiring them to locate factories in the host countries.

Businesses sometimes seek government regulation in order to enhance their competitive position. During an economic downturn, businesses are more likely to accept regulation in exchange for government assistance. At other times, firms within regulated industries may work with government bureaucrats and legislators to fix prices or eliminate competitors. These "iron triangles"—made up of business managers, regulators, and politicians—protect established firms at the expense of the consumer and any potential competitors.

In a competitive global economy, governments around the world have adopted industrial policies aimed at making their country's businesses more competitive with foreign companies. In Japan, for example, the ministry of international trade and industry has a long history of targeting industries believed to have potential for rapid growth. Through a mixture of promotion (subsidies, tariff protection) and regulation (restraints on competition), the ministry has tried to enhance the competitive position of Japanese industry at home and abroad. Whether industrial policy is successful is a matter of debate among social scientists. Advocates of industrial policy argue that government can pick tomorrow's business winners while critics doubt that government can or should do so.

Although government regulation of business has increased dramatically in the twentieth century, there have been cases where governments deregulated industry. Beginning in the 1970's, when economic growth slowed down in most industrialized nations, governments of the United States, Great Britain, and elsewhere removed restrictions on business activity. Governments also privatized some of their state-owned industries. Supporters of deregulation and privatization hoped that, once freed from governmental restrictions, businesses would become more efficient and productive.

Business attitudes toward government reflect the diversity of the business community. The managers of large corporations are more likely to accept regulation because they can spread its costs over a wider base. Small business owners, on the other hand, frequently complain that regulation imposes a disproportionate burden on them. The members of some industries seek government regulation, while others oppose government interference with their business decisions. Similarly, the business community has split over the merits of deregulation. Understandably, firms operating within iron triangles do not wish to lose their privileged position, and so oppose deregulation. Potential competitors, on the other hand, might favor deregulation because it would allow them to attract customers away from businesses that have grown lazy and inefficient.

Whatever their view of government, most businesspeople recognize how important it is to reach public officials who make decisions affecting business. In order to influence regulators and legislators, businesses often form trade associations to lobby the government on their behalf. These associations usually represent a single line of trade, but a few, including the U.S. Chamber of Commerce, claim to speak for the business community as a whole. Trade associations enhance their influence in the halls of government by hiring paid lobbyists, and by contributing money to the campaign funds of political candidates.

The relationship between business and government varies from country to country. In some countries, such as Germany and Japan, government encourages cooperation between businesses; while in other countries policymakers cast a suspicious eye on agreements between firms, fearing this might lead to price fixing. The relationship between business and government also changes over time. For example, in the nineteenth century the government of Great Britain placed relatively few restrictions on business. In the twentieth century this laissez-faire policy gave way to increased regulation and state control of key industries. Conversely, in many formerly communist countries, governments have begun to privatize state-owned industry and agriculture.

Applications

The debate over the deregulation of U.S. industry in the late 1970's and early 1980's highlights the complexity of the business-government relationship. The circumstances favoring deregulation varied by industry. Economic or technological change led some industries to support deregulation. In other cases, deregulators gathered political support to overcome strong industry opposition. Finally, some industries were able to totally defeat deregulation.

In the 1970's, after decades of growth, the U.S. economy suffered from "stagflation" (high inflation coupled with sluggish growth). Stagflation was blamed, in part, on excessive government regulations. Consequently, deregulation was taken up by presidents Gerald Ford, Jimmy Carter, and Ronald Reagan. These presidents promoted the deregulation of several industries, including: airlines, trucking, railroads, financial institutions, and interstate bus lines. They also took steps to reduce government paperwork and to speed up the regulatory process. New presidential task forces supervised the rule-making process and performed cost-benefit analysis on proposed regulations.

Before the 1970's, political scientists had assumed that systems of regulation were unchangeable. Many observers believed that iron triangles could always defend regulation from their critics. The deregulation movement, however, demonstrated the unstable nature of public support for government regulation of business.

Several factors fueled the demands for business deregulation. First, economists had produced an impressive body of literature showing the inefficiency and irrationality of many regulations. Second, deregulation had an intuitive, popular appeal, bolstered by real-life examples of the benefits of deregulation. Unregulated airline flights, for example, were cheaper than comparable regulated flights. Third, deregulation appealed to various interests: Liberals saw it as a way to benefit the consumer, while conservatives championed deregulation as a move toward freer markets. The intuitive appeal of deregulation aroused strong feelings—this was an issue on which politicians could display political courage by opposing entrenched business interests.

In some cases, the advantages of government regulation evaporated as new competitors emerged outside the regulatory system and took market share away from regulated firms. American banks, for example, experienced this. The federal government set a low interest-rate ceiling on savings deposits and prohibited banks from paying interest on checking accounts. Meanwhile, unregulated financial institutions, such as mutual funds, developed new investment vehicles which offered higher rates of interest. Bank executives responded by supporting the passage of legislation deregulating their industry.

In the U.S. telephone industry, the American Telephone and Telegraph Company (AT&T) held a government-approved monopoly of the nation's phone service, and, initially, the company opposed deregulation. But, in 1982 the company's president decided that the computer market was potentially more profitable than telecommunications; therefore, AT&T relinquished its telephone monopoly in order to gain government approval for entry into the computer industry.

Of course, some businesses did not favor deregulation. The U.S. airline industry, for example, resisted deregulation. The industry's trade association joined with labor unions to oppose deregulation. Political factors played an important role in overcoming the opposition of these special interests. First, presidents Ford and Carter promoted deregulation of the industry by appointing a reform-minded chairman to the Civil Aeronautics Board (CAB), the government agency responsible for regulating airlines. The new chairman relaxed the regulations governing price competition in the industry. Second, administrative deregulation created uncertainty and weakened industry opposition to reform. The airlines failed to maintain a united front in opposition to deregulation. United Airlines felt mistreated by the CAB and eventually the company supported deregulation. Other airlines could not agree on tactics. Finally, Congress passed the Airline Deregulation Act of 1978, which abolished the CAB. In the U.S. trucking industry, a similar chain of events led to passage of the Motor Carrier Act of 1980, which allowed new competitors to enter this line of business.

Still, there were limits to deregulation. Some special interests, such as dairy farmers, defeated deregulation proposals. In the 1990's, there were also renewed calls for reregulation of the airline industry following the failure of several major airlines. Predictably, the business community was divided over this issue.

Context

Social scientists have produced a vast literature discussing the relationship between interest groups and the state. Marxists believe that business interests dominate the governments of all capitalist societies. They point out that, in many authoritarian societies, business and government are closely intertwined. Although democracies appear to be more pluralistic, Marxists contend that government actions are nearly always motivated by a desire to promote or protect business. Marxists have documented that many government officials have backgrounds in business (either as owners, managers, or lawyers serving corporate interests). They also cite iron triangles as examples of the cozy relationship which exists between business and government. Other interest groups might achieve minor victories, but only if they do not challenge the dominance of business. In short, Marxists assert that the government reflects the interests of the business (or capitalist) class.

Opponents of this viewpoint maintain that the pluralism evident in modern democratic societies is genuine. They argue that other interest groups (such as labor unions, consumer advocates, and environmentalists) do exert considerable influence on government policy-making, and in many instances these groups are at odds with business. For example, labor unions have secured legislation requiring businesses to accept collective bargaining over wages and working conditions, while consumer advocates have convinced governments to regulate how businesses design their products. Indeed, much of the growth of government regulation in the twentieth century has come over the opposition of business interests.

Government officials are not merely the pawns of special interests. In fact, businesses that operate within iron triangles are just as dependent on regulators as the regulators are dependent on them. Political scientists speak of a "bureaucratic imperative" that motivates government officials to place the interests of their agency above that of the constituency the agency is designed to serve. Furthermore, in many cases, government agencies serve several constituencies; thus, officials can play one interest off against another. The existence of competing interest groups also allows politicians to act on their own conception of the public interest.

Social scientists have long debated the merits of interest-group politics. Some believe that a balance has been reached between business and other interest groups, thus ensuring the stability and legitimacy of democratic governments. These people consider the presence of many organized interest groups a reflection of a healthy state of democracy; the more interests, the better. Others fear that self-serving interest groups have created, piecemeal, large, unwieldy governments. The legitimacy of democratic governments is threatened when politics is viewed as no more than the interplay of interest groups, with no regard for the general welfare. This issue of "interest groups," among them business, is a frequent topic for discussion among politicians and political scientists, and will likely remain a subject of controversy in the future.

Bibliography

Friedman, Milton. *Capitalism and Freedom*. Chicago: University of Chicago Press, 1962. Critique of government regulation of business by a Nobel Prize-winning economist.

Galbraith, John Kenneth. *The New Industrial State*. 4th ed. Boston: Houghton Mifflin, 1985. In contrast to Milton Friedman, the author contends that social progress can only come through government planning.

Johnson, Chalmers, ed. *The Industrial Policy Debate*. San Francisco: ICS Press, 1984. Essays on both sides of the debate over industrial policy.

Marx, Karl, and Friedrich Engels. *The Communist Manifesto*. Translated by Samuel Moore. New York: Penguin Books, 1967. First published in 1848, when revolutions were sweeping across Europe, this polemical work argues that, under capitalism, governments serve business interests and not the workers.

Smith, Adam. *The Wealth of Nations*. New York: Penguin Books, 1982. Argues for a business world relatively free of government regulation, pointing out that too often businesses use government regulation to eliminate competitors and fix prices.

Steiner, George A., and John F. Steiner. *Business, Government, and Society: A Managerial Perspective*. 6th ed. New York: McGraw-Hill, 1991. Textbook covering nearly every aspect of the business-government relationship. Numerous case studies.

Wilson, James Q. *Bureaucracy: What Government Agencies Do and Why They Do It*. New York: Basic Books, 1989. Analysis of how government agencies interact with various interests, including business. Chapter 16 features an international comparison of government bureaucracies.

Jonathan J. Bean

Cross-References

The Arts and Government, p. 101; Capitalism, p. 197; Commerce Regulation, p. 357; Communications Management, p. 370; Corporatism, p. 452; Energy Management, p. 604; Food Politics, p. 706; Industrialization, p. 916; Interest Groups, p. 936; Iron Triangles, p. 981; Keynesianism, Monetarism, and Supply-Side Economics, p. 1032; Labor Relations, p. 1038; Lobbying and Lobbyists, p. 1130; National Economies, p. 1248; Political Action Committees, p. 1420; Political Economy, p. 1455; Public Policy, p. 1633; Regulatory Agencies in the United States, p. 1678.

CABINET GOVERNMENT

Field of study: Types of government

Cabinet government is government by a committee of legislators who control both the executive and the legislature, unlike the division of responsibility in presidential government. The cabinet is chaired by a prime minister who is responsible to parliament.

Principal terms

CONVENTION OF THE CONSTITUTION: standard procedure that is of constitutional importance but is not in a written constitution; enforced by politics and convenience, not courts

DEPARTMENT: largest unit in the executive branch; a major department is headed by a cabinet member

LOWER HOUSE: one house of a bicameral parliament; its members are elected

PARLIAMENT: legislature; a unicameral parliament is a single body; a bicameral parliament is composed of two bodies, a lower house and an upper house

PARTY DISCIPLINE: party solidarity in public and in parliamentary voting

PARTY WHIP: member of parliament who is responsible for the achievement of solidarity in a parliamentary party

PRIME MINISTER: person who chairs a cabinet and selects its members

UPPER HOUSE: one house of a bicameral parliament; its members are elected or appointed or otherwise selected; neither power nor status is implied by "upper"

Overview

Cabinet government is government by committee. The governing committee, the cabinet, controls the executive departments and the parliamentary process. Either the whole cabinet, or at least its chair, is responsible to parliament. Parliament can remove the cabinet at any time by passing a motion of "no confidence" in the cabinet or its chair, the prime minister. Cabinet government, thus, is often said to be "responsible government" or "parliamentary government." All this is quite distinct from the role of cabinets in systems of presidential government.

The cabinet is a committee of parliamentarians, that is, past, present, or prospective members of parliament. Its operation is characterized by secrecy and solidarity. While members may disagree in private, they must agree in public. Great Britain's prime minister Melbourne summed up this attitude in a famous remark regarding government policy on the price of grain. He said it did not much matter whether the cabinet supported raising or lowering the price, so long as its members all take the same position. A member who refuses to accept a decision of the cabinet is expected to resign from the cabinet.

The cabinet is responsible to parliament, but everyone—citizens, parliamentarians, bureaucrats—expects the cabinet to govern. This expectation is the basis of cabinet control of the legislative and executive branches. The cabinet's administrative control of the executive branch is marked by the appointment of cabinet members to head all major departments. A cabinet member who does not head a department is said to be a nondepartmental minister or "minister without portfolio." The prime minister is a nondepartmental minister.

The cabinet's administrative control of the executive branch depends, in practice, on the willing cooperation of career bureaucrats. In some countries, for example, Germany, cabinet members may reassign top bureaucrats for political or personal reasons; in others, such as Great Britain, they may not. In all cases, however, the executive branch is much larger than the cabinet. Cabinets vary in size, from fewer than ten members to more than forty, but approximately twenty members is common. Thus, there are too few cabinet members to oversee in detail the multitude of bureaucrats who are expected to accept direction from the cabinet.

The cabinet's political control of the legislative branch is based on political parties and party discipline. Cabinet government, thus, is often said to be "party government." Members of a parliamentary party may disagree in private, in caucus, but they are expected to agree in public, in parliament. The cabinet needs a reliable majority in parliamentary voting.

In two-party systems, such as Great Britain's, the cabinet's political control is usually straightforward. With occasional exceptions, there is a majority party in the lower house of parliament. The leader of its majority party becomes the prime minister and selects the other cabinet members from the majority party. Party discipline, with its block voting, ensures that the cabinet's agenda is passed in parliament.

In other party systems, the cabinet's political control is often complex. A variety of possibilities has been displayed in the last half of the twentieth century.

There might be no major party, as measured by the percentage of seats in parliament, in a multiparty system. When this is the case, a majority coalition involves the agreement of several parties, perhaps five or six. Such coalitions are often short-lived. This often occurred, for example, in postwar Italy.

In some cases, there is only one major party. When that party has a majority in the lower house, the cabinet is formed by that majority party, as in two-party systems. When there is no majority party in the lower house, the cabinet is based on a majority coalition, as in multiparty systems.

A third situation involves two major parties, neither of which has a majority, and few minor parties. A majority coalition then involves the agreement of a few parties, perhaps only two. Such coalitions are often long-lived, as in the case of Germany's Christian Democratic Union and Christian Social Union after World War II.

Party discipline is typical in systems of cabinet government, but agreement between or among two or more parties generally is more difficult to achieve than majority or consensus agreement within one political party. The leaders of all coalition parties must be satisfied by a coalition cabinet, and the prime minister must accommodate other parties' leaders. The prime minister, thus, usually has more influence in a cabinet based on a majority party than in a cabinet based on a coalition.

A disciplined majority—whether a majority party or a coalition—is almost certain to defeat a motion of "no confidence" in the cabinet or prime minister. Consequently, party discipline lessens the cabinet's responsibility to parliament.

Parliament's control of the cabinet is often rather slight. Parliament schedules time for its members to question ministers, and cabinet members must defend their policies and proposals in parliamentary debates. A member of the cabinet is expected to be coherent and consistent, at a minimum, and a minister's performance in parliament is monitored, particularly by opposition parties. For example, a committee of parliament was established to monitor the promises made by cabinet members in parliamentary debates in India. Critical questions usually are asked only by members of opposition parties, not by members of the governing party. A cabinet member who performs poorly in debate or "question time" may suffer not just embarrassment, but could even be required to resign.

Cabinet government had become bureaucratized by the last half of the twentieth century. Prime ministers and cabinets were assisted by cabinet secretariats of career bureaucrats. Cabinet committees were established in most systems of cabinet government. Proposals such as budgetary costs and personnel requirements were expected to be submitted to the cabinet via one of its committees, and in a standard form. These procedures have reduced the scope of discussion in cabinets and increased the influence of the prime ministers, who controlled the cabinet agenda.

Although cabinet government merges the leadership of the legislative and executive branches, it preserves the independence of the judiciary. The cabinet is expected not to control the judicial branch.

Applications

Terminology varies among systems of cabinet government. For example, the prime minister may be called the chancellor or premier; the parliament may be called the cortes or diet; cabinet members may be called secretary or minister; the cabinet may be called the ministry or government.

Cabinet governments have varying structures. Parliaments are usually bicameral but are sometimes unicameral, as in New Zealand. Cabinet members are usually from both houses of a bicameral parliament, but sometimes are from only one house, as in Germany. Cabinets are usually responsible to the lower house, but are sometimes responsible to both houses, as in Italy. Every member of the cabinet is usually responsible to parliament, but sometimes only the prime minister is responsible to parliament, as in Germany: Constitutionally, Germany's chancellor is responsible to the lower house, and the other members of the cabinet are responsible to the chancellor. This reflects the reality of practical politics but not the language of traditional politics, which in many systems of cabinet government asserts the cabinet's responsibility to parliament.

The legal basis of cabinet government varies. It may be based on the language of the constitution, as in Germany and several other European countries, or on the conventions of the constitution, as in Great Britain and some members of the Commonwealth. Acts of parliament are supplemental, not fundamental, as bases of cabinet government.

Methods of selecting cabinets and prime ministers have varied. Often, leaders have been elected by parliamentary parties and then became prime ministers. The selection of cabinet members and the allocation of departments to members were usually left to the political judgment of the prime minister. On the other hand, both cabinet and prime minister might be elected by a parliamentary party, with only the allocation of departments to members being left to the prime minister, as is done by the Australian Labor Party.

Cabinet government began before party discipline, but in the last half of the twentieth century, disciplined parties became political basis. A party's public solidarity may reflect its private unity or conceal its private disunity. Cabinet members usually can rely on party discipline in open meetings of parliamentary committees, but cannot necessarily rely on party discipline in closed meetings of parliamentary committees. Cabinets may lose votes in secret meetings of parliamentary committees. Such closed meetings may increase the degree of the parliament's control of the cabinet.

The cabinet or prime minister is responsible to parliament in principle. In practice, however, cabinet solidarity, through party discipline, is sufficient for cabinet control of parliamentary voting when the cabinet is based on a majority party or majority coalition. Parliamentary control of the cabinet is exercised within that majority, usually behind closed doors. These political realities can be illustrated by two notable controversies in Britain.

In May, 1940, the House of Commons debated the question of its confidence in Prime Minister Neville Chamberlain, who had failed flagrantly with his policy of appeasement of Nazi Germany. The debate was bitter, but party discipline held in the parliamentary voting. After Chamberlain appealed to his allies, party whips rationed permissions to abstain or vote no, and he won by 281 to 200. This margin of victory, however, was smaller than usual. The prime minister clearly had lost the confidence not only of country and Parliament but also of his own Conservative Party. Chamberlain resigned and Winston Churchill became prime minister.

In 1964, Edward Heath, former chief whip and future prime minister, was president of Great Britain's Board of Trade in a Conservative cabinet. Heath introduced a bill in Parliament to abolish the power of producers to fix the prices to be charged by retailers. The bill had been approved by the cabinet but was opposed by many members of Parliament, including Conservatives. Private consultations were normal as bills were drafted and compromises were normally made before a bill was approved by the cabinet. Conservative backbenchers—the rank-and-file members of Parliament— believed that their views had been ignored, and the minister had not tried to accommodate their opinions. This perceived arrogance provoked a backlash in the Conservative Party. Heath compromised, after the bill had been approved by the cabinet, in private negotiations with a committee of senior backbench Conservatives.

Context

Cabinet government began in Great Britain. The British constitution is uncodified (unwritten), so precise dates are rather obscure, but the first prime minister was Sir Robert Walpole, who served from 1721 to 1742. Cabinet government has been advocated, adopted, or adapted in other countries since then, and has continued to evolve in Britain.

From its inception, the cabinet was characterized by secrecy and solidarity; over time, its influence increased and that of the monarchy decreased. This evolution occurred not by laws, but by conventions of the constitution. The prime minister and cabinet have been mentioned only incidentally in statutory law.

Cabinet government was a political reality by the middle of the nineteenth century. With some exceptions, the pertinent conventions of the constitution were well established, by custom and usage, by the time of Walter Bagehot's *The English Constitution* (1867). This book is the classic description of cabinet government in Great Britain: The cabinet joins the legislative and executive at the top, and manages the bureaucracy, the Parliament, and the monarch. The prime minister, who is the leader of the majority in the House of Commons, chairs the cabinet and selects its members from Parliament. Cabinet members are responsible, individually as well as collectively, to the lower house of Parliament, the House of Commons.

Bagehot's account must be augmented to encompass the consequences of the rise of democracy in Great Britain. The Great Reform Act (1832) standardized the qualifications to vote and expanded the electorate; the electorate was expanded further by the Second Reform Act (1867). These reforms, particularly the second, stimulated the organization of constituencies by the two major parties as well as the rise of party discipline in the two-party system. The prime minister thus became the leader of the majority party in the House of Commons.

In 1923, the rise of democracy was used to rationalize the contentious selection of Stanley Baldwin, a member of the elected House of Commons, as prime minister, rather than Lord Curzon, a member of the hereditary House of Lords. This rationale so suited the times that it instantly became a convention of the constitution: The prime minister must be, or must promptly become, a member of the House of Commons.

By the last half of the twentieth century, the powers of Britain's prime minister had become so vast that the system of government had become prime ministerial government rather than cabinet government, according to the controversial thesis of former professor (then a member of Parliament) John P. Mackintosh's *The British Cabinet* (1962).

Bibliography

American Political Science Association, Committee on Political Parties. *Toward a More Responsible Two-Party System: A Report*. New York: Rinehart, 1950. Advocates the model of responsible government as a standard for the United States, as had been suggested earlier by Woodrow Wilson.

Bagehot, Walter. *The English Constitution*. London: Oxford University Press, 1928.

The seminal exposition of responsible government, first published in 1867.

Butt, Ronald. *The Power of Parliament.* New York: Walker, 1968. Chapter 9 analyzes the controversy over resale price maintenance within the British Conservative Party, describing the private negotiations between a cabinet minister and his party's rank-and-file in Parliament.

Jennings, Sir Ivor. *Cabinet Government.* 3d ed. London: Cambridge University Press, 1959. A standard work on its subject.

Mackintosh, John P. *The British Cabinet.* 3d ed. London: Stevens, 1977. Advances the controversial thesis that cabinet government had become prime ministerial government in Great Britain. First published in 1962.

Ostrogorski, Mosei. *Democracy and the Organization of Political Parties: England.* Chicago: Quadrangle Books, 1964. Describes the rise of the system of disciplined parties in late nineteenth century Britain. First published in 1902.

Wilson, Woodrow. *Congressional Government: A Study in American Politics.* New York: Meridian Books, 1956. Originally published in 1885. Takes Bagehot and Great Britain as models to be copied in the United States, but stresses that congressional committees rather than the president's cabinet are powerful in the United States.

Thomas W. Casstevens

Cross-References

Accountability in U.S. Government, p. 1; The British Parliamentary System, p. 146; The Canadian Parliamentary System, p. 190; Constitutional Governments, p. 432; Government Types, p. 785; Legislative Body Types, p. 1091; Monarchy in Constitutional Governments, p. 1215; Multiparty Systems, p. 1235; Parliamentary Government, p. 1377; Separation of Powers: Presidential Government, p. 1815; Two-Party Systems, p. 2033.

THE CANADIAN PARLIAMENTARY SYSTEM

Field of study: Comparative government

As Canada's federal lawmaking body, Parliament represents the national elector-ate. It sets public policy, approves expenditures, and provides a forum for debate on important public issues, while working under the close supervision of the prime minister and cabinet, whom it holds accountable to the nation as a whole.

Principal terms

CABINET: government body comprising departments headed by ministers, most of whom the prime minister selects from Parliament

FEDERALISM: system in which power is shared between national and regional governments

GOVERNMENT: in the context of a parliamentary system, the prime minister and cabinet, who effectively act as an executive branch

HOUSE OF COMMONS: elected and politically more powerful house of Parliament

PRIME MINISTER: head of the government and leader of the party holding the most seats in the House of Commons

PROVINCES: the ten most heavily populated administrative units into which Canada is divided, in contrast to the thinly populated northern territories; each province has its own semiautonomous government

REFERENDUM: policy decision put to a direct popular vote

RIDING: electoral district for a House of Commons seat

SENATE: nonelected house of Parliament made up of senators selected by the prime minister

VOTE OF CONFIDENCE: vote of approval by the House of Commons on a bill sponsored by the prime minister and cabinet, who resign if it fails to carry

Overview

In many ways the Canadian Parliament resembles that of Great Britain, which once governed Canada. It does, however, have characteristics that are distinctly Canadian. As in Britain, the Canadian Parliament is a two-house system. Also as in the British system, one of these houses is called the House of Commons; however, instead of a House of Lords, its upper house is called the Senate. Of the two Canadian law-making bodies, Commons plays the more important role. Its 295 members are elected by popular vote from single-member districts known as ridings. The heavily popu-lated eastern provinces of Quebec (whose residents are mostly French-speaking) and Ontario supply more than half of the representatives. The other eight provinces and the two northern territories supply the balance.

The Senate normally consists of 104 members who represent the provinces. During the Parliament's early years, senators received life appointments; since 1965 they have had to retire at age seventy-five. Twenty-four senators represent each of the country's four main regions: Ontario, Quebec, the Western Provinces (Alberta, British Columbia, Manitoba, and Saskatchewan), and the Maritime Provinces (New Brunswick, Nova Scotia, and Prince Edward Island) along the Atlantic coast. The remaining eight senators represent the province of Newfoundland (which joined Canada in 1949) and the lightly populated Yukon and Northwest territories. After senators are selected by the prime minister from the government's ruling political party they are officially appointed by the governor general. Although its members are not elected, the Senate's role in passing legislation is nearly equal to that of the House of Commons. In Canada a bill cannot become law until both houses of Parliament pass it in identical form. When the two houses disagree on the form of a bill, the Senate normally yields to Commons; under the Constitution, the governor general, who would do so only if requested by the prime minister, could also appoint four or eight additional senators. Nevertheless, the Senate has occasionally frustrated the will of the Commons, as when it blocked railway construction and when it forced the government to call an election in order to get approval of free trade in the late 1980's.

In contrast to the government of the United States, Canada's federal government does not differentiate sharply between its executive and legislative branches. This is, however, typical of parliamentary political systems. The Canadian head of state is the British monarch, who personifies the Crown. The Crown is represented in Canada by an appointed governor general, who signs all bills passed by Parliament. Since 1952, this office has always been filled by a Canadian. Neither the Crown nor the governor general normally exercises significant political power, however. Essentially symbolic, they serve as reminders of the country's historic ties to Great Britain and real executive power rests with the prime minister.

Always a member of the House of Commons, Canada's prime minister is not directly elected, except by the voters of the riding (electoral district) that the prime minister represents in Commons. The leader of the political party with the most representatives in Commons is selected prime minister. Since Canada was founded under the British North America Act of 1867, every prime minister has been the head of either the Liberal Party or the Progressive Conservative Party—both of which are truly national parties. Other, mostly regional, parties have been represented in Parliament since 1921, but none has been strong enough to provide the nation with a prime minister.

Because either the Liberals or the Conservatives have almost always controlled a clear majority of seats in the Commons, multiparty coalition governments have been rare in Canada. Minority governments, in which a prime minister's party has controlled fewer than half the seats, have been more frequent. As might be expected, Quebec and Ontario have contributed more prime ministers than other provinces.

The prime minister forms a government by selecting members of Parliament to serve as cabinet ministers. Aside from a few Senators and an occasional person from outside the Parliament, all cabinet ministers come from the House of Commons. Cabinet ministers head the various departments of the government such as finance, agriculture and agrifood, justice, national defense, Indian affairs and Northern development, health, and foreign affairs and international trade. Virtually always members of the prime minister's party, cabinet ministers normally have long service in Parliament and often have served in past governments.

Nearly all important Canadian legislation originates in the government ministries, whose career civil servants play major roles in writing legislation. After the prime minister and cabinet ministers decide what legislation is needed on an issue, its details are formulated in the appropriate ministry and introduced to Parliament by the prime minister or another minister. Various cabinet committees, such as those on social policy development and economic development, assist the cabinet in making policy. Each prime minister decides what cabinet committees will be organized. The prime minister, cabinet members, and cabinet committees meet regularly in order to develop policy and discuss the legislation that the government will present to Parliament. Although cabinet ministers are free to disagree during meetings, there is collective responsibility among members of the government for the decisions that are made. Any minister who cannot publicly support the prime minister and the rest of the cabinet is expected to resign.

Bills sponsored by the prime minister and the various ministries are known as government bills. Money bills, which deal either with taxation or the spending of government funds, must be first introduced in the House of Commons. Others may start the legislative process in either Commons or the Senate.

As in the United States Congress, the Canadian Parliament uses legislative committees to examine bills and consider possible amendments. The work of these committees is important, but because of the government's strong influence on Parliament their impact is normally less than in the U.S. system, in which power is sharply divided between the executive and legislative branches. After an appropriate committee makes its report, there is opportunity for debate and voting on proposed amendments.

When a government-sponsored bill comes up for a final vote of approval, voting is strictly along party lines, with all members of Parliament expected to vote with their own parties. Failure of members to vote with their parties can mean that they will not have party support in the next election. Party discipline is crucial because any time that a government loses a vote in the House of Commons amounts to a vote of no confidence—which requires that the prime minister and all cabinet ministers immediately resign. The governor general, at the request of the prime minister, then orders the House to dissolve and a new national election must be held—usually within about seven weeks. Canadian election campaigns are much shorter than their equivalents in the United States, but somewhat longer than in the British parliamentary system. Former members of the House of Commons—including the prime minister—who want their parliamentary seats back must run for reelection in their individual ridings.

So long as the prime minister's party enjoys a majority in Commons, no-confidence votes are unlikely. Such votes occur more frequently in coalition governments, or at the rare moments when a ruling party has formed a minority government (in which it controls fewer than half the seats). Although no-confidence votes are rare in Canada, they do happen—as governments discovered in 1963, 1968, 1974, and 1979. It may happen, however, that the electorate will return a party to power even after it has lost a vote of confidence.

Losing a vote on a bill in the Senate may embarrass a government, but it does not bring the government down as it does in Commons. The prime minister thus does not resign, and no new election is held. However, any bill defeated in the Senate is considered dead and its supporters must reintroduce it and go through the entire legislative process again if they still wish to see it become law.

The Canadian Constitution requires that a general election for the House of Commons be held at least once every five years. Elections take place at the discretion of the prime minister, but the pattern has generally been to hold a new election about every four years. Prime ministers can, however, call for the dissolution of Commons and new elections at any time that they believe it is favorable for their parties to do so.

Although most significant legislation originates with the government, a time known as "Supply Days" is allotted during which opposition parties can respond to government proposals and put forth ideas of their own. Proposals made by minority party members have little chance of becoming law, but the process helps to hold the government accountable and to present fresh alternatives to the voters at general elections. Parliamentary rules allow members to submit their own bills, which are known as private members' bills. These bills can deal with virtually anything that concerns the members who introduce them. Party voting on them is apt not to be as strict as it is with government bills, and their rejection does not bring down the government.

The government's positions may be scrutinized through the Oral Question Period. During this time, any House of Commons member may pose questions to the prime minister or any cabinet minister. The speaker of the house selects the questioners from lists furnished by party leaders, who are known as "whips"—as in the U.S. Congress. Another process, Questions on the Order of the Paper, permits members of Commons to submit questions in writing and receive written replies.

Applications

Members of Canada's Parliament have sometimes felt that the national legislative process is dominated by the prime ministers and their parties. Concerns of the particular constituency that a member of the House of Commons represents are likely to get less attention. The area of trade illustrates the dominant—but not total—role played by prime ministers in shaping Canada's legislation.

Canada's first national prime minister, Sir John Macdonald, served from 1867 to 1873 and from 1878 to 1891. Through his efforts Parliament enacted the National Policy, a program of protective tariffs largely designed to protect Canadian companies from U.S. competition. One of Macdonald's successors, Wilfrid Laurier (prime minister from 1896 to 1911), discovered that it was easier to influence Parliament than the national electorate as a whole. He moved to have Parliament reduce some tariffs and gave preference to British goods, but the Canadian electorate ultimately voted his party out of office because of later tariff policies.

At times, individual cabinet ministers have played major roles in determining business and trade policies. C. D. Howe, for example, dominated the Department of Trade and Industry for twenty-two years—including the period during World War II. Businessmen who needed anything from the government learned that they had to deal directly with Howe.

During the 1980's, the Progressive Conservative prime minister Brian Mulroney (in office from 1984 to 1993) decided to move toward a free trade agreement with the United States, despite Liberal Party opposition within Parliament. In January, 1988, Mulroney reached an agreement on trade policy with U.S. president Ronald Reagan. With Mulroney's party firmly in control of Canada's House of Commons, approval of the agreement there was reasonably certain; however, the nonelected Senate refused to give way to the House, although it looked to the House of Commons for clarification of what it should do. The opposition Liberal Party controlled most of the Senate's seats. Under the urging of the opposition leader in the House of Commons, leader John Turner, the Liberal Party senators rejected the legislation required to put the free trade agreement with the United States into effect. Mulroney had the final word, however. As was his right to do at any time, he called for the dissolution of the House of Commons and made the trade agreement with the United States the major issue in the 1988 national election campaign that followed. His Progressive Conservatives won, returning him to power, and Parliament bowed to the will of the people. The free trade agreement went into effect in January, 1989.

Shortly after his electoral victory, Prime Minister Mulroney again used the power of his office to make certain that Parliament gave formal approval to government policy. Still completely in control of the House of Commons, he asked the governor general to exercise his constitutional right to appoint eight additional senators. This meant there could be no Senate rebuttal of the government's controversial proposed new Tax on Goods and Services. Although Mulroney got this tax passed, the electorate demonstrated that it actually had the last say. Partly because of the unpopularity of his new tax, Mulroney was ultimately forced to step down as prime minister and as head of the Progressive Conservative Party in 1993. Later that year, his party went down to an overwhelming defeat, losing all but two of its seats in the House of Commons to the Liberals and other parties.

Context

The formal powers and responsibilities of the Canadian Parliament are enumerated in the Canada Act of 1982, which includes both the Constitution Act of 1867 (previously known as the British North America Act of 1867) and the Constitution Act of 1982. Under the Canada Act, the technical right of the British Parliament to amend

Canada's Constitution was finally abolished. This had been in effect since the country was founded in 1867, although in reality, Canada had been self-governing and completely independent for many years.

Consistent with Canada's evolution from the British political system, several Canadian governmental practices rest on custom and tradition rather than on formal constitutional provisions. Parliament's work is affected by some of these traditions. As in Great Britain, any prime minister who loses a vote of confidence in the House of Commons is expected to resign and ask the governor general to dissolve the House, even though no written constitutional provision says that the prime minister must do so.

Unlike Great Britain's Parliament, that of Canada functions under a federal system of government. Each of the country's ten provinces has its own legislative body and the constitutional right to act autonomously in several important areas. Canada's national government formed during the late 1860's, immediately after the U.S. Civil War ended. In order to avoid the kind of tragedy that the United States experienced in its violent struggle to resolve the question of whether states could secede from the Union, the British North America Act differed from the U.S. Constitution in reserving powers not specified in the document to the federal government, instead of giving them to the provinces. This was not changed by the Canada Act of 1982.

Canada remains a country in which regional interests are strong, not only in the predominantly French-speaking province of Quebec, but also in the Western Provinces, and among the aboriginal peoples and others. Consequently, there is a powerful impulse for the provinces to demand greater control over their own affairs. This impulse has tended to restrict the realm of the federal Parliament, as has the strengthening of provincial control over natural resources empowered by the Constitution Act of 1982. The Canadian Charter of Rights and Freedoms that is contained in the same document has had a similar restraining effect.

Other factors also limit the role of the national Parliament. Under certain circumstances, major issues can bypass Parliament and be taken directly to the people in the form of national referendums. In 1992, for example, a proposal known as the Charlottetown Accord was put to a national referendum. This measure, which would have modified the Constitution in order to help win its ratification in Quebec, failed to win approval. Although the measure was voted down, it stands out as an example of Canadian national politics that is unparalleled in the United States.

During the 1990's, many Canadians have questioned whether their national Parliament truly legislates, or if in fact, the prime minister, cabinet, and federal bureaucracy perform this function. Some Canadians believe that the struggle between Parliament and the government would be more equal if the Senate's power were to be strengthened. Proposals for the creation of a so-called Triple-E Senate would reform it into a body more similar to those in Australia and the United States. Its members would be elected by popular vote, with six senators from each province, and they would have effective legislative powers similar to those already enjoyed by the House of Commons. The Charlottetown Accord called for Senate reform along these lines.

Bibliography

Bell, David V. J. *The Roots of Disunity: A Study of Canadian Political Culture*. Rev. ed. Toronto: Oxford University Press, 1992. Penetrating examination of the multicultural and regional forces that tend to fragment Canadian politics and make the Parliament's task especially challenging.

Franks, C. E. S. *The Parliament of Canada*. Toronto: University of Toronto Press, 1987. Presenting a thorough analysis of Canada's national legislative body, this solid work is the ideal source for those seeking a complete treatment of the subject.

Hockin, Thomas A., ed. *Apex of Power: The Prime Minister and Political Leadership in Canada*. 2d ed. Scarborough, Ontario: Prentice-Hall of Canada, 1977. Excellent study of the dominant role played by the prime minister in the Canadian governmental system.

Jackson, Robert J., and Doreen Jackson. *Politics in Canada: Culture, Institutions, Behaviour and Public Policy*. 3d ed. Scarborough, Ontario: Prentice-Hall of Canada, 1994. Comprehensive study of Canada's political system, including detailed coverage of the organization and work of both houses of Parliament. Contains considerable information difficult to obtain elsewhere in a single source, as well as the complete text of the Canada Act of 1982.

John E. Santosuosso

Cross-References

The British Parliamentary System, p. 146; Bureaucracy, p. 164; Cabinet Government, p. 184; Commonwealths, p. 364; Congress, p. 412; Constitutional Governments, p. 432; Government Types, p. 785; Legislative Body Types, p. 1091; Legislative Functions of Government, p. 1098; Monarchy in Constitutional Governments, p. 1215; Multiparty Systems, p. 1235; Parliamentary Government, p. 1377; Political Parties, p. 1485; Regional Governments, p. 1672.

CAPITALISM

Field of study: Political philosophy

Capitalism, an economic system featuring private property ownership and free markets, has a controversial relationship to government in the view of three major schools of economists. The precise nature of the controversy depends on the school.

Principal terms

CLASSICAL (OR NEOCLASSICAL) ECONOMISTS: followers of Adam Smith who believe the greatest economic well-being emerges when private property is protected and prices of goods and services are set in free markets

MARKET: setting in which goods or services are sold between willing buyers and sellers

MARXIST ECONOMISTS: followers of Karl Marx who believe that by allowing owners of private property to sell goods at a profit, capitalism steals from the workers, who create all value

MONOPOLY: any economic entity that controls the entire supply of a good or service, thereby destroying free market exchange

PROLETARIAT: Marxist term for the most numerous and lowest class of people within capitalist societies consisting of workers who are exploited by capitalists

RADICAL POLITICAL ECONOMISTS: followers of Paul Sweezy and Howard Sherman who selectively adapt ideas from both neoclassical and Marxist economics

VANGUARD OF THE PROLETARIAT: proletariat group that leads workers to see their "true" interests and maintains a dictatorship over all in a communist society

Overview

Capitalism is an economic system in which free markets are used for all producers and consumers to exchange goods and services. Efficiency and overall economic well-being are said to result from the individual owners of private property making choices in a free market to buy low and sell high, keeping any difference between the buying and selling price as profit. Government is the virtually universal institution that attempts to reduce the amount of violence between individuals and groups in the world by providing a legitimate monopoly right to use force in order to control violence.

The relationship between capitalism and government falls within the larger debate over the relationship between economics and political science. In an earlier period the conflict between political science and economics was less pronounced because of the tendency to include both disciplines under the general name of political economy. More recent trends have both separated these two disciplines and given rise to a controversy over how the separated disciplines relate to each other. Even more striking is the debate among the three major schools of thought in economics. Neoclassical, Marxist, and radical political economists differ greatly over the relationship between capitalism and government. While all three schools have many features in common, each is sufficiently distinct that they can be treated as separate schools.

Classical (or neoclassical) economic thought is typically dated from Adam Smith's publication of *The Wealth of Nations* in 1776—the same year that America declared its independence from Great Britain. Classical economics was soon more fully developed by Thomas Malthus, David Ricardo, James Mill, Jeremy Bentham, and John Stuart Mill and was modified in the following century by Ludwig Von Mises and others in the Austrian school of economics. Because changes have taken place since Adam Smith's time, this school is now called neoclassical economics and is currently espoused by such Nobel Prize-winning economists as Frederick Hayek, James Buchanan, and Milton Friedman.

The second major school, Marxism, has many permutations but is perhaps best known as it is promulgated by economists schooled in the former Soviet Union and other communist countries. Although there are legitimate differences among economists within this school, the relationship between capitalism and government will be treated here as it would have been by Soviet Marxist economists.

The third school is a relatively new one generally known as radical political economics. Drawing on insights from classical economists (particularly David Ricardo) as well as from Marxist thought, radical political economics believes that it can establish a new set of principles (or a paradigm) that can develop the best of the other schools while avoiding their defects.

For neoclassicalists, the relationship between capitalism and government is rooted in the belief that economics can be understood apart from government and that it works better with minimal governmental intervention. Nevertheless, neoclassicalists hold that government is necessary to provide a stable political order in which capitalism's free markets can operate. Critical of what they call government interventionism (or "statism"), neoclassicalists believe that the greatest economic progress for all comes from the operation of the profit motive in a market system. Every person in the market system is considered to be a rational individual whose preferences are entirely his own. Always buying at the lowest possible price and selling at the highest possible price, everyone in the system seeks profits, creates a fair market price for every commodity or service, and thereby promotes the most efficient allocation of limited resources for all ("all other things being equal," as neoclassicalists are fond of saying). Because of their belief that this system can operate without government intervention, neoclassical economists are frequently accused of carrying to an extreme the notion first offered by Adam Smith that an "invisible hand" will operate the economic system to everyone's benefit.

Both Marxist and radical political economists are skeptical of this "invisible hand" notion and therefore challenge neoclassical thought at its very core. Both Marxist and radical economists insist that government must have a larger role in the management of economy than that allowed by neoclassicalists, who would restrict government to the limited role of maintaining the stable environment in which the market operates.

Marxist economics draws its main thrust from the insights of the economist Karl Marx and others who claim to follow his lead. In this century, the vast majority of these Marxists were trained in the Soviet Union and were heavily influenced by additional insights offered by Communist political leaders such as V. I. Lenin, Joseph Stalin, Fidel Castro, and Mao Tse-tung. Because these politicians have combined their economic insights with their control of the government apparatus in their countries, they have been able to articulate a system of economic thought generally acknowledged to be Marxist in its orientation though dominated by government officials. There have always been critics who pointed out significant deviations from Marxist thought on the part of these government-dominated economists. Soviet Marxist historians have generally been criticized for converting an open philosophical system into a dogmatic ideological posture.

The Marxist view of capitalism's relationship to government differs greatly from that of neoclassicalists. Marxism holds that all the value in the economic system comes from the so-called labor theory of value, in which only those who contribute labor actually add value to products. Since capitalism figures a profit into the price of any product sold in addition to the value contributed by labor, such profit represents a surplus payment or—in the Marxist view—a theft from the workers. Insofar as government supports capitalism, it supports theft. This capitalist governments naturally do—in the Marxist view—dominated as they are by those who have already reaped large profits and who own much private property. Because capitalists are interested in maintaining their advantages, they will try to dominate government, even if a capitalist government "pretends" (again, in the Marxist view) to be democratic.

For Marxists, the capitalist "mode of production" inevitably leads to capitalist control of whatever political structure may be used, even in so-called democratic countries. Democracies, such as the United States or Great Britain, are frauds because the capitalists use campaign contributions or bribe elected officials in order to perpetuate their political control, despite the apparent choices available to voters.

Indeed, voters do not even have a voice as consumers in the system (as the neoclassicalists would maintain) because consumers are forced to accept choices that are prepared for them by those who have already accumulated large quantities of private property and are making huge profits. These wealthy individuals often have formed monopolies which can dictate choices for consumers. These same owners of capital dominate the workers not only by stealing their property (in the form of profits) but also by forcing workers who are not politically pliable enough out of work entirely.

In the most fundamental sense, Marxism holds that economics runs every political system because dialectical materialism is the key operational force in history. Because of this belief, Marxists inconsistently answer how government would be treated under their preferred economic system which may be described as "communist." According to Marx, all government would "wither away" under communism, but governments under actual communist regimes tend to grow larger, not smaller, and none of them has voluntarily disappeared.

Under Soviet Marxism, once the workers have carried out a revolution against the capitalists and taken over the entire economic and political structure, they should be able to maintain a dictatorship of the workers (or proletariat) over the capitalists. In such a system, the government is said to control the mode of production so that the workers will not be harmed. Since the workers are the overwhelming majority in virtually every industrial society, this new economics system is said by Marxists to be the most "democratic," as the harmful influences of the private ownership of property and the profit motive would be eliminated from the system.

Although Marxists claim that communism is good for all workers, some workers have always resisted its adoption. Marxists acknowledge that worker resistance to communism exists but claim that many workers do not understand their own true interests. Marxists maintain that it is therefore necessary for a "vanguard of the proletariat" who represent true worker interests to exercise leadership both before and after the revolution. For Soviet Marxists, this vanguard of the proletariat became the Communist Party, which was granted a long-term leadership role that excluded any other political party (which might be dominated by capitalists) from competing with it. This vanguard of the proletariat led the dictatorship of the proletariat, which ensured that no capitalist would ever again undermine the system.

Neoclassical economists naturally view this "dictatorship of the proletariat" as a plain old-fashioned dictatorship that dominates and exploits everyone—workers as well as capitalists—while destroying the efficient allocation of resources in the name of a false equality. The neoclassical objection to Marxist solutions is echoed by the newer school in economics known as radical political economics.

Radical political economists have divisions in their ranks as well but enough cohesion to be recognizable as a new school of thought. They generally accept from neoclassicalists the importance of the market but differ by insisting that capitalism tends to breed strong monopolies that cannot be eliminated through the ordinary operation of the economy (as neoclassicalists believe). Radical political economists say that government has a role in eliminating monopolies; they share with Marxists a belief that monopolies lead to the accumulation of great wealth in the hands of a few, who then constitute an economic class that controls even democratic governments by outright ownership or bribery (or campaign contributions) in order to provide a favorable governmental climate for the perpetuation of their monopoly position.

Despite the Marxist tone of this argument, radical political economists do not accept the Marxists' necessity for a violent, bloody revolution, and they also are skeptical of the role that the government has played under the Soviet-style Marxist political system. Joining the neoclassicalists in calling the Marxist system evolved by Stalin "statism," radical political economists are skeptical that Marxist-planned economies can solve all economic problems. Respecting the market (so long as it is not dominated by monopolies), radical political economists believe that the intervention of government on behalf of worker interests can have positive economic effects. Furthermore, radical political economics attempts to reduce the massive accumulation of private property and profit making in the hands of a few individuals by promoting what they would call "workplace" democracy in corporations, so that workers would have a direct stake and become quasi capitalists themselves. For this system to be adopted, some substantial redistribution of wealth, perhaps through a strongly progressive income tax, might be necessary. If these goals cannot be achieved, radical political economists see the possibility of violent revolutions—especially if the gap between the rich few and the poor masses becomes too great.

Applications

How can one reach any clear practical proposals for political resolution among such widely differing views? Although it is always risky to attempt a synthesis or compromise among philosophical systems, some practical pointers may be useful so long as one recognizes that a final resolution of this debate may be impossible. One way to approach the question of the relationship of capitalism to government is to focus on the amount of free public choice that is available to the citizen, voter, or consumer. Assuming that a large number of individuals possess enough wealth to have a comfortable standard or living, one might assume that the capitalist free enterprise system would be compatible with acceptable government because there would be no massive inequality of wealth that might allow wealth to control the system. Alternatively, steps could be taken to mitigate or reduce substantially the influence of wealth through political campaign reform and corporate domination of the media. This might mitigate some of the concerns of the radical political economists, although the Marxists say that capitalists would never allow such reform.

Given the abandonment of the Stalinist form of Marxism in Russia and Eastern Europe in the early 1990's, many are now skeptical of the Marxist Leninist Stalinist claim that the vanguard of the proletariat is a safe repository for political power in a system that claims to have a dictatorship of the proletariat. Focusing on political issues alone, these people—along with the classical economists and the radical political economists—find that the dictatorship of the proletariat is simply a dictatorship. These same people might have some sympathy for the enlarged governmental role that is envisioned by the radical political economists. They might also favor it over both the accepted governmental role envisioned by the Marxists and the almost nonexistent governmental role envisioned by the neoclassical economists.

Context

There may be no way to overcome the great theoretical differences that separate the three schools, but trying to understand the debate from the perspective of political science or the practical operation of government might help. A political scientist who believes in a democratic system is most likely to focus on the issue of choice and to hold that a government is truly democratic so long as all people can make a meaningful choice between economic systems. Naturally, this point of view is not necessarily going to resolve the concerns of any of the particular advocates of the various economic schools discussed, but it might be a place to begin for any citizens who wish to resolve the debate as a practical matter in their own minds.

Someone with a more objective perspective, while acknowledging that economics is fundamental in any society, would suggest that any definition of democracy should be kept free of economic considerations (unless the political system were unduly influenced by special economic conditions). So long as a society retains the ability to choose among alternative economic systems, then a democratic society is possible.

Choice becomes particularly important when it is realized that no society can claim to be a perfect democracy. Democracy expresses a spirit that requires openness of mind and ability to see through demagoguery. It avoids absolute positions and rigid ideological postures and recognizes the necessity of compromise. It requires a tolerance for different ideas, an attempt to understand the beliefs and practices of others without necessarily accepting or sharing them. Democracy is nurtured by, and flourishes with, practice. It is not preserved in documents or rituals. Not something finished, complete, and possessed, it is something by which each person and each democratic society must continually live.

Bibliography

Friedman, Milton *Capitalism and Freedom.* Chicago: University of Chicago Press, 1962. This classic statement of neoclassical thought and its relationship to government remains an easily readable explanation of neoclassical assumptions.

Hayek, Frederich A. *The Road to Serfdom.* Chicago: University of Chicago Press, 1944. One of the finest critiques of the central planning that is necessary in socialist and communist regimes, this work underscores the neoclassical belief in the logic of the free market system.

Ozinga, James R. *Communism: The Story of the Idea and Its Implementation.* 2d ed. Englewood Cliffs, N.J.: Prentice Hall, 1991. Excellent analysis of Communist thought that carefully distinguishes its economic and political assumptions.

Sherman, Howard J. *Foundations of Radical Political Economy.* Armonk, N.Y.: M. E. Sharpe, 1987. One of the clearest statements of radical political economy, this work also clarifies underlying assumptions in both neoclassical and Marxist thought.

Smith, Tony. *Thinking Like a Communist.* New York: Norton, 1987. Perhaps the finest brief explanation of Communist thought, this book sets out the ideology's underlying logic in simple direct terms and explains its permutations in a variety of applications in different countries.

Richard L. Wilson

Cross-References

Burke's Political Philosophy, p. 171; Business and Government, p. 177; Corporatism, p. 452; Dialecticism, p. 540; Feudalism, p. 688; Funding of Government, p. 724; Industrialization, p. 916; Invisible Government, p. 975; Keynesianism, Monetarism, and Supply-Side Economics, p. 1032; Labor Relations, p. 1038; Marxism-Leninism, p. 1155; National Economies, p. 1248; Neo-Conservatism, p. 1281; Scientific Humanism, p. 1784; Social Democratic Parties, p. 1846; Totalitarianism, p. 1987; Utilitarianism, p. 2077.

CASTE SYSTEMS

Field of study: Politics

Caste is a component of a system of social stratification that severely limits contacts between groups and upward mobility of the lower levels of society. It evolved in its purest form in India, where Aryan peoples developed caste distinctions within the Hindu religious system to establish themselves as the region's dominant ethnic group.

Principal terms
ARYANS: Indo-European people who began entering India around 1500 B.C.E.; they occupied the upper levels of the caste system and provided the major impetus in developing Hinduism
CASTE: major level within a caste system
CLASS: group sharing a common economic or social status
DHARMA: Hindu concept of duty to parents, teachers, spouses, society, and God; such duties vary among castes
KARMA: Hindu and Buddhist concept that the force generated by one's actions leads to consequences that can affect one's next level of existence
POLLUTION: condition of ceremonial or moral impurity
UNTOUCHABILITY: condition adhering to persons or groups who are believed to defile other people through social contact

Overview

Deriving from the Portuguese word *casta*, the word "caste" was originally used to designate traditional divisions within the population of India—the logical starting point in any discussion of caste systems. In India, the system traditionally exhibited seven characteristics. It was endogamous, limiting marriage to partners of one's own caste. It was also hereditary and restrictive, limiting other kinds of social contact between members of different castes. It was a hierarchical system, in which only about 5 to 10 percent of the Hindu population occupied the highest caste. Members of the high castes could be polluted by touch or other association with persons from lower castes. The system centered on the prestige of the priests and traditional occupations were associated with most castes.

The four basic castes in India's Hindu society gave primacy to the Brahmans or priests, who were the spiritual and intellectual leaders. Second came the Kshatriyas, the ruling military class that also came to practice trading. Third were the Vaishyas, who were landed farmers, herdsmen, craftsmen, and traders. These three castes were considered "twice-born"; they could undergo initiation rituals and learn the Vedas, the scriptures of Hinduism. Only the Brahmans, however, could teach the Vedas. The fourth group formed the Sudras, the indigenous majority of the population that supported the three Aryan castes above them. They were peasants or workers. The work of some Sudras was considered so polluting they were eventually excluded from the system, forming the Pariahs, or outcastes. As outcastes, they formed their own hierarchy similar to that of the hierarchy above them.

It is not clear in which part of India the caste system originated. Scholars most often suggest the Ganges Valley, followed by the Indus Valley, but southern India may have exhibited better the diversity of population that the system presupposes. Perhaps several different regions contributed differing elements to the system at more or less the same time.

Theories of how caste originated also abound. As the term "varna" indicates, color played a role in caste, though the extent of that role is debated. At a minimum, caste distinguished light-skinned Aryan invaders from the indigenous dark-skinned Dravidians. Perhaps the Vaishyas stemmed from yellow-skinned Mongols. A second theory is that caste simply hardened from the class system that preceded it. Class differences that originally had been based on merit thus eventually became hereditary. A third theory holds that caste arose around hereditary occupations. None of these theories alone, however, nor the group of them together, fully explains the diversity of castes.

The demarcation of occupations into priests, military leaders, traders, and peasants proved insufficient to accommodate the proliferation of occupations. Nor was the growth of occupational castes uniform throughout India. Also, various tribes were assimilated partially or wholly into Hinduism over the centuries, resulting in new castes. Persons of other religious persuasion, such as Muslims, Christians, and Sikhs, typically are seen as belonging to their own religious caste and themselves exhibit some features of caste. For example, converts to Christianity from differing castes may continue to observe caste distinctions and even worship in different churches, and various Christian denominations may advocate marriage within that denomination. The consequence of all these developments was the emergence over time of more than three thousand subcastes.

Wherever and however caste arose, its four major divisions appeared as early as the Rig-Veda (approximately 1500-1200 B.C.E.), a hymn which described creation in terms of a sacrifice by the gods. From the mouth of the sacrifice came the Brahmans, from the arms the Kshatriyas, from the thighs the Vaishyas, and from the feet the Sudras. This hymn shows the relative prestige of the four, but the stringent caste system seems not to have emerged at that time. At the time of the rise of Buddhism in the sixth century B.C.E., Brahmans and Kshatriyas still vied for preeminence. Both the Buddha and Mahavira, the founder of Jainism, were Kshatriyas who rejected Brahmanic sacrifice. By about 200 B.C.E., however, the responsibilities of each caste were described in the Laws of Manu. This Hindu writing also emphasizes that there is no fifth caste, that therefore Pariahs or outcastes stood outside the caste system.

The Laws of Manu lists the duties of each major caste. The Brahmans were charged with six basic functions: teaching, studying, sacrificing for themselves, sacrificing for others, making gifts, and receiving gifts as a source of religious merit for the giver (Manu, 10.75). For the Kshatriyas, teaching, sacrificing for others, and accepting gifts are forbidden (10.77), but bestowing gifts on Brahmans, offering sacrifices, studying the Vedas, and holding themselves aloof from sensual pleasures were commanded. Further, the Kshatriyas were to bear arms (10.79) and to rule, with the responsibilities of punishing those who defied caste and order and of defending their people in war (7.18-35, 7.87-89). The Vaishyas were prohibited from teaching, sacrificing for others, or receiving gifts (10.78). In addition to religious duties, they were charged with vocations of cowherding, farming, working with jewelry, and trade. They could accumulate wealth, but had to be fair to their employees (9.326-333). The Sudras were denied any of the six acts of the Brahmans and were consigned to serving the upper castes (8.413) and imitating the behavior of the virtuous (10.128). In addition, all four castes were to practice self-control and to abstain from injuring others, from stealing, from lying, and from unchastity (10.63).

The whole life of the upper castes was legislated. First, a man would live as a student. The Brahmans especially would spend years studying Hindu scriptures as well as the laws for each caste. The second stage would be spent as a householder, practicing his caste occupation and producing children. The third stage commenced after the birth of a man's grandchildren and consisted of physical or psychological separation from his livelihood and the pursuit of religious enlightenment. He could pass to a fourth stage where he abandoned all attachment to worldly things and lived as a wandering ascetic. Women were not permitted to progress through these stages in the same way, but they could accompany their husbands into the forest or spend time at home under the care of a son seeking enlightenment.

According to Hinduism each deed carries the seed of its own reward. This is the law of karma. It is the duty or dharma of each person to live according to his caste rules. The Bhagavad Gītā (3.8) and the Laws of Manu (10.97) teach that it is better to discharge one's own dharma incompletely than someone else's perfectly. Further, caste was connected with reincarnation. One's birth into one's caste was determined, among other things, by following one's dharma in previous lives. Hence, there was nothing unjust about being born a Sudra instead of a Brahman. Rather, one could assure oneself of a higher rebirth in the next life by following one's dharma in this life.

Some mobility seems always to have been possible within the system. In the event an upper-caste person could not earn a living at his caste level, he could move down to the next rank in search of livelihood. If a higher-caste man wished to take a second wife, she could be from the next caste lower than his, so upward mobility was available to women through marriage. In addition, all members of a local subcaste might move up a notch in a community in which an insufficient number of practitioners of a higher occupation left a void to fill. Or a local subcaste might grow too large and split up. Such movement was possible because decisions about which rules and rituals to follow, as well as decisions to exclude and readmit rule breakers, were made at the local level.

The control that caste exercised over individual Indians and local groups mitigated against their uniting against foreign invaders. It also hindered their uniting behind rulers, foreign or domestic. Hindus could accept Indian rajas, Buddhist rulers, Muslim conquerors, or British administrators with equal ease and disinterest. The same was true of different types of government, whether monarchy or democracy. Instead, they gave ultimate allegiance to their own caste. In Indian society at large, they coexisted more than they cooperated.

In general, caste has had at least three main functions in Indian society. First, as a transmitter of custom, caste functioned to socialize the young in everything from table manners and taste in food to hereditary occupations and endogamous marriage. Caste control of individuals allowed castes to act as corporate bodies for mutual benefit. Castes collectively provided India with a sense of solidarity. Second, caste functioned as a means of economic control by establishing guilds, not only to train apprentices, but also to limit entrance into various occupations and to set prices for goods produced. Third, caste functioned to define priorities for Indian life and thus to fix the status of individuals: The holy man outranked the conqueror, the rich man, and the proletariat.

Caste, nevertheless, was an imperfect system. Efforts to reform it were spurred internally by its rigidity and externally by contact with the West. Castes split up and new occupations became available, particularly after the arrival of the British East India Company in 1602. British missionaries, educators, and social workers arrived in large numbers in the early nineteenth century. The *Brahmo Somaj* movement sought to abolish caste in response to Christian criticism, and the *Arya Somaj*, in response to both Christianity and Islam, succeeded in modifying some caste rules in North India. When India adopted a new constitution after independence from Great Britain, two sections addressed caste as the basis of employment. Section 16 prohibited racial discrimination for government employment, while section 19 permitted anyone to follow any occupation, trade, or business.

Those who had suffered the most from caste were the untouchables. Comprising about 15 percent of the Indian population, they had endured numerous restrictions such as being forbidden to draw water from wells used by people of caste or to use public roads in the vicinity of Hindu temples and being forced to bear such insults as having to wear bells, like cattle, to warn caste members of their presence. Having benefited little from Hinduism, they sometimes converted, especially to Christianity. Mohandas Gandhi championed their cause, calling untouchability Hinduism's greatest blight and renaming untouchables *harijans*, which means "children of God." He campaigned successfully to get thousands of Hindu temples opened to them. In the legal sphere, he attempted to gain political representation for them. Section 17 of the new Indian constitution abolished untouchability. The constitution also granted untouchables a quota of jobs in public service and the right to hold seats in legislative bodies. Occasionally an untouchable has even run for high office, but without success.

Applications

Caste certainly exists in a more complete form in India than anywhere else, but the question is often asked whether it truly exists elsewhere. Scholars sometimes point to India's island neighbor Sri Lanka, but it is a Buddhist nation without the strict division between priests and rulers that is crucial to caste. Indians migrated in the nineteenth century to Mauritius, Guyana, Trinidad, Surinam, Fiji, South Africa, and East Africa, but they did not form caste units, nor were intercaste relationships important. Many immigrants did not even know to which caste they belonged. Caste occupations were almost totally absent, at least partially because immigrants generally left India as indentured servants. On the other hand, caste restrictions seem strongest in connection with endogamous marriage and with defining one's status among Indians.

Scholars also point to other places where institutions analogous to caste are said to exist. The Burmese, when possible, tend to shun various occupations, including temple slaves, beggars, and jailers, and the Japanese have avoided becoming executioners, butchers, leather workers, cobblers, and grave diggers. Scholars point to taboo crafts in Somalia, endogamy in Rwanda and Zaïre, and an outcaste group among Nigeria's Ibo people. Ancient Egypt is sometimes said to have had a social system similar to that of India. Herodotus reported seven Egyptian occupations facing restriction: priests, fighters, cowherds, swineherds, traders, interpreters, and sailors. However, he reports nothing that resembles the society-wide restriction of contact such as that in Hinduism.

Still others point to the policy of apartheid in South Africa as an example of caste. It is true that apartheid was used as a means of economic exploitation of the black majority by the white minority. Thus, it had both economic and racial components. Is racial prejudice in the United States evidence that it has a caste system? Certainly blacks have been barred from certain occupations and from marriage with whites. The successes of the Civil Rights movement and the existence of a substantial and growing middle and professional class among blacks disprove such charges.

One's conclusion about whether caste exists outside of Indian communities may ultimately depend on how one defines caste. Sometimes scholars, particularly scholars writing apologetically on behalf of India, will treat caste as scarcely different from any other class system. Several features of caste, however, cannot be found outside of India. Caste encompasses the whole community, not just certain low-status groups. It creates a network of self-governing constituent groups. In caste, status and power are almost totally disassociated. Brahmans hold neither political nor economic power. Caste is tied to religious ideas such as reincarnation, to religious duties, and to rituals to a degree not known elsewhere. The absence of these features elsewhere suggests that caste does not exist outside the subcontinent.

Context

The future of caste systems is in doubt. The failure of caste to maintain significant influence on Indians outside the subcontinent and the reduction of its influence in India itself suggests that it will continue to decline in importance. On the other hand, it will probably continue to change, perhaps by sanctioning intercaste marriage and out-of-caste occupations. Under such conditions it will probably survive, largely as an impediment to rapid social change, especially in rural areas and among people attempting to hold out against the onslaught of Western thought and technology.

Bibliography

Dumont, Louis. *Homo Hierarchicus*. Translated by Mark Sainsbury, Louis Dumont, and Basia Gulati. Chicago: University of Chicago, 1980. Best book on Indian caste, both in terms of description and assessment.

Hutton, J. H. *Caste in India: Its Nature, Function, and Origins*. 4th ed. London: Oxford University Press, 1963. Survey of caste in India, its background, and origins. Contains a chapter on analogous institutions in Africa, Burma, and Japan.

Marriott, McKim. *Caste Ranking and Community Structure in Five Regions of India and Pakistan*. Poona, India: Deccan College Postgraduate and Research Institute, 1965. Discusses the impact of caste in five areas: Middle Indus and Upper Ganges in the north, Bengal Delta (now part of Bangladesh), and Coromandel and Kerala at the southern tip.

Radhakrishnan, Sarvepali. *The Hindu View of Life*. New York: Macmillan, 1968. Thin volume by a leading philosopher who was also president of the Republic of India. Two chapters provide an explanation and defense of the caste system.

Schwartz, Barton M., ed. *Caste in Overseas Indian Communities*. San Francisco: Chandler, 1967. Studies of the limited role of caste among Indian populations abroad.

Zinkin, Taya. *Caste Today*. London: Oxford University Press, 1962. Describes the caste system in India, its relationship to democracy, and how the Indian government has attempted to resolve issues between the two.

Paul L. Redditt

Cross-References

Buddhism and Government, p. 152; The Civil Service in the United States, p. 310; Feudalism, p. 688; Hinduism and Government, p. 823; Individual Versus State Rights, p. 910; Oligarchy, p. 1344; Social Darwinism, p. 1833.

CHARISMATIC LEADERSHIP

Field of study: Political philosophy

Max Weber's theory of leadership identifies three bases for authority: charismatic, traditional, and rational-legal. He defines the basic requirements for political legitimacy and offers a rational framework to analyze and predict shifts in authority systems.

Principal terms

COLLEGIAL BUREAUCRACY: transitional type of rational-legal authority in which some bureaucratic offices are occupied by committees

GERONTOCRACY: rule by elders who exercise authority solely on the basis of tradition

IMPERATIVE COORDINATION: directed action voluntarily accepted by a group regardless of individual preferences

LEGITIMACY: acceptance of the validity of leadership by the group that makes imperative coordination possible

MONOCRATIC BUREAUCRACY: rational-legal bureaucratic administration in which lines of authority flow from one official to another in a hierarchic pattern

PATRIARCHY: traditional rule through inheritance

PATRIMONIALISM: traditional rule with an administrative staff that makes large-scale compulsion possible

ROUTINIZATION OF CHARISMA: the absorption of a charismatic action into customary practice

Overview

Max Weber (1864-1920), a German sociologist and political scientist, used the concepts of charismatic, traditional, and rational-legal authority to explore the nature of legitimate rule. He investigated fundamental issues such as why a given group routinely accepts the validity of directions regardless of individual attitudes. Weber discounted factors such as physical intimidation, economic pressure, ideology, habits, or personal advantage, which he collectively termed "influence." While he recognized that these factors were present in power relationships, he did not believe they could consistently transform leadership directives into group action. Instead, he searched for a binding force that compelled obedience over time, one that continually transformed the will of the leader into the will of the led. That group cohesiveness, which Weber called legitimacy, made continuous, large-scale, directed action possible. He termed that voluntarily embraced directed action "imperative coordination" (*Herrschaft*) and examined its causes and characteristics.

Weber also investigated the issue of change in authority systems, asking why and how one kind of imperative coordination modifies itself or gives way to another. In doing so, he probed the consequences of altered patterns of legitimacy under various conditions.

In grappling with these questions, Weber posited three ideal types of authority: charismatic, traditional, and rational-legal. He did not claim that his models closely matched any given reality, for authority systems usually combined elements of two, and sometimes all three, types in endlessly shifting relationships. The ideal types were analytical reference points, for elements of one model of imperative coordination dominated over others at any given time. Consequently, every system resembled some ideal type, sharing many of its distinctive features and responding to external forces and internal dynamics in noticeably similar ways.

Charismatic leadership, the most dramatic type of imperative coordination, is rule under emergency conditions. This authority system, dating from hunter-gathering times, is produced by crisis. The anxiety generated by prolonged difficulties brings forth a leader whose qualifications set him apart from the commonplace. He is the bearer of charisma, a spiritual quality with religious or magical resonances, and guides the group because of a perceived duty to accomplish an extraordinary mission. The charismatic shaman, warlord, or prophet performs phenomenal deeds that supposedly prove charismatic endowment and divine preference.

Belief in divine favor is at the core of charismatic authority. If one believes that a supernatural force has manifested its will through its chosen instrument, withholding allegiance to that instrument would be blasphemy. On the other hand, failure signals the withdrawal of the divine presence and the end of the heroic quest. The followers' constant need for reassurance through wondrous proofs during perilous times makes charismatic authority unstable.

That shortcoming is compounded by administrative weakness, for the only requirements for government are the mission of the leader and its acceptance by disciples. In its ideal form, charismatic authority lacks a bureaucracy. Decisions are arbitrary, because legitimacy lies with the leader, not in formal rules, precedents, or principles. Each pronouncement is unique, the fruit of divine revelation. Since purely charismatic leadership is both irrational and erratic, it cannot generate a self-perpetuating system through its own resources.

Economic factors also shorten the life span of charismatic leadership. Since the leader arises during tumultuous times, operations are financed in a makeshift fashion. This is in keeping with the otherworldly mentality of charismatic figures, who typically disdain materialistic concerns and preoccupations. Group interests are poorly served by such neglect, however, and irregular financing (by booty, gifts, or confiscations) places severe limits on the long-term success of charismatic authority.

The defeat or death of the charismatic leader has often brought some variant of a different ideal type—traditional authority—to the forefront. Elements of the preceding system may linger, especially if the new ruler has "inherited" charisma through some formal procedure. The succeeding order emphasizes practices hallowed by time rather than revelation. In traditional authority, legitimacy springs from the way things are believed always to have existed. The ruler is chosen through precedent and exercises power through personal authority based on traditional status. Obedience is owed to the leader himself, not to his office or to a presumed mission, and followers are held by bonds of personal loyalty.

Weber identifies several versions of traditional rule. The most primitive ones, which lack a personal administrative staff, are gerontocracies (rule by elders) or patriarchies (preeminence solely through inheritance). Often found together, these are weak forms of authority that lack the machinery of compulsion. The development of personal administrative staffs, particularly military forces, transform patriarchy into a more potent form of rule called patrimonialism. Members of the group become subjects; authority, formerly exercised by the ruler on behalf of the group, is claimed personally. Patrimonialism that sheds the limitations of precedent and maximizes personal authority becomes sultanism.

Patrimonial officials, often called retainers, are distinguished by personal connections to the leader rather than by competence, training, or well-defined spheres of authority. They are unsalaried; their economic needs are met through their chief's personal resources, by allowances in kind, through seizure of fees or taxes, or by benefices such as fiefs. Thus feudalism, which is based on personal loyalty and military service supported by fiefholding, is a form of patrimonialism.

Traditional authority promotes stable "housekeeping" economic activities but discourages capital growth or economic expansion. Because financial self-interest encourages rulers to escape the limitations of custom, traditional rule tends to move toward rational-legal authority.

Rational-legal authority appears under the banner of increased efficiency. The ruler's administrative staff becomes a hierarchical bureaucracy of trained experts. There is a clear, rule-bound chain of command. Typically, individuals in authority occupy offices with specified functions; are salaried, full-time appointees; hold their positions through free contracts; and advance on a career ladder determined by merit. Power relationships are defined by deliberately created laws, obedience is owed to the office rather than to any particular individual, and authority is exercised through administration.

In the transitional collegial form of rational-legal authority, some offices are held by committee. In the monocratic form, each significant office has a single occupant. Ultimate power is held by the bureaucracy: its technical expertise determines policy; the results of its actions can be closely predicted; and its working relationships, animated by reason and duty, are efficient. According to Weber, rational-legal authority is superior to other forms of imperative coordination in terms of reliability, control, effectiveness, and adaptability in problem solving.

Applications

Variants of Weber's leadership categories are easily recognizable in all parts of the world, in ancient as well as in modern times. The great majority are either mixed or transitional forms, but a number of instances approach his ideal types. His system is useful in identifying specific kinds of imperative coordination, analyzing their dynamics, and predicting their likely transformations through time.

A good example of pure charismatic leadership is the brief ascendancy of a Plains Indian shaman, Sitting Bull, over large parts of the Sioux nation in the mid-1870's. His greatest success came in 1876 when, as described in considerable detail on buffalo hides that circulated among the Sioux, he prophesied the defeat of U.S. cavalry units and mobilized the forces that produced victory at the Battle of the Little Big Horn. Similar cases include the successful promotion of a burning form of nationalism by Adolf Hitler, the head of the German Nationalist Socialist Party, in the early 1930's, and the unique personal influence, gained through messianic oratory, of the populist lawyer Aleksandre F. Kerensky in the first phase of the Russian Revolution of 1917. Since Kerensky's and Sitting Bull's persuasive powers faded rapidly in the face of military setbacks, it cannot be determined if their authority systems could have evolved into more stable forms.

Hitler's example is more instructive. Under initially peaceful conditions, he built an aggressive warrior society that preserved strong charismatic elements within a rational-legal framework. When his perceived mission collided with the interests of other powerful rational-legal systems, large-scale warfare broke out. Six years of conflict, resulting in destruction throughout Europe, were required to halt Hitler's apocalyptic ambitions. Weber has pointed to the grave instabilities that are generated when rational-legal authority combines with charisma to undermine the social stability promoted by tradition. The history of Hitler's regime supports that analysis.

Hitlerian Germany was an extreme example of charismatic dislocation, for such episodes are usually temporary breaks in a slow progression from traditional to rational-legal authority. In most cases, charismatic effects are either quickly erased or harmlessly incorporated. One example of the routinization of charisma is the politically harmless Chinese belief in a "mandate from heaven" that endorses the current political order. Another can be found in the prerevolutionary French monarchy, where acknowledgment of the charismatic warrior-hero status of the Frankish leadership (preserved with Christian trappings by Clovis, a converted Merovingian king, in the fifth century C.E.) was eventually reduced to the ceremonial anointing of kings with sacramental oil. While that rite was still being faithfully practiced, the French crown passed from a patrimonial to a predominantly rational-legal authority system.

Weber's categories are as useful in understanding the accelerated dynamics of nomadic or seminomadic conquest regimes, such as the Mongols under Genghis Khan's successors or the Manchu Ch'in dynasty, as they are in tracing the growth of bureaucracy in long-established systems. Without a suitably analytical perspective, the rapid progression of tribal peoples from clan affiliations to the creation of stable, sophisticated empires would present a bewildering, conceptually impoverished picture.

This can be illustrated by applying Weber's leadership theories to early Islam, an unusually complicated example of a conquest dynasty. Applying legitimacy theory to the problem, it can be seen that the Prophet Muhammad (570-632 c.e.), the founder of the new religion, was born into a primarily patriarchal society, exercised charismatic rule in a remarkably pure form, and that he established a patrimonial conquest regime driven by an extremely strong religious mission. Upon his death, a process of charismatic inheritance legitimized his successors, the caliphs, who continued his expansionist policies and conquered a vast empire previously controlled by heavily bureaucratic states. Within decades of the Prophet's death, economic interests and the availability of conquered administrative resources moved the Umayyad caliphate from a mixed charismatic-traditional to a predominantly rational-legal authority system. Concurrently, the bedouin tribes spread Islamic rule because they were still influenced by charismatic factors—that is, they preserved the sense of divine mission that they originally possessed in Muhammad's lifetime. Thus, using a few powerful leading ideas coupled with the careful accumulation of data, Weber's system imposes conceptual order on an otherwise sprawling, confusing religious and political phenomenon.

Context

Although Weber developed a powerful leadership theory, his work has been slow to receive formal recognition for several reasons. First, he died unexpectedly, at the age of fifty-six, before fully developing his ideas. His most important work dealing with authority systems, *State and Society (Wirtschaft und Gesellschaft)*, was still in fragmentary form in 1920, when he died, and did not appear until 1925. In *State and Society*, he had intended to deepen his treatment of leadership types, particularly in regard to the special cases of Western feudalism and American democratic practice. His failure to elaborate his system, as well as the scattered and fragmentary nature of his writings, hindered full awareness of his work. Appreciation for Weber's theories was also retarded by a general decline in respect for German scholarship following World War I. Before 1914, the German scholarly tradition was dominant in the Western world. But in the emotional anti-German backlash after the war and the increased politicization of German academic life in the early 1930's, Weber's ideas failed to attract the careful scrutiny they deserved.

Weber's impact was also diminished by the spread of Marxism during and after World War I. Because he paralleled Marx in emphasizing the importance of economic factors in the transformation of authority systems, Weber was sometimes dismissed as derivative. Ironically, his observations on the importance of noneconomic values such as the significance of shared outlooks led to a different criticism. Although he was a foe of Marx, by including so many economic factors in his analyses, he was thought to have made unnecessary concessions to his adversary. Thus, some critics saw his system as a weak, and therefore invalid, response to Marxism.

The appeal of Weber's legitimacy theory was limited also by its inability to provide simple formulas. It was composed of a few powerful ideas that illuminated, but did not authoritatively describe, any given society. Each case required close historical examination, and predictions were dependent on meticulous individualized analysis. It was easy to generalize from a Marxist base; Weber's system required careful research and prudent qualification. In the ideological climate of twentieth century politics, that has often proven to be a handicap.

Despite the fact that portions of his work remain untranslated from the original German, Weber's views on authority have increasingly infiltrated scholarly activity. His ideas on leadership dynamics, though usually without attribution, permeate many broad-scoped historical works; in effect, they have become the common inheritance of modern scholarship. Two classic examples of Weber's pervasive, if unstated, influence can be seen in Ira Lapidus's massive and informative *History of Islamic Societies* (1988) and Franz Michael's elegant survey *China Through the Ages* (1986), which owe much of their perspective and cohesion to his views on authority.

Bibliography

Albrow, Martin. *Max Weber's Construction of Social Theory*. New York: St. Martin's Press, 1990. A thorough review of Weber's ideas, put into context with those of other sociologists. Readable prose, with many definitions. Includes references, an index of names, and a subject index.

Andreski, Stanislav. *Max Weber's Insights and Errors*. London: Routledge & Kegan Paul, 1984. Describes the personal and political background that underlies Weber's theory. Provides a thorough description of how feudalism and patrimonialism developed through traditional authority.

Bendix, Reinhard. *Max Weber: An Intellectual Portrait*. Garden City, N.Y.: Doubleday, 1960. Excellent treatment of Weber's life and interests by a fellow sociologist. Discusses his work on the sociology of religion and his leadership theories.

Dronberger, Ilse. *The Political Thought of Max Weber: In Quest of Statesmanship*. New York: Appleton-Century-Crofts, 1971. An interesting, comprehensive biography of Max Weber, integrating his political and scholarly interests. Includes notes and an index.

Mommsen, Wolfgang. *The Age of Bureaucracy: Perspectives on the Political Sociology of Max Weber*. Oxford, England: Basil Blackwell, 1974. A clear description of the three types of legitimate authority. Features a very detailed chart comparing the three systems in terms of the sources of authority, forms of legitimacy, and type of legal system that would apply to each one. Includes a useful bibliography.

Parken, Frank. *Max Weber*. London: Tavistock, 1982. A readable and interesting description of Weber's ideas, with clear examples and definitions of his terms. Provides a bibliographic sketch of Weber that puts his ideas into the context of the times.

Weber, Max. *Max Weber: Selections in Translation*. Translated by E. Matthews. Edited by W. G. Runciman. Cambridge, England: Cambridge University Press, 1978. Solid, gracefully translated sampling of Weber's work. Chapters four and five discuss charismatic domination and the formation of bureaucracy. Includes a preface, biographical summary, introduction, index, and bibliography.

_____. *Max Weber: The Theory of Social and Economic Organization*. Translated by A. M. Henderson and Talcott Parsons. Edited by Talcott Parsons. New York: Free Press, 1947. Selection of substantial parts of Weber's work, including his discussion of leadership types. Although somewhat stilted and occasionally convoluted, is essential reading for a firm grasp of Weber's ideas.

Wrong, Dennis, ed. *Max Weber*. Englewood Cliffs, N.J.: Prentice-Hall, 1970. A thorough analysis and critique of Weber's methodology, theory and philosophy. The chapter on charismatic leadership describes four actual political leaders and analyzes their charismatic authority according to Weber's criteria. Includes an introduction and a selected bibliography.

Michael J. Fontenot

Cross-References

Armed Forces, p. 89; Bonapartism, p. 140; Church Government, p. 241; Clientelism, p. 337; Comparative Government, p. 384; Cult of Personality, p. 477; Demagoguery, p. 507; Empires and Empire Building, p. 597; Fascism and Nazism, p. 656; Feudalism, p. 688; Government Roles, p. 778; Government Types, p. 785; History of Government, p. 829; Imperialism, p. 889; Islam and Government, p. 994; Leadership, p. 1066; Legitimacy, p. 1105; Nietzsche's Political Philosophy, p. 1300; Nomadic Peoples' Governments, p. 1306; Populism, p. 1551; Public Opinion Polling, p. 1627; Self-Interest in Politics, p. 1802; Statesmanship, p. 1898; Succession, p. 1909.

CHECKS AND BALANCES IN U.S. GOVERNMENT

Field of study: Political philosophy

Checks and balances are the principal means by which the U.S. Constitution prevents any one branch of the government from dominating the whole. The Constitution divides power in such a way as to require at least two, and occasionally all three, branches of the government to act before anything can be accomplished.

Principal terms

EXECUTIVE BRANCH: in the United States, the president and the major departments of the government such as state, defense, treasury, and justice

EXECUTIVE POWER: power to execute or administer the laws passed by the legislature

JUDICIAL BRANCH: federal judiciary, headed by the Supreme Court, and including courts of appeals, district courts, and a few specialized courts

JUDICIAL POWER: court's power to interpret the law by deciding individual cases

JUDICIAL REVIEW: power of courts to decide whether a statute or executive act is in accordance with the Constitution

JURISDICTION: court's power to decide a case; literally, the power to "say what the law is"

LEGISLATIVE BRANCH: Congress of the United States, which consists of the Senate and House of Representatives

LEGISLATIVE POWER: power to make laws

LIMITED GOVERNMENT: government whose structure prevents official acts that violate the rights of individuals or minorities

VETO POWER: president's authority to prevent bills passed by Congress from becoming law unless overridden by a two-thirds vote in each house

Overview

"Checks and balances" are the means by which the principle of separation of powers in the U.S. Constitution is executed. Separation of powers is the idea that the powers of government separate themselves naturally into three different kinds of activities: lawmaking, administration or enforcement, and judging. John Locke and Charles-Louis de Secondat, Baron de Montesquieu are the most influential political philosophers of separation of powers. Locke, in *The Second Treatise of Government* (1690), urged "balancing the power of government by placing several parts of it in different hands." In *The Spirit of the Laws* (1748), Montesquieu argued that "Where the legislative and executive powers are united in the same person, or in the same body of magistrates, there can be no liberty. . . . Again there is no liberty, if the judicial power be not separated from the legislative and executive. Were it joined with the legislative, the life and liberty of the subject would be exposed to arbitrary control; for the judge would then be the legislator. Were it joined to the executive power, the judge might behave with violence and oppression." As the text of the Constitution shows, the Framers were strongly influenced by these arguments. *The Spirit of the Laws* was repeatedly appealed to at the Constitutional Convention of 1787 and is also discussed at length in the Federalist Papers, an important series of essays that urged adoption of the Constitution.

The Framers devised a system of separation of powers in which each form of governmental power is exercised by a separate branch of government. The branches are not fully independent of one another, however; each has constitutional powers with which it can check and regulate the actions of the others to some extent. Moreover, the members of each branch are selected by different means or constituencies and tend to represent different groups, interests, or political ideas.

Congress can be limited by the president in several ways. Every bill or measure passed by Congress that is to have the force of law must be presented to the president for consideration. If the president does not approve of the measure, he may veto it by returning it to Congress with his objections. The president's veto, however, is not final. Congress may still force the bill into law, but it is necessary to pass it again with a two-thirds majority in each house. This is usually difficult, as the president has considerable political influence. Indeed, a president's ability to make a veto "stick" is one of the indicators used by press and public to judge the president's political strength. The president also has other influential legislative functions. Under the Constitution, he may make formal recommendations to Congress for action, and his program normally has great political weight. He submits an executive budget to Congress every year, and this proposal sets the legislative agenda for government spending and taxing.

The president's executive powers also helps him to check the legislature. He may be able to decide how much administrative weight to give a law. A program that is not enforced has little influence. Moreover, to the extent that a statute is ambiguous, the president's interpretation of it controls its execution and its meaning in practice. He can also call Congress into special or emergency session, although this constitutional power has been little used in the late twentieth century because Congress is in session most of the year.

The Supreme Court also has significant power over Congress. Lawsuits sometimes raise the issue of whether a particular law is constitutional or how it should be interpreted. If such a case arises within the Supreme Court's jurisdiction, it has the power to decide on the meaning of the law or to declare it unconstitutional. Although it is not found explicitly in the Constitution, this power—often called the power of judicial review—has existed since the Supreme Court's decision in *Marbury v. Madison* in 1803. In this landmark case, the Court held that the Constitution is superior to laws made by Congress. If the Constitution and a law conflict with each other, the law must give way.

The Supreme Court exercises the same power of judicial review over administrative acts, including some acts of the president. For example, the Court could decide that a particular executive action is unlawful because it is not authorized by legislation. Presidential acts may also be declared unconstitutional if they violate a provision of the Constitution.

Congress may also limit the president. First, Congress makes the laws, and, if there are sufficient votes, can override the president's veto. The president is bound by the laws, as he is charged by the Constitution to "take care that the laws be faithfully executed." Although he is given power to execute the laws, he must obey them. Thus by making law, Congress can tie the president's hands. A president who violates a statute can be impeached by the House of Representatives and removed from office if convicted by the Senate. The Senate must approve most executive appointments and all treaties. By enacting the budget, Congress controls the expenditure of all government monies and thus may prevent the president from executing particular programs.

Congress has a number of checks against the judiciary, which has been called the weakest or least dangerous branch of the government. Persons nominated to be federal judges must be confirmed by Congress. The power to reject judicial nominees was exercised frequently by the Senate during the second half of the twentieth century, often to prevent too sharp a shift in judicial ideology. If Congress dislikes the Court's interpretation of a law, it may alter or clarify the statute. Congress may also initiate constitutional amendments. Congress has power to set the size of the federal court system, including the size of the Supreme Court itself. The appellate jurisdiction of the Supreme Court is also subject to Congress' control to some extent. Congress removed certain cases from the Court's jurisdiction for a time after the Civil War. Federal judges, like the president, are subject to impeachment and removal from office.

The president also has some powers over the courts. He nominates all federal judges and can attempt to shape future decisions through appointment power. He may pardon people who have been convicted of criminal offenses. Court decisions that interpret a statute may require execution by the president, and his decisions can affect the implementation of the decision.

In a federal system, such as that of the United States, governmental power is divided between the central and state governments. James Madison wrote in Federalist No. 51 that a federal system is a superior form of limited government because power is divided between two governments, each of which has its separate branches. For example, in the United States, state governments have the greatest role in crime control, education, and general traffic and safety regulations. Many decisions are made locally, which helps prevent any branch of the federal government from becoming oppressive or tyrannical. The division of powers between the federal and state governments is, therefore, a further implementation of checks and balances.

Applications

There are many important examples of the operation of checks and balances in U.S. politics. The most noticeable and unusual feature of the system of checks and balances is the Supreme Court's authority to declare federal and state laws unconstitutional. Many profound political changes have been the result of Supreme Court decisions. In *Baker v. Carr* (1962), the Supreme Court held that the judiciary has the power to end malapportionment in Congressional districting. Subsequent decisions ended the pattern of rural overrepresentation in Congress, which had been characteristic of U.S. politics since the end of the nineteenth century. The implementation of the principle of one person, one vote brought about a political revolution in urban-rural balance in the United States.

The Supreme Court's decision in *Brown v. Board of Education* (1954) ended the era of legalized racial discrimination. Supporting court decisions during the following two decades almost entirely eliminated legal racial discrimination. By the end of the twentieth century, nearly all public schools were integrated, and legal support of racial discrimination in public accommodations had almost completely disappeared.

The flag-burning cases offer another example of the Supreme Court's willingness to play an antimajoritarian role, even in small cases. In *Texas v. Johnson* (1989) the Court struck down as a violation of the First Amendment guarantee of freedom of speech a Texas statute that prohibited desecration of the American flag. Congress almost immediately passed a federal flag-desecration statute, which was also declared unconstitutional by the Court in *Eichman v. U.S.* (1990). Congress's power had been checked.

Congressional checks against presidential power are also common, and some have been striking. Congress' refusal to fund additional military and paramilitary assistance to the Nicaraguan Contras during President Ronald Reagan's administration prevented the president from implementing a cherished foreign policy. The administration attempted to evade the law, thus bringing about a scandal that resulted in the dismissal and conviction of two of Reagan's aides and a congressionally mandated reorganization of the National Security Council.

Congress' power to pass on nominees for judicial and executive positions has also been used to check presidential power. Two of President Richard Nixon's appointees to the Supreme Court were rejected or forced to withdraw by the United States Senate. About a quarter of presidential nominees to the Supreme Court have been rejected since 1789.

Congress's impeachment power has also been used as a check on the judiciary. Since 1789, thirteen federal judges have been impeached by the House, of whom seven were convicted and removed from office. The only Supreme Court justice to be impeached—Samuel Chase, in 1804—escaped conviction in the Senate. No U.S. president has been impeached and convicted. Andrew Johnson was formally impeached in 1868 for his opposition to Congress's harsh reconstruction policies, but the effort to convict him in the Senate failed by one vote. The likelihood of impeachment and conviction led Richard M. Nixon to resign from the presidency in 1974 in the wake of the Watergate affair.

The president's check on the direction of the judiciary can be observed by scrutinizing judicial appointments. During the administrations of Ronald Reagan and

George Bush, the ideological direction of the Supreme Court was significantly altered by the appointment of six justices who proved to be much more conservative than their predecessors. A similar pattern of appointments was made in the lower federal judiciary during the same years.

The president's most influential check on Congress is the veto power. Congress can seldom muster the special majority required in each chamber to override a presidential veto. Thus the president often has the power, sometimes through the threat of a veto alone, to prevent passage of measures with which he strongly disagrees. When the Civil Rights Bill of 1991 was being debated in Congress, for example, President Bush announced that he would veto any bill that imposed hiring quotas on employers. Congress was forced to alter the bill to meet the president's wishes; the proponents of quotas could not muster enough votes to defeat a veto. The veto can be an effective restraint on Congress, though it does not help a president to force his proposals through Congress.

The pardoning power has not often been used as a check on the other branches of the government, although President Gerald Ford's pardon of Richard Nixon after the latter's resignation ended all legal action against him. President Jimmy Carter used the pardon power to grant amnesty to all who had resisted the draft during the war in Vietnam, thus helping to put to rest a potentially divisive political issue.

Context

The roots of the idea of checks and balances lie in the admiration of early American political thinkers for limited government. They had observed European nations in which the divine right of kings was accepted and in which subjects had little liberty. Their own heritage was English, but in England a system of rights had developed as well as a partial system of separation of powers. The English tradition of limited government was reflected in the form and powers of many of the colonial governments. When American independence came about and a new government was to be established, the ideal of limited government had taken firm hold in the United States. The theory of individual natural rights and limited government propounded by John Locke inspired the generation of American revolutionary leaders. The Framers of the Constitution sought to limit government, both textually and structurally. The structure they devised incorporated separate governmental branches sharing power by means of the elaborate system of checks and balances set out above. James Madison argued in Federalist No. 48 that "unless these departments be so far connected and blended as to give each a constitutional control over the others, the degree of separation which the maxim requires, as essential to a free government, can never in practice be duly maintained."

The limited government established by the Constitution has not always operated to protect minorities or minority opinions; even the Supreme Court acquiesced in state-mandated discrimination in *Plessy v. Ferguson* (1896) and in the imprisonment during World War II of United States citizens of Japanese ancestry. In contrast to countries in which brutality and mass murder by government is common, the United

States has been successful in restraining political power. Periods of severe repression have been rare and short-lived for the most part. In the United States, people live out their lives without the fear that the government will unjustly imprison, torture, or kill them.

The great challenge to the political institutions of the United States in the twenty-first century will be to make sure that the system of checks and balances does not paralyze government entirely. There are many veto points or checks within the structure. As public opinion has become more diverse and as special interests (Madison would have called them factions) have proliferated, positive political action has become harder to achieve.

Bibliography

Becker, Carl L. *The Declaration of Independence: A Study in the History of Political Ideas*. New York: Knopf, 1966. Discusses the Declaration of Independence and the events which inspired it.

Hamilton, Alexander, James Madison, and John Jay. *The Federalist Papers*. Edited by Clinton Rossiter. New York: New American Library, 1961. Originally published in 1788 to promote ratification of the U.S. Constitution, these essays are among the most brilliant expositions of American political theory ever published. Numbers 47 and 48 are particularly relevant to the system of checks and balances.

Locke, John. *The Second Treatise of Government*. Edited by Thomas P. Peardon. Indianapolis: Bobbs-Merrill, 1952. Originally published to justify the Glorious Revolution of 1688, this immensely influential essay provides a powerful argument for limited government and individual natural rights.

Montesquieu, Charles-Louis de Secondat, Baron de. *The Spirit of Laws*. Translated by Thomas Nugent. Rev ed. Cincinnati: R. Clarke, 1873. Montesquieu's 1748 study of the English constitution is justly celebrated for his defense of separation of powers and for his sense that the "beautiful" English constitution arose as a result of experience and history rather than logic.

United States. Constitutional Convention (1787). *The Records of the Federal Convention of 1787*. Edited by Max Farrand. Rev. ed. New Haven, Conn.: Yale University Press, 1966. Includes all the important records of the Philadelphia convention; especially useful for understanding the range of opinion on the new governmental structure.

White, Morton. *Philosophy, the Federalist, and the Constitution*. New York: Oxford University Press, 1987. Analysis of the theoretical ideas of the Federalist Papers, including their connection to John Locke's ideas.

Robert Jacobs

Cross-References

Congress, p. 412; The Constitution of the United States, p. 425; Constitutional Law in the United States, p. 439; The Electoral College, p. 584; Federalism in the United

CHINESE COMMUNISM

Field of study: Comparative government

The Chinese Communist Party (CCP), ideologically based on Marxism-Leninism, was formed in 1921. After defeating the Kuomintang, or Nationalist Party, in 1949, it established the People's Republic of China and totalitarian power, allowing no political opposition.

Principal terms

CULTURAL REVOLUTION: power struggle launched by Mao Tse-tung, his wife Jiang Qing, and her radical allies against the pragmatists led by Liu Shaoqi and Deng Xiaoping, resulting in widespread chaos from 1966 to 1976

FIRST UNITED FRONT: period during the mid-1920's when members of the Chinese Communist Party (CCP) were admitted to the Kuomintang (KMT), which was reorganized with Soviet help; it ended when the Kuomintang purged Communist members and expelled the Soviet advisers

GREAT LEAP FORWARD: Mao's failed attempt to gain instant modernization and to overtake the Soviet Union ideologically by instituting communes in both urban and rural China and backyard furnaces to make steel during the late 1950's

LONG MARCH: 6,000-mile retreat by the CCP from Jiangxi to Yanan, pursued by the Kuomintang army; an epic of survival that lasted from October, 1934, to October, 1935

SECOND UNITED FRONT: alliance between the KMT and CCP to fight against Japanese aggression during World War II

Overview

The Chinese Communist Party (CCP) was formed secretly in Shanghai in 1921 by twelve men who were disillusioned with Western democracies. The men were disappointed with China's diplomatic reverses in the Paris Peace Conference that ended World War I, and attracted by the ideals of social and economic revolution and by the new world order promised by Marxism-Leninism. Chen Duxiu and Li Dazhao, two leading intellectuals, were cofounders of the party; Mao Tse-tung was also a founding member. An agreement between Sun Yat-sen, leader of the Nationalist Party (Kuomintang, or KMT), and Adolf Joffe, representative of the Soviet Union and the Communist International (Comintern) in China in 1923, allowed the four hundred members of the CCP to join the established and much larger KMT to form a United Front (the First United Front, in retrospect). The Soviet Union's goal in participating in the United Front was to use the KMT to nurture the infant CCP, and, when the opportune moment arrived, to discard the KMT, as Joseph Stalin said, like "squeezed out lemons." After Sun Yat-sen's death in 1925, the KMT split between those who advocated continuation of Sun's policies and those who opposed it, with the former in ascendancy.

With Soviet organizational and financial aid, the KMT launched a Northern Expedition in 1926 from its base in Canton. The object of the expedition was to rid warlord domination and to unify the country. In 1927 Chiang Kai-shek, the victorious commander in chief of the Northern Expedition, successfully moved to expel the Soviet advisers and purged the CCP, ending the United Front.

The Communists who escaped the KMT purge fled to the hills of Jiangxi province in southeastern China and established the Chinese Soviet Republic in 1928. It carried out violent land reform in areas it controlled. The KMT government launched sporadic campaigns to eliminate the CCP. Faced with certain defeat in 1934, the remaining CCP fled Jiangxi in a Long March that lasted from October, 1934, to October, 1935. It began with approximately 100,000 soldiers and civilians and covered six thousand miles; around 20,000 survivors reached sanctuary in northern China, where they joined with local Communist guerrillas and eventually established their headquarters in Yanan. Mao Tse-tung emerged supreme within the party as a result of the Long March.

Accelerated Japanese aggression against China that began with its conquest of the Northeastern Provinces (Manchuria) in 1931 solidified Chinese public opinion against the KMT's continuing anticommunist campaigns and domestic consolidation policy in favor of another united front against Japan. Conversely, fear of Chinese unity and the KMT's successful modernization programs had been influential in leading Japan's militarists to collaborate with Fascist Italy and Nazi Germany in an anti-Comintern pact.

On July 7, 1937, Japanese militarists provoked an incident in China that began the Sino-Japanese War. As the KMT government prepared for a long fight, it moved to formalize the formation of a united front, with the CCP, against the Japanese. In the agreement for a Second United Front, concluded in September, 1937, the CCP agreed to stop designating as soviets the areas under its control, to abolish the name Red Army for its military force, to obey the military orders of the KMT government, to cease implementing Marxist programs in its areas, and to obey Sun Yat-sen's ideology of the KMT. In return, the KMT formally called off its military campaigns against the CCP, elected Mao and other leaders to participate in the newly created People's Political Council, and took other measures to ensure collaboration between the two parties in resistance against Japan.

CCP policy objectives doomed the Second United Front. As Mao Tse-tung told his cadres in 1937: "Our fixed policy should be 70 percent expansion, 20 percent dealing with the Kuomintang, and 10 percent resisting Japan." The Sino-Japanese War, which expanded into World War II after Japan's attack on the United States naval base at Pearl Harbor in 1941, gave the CCP an opportunity to recoup and expand. Superior Japanese armed forces inflicted heavy losses on the KMT army and forced the KMT government to retreat inland from its coastal bases. Eight years of war wore down the morale of the KMT troops and the economy of the interior regions it controlled, resulting in high inflation, corruption, and public disaffection.

While Chiang Kai-shek was preoccupied with conducting the war, Mao spent much of the wartime writing and developing his blueprint for a Marxist program suited to primarily agrarian China. This blueprint would later be enshrined as the thought of Mao Tse-tung. It was a creative adaptation of Marxism-Leninism to conditions in China, and by implication, to all nonindustrialized, non-Western countries. The CCP also skillfully organized peasants into guerrilla units that simultaneously resisted the brutal Japanese military while expanding the CCP power base. Mao also wrote that in this transitional period, the CCP would collaborate with noncommunist political parties and nonproletarian but patriotic social classes. It also stopped its earlier class struggle policies, gaining the support of many segments of society. The CCP, however, retained complete control of the government in its territories. The Yanan period, thus, was one of growth and preparation for the final seizure of power. By 1941, the United Front had broken down in all but name; by the end of the war, the KMT was reserving some of its best forces to blockade the CCP.

While the relatively open KMT-controlled areas were exposed to the critical evaluation of Western diplomats and reporters, the rare, short, and closely supervised visits of Westerners to CCP-held areas allowed the Westerners to see only what their hosts wanted them to see. As a result, while Westerners wrote critically of conditions in KMT-held areas, they were enthusiastic about what they were exposed to in CCP-ruled regions, often extolling the "Yanan way."

With the defeat of Japan in 1945, China's civil war resumed. Whereas the CCP had approximately 30,000 soldiers scattered in several guerrilla bases in northern and southeastern China in 1937, in 1945, it counted more than 900,000 regular soldiers and about 2 million guerrillas and controlled large regions in northern China.

The United States, which had become China's ally in World War II, attempted to mediate a peaceful settlement and the establishment of a coalition government at war's end, but failed. The United States withdrew its support from the KMT government. The Soviet Union, on the other hand, supported the CCP covertly and diplomatically. Numerous factors resulted in the military defeat of the KMT, which fled to the island province of Taiwan (Republic of China or ROC), and the establishment of the People's Republic of China (PRC) on October 1, 1949. Mao Tse-tung became the chairman of the Chinese Communist Party and the People's Republic, holding the former post until his death in 1976.

Whereas the Soviet Union's government was called a dictatorship of the proletariat, the PRC's calls itself a "democratic dictatorship" led by the CCP, which had 4.5 million members in 1949, 17 million in 1961, and 46 million in 1988. The difference between the two Communist powers is that whereas the Soviet Union was a one-party state, several parties friendly to the CCP were allowed to exist in China, as window dressing.

Although several constitutions have been enacted since 1949, they all have endorsed a central government under a premier and cabinet that is "elected" by a National People's Congress that is supposed to meet once a year to endorse major policy decisions. Unlike the Soviet Union, which was a federation, China's government was centralized. Provinces and counties have remained the local government units. In addition, several areas with significant ethnic-cultural minority populations (such as

Tibet) have been established as autonomous regions. The CCP structure has paralleled that of the government. For example, the National Party Congress, elected by party members every five years, has paralleled the National People's Congress.

The party and government are closely intertwined at every level, and key party leaders also fill the top government positions. The CCP also controls the trade unions, farmers' groups, women's groups, youth groups, and all other mass organizations, thus extending its control to all areas of society. The almost total integration of the CCP with the government and with mass organizations and the CCP's absolute control over the media, education, culture, and other aspects of society made the PRC a totalitarian state similar to the Soviet Union. Entire classes of people, suspected of disloyalty by the party, were designated enemies of the people and deprived of political and civil rights. Children and grandchildren of former landlords, born after land reform, continued to be so designated. The party, moreover, can newly declare given groups enemies of the people. There are no appeals against the party's decisions.

The total domination of the CCP in all aspects of the government, military, judiciary, and society of China is characteristic of a totalitarian form of government. This form of government is clearly different from the democratic government that exists in the United States, where there are free elections, a separation of powers, an independent judiciary, a military that is accountable to no political party, and where press and other basic freedoms are guaranteed by the Constitution and safeguarded by law.

Another significant difference between a totalitarian system of government, such as the PRC's, and a democratic one, as in the United States, is political succession. The U.S. Constitution provides for peaceful transfers of power from one party to another as mandated by the people in elections, and a smooth succession in case of the death or incapacitation of the president. None of China's several constitutions since 1949 has provided for a smooth transfer of power within the Communist leadership. This omission has resulted in intrigues and power struggles that have crippled the CCP and devastated the nation. Mao Tse-tung installed and unseated a succession of heirs, and power struggles and an attempted coup rocked China after Mao's death. The power struggles continued under Deng Xiaoping during the 1980's and 1990's.

These power struggles had parallels in the Soviet Union, as evidenced by events before and after the death of Vladimir Lenin, after the death of Stalin, the ouster of Nikita Khrushchev, and the death of Leonid Brezhnev. The totalitarian form of government in both countries was augmented by the creation of personality cults of Stalin in the Soviet Union and Mao in China, which obliged the people to venerate their leaders. These practices contrast with the dynastic governments of pre-twentieth century China and with the government of the ROC. In imperial China, each dynasty clearly spelled out laws of succession, which generally precluded power struggles at the death of an emperor. In the ROC, Chiang Kai-shek and his son Chiang Ching-kuo dominated politics and were elected to the presidency by docile national assemblies. Chiang Ching-kuo, however, began a process of democratization in the late 1980's that made the ROC a multiparty democracy in the 1990's. In further contrast with democratic governments, power in the PRC is often exercised from behind the scenes and under tight secrecy. It has been a rule of men rather than rule of law.

Until the early 1960's, the PRC's foreign policy favored the Soviet Union and other Communist states and was anti-Western. With the souring of relations with the Soviet Union in the 1960's, China and the United States moved toward a rapprochement that culminated in the first visit to China by a U.S. president (Richard M. Nixon in 1972) and the establishing of full diplomatic relations in 1979. China sent troops in 1950 to rescue its North Korean communist ally from the United Nations' forces. China also helped Communist North Vietnam materially in its war against France and later against the United States and South Vietnam. China also fought a border war against India in 1960, clashed with the Soviet Union over border disputes in 1969, and launched a brief punitive war against its former (North) Vietnamese ally in 1979. A nuclear power since 1964, the PRC was admitted to the United Nations in 1971 and holds one of the five permanent seats on the U.N. Security Council.

The CCP followed the Soviet Union's example in instituting violent land reforms that eliminated the gentry and landlords as a class. It forcibly enrolled all peasants in collective farms. Soviet-style plans of economic development that favored industries over agriculture were also adopted. In 1958, Mao Tse-tung replaced the Second Five Year Plan with an unrealistic economic program called the Great Leap Forward. Its inevitable failure resulted in widespread economic dislocation and famine. Mao as a result lost the state chairmanship to a pragmatist, Liu Shaoqi, in 1960. Mao's revenge led to the Cultural Revolution, which resulted in the ouster of Liu and his assistant Deng Xiaoping. The struggle for succession led to the rise and fall of Minister of Defense Lin Biao, and, after Mao's death, of his widow Jiang Qing and her supporters (the Gang of Four). The struggle culminated in Deng's return to power in 1980. The quest to succeed the aging Deng resulted in turmoil within the CCP in the 1980's and was partly responsible for the slaughter of student demonstrators in Tiananmen Square in Beijing and in other cities in 1989, and that has continued in covert power struggles in the 1990's.

After 1980, Deng Xiaoping dismantled most of Mao's Marxist economic programs. All farming returned to private hands, as did most trade and many industries, except for strategic and heavy industries. After 1991, as communism crumbled in the former Soviet Union and Eastern Europe, China, Vietnam, North Korea, and Cuba remained the surviving communist states. In China, communism survived not as a viable economic system or social order, but solely as an instrument of an authoritarian, one-party government.

Applications

The primary goal of the CCP since its inception in 1921 has been to seize and hold power by force, although it made compromises when necessary, as evidenced in the First and Second United Fronts. Once in power, the CCP eliminated opposition and used its control of the military forces to monopolize power, maintain control, and implement its economic and other programs. China was near bankruptcy and many of its people were on the verge of starvation in 1976, so Mao's successors abandoned

Marxist economic programs and models in favor of a "socialist market economy." They vowed to turn China into a leading modern state by the year 2000 through the Four Modernizations—of agriculture, industry, science and technology, and defense. To do so, they tentatively opened China to the world, privatized agriculture, and also returned the private sector to the urban economy. These moves dramatically improved the standard of living of many Chinese, but they also resulted in serious problems for the party, undermining its ideology, widening the gap between rich and poor, and leading to widespread corruption among party and government officials. Opening China to the outside world has led many Chinese—notably students and intellectuals—to demand a fifth modernization as a must for a modern nation—political modernization through democracy. The demand for democratization and against corruption was the main force behind student demonstrations in 1989 that led to the Tiananmen Square massacre. With its abandonment of Marxist economic theories, the Chinese Communist Party retains exclusive political power with no real ideological justification.

Context

The Chinese Communist Party was formed in 1921 in the wake of World War I and soon after the establishment of a communist state in Russia. It developed in response to both China's domestic economic problems and the rising crisis in its relationship with Japan and was saved from destruction by the Kuomintang by the eight-year Sino-Japanese War, which fatally weakened the KMT. Just as World War I brought about the triumph of communism in Russia, World War II did so in China. Communist China followed the Soviet Union's model in instituting a one-party totalitarian state, in state economic planning, and in adopting a Marxist economic system. The Soviet Union and China fell out with each other, however, over disputes on the correct interpretation of Marxism-Leninism, over the contributions of Mao Tse-tung's thought, over leadership in the Communist world, and over territorial disputes.

The corruption of the Communist Party and the bankruptcy of the communist economic system has led to the collapse of the Soviet empire in Eastern Europe and of the Soviet Union. Mikhail Gorbachev's policy of glasnost (openness) and perestroika (restructuring of the communist system) could not avert this collapse. China's Deng Xiaoping, on the other hand, refused to restructure the Chinese political system and limited the degree to which China is opened to the outside world. His tough stance in these regards, plus his timely economic reforms, saved the Chinese Communist Party from a fate similar to that of European communist parties. As a result China remained a Marxist-Leninist state.

Bibliography

Barnett, A. Doak, and Ralph N. Clough, eds. *Modernizing China: Post-Mao Reform and Development.* Boulder, Colo.: Westview Press, 1986. Many experts deal with problems and prospects in China after 1976.
Brzezinski, Zbigniew. *The Grand Failure: The Birth and Death of Communism in the*

Twentieth Century. New York: Charles Scribner's Sons, 1989. Panoramic view of the rise and fall of communism worldwide.

Feigon, Lee. *Chen Duxiu: Founder of the Chinese Communist Party.* Princeton, N.J.: Princeton University Press, 1985. Account of the founder and early leader of Chinese Communism and of the intellectual and political climate in China that explain why some intellectuals embraced Marxism.

Fitzgerald, Charles P. *Revolution in China.* New York: Praeger, 1952. Focuses on the indigenous forces and economic problems that led to the rise of Chinese Communism; also traces the progress of the CCP until its victory.

Kataoka, Tetsuya. *Resistance and Revolution in China: The Communists and the Second United Front.* Berkeley: University of California Press, 1974. Describes the importance of the Sino-Japanese war as the turning point in the development of Chinese Communism and how the CCP's ability to mobilize the people to resist Japan led to its final triumph.

Li, Zhisui. *The Private Life of Chairman Mao.* New York: Random House, 1994. Mao's personal physician details the corruption among the Communist leadership, their abuse of power, and the lack of institutional controls in the exercise of power by Mao and other Communist leaders.

Loh, Pichon P. Y., ed. *The Kuomintang Debacle of 1949: Collapse or Conquest?* Boston: D. C. Heath, 1965. Experts' and participants' views on the Communist takeover of 1949. Contains firsthand accounts and incorporates theories regarding the Chinese revolution of 1949.

Salisbury, Harrison E. *The New Emperors: China in the Era of Mao and Deng.* Boston: Little, Brown, 1992. Recounts the exercise of power in China after 1949 and details how power has corrupted Chinese Communist leaders.

Schwartz, Benjamin I. *Chinese Communism and the Rise of Mao.* Cambridge, Mass.: Harvard University Press, 1961. Account of the early years of the communist movement in China and Mao's early rise to power.

Wilson, Dick. *The Long March, 1935.* New York: Penguin, 1977. Account of the epic of the Chinese Communists' survival as they fled the pursuing KMT army and made their way to Yanan.

Jiu-Hwa Lo Upshur

Cross-References

Communist Parties, p. 377; Confucianism and Government, p. 405; Cult of Personality, p. 477; Empires and Empire Building, p. 597; Geopolitics, p. 759; Government Roles, p. 778; History of Government, p. 829; Marxism-Leninism, p. 1155; One-Party Systems, p. 1350; Political Parties, p. 1485; Political Party Roles, p. 1499; Power in Politics, p. 1584; Revolutionary Governments, p. 1725; Revolutionary Parties, p. 1731; Russian Political History, p. 1770; Succession, p. 1909; Superpowers and World Politics, p. 1916.

CHURCH AND GOVERNMENT IN HISTORY

Field of study: Religion and government

Relationships between church bodies and governments take three basic forms: government over church, as in Communist-controlled Europe; church over government, as in medieval Europe; or mutual accommodation.

Principal terms
  BULL: papal document appointing bishops, canonizing saints, or
    defining doctrine
  CHURCH: organized body of adherents to a set of religious beliefs
  CONCORDAT: agreement between a pope and a ruler or a government
    concerning the regulation of church affairs
  COUNCIL: assembly of bishops convened to make decisions regulating
    Christian belief and practice
  PATRIARCH: bishop of an Eastern Christian church
  POPE: head of the Roman Catholic church
  STATE: politically organized body of people with a territory
  SYNOD: in Eastern Christianity, a council; used interchangeably with
    "council" in the West after the Council of Nicea (325)

Overview

The relationship between church and state may take three forms. First, some governments and theorists have held that the state is absolute and that its function is to preserve and enhance itself. In such a context, there might be little tolerance for a church. It might be allowed to exist but not to make efforts to expand its power and certainly not to criticize the state. Such a relationship existed for much of the twentieth century in the Soviet Union. In totalitarian states there is still sometimes room for the church. A church might be allowed to exist for the purpose of helping preserve the state, most likely by supporting the status quo.

A second possibility is the opposite, in which the church attempts to replace or at least direct the state. Muhammad, the founder of Islam, became the ruler of Medina after the hegira, his flight there from Mecca in 622, and the Ayatollah Ruhollah Khomeini took control of Iran after he returned there in 1979. In fact, Khomeini's hope for a modern Islamic state envisioned a society in which political and religious actions alike were parts of the larger entity of Islam. Similarly, the Protestant reformer John Calvin exercised civil authority over Geneva after 1541 through his seat on the city council, and Oliver Cromwell attempted to enforce his view of piety on England during the 1640's.

The third type of relationship is accommodation or mutual cooperation between church and state, in which the two institutions tacitly agree to share power. This relationship may take the form either of an established church or of the recognition of the right of the church to operate independently of the government.

All three of these types of relationships have appeared in the history of Christianity. After centuries of outright persecution of the Christian church, the Roman Empire first officially recognized Christianity in 311 with the Edict of Toleration promulgated by Emperor Galerius and in 313 with the agreement between Constantine and Licinius known as the Edict of Milan, which permitted full religious freedom for Christians.

The first church father to articulate his view of the proper relationship between church and state was Augustine in his book *The City of God*, written between 413 and 426. He argued that human beings had formed an earthly city, represented by Babylon and Rome but embodied in all civil states. The earthly city, though founded upon self-love and opposition to God, nevertheless preserved peace and order. That city, however, must pass away and be replaced by the city of God, made up of all true believers, who more and more would come to rule the world through the visible church by means of the Christian state. That state exists to preserve peace and, more important, to promote the worship of God. Hence, the church and the ideal Christian state would be mutually dependent and share reciprocal obligations.

Augustine charted the course for the relationship between church and state during the Middle Ages. Efforts to establish a Christian state took a long stride toward fulfillment in 751, when Pope Zacharias appointed Pepin the Short as king of the Franks. Pepin in turn aided Pope Stephen II by invading Italy (754 to 756) and requiring the Lombards to return Ravenna and other territories to the pope's control. The implication of these events was that the pope had the power to grant or withhold kingdoms. Another step toward the Christian state was taken when Pope Leo III placed the imperial crown on the head of Charlemagne on Christmas Day, 800, in St. Peter's Cathedral, thus founding the Holy Roman Empire. In the centuries that followed, the papacy and various emperors vied for supremacy.

Between 1450 and 1500, the struggle swung in the favor of rising national states under monarchs in England, France, and Spain. The Protestant Reformation divided the church and further limited the pope's sphere of influence. If the crowning of Charlemagne marked a high point of papal control, Napoleon's self-coronation marked a final low one.

With the rise of national states, the church established two new patterns of accommodation with governments. The first was that of the established church. Usually, an established church has not only government endorsement but also official status and prerogatives. A national government may, in collaboration with an established church, collect taxes, pay pastors and church expenses, support Christian education, and even name church officials. Examples of this pattern are the Church of England, the Church of Sweden, the Greek Orthodox church, the Ethiopian Orthodox church, and the Roman Catholic church in some areas, particularly in Latin American countries. This relationship also exists in virtually every Muslim country except Turkey and in some Buddhist countries. Less frequently, national governments recognize more than one official church. Finland, Germany, and Switzerland recognize two, Indonesia four, and Belgium five.

The functions of government-sponsored churches number at least four. The most obvious is to bless the actions of the civil government, a function that stands in tension with the other three. An established church may serve as a nation's conscience, advising against, or even actively protesting, government policies that violate church doctrine. An established church may attempt to correct moral failures of a nation's society at large. Finally, it may attempt, largely through education and moral persuasion, to prepare its nation for the coming of the kingdom of God.

The other basic pattern of accommodation to modern states, increasingly more prevalent since its adoption in the United States Constitution, is the separation of church and state. This pattern is found also, among other places, in Canada and Mexico in North America; in Brazil, Chile, and Ecuador in South America; in France, The Netherlands, and Italy in Western Europe; in some former communist countries, including Bulgaria and Hungary; in some African countries, including Chad, Gambia, and Kenya; and in some Asian countries, including India, Japan, and South Korea.

Applications

The struggle to find the proper relationship between church and government has affected all three branches of Christianity: Roman Catholicism, Eastern Orthodoxy, and Protestantism. In the case of Roman Catholicism, one effort at a proper relationship was the Holy Roman Empire. Charlemagne, its founder, united territory from France in the west to Croatia in the east, from Denmark to the north to Rome in the south. His empire disintegrated in 887, to be revived—minus most of France—by Otto I (reigned 936-973). Otto I named his supporters as bishops and abbots of the large monasteries, who together controlled large areas of German territory. Thus, imperial power was based on control of appointment to church offices. Otto twice invaded Italy at the behest of Pope John XII (955-964), who crowned him emperor in Rome in 962. When John turned against Otto, the latter deposed John and forced the Roman people to choose no pope without his consent. His choice for the next pope was Leo VIII (963, 964-965), whom he had to restore to power once, and then John XIII (965-972).

The empire reached its peak under Henry III (1039-1056). In 1035, the scandalous situation arose that three different men claimed to be pope. Henry convened two synods, one in Sutri, the other in Rome, to depose two and force the third to resign. He named Clement II (1046-1047) in their place. In the next few years, he also named Damasus II, who lived but a few more months; his own cousin Bruno, who took the name Leo IX (1049-1054) and Victor II (1055-1057). When Henry III and Victor II died about a year apart, the stage was set for wresting control of the papacy from the emperor's hands, since the new emperor, Henry IV (1056-1106), was only seven years old.

The pope's chance came in 1075, when Pope Gregory VII (1073-1085) opposed investiture by laypeople, thus denying to Henry IV a voice in naming bishops. Henry responded by holding a council in Worms, which rejected Gregory's authority as pope. Gregory, in turn, excommunicated Henry in 1076, and released Henry's subjects from allegiance to him as emperor. Their confrontation ended in the Alps, with Henry standing barefoot in the snow for three successive days asking for pardon, which Gregory granted in January, 1077. This event became the symbol of state submission to the church, but Gregory's victory was not to last. In March, civil war broke out, and Gregory sided with Henry's enemies. Henry named a new pope and marched on Rome. In 1084 Pope Clement III was enthroned and named Henry emperor. The issue of investiture was not resolved until 1122, with the Concordat of Worms, in which it was agreed that church officials would elect bishops, but in the presence of the emperor or his representative.

Not all the church followed Rome, however. Indeed, the early church knew a number of leading churches, including Jerusalem, Antioch, and Alexandria. After Constantine moved the capital of the Roman Empire to Byzantium in 330, renaming the city Constantinople, the city's patriarch grew in prestige. Disputes between the eastern and western church led to a break in 1054. In Russia, the eastern church prevailed beginning with Vladimir I, the grand prince of Kiev, who was baptized in 988, and who sided with Constantinople in 1054. At first, Russian orthodoxy's center was Kiev, but after the Tatars destroyed it in 1240, the center moved to Moscow. When Constantinople fell to the Turks in 1453, Moscow began calling itself the third Rome—the final, true center of Christianity.

Founded and aided by governments in Kiev and Moscow, the Russian Orthodox church became the servant of the government under Peter the Great (1672-1725) and subsequent czars. The patriarchate became vacant in 1700, and Peter declined to name a successor. In 1721 he instead appointed a holy governing synod consisting of a few bishops and priests. Its leader was a layperson called the Over-Procurator, who was nevertheless a political appointee responsible to Peter. Subsequently, authorities forbade the convening of church councils, seized church property, and propagated Roman Catholic or Protestant doctrines. Not until 1918 was the patriarchate restored. Under the Soviet regime, the patriarchate cooperated with the government in political affairs in exchange for permission to open churches and publish literature, including Bibles. With the fall of communism in the Soviet Union, the Russian Orthodox church became a denomination approved for religious freedom.

In the West also some Christians broke with Rome. The Reformation left the Holy Roman Empire and the modern state of Germany with not one, but two established churches. At the turn of the sixteenth century, Germans resented papal "interference" in the appointment of church officials, some monks and priests led worldly lives, and peasants resented the land and wealth controlled by the church. The Renaissance was reaching Germany, and humanism began to influence the universities in Vienna, Basel, Tübingen, Heidelberg, Ingolstadt, and Erfurt.

The man who articulated the need to reform the church was Martin Luther (1483-1546), an Augustinian monk and priest, and also a professor at the newly founded university in Wittenberg. In 1517 he posted on the door of the castle church there his Ninety-five Theses, a document setting forth topics for scholarly debate. The discussions that ensued eventually led to Luther's being condemned for heresy in a papal bull issued on January 2, 1521, and being tried by the Emperor Charles V and the

Reichstag on April 17, 1521. He was convicted by the Reichstag but was protected by Elector Frederick III.

When the peasants began revolting in 1524, Luther determined that their social and economic demands threatened his movement and wrote a pamphlet against them, imploring the princes to crush the revolt by force. While his writing cost him peasant support, and his enemies within the Roman Catholic church blamed Luther for the revolt, its repression set the stage for religious and political realignment in Germany. The Peace of Augsburg (1555) reached the compromise *cujus regio, ejus religio*, a Latin phrase translated "whose region, his religion." This compromise meant that areas ruled by Lutheran princes would have a Lutheran state church, with all baptized citizens as members, while areas ruled by Roman Catholic princes retained the bishop-ruled order.

Such arrangements between church and government resulted in the enfranchisement of various groups, for example, Lutherans in Germany and Scandinavia, Anglicans in England, Presbyterians in Scotland, as well as Catholics and Orthodox members in many states. Those arrangements also left outside the power structure many persons or communities, some of whom suffered persecution at the hands of various governments on behalf of established churches. Since colonization was also beginning, both established churches and disenfranchised groups looked to new shores. Hence, the United States was settled by people with varied religious agendas. Puritans came to Massachusetts to practice their own form of orthodoxy. Roger Williams fled to Rhode Island in 1635; Anne Hutchinson and her supporters followed in 1638 and 1639. Catholics settled in Maryland, Quakers in Pennsylvania, Anglicans in Virginia. More and more American Christians came to think that church and government should be separated, a view shared by secular thinkers who feared corruption of the state by the church. Hence, separation was written into the First Amendment to the U.S. Constitution.

This separation was and remained controversial. In July, 1812, Timothy Dwight, speaking at a public fast at the Yale University Chapel, complained that the Constitution was non-Christian. The celebrated visitor Alexis de Tocqueville remarked in his *Democracy in America* that religion exerted little influence on laws and public opinion in the United States, but directed the domestic life of Americans and thereby directed the state. Over the years the problem of how to construct "the wall of separation" between church and state has vexed the legislatures and courts of the United States.

Context

All humans have basic physical needs, such as those for food, shelter, safety, growth, and reproduction, which must be met if life is to continue. They also experience the need for companionship, intellectual and aesthetic expression, recreation, and a sense of meaning to make life fulfilling. Societies establish economic, political, educational, legal, artistic, and familial institutions to meet those needs. Two such institutions are church and state. In theory, the church exists to stir human belief in the divine and to organize and perpetuate the behaviors to assure the continuation of the relationship.

The state, by contrast, exists to direct and govern mundane matters such as a society's collective efforts to meet physical needs and to ensure personal or group rights. In actuality, however, these domains overlap. Both church and state, for example, may take an active interest in how persons meet their sexual needs or in defining the equitable or appropriate division of food, housing, or other goods. They may not agree, however, on how best to meet human needs or even on which needs are most important. While they share a common concern for order in society, their agendas may conflict.

Given this mutual interest in the conditions of life within a state, both church and government will continue their sometimes harmonious, sometimes antagonistic relationship. The issues of the establishment of religious bodies, the protection of human rights, and the guarantee of social justice, among others, will stand in the forefront of that relationship.

Bibliography

Barrett, David B., ed. *World Christian Encyclopedia: A Comparative Study of Churches and Religions in the Modern World, A.D. 1900-2000.* New York: Oxford University Press, 1982. Thousand-page compendium of historical and demographic information on churches and religions worldwide.

Herzstein, Robert E., ed. *The Holy Roman Empire in the Middle Ages.* Lexington, Mass.: D. C. Heath, 1966. Thirteen articles on Charlemagne and the relationship between the papacy and the Holy Roman Empire.

Hunt, George L., ed. *Calvinism and the Political Order.* Philadelphia: Westminster Press, 1965. Ten Woodrow Wilson Lectures of the National Presbyterian Church and Center covering not only Calvin but also other Calvinist figures of significance.

Jansen, Godfry H. *Militant Islam.* New York: Harper & Row, 1979. Examination of Islam from 1800 to 1979, concluding with a survey of the diverse views on the Islamic order and the Islamic state.

Noll, Mark A., ed. *Religion and American Politics: From the Colonial Period to the 1980's.* New York: Oxford University Press, 1990. Seventeen essays discussing the history of religion and American politics.

Stroup, Herbert. *Church and State in Confrontation.* New York: Seabury Press, 1967. Review of church and state relations from biblical times to the twentieth century.

Warren, Max. *The Functions of a National Church.* London: Epworth Press, 1964. Brief discussion of the functions of the national church.

Paul L. Redditt

Cross-References

Augustine's Political Philosophy, p. 121; Church and State Relations in the United States, p. 236; Church Government, p. 241; Dante's Political Philosophy, p. 483; Deism, p. 495; Hooker's Political Philosophy, p. 842; Islam and Government, p. 994; John of Salisbury's Political Philosophy, p. 1006; Liberation Theology, p. 1124; Religion and Politics, p. 1685; Theocracy, p. 1968; The Vatican, p. 2091; Zionism, p. 2192.

CHURCH AND STATE RELATIONS IN
THE UNITED STATES

Field of study: Religion and government

The issue of separation of church and state, which is based on the First Amendment to the Constitution, has had a profound effect on politics in the United States. Of particular interest has been religion in the public schools and political pressures on government from religious organizations.

Principal terms
  ANABAPTISTS: religious sects (including the Amish and the Mennonites), which believe in adult, as opposed to infant, baptism
  CHAPLAIN: religious practitioner serving in a nonsectarian organization such as a legislature or the military
  DEIST: believer in a single supreme being as creator of the world rather than the Christian Trinity
  HOME SCHOOLING: education of children by parents or other adult members of their families
  PAROCHIAL SCHOOL: school owned, staffed, and operated by a sectarian organization that offers nonreligious school curricula and religious instruction
  RELEASE TIME: time during the school day during which students are allowed to go elsewhere for sectarian religious instruction
  SCHOOL PRAYER: religious prayers as part of the school day, usually discussed in the context of formalized or mandatory use of a part of the school day for prayer
  SECTARIAN: of or pertaining to religious denominations or sects

Overview
  Many issues pertaining to the relationship of government to religion arose early in the history of the United States because many colonies had more or less official religions. In many of the colonies, taxation for a specific religious denomination was not only accepted but also encouraged. Deists such as Thomas Jefferson and George Washington, for example, outside the generally accepted Trinitarian Christian fold, would have been obliged to pay for the church of the majority. Accordingly, the First Amendment was of vital importance to the Founders. While the U.S. Constitution was in creation, some of the colonists were already considering entering free religion clauses into their constitutions. Jefferson had, in fact, written such a clause for the Virginia constitution:

> All persons shall have full and free liberty of religious opinion; nor shall any be compelled to frequent or maintain any religious institution.

It was natural, then, that when the Bill of Rights was created for the Constitution of the United States, the First Amendment would begin:

> Congress shall make no law respecting an establishment of religion or prohibiting the free exercise thereof.

Subsequently there were defenses in lawsuits about the separation of church and state that were based on the fact that the issues involved had nothing to do with Congress. To address some of the legal and social problems following the Civil War, the Fourteenth Amendment was created in 1868:

> No state shall make or enforce any law which shall abridge the privileges or immunities of citizens of the United States; nor shall any state deprive any person of life, liberty or property, without due process of law; nor deny to any person within its jurisdiction the equal protection of the laws.

By this rule, any action of the states on religious bodies within them was required to meet the same tests as if Congress had in fact been the governing body. Implicit in this new thinking is the corollary, that the action of religious bodies on the various governments was also forbidden if the action afforded the religious body any advantages over others. From the time of its ratification until early in the twentieth century the Fourteenth Amendment had little effect on religion in American society. Then, in a series of suits, the battle between religious bodies and advocates seeking to protect the Constitution began.

There are several areas of dispute in the debate on religious freedom. First, most religious institutions receive tax breaks or immunity from taxation. For many years this was ignored by governments. The loss to the taxing bodies from the small and poor church properties was not thought to be important. Also, churches of all kinds were exempt equally, in the spirit of the First Amendment. As religious bodies built greater edifices on more valuable property that could produce huge revenues if secular, this loss to the taxing bodies grew. Church-owned properties kept for nonreligious use are, in fact, usually taxed. Defense of the exemption of most church property rests upon the fact that the benefit is not applied unfairly among the various denominations.

Another issue is that of religious instruction in public schools. In many suits the decision has been to ban any sort of religious instruction in buildings owned by the public and staffed at the public expense. Some schools sought to accommodate this by releasing those students who wished to receive their sectarian education outside. When this became a problem for the students who remained behind and were made to feel different, such arrangements were challenged and discontinued.

In most public schools at one time, the day was begun with a ceremony which included the pledge of allegiance, a short Bible reading, perhaps a patriotic song, and, in some cases, the Lord's Prayer. Those students who were not Christians were offended and their parents sought to have the practice banned. One youngster was repeatedly beaten with a cane to make him agree to repeat the Protestant version of the Ten Commandments. Such abuses were rare, but students not of the denomination of the majority were either forced by public opinion to conform or were taken by their parents from the offending schools.

Use of the Bible as a textbook had its proponents and detractors, and this has been decided on individual situations. The presence of the Bible and other religious texts in school libraries has, for the most part, been allowed.

In most of the country there are parochial schools, private schools operated and staffed by religious institutions. Tax benefits, publicly funded transportation, and direct government grants have traditionally been provided to these institutions. After many local suits, these issues have been decided in favor of continued support of the sectarian schools with the requirement that the instructional content of their curricula be parallel and comparable to that provided in the public schools. In some places nuns from nearby parochial schools have been employed in the public schools, although litigation against this practice has occurred, particularly if the nuns wore their habits.

Home schooling is yet another issue. Many fundamentalist sects, particularly the Anabaptists, prefer to teach their children at home to protect them from the worldly influence of the public schools. This is permitted in every state, with the requirement that records be kept to show that attendance and accomplishment are acceptable. Several states, in response to liberal pressures, have attempted to introduce a system of licensing or qualifying home teachers (usually female adults in the families).

Some religious sects believe that a child's education is complete enough at age fourteen for him or her to take his or her place as an adult in their primarily agricultural society. The states have disagreed, arguing that home schooling should be compulsory until age sixteen or eighteen, as it is in the public schools. This issue was solved in two ways. In one case, the parents were able to convince the courts that the child's truncated education was sufficient for their society. In others, the parents were required to continue the children's education at home until the children were of age.

Religious symbols such as Nativity scenes and Christmas trees set upon public property have been challenged repeatedly by those who see in this a support by the public trust of the religious traditions involved. In most cases these issues have died under public pressure on the basis that such displays are traditional. Issues such as whether there should be chaplains in the Congress and the military have been set aside in the past, but increasingly militant advocacy for separatism may yet cause these institutions to be dissolved.

Applications

The issue of the use of prayer and Bible reading in the schools was treated in a landmark case, *Engel v. Vitale*, in 1962. The Supreme Court declared that state laws allowing or requiring prayer in the public schools were forbidden by the Constitution. Two more cases, decided in 1963, forbade the required reading of Bible verses in public schools. One case was brought by a Jewish parent who objected to the use in a public school of the Bible that contained language that Jews may find blasphemous. The other case was brought by an atheist mother who objected to Bible reading in the

Baltimore schools. With these decisions, the required use of religious material in schools was denied.

Since those decisions the Bible and other religious texts have been barred from mandatory use as curriculum in public schools. Prayer, given voluntarily, has been permitted by Supreme Court decisions, although local challenges to this practice are sometimes mounted.

Direct aid to parochial school is given in the form of free textbooks and school lunch assistance, both of which are deemed to be of no assistance to the denominations. In return for these and other publicly funded grants, the parochial schools have had to give up their autonomy, yielding to state and federal requirements relating to quality of education and to student health and welfare issues.

Tax funding of parochial school transportation was opposed in a suit by a taxpayer, Arch Everson, in 1946. The town of Ewing, New Jersey, had passed a statute to allow the parents who paid for public transportation of their children to parochial schools to be reimbursed by the board of education. The statute was held to be valid by the Supreme Court and the action became precedent. Other tax-exemption issues have been raised and defeated despite the growing value of exempt property.

Legislation introduced to force qualification and licensing of parents practicing home schooling has been defeated repeatedly. Religious groups seeking to continue home education are now joined by many who educate their children at home in order to give them a better education than is available in the public schools, not merely to respond to religious convictions.

Context

Most issues of church-state interactions in the United States have been conclusively settled by court actions and are a part of the law of the United States. Pressure continues to be brought by groups to permit religious practices that are in violation of laws not related to the church-state issues. For example, should the use of illegal drugs in religious rituals continue to be prohibited for public health reasons? A few cults have been forced to give up practices that threaten the health of children. Beyond these issues, the church-state question has reached a legal standing of relative stability.

Public aid to religious schools is limited to those situations in which the public funds are provided for similar services in secular education. With such aid there is implicit the right of the public to oversee the use of such aid to prevent abuse. Tax exemptions have been sustained by court action except where the acquisition of large and valuable properties for nonsectarian commerce has been made, in which cases the taxing bodies involved have been permitted to make division of the property into exempt and nonexempt portions on a case-by-case basis.

Religious decorations on public land are for the most part banned if any objection is raised. Mandated religious expression in public schools is banned, although private, voluntary prayer is allowed. Religious mottoes on United States currency and documents have been retained as historical rather than religious expressions. The historical artifact of the post of chaplain in the federal government has also been allowed to continue. Chaplains in the military are allowed by the argument that people in military service are unable to attend church and the government is thereby prohibiting their free expression unless an alternative access to religious support is allowed.

Sects have introduced practices unfamiliar to many Americans, and the threshold across which a religious ritual becomes a cultist crime is sometimes decided in the courts. It is seldom, however, that such a ritual is controlled by law unless it threatens the safety or health of the general public. Beyond these issues and some localized problems involving use of public resources for sectarian applications, the church-state problem is fairly well settled in the United States.

Bibliography

Antieau, C. J., P. M. Carroll, and T. C. Burke. *Religion Under the State Constitutions.* Brooklyn, N.Y.: Central Book, 1965. Compendium of references to constitutional provisions and amendments regarding church-state conflicts.

Cousins, Norman, ed. *"In God We Trust": The Religious Beliefs and Ideas of the American Founding Fathers.* New York: Harper & Row, 1958. Letters, speeches, and private writings of a number of the Founders of the United States.

Finney, R. L. *A Brief History of the American Public School.* New York: Macmillan, 1946. Definitive history of the American public school system from its roots in the colonial religious schools.

Mechling, Jay, ed. *Church, State, and Public Policy.* Washington, D.C.: American Enterprise Institute for Public Policy Research, 1978. Lectures by leading educational and religious leaders on the subject of church-state relations.

Pfeffer, Leo. *Church, State, and Freedom.* Boston: Beacon Press, 1953. Legal history of church-state affairs in the United States, including an index of hundreds of court decisions.

Loring D. Emery

Cross-References

The Bill of Rights, p. 134; Church and Government in History, p. 230; Civil Rights and Liberties, p. 298; The Constitution of the United States, p. 425; Constitutional Law in the United States, p. 439; Education Management, p. 565; Grants-in-Aid, p. 791; The New Right, p. 1293; Religion and Politics, p. 1685; The Supreme Court: Role in Government and Law, p. 1935; Taxation and Appropriation, p. 1941.

CHURCH GOVERNMENT

Field of study: Religion and government

The formal organization of Christian religious bodies at local, regional, and world levels, church government is one of the two major areas of disagreement blocking modern Church reunion.

Principal terms

BISHOP: clerical official responsible for a district in episcopal forms of church government

CONGREGATIONALISM: form of church government in which the seat of authority is held to reside within individual believers and is exercised as a part of the congregation as a whole

DEACON: lay church official in congregational polities

EPISCOPACY: church government in which authority for ordaining new officers and doing ministerial work rests in bishops

POLITY: any politically organized unit

PRELACY: episcopal church government

PRESBYTER (ELDER): office held by a minister or layperson, depending upon the polity

PRESBYTERIANISM: church government in which the seat of authority resides in a collegial body of elders, or presbyters

SESSION: first level of government in local Presbyterian churches

SYNOD: general governing assembly of a church

Overview

Despite their common roots, Christian churches exhibit a wide diversity of government forms that have become impediments to modern unity. These differences can be traced back to the origins of the church. Jesus Christ, the ostensible founder of the church, articulated no code of rules to define his church's institutions. Forms of government nevertheless developed in the early church; however, the New Testament does not explain how they arose. Nor does the New Testament thematically develop a doctrine of polity. What is known about early church government is that Jesus appointed twelve Apostles to the church. In ways that remain unclear, the Apostles either appointed or confirmed the election of presbyters and deacons, and perhaps bishops. After the Apostles died, their successors built the church upon the Apostolic foundation of officers and practices.

In the New Testament the main terms for officers are bishop, presbyter, and deacon. Each term represents a cluster of words taken from both the Old Testament period and the wider Hellenic worlds. While each of these terms was common in the ancient world, they usually had general rather than technical meanings. When taken up by the new church these terms acquired new and rich meanings. The term bishop, which comes from *episcopos*, for example, means someone who "visits or watches." In the old and new testaments it is applied to both God and those responsible for the exercise of the care of souls. A bishop therefore is charged with responsibility for watching over the welfare of the souls of his spiritual flock. Because only a bishop can ordain another bishop, this points to a hierarchical principle.

The term *presbuteros* (presbyter or elder) implies an older member of the community. Presbyters were responsible for the life of the community and for the ordering of worship. The word presbyter was used by the pre-Christian rabbinical translators of the Old Testament version known as the Septuagint. It also had various uses in the ancient pre-Christian world. Because elders function in groups, a collegial, or representative, principle of polity is present.

The term deacon derives from a cluster of words associated with the word *diakonia*. It literally means someone who "waits on tables." In the Book of Acts the Apostles ordained seven godly men to serve the community by distributing food to the poor widows. Since the food was probably received at the common meal of the Jerusalem community, the first deacons were literally waiters.

Several conclusions can be drawn about early church government. First, the officers were either appointed by other officers, or elected by the people of the church. Appointment is a hierarchical principle, while election is a democratic principle. Second, all were ceremonially "set apart," or ordained, by the Apostles. Third, sometimes governing is a monarchical pastoral act, and sometimes it is collegial. Finally, there is an overlapping division of labor. The deacons have the responsibility to serve the bodily welfare of the needy. The presbyters teach and order the life of the congregation. The bishops in contrast are to oversee the spiritual welfare of the community of faith. From this rough division of labor can be seen practices that receive a rich development.

Historically the church has often been structured to meet changing circumstances. The early church, located in the office of the bishop, arose in the period of persecution during the Roman Empire. The need to resist false teaching aided the tendency to rally around the bishop in the face of persecution. By the end of the Roman Empire a monarchical bishop with consolidated power became the chief spiritual leader in the church until the Reformation began in the sixteenth century. The Reformers (Martin Luther, John Calvin, and many others) rejected the monarchical bishop form of polity. Most Protestant groups adopted presbyterial or congregational systems of church government. These alternative polities were viewed as a restoration of the New Testament church. The Reformers thus believed they were restoring the church to her original purity from the corruption created by prelacy, or episcopal church government.

Like the Reformers, other theologians over the centuries have claimed that one form or other of church government is the divinely intended form. These claims have produced serious conflicts. Those who would argue that the New Testament prescribes a particular form are in the minority. Others see the lack of a prescribed form as a useful providential blessing that allows freedom to respond to new situations. Three principal forms of church government exist. Within each form are wide variations. These three forms are the episcopal, the presbyterial, and the congregational, each of which finds its roots in the New Testament. Each derives its officers from the three ministries of the *episkopos* (bishop), the *presbuteros* (elder), and the *diakonia* (deacon). Each reflects ideas about polity including hierarchy, democracy, and representation. Ultimately all churches are seeking to do almost all the same things in ministry. This forces each to move toward a similar structure informally despite external differences.

A few churches have mixed types of polity. The Assemblies of God, for example, has a polity that is both presbyterial and congregational. Among Lutherans, the polity may be episcopal in one country (Sweden) and congregationalist in another. Some churches have nongovernmental forms. Quakers, the Plymouth Brethren, and some others believe that the church should have no visible form because it is the invisible body of Christ. Consequently, they see no need for a visible ordained clergy. Some few groups have alternative forms. The Salvation Army, for example, has dropped traditional ecclesiastical polity for a military organizational pattern.

Since the Council of Nicea in the fourth century the church has been described with four marks: "one, holy, catholic and apostolic." These marks have been influential in the development of polity. The Church is described as "one" because it is united. Nineteenth century Christian missionaries to non-Western regions found the historical divisions of the churches since the Reformation irrelevant to their mission fields. The Ecumenical Movement arising from this experience has stimulated reunion efforts to restore visible unity. The Church is described as "holy" because it aims to produce holy lives. Church discipline is a process for correcting evil ministers or erring laity. This power derives from a doctrine called the Power of the Keys. The mark "catholic" points to the universal (ecumenical) nature of the Church. The National Council of Churches, the World Council of Churches, and other bodies, such as the World Alliance of Reformed Churches, have grown out of efforts to extend fellowship or to minister on a large scale. Each of these new forms of organizations expresses the nature of a single universal Church. "Apostolic" means that the Church has continuity with the Apostles. The doctrine of Apostolic succession has two main interpretations which contribute to polity. For many churches, mostly of the episcopal form, the ordination of officers by the ritual of "laying on of hands" in an unbroken chain of generations from the Apostles to today constitutes the meaning of the term. For others the Church is Apostolic because it has received and transmits the teachings of the Apostles faithfully. The issue of ordination is now a major stumbling block to church reunion. The different meanings of Apostolic succession make mutual recognition of ministries difficult. Furthermore, disagreements about ordaining women and homosexuals add to the difficulty.

Applications

Within each of the three major forms of church government there are such a wide variety of forms that precise description in a brief space is difficult. All forms have benefits and problems. The many episcopal forms house the largest number of Christians. The chief officer is the bishop who is the seat of authority. A major difference among episcopal forms is the number of levels of bishops. Some churches, such as the Methodists, have only one level. Roman Catholics, Orthodox churches, Episcopalians, and others have multiple levels. Authority flows downward from the highest ranking bishop—the pope, patriarch, or archbishop—who heads the whole church. Usually an archbishop oversees a province, composed of several dioceses. A bishop is the head of a diocese, which is composed of several parishes. The bishop appoints priests to the local parish and then supervises their work. Priests (presbyters) serve as the pastors of particular churches. The first step in ordination is that of deacon.

Parish priests may be assisted by a parish council (Roman Catholic) or vestry (Episcopal). The members are all laypeople who belong to the local church. Both parish council and vestry are typically organized in a committee system. A church treasurer may be a member too. The chief lay officer of the vestry is the senior warden.

Methodists have only one level of bishop, but collectively these meet at times in assemblies. Methodist ministers are officially presbyters. The first step in ordination is that of deacon. The minister of the local church is usually assisted by a group of lay members. Both deacons and ministers belong to the Conference with the bishop. The Conference is composed of districts governed by district superintendents.

Presbyterian polity is a representative form composed of governing bodies in "regular gradation." The chief officers, or elders, act collegially rather than individually. Presbyterian, Reformed, and a few other denominations use this form of polity. The congregation of a particular church has limited rights but is not a governing body. It may call its own pastor, elect elders and deacons, and decide about major property transactions. The first level of governance is the session (Presbyterian) or consistory (Reformed) of the local church. It is composed of the minister, who moderates the meetings, and the elders.

Many larger congregations have boards of deacons, which may handle charity, property, and other matters. The deacons are elected by the congregation but operate under the supervision of the session. Many deacons eventually become elders. The session elects elders from among its number to be commissioners to attend presbytery meetings. Ministers, as members of presbytery, attend automatically. At all levels the ministers and elders follow a trustee theory of representation. This means that they make decisions based on their best understanding of the issues in the light of a good conscience.

The presbytery (Presbyterian), or classis (Reformed), is the main seat of authority, but its actions can be overturned by the synod or the general assembly in a limited number of ways. It ordains and installs ministers, promotes the common work in camps and retirement centers, tries cases, and does many other things. The principle of the parity of the laity and clergy requires that the presbytery comprise equal numbers of ministers and elders from the churches of its region. This principle applies to meetings of synods and the general assembly as well. The presbytery elects equal numbers of clergy and laity to be commissioners to attend synod meetings. A synod is composed of at least three presbyteries. If the denomination is small in numbers this may be the highest governing body. Typically in the United States this body is mainly concerned with the administration of schools, orphanages, retirement centers, hospitals, and other institutions. It also hears administrative disputes and judicial cases involving miscon-duct. The presbytery will also elect commissioners to the General Assembly. This highest governing body proposes amendments to the constitution, acts as a court of last resort, develops social pronouncements, and administers church-wide programs among other tasks. It has a permanent bureaucratic staff.

The congregationalist form locates the seat of authority in the people of the congregation acting as a whole. Baptists, Congregationalists, and others practice this form of polity. Because each local church is autonomous, a rich variety of local practices has developed. Each congregation is a direct democracy which votes on all matters. This includes calling pastors, electing deacons, or making decisions, such as whether to give money to a cause. In larger congregations a committee system may assist the church in its program. All officers are simply functionaries of the church and have no governing authority. Some congregationalist churches are independent and have no formal ties with other churches. Others form organizations called associations, conferences, or fellowships to promote mutual concerns of their ministries. Delegates to such meetings, whether local, regional, or general, are considered to be "messen-gers" who do not act independently but only express the views of those who sent them.

Context

With regard to polity, there have been at least three formative eras in the history of the Christian church. The founding period encompassed the work of the Apostles and several generations of their successors. During the era of the primitive church, the basic images and forms of the church were deposited in the life of the faithful and expressed in the words of the New Testament. Among the first fruits of this early development of the church was the rise of the monarchical bishop in response to the dangers and doctrinal controversies of the early church. This period's modern mani-festation is the Roman Catholic church.

The second major period of development came with the Reformation. The rejection of the corrupted prelacy of the medieval church led to the development of constitu-tional and democratic forms of church government in the presbyterial and congrega-tional forms among Protestants. The spread of Protestantism in places they mission-ized, especially in the United States, saw the further development of these forms.

The third great formative era began with Vatican II, a great ecumenical council that was preceded by the rise of the ecumenical movement among Protestants and the development of the World Council of Churches and its member bodies. These developments in the ancient Western heart of the church were directly stimulated by the concerns of missionaries in the nineteenth century laboring in mission fields in the non-Western world.

Both ecumenical concerns and the vast changes in the modern world have presented Christian churches with new challenges, and a growing body of literature reflects the spiritual struggle of Christians over the nature and form of the church. By the 1990's, the younger churches of the Third World, often guided by Liberation Theology, composed the majority of Christians. The new understandings and forms that these maturing churches will bring to the church will inevitably have a major impact. Meanwhile, the issue of church government that most affects the church is the question of ordination. The nature of the ministry and who is properly ordained remains a major stumbling block to the efforts at reunion of all Christian bodies.

Bibliography

Jay, Eric G. *The Church: Its Changing Image Through Twenty Centuries.* Atlanta, Ga.: John Knox Press, 1978. Readable study of the nature and forms of the Church in its historical perspective, with significant attention to current issues.

Kung, Hans. *The Church.* Garden City, N.Y.: Image Books, 1976. Influential historical study by a Roman Catholic scholar emphasizing the nature and forms of the Church.

McNutt, William Roy. *Polity and Practice in Baptist Churches.* Rev. ed. Chicago: Judson Press, 1959. Description of Baptist practices and polity, which resemble those of other congregationalist bodies.

Mead, Frank S., ed. *Handbook of Denominations in the United States.* 7th ed. Nashville, Tenn.: Abindgon, 1980. Description of the historical development, doctrines, and polities of more than 250 religious bodies.

Piepkorn, Arthur C. *Profiles in Belief: The Religious Bodies of the United States and Canada.* 4 vols. New York: Harper & Row, 1977. Broad survey of most of the Christian denominations found in the United States and Canada, with descriptions of their beliefs and sketches of the governments of most bodies.

Presbyterian Church. *The Book of Common Worship.* Louisville, Ky.: Westminster/ John Knox Press, 1993. Second part of the constitution of the largest Presbyterian body in the United States.

Schaver, John Louis. *The Polity of the Churches.* 2 vols. Chicago: Church Polity Press, 1947. First volume describes church government generally; second volume focuses on the Christian Reformed church.

United Methodist Church. *The Book of Discipline of the United Methodist Church, 1992.* Nashville, Tenn.: United Methodist Publishing House, 1992. Laws of the United Methodist church, setting forth the polity and process for governing the church.

Vatican Council. *The Sixteen Documents of Vatican II and the Instruction on the Liturgy.* Compiled by J. L. Gonzalez and the Daughters of St. Paul. Boston: St. Paul Editions, 1966. Several documents in this collection detail Roman Catholic views on episcopacy.

Winter, Gibson. *Religious Identity: A Study of Religious Organization.* New York: Macmillan, 1968. Sociological study of Jewish and Christian religious organizations in the United States. Contains references to further studies.

A. J. L. Waskey, Jr.

Cross-References

Charismatic Leadership, p. 209; Church and Government in History, p. 230; Church and State Relations in the United States, p. 236; Democracy, p. 513; Feminist Politics, p. 682; Gay and Lesbian Politics, p. 732; Monarchy in Constitutional Governments, p. 1215; Oligarchy, p. 1344; Polity, p. 1545; Theocracy, p. 1968; The Vatican, p. 2091.

CITIZEN MOVEMENTS

Field of study: Politics

Citizen movements are the organized efforts by people sharing common goals and values who engage in collective political action to change, or to resist change in, some aspect of society.

Principal terms

CHRISTIAN RIGHT MOVEMENT: movement formed in the late 1970's and early 1980's by Christians who opposed legal abortion and homosexuality and supported prayer in public schools and "family values"

CIVIL RIGHTS MOVEMENT: predominantly black-led movement based in churches and legal-action groups that worked to extend full social and political rights to all Americans

CONVENTIONAL POLITICS: political tactics that include voting, lobbying elected officials, and joining an interest group

POPULISM: political movement of farmers in the South and West in the 1880's and 1890's that sought to increase democratic control over banks and railroads

UNCONVENTIONAL POLITICS: disruptive and often controversial tactics employed by citizen movements that include marches, political protests, and acts of civil disobedience

UNITED WE STAND: organization founded in 1992 by billionaire businessman H. Ross Perot that sought to increase citizen control over elected officials

WOMEN'S SUFFRAGE MOVEMENT: late nineteenth and early twentieth century movement that worked to extend full voting rights to women

Overview

Citizen movements form among people dissatisfied with the status quo who want to make reforms in the political process. Such movements appeal to political outsiders, to citizens whom the political system has disadvantaged or disenfranchised, and to groups whose interests and needs have been neglected. Such movements combine conventional forms of political participation such as voting, interest group pressure, and lobbying of elected officials with unconventional political activities such as protests, sit-ins, demonstrations, and rallies. Citizen movements attract people deeply committed to causes and willing to spend considerable time and resources to try to bring about political and social change. They have been an important means of participation by political outsiders and have had a dramatic impact on politics, particularly in the United States, where they have attracted more followers than in any other democracy. Some of the most important citizen movements in American history include the abolitionist movement, the temperance and prohibition movements, the labor movement, the women's suffrage movement, the Civil Rights movement, and the Christian right movement.

Shared values provide the basis for the formation of a citizen movement; people join movements to defend or promote values threatened or ignored by public policy makers. Not every political grievance, however, leads to the formation of a citizen movement; there are always many more people upset with conventional politics than there are movements to represent them. Successful movements are ones that have the resources—money, leaders, organizations—to translate citizen disaffection with politics into a dynamic movement. This is not an easy task. People might be aware that there is something wrong in their lives, they might even know that there are many other people who share their feelings, but they do not automatically form organizations to press for political change.

To succeed, a citizen movement needs effective leaders to persuade people to act on the social and political problems that they perceive. Among the most important leadership qualities are charisma to inspire citizen participation, communication skills to publicize the cause, and organizational ability to raise money. Citizen movements are often associated with the work of dynamic leaders. Martin Luther King, Jr., and Ralph Abernathy were prominent leaders of the Civil Rights movement, Pat Robertson and Jerry Falwell helped organize the Christian right movement, and H. Ross Perot founded United We Stand. Individual leaders are important, but citizen movements rely on hundreds of leaders at local, state, and national levels to keep people involved and convince them that collective action can bring about political change. Leaders often take advantage of existing organizations within the community to mobilize citizen activism. The Civil Rights movement organized groups through black churches and colleges; the Christian right movement similarly used the existing network of conservative evangelical and fundamentalist churches, television programs, and schools to mobilize their movement.

A citizen movement is a grassroots phenomenon; its power comes from the number, commitment, and energy of the people who join the movement. Citizen movements often use unconventional strategies to attract attention to their cause because often the political change that a movement desires is hard to accomplish through the usual political channels of voting and interest group activity. For example, until the ratification of the Nineteenth Amendment in 1920, women could not vote, so it was impossible for them to effect change through voting. The women's suffrage movement used tactics such as rallies and political protests to highlight the plight of American women. The Civil Rights movement of the 1950's and 1960's used boycotts, sit-ins, and nonviolent civil disobedience to make itself heard and in order to win civil and political rights for black Americans. Gay rights organizations have staged rallies in front of Saint Patrick's Cathedral in New York City to protest the Roman Catholic church's position on homosexuality. Christian right activists blocked the entrance to health clinics to protest legal abortion. Citizen movements raise public awareness about issues to which policymakers are not responding.

Political leaders often complain that a citizen movement's goals are too uncompromising and its tactics too confrontational. According to people in a citizen movement, that is precisely the point: They want to draw attention to issues about which they feel strongly and which they believe political leaders have disregarded. While unconventional tactics are not always popular, they are newsworthy; they draw attention to the movement and can help to promote change. The Civil Rights movement used sit-ins and marches to protest the segregation of public accommodations and schools; leaders hoped that the publicity would increase public awareness of the fact that many communities denied blacks social and political rights. Police brutality against peaceful marches shocked people across the nation and generated sympathy for the movement. The strategy succeeded at helping to speed up the process of political reform as Congress passed the landmark Civil Rights and Voting Rights acts in 1964 and 1965.

Citizen movements, however, rarely rely on unconventional tactics alone. There often are different factions of a movement that advocate different kinds of political action. These factions can threaten a movement's vitality as adherents clash over the issue of strategy. The Civil Rights movement became fragmented between radical and moderate factions on whether the movement should remain committed to the strategy of nonviolence. The radicals renounced nonviolence while the moderates retained it. Successful movements strike a balance between conventional and unconventional strategies and keep public attention focused on the issue without alienating the public.

Citizen movements are difficult to sustain for long periods. It is hard to sustain the high level of commitment that is necessary for an effective movement; people tire of the time and financial dedication that a movement demands. Political failure or success can also undermine a movement. The Populist movement faded away because farmers were unable to win political concessions on the issues they cared most about: changing the monetary standard from gold to silver and getting greater public control over the railroads and banks. Farmers lost enthusiasm for a movement that seemed unable to have a direct impact on politics. The abolitionist movement, by contrast, disappeared with the ratification of the Thirteenth Amendment outlawing slavery. Victory ended the movement.

Other successful citizen movements are eventually transformed from political outsiders to political insiders. The labor movement changed from a politically militant organization in the 1930's to a moderate and bureaucratic group of labor unions by the 1950's. Politically liberal civil rights organizations of the 1970's and 1980's replaced the grassroots insurgency of the movement in the 1950's. This transition from social movement to interest group is on the one hand a sign that the movement has gained political status. Civil Rights organizations and labor unions are important factions within the Democratic Party. On the other hand, the price of political access for a citizen movement is a loss of urgency and a dampening of the enthusiasm that originally propelled the movement. In the American political system, insiders learn the need for and the value of political compromise, consensus, and moderation—the very values that the citizen movement originally derided. In order to get things accomplished, interest groups have to moderate their long-term goals in exchange for short-term victories. Citizen movements may endure and continue to have an impact, but in a different political form and using different strategies.

Applications

The Christian right movement exemplifies how a citizen movement forms, behaves, and changes over time. Conservative Christians objected to what they viewed as America's moral decay in the 1960's and early 1970's; they opposed the legalization of abortion, the U.S. Supreme Court's decisions against prayer and Bible reading in public schools, the proliferation of pornographic materials, and the more open expression and acceptance of homosexuality. Conservative Christians perceived a threat to their religious values as American society condoned practices that violated their religious beliefs; they were, however, political outsiders. Policymakers neglected their religious and political values because these Christians were not an organized movement nor were they recognized as a potentially powerful and cohesive voting bloc.

Evangelical and fundamentalist Christian leaders transformed this amorphous religious discontent with public policy into dynamic organizations in the late 1970's and early 1980's. Jerry Falwell formed the Moral Majority; Pat Robertson founded the Christian Coalition; and dozens of other Christian leaders formed groups to oppose abortion, pornography, and homosexuality and to support a more prominent place for their religious values in policy-making. Group leaders used existing organizations within Christian communities to raise resources and attract group members. Falwell and Robertson both had religiously themed television shows with large audiences to which they could appeal for support. Other leaders sent direct-mail solicitations to members of sympathetic churches throughout the nation. The Christian right movement expanded rapidly.

As membership grew, so too did the movement's political efforts. Groups organized marches on Washington, D.C., and acts of civil disobedience at health clinics that provided abortion services. They combined these unconventional tactics with more conventional forms of participation such as voter registration drives among unregistered conservative Christian voters. These tactics increased public awareness of the Christian right movement. The movement enjoyed the fruits of its adherents' enthusiasm, dedication, and fervor for the cause as political leaders began to respond to the political claims of the Christian right. In 1980, the movement found a sympathetic and politically powerful spokesman for its causes in Ronald Reagan, the Republican Party nominee for the presidency. Reagan, who won the presidential elections of 1980 and 1984, appealed to Christian voters on the issues of abortion, prayer, and pornography. He provided the movement with access to government officials, publicity, and legitimacy in the public eye. Conservative Christians were no longer political outsiders; they formed interest groups that lobbied for political change and worked within the Republican Party to affect public policy.

Abortion, family values, and prayer in public schools became national political issues in the 1980's. In terms of policy, however, very little changed during Reagan's eight years as president. Abortion remained legal, although more difficult to obtain, and the efforts to pass a constitutional amendment to allow prayer in public schools failed. Conservative Christians became a divisive force within the Republican Party in the 1990's as they worked to increase their influence and control of state party offices. The movement faced an internal struggle in the early 1990's between a radical faction that contended that Christian groups had become too accommodating and closely tied to the Republican Party and a more moderate wing, which argued that working within the party and the political system offered the best hope for change.

Several features of the Christian right movement characterize citizen movements more generally. First, the movement arose because a large number of people wanted a dramatic change in public policy. Conservative Christians believed that America had become morally bankrupt and that political leaders were doing little to change it. Second, charismatic leaders used existing organizations within the Christian community to mobilize discontented believers into a citizen movement. Religious schools, churches, and television programs enabled leaders to raise resources and attract followers for the Christian right movement. Third, the movement used conventional and unconventional strategies to draw attention to the cause and effect political change. Conservative Christians combined acts of civil disobedience with voter registration drives to bring political attention and power to the movement. They raised public awareness about a series of issues that had not been on the national political agenda before the movement arose. Finally, as with many other citizen movements before it, the Christian right movement changed from a political outsider to an insider and traded some of its independence and fervor for organization and stability.

Context

Citizen movements are important for a democracy because they get people involved in politics, raise issues formerly excluded from the policy process, and help make fundamental and dramatic political changes. They are one of the most effective means for political outsiders to enter American politics. America's democratic polity needs to have citizens actively involved in politics. These movements encourage meaningful citizen participation and allow people to see the reward for and the value of the U.S. democratic system.

Citizen movements also shake up political institutions. This is important because the checks and balances of America's political system can make it difficult to get anything done at all. Movements bring public attention to issues that policymakers have ignored but that are important to a large number of people. Some of the most significant social and political reforms in America's history—the ending of slavery, citizenship rights for blacks, the right of women to vote, and raising the moral issues of abortion and family values—would not have been possible without citizen movements.

Citizen movements are also controversial. Because they use unconventional tactics and are politically immoderate, citizen movements invite conflict and disrupt American politics and society. Citizen movements have helped to fuel the most divisive crises in American history—the Civil War, the struggle for civil rights, and the battle over abortion. People usually have very strong feelings for or against a citizen movement, and it is only natural to question if they do more harm than good for democracy and social order.

Despite this question, citizen movements will likely be an enduring presence in American politics. They have helped to accomplish much in the past, and political outsiders will turn again to citizen movements for legislative change in the future.

Bibliography

Bruce, Steve. *The Rise and Fall of the New Christian Right.* Oxford, England: Clarendon Press, 1988. Account of the genesis of the Christian right movement. Somewhat dated; does not include developments of the early 1990's.

Evans, Sara M. *Born for Liberty: A History of Women in America.* New York: Free Press, 1989. History of the women's suffrage movement and the equal rights movement.

Gamson, William. *The Strategy of Social Protest.* 2d ed. Belmont, Calif.: Wadsworth, 1990. Overview of how citizen movements raise resources and select political strategies that will benefit the movement.

McAdam, Doug. *Political Process and the Development of Black Insurgency.* Chicago: University of Chicago Press, 1982. Review of the Civil Rights movement that focuses on how organizations and leaders in the black community sustained the movement.

Wallis, Roy. *Salvation and Protest: Studies of Social and Religious Movements.* New York: St. Martin's Press, 1979. Somewhat dated, still one of the best accounts of why a group's beliefs and values are important for a citizen movement.

J. Christopher Soper

Cross-References

CITIZENSHIP IN WORLD GOVERNMENTS

Field of study: Comparative government

Citizenship is the conception by which individuals are given membership, rights, and responsibilities in a political community, particularly a city or a nation-state. It is conferred upon individuals by governments, which have the sole authority to determine the criteria for citizenship and the benefits that flow from that status.

Principal terms
ALIEN: person who resides or travels outside of the country of his or her citizenship or nationality
ASYLUM: legal process by which a government extends temporary or permanent haven to people who have fled their countries of origin because they fear persecution, thus losing the protective benefits of citizenship
JUS SANGUINIS: "the law of blood ties," whereby individuals receive at birth the citizenship of their parents
JUS SOLI: "the law of soil," whereby individuals acquire the citizenship of the country in whose territory they are born
NATIONALITY OF CLAIMS: mechanism by which citizens may seek redress of injuries against the government of another country by appealing to their own government to press suit
NATURALIZATION: legal process by which a person can acquire a new nationality or citizenship

Overview

Citizenship is an important ingredient in the formation and operation of political communities. When communities form to provide security and extend the benefits of social and economic interaction, such questions arise as: Who shall be a member of the community? Who shall have the right to participate actively in the decision-making processes that affect the people at large? Who shall rule and how shall they be chosen? Who has the right to vote or hold office? Who has the duty to pay taxes and to protect and defend the community? These questions point to the crucial role of citizenship in the state. Through citizenship a state seeks to pass on its culture, lore, and traditions to its citizens, raising their patriotic sensibilities, and providing a context in which its individuals and families will become a solid foundation for the community's survival and growth.

In the twentieth century, citizenship is bestowed by nation-states, as in ancient times it was bestowed by city-states or empires. Under modern international law, each state is the sovereign legal authority within its territorial jurisdiction, and may decide who can become a citizen and how. Therefore, the laws of citizenship vary from one country to another. By defining who its citizens are, a government establishes a distinction between its citizens and aliens. The former have special civil rights that do not extend to the latter, especially the rights of voting and political participation. Even aliens, however, are expected to have basic rights and freedoms, including equal access to the justice system when they have been injured or entangled in violations of local law. In some countries, aliens receive the full rights of educational and welfare benefits; in others, they do not. In all cases, aliens are obliged to observe the laws of the nations in which they reside or through which they travel (unless they are certified diplomatic officers).

Despite the variation of national approaches to the acquisition of citizenship, there are three basic means for attaining citizenship. First, virtually all nations bestow citizenship based upon the circumstances of birth. Some governments, using the *jus soli* (law of soil) principle, extend citizenship to all persons born on their territory. The United States follows this principle. Other governments, using the *jus sanguinis* (law of blood) principle, extend citizenship to all persons born to parents who are citizens. France, Germany, and many other European states follow this principle. Many states employ some combination of these two principles. The United States, for example, principally recognizes the *jus soli* rule, but accords citizenship to children born to U.S. citizens who are living or traveling abroad.

Most governments also provide naturalization processes by which citizens of another country may acquire citizenship in the new country. Laws of naturalization vary considerably from one country to another as regards who is eligible, how long it takes to become naturalized, and what special requirements must be met during the process of naturalization. Countries routinely administer oaths of allegiance prior to conferring citizenship on naturalized citizens.

Finally, persons may become citizens derivatively, as happens in the case of children who have not attained the age of majority when their parents are naturalized. Typically in such cases, the citizenship of the children follows that of the parents.

The rights and responsibilities that accompany citizenship are normally stipulated in the written constitution, bill of rights, customs and traditions, or statutory law of a country. In virtually every country, citizens have a right to vote. In authoritarian countries, however, the right to participate freely in the political system beyond voting may be severely circumscribed, and even voting may have little substantive meaning. Democratic governments generally encourage and protect a citizen's right of association, freedom of speech, and expression and right of dissent. Democratic governments usually extend rights to freedom of religion, freedom from unreasonable searches and seizures, due process, and access to legal protection through the courts. In authoritarian regimes, these rights and freedoms may be substantially curtailed; even in democratic states the government may take steps to curb such rights during times of national exigency or war. The rights to vote and to political participation have not always been broadly construed, even in democratic states. Suffrage did not extend to all people in the early phases of the development of parliamentary and democratic governments. Unpropertied males, freed slaves, and women were extended suffrage only gradually in the nineteenth and twentieth centuries.

Governments usually wish to imbue their citizens with values and skills that will make them useful and loyal members of the community. Virtually all governments encourage the development of educational systems and curricula that pass along the community's history, language, and culture. Some form of civic education, which helps to develop citizens who have a strong sense of their obligations, duties, and responsibilities, is promoted by all governments. This education may emphasize both the rights and the duties of citizens, as in democratic systems, or it may emphasize the duties more than the rights, as in more authoritarian or traditional regimes.

The duties of citizens generally involve the preservation and protection of the state, and the responsibility to pay their fair share of expenses for public programs, usually through taxes. Many governments require able-bodied male (and in some countries female) citizens to serve in the armed forces. Others, such as the United States, make this a voluntary option during peacetime, although requiring males to register for the draft or selective service. Citizens of all countries are presumed to have a duty not to commit treason against their government, and all governments specify penalties for those who commit crimes against the state, such as committing treason, failing to observe their mandatory service obligation, or not paying their taxes. Enforcement of these penalties, however, is often highly variable.

Applications

When applying the laws of citizenship, numerous complications arise for both individuals and governments. A person who is born in a country recognizing the *jus soli* principle but whose parents are citizens of a country recognizing the *jus sanguinis* principle, will have dual citizenship. Some countries, such as Ireland, allow new citizens to retain their previous nationalities. Other countries, such as the United States, regard naturalization as a citizen as a formal renunciation of prior citizenship. Some countries, for example France, hold to the doctrine of indelible allegiance, that is, no French citizen may renounce his or her citizenship. Thus, a young Frenchman who becomes a naturalized American citizen is still required by French law to perform his mandatory service in the French armed forces. Other countries recognizing the indelible allegiance principle include Egypt, Greece, Iran, Poland, Romania, Syria, and Turkey.

The problem of dual nationality can be even more complicated if two countries are at war with each other, as were the United States and Japan during World War II. Japanese Americans who happened to be in Japan (which recognizes the *jus sanguinis* principle) during the war were required by Japan to serve in its armed forces or face heavy penalties, but in the United States, which holds to the *jus soli* principle, such acts constituted treason. As early as 1930, some governments recognized the need to deal with such problems and promulgated the Convention on Questions Relating to Conflict of Nationality Laws. The United States never became a party to this treaty, but its provisions concerning dual nationality are recognized by many nations.

The opposite problem occurs when parents of a country recognizing only the *jus soli* principle have children in a country recognizing only the *jus sanguinis* principle.

Normally, states make provision for citizens facing these circumstances. When the normal ties of nationality are broken, however, such as when people flee persecution as refugees and then have children in exile, the children run the risk of being stateless. Several international conventions, including the 1951 Convention on the Status of Refugees and the 1967 Protocol to the 1951 Convention, have attempted to provide a legal basis for intercession on behalf of refugees and stateless persons, assuring that they receive protection and assistance, and providing mechanisms for refugees to obtain a new citizenship.

Another complicated issue over the years has regarded the nationality of women. In some countries, the marriage of a woman to a foreign national has no effect on the woman's nationality; in other states, a woman's nationality automatically follows that of her husband. In the mid-1800's, the United States passed legislation conferring citizenship on alien women who married U.S. citizens. In 1907, Congress passed legislation that forced U.S. women who married foreign nationals to acquire their husband's nationality, thus losing their U.S. citizenship. Many other countries adopted similar rules. Although women could resume their original nationality on the termination of marriage to an alien, these rules created many complicated situations. The United States, attempting to regularize the status of women regarding nationality, later passed the Cable Act (1922), which reversed the earlier law and provided that women who married aliens would retain their U.S. citizenship unless they officially chose to renounce it in favor of their husband's nationality.

Governments routinely enact immigration and naturalization legislation to regulate entry into the state's territory. Growing up around the establishment of citizenship ties, then, is a body of exclusionary law that seeks to regulate immigration. Individuals have no inherent right to visit or reside in other lands, nor may individuals demand to be made citizens of another state. Individuals who illegally enter the territory of another state may be deported. An exception to this rule concerns cases of asylum, where individuals fleeing from persecution are protected from being forcefully repatriated to the country of nationality from which they fled. On the other hand, no state is obliged to offer asylum or citizenship, although they may choose to do so.

The chief problem in asylum cases is to determine whether individuals have a valid asylum claim. Each country has its own rules regarding the extension of asylum. These rules may be generously or restrictively construed and applied. Some countries, such as France, the United States, and the United Kingdom, have been generous in extending asylum to refugees from other countries over the years, and often these asylum seekers eventually became naturalized citizens. Generous temporary asylum policies have also been practiced widely among African states. In Southeast Asia, however, governments, fearing ethnic destabilization and economic hardship, have tended to be highly restrictive in granting asylum. In the late twentieth century, Vietnamese and Cambodian refugees often sought resettlement and citizenship in the United States, Canada, Australia, or Western Europe. Attitudes toward asylum in these countries, however, grew more restrictive in the 1980's and 1990's. Most governments view themselves as protectors of the existing citizen body and are reluctant to become targets for large or uncontrolled movements of people seeking entry in order to enjoy the benefits of citizenship in wealthy and democratic states.

Context

Citizenship has always been an integral part of the political life of nations. Questions surrounding who may be a citizen and what privileges the status of citizenship accords are at the heart of politics. In democracies, citizens are the ultimate sovereigns who select those who make decisions for them. Citizens are obliged to obey the laws of their country, and may be punished when they do not. In less democratic societies, citizens usually have less extensive rights. Citizens are an essential ingredient of all societies, however, and authoritarian regimes, if they are to survive, must command the support of the citizen body. Without legitimacy in the eyes of citizens, governments run the risk of rebellion, revolt, and revolution. Citizens, however, need government to provide security and promote prosperity. The relationship between individuals and the state, then, involves a dynamic tension of mutual rights and responsibilities.

In the late twentieth century, an increasing demand for human rights was heard. The elevation of human rights' debates suggests that eventually governments should be held accountable for mistreatment of their own citizens, and indeed, sometimes international pressure has encouraged governments to treat citizens and resident aliens with greater dignity and respect. Unless the sovereign state system is replaced by some other, perhaps global, form of government, which seems unlikely from the perspective of the 1990's, governments themselves will be responsible for ensuring that the fundamental rights and freedoms of persons are respected and enforced.

The prospect of a more global conception of citizenship has long been a hope of humanitarians and visionaries. With the resurgence of virulent and highly particular nationalistic claims in the latter half of the twentieth century, this hope appears to be a distant dream. The very division of peoples into national units that confer specific citizenship rights is a divisive feature of the modern world, which militates against the creation of a wider, more cosmopolitan conception and practice of citizenship.

Bibliography

Bookchin, Murray. *The Rise of Urbanization and the Decline of Citizenship.* San Francisco: Sierra Club Books, 1987. Critical appraisal of the possibilities for genuine civic action and citizen involvement in large, urban, capitalist environments. Its historic and economic analysis leads to the conclusion that noncorporate, locally controlled municipalities should replace our corporate, capitalist, centralized culture, if genuine citizenship is to be made possible.

Fustel de Coulanges, Numa Denis. *The Ancient City: A Study on the Religion, Laws, and Institutions of Greece and Rome.* Garden City, N.Y.: Doubleday, 1956. Classic study of the ancient origin of cities and the role of citizenship in them. Explores the earliest roots of the practice of citizenship, particularly in ancient Greece and Rome.

Merriam, Charles. *Civic Education in the United States.* New York: Charles Scribner's Sons, 1934. A dated but insightful critique of social studies curricula, this report of the Commission on the Social Studies gives a sense of the kinds of skills, knowledge, and values about citizenship that a society seeks to inculcate into its youth.

Schuck, Peter H., and Rogers M. Smith. *Citizenship Without Consent: Illegal Aliens in the American Polity.* New Haven, Conn.: Yale University Press, 1985. Discusses various conceptions of citizenship, arguing in favor of a consensualist approach, which would interpret *jus soli* to apply only to children of citizens and legal resident aliens, not to children of illegal immigrants.

Von Glahn, Gerhard. *Law Among Nations: An Introduction to Public International Law.* 6th ed. New York: Macmillan, 1992. Contains excellent discussions on the role and status of citizenship, national jurisdiction over aliens, the law of state responsibility toward aliens, and asylum law. Provides comparative examples of citizenship practices in a number of countries.

Walzer, Michael. *Obligations: Essays on Disobedience, War, and Citizenship.* Cambridge, Mass.: Harvard University Press, 1970. A thoughtful and thought-provoking analysis of the duties that individuals have as citizens of states, especially states that are at war. Touches on the dilemmas of civil disobedience, conscientious objection, and alienated minorities.

Robert F. Gorman

Cross-References

The Bill of Rights, p. 134; Citizenship Rights and Responsibilities, p. 260; Civil Disobedience, p. 285; Civil Liberties Protection, p. 291; Civil Rights and Liberties, p. 298; Civil Rights Protection, p. 304; Individual Versus State Rights, p. 910; International Law, p. 956; The Nation-State, p. 1241; Naturalization, p. 1275; Patriotism, p. 1384; Voting in History, p. 2116.

CITIZENSHIP RIGHTS AND RESPONSIBILITIES

Field of study: Political philosophy

Citizenship is membership in a political state. Citizens in representative democracies have both rights and responsibilities as active participants within the civil community.

Principal terms
    CIVIL LIBERTIES: guarantees protecting citizens from government interference and restraining governmental powers
    CIVIL RIGHTS: explicit acts of government, either constitutionally derived or promulgated as statutory law, that protect citizens from unfair, arbitrary, and discriminatory treatment at the hands of government or other citizens
    DEMOCRACY: rule by the people in a system that encourages public participation
    POLITICAL RIGHTS: rights to participate and influence public policy and the management of government by voting, joining political parties, and expressing opinions
    REPRESENTATIVE GOVERNMENT: political system in which citizens elect representatives as their agents for lawmaking, law enforcement, and decision making

Overview

Political systems enable people to come together, resolve conflicts, promulgate the society's values, and create processes by which some people are authorized to make decisions and enforce the rules. In politics there is conflict and competition, but human beings have devised governments and rules by which to play the political game. Governments represent peoples and societies, their customs and cultures. Citizens are the participants and stakeholders in politics.

Citizenship is defined as recognition that an individual is a legal member of a state. Here the word "state" refers to all the institutions of government and society within a single country or nation. Thus, national citizenship can be narrowly construed as membership in a country. For example, anyone who is born in the United States is a natural-born citizen with all the privileges of that position. People of foreign birth and citizenship (aliens) may become U.S. citizens by the process of naturalization. The rules for naturalization are spelled out in Article 1, section 8, of the U.S. Constitution. Although rights and responsibilities are implicit in the acceptance or recognition of citizenship, this narrow usage of the term ignores more philosophically significant understandings of the ideal of citizenship.

The ideal notion of citizenship extends beyond simple state membership. For centuries, human societies have imbued the concept of citizenship with special meaning: an identity as a part of a group that shares a common heritage, destiny, and country. States and societies are reflections of the people, and the citizen has a special place in the social relationships that integrate the community. For example, a person's recognition as a citizen of ancient Athens gave the person an exclusive place within society. Citizenship was so important in the ancient Roman state that, as the empire expanded, citizenship in the Roman Republic was granted as a reward throughout its dominions.

Citizenship grants rights and privileges, but also implies that the state has a right to make certain demands upon the individual. Citizenship was regarded as fundamentally exclusive in ancient societies, and citizens are tightly controlled in modern authoritarian or autocratic systems. Citizens in those systems are bound to perform duties and provide services, and the real authority in the system comes from the top down. Citizens have relatively little control over the demands that the ruler can make, and citizenship is often restricted to a very few. Only in the evolution of representative and participatory democracies did citizenship develop greater significance and power, especially in the context of twentieth century nationalism.

The examples of ancient Athens and the Roman Republic are instructive because contemporary society has inherited many of its ideals about citizenship from these two civilizations. Even so, the ideals were not fully achieved in practice in those societies. Athenian democracy was a form of direct democracy; common citizens participated in active governance and were allowed to participate in the assembly, and many public offices of importance were chosen by lot. The Greeks believed that ideally people must be governed by laws, not by kings or despots who ruled through arbitrary, personal judgments.

There is little dignity in being the servile subject of another man, according to the Greek ideal. This ideal led the fourth century B.C.E. philosopher Aristotle to conclude that only in politics can the human individual perform immortal acts that are remembered for their selflessness and public spirit. Aristotle emphasized the role of the citizen as a participant in government, who acts in the public interest and the dictates of human reason. Citizenship was a high calling, made more meaningful in the context of democracy.

Despite these Greek ideals, ancient Athens did not have representative government, and Athenian citizenship was held only by sons of free Athenian parents. Only those who lived within the city itself had the time, education, and wealth to participate, and all foreigners, women, and slaves were excluded. In fact, slavery was a key in allowing Athenian citizens to play an active role in government, and Aristotle defended its existence. Therefore, the civil rights of citizenship were held exclusively by a citizen caste in Athens. Athenian democracy and the powerful ideals passed down from the Greeks were based on an antidemocratic society.

The same was true of the Roman Republic. Citizens of Rome were given special status and civil rights, and citizenship was a coveted recognition. Although this recognition was granted to certain members of the expanded empire, true participation was only available to those who lived within the walls of the city of Rome itself. Within the city, powerful patrician and plebeian classes dominated the society. The large slave population in Rome had no hope of achieving citizenship. Since the rights of citizenship were not extended to broader classes of people, the republic was established on a fundamentally antidemocratic foundation.

Twentieth century citizens have inherited an ideal concept of citizenship from Rome and Athens, emphasizing empowerment, participation, and selfless obligation to the community, and live in societies where the reality has the potential to approximate more closely the ideal. Citizenship is more significant in representative democracies, because of their inclusive character. Citizenship in twentieth century democracies is based on ancient ideals set into new contexts.

Citizenship gained its full democratic significance as the idea of nationalism grew. Twentieth century nationalism requires that citizens embrace a political identity, based on common ideals, culture, and history, that personally identifies the individual with the state and its society. To be a citizen of a country substantially defines who people are in a personal way, and what they believe about the world around them. Modern democracies expanded on the idea of "rule of the people" in the modern nation-state.

Twentieth century states are complex organizations, with many institutions of government and society that integrate the nation over large territories and populations. These complex institutional structures—which usually include standing armies, highly developed police and judicial structures, and many public agencies that manage political, social, and economic affairs—require the participation of the masses of people to work properly. Nation-states have become more expansive because society—including industry, science, education, transportation, and communications— integrates the contributions of millions of people. Many authoritarian dictatorships have developed in the twentieth century, which have forced the masses of people to participate in their enterprises and government, and used expanded notions of national citizenship. Nevertheless, representative democracy has had the greatest impact in expanding the idea of citizenship, while organizing masses of people for the enormous mission of the modern state.

In representative democracy, the citizens choose representatives to act as their agents in government. Voters may select individuals to represent them in legislatures, in local governments, or as chief executives. Representative government is necessary because direct democracy would be impossible in large nations with millions of people. Representative democracy is based on rules and laws that allow citizens freely to elect and replace their rulers. Thus, representative democracy has allowed society to expand democratic participation to more people.

Participatory democracies differ from political democracies. A political democracy is a system of government that encourages citizens to participate, but this participation is optional. Political democracy is based on political rights, which are derived from civil rights and liberties, but are specifically related to participation in the political process. Political rights include the right to vote, join political parties, and engage in activities that influence government, elections, and lawmaking.

Civil rights and liberties are important, but often overlooked, aspects of citizenship.

Civil rights and liberties form the basis for the powers of citizenship, but are meaningless unless people actively work to make them effective. Although political democracy does not force citizens to participate, citizenship in a democracy becomes useless unless the citizens are educated and aware of their political world, understand the rules of the system, and take an active part in political life. Thus, citizenship is directly linked to participation. Civil rights—positive acts of government to defend against violation of liberty—will only be maintained when citizens actively exercise their civil liberties.

Citizenship in a representative democracy is empowering and liberating, but carries significant responsibilities with it. Citizen participation must go beyond occasional visits to the ballot box to include public service; volunteer activity; involvement in campaigns; and active membership in political groups, associations, and lobbies. The Greek and Roman ideals of commitment are necessary to realize the greater opportunity of empowerment, influence, and dignity offered in twentieth century political democracy.

Applications

There are many forms of representative democracy and types of citizen participation defining differing kinds of citizenship. Political and representative democracies differ from other systems, for example dictatorial regimes in which people are forced to engage in government-sponsored political activities. Participation in electoral politics in the former Soviet Union, for example, did not empower citizens, because their freedom of choice was removed: Universal participation is meaningless when the candidates are selected by the ruling party. Political democracy grants the power to engage in politics by choice, and thus enhances the responsibilities of citizenship.

Different representative democracies emphasize varying patterns of participation. For example, the parliamentary system of Great Britain is strictly representative, in contrast to systems that allow direct democracy or plebiscitarian participation. In Britain, elected representatives (for example, members of the House of Commons) make decisions; the public does not vote directly on the passage of law. The British prime minister is selected by the ruling party in Parliament, and the British people only vote for representatives from their districts. In the representative system of France, however, there are many examples of direct democracy where citizens vote on law and policy in national referendums, also called plebiscites. The French president also is elected by a direct national vote of all citizens.

Another example that shows the differences between Great Britain and France was the passage of the Maastricht Treaty, an agreement to the first steps for creating a more united European community, in the 1990's. In Great Britain, this treaty was passed by Parliament alone—the representatives elected to the House of Commons. In France, citizens voted directly on the treaty in a national referendum. Both the British and French systems are representative democracies, but each provides its citizens with different political rights.

The ideal of the modern citizen has been pivotal in the philosophy behind establishing modern democracies. Leaders of the American Revolution, such as James Madison and Thomas Jefferson, emphasized that public spiritedness and social responsibility were required if democracy were to work. Public service and political education are necessary to develop a responsible citizenry that engages in political affairs, and is even willing to die for its country in a national cause. Education is so important that it was one of the first things that the new West German government required of citizens after the fall of the Nazi government in World War II. Education in democratic values was believed to be necessary for West Germany to establish democracy. Thus, the potential for modern democracies to establish societies based on freedom and human creativity is dependent on a modern ideal of citizenship emphasizing responsibility, commitment, and education in a context of protected civil rights and liberties.

Context

Political democracy can succeed only where the political arena represents as many ideas as possible. Citizens of political democracies concentrate on their opportunities to influence the system—hence law, policies, and distribution of values. No modern state can survive for long unless the masses of people are committed to and identify with the common enterprise. In this there is a requirement for an enhanced role of the citizen, but there is no guarantee that this will be liberating. Modern states integrate their citizens into their projects either by force or by choice. Representative democracies offer the opportunity for citizenship to be empowering and liberating, and grant the ability for citizenship to be creative and dignifying.

A great danger to democracy emerges when people ignore their responsibilities as citizens. When the public is uninterested in elections and political affairs, and is preoccupied with the business of survival or narrow self-interest, citizens in a political democracy are in danger of losing their power. Citizens must empower themselves, and civil rights and liberties will lose their significance if not given constant attention by the people.

A key to the success of democracy is in the education of its citizens. In an age of high-speed information through electronic media, it becomes easy for citizens to believe they are well informed when they may have only the most superficial understanding of their political world from the media. Modern citizens must make a powerful effort to learn about politics and the world, to cultivate understanding and tolerance, and to analyze events and information critically. Intelligent, well-educated citizens are then responsible to step forward and make themselves heard in the public arena.

Bibliography

Barber, Benjamin. *Strong Democracy: Participatory Politics for a New Age.* Berkeley: University of California Press, 1984. Analysis of democratic ideologies and frameworks accompanies a proposal for a new concept of citizen participation in the United States.

Dalton, Russell J. *Citizen Politics in Western Democracies: Public Opinion and Political Parties in the United States, Great Britain, West Germany, and France.* Chatham, N.J.: Chatham House, 1988. Comparison of citizen participation, values, and elections in the United States, Great Britain, West Germany, and France.

Key, V. O., Jr. *The Responsible Electorate: Rationality in Presidential Voting, 1936-1960.* Cambridge, Mass.: Harvard University Press, 1966. Classic study of the American electorate demonstrating how citizens formulate policy preferences, evaluate the actions of government and the parties in power, and then utilize these preferences when casting their ballots in elections.

Lasswell, Harold. *Politics: Who Gets What, When, How.* Cleveland: World, 1958. Classic statement on the nature of the political game and the role of citizens in the process.

Sartori, Giovanni. *The Theory of Democracy Revisited.* Chatham, N.J.: Chatham House, 1987. Thorough analysis of the evolution of democracy and democratic ideals, with an objective approach to the meaning of democratic theory.

Schulz, Donald E., and Jan S. Adams. *Political Participation in Communist Systems.* New York: Pergamon Press, 1981. Collection of articles concerning political participation in communist regimes, demonstrating that even in communist systems autonomous roles for citizens evolved.

Anthony R. Brunello

Cross-References

Activist Politics, p. 7; The Bill of Rights, p. 134; Burke's Political Philosophy, p. 171; Citizen Movements, p. 248; Civic Education, p. 278; Civil Rights and Liberties, p. 298; Government Roles, p. 778; Legislative Body Types, p. 1091; Liberal Nationalism, p. 1111; Mill's Political Philosophy, p. 1204; Naturalization, p. 1275; Patriotism, p. 1384; Political Participation, p. 1479; Voting Processes, p. 2123; Woman Suffrage, p. 2141.

CITY GOVERNMENT IN THE UNITED STATES

Field of study: Local and regional government

Municipalities are political subdivisions created by states. Twentieth century U.S. cities are governed either by an elected mayor and council, elected commissioners, or an elected council and an appointed city manager. Approximately three-quarters of the U.S. population lived in cities near the end of the twentieth century.

Principal terms
CHARTER: legal document granted by a state that creates a municipality
   and defines its legal status
CITY MANAGER: appointed officer who carries out the executive duties
   of a municipality in a council-manager form of government
COMMISSIONER: elected official who performs both executive and
   legislative functions in the commission form of government
COUNCIL: unicameral legislative body for municipalities
MAYOR: chief executive, normally elected, of a municipality
NONPARTISAN ELECTION SYSTEM: election system in which only the
   names of the candidates appear on the ballot
POLITICAL MACHINE: tightly disciplined party organization, run by
   professional politicians, that dominated big-city politics in the
   United States in the last quarter of the nineteenth century
WARD: geographical subdivision of a city that is used to elect city
   council members

Overview

The structure of municipal government in the United States is primarily based on English precedent. In the colonial era, municipal governments generally followed the British model of a common council consisting of a mayor, a recorder, and aldermen. In New England, town meetings were widely used in local communities. Most cities, however, were overshadowed in this era, because the colonies were primarily rural and agriculture-based. After the revolutionary war, many cities were governed through a borough system, in which unelected town leaders volunteered to make decisions for the community. The average citizen was not involved in this decision-making process.

In the 1820's and 1830's, the reforms of Jacksonian democracy resulted in more nearly universal male suffrage and mass-based political activity. As a result, a new generation of municipal leaders emerged. More formal governmental systems were also created, most notably the mayor-council arrangements. Until the middle of the nineteenth century, the councils were the dominant actors and mayors played a secondary role. In the mid-nineteenth century, some cities created independent boards and commissions to perform administrative functions. These governing structures were dominated by the business interests in the community.

The Industrial Revolution and the development of mass democracy transformed the character and politics of United States cities in the post-Civil War era. Factory districts developed in the cities, and their populations grew rapidly as immigrants from Europe and migrants from the rural areas moved to urban areas seeking employment. Rather than being run by business elites, cities began to be controlled by politicians who used the political system for personal advancement. In the last quarter of the nineteenth century, political machines evolved in most large cities in the United States. Machine politicians relied on two constituencies, voters and business, to maintain their position of power. They traded jobs and business contracts for electoral and financial support. Few people benefited from this arrangement, and opposition to the corruption and excesses of the machines resulted in a reform movement at the turn of the century.

In 1894, the National Municipal League was organized to reform the corrupt practices of the cities. By 1896, there were 180 local chapters of the organization; by the beginning of the twentieth century, all large cities were members of the organization. Reforms advocated by the National Municipal League included at-large elections, nonpartisan elections, unicameral city councils, a strong mayoral system of government, civil service appointments for most administrative positions in city government, and home rule charters. New forms of urban government began to appear, including the commission system and the city-manager system. In the 1990's, cities in the United States were governed by either the mayor-council system, the commission system, or the council-manager system.

The mayor-council system was the most common form of city government in the United States in the 1990's. Mayor-council systems have an independently elected mayor whose primary responsibility is to implement ordinances or laws passed by councils. A council is composed of council members or aldermen, and can range in size from fewer than ten to more than forty members. Mayor-council systems may have a strong or a weak mayor. In strong-mayor systems, the mayor generally serves a four-year term, prepares a city budget and submits it to the council, appoints and removes agency heads, defines administrative duties, can transfer monies without council approval, and possesses a veto power. In a weak-mayor system, the mayor has few duties other than presiding over council meetings and attending ceremonial functions. The council or public boards appoint and supervise department heads. The mayor has no veto power and may serve a term as short as two years with no opportunity for reelection. In most mayor-council systems, the distribution of power falls somewhere between these two illustrations. In general, the larger the city, the stronger the mayor.

In the commission form of government, the only elected officials of the city are commissioners, who are normally elected at large on a nonpartisan ballot. Collectively, they perform both policy and legislative functions, including enacting laws and approving budgets. Each commissioner also heads an administrative department. Assignment of departments may be by election or by commission appointment. One of the commissioners serves as mayor. The mayor may be chosen by the people or by the commission; however, the functions of this position are ceremonial. The mayor presides over commission meetings and represents the city at official functions.

In the council-manager form of city government, there is an elected city council and a mayor. The council acts as the city's legislature and appoints a professional city manager. The mayor may be elected by the people or selected by the council from its own membership. The duties, however, are ceremonial; the mayor possesses neither a veto nor appointment power. The city's executive functions are performed by the manager, who proposes a budget, appoints department heads, and supervises their activities. In theory, the council makes policy and the city manager executes it. In practice, city managers frequently make policy recommendations to council. Managers serve at the pleasure of council, however, and must be sensitive to the political environment of their city.

The system used by municipalities to elect city council members varies. In the 1990's, approximately 13 percent used a ward system, in which each council member is elected from a geographical subdivision of the municipality. Sixty percent of municipalities used an at-large system, in which each council member is elected by all the voters in the city and represents the entire city. Approximately 27 percent of council elections used a combination of ward and at-large systems. Almost three-quarters of municipal elections were nonpartisan; that is, only the candidate's name appeared on the ballot, without party affiliation being identified.

Applications

The most common form of municipal government in the United States in the 1990's was the mayor-council plan, which was in use in more than half of the cities. Weak mayors were more likely to be found in cities with populations of fewer than ten thousand. Larger cities had moved to a strong-mayor-council system, as had been recommended by the reform movement in the early twentieth century. Reformers had argued that under a weak-mayor system authority was in the hands of too many people—council members, boards, and commissions—so no one person could be held accountable for public policy. They argued for a strong executive with sufficient power to run city government. The National Municipal League recommended a strong-mayor-council model in 1899. Their proposal was for a city council of five to nine members elected at large along with a mayor with broad appointment and veto powers. Large cities began to adopt this system. By 1990, almost 80 percent of all cities in the United States with a population of more than 500,000 had a strong-mayor system, and all cities with a population of more than one million had this arrangement. In many large cities, including New York, Chicago, Boston, Philadelphia, and San Francisco, the mayor had a chief administrative officer (CAO) to serve as second-in-command, which further strengthened the mayor's power. The CAO is appointed by the mayor, and handles staff and administrative duties such as routine supervision of departments. This enables the mayor to spend more time on policy questions. Politically, the strong-mayor-council arrangement gives the mayor a local status equivalent to the governor at the state level or the president at the national level.

The commission form was first used in Galveston, Texas, in 1900. When the existing mayor-council system was unable to rebuild the city following a devasting hurricane, citizens petitioned the Texas state legislature for a new form of city government. The legislature approved the commission form, and the new government's success in rebuilding Galveston resulted in adoption of this form of government by other cities. Des Moines, Iowa, adopted a commission system in 1908 that included a five-member commission; nonpartisan, at-large elections; a civil service system; and three direct democracy entities—the initiative, referendum, and recall. This reform package led to a widespread adoption of the commission system. By 1915, at least 465 cities had adopted this form, and by 1920, an estimated 20 percent of all cities with a population of more than 5,000 had a commission system.

The commission system was touted as a cure-all for municipal government; however, in time, problems with the arrangement became apparent. The major problem was fragmented leadership. A commission did not operate like a board of directors; each commissioner headed a separate department and commissioners often refused to cooperate with each other. In addition, persons not qualified to operate a department frequently were elected as commissioners. The commission system began to decline in popularity in the 1920's. By 1970, only two hundred cities still used this form. By the early 1990's, fewer than 3 percent of United States cities used a commission system, including only seven cities with a population of more than 100,000.

The council-manager form was another attempt at reform of municipal government. While Staunton, Virginia, experimented with this form as early as 1908, Sumter, South Carolina, was the first city to adopt this system, in 1912. In 1913, Dayton, Ohio, adopted the council-manager form of city government following a flood, with spectacular results. The National Municipal League then recommended that cities replace the commission form with the council-manager system. Soon thereafter, the Dayton Plan began to be adopted throughout the United States. By 1923, 240 cities had adopted this system; within the next five years, another 84 cities had adopted it. This system proved to be popular and successful in newer, fast-growing cities with mobile populations. This description fits many suburban communities, especially in the Sun Belt region of the United States, where planning for urban growth is important. More than half of U.S. cities with a population between 25,000 and 250,000 had a council-manager system in the 1990's. At the same time, more than two-thirds of cities with a population between 100,000 and 200,000 had this arrangement. Overall, between 35 and 40 percent of U.S. cities had a council-manager arrangement.

Context

When the United States Constitution was adopted in 1789, only 5 percent of the population lived in urban centers with a population of twenty-five hundred or more. Throughout the United States there were only twenty-four such communities at that time. Only New York, Philadelphia, Baltimore, Boston, and Charleston, South Carolina, had populations of more than ten thousand. During the nineteenth century, the growth of urban areas was steady. Between 1820 and 1860, as German and Irish immigrants came to the United States, city population increased at a rate three times faster than the population as a whole. By 1860, one hundred cities had populations of more than ten thousand, and nine cities had populations exceeding one hundred thousand. Altogether, almost 20 percent of the American population lived in areas classified as urban in 1860. This percentage doubled in the next forty years, and by the beginning of the twentieth century, 40 percent of all Americans lived in cities with populations of more than twenty-five hundred. When the 1920 census was taken, 51.2 percent of the population lived in urban areas. In the 1990's, more than 75 percent of the population in the United States lived in urban areas.

Despite the growing importance of the city in American life, urban areas were limited in their decision-making authority and influence. Cities, generally governed by a business elite, were ignored by rural-dominated state legislatures in the nineteenth century. As immigrants flocked to the cities in the last half of the nineteenth century, restrictions on the city's authority became the rule. Courts have ruled consistently that cities were creations of the states and, as such, had limited authority beyond that granted by the state.

A city operates under a charter granted by a state. The charter defines the city's boundaries, structure, functions, methods of finance, and powers of election and appointment. In general, the larger the city, the greater the discretionary authority. Legally, cities have an inferior status to the states that issue their charter. As early as 1819, the United States Supreme Court held that states could amend or rescind city charters at will. In an 1868 court case, the chief justice of Iowa's state supreme court, John F. Dillon, offered what became the definitive interpretation of the relationship between city and state. His decision described cities are mere tenants at the will of state legislatures. His *Treatise on the Law of Municipal Corporations* (1872) became the defining edict on municipal law in the United States. "Dillon's Rule," as it is called, said that any conflicts concerning the powers of the city were to be resolved in favor of the state.

Cities also faced obstacles in dealing with rural-dominated state legislatures from the nineteenth century until the mid-1960's. Urban areas were grossly underrepresented in most state legislatures during that era of growth. Hence the problems of the cities, ranging from traffic congestion to slums, were largely ignored by the states. In 1964, the U.S. Supreme Court ruled that both houses of state legislatures must be apportioned based on the principle of "one man-one vote." As a result, state legislatures became more responsive to urban needs and problems. In the 1990's, cities performed a variety of services including public safety, public works, and parks and recreation. With more than 75 percent of the population of the United States living in cities, they have become central to U.S. political, social, and economic life.

Bibliography

Goldfield, David, and Blaine Brownell. *Urban America: A History.* 2d ed. Boston: Houghton Mifflin, 1990. Thorough, one-volume overview of urban history and politics in the United States.
Judd, Dennis R., and Todd Swanstrom. *City Politics: Private Power and Public Policy.*

New York: HarperCollins, 1994. Discusses city politics as a complex interaction among private and public institutions, actors, and resources.

Pohlmann, Marcus D. *Governing the Postindustrial City.* New York: Longman, 1993. Excellent analysis of contemporary urban politics. Examines both the political processes and the social and economic contexts within which decisions are made.

Royko, Mike. *Boss: Richard J. Daley of Chicago.* New York: New American Library, 1988. Short, easy-to-read, humorous description of one of the last political machines in the United States.

Savitch, H. V., and John Clayton Thomas, eds. *Big City Politics in Transition.* Newbury Park, Calif.: Sage Publications, 1991. Examines changes in thirteen of the largest American cities in terms of demographics, economics, government, and decision making. In general, the authors conclude that most cities discussed are the products of external influences and the decentralization of decision making.

Stone, Clarence N. *Regime Politics: Governing Atlanta, 1946-1988.* Lawrence: University Press of Kansas, 1989. A case study of politics in Atlanta, which concludes that its governance is an informal partnership between elected city officials and the business elite of the community.

William V. Moore

Cross-References

County Government, p. 458; Education Management, p. 565; Elected Versus Appointed Offices in the United States, p. 572; Entitlements, p. 610; Federal Mandates, p. 662; Fire Protection, p. 700; Funding of Government, p. 724; Grants-in-Aid, p. 791; Initiatives and Referendums, p. 923; Local Governments, p. 1136; Nonpartisan Political Organizations, p. 1326; Political Machines and Bosses, p. 1468; Public Works, p. 1647; Rural Community Government, p. 1763; State and Local Government, p. 1885; Urban Governments, p. 2052; Urban Renewal and Housing, p. 2064; Urbanization, p. 2071.

THE CITY-STATE

Field of study: History of government and politics

From at least the fifth century B.C.E. through the nineteenth century, the independent city-state proved a successful, often powerful form of government in Western civilization as well as a vital focus for the development of political practice and theory.

Principal terms
ABSOLUTISM: government by absolute rulers or authorities
AUTOCRACY: government by one person wielding absolute authority
CITY-STATE: small, independent political entity composed of a city and the surrounding countryside
DEMOCRACY: direct or indirect government by the people, sometimes rule by the majority
ELITE: powerful minority
EMPIRE: political consolidation of vast territories and disparate peoples under one rule
NATION-STATE: large sovereign political organization containing a relatively homogeneous population
OLIGARCHY: rule by the few
POLIS: independent Greek city-state

Overview
From the fifth century B.C.E. until the last quarter of the nineteenth century—2,500 years—independent city-states were workable forms of government and community in the Western world. As empires and nation states rose and fell around them, individual city-states collapsed, were absorbed, disappeared, and endured. The types of government and community manifested by various city-states throughout these years made profound and indelible contributions to Western political practices and political theories. Experiences gained within city-states deeply affected evolving concepts of individualism, heroism, and leadership. They shaped the meanings of freedom, free speech, and loyalty. They influenced ideas about the nature of citizenship and civic virtue, and they brought understanding to discussions of absolutism, autocracy, democracy, elites, law, liberalism, oligarchy, and sovereignty.

Several millennia before the Christian era, city-states appeared in ancient Sumeria, notably the cities of Erech, Kish, and Ur. Sumerian city-states, however, transmitted little of lasting importance to Western political culture.

On the other hand, the Greek city-states, which reached their cultural apogees during the fifth and fourth centuries B.C.E., have influenced Western politics and culture tremendously. There were scores of Greek city-states, the most famous of which were Athens, Sparta, Corinth, Megara, Miletus, Mytilene, Argos, and Thebes. Their forms of government varied: Some were tyrannies, some were autocracies, and others were oligarchies. None was more important to the realm of political ideas than fifth-century

Athens, the epitome of the classic polis. Under the leadership of Pericles (c. 495-429 B.C.E.), Athenians established what may have been the world's first, if limited, democracy. The philosophies of Socrates (c. 470-399 B.C.E.), Plato (c. 427-348 or 347 B.C.E.), and Aristotle (384-322 B.C.E.), who all lived in Athens, laid the foundation of Western political thought.

The influence of independent Greek city-states declined after 339 B.C.E. when many of them were brought under the authority of the Macedonian Empire of Philip II and his son Alexander the Great. Others that survived independently, in some instances even prospered, were incorporated eventually into the Roman and Byzantine empires. Their cultural legacies, nevertheless, proved durable. Starting in the eighth century B.C.E., for example, Greek colonies were planted in Sicily (for example, Syracuse, Messina, and Catania) and in southern Italy. As conveyors of Greek culture, these city-states, by the fourth century B.C.E., had begun modifying the cultures of early Italian city-states, the most impressive of them being Rome.

Founded around the mid-eighth century B.C.E., Rome previously had been the dependency of a confederation of Etrurian city-states, among them Arezzo, Perugia, Cortona, Volterra, Tuscania, and Chiusi. In the sixth century Rome itself served as the center of an Etrurian monarchy. Etrurian rule was overthrown by 500 B.C.E., and for the next three centuries Rome and surrounding Latium was governed as a republic dominated by oligarchies or elites drawn from aristocratic families. This remarkable city-state was transformed after 151 B.C.E. into the center of a vast imperial establishment which lasted until 395 C.E., the beginning of the end of the devolution of the Roman Empire.

City-states reemerged as vital political entities during the Middle Ages. This was particularly notable on the Italian peninsula and within the complicated political arrangements that characterized Germany. In Italy, Venice had achieved urban independence by the ninth century and soon spread its political influence from the scores of islands on which it was founded to nearby coasts and to Dalmatia. By the fourteenth century, the Venetian city-state, an impressive center of commerce, industry, and finance, had become an international power.

Venice was not alone; by the tenth century Italy had become a mix of ambitious, quarrelsome city-states, among them, Florence, Milan, Bologna, Siena, Pisa, the Papal States, Genoa, Perugia, and Amalfi. By the thirteenth century, the Italian city-states were nurturing the Renaissance.

Elsewhere in Europe, along the Schelde and Rhine rivers as well as farther north along the coast of the Baltic Sea, a number of cities successfully bargained with, or fought against, local princes and prelates to win urban independence by the twelfth century. In Flanders, for example, Bruges, Ypres, Ghent, Antwerp, and Douai, thanks to the excellence and extent of their industry and international commerce, soon dominated their various hinterlands. Autonomous Rhenish cities, such as Cologne, their independence also underwritten by trade, sometimes formed alliances such as the Rhenish League to further their political and territorial ambitions. Similarly, along the Baltic, other city-states whose wealth and autonomy were based upon powerful mercantile classes and long-distance trade, flourished between the twelfth and fifteenth centuries. These were the Hansa towns (subsequently members of the Hanseatic League), most prominent of which were Lübeck, Hamburg, Bremen, Rostock, Visby, Riga, and Dorpat. Though the Hanseatic League collapsed in the sixteenth century, Lübeck and Hamburg continued as city-states until they were absorbed in the unification of Germany in 1870.

Some authorities maintain that the city-state made its last contributions to political history during the Swiss Reformation in the sixteenth century. This view is especially pertinent in regard to the development of Zürich and Geneva, each of which had either revolted against the Swiss Confederation or had managed to remain outside of it. Protestant reformer Huldrych Zwingli transformed Zürich into the center of the Swiss Reformation until its defeat by Catholics in 1531. Equally important, from 1540 to 1564, John Calvin, a leading protestant reformer, converted Geneva into a city-state tightly organized around a body of believing Christians, one that became the focal point of the European Reformation. What these two city-states contributed was the model of their own organization and spirit: the church-society and government by councils, as well as political combinations of secular and spiritual concerns.

City-states were characterized by nearly every type of political organization. Some were autocratic, some tyrannical, some oligarchic, some theocratic, and some republics. They serve the historian as political laboratories in which eternal political questions were probed. They raised issues about ideal forms of government and the quality of life that might be achieved through political association. They posed the problem of the effective boundaries of political space: that is, how extensive these boundaries could be before common interests and a sense of community were overly compromised. They questioned how many people a community might include before government by citizen participation ceased to be meaningful.

Applications

For two and a half millennia, from Greece to the Baltic, city-states fashioned their political institutions and concepts of citizenship from a wide spectrum of possibilities. None of these choices gained more enduring prominence in Western political literature than the ones made by the Athenian city-state from the fifth century B.C.E. to Roman times. Athens and its surrounding territory of Attica constituted the classic polis; "political" means "concerning the polis." The singular status accorded Athens results from the political writings of Athenian philosophers, foremost among them Socrates, Plato, and Aristotle. It also owes much to the additional writings, orations, or histories of men such as Gorgias, Isocrates, Demosthenes, Herodotus, Thucydides, and Plutarch.

These people's histories illuminate the political, social, and economic structure of an evolving city-state that became—and for centuries remained—a successful democracy. Athenian democracy was tainted by a continuation of slavery, by class and familial conflict, by demagoguery, as well as by the acquisition—and frequent misuse—of empire. What is more, its early history was characterized by a succession of tyrants. Nevertheless, Athens organized its political life around a constitution, law, and elective institutions: a Council of Four (later Five) Hundred, the archonship, and large juries on which all citizens served. Of more fundamental importance, these elective institutions arose within a society that highly valued private and personal freedom, as well as equality of opportunity (for male citizens) in holding public office, and education that fostered the adaptability believed essential to civic life. Athenians, in short, conceived of their democracy as a way of life.

Politically very different from Athens, sixteenth-century Geneva under protestant religious reformer John Calvin became an ecclesiastical city-state based on Calvin's understanding of the "visible church." Calvin's Geneva, with its emphasis on order and obedience, perceived the community as a school of virtue, as a halfway house between earth and Heaven. Geneva's institutions were seen as agencies working toward the realization of human perfection within God's universe. Geneva's religious affairs were dominated by pastors and lay elders who, while directly elected by the citizenry, thereafter merely had their leadership confirmed or rejected by the citizenry. Pastors' and lay elders' authority was reinforced by chosen civil magistrates, whose depersonalized role was to speak the law. The functions of magistrates and pastors were never separate; both authorities formulated policy. Citizens could only affirm or negate them.

After Calvin, Geneva gained fame as a protestant refuge. Another protestant zealot, John Knox, also preached there in the sixteenth century. The city was a sanctuary for many French Huguenots during their seventeenth century persecutions by the French Bourbon monarchies of Louis XIII and Louis XIV. By the eighteenth century, Geneva's theocracy had become a patriciate and the city-state an intellectual center that variously hosted Voltaire, Jean-Jacques Rousseau, Albert Gallatin, Henri de Saussure, and others.

The Italian city-states, in which the Renaissance originated and flourished between the thirteenth and sixteenth centuries, fall somewhere between the Athenian polis and Calvin's Geneva on the political spectrum. Most were dominated by wealthy and powerful noble families such as the Medici in Florence, the Visconti and the Sforza in Milan, the Petrucci in Siena, the Doria and Fieschi in Genoa, the Peppoli, the Visconti, and the Bentivoglio in Bologna, and the Dandolo in Venice. Frequently, and often for extended periods of time, nearly all the Italian city-states were rent by factional struggles and class warfare. Their political complexions varied. Some became oligarchies, some patriciates; some, like the Papal States, were theocracies, while others, such as Florence, maintained republican forms but were de facto autocracies.

Context

City-states pre-dated imperial establishments. The early city-states of the ancient Middle East were absorbed by a succession of empires. Centuries later, the Greek city-states were merged into the Macedonian, Roman, and Byzantine empires. The Italian city-states were variously conquered by the papacy, by France, by Spain, and by the Hapsburg rulers of the Holy Roman Empire. The last of the Hanseatic city-states were absorbed by the unification of Germany in 1870, while the Swiss city-states were eventually incorporated into the Swiss Confederation.

Toward the close of the twentieth century, in a world dominated by more than 150 sovereign nation-states, city-states had all but disappeared from the political map. One exception is Singapore, an Asian nation 225 square miles in area that embraces Singapore Island and several smaller islands at the southern end of the Malay Peninsula. Both the city of Singapore and its contiguous areas are governed as a republic. It is one of the busiest, most prosperous, and orderly of the world's polities.

If all but extinct at the close of the twentieth century, city-states nevertheless have left an immense legacy of political experience and political literature behind them. Historically, they proved to be extraordinarily fertile ground for distinguished intellectual and cultural achievement.

Moreover, despite territorial dimensions that were usually modest—seldom more than a few hundred square miles—a number of city-states periodically possessed substantial power, based in most instances on their remarkable economic performances and their citizens' acquisition of extraordinary wealth. Athens, for example, first dominated all of Attica and eventually, through alliances and seapower, nearly all of Greece, along with adjacent areas of the Mediterranean. Similarly, the expansion of the Roman city-state from the few square miles of Latium to all of Italy transformed it into one of the West's greatest powers between the fourth and first centuries B.C.E., even before the Roman Empire became the world's largest during ensuing centuries. Venice, too, in the fourteenth and fifteenth centuries, ranked first among the great sea powers, and was a center of international finance. Venice, along with other Italian city-states, invented banking, double-entry bookkeeping, bills of exchange, letters of credit, and other elements of modern finance, creating Europe's chief financial center from the thirteenth to the sixteenth century.

Bibliography

Hibbert, Christopher. *The House of Medici: Its Rise and Fall*. New York: William Morrow, 1975. Excellent study of a remarkable Florentine family and Florentine life from 1464 to 1753. Contains maps, illustrations, notes, and an extensive bibliography.

Jones, A. H. M. *Athenian Democracy*. Baltimore: The Johns Hopkins University Press, 1986. Covers all aspects of Athenian democracy: its economic base, its social structure and political organization, and the way it actually functioned.

Pallottino, Massimo. *The Etruscans*. Rev. ed. Edited by David Ridgway. Translated by J. Cremona. Bloomington: Indiana University Press, 1975. Readable analysis of Etruscan origins, culture, and city-states, and the city-states' relationship to the Roman city-state.

Rörig, Fritz. *The Medieval Town*. Berkeley: University of California Press, 1967. Covers medieval towns, their origins, economic, social and political development, and their interrelationships.

Scullard, H. H. *The Etruscan Cities and Rome*. London: Thames and Hudson, 1967. Covers Etruscan city-states and the Roman city-state. Not intended for laypeople.
Sealey, Raphael. *A History of the Greek City-States, ca. 700-338 B.C.* Berkeley: University of California Press, 1976. Thorough examination of the subject from 700 to 338 B.C.E. It is the best work of its kind in English.
Starr, Chester G. *The Emergence of Rome as Ruler of the Western World*. Ithaca, N.Y.: Cornell University Press, 1968. Brief scholarly survey from 5000 B.C.E. to 180 C.E. Useful for understanding the development and expansion of the Roman city-state.
Wolin, Sheldon S. *Politics and Vision: Continuity and Innovation in Western Political Thought*. Boston: Little, Brown, 1960. Lucid analysis of continuity and change in Western political thought, in which the political practices and theories developed in city-states played a major role for nearly three millennia.

Clifton K. Yearley

Cross-References

Aristocracy, Oligarchy, and Plutocracy, p. 78; Aristotle's Political Philosophy, p. 83; Democracy, p. 513; Despotism and Tyranny, p. 527; Empires and Empire Building, p. 597; Federations, p. 675; Government Types, p. 785; History of Government, p. 829; Machiavelli's Political Philosophy, p. 1148; The Nation-State, p. 1241; Ochlocracy, p. 1338; Oligarchy, p. 1344; Plato's Political Philosophy, p. 1396; Rousseau's Political Philosophy, p. 1756; Stoic Political Philosophy, p. 1904; Theocracy, p. 1968; Urban Governments, p. 2052.

CIVIC EDUCATION

Field of study: Functions of government

All societies, whether democratic or totalitarian, must convey to their citizens certain values, goals, and objectives in order to sustain themselves. Civic education seeks to gain support for political systems through a variety of means and is an integral part of the process of political socialization.

Principal terms

AGENTS OF SOCIALIZATION: people and institutions that carry out the process of socialization, influencing the individual's attitudes, beliefs, self-image, and behavior

CITIZENSHIP: legal status or relationship that exists between an individual who owes allegiance and a political society that provides protection

CURRICULUM: course of formal study

POLITICAL SOCIALIZATION: process by which a person acquires political knowledge, beliefs, and attitudes

PROPAGANDA (INDOCTRINATION): systematic attempt to convert individuals to a belief system that conceals the flaws of the preferred system and rules out alternative positions

Overview

In democratic political systems, civic education is considered essential if the systems are to survive. In a direct democracy, every voter participates directly and personally in the decision-making process. In a representative democracy, citizens participate indirectly by electing others to represent them. In either system, there is an assumption that the citizens are informed enough, not only to debate the issues, but also to decide on the basis of what is best for themselves and what is best for the society as a whole.

Eighteenth century philosophers such as John Locke believed that humankind is rational enough to participate in governing with few limitations. Locke's belief that the people are capable of governing themselves became a basic principle of American democracy. Thomas Jefferson, who believed that a nation cannot be both ignorant and free, argued that education should help prepare citizens to make informed political choices and instill in citizens a strong sense of democratic values.

British writer Thomas Hobbes and others argued that the only individuals qualified to decide public policy are the wise and benevolent, since people are generally too apathetic or irrational to govern themselves effectively. There is ample evidence to support this view. Voters often choose on the basis of a candidate's appearance, ethnic background, religion, or some other characteristic that defies rationality. It has been proven, however, that education reduces prejudice, creates open minds, and promotes respect for the rights of others.

Citizens in a democracy must ask themselves what they expect from their government and how they can get the government to implement their wishes. These questions require a fundamental background in how the political and legal systems work. Citizens must be able to sort through alternatives, which may be numerous in a complex society. This requires a level of political education that goes beyond facts alone. Schools must educate with the goal of responsible participation as the outcome.

Civic education is part of the overall process of political socialization. Within totalitarian societies, such education might be viewed as indoctrination or propaganda. The goal of totalitarian regimes generally is to maintain a compliant and obedient citizenry. Within democratic societies, civic education is seen in terms of creating knowledgeable citizens committed to their societies by their own free will.

To have an informed citizenry requires socialization in the political world during childhood and continuing throughout adult life. The individual's reaction to politics is rooted in personal experiences. Some individuals will be active in politics, some will be hostile, some will be indifferent. The various agents of socialization—the family, schools, religious organizations, and economic institutions—influence and educate the citizenry. Educational institutions have a central role in this process.

Civic education is a multidimensional concept directed toward instilling fundamental knowledge about the political society, about preparation for participation in both the direct and indirect governance of the society, and, in general, about being a good citizen. The main goal of civic education in the United States is the teaching and learning of the sustaining concepts of the nation, such as liberty, equality, respect for the law, individual rights, and patriotism. Whether civic education should include such issues as morality, the right to dissent, and social responsibility has continued to be controversial.

The major focus of civic education in the United States has always been to foster understanding of the principles set forth in the Constitution. The curriculum generally has included knowledge of and respect for the law. It could be argued that what is taught and the manner in which it is taught could be construed as indoctrination, leading to blind obedience. The instructional emphasis, however, has been toward the benefits of participation by choice, rather than a demand that the citizenry accept the promulgated policy.

A citizen in a democratic society is considered to have certain responsibilities. Government is said to be the product of the will of the people. Citizens are expected to participate by voting directly for legislators or by electing representatives to act in their behalf. All the goals the society hopes to achieve, such as security, clean air, health care, or equal employment opportunities, are only possible if the people support them. In addition, individual goals of economic gain, personal enrichment, and personal freedom are sustained only in a free and open society.

A well-educated and informed citizenry is said to be essential to the success of a democratic society by preparing young people and adults to be active in their government. It has generally been agreed that citizens need not be versed in the technical issues, only that they be able to select competent and qualified individuals who can represent them on such issues.

The civic education curriculum is one source of information needed by a citizen. Children and adults learn how to become good citizens through a variety of educational programs. There is no set national curriculum; each public school system has adopted a program that offers what it believes students will need to know. Most states require that a course in civics be passed as a high school graduation requirement. Some activities, such as the pledge of allegiance to the flag and the singing of the national anthem, are not part of the curriculum, but are still a daily occurrence in many schools. Other aspects of political socialization are part of the curriculum, such as courses in government or civics. Courses that have aspects of civics embedded in them include American history and literature.

In elementary schools, students learn about the events and people who shaped the nation. The Declaration of Independence, the United States Constitution, the presidents of the United States, and the process of how a bill becomes a law are essential topics to be studied. In high school and college, students are encouraged to debate issues. This helps instill a sense that a certain amount of dissent is healthy in a democratic society.

Civic education curricula may include the consideration of ethical issues, moral issues, and value judgments, such as whether the death penalty should be abolished, whether physicians should assist suicides, or whether tax dollars should be spent on weapons of war or on social programs. This new curriculum creates a dilemma for educational institutions: The topics cannot be discussed without alienating some individual or group, or appearing to advocate a certain position. To eliminate such discussions from the curriculum, however, denies the responsibility of the educational system to inform.

Applications

In 1975, the Danforth Foundation and the Institute for Development of Educational Activities embarked on a project to improve civic education. The members represented educators from the elementary school level through universities, elected government officials, governmental staff, students, and social sciences researchers. The findings of this project had implications for the future of civic education.

The report concluded that civic education was lacking in quality and that young people had seriously lost sight of important values. Traditional family values were missing, there was a growing lack of respect for the law, and a general feeling of alienation from the political institutions was evident.

The report also noted a lack of information that previously had been considered basic in the American civic culture. Citizenship education was being replaced with drug education, sex education, and career education. All too often civic courses were assigned to athletic coaches who needed to fill out their contracts.

The schools could not take all the blame or responsibility, the report stated. The home environment had changed as had the role of religious institutions. Television and other media had become an integral part of the total educational environment. The demographic makeup of the schools also had changed. Poor, inner-city children experience a different educational environment than students in more affluent suburbs. Schools also had to deal with multilingual arrangements and attention to cultural diversity in an increasingly multicultural society.

Such events as the Vietnam War, Watergate, and the Iran-Contra affair have made citizens skeptical, even cynical, about their government. The task of civic education is to reestablish a sense of trust and patriotism, but, the report suggests, many educators had stopped trying.

One of the more enduring arguments that surfaced in the report was whether the fundamental concept of democracy in the United States is threatened by a lack of education in politics, and a corresponding lack of participation in politics. Statistics continue to show that young people between the ages of eighteen and twenty-one are the least likely to vote or to participate in politics.

Civic education during the colonial period was not a specific curriculum but was incorporated in spelling, reading, and grammar lessons. Thomas Jefferson was a leading proponent of teaching a specific civic education curriculum, particularly at the university level. It was Jefferson who first raised the issue of teachers indoctrinating students to a particular point of view and of the inclusion of a person's political values in his or her teaching.

Although most of the Framers of the Constitution argued for free public schools, until the mid-1800's most education, and therefore civic education, was private and much of it was ideologically conservative; that is, the emphasis was on national preservation and unity rather than on the development of the individual. By the 1820's, public schools, called common schools, were operating in many communities. In 1821, the first public high school in Boston included a course in civic education.

The conservative values carried through to the mid-nineteenth century. The Civil War split the country, and both sides began to teach their values through civic education. The post-Civil War period moved civic education into a new role, that of instructing the poor, both black and white, and immigrants from Europe, Asia, and Mexico who began to fill the classrooms.

By the beginning of the twentieth century, a new tone began to emerge. The various factions began seeking a measure of the "good life" promised by the United States. More than ever, the schools were given the tasks of instilling a strong sense of loyalty to country and promoting social cohesion. The 1916 Report of the Committee on Social Studies of the Commission on the Reorganization of Secondary Education, sponsored by the National Education Association, marked the point at which social studies was officially recognized by a national body. Much of the report reflected an investigation into the teaching of civics, and the conclusion was that what had gone before had not worked. The committee argued that civic education was more than history and more than a discussion of topics such as the branches of government, lawmaking, or voting and political parties.

The 1916 report recommended the establishment of a civics curriculum that would replace the previous course, called civil government. It called for inclusion of civics at three levels. Beginning in ninth grade, a specific course in civics would be taught, which would emphasize social problems. Courses in history, particularly ancient history, would be reduced at all grade levels. All history courses from the ninth grade on would emphasize the relationship between history and the present, culminating in a twelfth-grade course on problems of democracy, in which issues relating to citizenship would be addressed with a view toward problem solving. The overall concept would be referred to as community civic.

The 1920's through the 1970's were tumultuous years for civic education. In 1934, the American Historical Association (which had been a part of the 1916 commission) published a report suggesting that civic education needed to be more realistic. The report recognized the pluralistic nature of the society and the world where students may confront competing allegiances. Students should be provided with what the commission report referred to as disciplined knowledge in order to make informed choices, but should not be forced to adopt a particular orientation. Generally, the commission's recommendations were seen as espousing an unstructured curriculum. Educators attempted to adopt the recommendations, but the state of civic education became confused in the process.

World War II was a major event that caused another reexamination of civic education. The decidedly liberal emphasis of the 1900's came to an abrupt end. Patriotism and unity were to be emphasized once again. The Depression period, however, found many people in a condition they never expected: poor, unemployed, even starving, and turning toward the government for help.

The concerns of the post-Depression period were reflected in the curriculum. Educators began to talk about social and economic inequality, wasted national resources, and a rising crime rate. Citizenship was being redefined. To the basics of equality, liberty, and a respect and adherence to the law, were added family, a sense of community, and an understanding of the United States' role in international affairs.

The Cold War, the Civil Rights movement of the 1950's through the 1970's, and the Vietnam War complicated civic education. The schools had to encourage simultaneously the development of the individual with the need to maintain unity. Support for the system had to be balanced against the right to dissent.

Context

Based upon recommendations by various educational research organizations, American curricula now include emphasis on how the system works in reality and on the specific skills needed to participate in the civic environment. Students are encouraged to become aware of the social and political world, and the interdependence of local, state, national, and international communities. Schools regularly promote school elections for student government, organize mock national presidential elections, or promote programs in which students replace an elected official for a day. Some schools work with social services agencies to provide students with hands-on experience in program administration.

Civic education for adults is also provided, particularly for the assimilation of immigrants. Thousands of immigrants work during the day and attend classes in the evenings or on weekends in order to obtain citizenship. Adult civic education plays a major role in the development of an informed citizenry.

Research on civic education not only has provided information about the subject, but also has contributed to the development of curriculum. Most of the research focuses on children. Findings of research projects demonstrate that the basic political and civic orientations are established by twelve or thirteen years of age. Schools were found to be significant socializing agents, but parents, the mass media, church, and peers also were influential factors. Research supports the idea that the direct teaching of civic attitudes and values does not occur independently from other sources. The most favorable results in teaching civic attitudes were achieved through mutually supportive experiences in the home and other sources outside the school.

Research has found that children become socialized to support positively the system early in childhood, but that the child's image must harmonize with the adults with whom they come in contact. The central political figure in the child's political life is the president of the United States. Gradually, other more complex images are incorporated. The child begins to recognize what is inside and what is outside the realm of government.

Bibliography

Boggs, David L. *Adult Civic Education*. Springfield, Ill.: Charles C Thomas, 1991. Contains a history of adult civic education; also reflects on civic education for both adults and children in a democratic society.

Butts, Freeman R. "The Revival of Civic Learning." In *Voices of Social Education, 1937-1987*. Edited by Daniel Roselle. New York: Macmillan, 1987. Summarizes changes in civic education and offers suggestions on improvement.

Easton, David, and Jack Dennis. *Children in the Political System: Origins of Political Legitimacy*. New York: McGraw-Hill, 1969. Significant and often-cited study on the political socialization of children.

Ichilov, Orit. *Political Socialization, Citizenship Education, and Democracy*. New York: Teachers College Press, 1990. Essays on various topics in the research of citizenship in a democratic society. The chapter on political socialization research is particularly useful.

Jenness, David. *Making Sense of Social Studies*. New York: Macmillan, 1990. Charts the development of social studies, including civic education, dating back to the colonial period. Also discusses issues surrounding citizenship education and political education.

National Task Force on Citizenship Education. *Education for Responsible Citizenship: The Report of the National Task Force on Citizenship Education*. New York: McGraw-Hill, 1977. Collection of reports covering the historical, analytic, and prescriptive aspects of citizenship education.

William J. Mark

Cross-References

Citizenship in World Governments, p. 254; Citizenship Rights and Responsibilities, p. 260; Communications Management, p. 370; Democracy, p. 513; Education Management, p. 565; Immigrants and Politics, p. 861; Mill's Political Philosophy, p. 1204; Naturalization, p. 1275; Patriotism, p. 1384; Political Participation, p. 1479; Propaganda, p. 1615.

CIVIL DISOBEDIENCE

Field of study: Civil rights and liberties

Civil disobedience is a form of political activism characterized by intentional violation of the law. Nonviolent disruptive actions, usually based on moral principles, are used to emphasize presumptive injustices.

Principal terms

CIVIL DISOBEDIENCE: intentional disobedience to governmental authority, usually for the sake of moral principle

NONVIOLENT DIRECT ACTION: method of protest in which the protagonist initiates conflict nonviolently by doing or refusing to do certain things

PACIFISM: refusal to settle disputes with violence, usually based on moral or religious grounds; often used interchangeably with passive resistance and nonviolent resistance

PASSIVE RESISTANCE: nonviolent resistance, usually characterized by acts of noncooperation by individuals or groups despite physical threat or pressure

Overview

Civil disobedience is a concept that encompasses a wide range of interpretations. The term frequently is used interchangeably with similar concepts, such as nonviolent resistance, nonviolent direct action, passive resistance, and pacifism, in discussions of structured opposition to laws or governmental policies that are perceived to be unjust or immoral. The fundamental tenet of civil disobedience is the purposeful, nonviolent opposition to laws or policies enacted by the state. In the United States, civil disobedience is associated with the intentional disregard for laws or policies enacted by the federal government, individual states, or local municipalities that individuals, groups, or specific populations find objectionable on moral or ethical grounds. Opposition to such laws is demonstrated in a variety of ways—from mainly verbal antagonism to outright disobedience. Some argue that civil disobedience must involve the willful resistance to laws, statutes, or social norms that are perceived to violate the ethical or moral ideals of certain segments of society. Others perceive civil disobedience to be the right of the individual or group to oppose the authority of the state when the state infringes upon civil liberties. Still others view civil disobedience and other forms of resistance merely as unlawful activity.

By most definitions, civil disobedience fulfills five specific conditions: the action taken by the protagonist is clearly illegal; it is done openly, rather than clandestinely; it is intended to call attention to a law, policy, or social condition; its intent is to improve the condition or change the law or policy; and the protagonist is willing to suffer the consequences for the act of defiance. Much attention has been given to the last condition. For some, civil disobedience requires the protagonist's willingness to endure whatever sanctions are forthcoming from the state for violating the law; any attempt on the part of the protagonist to avoid sanctions changes the violation from civil disobedience to merely breaking the law. Many people believe that if individuals or groups are found guilty of violating the law, they should suffer the consequence, regardless of their belief that the law is unfair. These people argue that illegal acts perpetrated during student rebellions, civil rights demonstrations, war protests, or antiabortion activities should culminate in the protagonists being prosecuted despite their claims that the law they broke or social policy they were protesting was unjust.

In some circumstances, the protagonist has no intention of avoiding the penalty for disobedience; in such instances, civil disobedience may be in consonance with nonviolent resistance and nonviolent direct action. In such cases, the goal may be to raise the level of consciousness regarding what the protagonist believes to be an immoral or unethical law. In other cases, the protagonist's intention is to fight the penalties for disobeying the law in the court system, with the aim of tying up the courts and judicial system, further dramatizing the initial concern. This strategy may be accompanied by the protagonist's insisting on a trial by jury, entailing lengthy litigation.

Civil disobedience also has been closely tied to the idea of nonviolence. While it has not been exclusively identified with nonviolent resistance, it has come to be seen as a nonviolent mode of protest. Relatively few would argue that social reform is undesirable; many citizens probably believe that reform would be beneficial in areas such as social welfare, health care, or the way political campaigns are financed. Many would insist, however, that reforms be pursued without violating the law, and particularly without the use of violence.

Proponents of the view that citizens have the right to disobey unjust laws or policies argue that it is good to disobey any law that encroaches upon human rights, particularly if, in the public's mind, it is always to be obeyed despite its unhealthy impact upon the growth of democracy. In such instances, civil disobedience is the organized expression of opposition to an existing evil (the law); civil disobedience did not create the evil, but directs resistance in a rationalized manner. Accordingly, civil disobedience may provide an organized outlet for opposition that is more acceptable than outright rebellion or some other form of unrestrained resistance.

Applications

Civil disobedience is often used in issues involving the perception of what is just and moral. The issue of abortion, for example, has generated many debates over civil liberties and morality. Opposition to abortion has largely been predicated on certain moral views, for example: it is immoral to take any life; it is especially wrong to take the life of an unborn, defenseless human; abortion is cruel and painful; and the mother eventually will regret her decision to take her unborn child's life. This has prompted several forms of civil disobedience, and sometimes outright lawlessness, including passing out literature beyond boundaries established by the courts; picketing hospitals and clinics that perform abortions; blocking entrances to abortion clinics; harassing or attacking potential clients; destroying abortion clinics; and physically assaulting or killing medical personnel. The abortion controversy has often gone beyond the nonviolent posture that many believe to be an integral component of civil disobedience. There are many other issues where nonviolent civil disobedience has had a tremendous impact on society. The magnitude and consistency of civil disobedience sometimes have succeeded in changing laws that even the Supreme Court had at one time maintained were constitutional. It could be argued that without sustained civil disobedience, many of the unjust laws that existed in the South before the Civil Rights movement might not have been changed.

During the legal segregation in the United States, from 1896 following the U.S. Supreme Court's *Plessy v. Ferguson* decision to *Brown v. Board of Education* in 1954, segregationists in many states had a legal right to discriminate against minorities. Viewed from a historical perspective, discrimination based on race was initially a moral issue because the "separate but equal" conclusion reached by the Supreme Court in *Plessy v. Ferguson* legally permitted it. It was later changed to a legal issue, following the reversal of that doctrine in *Brown v. Board of Education*. Consequently, the segregationist could no longer legally discriminate. The shift from segregation as a moral issue to one embroiled in legality was prompted in large part by civil disobedience, especially the sit-ins, jail-ins, and demonstrations subsequent to the *Brown* decision. While many would argue that laws that permit differential treatment based solely on race clearly should be illegal, for at least fifty-eight years segregation—along with all of its pernicious effects—was the law in much of the country.

Civil disobedience may involve the assertion of certain basic constitutional rights. For example, asserting the right to equal protection of the law may require denying the legitimacy of another law to some degree. For example, if some members of society are permitted to ride in the front of a bus, to deny the same right to others for some arbitrary reason, such as race—which was legal in some parts of the South into the 1960's—was a denial of the equal protection of the law. Consequently, denying the legitimacy of the law through civil disobedience was actually the exercise of a constitutional liberty.

Although the Montgomery, Alabama, bus boycott of 1955, in which Martin Luther King, Jr., first gained national prominence, is considered the catalyst for the Civil Rights movement, the initial act of civil disobedience was carried out by Rosa Parks when she disobeyed a local law by refusing to give up her bus seat to a white man when ordered by the driver. The subsequent boycott was not an act of civil disobedience, but an organized effort to force the white power structure in Montgomery to desegregate the local transit system. Although the boycott challenged a law, it fell within the limits of the law.

The student sit-ins of the 1960's, on the other hand, utilized civil disobedience to confront racial discrimination in the South. Three African American students from North Carolina Agricultural and Technical College in Greensboro, North Carolina, set in motion what is considered the modern "sit-in." On February 1, 1960, they quietly seated themselves at an F. W. Woolworth's lunch counter with the intent to draw attention to the practice of refusing to serve African Americans seated in public restaurants. Local custom dictated that African Americans must remain standing if they wished to be served. The three students were asked to leave because of their actions. When they refused to obey, they were summarily arrested. The sit-ins spread to stores that had similar segregation policies. By February 16, 1960, the sit-ins had spread to fifteen cities in five Southern states. Sit-ins slowly moved beyond Southern cities. At first they were aimed at affiliates of F. W. Woolworth and S. H. Kress, but soon targeted other variety stores.

The sit-ins began as a spontaneous act by three students, but by September, 1960, they involved nearly seventy thousand students, almost thirty-six hundred of whom were arrested at one time or another. Some sit-in demonstrators refused to post bail. This not only drew attention to the issue of racial discrimination, but caused financial and judicial problems for local municipalities. An unmistakable message was being sent by young civil rights activists: Civil disobedience would become a powerful tactic in the campaign against unjust laws based on race.

Civil disobedience in the form of sit-ins, demonstrations, and other modes of nonviolent direct action drew attention throughout the United States during the 1960's. As a result, the inequities of many Southern practices came under scrutiny by many white citizens who had been oblivious to such practices. Drawing attention to per-ceived injustices has been a major goal behind many acts of civil disobedience.

Context

Civil disobedience has been an invaluable tool for oppressed groups around the world. In most instances, the oppressed group or marginalized population did not have the political power to bring about social change. Violence or physical confrontation would merely legitimize the existing power structure's use of force to eliminate any opposition to the status quo. Civil disobedience through nonviolent direct action— either disobeying unjust laws, refusing to carry out some perceived unjust function, or actual protest over some policy or law—has in many instances forced the power structure to use alternative methods for dealing with the perceived threat. Civil disobedience draws attention not only to the action itself, but also to the reason for disobedience. It is conceivable that the continued existence of a policy or law perceived as unjust or immoral could have been the result of a lack of awareness or understanding regarding its impact on the powerless or oppressed group.

Civil disobedience has a long and storied history in the development of American society. Credit for the birth of civil disobedience in the United States is often given to Henry David Thoreau, the nineteenth century American writer who wrote the essay "Civil Disobedience" after spending a night in jail in 1846 for refusing to pay the Massachusetts poll tax. Nevertheless, one of the best examples can be illustrated by the struggles of Mohandas Gandhi against the British governments in South Africa and India.

Gandhi studied Western philosophy and law in England, where he became familiar with Thoreau's views that later became the foundation on which he built his nonviolent strategies. From 1893 to 1914, Gandhi fought against oppressive legislation and the discriminatory treatment of Indians in South Africa. During this period he developed his moral doctrine of Satyagraha and the nonviolent techniques that eventually were so successful in India. He was instrumental in getting the Indians' Relief Bill passed, which improved the political, social, and economic conditions of Indians in South Africa.

Following World War I, Gandhi returned to India where he began the struggle of seeking independence from Great Britain. He used civil disobedience as a nonviolent political tactic to challenge the legitimacy of the British sovereignty over India. He led strikes, boycotts, and nonviolent direct action strategies against the British. Gandhi encouraged Indians to discard their foreign clothing and to wear only garments made of Indian fabric. He was jailed on many occasions because of his actions. He always refused to eat when jailed, and because of his status, forced the British to capitulate to many of his demands; more important, he forced them to respond to Indian resistance with strategies other than violence. India was successful in winning its independence in 1947. Much of the credit is given to Gandhi and his insistence on nonviolent civil disobedience.

Civil disobedience and other forms of nonviolent resistance have proved to be effective tools for effecting social change. This is particularly critical when the protagonists are politically powerless and seek to bring about profound and systemic change. Regardless of the social arrangement in a society, whether the situation involves the suppression of a numerical minority, or a numerical majority, or marginalizing an ethnic or religious population, any attempt to effect change through force or physical violence typically results in the oppressed group being further oppressed. Civil disobedience allows the protagonist to challenge unjust laws or social conditions without experiencing the full might of the state. Public opinion serves to restrain the state from using undue physical force to terminate nonviolent opposition.

Bibliography

King, Martin Luther, Jr. "Pilgrimage to Nonviolence." In *Nonviolence in America: A Documentary History*, edited by Staughton Lynd. Indianapolis: Bobbs-Merrill, 1966. Compilation of historical figures in American history who have advocated or used civil disobedience or other forms of nonviolent resistance to protest a wide range of social and political issues.

Oppenheimer, Martin, and George Lakey. *A Manual for Direct Action*. Chicago: Quadrangle Books, 1965. Manual detailing how to organize and carry out specific strategies, and a survey of the history of student nonviolent resistance activities.

Pelton, Leroy H. "Noncooperation." In *The Psychology of Nonviolence*. New York: Pergamon Press, 1974. Explores the types of noncooperation that individuals and groups can utilize, and the moral responsibility that individuals have for the administration of justice.

Sharp, Gene. *The Politics of Nonviolent Action*. Boston: Porter Sargent, 1973. Penetrating analysis of the types of nonviolent resistance and the methods that have been used to bring about social and political change around the world.

Smith, Michael P., and Kenneth L. Deutsch, eds. *Political Obligation and Civil Disobedience: Readings.* New York: Thomas Y. Crowell, 1972. Excellent collection of philosophical positions and personal reflections of historical figures who used civil disobedience in the struggle for a particular cause. Includes Thoreau's essay on civil disobedience.

Stiehm, Judith. "Social Change and Nonviolent Power." In *Nonviolent Power: Active and Passive Resistance in America.* Lexington, Mass.: D. C. Heath, 1972. Explores the rationale for, problems with, criticisms of, and justification for nonviolent resistance.

Zinn, Howard. *Disobedience and Democracy: Nine Fallacies on Law and Order.* New York: Random House, 1968. Discusses some of the misconceptions about civil disobedience, and the analyses that have led to much of the confusion.

_____. *SNCC: The New Abolitionists.* Boston: Beacon Press, 1964. Insightful look at one of the most influential and controversial organizations of the Civil Rights movement era, the Student Nonviolent Coordinating Committee. Details its growth from a disorganized group of committed youths to one of the most powerful civil rights organizations of the 1960's.

Zwiebach, Burton. *Civility and Disobedience.* Cambridge, England: Cambridge University Press, 1975. Scholarly, but readable treatment of civility and disobedience. Raises a fundamental question about whether the individual has the right to disobey certain laws.

Charles C. Jackson

Cross-References

Activist Politics, p. 7; Augustine's Political Philosophy, p. 121; Civil Liberties Protection, p. 291; Civil Rights and Liberties, p. 298; Civil Unrest and Rioting, p. 317; Individual Versus State Rights, p. 910; Legitimacy, p. 1105; Political Violence, p. 1539; Protest Movements, p. 1621; Race and Ethnicity, p. 1654; Reproductive Politics, p. 1692.

CIVIL LIBERTIES PROTECTION

Field of study: Civil rights and liberties

Civil liberties are personal freedoms possessed by individuals, such as freedom of speech, protections against arbitrary criminal punishments, and opportunities to own and sell property. The existence, definition, and protection of these freedoms vary among countries, depending on each nation's societal values and the structure of its government.

Principal terms
 CONSTITUTION: fundamental document that defines the structure and
  powers of government; it may include limitations on governmental
  powers, such as descriptions of individuals' civil rights and liberties
 DEMOCRACY: form of government in which citizens can protect their
  own freedom by electing new officials if the government infringes
  on civil liberties
 SEPARATION OF POWERS: structural element in some governing systems
  that gives the judicial branch sufficient power to protect civil
  liberties from encroachment by the other branches of government
 TOLERANCE OF DISSENT: distinguishing feature of societies and
  governing systems that provide protection for free speech and other
  civil liberties

Overview

Civil liberties are the personal freedoms possessed by members of a state that protect them from having their words and actions controlled by their government. The ability of people to speak freely and criticize their own governments depends on the existence of laws and government structures that will protect the exercise of such freedoms. The same is also true of people's abilities to practice freely their religious beliefs. Similarly, freedom from arbitrary criminal prosecution and from government control over people's property and economic decisions depends on the existence of mechanisms to prevent governments from having complete control over individuals. Although citizens of the United States, Canada, and other Western democracies take for granted their entitlement to protected civil liberties, the exercise of individual freedoms depends on two critical factors. First, the historical traditions and political values of a society must favor individualism and the existence of protected liberties. Second, the governing system of a society must contain mechanisms that limit the power of government to interfere in individuals' lives.

Not all societies favor individualism and the existence of protected liberties. In many traditional societies, for example, individual residents of a town or other geographic area were obligated to obey kings, chiefs, religious leaders, or other authority figures. Such leaders were often presumed to possess divine authority to control the lives of their subjects and to determine what rules were best for the community or nation. In such contexts, individuals are expected to serve their leaders' visions of society. Instead of being able to think and speak freely, people in such societies risk punishment if they criticize their leaders or their leaders' visions. Ownership of property and decisions about matters such as appropriate agricultural activities and commercial transactions are determined by the leaders' rules. Such rules may vest leaders with complete power or ownership rights over the means of economic production. In addition, crimes and punishments may be defined by the leaders or by religious or other historical traditions. These traditions typically do not include protections for persons accused of crimes against arbitrary prosecutions or excessive punishments.

Although citizens of modern democracies may view the above conditions as describing feudal societies, many modern countries embody aspects of these characteristics. In countries in which a single religion is dominant, for example, the people's shared beliefs may place significant authority in the hands of religious leaders who may or may not also control the country's civil government. Religiously based societal values may include the belief that certain behaviors merit punishment by the government. In some societies, the definition of personal freedoms may reflect societal values about the respective roles of men and women in society, or about the entitlement of certain ethnic or social class groups. For example, men often have more freedom than women in some societies. Whether or not they are based on religion, widely shared beliefs in a society can define which civil liberties, if any, are expected to exist and remain free from interference by authorities.

Alternatively, a dominant political ideology that is accepted by a majority of people within a society can also shape expectations about civil liberties. In communist countries, for example, people are taught to believe that they should act for the benefit of the entire society. Thus many people in such societies may genuinely accept government control over private property and the imposition of punishment upon individuals who criticize the government.

By contrast, citizens of the United States, Canada, and other Western democracies are taught to value individualism. Individualism, personal autonomy, and freedom to make decisions are at the heart of the political and economic systems in such countries. In the United States, these beliefs were shaped by a vision of natural law articulated by philosophers whose works influenced the country's Founders. Under their conception of natural law, every human being automatically possesses certain freedoms. Thomas Jefferson enunciated this principle in the Declaration of Independence, which states "We hold these truths to be self-evident, that all men are created equal, that they are endowed by their Creator with certain unalienable rights, that among these are Life, Liberty, and the pursuit of Happiness." This characterization of individual freedoms differs greatly from that which dominates communist countries and some religiously dominated societies. Thus people in Western democracies and many other countries develop shared values and high expectations about civil liberties and they seek to design governmental mechanisms to protect individual freedoms.

Strong values favoring individual liberty are not sufficient by themselves. There must also be mechanisms to protect that liberty. A country may make formal statements about the freedoms that its citizens possess, but if there is no mechanism that actually protects those freedoms, they remain merely words on paper. Countries that seek to define and protect civil liberties confront a difficult paradox: They want to protect individual freedoms from infringement by government, yet government itself is the only entity with sufficient power and authority to protect those freedoms. For example, citizens of a country may desire freedom of speech, rights for accused defendants, and freedom to own and sell property. If a dictator, however, controls their government and uses military force to restrict civil liberties, how will the people's values and expectations be fulfilled? Tolerance of dissent is a key attribute that indicates whether a society's government will accept and support civil liberties. Dictatorial governments based on military power rarely permit opposing viewpoints to be expressed. They limit the exercise of personal liberty by jailing political opponents, usually without the benefit of fair and open trials.

The negative example of dictatorial military governments demonstrates that the constitutional design and operation of a governing system is an essential element for the existence and protection of civil liberties. Countries can most readily protect civil liberties through a constitutional democracy. Constitutions are fundamental documents that are written to define a government's structure and powers. They can also describe the civil liberties protections to which citizens are entitled. A constitution can both define civil liberties and authorize the governmental powers to limit the opportunities for government to infringe upon the freedoms enjoyed by the citizens. While a constitutional government provides this opportunity for coordination, democracy provides the means to enforce compliance with the constitution. For example, if a democratically elected government violates its fundamental document by limiting freedom of speech that is guaranteed in its constitution, its citizens can vote in new leaders who will be more responsive to their values.

While the existence of a constitutional democracy creates favorable conditions for the protection of civil liberties, it does not automatically ensure that individual freedoms will be protected. The experiences of the United States, Canada, and other Western democracies show that significant problems can exist in ensuring the protection of civil liberties for individuals whose views and behavior differ from those of a majority of citizens. Members of minority groups—whether those groups are religious, political, ethnic, or racial—may find it more difficult than other people to speak freely, practice their religions, or receive fair trials if a government directs it policies against them. Because a majority of citizens may support the government's actions which discriminate against the civil liberties of selected groups, the mechanisms of democracy and citizen voting will not necessarily bring the government back into line with its constitution's principles. For example, African Americans in the United States historically did not receive fair treatment by police and prosecutors, yet the white majority in many states supported this denial of civil liberties.

An additional governmental mechanism that can help to protect civil liberties is separation of powers. If the judicial branch of government is given the authority to overrule actions taken by the executive and legislative branches, then one independent governmental voice may exist to make sure that the other components of government do not unlawfully deprive people of their freedom.

Many scholars who compare governments around the world believe that there is a relationship between protection of civil liberties and the adoption of democratic governing structures and free enterprise economic systems. Many people believe that personal freedom can be better appreciated and protected when individualism, including the ability to express political dissent and to own property, is incorporated into values throughout a society.

Applications

The exercise of government functions for the protection of civil liberties can be illustrated by comparing several countries. The government of Iran, for example, fell under the control of religious leaders after the revolution of 1979. Although Iran's religion-dominated government did not abolish all civil liberties, the dominant values of its leaders and their many followers limited the definitions of personal freedoms. For example, their values precluded expressing opinions contrary to the dominant religious principles and they denied protections for accused persons in the revolutionary courts, which conducted summary trials and imposed punishments. In addition, under religious rules for proper conduct, there were substantial differences between the degree of personal freedoms enjoyed by men and women. The people in this society did not define and protect civil liberties in the same manner as people in most constitutional democracies.

Comparison of the constitutions of the United States and the former Union of Soviet Socialist Republics shows that a written constitution by itself does not guarantee protection of civil liberties. Basic civil liberties protections for freedom of speech and free exercise of religion were written into both constitutions. Opponents of the Communist Party that governed the Soviet Union, however, were frequently imprisoned for criticizing the government, and the government sought to prevent Jews, Christians, Muslims, and others from freely practicing their religious beliefs. The Soviet Constitution contained words that guaranteed civil liberties, but there was no governmental mechanism to enforce these guarantees. Governmental power was consolidated into the hands of the leaders of the dominant political party and no other executive, legislative, or judicial officials could overrule their decisions. Civil liberties existed only as words on paper and the government did not fulfill its function of upholding all the provisions of its own constitution.

By contrast, under the U.S. Constitution, federal judges are given life tenure and the power to review actions by other branches of government. The justices on the U.S. Supreme Court have used their protected status and genuine power to ensure that Americans enjoy equal opportunities to speak freely, practice their religions, control private property, and receive fair trials without undue interference from government. Historically, the judicial branch did not always protect free speech for communists, ensure fair trials for members of racial minority groups, or protect certain other freedoms; however, the Supreme Court began regularly to prevent government infringement of various civil liberties during the 1950's. For example, the Court clashed with the viewpoints held by a majority of Americans in declaring that political radicals could burn American flags as a means of expressing their political beliefs (*Texas v. Johnson*, 1989). Because the justices possessed actual power and secure tenure, they could act to protect the freedom of an unpopular political minority in the face of opposition from the other branches of government and even a majority of citizens.

In other constitutional democracies in which the judicial branch is less powerful, judicial decisions adverse to the government may help protect civil liberties by mobilizing opposition to the government in the legislature and among the voters, rather than by overruling a government action by its own force. The House of Lords in Great Britain, for example, has limited direct authority to counteract actions by the government, but its decisions can publicize improper actions and thereby mobilize democratic political opposition on behalf of protecting civil liberties.

Context

Governmental protection of civil liberties is regarded as an important priority by citizens and governments in the constitutional democracies of Western Europe, North America, and elsewhere. Because many of these countries are the dominant economic and military powers of the world, they can assert their desires to protect civil liberties when they interact with other countries. As dominant actors in the United Nations, these countries can have their conceptions of civil liberties and human rights placed in declarations made by the United Nations, the world's largest forum for international interaction and discussion. U.S. declarations often advocate freedom of speech and press, religious liberties, and protections for those accused of crimes. The democratic countries can also make their foreign aid and trade activities contingent on other governments' protection of civil liberties. This pressure is frequently focused specifically on civil liberties issues; however, it carries with it the suggestion that civil liberties could be better protected through the adoption of democratic governing structures and free enterprise economic systems. The United States, for example, regularly pressures countries to permit freedom of the press and to stop the use of child and prison labor under conditions that are akin to slavery. Although the powerful countries may reduce foreign aid or impose limited trade sanctions against countries that violate their citizens' liberties, there is generally a reluctance to follow through on threats to end all contacts with repressive governments.

Although the values of these powerful democracies have made the protection of civil liberties an issue of international scope, these countries are selective in applying pressure to advance this goal. Countries that have strategic military importance or economic importance, such as oil-producing states, can often maintain beneficial interactions with Western democracies whether or not they share the values and governmental structures that foster protection of individual freedoms. Much to the disappointment of political pressure groups, such as Amnesty International, which advocate the expansion of civil liberties protections throughout the world, governmental commitments to civil liberties are rarely top priorities, even among the constitutional democracies that encourage other countries to follow their example.

Bibliography

Andrain, Charles F. *Foundations of Comparative Politics: A Policy Perspective.* Monterey, Calif.: Brooks/Cole, 1983. Compares political systems around the world, analyzing the political values relevant to civil liberties that characterize various systems.

Curtis, Michael. *The Great Political Theories.* New York: Avon, 1961. Collection of excerpts from famous philosophical works concerning government and individual freedom. Of special interest are the excerpts from John Locke's writings, which had a strong influence on the development of concepts of individual liberty in Western constitutional democracies.

Duchacek, Ivo D. *Rights and Liberties in the World Today: Constitutional Promise and Reality.* Santa Barbara, Calif.: ABC-Clio, 1973. Comparative analyses of the civil liberties protections contained in various national constitutions.

McColm, R. Bruce. *Freedom in the World: Political Rights and Civil Liberties.* New York: Freedom House, 1978-. Annual volume that compares how civil liberties are protected in every country of the world. Each volume also provides an overview of conditions throughout the world as a whole and a review of the previous year's developments.

Mill, John Stuart. *On Liberty.* Reprint. New York: Appleton-Century-Crofts, 1947. First published in 1859, this classic philosophical work helped to shape the views of political leaders in Great Britain, the United States, and elsewhere who advocated broad liberty of thought and action for individuals.

Nagle, John D. *Introduction to Comparative Politics: Political System Performance in Three Worlds.* Chicago: Nelson-Hall, 1985. Analysis of democracy, liberty, and economic development in political systems throughout the world, with greater attention to non-Western countries than is usually found in books on comparative politics and government.

Patel, Satyavrata. *World Constitutional Law and Practice: Major Constitutions and Governments.* Delhi: Vikas, 1970. Basic, readable comparison of the constitutional provisions in the governments of thirteen countries, with particular attention to civil liberties issues.

Christopher E. Smith

Cross-References

The Bill of Rights, p. 134; Civil Disobedience, p. 285; Civil Rights and Liberties, p. 298; Civil Rights Protection, p. 304; Comparative Government, p. 384; The Constitution of the United States, p. 425; Constitutional Governments, p. 432; Constitutional Law in the United States, p. 439; Courts: U.S. Federal, p. 471; Human Rights and International Politics, p. 848; Individual Versus State Rights, p. 910; Liberalism, p. 1118; Locke's Political Philosophy, p. 1142; Mill's Political Philosophy, p. 1204; Political Pragmatism, p. 1519; The Supreme Court: Organization and Purpose, p. 1929; The Supreme Court: Role in Government and Law, p. 1935; Totalitarianism, p. 1987.

CIVIL RIGHTS AND LIBERTIES

Field of study: Civil rights and liberties

Civil rights and civil liberties are closely related concepts pertaining to the individual rights that citizens are entitled to enjoy under law. The concept of civil liberties pertains to individual behaviors, such as free expression. The concept of civil rights pertains to equal treatment of groups or categories of citizens.

Principal terms

AFFIRMATIVE ACTION: description of a program designed to redress the negative effects of past discrimination by giving special consideration to persons representing groups traditionally victimized

BILL OF RIGHTS: first ten amendments to the U.S. Constitution, which list the basic liberties that the federal government cannot abridge; these include freedom of expression, property rights, and the rights of citizens accused of crimes

CIVIL DISOBEDIENCE: deliberate violation of a law that one finds reprehensible for the purpose of challenging its constitutionality—a process widely used in the Civil Rights movement

DUE PROCESS OF LAW: principle articulated in the Fifth and Fourteenth amendments of the U.S. Constitution declaring that government cannot infringe upon individual liberties or deprive citizens of "life, liberty, and property" without following carefully applied procedures

EQUAL PROTECTION CLAUSE: principle articulated in the Fourteenth Amendment to the U.S. Constitution declaring that individual state governments must grant the same civil rights to citizens that are protected by the federal Constitution

EXCLUSIONARY RULE: concept established by the Supreme Court that prevents evidence obtained in violation of a citizen's civil liberties from being introduced in a court of law

FREEDOM OF EXPRESSION: right of citizens to speak or write what they wish, and to assemble to make their ideas known, without interference from government

JIM CROW LAWS: laws mandating or supporting the physical segregation of African Americans from European Americans; they were particularly characteristic of Southern states

RIGHTS OF THE ACCUSED: based on the idea that citizens are innocent of crimes until they are convicted, these rights guarantee procedures that will protect the accused

Overview

The rights that individuals have as citizens in a nation are often hard to define.

Indeed, one of the most difficult arrangements that governments have is to balance the need for authority with the rights of individuals to be free from undue government interference. Constitutional governments, such as that of the United States, have as a central purpose the defining of the limits of governmental power. It is therefore no surprise that the most controversial amendments to the Constitution pertain to civil rights and liberties.

The Framers of the U.S. Constitution were concerned primarily with outlining the duties of government—separating powers among the three branches of government and dividing powers between national and state governments. As the finished Constitution was being ratified, however, another set of issues came forward. How would average citizens be protected from the intrusive power of the newly created strong government? The answer seemed to lie in attaching amendments to the Constitution that would specifically describe the limits of government with regard to the freedom of religion, the freedom of other forms of expression, the property rights of citizens, and the rights of individuals who have been accused of crimes. Because of the deficiencies of the new Constitution in defining such limitations on government, leaders in several states would ratify the document only if it contained a "bill of rights." When Congress first met following the ratification of the Constitution, the issue of writing a bill of rights arose almost immediately, and the first ten amendments to the Constitution were soon adopted.

These amendments, known as the Bill of Rights, became the defining limitations on federal government power. The Supreme Court has come to regard these limitations as so essential to the nation that almost the entire first ten amendments have been incorporated to apply to state and local governments, as well as the national government. These amendments define civil liberties in the United States; they explicitly limit the government's power to ban freedom of religion and of political expression. They also list the rights of citizens who have been accused of criminal behavior. Finally, they assure citizens that they cannot be deprived of life, liberty, or property without the due process of law.

The first ten amendments did not solve all the problems of citizens in the United States with respect to civility, and in fact the original document avoided confronting a primary social problem that differentiated citizens from one another—the institution of slavery. It was not until the Civil War that the nation found itself unable to compromise on the issue of civil rights and confronted the issue head-on. Three constitutional amendments—the Thirteenth, Fourteenth, and Fifteenth—were designed to extend to all citizens in the nation the same civil rights. Collectively, these amendments abolished slavery, provided for the equal protection of the laws, and removed race and former servitude as impediments to the right to vote. As is the case with all laws, they are only as important as the people who enforce them believe them to be, and important elements of the Civil War amendments were limited in their impact from the end of the Reconstruction era following the Civil War until the 1950's, when the Supreme Court began to interpret them in ways that were meant to put teeth into the meaning of the amendments. Congress also became interested in using legislation to fill out the meaning of civil rights and passed three landmark laws in 1957, 1964, and 1965 designed to make civil rights a reality. It is fair to say that the primary impetus for the passage of legislation was the activity of the Civil Rights movement, led by Martin Luther King, Jr., and others who conducted marches and engaged in acts of civil disobedience to bring the issue of civil rights to the attention of the general public and to make the public react to the obvious discrimination that African Americans were suffering.

Substantively, civil liberties and civil rights encompass a few core concepts. The U.S. Bill of Rights defines civil liberties that fall into the following categories: freedom of religion, freedom of expression, rights of persons accused of crimes, and, arguably, the right of privacy. Such rights have specific technical definitions and are not absolute, but they follow some general guidelines. There are two aspects to the freedom of religion in the United States: freedom to practice the religion of one's choice (or no religion at all) and freedom from government establishment of any religion. Freedom of expression includes the right of citizens to say what they want and to publish what they want and to assemble to seek government action. Although the freedom of expression is not an absolute one, it is often seen as the most essential one to democracy. Persons accused of crimes are entitled to certain specific protections provided in the Bill of Rights, including being free from searches and seizures by government unless the police can show good reason (known as probable cause) and not having to testify against themselves. Evidence that is collected through violations of these rights is subject to the exclusionary rule, which prevents tainted evidence from being introduced in court. Persons accused of serious crimes also have the right to be represented by lawyers and to have trials by jury. Finally, once convicted of a crime, persons cannot be subjected to "cruel and unusual punishment." A final liberty that has been inferred by the Supreme Court from other rights in the Bill of Rights is privacy, which limits the right of government to regulate private behavior, including the rights of women to obtain birth control or to have an abortion. The general rules listed here have been interpreted many times by the U.S. Supreme Court, whose decisions help to give technical applications of the general principles.

Civil rights have been defined in the United States through actions of each of the three branches of government. The judicial branch has, for example, interpreted the Fourteenth Amendment to require that "the equal protection of the laws" means that public schools cannot be segregated by race. For its part, Congress passed three important civil rights laws in the 1950's and 1960's, the Civil Rights Acts of 1957 and 1964 and the Voting Rights Act of 1965. Combined, these acts were designed to give people equal access to public accommodations such as restaurants and motels and to give citizens equal access to participation in politics. The president engaged in civil rights policy-making by executive order, such as when President Harry S Truman desegregated the military or when President Lyndon B. Johnson required contractors doing business with the national government to have "affirmative action" plans that required giving special consideration to minority groups in hiring decisions. These governmental decisions, as a group, had the effect of transforming civil rights.

Applications

Civil liberties protect all citizens. They become controversial when they are applied to protect those who hold ideas deemed dangerous to the nation or when they protect reprehensible citizens in addition to those who are innocent. Civil rights, similarly, find broad acceptance in the general public in the abstract, but can be quite unpopular when they appear to threaten majority groups. This section will consider an example of the way in which all are protected by civil rights and liberties and also an example that shows their more controversial nature.

Perhaps the most cherished of civil liberties is the freedom of speech. Because governments historically have been afraid of those who would change them, they have often been suspicious of those who speak or write against them. At one time, for example, people who were deemed sympathetic to communist principles were seen as threats to American government and society who should be punished. During the 1950's, Minnesota's Senator Joseph McCarthy received public accolades for advocating ridding the nation of the "communist threat" when he announced that there were communists working in the State Department. What followed, however, was more of a random witch hunt than an attempt to rid the nation of communists. The freedom of speech is designed, in contrast to the feelings engendered during the McCarthy era, to protect even communists from having their beliefs silenced—even if in the abstract those beliefs include overthrowing the national government.

Another set of civil liberties has to do with the rights of people accused of crimes. Perhaps the most important case that the Supreme Court has decided in this field occurred when it ruled that states must provide attorneys for people accused of serious crimes. The case involved a man named Clarence Earl Gideon, who had been convicted in Florida of robbery. Without an attorney representing him, Gideon had been unable to put on an adequate defense. After the Supreme Court's ruling, Gideon was acquitted of the crime because the attorney was able to show conclusively that Gideon had not been the robber. Had Gideon not had an attorney, as guaranteed by the Sixth Amendment, he would have served a prison term for a crime that he did not commit.

Another side of the rights of the accused is that they can have the impact of protecting the guilty as well as the innocent. The case of Ernesto Miranda is an example. Miranda was a truck driver convicted of the kidnapping and rape of a teenager. At issue from a civil liberties perspective was his confession, one that Miranda claimed was coerced. The Supreme Court found that under such circumstances, the confession could not be used in court and that in the future, all persons accused of crimes would have the right to be told what their individual liberties are. Although Miranda may have been reprehensible as a person, his case became a symbol of the concept that civil liberties should protect everyone—even the most undeserving of citizens.

One of the most famous assertions of civil rights came from a woman named Rosa Parks who challenged a "Jim Crow" law requiring that black riders sit at the back of the bus. Although she later said that her protest came simply because she was tired and did not want to get up from her seat, her simple act of civil disobedience helped launch a challenge to laws in the Southern United States that required the segregation of the races in public transit, in public accommodations, and in public facilities. The Civil Rights movement of the 1950's and 1960's forced government action to assure that segregation practices would end.

Civil rights are more controversial, though, when applied to groups other than racial minorities or when they involve special treatment of minorities as a remedy for past discrimination. For example, homosexuals have made the claim that there should be no discrimination against them based upon their sexual orientation, but courts have failed to rule that states must recognize single-sex marriages. Similarly, women have claimed that they should not be excluded from combat by their gender, a claim that has met with much controversy. Civil rights programs such as affirmative action have long been the subject of debate. Affirmative action programs are designed to give special consideration to people who have been discriminated against in the past in such areas as admission to universities or employment. Critics have charged that affirmative action is wrong because it encourages the very type of behavior—treating people unequally—that the Civil Rights movement was designed to combat.

Context

Civil rights and liberties are among the most cherished symbols of the rights of individual citizens in the United States. Other nation's citizens stand in open envy of the amount of protection that these rights afford individual Americans. Indeed, one of the driving forces in the revolutions of the 1980's, including the falling apart of the Soviet Union, came about because of the perception in those nations that there was not adequate protection of the individual. Most other nations in the world do not have the tradition that the United States has of trying to protect its individual citizens from the government through the elaborate language of a constitution or the constant vigilance against government intrusion by an independent judiciary.

Yet, notions of civil rights and liberties always remain controversial because they may involve allocating protections and resources to groups with which we may disagree or giving criminals protection from law enforcement. Or, in the case of civil rights, the movement may involve having special programs to attempt to rectify past inequalities. There has also been resistance to defining civil rights in a way that would apply them to groups other than racial minorities, such as women or homosexuals. To the extent that such controversies exist, civil rights and liberties can never be taken for granted. They will always engender debate, for they are designed to protect political speech, and in so doing, they protect even reprehensible political ideas. They are designed to protect the innocent, and in so doing, they also serve to protect the guilty. They are designed to promote equality, and they may do so even when they protect those with lifestyles others in the society may not like. Without constant vigilance, these cherished values cannot be assured. Even the powerfully written language in the Bill of Rights and in the Civil War amendments cannot, without the active participation of citizens, be a protection against infringement on the individual.

Bibliography

Abraham, Henry J. *Freedom and the Court: Civil Rights and Liberties in the United States*. 6th ed. New York: Oxford University Press, 1994. Standard textbook concerning the application of civil liberties and civil rights law to the government by the Supreme Court.

Branch, Taylor. *Parting the Waters: America in the King Years 1954-63*. New York: Simon & Schuster, 1988. Well-written historical narrative about the most dramatic events of the Civil Rights movement led by Martin Luther King, Jr.

Graham, Hugh Davis. *The Civil Rights Era: Origins and Development of National Policy, 1960-1972*. New York: Oxford University Press, 1990. Perhaps the best single-volume historical treatment of the Civil Rights movement and the development of national civil rights policy.

Lawson, Steven F. *Running for Freedom: Civil Rights and Black Politics in America Since 1941*. Philadelphia: Temple University Press, 1991. Definitive discussion of the roles of black leaders in the Civil Rights movement.

Morgan, Richard E. *The Law and Politics of Civil Rights and Liberties*. New York: Alfred A. Knopf, 1985. Useful summary of the interaction between law and politics in the arena of civil rights and liberties in the United States.

Tedford, Thomas L. *Freedom of Speech in the United States*. New York: McGraw-Hill, 1993. Beautifully written book that focuses on the most prized of civil liberties—the freedom of expression.

James W. Riddlesperger, Jr.

Cross-References

African American Politics, p. 28; Asian American Politics, p. 115; The Bill of Rights, p. 134; Civil Disobedience, p. 285; Civil Liberties Protection, p. 291; Civil Rights Protection, p. 304; Constitutional Law in the United States, p. 439; Feminist Politics, p. 682; Gay and Lesbian Politics, p. 732; Human Rights and International Politics, p. 848; Individual Versus State Rights, p. 910; Latino Politics, p. 1052; Political Correctness, p. 1441; Protest Movements, p. 1621; Race and Ethnicity, p. 1654; Reproductive Politics, p. 1692; Right to Bear Arms and the Second Amendment, p. 1750.

CIVIL RIGHTS PROTECTION

Field of study: Civil rights and liberties

Civil rights protection as a function of government is an important political issue in the United States and around the world. Civil rights are generally regarded as affirmative promises governments make that they will protect all persons including various racial, ethnic, or gender groups previously denied rights.

Principal terms
AFFIRMATIVE ACTION: idea that government should use its coercive power to redress past wrongs done to recognizable disadvantaged groups
FOURTEENTH AMENDMENT (1868): amendment to the U.S. Constitution that requires states to provide all persons within their jurisdiction "due process" and "equal protection" under law
SEGREGATION: practice, especially widespread in the American South, in which legal and nonlegal means forced physical separation of the races
SEPARATE BUT EQUAL: doctrine used to justify inferior facilities provided for African Americans under the guise of providing for the "equal protection" requirement of the U.S. Constitution's Fourteenth Amendment

Overview

Civil rights are generally regarded as affirmative promises governments make that they will treat all individuals fairly. Insofar as they have failed to do so in the past, governments promise to take active steps to reduce or eliminate discrimination against various racial, ethnic, or gender groups whose rights have been denied by other individuals or groups in society. Generally, such protected groups are recognizable minorities which have previously suffered because of government inaction in the past and whose safety or equality might be threatened in the future.

Such civil rights are typically distinguished from civil liberties, which are regarded as negative promises that governments make that they will not do certain things that are harmful to the interests of citizens. While civil rights and civil liberties can be distinguished, there is always an overlap between the two. For example, a negative promise that the government will not interfere with the free expression of ideas carries with it an affirmative promise that the government will set conditions that allow individuals to express their opinions even in the face of majorities which may wish to silence them. Nevertheless, making a distinction between the affirmative characteristics of civil rights and the negative characteristics of civil liberties is useful.

The distinction between civil liberties and civil rights can be traced to different philosophical and historical traditions. The United States has honored civil liberties more consistently for a longer period of time because they are based on the idea of limited government set out in the Declaration of Independence (1776) and reaffirmed in the U.S. Constitution, particularly in Article 1, sections 9 and 10, and in the Bill of Rights. Civil rights are more frequently traced back to the French Revolution with its call for "fraternity and equality," in addition to "liberty," and to the Russian Revolution, with its Marxist concern for economic equality. In fact, communist constitutions are frequently criticized for providing only affirmative promises or "civil rights" (purportedly promoting economic equality) while making no provision for negative restraints on government, or "civil liberties."

Both civil rights and civil liberties must be provided. Civil rights are indeed a part of the responsibility of even limited governments such as the United States. For example, if civil liberties are found principally in the Bill of Rights, then civil rights are based mainly on the Fourteenth Amendment's promise of "equal protection of the law." From a global perspective, the idea that civil rights protections are a governmental function rests on the notion that there are some rights so basic that all persons are entitled to them by virtue of being human beings. While the "natural rights" theory is no longer widely accepted, there is a residual assumption that each individual has certain basic human rights, which are the basis for the worldwide human rights movement.

Before any rights or liberties can be protected effectively, there must be a government committed to the rule of law. Although the rule of law is possible in nondemocratic regimes, it is absolutely essential for any government that calls itself democratic. One element in the rule of law is the notion that the government should provide effective enforcement of laws against private violence. All governments, whose very existence is justified by their promise to substitute a monopoly of the legitimate use of force for random violence, make and enforce laws prohibiting private violence by individuals. The rule of law cannot prevail if the law is not enforced against individuals and groups which engage in private violence (such as the Mafia in Sicily, street gangs in the United States, and drug cartels in Colombia).

Americans may respond positively to the Wild West image of a posse of vigilantes catching bad guys and stringing them up from the nearest tree, but this notion of frontier justice is the opposite of what the rule of law seeks to achieve. An idea that the film industry can turn into a box-office hit is not necessarily the basis for sound government. The rule of law calls on the government to resolve, through its public court system, all serious conflicts that might result in violence. It is only when the government fails to provide effective enforcement of laws against private violence that the call for vigilantes arises. These vigilantes are, at best, dysfunctional since they have punished (perhaps accidentally) the innocent along with the "guilty." Insofar as vigilantes are allowed to use force against individuals, they may also advance their own interests over some minority they dislike.

Mob violence or discrimination of private groups previously has given rise to modern demands that governments provide civil rights protections to disadvantaged groups and even redress wrongs which it did not prevent in the past. The Ku Klux

Klan, acting in conjunction with Southern state authorities, enforced a racially segregated system and engaged in violence against African Americans, Jews, Roman Catholics, and other groups. Such activities effectively negated the promise of the U.S. Constitution's Fourteenth Amendment that no state shall "deny to any person within its jurisdiction the equal protection of the laws." This implicated the federal government in the wrongdoing, as Congress was given the power to enforce the amendment and did not do so for almost a hundred years.

Insofar as acts of violence occur against any disadvantaged group, the government also fails to fulfill its responsibility. While Klan violence against African Americans has abated, gays, lesbians, and some ethnic groups continue to complain of violent assaults and death as a result of mob action in various localities. Comparable cases abound in other countries. Before coming to power in Germany, Adolf Hitler used a gang of thugs known as "Brown Shirts" to terrorize Jews and others. Some Latin American countries also tolerate private "death squads" against groups.

Beyond violence, other forms of discrimination exist. All the above mentioned groups, and women as well, claim that discrimination has existed for a long time and has used tacit government support to advance advantaged groups or individuals over individuals from disadvantaged groups. Lacking government protection, the minorities, if strong enough or desperate enough, may resort to violence to defend themselves, frequently setting off new rounds of violence and undermining the government's basic justification for being granted a monopoly of legitimate force.

That this would be the case especially for the case of African Americans was recognized by no less a figure than President Abraham Lincoln. In words that can be understood from either a liberal or conservative perspective, Lincoln provided a justification for civil rights protection as a function of government, and even arguably, for affirmative action in his Second Inaugural Address. He said that the United States might have to endure conflict "until all the wealth piled by the bonds man's two hundred and fifty years of unrequited toil shall be sunk, and until every drop of blood drawn with the lash shall be paid by another drawn with the sword." Although Lincoln may have hoped that the problems of slavery would be resolved within the century that was to follow, the issue of a fair treatment for all citizens is still not resolved to everyone's satisfaction.

The applications of this theoretical statement remain thorny and unresolved, but there is a growing awareness globally that civil rights protection is a proper function of governments. The human rights movement has even succeeded in expanding the arena in which international law operates by including human rights through such international agreements as the Helsinki Accords.

Applications

It is widely acknowledged that governments do have an obligation to protect civil rights for all persons from this time forward. The real difficulty comes when the question arises of how much, if at all, government should compensate those who have been denied civil rights protection in the past. There are at least two levels to the problem and the second is much more difficult than the first.

First, while there are always problems of calculating the exact amount of repara-tions, in principle, it is simple to determine that governments do have a responsibility to pay damages to any clearly identifiable victims of specific government programs in the past. To take one case, the U.S. government in World War II rounded up many native-born Americans of Japanese descent and interred them in concentration camps, solely because they were Japanese. During the Japanese American incarceration, their businesses were destroyed and their homes, personal property, and businesses were seized by the government or looted by neighboring groups. Clearly, the U.S. govern-ment had acted in such a way as to deny these people both the "due process" and the "equal protection" promised by the Fourteenth Amendment. After decades of delay, Congress voted a token compensation to those who could be clearly identified as having suffered from this tragedy. It was the least the government could do, and it follows a widely, but not universally, accepted principle.

Second, many times grave wrongdoing has taken place, but there is no way to identify those who suffered directly. The history of African slavery in the United States was morally wrong and obviously contrary to the democratic principles of the Declaration of Independence and the U.S. Constitution. Arguably, even the Framers recognized this, refused to use the word "slavery" in the document, tried to mitigate it by prohibiting further slave importation after 1808, but were unable or unwilling to eliminate it. After the Civil War, slavery was abolished by the Thirteenth Amend-ment, and full citizenship was granted African Americans (and others) by the Four-teenth Amendment. After a brief attempt to implement the Fourteenth Amendment, its words were largely ignored, and segregation and private group violence against African Americans continued, often with only perfunctory government attempts, if any, to stop it.

After an exceedingly long delay, this practice was reversed. The famous *Brown v. Board of Education* (1954) overturned an earlier case by deciding that "separate but equal" was an impossibility and that segregated facilities were inherently unequal. Southern states had been taxing all of their citizens, black or white, but had been using that tax money to benefit whites far more than blacks. This was aggravated by the difficulty that African American citizens had in exercising the right to vote so they had no political remedy to use against their discrimination. It was this abusive use of the coercive power of the state that gave the Supreme Court its greatest moral claim to set aside segregation in schools and the other affected facilities.

In *Brown*, the Court was seeking not to persuade an individual but to persuade large masses who could use the federal system and their state governments as a counterpoise against the Supreme Court. Many Southern states responded by erecting local legal and constitutional barriers against the *Brown* decision, continuing to use their coercive power to deny African American citizens equal protection. They also frequently continued to withhold protection of African American citizens from the Ku Klux Klan.

In the end, the Court's power alone was not sufficient to end segregation. From the *Brown* decision to the passage of the 1964 Civil Rights Act, the courts decided numerous cases striking down laws in Southern states denying equal protection, a process so tediously slow that, a decade later, only one percent of Southern students were attending integrated schools. The Court lacked the support of the executive and legislative branches of the United States government. Only with the passage of the 1964 and 1965 Civil Rights acts did all three branches of the national government begin providing for equal protection of the laws for African American citizens.

The problem was more difficult because it was not a question of only striking down specific laws that gave whites preference over African Americans, but a whole fabric of protected privileges acquired over decades of discrimination. Without equality, a sense of legitimacy of the law will erode, and there is a potential for violence from those who feel aggrieved, as did African American urban rioters in the 1960's.

The attempt to redress all the problems caused by segregation was still more difficult because many discriminatory acts were in the domain of activities long regarded as private and beyond the legitimate scope of government activity. The Supreme Court could strike down state constitutional provisions one after the other; but they would still find schools largely segregated because of the pattern of segregation based on residential housing patterns. The Court could do far less when discrimination was not the result of deliberate governmental action.

Affirmative action (which idea asks government to use its coercive power to redress wrongs in the past) is one of the most controversial issues in contemporary American political life. It is favored by those who see clearly the continuing legacy of the wrongs done in the past, and opposed by those who see it as excessive government actions which bring about a new inequality.

It is clear that affirmative action has not received the kind of overwhelming support from the Supreme Court or in society at large as the earlier *Brown* decision, and the existence of people who have not yet accepted the fairness of the U.S. legal system creates an enduring political crisis yet to be resolved. One problem with affirmative action for proponents is that they are seeking a retroactive change in a legal system that frowns on retroactive laws. Seizing on the dangers of retroactivity, opponents ignore the dangers of inequality continuing to flow from past discrimination, for existing laws should not support ill-gotten gain. When the police and the courts apprehend a bank robber, they do not merely advise the robber not to do it again, they also demand the money back. Still affirmative action probably will not be persuasive until proponents can fashion laws more precisely tailored to redressing very precise prior wrongs. The legal system forces robbers to return the money they steal but does not insist the robbers repay every penny ever stolen by all previous robbers. To the extent that existing laws protect unfairly received benefits, the justification for affirmative action is appropriate.

Context

Civil rights protection as a function of government rests on the notion of the rule of law. While a rule of law analysis is useful in framing the issue, the controversies over affirmative action point out the limits of law. The rule of law is not a substitute for human ingenuity in finding political answers to contemporary problems. Moreover, other groups besides African Americans claim to have suffered discrimination in the past (and no group more obviously so than women) who were similarly not granted equal protection of the laws in the late 1800's despite their pressing claims at that time. Other groups make claims with a less obvious claim for relief from past discrimination, and the clarity with which the claims are advanced leaves much to be desired if the goal is to be persuasive to all Americans.

Bibliography

Finnis, John. *Natural Laws and Natural Rights*. Oxford, England: Clarendon Press, 1980. Discusses Anglo-American legal principles from the perspective of trying to reinvigorate the notion of "natural law" from a nonreligious perspective. Argues against legal positivism but ends up not far from the position of legal positivist Joseph Raz.

Fiscus, Ronald J. *The Constitutional Logic of Affirmative Action*. Durham, N.C.: Duke University Press, 1992. Perhaps the most compelling argument yet written in support of the concept of affirmative action as a component of "civil rights." The very title suggests the tightness of the argument used to provide a reasoned basis for affirmative action.

Greenawalt, Kent. *Discrimination and Reverse Discrimination*. New York: Alfred A. Knopf, 1983. Excellent book on the subject of civil rights, which, if read in conjunction with Ronald Fiscus' book, gives a good overview of the debate.

Raz, Joseph. *The Authority of Law*. Oxford, England: Clarendon Press, 1979. Analyzes Anglo-American principles from a legal positivistic perspective, but ironically arrives at principles not far removed from those of John Finnis. Defines the rule of law especially succinctly on pages 210-229.

Walker, Geoffrey de Q. *The Rule of Law*. Carlton, Australia: Melbourne University Press, 1988. Describes the extent to which the concept of the rule of law and other Anglo-American legal principles can be used as objective standards by which governmental and legal systems may be evaluated.

Richard L. Wilson

Cross-References

African American Politics, p. 28; Citizenship in World Governments, p. 254; Civil Disobedience, p. 285; Civil Liberties Protection, p. 291; Civil Rights and Liberties, p. 298; Civil Unrest and Rioting, p. 317; Constitutional Law in the United States, p. 439; Courts: U.S. Federal, p. 471; The Democratic Party, p. 520; Equality and Egalitarianism, p. 630; Federal Mandates, p. 662; Feminist Politics, p. 682; Gay and Lesbian Politics, p. 732; Gender Politics, p. 738; Human Rights and International Politics, p. 848; Latino Politics, p. 1052; Political Correctness, p. 1441; Race and Ethnicity, p. 1654; Slavery and U.S. Political History, p. 1821; Voting in History, p. 2116; Woman Suffrage, p. 2141; Women in Politics, p. 2147.

THE CIVIL SERVICE IN THE UNITED STATES

Field of study: Functions of government

As the primary personnel system of government in the United States the civil service is expected to provide governmental services in a competent, efficient, and politically neutral manner in accordance with the principles of merit. It has been shaped largely by periodic reform movements.

Principal terms

CIVIL SERVICE REFORM ACT OF 1978: act of Congress that abolished the Civil Service Commission and created a new governing structure for the federal civil service

MERIT SYSTEM: selection and advancement in public employment based on competitive examinations and ability, knowledge, and skills

PATRONAGE: selection and advancement in public employment based largely on political loyalty and service

PENDLETON ACT: act of Congress that created the Civil Service Commission in 1883 and gave rise to the modern civil service

SPOILS SYSTEM: granting of government jobs to political supporters by elected officials

Overview

The civil service is the primary personnel system of federal, state, and local governments in the United States. While not all the seventeen million workers employed by these governments work in a civil service system, the principles and practices of the civil service embody many of the core values and contradictions that define public sector employment and the nature of the larger governmental system. The civil service is an institution that has developed over time and reflects the growth and development of the nation. Government employment has expanded from an insignificant number in the early years of the republic to constitute a major segment of the labor market in the decades following World War II. As late as 1816 there were fewer than five thousand employees in the federal government and even fewer in state and local governments. Spurts of growth in federal employment occurred after the Civil War, during the Depression, and after World War II, with total employment stabilizing between two and three million employees. State and local civil service employment has also seen dramatic growth since World War II, to the point where both outnumber those in the federal service (four million for state governments, ten million for local), with 60 percent of government employees working for local governments in 1985.

As the number of individuals employed by government has expanded, so has public concern over how this large workforce is managed. This concern is reflected in periodic reform movements aimed at eliminating perceived abuses and corruption or at improving the effectiveness and efficiency of governmental services. The civil service owes its form to these reform efforts.

The history of civil service reform falls into three main periods: from 1792 to 1829, when appointment to governmental positions was based on the qualifications of individuals or "fitness of character"; from 1829 to 1883, when government employment was dominated by the patronage system; and the period beginning with the passage of the Pendleton Act in 1883 that led to the primacy of merit principles and the permanent civil service. Each of these periods is characterized by its own set of values and practices that continue to influence the nature of the civil service.

A critical factor in the development of the civil service is that the U.S. Constitution provides little guidance on how to appoint and organize governmental employees except for the required appointment and confirmation by the Senate of cabinet officers. This meant that George Washington, the first chief executive, had the opportunity to set an important precedent for the nature of the nation's public service. He used the standard of "fitness of character" in making appointments, which referred more to personal integrity and social standing than it did to technical competence. Thus he sought honest individuals from the elite of society to serve in governmental positions. This approach was generally followed by other presidents during the first four decades of the republic.

The emergence and strengthening of political parties and mass voting led to the open use of patronage and the beginning of a new era in the development of the civil service following the election of President Andrew Jackson in 1828. Jackson attacked the elitism of government service and maintained that government service was the domain of the common man. Also, the expansion of the electorate during the early nineteenth century required a large pool of party workers at election time to disseminate information and recruit voters. These party workers sought government jobs as a reward for their efforts. By mid-century the "spoils system" had spread throughout the federal government and to most state and local jurisdictions.

Widespread use of patronage for appointments to government positions had both positive and negative consequences. On the positive side, the benefits of patronage included the support of political parties by providing rewards for loyal party workers, greater responsiveness and loyalty of administrators to political leaders, and the creation of a more open, nonelitist public service. The patronage system thus supported mass participation in electoral politics and greater egalitarianism in government employment.

The negative consequences of patronage, however, came to outweigh its benefits. An ever-expanding number of government positions filled by political appointment led to massive turnover and chaos at each change in political leadership. Whereas public service had once been seen as the domain of personal integrity and honesty, it came to be associated with political corruption and incompetence as numerous unqualified political appointees populated government offices. The chief executive found his time increasingly taken up by requests for appointments, even to the lowliest clerk positions. President Abraham Lincoln, when suffering from an attack of smallpox, asked one of his assistants to invite all the job seekers in, "for at last I have something to give to all of them."

Calls for reform of the public service began before the Civil War and intensified afterward. The reform movement gained strength when Great Britain implemented recommendations of the Northcote-Trevelyan report in the Order of Council of 1870, which mandated competitive examinations for the Home Civil Service and instituted a hierarchy of careers staffed under strict rules integrating educational level, type of work, and relative status in society. A study of the British system by New York lawyer and founder of the National Civil Service Reform League, Dorman P. Eaton, was ordered by President Rutherford B. Hayes. While the elitism of the British system did not appeal to American sensibilities, the notion of a merit-based, politically neutral civil service began to take hold. In the absence of any strong political will, however, little was accomplished until President James Garfield was assassinated by a disappointed office seeker in 1881. This violent act brought the campaign against the evils of the spoils system to a head and provided the impetus for the passage of the Pendleton Act in 1883. The act created the Civil Service Commission—a three-member, bipartisan panel to advise the president on personnel matters—and established the civil service. This meant that some positions in the federal government would be protected from political influence, with selection and advancement based on the knowledge, skills, and abilities of qualified individuals. Selection for these positions would be determined by performance on written examinations, not by political loyalty, and individuals could not be removed from their jobs for political reasons.

The Pendleton Act contained two key provisions that helped to distinguish the American civil service from its British counterpart. First, qualifying examinations were to be practical in nature, related to the requirements of the job, rather than focused on general intelligence. Second, provision was made for lateral entry (direct access to middle to higher range positions) in contrast to the British careerist system. These provisions helped to create a uniquely American system characterized by greater openness, opportunity, and pluralism. It is important to understand that the Pendleton Act does not represent a sharp break with the past, but rather a change in direction. It was a negative reaction against the perceived evils of the spoils system. The act did not create a universal system of governmental employment, nor did it do away with patronage. Instead, it provided for the president to designate a percentage of positions as within the "protected" civil service. Little thought was given to the nature of the replacement system beyond the use of competitive examinations for selection. It is not surprising, therefore, that the public service came to resemble more of a patchwork quilt than a seamless, logical system. Over time, the civil service, careerists, political appointees, unionized employees, and contract professionals all came to work together under the governmental umbrella.

While the Civil Service Commission was originally conceived of as a staff aid to the president it soon became a more independent power, presiding over the merit system and watching for transgressions of merit principles. The consequences of this development were a continued emphasis on morality in the public service and the separation of personnel administration from general management. It was the latter consequence that led to new calls for reform, this time in the cause of greater effectiveness and efficiency in the delivery of governmental services. The fundamental dilemma confronted by these reformers centered on how to balance the desire to give more control over personnel policy and practices to agency managers with the need to ensure accountability and responsiveness to political authority. The approach that developed during the first half of the twentieth century was to promote political responsiveness by allowing political appointments to key positions and protect the merit system by administering it through the centralized authority of the Civil Service Commission. It soon became clear to many that the single administrative vehicle of the Civil Service Commission was not able to manage effectively the dual role of advising the president on patronage and management policy on the one hand and protecting the merit system on the other. While the application of the principles of scientific management helped to develop the civil service into a more rationalized system (with position classification, job descriptions, and performance appraisals), the lack of managerial control over these systems was criticized by the Brownlow Committee in the 1930's and by the Hoover Commissions of the 1940's and 1950's. Also, the increased size and complexity of the federal service and demands for greater diversity and affirmative action exceeded the limits of an administrative structure designed for the relatively small, homogeneous federal workforce of the late nineteenth century. Further reform was needed, but had to await a receptive political climate before it could occur. The 1976 election of President Jimmy Carter, a Washington outsider, in the wake of the Watergate scandal provided the opportunity for civil service reform.

Applications

The Civil Service Reform Act of 1978 created a new administrative structure for the federal civil service which acknowledges its complexity and the competing values of merit, performance, political responsiveness, executive leadership, and equal employment opportunity. The act abolished the Civil Service Commission and replaced it with a multiagency structure. The Office of Personnel Management was created to administer a more decentralized, management-focused personnel system, while the Merit System Protection Board took on the watchdog function of assuring that merit principles are followed for all public employees. These principles are explicit in the act and include: recruitment of qualified individuals based on knowledge, skills and abilities; fair and equitable treatment—no discrimination on the basis of race, sex, religion, or disability; equal pay for work of equal value; high standards of integrity, conduct, and concern for the public interest; effective and efficient use of the workforce; emphasis on performance standards; and ongoing training and education for public employees.

The act also created the Federal Labor Relations Board (to oversee collective bargaining in the federal government) and the Senior Executive Service (to provide a corps of highly trained generalist administrators). It set aside funds for experiments with administrative innovations such as pay banding and broader job classifications, and mandated recruitment from all segments of society, reflecting the value that the public service be representative of society as a whole.

Despite its ambitious agenda, the Civil Service Reform Act of 1978 did little to end calls for reform of public employment. The spirit of the 1978 reform was not unlike that of the Pendleton Act—a negative movement to rid the system of perceived evils and abuses. This time the evil was not the spoils system, but the perceived incompetence of civil service employees and their lack of responsiveness both to the public and to political leadership. The reform did not create a new personnel system, only a new administrative structure designed to allow for more managerial influence and executive leadership over the civil service. Some critics of the reform charged that it opened the door to political manipulation of the civil service, while others maintained that reform did not go far enough to make the civil service responsive to demands for greater effectiveness and efficiency.

Within a decade of the 1978 reform a commission was appointed, headed by Paul Volcker, to make recommendations for the revitalization of the federal civil service, which spawned a number of similar commissions at the state level. Volcker's commission found that the civil service lacked public respect, suffered from low morale, had too many political appointees, contained few incentives for high performance, and found it increasingly difficult to attract talented newcomers. The commission generated numerous recommendations for revitalizing the civil service without calling for fundamental changes in the system. Despite a high profile and prestigious membership, the commission did not lead to an active legislative agenda on behalf of the civil service.

A more comprehensive reform of the civil service was proposed by the 1993 report of the National Performance Review, headed by Vice President Al Gore. Subtitled "Creating a Government That Works Better and Costs Less," the review sought to reinvent government on the basis of four key principles: cutting red tape, putting customers first, empowering employees to get results, and producing better government for less. The report recommended a radical decentralization of personnel policy, specifically, that all departments and agencies be given the authority to conduct their own recruiting and examining for all positions, that all central registers and standard application forms be abolished, and that the classification system be greatly simplified to give agencies greater flexibility in how they classify and pay their employees. Given the history of civil service reform, it seems certain that the civil service is destined for further changes.

Context

The civil service does more than merely provide a structure for government employment. Also, and more important, it embodies and reflects many of the values that define and invigorate a society and its system of governance. The fact that these values are not always consistent, and are often in conflict with one another, makes it difficult to achieve consensus on the nature and structure of the civil service in a complex society that espouses democratic principles. The central problem is how to reconcile a permanent, professional civil service—which citizens depend on for many services but whose membership citizens cannot vote out of office—with the principle of government by the people.

This dilemma results in a profoundly ambivalent relationship between citizens and the public service. Civil service employees are expected to be highly competent and to uphold high standards of integrity as they manage public money and provide essential services, yet they are also viewed as inferior to private sector workers and as hiding behind civil service protections. In addition, the civil service also must balance the principle of merit and finding the best person for each job with the demand for equal employment opportunity and an open and representative public service.

It could be argued that standards for the public service have been set so high, with so many competing values, that dissatisfaction with its performance is inevitable. Indeed, there is considerable evidence that public perceptions of the civil service have become increasingly negative, fueled by bureaucrat bashing by politicians. Despite these negative views of civil servants, they are increasingly expected to do more with less as governments downsize, cutting budgets while the demand for services continues to increase.

The future of the civil service and the quality of government depends on the willingness of the public and their elected representatives to move beyond negative reforms to initiatives that create a positive and effective working environment for public servants at all levels of government. The extent to which the public supports or neglects its civil service is reflective of the capacity for and interest in effective constitutional governance.

Bibliography

Ban, Carolyn, and Norma M. Riccucci, eds. *Public Personnel Management: Current Concerns, Future Challenges.* New York: Longman, 1991. Essays and studies on a range of contemporary issues in public personnel management.

Chandler, Ralph C., ed. *A Centennial History of the American Administrative State.* New York: Free Press, 1987. Summarizes how American public administration has evolved, using 1887 as a focal point.

Lee, Robert D., Jr. *Public Personnel Systems.* 2d ed. Rockville, Md.: Aspen, 1987. Basic text in public personnel administration that applies systems theory to the history and functions of the civil service.

Mosher, Frederick C. *Democracy and the Public Service.* 2d ed. New York: Oxford University Press, 1982. Authoritative history and analysis of the development of the American civil service and its relationship to constitutional government.

National Commission on the Public Service (U.S.). *Leadership for America: Rebuilding the Public Service.* Lexington, Mass.: Lexington Books, 1990. Paul Volcker's National Commission of the Public Service report.

National Performance Review (U.S.). *From Red Tape to Results: Creating a Government That Works Better and Costs Less.* New York: Times Books, 1993. Vice

President Al Gore's National Performance Review report. Recommends substantial restructuring of the federal civil service along with a number of other reforms.

Danny L. Balfour

Cross-References

Accountability in U.S. Government, p. 1; Bureaucracy, p. 164; Civic Education, p. 278; Constitutional Governments, p. 432; Executive Functions in U.S. Government, p. 636; Government Agencies, p. 765; Local Governments, p. 1136; Political Machines and Bosses, p. 1468; Postal Service, p. 1563; State Government, p. 1891.

CIVIL UNREST AND RIOTING

Field of study: Civil rights and liberties

Societies throughout the world have periodically contended with outbursts of civil unrest. Often violent affairs, some conflicts have produced substantive changes; however, they have seldom accomplished intended goals.

Principal terms
> INTIFIDA: popular Arab resistance to Jewish occupation of the Jordan River's West Bank
> JACQUERIE: revolt of French peasants against the nobility
> LUDDITISM: British labor violence named for a legendary labor activist, Ned Ludd
> PEASANT: small-scale European farmer or farm laborer
> RIOT: violent public behavior or disorder

Overview
Nations throughout the world have historically contended with occasional civil disturbances. Often inflamed by unpopular governmental policies or the failures of authorities to address public grievances, interest groups such as farmers, laborers, racial and ethnic minorities, immigrants, and youths have periodically sought redress through threatening or violent ways. Sometimes such groups railed against one another. Economic factors typically provoked the conflicts, but the outbursts frequently spotlighted the volatile interplay of political, racial, religious, and moral cleavages among diverse peoples. Fueled by an intense emotionalism, such uprisings seldom produced the results that their participants sought. The fact that they occurred at all, however, determined that the instigators' frustrations and demands could not be ignored by the government forces capable of addressing them.

These disturbances appear early in the experiences of both Western and Eastern civilizations. For example, uprisings regularly occurred in the Roman Empire and in the ancient Far Eastern cultures of China, Japan, and Korea. In these primarily agrarian societies the disruptions largely manifested themselves as peasant rebellions in which farmworkers reacted violently to changes in provincial or aristocratic land and labor edicts.

Well into the eighteenth century, peasant unrest persisted throughout Europe and Asia. Areas of the Western Hemisphere were also affected. In colonial Latin America and in the United States, rural discontent arising from burdensome governmental policies—especially taxation measures—and class conflicts spawned occasional flare-ups. In colonial Peru and New Granada, for example, the unrest caused thousands of deaths, but few reforms. In the United States fewer deaths typically resulted, but property damage was often considerable.

Urban artisans frequently imitated the examples of their rural counterparts. In fifteenth century Japan, confrontations frequently took on the appearance of city versus countryside conflicts, but many of the European affairs resulted from efforts of independent town artisans to break the control of powerful guilds. Like the various rural uprisings in the preindustrial world, these urban conflicts generally failed after being brutally suppressed.

Indeed, the pattern of civil unrest and rioting has been most prevalent in urban settings. In the industrialized nations, labor discontent has been at the center of many of these problems. The transition from rural to urban life, through which virtually all participants of the Industrial Revolution passed, changed the ways of life in practically all aspects. In the cities, workers labored and employers owned; often the two saw little compatible in their relationships. As the conflicts of interest widened between the two sides, occasionally exacerbated by economic depression, workers sometimes responded with acts of protest, sabotage, and bloodshed. These could be especially violent affairs in nineteenth century England and the United States, but no area of the industrialized world has escaped occasional convulsions from labor unrest and rioting.

Dissatisfaction over the nature of political life has historically precipitated some of the world's most serious internal disturbances. In the twentieth century, oppressive political regimes in countries such as South Africa, East Germany, Hungary, Haiti, Chile, and China have trampled basic human rights and provoked bloody internal uprisings. Brutal suppressions of these political conflicts occurred when authoritarian leaders sought to establish their control, consolidate their personal power, or solidify the domination of a political ideology. In Fascist Italy and Nazi Germany of the 1920's and 1930's, private party armies became instruments of terror and intimidation provoking street brawls and massive property damage during Benito Mussolini's and Adolf Hitler's rise to power. Following the intervention of the Soviet Union, which saw the deaths of millions of political dissidents in the 1930's under Joseph Stalin's reign of terror, political unrest in Hungary in 1956 and Czechoslovakia in 1968 was arrested viciously by the Soviet military.

Occasionally, these twentieth century political problems have been intensified by religious discord, resistance to modernism, and the influence of Western culture, and nationalist movements. China's antiforeign, anti-Christian Boxer Rebellion of the late 1890's and early 1900's; India's nationalist independence struggle and continuing Hindu-Moslem struggles; the fervent 1978 Iranian fundamentalist Islamic revolution and deposal of the Western-influenced shah; and the persistent conflict between Catholics and Protestants in Northern Ireland are examples of how various combinations of factors have interacted to kindle often paralyzing social disorders.

In the modern world, racial and ethnic dissensions have perhaps precipitated the most deadly and widespread social upheavals. In the United States sporadic racial confrontations between black and white Americans, first appearing during the slave era, continued to affect twentieth century America generating serious questions about the nation's willingness to integrate racial minorities. In Eastern Europe in the 1980's and 1990's, ethnic troubles riddled Czechoslovakian, Hungarian, Romanian, and Bulgarian societies. Few troubles, however, have proved more intractable than those caused by festering differences in the former Yugoslavia or in the Middle East.

Applications

Social turmoil initiated by agrarian peoples has regularly occurred throughout world history. The French uprisings of the mid-thirteenth century, the Jacquerie, marked by the spontaneous killing of nobles and their families, and the burning of their homes and castles, set the pattern of similar revolts across medieval Europe. The largest was Germany's great sixteenth century Peasant Revolt. Despite being ruthlessly suppressed, these conflicts continued to occur, disrupting domestic peace, for example, in eighteenth century Russia and modern Vietnam.

Although different in motivation and goals, these rural European and Asian uprisings parallel disruptions in the American national experience. Problems occurred throughout the colonial and early national periods. Poor economic conditions threatened to undermine the democratic experiment in the post-revolutionary war era. Western Massachusetts farmers faced the greatest problems. Burdened by heavy taxation and the inability to acquire credit, many farmers saw their lands confiscated and their livelihoods jeopardized. In 1786, Daniel Shays led them in armed protest to prevent Massachusetts courts from foreclosing on their farms. The outbursts were easily quelled, but to conservatives, Shays's Rebellion raised the alarming specter of widespread mob rule. Ultimately, the rebellion helped strengthen the movement for a new constitution to strengthen the national government against future uprisings.

Until the twentieth century, no form of civil disturbance proved more unsettling to Americans than labor unrest. The late nineteenth century experienced hundreds of confrontations between labor and management and law enforcement agencies. In the mid-1880's, unrest in Chicago gave labor its blackest eye. McCormick Harvester workers, already haggling with management over job and pay cuts and the employment of replacement workers, joined a general strike already underway. On May 3, 1886, following a mass meeting near the plant, fighting erupted between strikers and new hires. Policemen, attempting to maintain order, fired into the crowd, killing two workers and wounding several others.

The following night, workers rallied in Haymarket Square to denounce the police atrocities. When policemen suddenly appeared, someone tossed dynamite at them, fatally wounding one policeman. The officers quickly regrouped, and fired into the fleeing crowd. Others wielded their nightsticks. The ugly melee was brief, but its human toll was costly. Seventy-three policemen were wounded, six of whom later died. The workers mourned four dead and twelve severely wounded.

Americans lamented the radicalism arising out of the maturing labor movement as problems continued into the twentieth century. These were problems with which European society was already familiar. Major worker riots, for example, had gripped seventeenth and eighteenth century England, one of the most serious being the Gordon Riots of 1780, when London burned. The most sustained period of ferment also occurred in England, beginning in the first decade after 1815, when masked gangs of unemployed and striking textile workers terrorized Manchester and other cities. This violence, called Ludditism, eventually spread to other parts of the continent.

As a nation of immigrants, the United States has often struggled with problems arising from pluralism. Native-born Americans, especially during the nineteenth century, occasionally clashed bitterly with immigrants. One of the bloodiest confrontations, the so-called Bible Riots, occurred in Philadelphia in June, 1844, between Irish Catholic immigrants and native-born Protestants over issues such as job competition, temperance, and which Bible version to use in the public schools.

In many ways, the most severe civil disorders in the United States have been those inflamed by racial, rather than ethnic conflicts. No group has been more affected by this kind of stress than African Americans. Throughout much of American history, prejudice and discrimination limited black progress, denying African Americans the full benefits of citizenship and human dignity. Sometimes their aspirations for economic and social justice clashed with the interests of white Americans and led to bloody upheavals; on other occasions, pent-up frustrations from the cumulative effects of racism precipitated raging furies against life and property.

A culture of mass violence against African Americans first appeared in the post-Civil War South. During Reconstruction, white bitterness over the war's results and black aspirations as freed people inflamed the racial atmosphere. In 1866, Memphis, Tennessee, and New Orleans, Louisiana, exploded in bloody rioting when white mobs invaded the black neighborhoods, killing, beating, robbing, raping, and burning homes, churches, and schools. In forty hours of terror, Memphis' riot left forty-eight persons dead—forty-six of whom were black. Similar numbers died in New Orleans' riot.

The white South used the riots with telling effect to help topple the hated black-supported Republican state and local governments. In addition, much of the South's "riotous" behavior manifested itself in the lynching of blacks for either imagined or real transgressions against white supremacy. Between 1884 and 1914 more than thirty-six hundred persons, mostly blacks, became lynch victims. Some of these atrocities were followed by acts of terrorism against black communities to ensure further the maintenance of white supremacy.

Sensational manifestations of hostility toward blacks opened the twentieth century, but after World War I, relations worsened. During the war, many blacks left the agricultural South, beginning the "Great Migration" to northern industrial areas. Thousands more donned uniforms to fight overseas for democracy. Black expectations of substantive gains from contributing to the war effort, coupled with their new urban orientation, won little support among whites. In the summer of 1919, rioting erupted in twenty-five cities over such issues as jobs, housing, and recreational opportunities. Chicago experienced the most serious trouble; thirteen days of strife there left fifteen whites and twenty-three blacks dead, more than five hundred injured, and more than a thousand families homeless.

Sometimes called "Red Summer" because of the massive bloodshed, the racial strife of 1919 occurred in a charged atmosphere of postwar intolerance. In other twentieth century wars, however, racial disorders did not wait for the conflicts to end. In June, 1943, during World War II, months of tension in Detroit exploded into street battles between blacks and whites. President Franklin Roosevelt proclaimed a state of emergency and sent federal troops to patrol the city, but not before the rioting had killed 25 blacks and 9 whites.

In the 1960's blacks in the Civil Rights movement sought to change the nation's historic pattern of racism. Significant gains occurred in the South, but the activism hardly affected urban ghetto conditions. The poverty, squalid housing, and high unemployment spawned hopelessness, frustration, and anger.

In the summer of 1965, these emotions spilled over in Watts—the largest black district in Los Angeles—and ignited the most destructive riot in more than two decades. For nearly a week, African Americans rampaged through the city, looting white-owned stores, firebombing buildings, and sniping at police, firemen, and National Guardsmen. Thirty-four persons died in the affair and nearly nine hundred were injured. Police arrested nearly four thousand persons, many of whom had helped to destroy some thirty million dollars worth of property.

Angry and frustrated blacks in other cities followed Los Angeles' example. In the hot summers of 1966 and 1967, rioting exploded in more than fifty cities. Of the forty disorders in 1967, those in Newark and Detroit were the most destructive. In 1968, one of the most eventful years in American history, the assassination of civil rights leader Martin Luther King, Jr., provoked another rash of disturbances. Blacks vented their rage over the fallen apostle of nonviolence by taking to the streets in some one hundred cities.

Understandably, the turmoil of the 1960's sent danger signals about the state of American race relations. The government's National Advisory Commission on Civil Disorders recognized this in its report to the nation, but many African Americans had long been aware of their findings: that America was essentially two societies, one black, one white—separate and unequal.

The commission's recommendations for improvement went unheeded. Miami, New Orleans, and Washington, D.C., became flash points after 1970. Police brutality lay at the bottom of many black grievances and none seemed more valid than those coming from Los Angeles. The 1991 brutal beating of black drunken driver Rodney King prompted the most serious crisis there since the 1960's. A passerby captured the affair on a video camera, but a Los Angeles County jury of eleven whites and one Hispanic still acquitted the responsible officers of criminal charges. In the spring of 1992, blacks and other minority groups responded to what they considered a miscarriage of justice—rioting, burning, and looting throughout the south-central portions of the city. Thirty-eight deaths, four thousand arrests, thirty-seven hundred fire-gutted buildings, and an estimated five hundred million dollars in property damage resulted from the four-day affair.

Even greater civil disturbances have occurred elsewhere. In 1991 centuries of bitter ethnic hatred in Yugoslavia erupted in civil war between Serbs, Slovenes, and Croats.

Bosnian Serbs, intent on dismembering Bosnia, have also sought the "ethnic cleansing" of the area's Muslim minority. In the Serb's efforts, the region suffered from rampant violence, including the systematic rape of civilian populations. The conflict challenged the effectiveness of the interventionist and mediation efforts of the United Nations.

In the Middle East, bitter Arab-Israeli differences, incited fundamentally by the question of land ownership between Jews and Palestinians, but complicated by religious and ethnic factors, have on four occasions erupted into general warfare. During the intervals, bloody street violence, acts of terrorism, and massive arrests have transpired between Israelis and Palestinians over the presence of Israel in occupied Arab territories. The most active and sustained resistance to the Israeli West Bank occupation, Intifida (Shaking Tremor), began in December, 1987, and lasted for more than two years. A 1994 agreement between the two sides promised for the first time to bring real peace to the region.

Changes in South Africa's black-white relationships have also virtually resolved one of the most serious racial quagmires affecting the international community. Until the 1990's, however, there seemed little willingness for this country's 4.5 million whites to make concessions to the more than 21 million blacks. The Afrikaner white supremacy policy of racial apartheid legally and strictly segregated blacks, and reserved virtually all political power for whites. Repressive police and military measures sought to throttle the African National Congress' (ANC) civil disobedience campaigns against the system. But as violence and repression in the 1970's and 1980's escalated, the international community aided the black cause, responding with censure, economic boycotts, and other activities abroad. The sanctions isolated the white racist regime and hastened substantive constitutional changes. Apartheid has been dismantled, and power has been transferred to the black majority, including the presidency held by former ANC political prisoner Nelson Mandela.

In the turbulent 1960's and 1970's, confrontations involving young people often diverted attention from international racial and ethnic turmoil. In the United States, for example, critics of the war in Vietnam caused the greatest distress. Young peace advocates publicly demonstrated through inflammatory speeches and by burning the American flag and their draft cards. Sometimes policy forcibly removed them from street demonstrations when their rallies violated local laws. Violence outside the 1968 Democratic National Convention in Chicago stretched the political dimensions of this youthful idealism. Peace zealots, many of whom were members of the radical Students for a Democratic Society (SDS), clashed with law officials on national television.

Realizing themselves an important force for social and political change, students in other parts of the world paralleled the upsurge of youthful American unrest. In some cases, as in London, Paris, and Tokyo universities in the 1960's, student outrage over U.S. involvement in the Indo-China War coalesced with other concerns to cause disruptions. Brutal police suppression of riots and other forms of unrest was common in West Germany's Free University radical student movement of the same period. When a 1968 student protest in Mexico City turned violent, several hundred people died in the army's ruthless quelling of the disturbance.

Nowhere, however, have numbers matched the human toll of Beijing's June, 1989, student uprising. The Communist regime met student demands for democracy and other reforms with deadly resistance. Army tanks descended on student demonstrators at Tiananmen Square, Communist China's chief parade ground, and killed perhaps as many as a thousand of them. Few reforms resulted.

Context

In the 1990's worldwide social turmoil was sparked by diverse emotional issues. Germany has contended with immigration conflicts and confrontations from youthful neo-Nazi groups. In the United States, perhaps the most serious problem has been antiabortion violence marked by occasional street sparring with police, the fire-bombing of clinics, and other acts of violence. The resulting bloodshed and wanton property destruction of the historical problems of social unrest and rioting have understandably alarmed peace-loving citizens and have often led to condemnation of the participants as criminals or dangerous extremists.

In some cases, the legitimacy of the participants' concerns was recognized, though the method of resolution might have been disapproved. Hence, in the aftermath of the hysteria, there occasionally occurred important dialogue between the antagonists, and perhaps, major or acceptable reforms. Generally, however, acts of social ferment have seldom produced substantive changes. Indeed, in cases where eruptions occurred in authoritarian societies, positive results were much less likely to happen. Even in more democratic societies, disturbances were often brutally crushed and survivors severely punished. Nevertheless, social unrest remains a frequent and recurring worldwide problem and serves as a constant reminder of the difficulty inherent in all human societies.

Bibliography

Dubofsky, Melvyn. *Industrialism and the American Worker, 1865-1920*. New York: Crowell, 1975. Perhaps the most focused and useful overview of post-Civil War workers and activism.

Lipset, Seymour M. *Rebellion in the University*. Chicago: University of Chicago Press, 1976. Study of the varieties of student radicalism in the United States.

McPherson, James M. *Ordeal by Fire: The Civil War and Reconstruction*. New York: Alfred A. Knopf, 1982. Comprehensive study of two crucial periods in American history.

Rothschild, Joseph. *Return to Diversity: A Political History of East Central Europe Since World War II*. New York: Oxford University Press, 1989. Survey of countries including Czechoslovakia, Hungary, and Yugoslavia prior to the changes that swept Europe in 1989.

Smith, Charles D. *Palestine and the Arab-Israeli Conflict*. 2d ed. New York: St. Martin's Press, 1992. Examination of the effects of the new world order on the Middle East conflict.

Tuttle, William M. *Race Riot: Chicago in the Red Summer of 1919.* New York: Atheneum, 1970. Thorough and readable description of the violence that gripped Chicago after World War I.

Robert L. Jenkins

Cross-References

Civil Disobedience, p. 285; Civil Rights and Liberties, p. 298; Civil Rights Protection, p. 304; The Civil Service in the United States, p. 310; Legitimacy, p. 1105; Political Violence, p. 1539; Protest Movements, p. 1621; Race and Ethnicity, p. 1654; Urbanization, p. 2071.

CIVIL WARS

Field of study: Military

Civil wars are armed conflicts occurring within nations. In a civil war, armed groups within a governed society fight over the future of that society and usually over control of the central government.

Principal terms

GUERRILLAS: irregular soldiers who engage in surprise raids and hit-and-run attacks

LEGITIMACY: state of being considered politically lawful, just, moral, and/or acceptable

NONSTATE ACTOR: organization not recognized by the international community as the highest authority over a particular territory

REVOLUTION: overthrow of a government or social system by some among those governed, usually by forceful means

SEPARATISM: advocacy of separation of a group, often ethnically defined, from another political unit or region

TERRORISM: use of violence, or threat of violence, especially against an innocent population, in order to achieve political goals

Overview

A civil war is a war taking place within the borders of a single nation. It usually involves different factions within the state trying to create (or prevent) a new government for the entire state, or some territorial part of it, or simply trying to take control of the existing government. Some groups in civil wars seek to alter the government, while others are simply out to replace the people in it. At least one of the groups in a civil war must be a nonstate actor. A nonstate actor is an organization that is not recognized by the international community as a nation-state with the sovereign right to rule a territory. The other actor may be the state government (recognized by the international community), or other nonstate actors.

Civil wars most commonly involve conflict between an established government and an antigovernment group or groups. The Salvadoran civil war, for example, was fought between leftist rebels (nonstate actors), who sought to overthrow the government, and the government of El Salvador. Civil war may also take place among several nongovernment groups fighting to establish power and legitimacy over a new government. After Portugal left Angola in the 1960's, for example, several groups fought for control of the newly independent nation.

Civil wars are not to be confused with civil disorder. In contrast to simple civil disorder, the insurgents in a civil war generally control an area of the nation's territory continuously. Civil disorders tend not to endure, and if they do they are civil wars.

Civil wars involve groups that are more highly organized and purposeful than those in civil disorders.

Civil wars share many characteristics. They are often quite brutal. According to one study of war, ten of the thirteen deadliest conflicts in the nineteenth and twentieth centuries were civil wars. Civil wars rarely have clearly defined front lines, meaning that noncombatants are often drawn into the conflict and violence. Civil wars, especially during the Cold War conflict between the United States and the Soviet Union, often have international dimensions, either because one side receives support from external actors, or because an external actor is vitally concerned with the outcome of the war. Ideology, economics, political power, and religion are among the factors that lead to the internationalization of civil war.

Civil wars also often tend to be protracted. They usually last for many years, or erupt repeatedly over even longer periods. This is because the battlefield, in civil wars, is the nation itself. Relations broken between countries may be restored; intransigence within a country, once it has led to war, is almost impossible to negotiate away. A civil war is a final break between two or more elements of a nation.

Civil wars may be massive upheavals involving millions of people, such as the U.S. Civil War or the Chinese Revolution. Civil wars can also be isolated, guerrilla skirmishes, such as the Contra rebellion against the Sandinista government in Nicaragua during the 1980's.

Civil wars can be classified by such variables as the goals of the groups and the sources of the conflicts. One of the most common types of civil war is a secessionist war, in which at least one group is separatist in nature. One fighting organization represents a region that seeks to separate itself from the nation and establish a new nation-state, or at least autonomy from the central government.

A second type of civil war is a territorial one. In this type, each of the opposing groups seeking control of the whole nation occupies a fairly well-defined geographic area of the country. In this type of conflict regional groups seek to establish a new government based on the hegemony of their own regional or ethnic group. This type of civil war may also take place when there is no clear successor to a powerful leader. Various factions may take up arms to determine the new leader or to seize territory.

There is also revolutionary civil war. In this type of conflict, one group seeks to overthrow the present government and establish itself as the decision maker for the nation. This type of war is different from territorial civil war because the impetus to overthrow the government is not based on ethnic or regional factors (at least not entirely) but rather on ideology. The Chinese civil war, fought between the nationalist government and the communist insurgents, is a good example. When the insurgents win this type of war, the usual result is a complete transformation of the government, and often the society and economy as well, as took place in China in 1949.

There are several preconditions for civil wars to take place. First, there must be some type of collective frustration within the society. This usually means that there is something that separates sectors of society. This division may take many forms, including ideological, religious, ethnic, or economic. For example, in many developing nations wealth and economic opportunity are distributed in a highly unequal fashion. When this inequality coincides with other differences—such as religious, ethnic, or regional differences—a sense of frustration begins to build up. Many nations, for example, include peoples within their borders who do not think of themselves first as members of that country (the Kurds in Iraq, Iran, and Turkey, for example).

Frustration may lead outsider groups to question the legitimacy of the ruling authorities. The absence of legitimate formal and informal channels for settling the political and other grievances of alienated groups may lead the groups to consider taking up arms to solve their problems. A sense of futility or fear of reprisals in raising grievances may also lead to such considerations.

In order for a civil war to occur, however, there must also be within the group an assumption or conviction that there is no recourse other than violence for securing the resolution of the problems facing the group. There also must be the capacity to take up arms. This is where the international dimension of civil wars often becomes important. Over the years imperialism (and the response to it), decolonization, the Cold War and its aftermath, along with the global arms trade, both official and black market, have all contributed to making it possible for frustrated groups to acquire the military tools necessary to wage a civil war. Other technological developments, such as devices for duplicating printed and recorded materials, as well as tactical developments, such as guerrilla warfare, have given those dissatisfied with a government and its policies a much greater opportunity to promote rebellion.

There are several possible outcomes to civil wars, in terms of unification or dissolution. One outcome in a government versus antigovernment civil war is for the government to emerge victorious. Unless this outcome is accompanied by some concessions to the aims of the insurgents, the seeds of the conflict may give rise to renewed civil war at a later time. This was the case in Cuba, when Spain's victory over Cuban independence fighters in 1868 was followed by a renewed, and more severe, conflict in 1895. For a civil war in which the government defeats the insurgents to result in unification, the victorious must give something to the defeated.

Another outcome is that the insurgents emerge victorious (or that one group wins over several). Quite often after a victory the forces of a renewed war are still present. There are always going to be some groups who are not satisfied with the outcome. Moreover, the precedent has been established that violence is an acceptable way to achieve political goals. Therefore, whether the insurgents or the governments win, the only civil wars that result in unification are those that end with some type of negotiated settlement in which all or most warring parties are involved.

A third outcome may occur in those civil wars that are fought between a group seeking separation from the political unit and the government of that unit. If the separatist movement wins, the result is dissolution. The winning movement establishes a new sovereign state in the international system. This is how many new nations are born. The old government moves to consolidate its authority in the area it has left.

Lasting resolutions to civil wars that end in unification are fairly exceptional. Either an agreement which is acceptable to all sides must be reached, or one side must achieve such military dominance in the field that it can impose both its program in the government and its version of history on following generations.

Applications

A first stage of a civil war, once a group has, in its view, exhausted its alternatives, usually involves an effort to establish a safe zone from which to build its organization. An insurgent organization must be capable of carrying out operations against the government or rival groups. The most important goal during this stage is simply to ensure the survival of the group. Tactics during this period often include terrorism, covert political action, and propaganda. Insurgent organizations are heavily dependent on the support of sympathizers for basic resources such as food and shelter, as well as more substantial resources such as finances and weaponry. Efforts to rally the support of the population are therefore important.

The next stage is characterized by strategic stalemate. The rebel group has begun to assert effective control over particular areas, dividing the nation between the opposing sides. During this phase the organization begins to pursue more advanced military strategies, such as raids and small-scale operations against government targets.

The final stage occurs when the insurgents develop organizations capable of waging large-scale battles with enemy forces. During this period the insurgents may attempt organized attacks to take control of the capital or other strategic parts of the country in order to establish a new government.

One of the most important civil wars of the twentieth century was the Spanish Civil War, which began with a military uprising in July, 1936, and ended with the defeat of the Spanish republic in March, 1939. As with most civil wars, numerous actors were involved. The Nationalist side was supported by the military and conservatives from a variety of political parties, as well as extreme rightists. On the republican, or "loyalist," side were socialists, communists, certain trade unions, and those who generally supported the republican government.

Increasing polarization characterized Spanish politics from 1931 until the start of the war. First, a mildly reformist government alienated landowners, military officers, and clergy. Then a conservative government reversed the reforms of the earlier government, and imposed restrictions and repression upon workers. After that, a leftist popular front government threatened to bring about a social revolution. This series of governments undermined the legitimacy of the republican government for a number of significant groups in society.

The war began with a military uprising in Spanish Morocco led by General Francisco Franco. This rebellion quickly spread to garrisons on the mainland. By the end of July, 1936, the nationalist insurgents had established a zone in the agrarian provinces of western Spain and effectively had split Spain into two. The leftist parties and labor unions successfully kept the nationalists from capturing Madrid. The fighting became stalemated.

As is frequently the case with civil wars, Spain's conflict very early acquired international political and ideological significance. Fascist Italy sent about seventy thousand troops to support the nationalists, while Nazi Germany provided planes, pilots, arms, and technicians. The Soviet Union sent weapons and advisers to the republicans and organized international brigades to help in the fight against fascism. Spain represented, in microcosm, the polarization of the Western world into left- and right-wing camps. Many call the Spanish Civil War a rehearsal for World War II.

The nationalists soon began to make significant gains, capturing more provinces and further encircling Madrid, Spain's capital. The loyalist side was characterized by internal strife, while the nationalists were well disciplined and organized under Franco's authoritarian hand. Soviet supply shipments began to decrease in 1938, allowing the nationalists to develop a substantial military edge, and in February of 1938 the nationalists split the loyalist forces by successfully driving through them to the Mediterranean. Barcelona was captured in January, 1939, and Madrid in March, effectively ending the war. Both sides were accused of sickening atrocities: The loyalists were charged with the murder of hundreds of members of the clergy and political enemies, and the nationalists' systematic bombing and strafing of nonmilitary objectives was, at that time, an unthinkable act. Bombing and strafing civilians became routine in World War II.

In order to consolidate his authority (and thus prevent dissolution) Franco authorized only one political party, the Falange Española Tradicionalista, and made himself chief of state, commander in chief of the armed forces, and head of the Falange. He was also granted emergency war powers, which made harsh repression by military tribunals and political purges possible. All potential opposition to Franco's regime was effectively checked and the new government lasted until Franco's death in 1975.

Context

The distinction between external and internal wars dates to the nineteenth century, although civil wars have existed since at least as early as the Roman Empire. Over the years, a common way that new nations have entered the political system is through secessionist civil wars. Since the end of World War II, civil wars have actually erupted more frequently than have wars between states. According to one study, between 1900 and 1941 over 80 percent of wars involved two or more nation-states fighting each other. From 1945 to 1976, by contrast, 85 percent of wars were civil wars.

It is likely that civil wars will continue to be a prominent feature of the international system. Much unrest and discontent that was held in check by the forces of the Cold War were released when it ended, and some of this strife has erupted in civil wars, as in the former Soviet republic of Georgia, in 1993. Much of this unrest and discontent, in the former Soviet republics as well as elsewhere in the world, is based on ethnic differences and other societal divisions as noted earlier. The most significant challenges to state authority are likely to continue to come from inside rather than outside, and civil war will continue to be an important area of concern.

Bibliography

Ali, S. Mahmud. *The Fearful State: Power, People, and Internal War in South Asia.* Atlantic Highlands, N.J.: Zed Books, 1993. Examination of five insurgencies in South Asia, with some general conclusions.

Bolloten, Burnett. *The Spanish Civil War: Revolution and Counterrevolution.* Chapel Hill: University of North Carolina Press, 1991. The author, one of the preeminent scholars of this conflict, served as the United Press correspondent covering the war. Although the volume is quite lengthy, with great detail, it is also highly readable.

Gurr, Ted Robert. *Why Men Rebel.* Princeton, N.J.: Princeton University Press, 1970. One of the most important works in this area.

Licklider, Roy, ed. *Stopping the Killing: How Civil Wars End.* New York: New York University Press, 1993. Theoretical considerations and seven case studies. The cases are limited, but they make for fascinating reading, and the theoretical chapters stimulate interesting ideas.

Vulliamy, Ed. *Seasons in Hell: Understanding Bosnia's War.* New York: St. Martin's Press, 1994. Firsthand reporting of the civil war involving Croats, Serbs, and Muslims in Bosnia. Provides a complete understanding of the context for this brutal conflict, including the words of the participants on all sides.

Eduardo Magalhães III

Cross-References

Colonialism and Anticolonialism, p. 351; Genocide, p. 752; Independence Movements and Transitions, p. 896; Insurgencies and Coups d'État, p. 930; Legitimacy, p. 1105; Marxism-Leninism, p. 1155; National Liberation Movements, p. 1255; Nationalism, p. 1268; Political Violence, p. 1539; Revolutionary Governments, p. 1725; Revolutionary Parties, p. 1731; Revolutions, p. 1738; Right of Revolution, p. 1744; Secessionism, p. 1790; Terrorism, p. 1962.

CLASS CONFLICT

Field of study: Politics

According to Marxist social theory, class struggle is the motive force behind history. It characterizes all social epochs, except the most primitive, because all societies are divided into two classes—the ruling class and the oppressed class. The struggle between these classes accounts for social change and historical development.

Principal terms

BOURGEOISIE: also known as the capitalist class, owns the means of production, employs wage labor, and has profit as its source of income

CLASS: group determined by its economic relationship to the means of production

CLASS CONSCIOUSNESS: awareness of belonging to a definite class and a conscious knowledge of the political interests of that class

CLASS STRUGGLE: historical conflict between the oppressors and the oppressed

PROLETARIAT: the working class, which produces commodities and derives its income from wages

Overview

The early Greeks recognized the existence of class differences and class conflict in their society. Plato, in the *The Republic* and *Timaeus*, distinguishes between the class of farmers and artisans from the class of guardians (rulers and warriors). In *Laws* Plato strictly forbids farmers and artisans from participating in politics. Likewise, Plato argues that the guardians are to be prohibited from working with their hands. By Plato's reasoning, politics requires diligent study and single-mindedness. Aristotle, in *The Politics*, agrees with Plato and insists that free citizens refrain from the trades and crafts, because otherwise there would be no distinction between masters and slaves. According to Aristotle, farmers and artisans provide society with the basics of life, but the free citizens provide society with higher ends, furthering the greater good. Aristotle also deemed the master craftsman more honorable and wiser than the manual laborer because of the former's greater knowledge.

Karl Marx did not originate the theory of social classes or class struggle. Although Marx did not systematize a theory of social classes, he did begin to elaborate such a theory at the end of volume 3 of *Capital* (1867) where he states, following established theory on political economy, that modern society is made up of three classes: wage laborers, capitalists, and landowners. They are differentiated by their respective sources of income—wages, profit, and rent. Laborers live off wages, capitalists on profit, and landlords on rent. Marx goes on to say that class differentiation based on sources of revenue would result in an unnecessarily complicated categorization of classes. Marx offers a provisional definition of class that emphasizes conflict, defining class in terms of separation, division, and opposing interest. Class is not a political category for Marx but rather an economic one. Economic position in the productive structure of society determines class membership—not political partisanship.

Marx defines classes in terms of two economic principles. First, there is the question of ownership or nonownership of the means of production. Second, the division of labor relegates some to the class of workers or producers and others to the class of nonproducers. Class conflict, then, boils down to the hostile and antagonistic divisions between the nonworking owners of the means of production and the nonowning workers. By Marx's reasoning the real foundation of society is the relation between owners of productive means and workers.

Class differences, therefore, are determined by patterns of property ownership and the social organization of producers and nonproducers. Marx and Engels pointed out the presence of class conflict in ancient Greece and Rome, feudal Europe, and modern capitalist society. Ancient society was divided into slaves and slave owners, feudal society was torn between serfs and feudal lords, capitalism is split between the wage workers and the capitalists.

In general terms, class conflict means that societies are divided into two major classes: the oppressors and the oppressed. In the *Manifesto of the Communist Party* (1848), Marx and Engels assert the idea that class conflict was the driving force of history. Class struggle is the essential relationship between oppressors and oppressed. In modern society the struggle is the antagonistic relation between the bourgeoisie and the proletariat. In the *Manifesto*, Marx and Engels claim that in the modern era, the antagonisms of class are simplifying. With greater and greater clarity, the different layers and groups of class are coalescing into two hostile camps: the bourgeoisie and the proletariat.

The essential interests in this conflict are those involving exploitation and resistance to exploitation. The political interests of the bourgeoisie seek to preserve the social structure, which is based on economic exploitation. On the other hand, the interests of the proletariat are to resist the exploitation of the bourgeoisie and to overthrow a society based on the division of classes. According to Marx, in modern bourgeois society, the state is an instrument of the bourgeois class used for maintaining its power.

Marx intended to study the different forms of the state in relation to their different economic structures. Marx, however, never developed a systematic theory of the state, but his ideas of the state revolve around economic principles, especially ideas of class differentiation and class struggle. In his 1859 preface to *A Contribution to the Critique of Political Economy*, Marx states a general theory that different forms of the state have their origins in economic conditions. More particularly, in the *Manifesto* he refers to the state as an executive committee for managing the affairs of the bourgeoisie. The latter idea grows out of his earlier comments made in *The German Ideology* that the ideas of the ruling class are the ruling ideas in a society. In effect, the class that wields political power controls the state. Engels makes this idea clear in *The Origin of the Family, Private Property and the State* (1902), in which he states that the state is a medium by which the economically powerful become politically dominant. Engels also says in *The Housing Question in Germany* (1872) that the kaiser is a servant of the capitalist class.

Several questions come to mind regarding the orthodox Marxist theory of class conflict. Can all state action be said to be the will of the bourgeoisie? Is it realistic to claim that the state is made up of members of the bourgeoisie? Given competition among capitalists, how can the state be an instrument for the capitalists as a whole? One answer is that the state enjoys a degree of autonomy from the dominant class that it serves. Another argument holds that the state mediates class conflict, making concessions to the dominated class in order to pacify any potential revolutionary fervor. The bourgeoisie influence state power through direct policy decisions of the members of the state sympathetic to their interests. Interests of the bourgeoisie often coincide with the interests of the state. The bourgeoisie, moreover, are capable of bringing down the state should it not conform to their interests.

Later Marxists followed the lines of thought opened up by Marx and Engels. Vladimir Ilich Lenin argued for a proletarian party because there can be no middle road between socialism and capitalism. Mere trade unionism, Lenin argued, amounts to a capitulation to capitalism. The question for Lenin was that of creating class consciousness. For this a vanguard of professional revolutionaries was needed. They could provide organization, professionalism, and leadership. Lenin also called for centralization of the organization in order to safeguard the revolution.

Class struggle, for Lenin, is necessary in order to wrench state power from the bourgeoisie. In Lenin's theory of the state, the state will eventually wither away. As Lenin explained it, the state is based on class division. With the elimination of classes the state will logically wither away into the higher stage of communism.

Applications

Rosa Luxemburg (1870-1919) advocated the conquest of state power but conceded the need for democratic participation through trade union struggle and parliamentary activity. The former is needed to socialize the economy, the latter to raise working-class consciousness. Mere legislative reform would lead not to socialism but to reformed capitalism. Democracy does not take the place of the conquest of power but makes the conquest of power possible.

This goal implies struggle, but the proletariat will not struggle unless it attains a certain level of class consciousness. More than any other Marxist theoretician, György Lukács (1885-1971), a Hungarian Marxist philosopher, attributed crucial importance to the development of class consciousness in his important work, *History and Class Consciousness* (1923). In this book he makes a significant distinction between actual class consciousness and imputed class consciousness. By actual class consciousness, Lukács means what members of a definite class really think. By imputed class consciousness, Lukács means what the working class would think if it had all the facts. Class consciousness refers to the conscious interests shared by members of a class by virtue of their class position.

Class consciousness is absolutely indispensable for organization, mobilization, and political activity. The absence of class consciousness is referred to as false consciousness. Trade union activity is the best way to instill class consciousness and to get workers to participate in class struggle. There is a debate in Marxism as to whether class consciousness is a necessary feature of class definition or of class conflict.

Antonio Gramsci (1891-1937), founder of the Italian Communist Party, formulated the concept of "hegemony" to express the ideological forces of the modern bourgeois state. Hegemony refers to the power and authority attained and maintained by the ruling classes through the coercive apparatus of the state and through the consent gained by the cultural institutions of civil society. Louis Althusser, a French Communist philosopher, developed the idea of ideological state apparatus. Briefly put, in order for society to maintain the status quo, it must also maintain across generations the fundamental economic social relations. That is, it must reproduce workers who submit to the bourgeois social control. This submission is made possible by the ideological state apparatuses, such as schools and churches, that propagate the ideas of the ruling class.

To begin to criticize Marxist thought, it is only necessary to ask questions. To what extent does theory of class and of class conflict help explain historical changes? Does Marxist theory of social classes correspond to the actual form of social stratification in modern society? Does the Marxist theory of class conflict apply to all historical epochs or only to modern capitalist society? Are historical changes best explained by the theory of class conflict? Do the bourgeoisie and the proletariat constitute the two major social classes in modern society? What about the middle classes? What about other social forces that account for historical changes such as nationalism, racism, imperialism, or the women's movement?

To be fair to Marx, however, one must realize that Marx had a very sharp focus and a clear aim. He wanted to uncover the logic of capitalism. Many would say he succeeded. As a result, however, his class analysis is basically applicable only to modern capitalist society. After all, the bourgeoisie and the proletariat are products of the modern era.

Critics are quick to point out, however, the improved lifestyles of the proletariat. It is believed that Marx claimed that the working classes would become more impoverished as capitalism progressed. Not only has the gulf between rich and poor not widened, say the critics, but the working classes are better off than ever. Marx, however, was not speaking in absolute terms, nor was he speaking solely in materialistic terms. He was speaking in relative terms and in spiritual terms. His argument was that relative to the output of the working class, their return in the form of wages would decrease. Also, the world of commodities created by capital does not allow for the full development of human beings as human beings. Instead, workers become alienated, making things so that they may buy things.

Along similar lines, critics claim that Marx's theory cannot adequately account for the rise of the middle class. On the contrary, in *Capital*, volume 3, in the unfinished manuscript on social classes, Marx does recognize other strata besides the major social classes. Also, in *Theories on Surplus Value*, Marx claims that bourgeois society tends to give rise to new middle classes. In a few places Marx and Engels made claims that the intermediate strata between the bourgeoisie and the proletariat would disappear. According to Tom Bottomore, the growth of the new middle classes, including office workers and technicians, interposes between the bourgeoisie and the proletariat a whole continuum of status groups. Such a continuum, according to Bottomore, being based on factors other than property ownership, would deflate the theory of class conflict. Bottomore, however, believes that Marx's theory of classes is less falsifiable than other theories of social stratification. In other words, while Marx did not get the whole picture, he got more of it than other thinkers did.

Also, property ownership, in Marxist analysis, becomes a thorny issue. It is not so simple to divide up society into property owners and the propertyless. Corporate property, profit sharing, and other distributions of property pose problems. Do stockholders own property or do they only have entitlements to shares of dividends? Is the source of power in the ownership of property or in the management of property? While these questions do raise sticky issues, it cannot be denied that Marx's fundamental principle is incontestable—the masses of people can survive only by selling their labor on the market. As long as this remains true, Marxist theory is applicable.

Context

As noted above, Marx did not invent the term "classes" or the idea of class struggle. The idea of social class division was rooted in the classical political economy of Adam Smith and David Ricardo, on the one hand, and in the socialist literature of Robert Owen, Charles Fourier, and Pierre-Joseph Proudhon, on the other. Although classical Greek and Roman historians did not use modern terms, they did make a distinction between free citizens and slaves, patricians and plebians, aristocrats and the hoi polloi, and so on.

In their respective analyses of political economy Adam Smith and David Ricardo divided modern society into three major classes—the capitalists, the landowners, and the laborers. Neither, however, elaborated on the relationship existing between the ruling classes and the state. This was left to Marx.

While agreeing with the analysis of political economy that society falls into two classes—the property owners and the propertyless workers—Marx criticized political economy for failing to consider the direct relationship between the state and the economy. In this relationship is found the core of capitalism—the antagonism between the capitalist class and the working class. In *Wage Labor and Capital* (1847), Marx asserts that the capital-labor relationship is the inner contradiction of capitalist society that will eventually culminate in the dissolution of that society.

Max Weber, believing that Marx's notion of class was inadequate, substituted his own notion of the status group. The status group designates social rank and explains collective action in ways that class alone cannot. Collective action cannot be explained by economic factors alone. Other factors like custom, tradition, lifestyle, religion, and culture must be taken into account as explanatory factors. The latter account for the rise of ideas and explain group behavior on the basis of honor, privileges, and distinctions accorded to different types of social status. As Weber sees it, class is only an economic category and can only account for market behavior. Dissatisfied with class as the sole explanatory force of social conflict, Max Weber connected religious traditions to different social classes. The privileged classes develop religious traditions justifying their social privileges. On the other hand, the oppressed turn to religious traditions that compensate for their misery.

Bibliography

Bottomore, Tom. *Classes in Modern Society*. New York: Vintage Books, 1966. Study of social classes in modern industrial society. Inequality and social hierarchy are considered from a Marxist perspective.

Draper, Hal. *The Politics of Social Classes*. Vol. II in *Karl Marx's Theory of Revolution*. New York: Monthly Review Press, 1978. Studious and comprehensive look at Marx's theory of a proletarian revolution.

Marx, Karl, and Friedrich Engels. *The Marx Engels Reader*. Edited by Robert C. Tucker. New York: W. W. Norton, 1978. Best anthology in paperback form of the writings of Marx and Engels. Contains letters, economic writings, political analyses, and philosophical treatises.

Weber, Max. *The Protestant Ethic and the Spirit of Capitalism*. Translated by Talcott Parsons. New York: Charles Scribner's Sons, 1958. Discusses the power that religious ideas have in influencing social and economic forces.

Michael R. Candelaria

Cross-References

Anarchism in Marxist Thought, p. 72; Aristocracy, Oligarchy, and Plutocracy, p. 78; Capitalism, p. 197; Dialecticism, p. 540; Elitism, p. 591; Feudalism, p. 688; Industrialization, p. 916; Insurgencies and Coups d'État, p. 930; Invisible Government, p. 975; Liberation Theology, p. 1124; Marxism-Leninism, p. 1155; Ochlocracy, p. 1338; Political Violence, p. 1539; Revolutions, p. 1738; Socialism, p. 1865.

CLIENTELISM

Field of study: Political philosophy

Clientelism describes a relationship between governmental or political elites ("patrons") and groups of privileged "clients" within the polity or society. The clientele relationship is one of mutual (though not equal) benefit, whereby the patron allocates jobs or other material rewards in exchange for political support from clients. In some countries, clientelism strengthens the basic political or societal structures.

Principal terms

AUTHORITY: right to issue commands or take actions in behalf of a recognized governmental body

FEUDALISM: economic and social order, characteristic of medieval Europe, in which a strict hierarchical organization defines the relationships between the serfs who work the land and the lords who own it

HIERARCHY: arrangement of the members of a political community in a series of graded ranks with those in the top ranks holding the most political power

LEGITIMACY: quality of having one's authority accepted as right and proper

NOBLESSE OBLIGE: presumed duty or responsibility of the higher classes to assist the lower classes, materially or otherwise

PATRONAGE: jobs and other material rewards provided in exchange for political support

SOCIAL CONTRACT: presumption that there is an implied agreement between a state and the people whom it governs

Overview

Clientelism is a symbiotic relationship between political elites and members of society, whereby the elites receive political support in exchange for material or political rewards. Although clientelism can enhance popular support for governmental authority, governments also maintain authority in other ways. In the ideal of the United States, for example, the authority of the federal government is generally respected by virtue of its selection by regular, free, and competitive elections. Truly free and competitive elections lend legitimacy to governmental authority. However, most of the world's countries do not meet this democratic ideal. The leadership's authority instead is based on other mechanisms, often seen by Western—and especially American—observers as less legitimate. One such mechanism is "clientelism."

As a socioeconomic arrangement clientelism has antecedents that predate the advent of the nation-state, going back even thousands of years. Traditional villages in various parts of the world often were structured as manorial patron-client systems.

Such systems were essentially self-sufficient communities headed by "patrons"—wealthy and powerful persons who provided for the security and basic needs of the people who lived and worked on their land. In return, these "clients" supported patrons with their allegiance and with their work: farming and producing goods, carrying out basic services, and even defending the manor against outside attack when necessary. Such arrangements were prevalent in Europe between the ninth and fifteenth centuries, and often are defined as "feudalism."

In its modern form, clientelism is integrated within developed governmental structures, although usually it is not acknowledged as a formal or legally sanctioned characteristic of the system. In many cases a modern governmental system has been grafted onto a preexisting patron-client structure in the society. Political scientists discuss modern clientelism under a number of different guises, including patrimonialism (or neopatrimonialism) and patronage. Subtle distinctions separate the various terms, and these distinctions represent variants found in different parts of the world. In essence, all convey a sense that political power is wielded by an elite group of leaders who are supported by key elements of society not because of respect for some recognized electoral procedure (hence legitimacy), but rather because of mutual—though not equal—benefit. Clientelism is thus based on the principle of reciprocity. Patrons, or governmental elites, provide desirable jobs and job security, or various other kinds of political favors (such as preferential treatment by governmental agencies) in exchange for political and material support.

Clientelism may be viewed as a form of contract between the governmental leaders and select members of the polity. In contrast to more democratic forms of "social contract" between a society and its government, however, clientelism does not presume even indirect societal involvement in the making of policy. Instead, a large measure of deference is expected of clients with regard to policy-making, which is seen as the exclusive responsibility of the patrons. This deference generally pervades the social structure. Social relations themselves thus are usually structured hierarchically in clientele systems, with deference and a measure of obedience paid to those of higher status. Such hierarchies are especially prevalent in Latin American countries. In other countries, such as nineteenth century Britain, class structures reflected a sense of "noblesse oblige," whereby those higher on the social ladder felt a duty to alleviate some of the effects of poverty and misfortune on the "lower classes." In return, people were expected to defer to the presumed wisdom of their societal superiors on political and other matters. It should be noted, however, that noblesse oblige is not meant to imply mutual benefit; rather, it assumes responsibility and obligation on the part of the higher classes. In contrast to patron-clientism, noblesse oblige is infused with paternalism.

Also in contrast to other versions of social contract, patron-client systems are necessarily more selective about who receives benefits. Certain benefits are provided primarily as a reward for political support. So long as enough of the important members of the society are co-opted into the system through patron-client structures, there is an adequate base of support for the government. It should be noted, in fact, that the majority of the populace in most clientele systems are not directly integrated either as patrons or as clients. It is concern with political stability (for the government) and personal gain (for the patron), rather than public interests, that drives the allocation of benefits in a clientele system.

Not only are distinctions drawn between the political leadership and their subordinate clients, but clientele relations also exist at intervening levels. Mid-level government bureaucrats, well-connected entrepreneurs, and even military officers can also provide political favors or other benefits to relevant "clienteles" in return for political support or cooperation. In fact, clientelism can extend throughout a society at any number of levels: Patrons at the lower levels of society might simultaneously serve as "clients" to higher-up "patrons." In this way, an extensive hierarchy of communication channels at once preserves governmental authority and political stability, while distributing political and material benefits within the society. It should be noted, however, that the patron-client network of clientele systems creates a source of power independent of the top governmental leaders who hold formal power. That is, by threatening to withhold political support, the patrons and clients within the bureaucracy (or in business or the military, as applicable) can extract concessions from top governmental leaders (for example, a prime minister). In this way, clientele systems tend to be less stable than governments which rest on popular legitimacy.

It is important here to distinguish between authority and legitimacy. The German sociologist Max Weber identified three broad bases for governmental authority: custom or tradition, the charisma of particular leaders, and established "legal-rational" procedures. Western liberal democratic governments generally are placed in the third category; clientele systems might best be placed in the first. Clientele systems achieve authority by "buying off" key citizens rather than by gaining reputations for "right and proper" power. Thus, to the liberal, clientelism can be viewed as a means for conferring authority with little regard for legitimacy. In most cases, modern clientelism, as a basis for governmental authority, is associated with authoritarian governments.

Applications

Examples of clientelism can be found, in different incarnations, in various parts of the world and at different times. Two features of clientelism are familiar to Americans. "Patronage" is a classic feature of the so-called political machines in American cities of the late nineteenth and early twentieth centuries. Machine patronage relates to clientelism, in that the clients—who were typically working-class and immigrant voters—supported the political patrons ("bosses") who in turn provided jobs and political favors. As with the broader definition of clientelism, patronage addressed the material needs of political supporters without necessarily making public interest in the larger sense a criterion for public policy. In Chicago from the mid-1950's until the mid-1970's, for example, the political machine of Mayor Richard Daley managed to retain power with an unlikely coalition of white and black voters and other diverse groups which supported it in exchange for the many jobs and other benefits at the disposal of the machine. Daley's was one of the last machines, however, and after his death in 1977 the voting coalition fragmented into competing racial and ethnic groups. The demise of machines and patronage in America is due in large part to progressive reforms which stressed allocating public jobs on the basis of merit, protecting the secrecy of ballots, and improving public access to the government generally.

"Iron triangles" in governmental regulatory relationships can be considered a variant of clientelism. In such cases, legislators draft laws that favor those industries and trades which support them, usually with campaign contributions. Thus, a patron-client relationship may develop between members of Congress (usually within a relevant committee or subcommittee) and representatives of wealthy or powerful interest groups. The third point of the triangle comes in the form of government regulators, who avoid strict enforcement of regulations upon those same industries or businesses, usually as a tacit exchange for continued funding or other benefits controlled by those same congressional committees. Iron triangles are thought to be quite prevalent in contemporary American politics.

Even more pervasively, patron-client relations can be found in Japan. Throughout the society, relationships are structured along the principle of *oyabunkobun*, which means literally "parent-role, child-role." The deference and hierarchy which charac-terize modern Japanese society in large part reflect Japan's past history of feudalism. Clientelism also characterizes a dimension of Japanese politics, in that exchanges of political favors and money pervade the system. Individual members of the Japanese Diet (parliament) tend to rely on their own personal patron-client networks (*koenkai*), which are similar to the American political machines discussed above. These networks have been highly effective. Although there are a number of different factors at play in Japanese politics, the fact that the Liberal Democratic Party maintained uninterrupted power in Japan from the time of its creation in 1955 until 1993 reflects more the effectiveness of clientelism than the popularity of its policies and ideology.

Although features of clientelism appear in some of the most modern and industri-alized countries—even those typically thought of as "democratic"—clientelism in these countries is not seen as a fundamental bulwark of governmental authority. In the field of political science "clientelism" more often refers to national governmental systems whose very authority depends on patron-client relations. These countries are typically less-developed, authoritarian states in Africa and Latin America. One reason for this is that clientelism thrives best where resources are most scarce. Scarcity drives clients to comply with the wishes of their patrons, rather than "go it alone" outside of the clientele system. In these countries, opportunities for securing rewarding jobs, decent housing, adequate incomes, education, health care, and so forth are few outside of the patron-client network.

Nigeria is one such country. Its economy is highly dependent upon the export of raw materials—particularly oil, whose prices became exceptionally unstable in the late twentieth century. Much of Nigeria's population lives in poverty, and the figures for life expectancy, infant mortality, caloric intake, and other indicators of quality of life are despairingly low. The country also has one of the world's most fragmented societies, with deep ethnic divisions that lead to chronic instability. Like many poor tropical countries, Nigeria is a creation of European colonization and thus is viewed as an "artificial" creation whose various peoples are not bound together by a sense of common nationalism. As a result, Nigeria's political system has been highly unstable since the country gained independence in 1960. Most often only military regimes have been able to hold power. In such a setting, clientelism has been one of the few mechanisms capable of maintaining a semblance of order in the society, even amid coups and civil wars.

Modern clientelism builds upon a particularly salient characteristic of colonial Nigeria: the division of the population into regional fiefdoms ruled by relatively strong leaders playing ethnic and tribal politics. During the colonial era, the British used rural elites to maintain order over various regions of Nigeria. After independence, those elites used their authority to build relatively powerful patron-client networks. No national government in independent Nigeria could hope to maintain power without their cooperation (or co-optation). With neither a sense of governmental legitimacy nor of nationhood, Nigeria perhaps needs clientelism to function. Yet clientelism also impedes Nigeria's hopes for progressive governmental and economic reform, and thence improved standards of living for the population as a whole.

In all these ways—as corrupt aspects of otherwise democratic states such as the United States, as a foundation for entrenched one-party rule in countries such as Japan, or as the only real source of political order in less developed countries such as Nigeria—different forms of clientelism are visible in political systems throughout the world. As a political philosophy it may have few advocates, but as a practical system of keeping governments functioning, it has its apologists.

Context

Since the demise of Leninist-style authoritarianism at the end of the 1980's, political systems have been increasingly measured by the ideals of Western liberal democracy. Clientelism is seen to fall short on a number of grounds. For example, clientele systems by definition favor political supporters, thus violating the equality principle of democracy. To the extent that their political decisions ignore the wishes or interests of the polity at large, clientele systems violate democratic notions of popular sovereignty. Thus, whereas most contemporary political systems are self-described as "democratic," those with a feature of clientelism (among others) necessarily fall short of that ideal. Clientelism also clashes with Western liberal values in other ways. It deviates from the Weberian ideal of bureaucracy in that governmental and quasi-governmental positions are allocated on the basis of patronage rather than merit. Beyond this, clients within hierarchies place the interests of their immediate patrons above those of the government or country as a whole. Even the principle of rule of law is consistently ignored in practice, for governmental services and even the administration of justice are conducted largely on the basis of what amounts to bribes.

Such criticisms notwithstanding, clientelism is explained, and sometimes defended, as consistent with the culture of the nation in question. Democratic liberal governments, with their emphasis on individualism and responsibility, it is argued, are ill-suited to hierarchically structured, deferential societies. Patron-client systems are effective, stable, and appropriate societies "where they are." In other words, the very values that ground liberal democracy are sometimes challenged as "Eurocentric" or otherwise not universally applicable. Nevertheless, many of those who defend governments which rest on patron-client relations concede that clientelism (and even authoritarianism) should be viewed as justifiable temporary expedients along the path to democracy, rather than as ideals in themselves.

The debate is really one between idealism and pragmatism. The ideal of governmental legitimacy based on popular sovereignty and free elections is given lip service around the globe. But the reality of ethnic divisions, illiteracy, scarcity of goods, foreign and domestic enemies, and other threats to a people may make democratic ideals seem out of reach, or, worse, may make trying to achieve such ideals dangerous. Clientelism may thus be better suited to the realities of many states, particularly in the less developed world. But certainly it is neither more efficient nor more equitable than many of the alternatives.

Bibliography

Achebe, Chinua. *The Trouble with Nigeria*. Exeter, N.H.: Heinemann Educational Books, 1984. Compelling though brief book that discusses both the political and social issues in Nigeria. A novelist, Achebe has also written powerful fictional works, such as *A Man of the People* (1966), that explore clientelism.

Blau, Peter M. *Exchange and Power in Social Life*. New York: John Wiley & Sons, 1964. Blau discusses a variety of aspects of social organizations. His examination of reciprocity, legitimacy, and authority are particularly relevant to clientelism, although he does not focus on this subject itself.

Fiorina, Morris P. *Congress: Keystone of the Washington Establishment*. New Haven, Conn.: Yale University Press, 1977. The classic study of iron triangles in the American political system, this short book offers a provocative and compelling indictment of a U.S. Congress "captured" by special interests.

Gamer, Robert E. *The Developing Nations: A Comparative Perspective*. 2d ed. Dubuque, Iowa: William C. Brown, 1988. Chapter 4 of this textbook provides an excellent discussion of clientelism that includes several case studies.

O'Donnell, Guillermo A., Phillippe C. Schmitter, and Laurence Whitehead, eds. *Transitions from Authoritarian Rule: Latin America*. Baltimore: The Johns Hopkins University Press, 1986. Provides case studies of Latin American countries attempting to move from authoritarianism to democracy. Although the authors address clientelism only sparingly, patron-client relations are a central issue in these studies.

Olson, Mancur. *The Logic of Collective Action: Public Goods and the Theory of Groups*. Cambridge, Mass.: Harvard University Press, 1971. Classic work explaining why groups associate and cooperate.

Powell, John Duncan. "Peasant Society and Clientist Politics." *American Political Science Review* 64 (June, 1970): 412-425. Discusses clientelism as a "basic pattern of social relations" for coping with scarcity in peasant societies, offering a brief, scholarly overview of patron-client relations.

Steve D. Boilard

Cross-References

Accountability in U.S. Government, p. 1; Charismatic Leadership, p. 209; Corporatism, p. 452; Feudalism, p. 688; Iron Triangles, p. 981; Legitimacy, p. 1105; Political Machines and Bosses, p. 1468; Self-Interest in Politics, p. 1802.

COLONIAL GOVERNMENT

Field of study: Types of government

When colonists from the home country are the majority, their governments can have considerable autonomy. If colonists are a minority ruling over an indigenous majority, the government is more likely to resemble a political and military dictatorship.

Principal terms
CONQUEST COLONY: formed when an alien majority conquers and rules over the majority population of a territory
DOMINION: colony that has become autonomous and whose ties to the home country are primarily cultural and sentimental
SETTLER COLONY: formed when large numbers of people from the homeland emigrate to a colony and retain close economic and political links to the land of origin; likely to become a dominion

Overview

English terms such as "colonial" and "colony" derive from the Latin word for farmer, *colonus*. The connection is more than a matter of vocabulary. The founding of colonies was one of the strategies the ancient Romans employed in establishing their empire. Imperial governments encouraged, even ordered, bands of settlers to occupy new lands and bring them under the plow. If a territory was already inhabited, the colonists either drove off or subjugated the indigenous peoples. To facilitate that process, groups of farmers often included retired soldiers who were expected to use their training to defend and expand a colony.

The colonies of the ancient world were located relatively near their homelands. The age of European exploration, which began in the fifteenth century, expanded the possibilities of colonization. Using sea routes, the emerging nation-states of Europe— Spain, Portugal, The Netherlands, France, and England—were able to extend their influence to places many thousands of miles away. Asia, North America, South America, the islands of the Pacific, and sub-Saharan Africa became open for colonization.

In some cases, exploration led rapidly to the conquest of large indigenous populations by tiny groups of Europeans. The Spanish conquest of Mexico is an example. Hernán Cortés had only a few hundred soldiers and horses with him, but as an outsider, he was able to discern that the Aztecs who ruled over the central plateau of Mexico were unpopular with the majority of the Indian communities that they had conquered. Using the discontent of subject tribes and his meager supply of gunpowder weapons, Cortés managed to overthrow the Aztec ruler in 1520, making the Spaniards dominant in Mexico.

Soldiers such as Cortés made their conquests in the name of the kings of Spain. The governments created by him and such others as Francisco Pizarro, the conqueror of the Incas, were modeled on the institutions of their Spanish homeland. Royal governors controlled the governments' military and police activities, and notaries and judges handled matters of civil law. The number of Spaniards was small compared to that of Indians. The Spaniards were able to control the Indians, however, by brutalizing them. Notions of law and order or the rights of royal subjects in practice applied only to the Spaniards, not to the majority of Amerindian inhabitants. Ultimately, government was of, by, and for the Spanish.

European colonies established in Africa and Asia most often followed the Spanish pattern. Comparatively few Europeans arrived in the colonies. Most were soldiers, government administrators, merchants, missionaries, and those interested in commercial farming. They governed themselves according to the customs prevalent in the countries of their origin. They claimed as few or as many legal protections as their own traditions gave them. The indigenous people, who usually outnumbered the colonizers by hundreds or thousands to one, were not given a share in the government except on clearly subordinate levels. The "natives" could be recruited as soldiers and petty officials. They assisted, thereby, in controlling the majority of their compatriots, but they possessed few, if any, inalienable rights. Not every colonial regime was as brutal as that of the early Spanish conquerors. Even so, Europeans who went to the conquest colonies of Asia, Africa, and the Pacific Islands had a tendency to apply force, rather than persuasion, in ruling subjugated majorities.

A somewhat different situation prevailed in the seventeenth century, when North America was colonized by groups from France, Britain, and The Netherlands. The Indians of North America did not live in densely populated agricultural societies like those of Mexico or Peru. Colonists were able to drive away the Indians or subordinate them comparatively easily. European immigrants were, within a few years of their arrival, the dominant population in any given North American colony.

Several forms of government emerged in the British colonies. Some of them had been settled by religious dissidents, for example, Massachusetts by Puritans and Pennsylvania by Quakers. In those places, the governor was appointed by the king or queen of England, but invariably he was a member of the sect that had founded the colony. In the colonies of New England, the residents of cities, towns, and villages had the opportunity to participate in government on the local level by electing mayors and aldermen or by holding town meetings to discuss common problems. In Virginia, a royal governor ruled, but his powers were limited by the presence of a colonial assembly, the House of Burgesses. Virginians who owned sufficient property—big landowners and wealthy merchants—elected representatives to that body.

Because most settlers in the North American colonies were British, they enjoyed significant autonomy. The thirteen British colonies of North America became, in effect, dominions, places that governed themselves with only occasional interference from the homeland. That habit of independence led the British colonies in North America to resent all attempts to impose a regime directly controlled by the government in England. When the British parliament tried to levy additional taxes in the mid-eighteenth century, it brought on a rebellion that began in 1775 and ended successfully in 1783.

In Canada, the demand for complete independence was less strong, and the transformation from settler colony to dominion took more time. The British had conquered the French colony of Quebec in 1759. Because the government of France had never devoted great resources to the maintenance of its North American holdings, the British won an easy victory. The Quebecois, however, continued to employ the French language in the conduct of their own affairs. The Quebec Act of 1774 guaranteed them the right to practice Roman Catholicism.

In the eighteenth and nineteenth centuries, however, more and more settlers began to arrive from the British Isles. People from places such as New York and Virginia who had opposed American independence migrated to Canada after 1782. Other, non-British Canadians included former slaves who had fled servitude in the United States and Amerindians, such as the Iroquois, who were loyal to the British. English-speaking Canadians came to outnumber the Quebecois. The Constitutional Act of 1791 recognized the distinction between the cultural groups by dividing Canada into upper and lower portions, with the Quebecois having special autonomy in lower Canada. In 1867, the British North America Act created a dominion out of a collection of British settler colonies and Quebec. Although living in a dominion, Canadians, especially those of British ancestry, harbored emotional and cultural ties to the motherland. Canada provided troops and supplies for Britain during both World War I and World War II.

Applications

India and Australia are examples of two different ways in which colonial governments could develop. Both became part of an expanding British empire in the eighteenth century. Both maintained links to Britain through seaborne transport. India's colonial government was dominated by the military and political arms of the empire, which severely limited Indian participation in the government. Australia gradually became a self-governing settler colony that attained dominion status in the early twentieth century. India's and Australia's experiences were similar to those of other territories colonized by the French (in Algeria), Dutch (in Indonesia), Spanish (in the Philippines), and Portuguese (in Angola).

Following the lead of Portuguese and Dutch traders, British merchants arrived in India in the early years of the seventeenth century. For a century and a half, British interests were purely commercial. Until 1859, British interests in India were represented by the East India Company. The British bought Indian manufactures, particularly cotton cloth, for importation to the British Isles and the European continent. The cloth was also important in other economic enterprises. For example, Indian cloth was used to purchase slaves in West Africa.

Toward the middle of the eighteenth century, the political situation in India became unsettled. The power of the Mughal (Mogul) emperors began to fade. Local leaders who took control in the provinces were unwilling to recognize the trade concessions granted to the British by the Mughal emperor. These new power holders were also interested in creating their own trading networks, which would have undercut the British advantage in international business.

Partly to protect their commercial monopoly, the British involved themselves in the fluid politics of India. The East India Company began to recruit and train soldiers. A few regiments were made up of Britons and other Europeans, often sailors who had deserted their ships. Most of the company's army consisted of Indian troops commanded by British officers. Slowly the British emerged as the most powerful among several forces competing for dominance in the subcontinent. After an initial victory at Plassey in 1757, the British expanded their authority. In the early 1840's, the British annexed the Punjab and Sind regions. Apart from 125 "native princes," who were allowed some control over the internal politics of their kingdoms, the British controlled the whole of South Asia.

After the revolt of 1857, direct imperial rule replaced the more indirect style of government exercised by the East India Company. Higher administrators were always British. They tended to come from middle-class backgrounds and were educated in the public schools of Great Britain. Many of them had Scots or Irish ancestry. As young men of nineteen, they took examinations for the Indian Civil Service and began a two-year short course in the basics of the law and administration; they were sent out to India at about the age of twenty-one. After a two- or three-year apprenticeship, they moved into either the field of district administration or the judiciary. Employing about twelve hundred staff members, the Indian Civil Service made all major political decisions. Everything from taxation to public sanitation was in their control. Colonial officers were supposed to seek advice from Indians, but invariably administrators listened most closely to men who had received British-style educations or who were local notables such as landlords.

Indians took part in the government of their country primarily as soldiers and subordinate officials. When the Indian National Congress was founded in 1885, the organization sought modest reforms. For example, it requested that the examinations for the Indian Civil Service be held in India as well as in England so that Indians might have a chance to join that administrative elite. The earliest Indian politicians sought dominion status, believing that one day their country would have a place in the British Empire similar to that of Australia and Canada.

During World War I, Indians supported the British cause. Even Mohandas K. Gandhi, who eventually became known as the Mahatma, encouraged Indians to enlist in the armed forces or buy war bonds. He and other leaders expected that following the war real progress toward dominion status would occur. Instead, the British became more repressive, limiting the freedom of the press and public assembly, while imprisoning Gandhi and most other politicians. Independence then became the goal of the nationalist movement. It was finally attained in 1947.

Australia was founded in 1788 as a prison of continental dimensions. People convicted of both major and minor offenses were shipped to Australia, where they were expected to build their own dwellings as well as feed and clothe themselves.

Guards and their families were sent along with the prisoners. A unique kind of society grew. Only the most persistent criminals were kept locked up; other convicts began to build new lives for themselves. At the end of their sentences, many decided to stay in Australia and bought land for farms or established shops to serve the needs of the guards and prisoners.

The indigenous peoples of Australia, the so-called aborigines, lived in small bands scattered throughout that vast island continent. They could not effectively resist the colonists so tried to avoid them by moving ever deeper in the dry wastelands of the outback. Only in recent times have the aborigines attempted to have their claims to land and equal status recognized by the government.

Immigration to Australia began in the nineteenth century. The British government urged people to migrate in hopes that this would relieve the overcrowding that was making bigger cities in England unpleasant. By 1809, less than half of the ten thousand inhabitants of New South Wales were convicts. By the middle of the nineteenth century, each of Australia's provinces had two legislative houses. The legislative assembly was elected by nearly universal male suffrage, and a legislative council consisted of people either appointed by the governor or elected by the wealthiest landlords and merchants. In the 1890's, Australian politicians started a series of meetings that culminated in the drafting of a constitution for a united country. In 1900, the constitution was ratified by all the provinces and approved by the British government.

The comparative ease with which Australia became a dominion reflected the difference in the political fates of conquest and settler colonies. Britain acquired control of India through war and political maneuver. Indians never attained much influence over their government in part because they had an ethnic and cultural heritage different from that of their rulers. Australians, although many were of Scots or Irish descent, belonged to the same race as the British and used the English language. They were quickly entrusted with the power to run their own governmental institutions.

Context

Colonial governments have existed throughout history. In the ancient world, colonies tended to be small and located relatively close to the colonists' place of origin. From the sixteenth century onward, two processes changed the character of colonies as well as their governments. Improved technology, especially in shipbuilding and weaponry, made it possible for small groups of Europeans to travel across the seas to subdue majority populations in Asia, Africa, and the Pacific. The second trend involved the development of a capitalist world market. Having colonies enhanced the political prestige of the home country, and colonized territories also became the sources for vital raw materials as well as new markets for the sale of products manufactured in Europe.

Technological progress and the chance for profit combined to shape the colonial governments that emerged from the eighteenth to the twentieth century. As the scramble of the European powers to take over Africa in the second half of the nineteenth century showed, modern colonialism was probably more aggressive than its ancient models. Moreover, as the contrasting political histories of India and Australia demonstrated, modern colonial governments were more obviously racist. Australia, populated by English-speaking whites and despite its origins as a penal colony, moved rapidly to dominionhood. India, by contrast, remained under the control of a small core of British administrators until 1947. Modern colonialism, especially in the conquest colonies, was synonymous with imperialism.

Conquest as well as settler colonies did not survive the twentieth century. The French withdrawal in 1962 from Algeria, which had been ruled as a province of continental France, marked one of the last great independence struggles. Puerto Rico, a commonwealth of the United States, and the British West Indies were among the few places to retain colonial-style regimes. Some peoples, especially those in the Third World, argued that although nineteenth century colonialism had faded, a new style of colonial government had appeared. Neocolonialism did not feature the direct conquest or settlement of a territory; instead, the great powers of Europe and North America manipulated the economies of Asian and African nations. Most of the profits went back to Northern Europe and North America so that Asia and Africa would not be able to develop advanced economic systems. In that way, the heritage of colonial governments continued to influence the conduct of politics and economics in the contemporary world, but as in the past, the quasi colonies developed the strength to break away.

Bibliography

Baumgart, Winfried. *Imperialism: The Idea and Reality of British and French Colonial Expansion, 1880-1914.* New York: Oxford University Press, 1982. Based on extensive reading of scholarship on colonialism and imperialism, this work explores the relationship between the ideas and ideals of colonialism and the actual practice of colonial governments.

Bayly, C. A., ed. *Atlas of the British Empire: The Rise and Fall of the Greatest Empire the World Has Ever Known.* New York: Facts on File, 1989. More than a book of maps, this work summarizes the history of Britain's colonies, both conquest and settler dominions, from their earliest moments until the end of the empire.

Fieldhouse, D. K. *The Colonial Empires: A Comparative Survey from the Eighteenth Century.* 1965, Reprint. Houndsmills, England: Macmillan, 1991. Fieldhouse explores the colonies founded by the British, Spanish, and French, showing the ways in which their colonial governments were similar and different.

Hughes, Robert. *The Fatal Shore: The Epic of Australia's Founding.* New York: Alfred A. Knopf, 1987. Hughes is a writer with the rare ability to be both interesting and thought provoking. He describes the lives of ordinary Australians and discusses the transition from penitentiary to settler colony.

Kiernan, V. G. *America, the New Imperialism: From White Settlement to World Hegemony.* London: Zed Press, 1978. Nineteenth century colonial governments disappeared in the late twentieth century, and neocolonialism may have taken their place. This book is worth reading for that alternative perspective.

Said, Edward W. *Culture and Imperialism*. New York: Alfred A. Knopf, 1993. Said is very subtle in revealing the ways in which the literature and fine arts of Europe and America are connected to colonial realities. Governments and art, according to Said, cannot be separated easily.

Gregory C. Kozlowski

Cross-References
Africa: Politics and Governments, p. 21; Asia: Politics and Governments, p. 108; Capitalism, p. 197; Empires and Empire Building, p. 597; Hegemony, p. 817; Mercantilism, p. 1173; National Liberation Movements, p. 1255; Pacific Islander Governments, p. 1362; Pan-Africanism, p. 1369; Race and Ethnicity, p. 1654; Social Darwinism, p. 1833.

COLONIALISM AND ANTICOLONIALISM

Field of study: Political philosophy

Colonialism and anticolonialism are two major movements that peaked in the nineteenth and twentieth centuries, respectively. They left in their wake a highly unbalanced form of international interdependence.

Principal terms
ANTICOLONIALISM: opposition to colonialism
COLONIALISM: political and economic process of discovery, acquisition, settlement, and exploitation. The Western nations, in modern history, did this to large areas of the world in Africa, Asia, Latin America, and elsewhere
DECOLONIZATION: replacement of colonial empires by politically independent states
IMPERIALISM: extension of a nation's power and influence, domination of a weaker by a stronger society
INFORMAL EMPIRE: arrangement in which the older colonial relationship perpetuated, the former colonial power supplying manufactured goods and services and the formerly colonized state providing cheap labor and raw materials

Overview

Colonialism was originally a morally neutral term. In the twentieth century it acquired a negative connotation as democracy and the striving for self-determination signaled its end. Former possessions became independent, a large number after World War II. Following the conclusion of the formal colonial system, neocolonialism is alleged to have replaced it. In this view, neocolonialism continues the subordination and exploitation of what have become independent states. Neocolonialism describes the conditions under which former colonies continue to serve the economic, political, military, and other interests of powerful, mostly Western, countries.

As one historian has put it, ambition, avarice, the love of change, and the morbid spirit of discontent drove the Westerners to seek colonies in the fifteenth century and thereafter. Whether for raw materials or trading advantages, for slaves, for a place for white settlers, for strategic reasons, for religion or prestige, or for no other reason than that it had become fashionable, imperialism and its colonial application became a distinctive feature of the world order. Most often, nationalism and mercantilism provided the ideological underpinnings.

Portugal, Spain, The Netherlands, England, France, and later Belgium, Germany, Italy, Japan, and the United States led the cavalcade of colonizers. After World War I, the victors absorbed the possessions of the defeated German and Ottoman empires.

The administration of the colonies varied as greatly as the reasons for securing them.

There was direct rule of the colonizers and indirect rule through native surrogates. Some colonizers centralized their powers in cities, others spread their influence thinly over wide areas. Sometimes the colonial power wished to assimilate the natives into European civilization; more commonly, it sought to perpetuate their segregation and subordination. The ruling power may have sought to prepare the natives for self-determination or independence; it may have ignored or forestalled, or never considered, the issue. With few exceptions—for example, in the British mandate of Palestine after World War II—little thought was given to the future of colonies until anticolonialism became strong. Violent national liberation movements arose in the Dutch East Indies, French Indochina and Algeria, Portuguese Angola and Mozambique, among many other places.

Nationalist movements often arose under the leadership of Western-educated colonial subjects, for example, Mohandas Gandhi in British India, Félix Houphët-Boigny in the French Ivory Coast, and Ho Chi Minh in French Indochina. The expressed ideology of many of the Western powers—freedom, equality, independence—also found its way back to the colonies by other means. The leaders and the people of Western powers at times themselves opposed colonialism. The Atlantic Charter of 1941 includes the Four Freedoms; the United Nations Charter of 1945 has subtly anticolonialist provisions; and the Cold War obliged both the United States and the Soviet Union to oppose colonialism (as, for example, in the Suez crisis of 1956) for various reasons, one of which being the two powers' struggles in the theater of public opinion.

National liberation movements, once begun, met various forms of resistance. Great Britain made an unqualified unilateral declaration of Egypt's independence in 1922; this may be contrasted with the fierce anticolonial war in French Indochina that ended in 1954. Independence and decolonization generally have not come without heroic struggle, sacrifice, and resistance—often armed.

Applications

A successful but at times turbulent anticolonialist movement leading to independence was made by Zaïre (formerly the Belgian Congo), which became sovereign on June 30, 1960. It was only in January of that year that the colonizing power had publicly decided to grant its possession for the previous eighty or so years its freedom. There had been serious anti-Belgian riots in 1959 and some domestic and international public opinion began to advocate independence for the African nation. A conference between Belgian representatives of all three major political parties (including the governing party) and Congolese leaders was held in Brussels. A date for independence was set and a new constitution drafted. The Congolese leaders, while sharing strong nationalist feelings, were divided by tribal animosities, policy conflicts, and personal ambitions. As a result, a Congolese government could barely be put in place before independence day, with rivals uncomfortably sharing power.

Subsequent events demonstrated how such haste and lack of preparation could lead to crisis. The Belgian colonial authorities also did very little about transferring power to the Congolese until after independence. A crisis broke out within days when Congolese soldiers in the colonial army mutinied against their Belgian officers. In the meantime, Katanga, the richest province, declared its secession from the central government, soon followed by South Kasai. A breakdown in law and order precipitated a massive flight of Europeans, mostly Belgians, leaving the new country with few competent administrators. As in the army, there had been no Congolese serving in the higher ranks of the civil service. The same was true of the professions in the private sector. Long-repressed tribal violence exploded. Outside powers, especially the Soviet Union but also Belgium, perceiving a political vacuum, pursued their own political agendas within the country. While the country was unraveling, the Congolese leaders—most notably Patrice Lumumba, Joseph Kasavubu, Joseph-Desiré Mobutu, Moise Tshombe, and Antoine Gizenga—engaged in a political power game, enlisting eager outsiders in the process.

To prevent the new state from falling into chaos, the Congolese government appealed, less than two weeks after independence, to the United Nations for military and economic assistance. To some extent, both of these needs were met by the United Nations. The United Nations was ultimately unable to carry out the neutralist, non-interventionist mandate that the world body's leadership, especially U.N. secretary-general Dag Hammarskjold, had at first insisted upon.

Among those Congolese who would attend, numerous constitutional conferences took place. Numerous, often broken, promises to work for a united Congo were made. Fighting among central and provincial government troops, tribesmen, and foreign mercenaries finally provoked the active involvement of the twenty thousand-troop peacekeeping force. The bloodshed continued. Former premier Patrice Lumumba was assassinated by unidentified perpetrators and Hammarskjold and his aides were killed in a somewhat mysterious plane crash. Only when Mobutu, a former sergeant-major in the colonial force, finally asserted his political control—in effect in September, 1960, but officially as the country's president in 1965—was a federal constitution finalized and the dissident provinces reintegrated.

Nearly four decades later, the country, still ruled by Mobutu Sese Seko (his Africanized name), continued to be a turbulent one. Despite its extensive natural resources, it remained impoverished and indebted, still suffering from tribal conflict and widespread violations of human rights.

Despite the strife and grief in the post-World War II era, the end of colonialism became an irreversible trend. The Conference of Nonaligned Nations in Bandung, Indonesia, in 1955, called for the end of colonialism. The United Nations Declaration on the Granting of Independence to Colonial Countries and Peoples in 1960, and subsequent United Nations actions, amounted to the end of the era of colonial expansion that had begun with the explorations of the Portuguese and Spaniards in the late fifteenth century. These declarations had the effect of transforming independence from a privilege into a right. France's military defeat in Indochina in 1954 and its failure in Algeria in 1962 provided an object lesson to the still dependent peoples and marked a watershed between the historical processes of colonialism and decolonization. Attempts to turn the colonial clock back, most notably by the British and French in their Suez attack in 1956, proved unsuccessful.

The colonizers themselves may have contributed to the end of colonization. It became evident that empire-building was not cost-effective, given the expensive military and civilian administrations mandated by its continuation. The high economic costs of military and political empire have been elevated into a theory to explain the rise and decline of great nations. There may also have been a growing feeling among the colonizers that in an age of free trade and great interdependence, physical control of colonies was no longer necessary. Domestic and especially international public opinion had also turned against the perpetuation of so-called non-self-governing territories and other dependencies.

Context

Western colonialism left its mark. The colonizers brought political, economic, technological, religious, and cultural change. Conversely, the colonized provided raw materials and slaves to the Westerners. Some became prosperous, others very prosperous from the two-way flow between colony and parent state. Demographic changes also resulted from colonialism as mixed-race populations arose, in the case of at least one country even becoming the majority. This fact in turn often had political consequences as different ethnic and racial groups eventually vied for power.

Generally speaking, peoples who were colonized shared feelings of humiliation, manipulation, and exploitation. The mostly white colonizers often exhibited attitudes of racial and cultural superiority. All of this helped to create lasting resentment in the Third World.

Critics charge that as a result of colonial exploitation, much of the current Third World continues under Western control by other means and thus in a state of vulnerability and poverty. Others point to the civilizing influence and progress made available by the empire-builders. Admittedly, the overreliance on one or a few commodities as the basis of the colonial economies and colonizers' protections against local manufacture have continued to render recently independent states exposed to world market prices for raw materials over which they have little control. The terms of trade continue to tend against primary producers. The insistence by the former parent countries on processing colonial raw materials at home prevented the colonies from obtaining industry-related value-added income. Unquestionably, also, colonialism brought a stifling of political and human rights and an undermining of traditional authority. The artificial borders drawn by the colonial powers brought a bitter harvest of political, ethnic, and religious conflict across wide areas.

Apologists for colonialism list the projects built by the colonizers—railroad and telegraph lines, ports, dams, oil wells, mines, hospitals, schools, and clean water supplies. Although these endeavors were not necessarily motivated by concern for the well-being of the natives but rather by the interests of the white planters, miners, troops, and civil servants, the local populations nevertheless benefited from them, directly or otherwise. The empire-builders also brought some measure of law and order into the colonies and may have facilitated the integration of the colonies into the global system, though some say that this has been a destructive contact. Moreover, in some cases—China or Japan, for example—similar benefits were achieved without direct colonial rule.

For the colonizer, final assessment must weigh the high financial and human cost of colonialism against the opportunities for gain that overseas possessions created for whites in the public and private sectors. Ultimately, however, historical processes such as colonialism and its aftermath have their own internal logic, whether good, bad, or indifferent.

Bibliography

Barraclough, Geoffrey. *An Introduction to Contemporary History*. New York: Basic Books, 1964. Describes how the ideas, infrastructure, and institutions exported by the European colonizers to their possessions were used by the latter to undo colonial rule.

Betts, Raymond F. *Uncertain Dimensions: Western Overseas Empires in the Twentieth Century*. Minneapolis: University of Minnesota Press, 1985. Describes the interwar period, when the business of empire, especially that of the British and French in Africa and Asia, was to perpetuate peace through the often inconsistent goals of stable government and economic development.

Césaire, Aimé. "On the Nature of Colonialism." In *African Politics and Society*, edited by Irving L. Markovitz. New York: Free Press, 1970. A former deputy from Martinique denounces colonialism.

Fanon, Frantz. *Toward the African Revolution: Political Essays*. Translated by Haakon Chevalier. New York: Grove Press, 1988. The author, using Algeria as an example, urges the complete destruction of colonial structures, by force if necessary.

Fieldhouse, David K. *Colonialism, 1870-1945: An Introduction*. New York: St. Martin's Press, 1981. Simple and short account by a British scholar focusing on pertinent central issues, such as the economics of colonialism.

Gann, L. H., and Peter Duignan, eds. *Colonialism in Africa, 1870-1960*. 5 vols. New York: Cambridge University Press, 1969-1975. Includes a masterly account of the new imperialism in the continent.

Knight, Franklin W. *The Caribbean: The Genesis of a Fragmented Nationalism*. New York: Oxford University Press, 1978. Useful survey of the rise and fall of colonialism in a wide area.

Riley, Philip F., et al. *The Global Experience*. 2 vols. 2d ed. Englewood Cliffs, N.J.: Prentice Hall, 1992. Includes short but excellent selections on colonization and decolonization across the world.

Rodney, Walter. *How Europe Underdeveloped Africa*. London: Bogle-L'Ouverture, 1972. Tries to establish a direct correlation between development in colonial European nations and the lack of it in their African possessions and how these patterns of economic and human exploitation persist.

Peter B. Heller

Cross-References

Africa: Politics and Governments, p. 21; Asia: Politics and Governments, p. 108; Colonial Government, p. 344; Developed and Developing Nations, p. 533; Empires and Empire Building, p. 597; Hinduism and Government, p. 823; Imperialism, p. 889; Independence Movements and Transitions, p. 896; Indigenous Peoples' Governments, p. 903; Mercantilism, p. 1173; National Liberation Movements, p. 1255; Nationalism, p. 1268; Social Darwinism, p. 1833.

COMMERCE REGULATION

Field of study: Functions of government

Governments regulate commerce to protect consumers against fraud and monopoly; to protect sellers against competition and entry of new businesses into the marketplace; to raise revenue; and to provide government officials with opportunities for personal gain.

Principal terms
CLIENTELE GROUP: beneficiaries of a particular government, usually organized; often a pressure group closely associated with a particular government agency
COMMERCE: buying and selling of goods and services, primarily those currently produced
CONTRACT: legally binding agreement to do something, usually in exchange for something of value
EXCISE TAX: tax levied on production or sale of a product
EXTERNALITY: significant cost or benefit from a decision that is not experienced by the decision makers
FRANCHISE: grant of permission to enter some activity from which the general public is barred
NATURAL MONOPOLY: type of production for which efficiency seems to be best achieved if there is only one producer
PRICE DISCRIMINATION: charging different prices to different buyers in situations where there is no comparable difference in the cost of supplying the different buyers
RENT-SEEKING BEHAVIOR: action aimed at increasing a group's share of the national income through government favoritism in ways that tend to decrease rather than increase the national income

Overview
A society's economic well-being depends to a great extent on buying and selling goods. The economic productivity of developed economic systems rests on specialization. Individual workers who concentrate on a specific craft or occupation can develop great skill in it. Business firms focus on certain products and processes, enabling them to develop highly specialized technology and equipment. Specialization is necessary for efficiency, but can not benefit the public unless there is effective exchange of the resulting goods and services. Consumers want a variety of goods and services. Buying and selling is the link that enables a person to receive a money income by supplying specialized services, and then to spend that income to purchase the specific items of food, clothing, shelter, transport, and entertainment that the person desires.

Although most people participate in the economy as both buyers and sellers, and share a common interest in having the economy work efficiently, particular buyers often confront particular sellers with a sense of conflict of interest. Individual consumers may feel powerless as buyers from large firms and may enlist the aid of government. Sellers depend on their sales revenues for their employment and their incomes. They are likely to try to persuade government to buy, promote, or subsidize their goods and services, or to impede the efforts of competitors to take away some of their business. Government's interest in commerce includes securing funds from the world of commerce by taxation or borrowing, along with the need to buy goods and services to support their operations. Government officials also may seek to advance their own welfare by intervening in market relationships.

In a market economy, government advances a favorable environment for commerce through the maintenance of law and order. Buying and selling operations work best when free from force and fraud. The legal system can prevent theft or extortion and limit opportunities for false and misleading information. The legal system helps to define and enforce appropriate contracts and property rights.

Commerce is a convenient area from which to collect taxes. The U.S. government levied its earliest taxes on goods imported from overseas (the Constitution forbids taxing exports), soon following with excise taxes on alcohol and tobacco products. Since taxing these items tends to reduce their consumption, there is a regulatory dimension to such taxes.

Governments are likely to impose outright prohibitions against goods and services deemed harmful. Between 1919 and 1933, the federal government attempted to prohibit the production and sale of alcoholic beverages, without notable success. In the early 1990's, the most prominent contraband goods were addictive substances such as marijuana and cocaine. Traditional prohibitions against vices such as prostitution, pornography, and gambling have lost much of their vigor and support.

Governments often regulate a commercial activity by requiring a license, franchise, or permit to engage in it. This is usually defended as a method of quality control, as with doctors. Companies providing electric power, telephone or cable television service, and other public utilities have been franchised because they were thought to be natural monopolies, that is, services for which it is inefficient to have many firms operating in one area. Public utilities have been subjected to direct government control of their rates and service. All programs to prevent entry into an activity can turn into methods of suppressing competition and limiting opportunity for the benefit of the existing suppliers.

Government often regulates commerce through specialized administrative boards or commissions. Most states have one or more commissions that regulate public utilities, and others that regulate banks and financial institutions. An important role for government regulatory agencies is inspection and examination of private firms. Operations involving food sale and preparation, for example, are subject to sanitary inspection. State and local governments commonly have agencies concerned with establishments that sell and serve alcoholic drinks.

Governments also influence commerce through promotional activity. The U.S. Department of Commerce conducts many activities designed to help business firms, in part through collecting and publishing business information. State and local governments have agencies that try to attract businesses to locate within their borders. More generally, governments assist commerce by providing a stable and unified monetary system, a suitable system of weights and measures, and such infrastructure facilities as highways and airports.

Applications

The historical evolution of commerce regulation in the United States has been closely bound up with the federal Constitution. The Constitution directly authorized Congress to regulate commerce with foreign countries, among the states, and with Native American tribes. States were forbidden to regulate interstate commerce, except as needed for their inspection laws. Regulation of intrastate commerce was among the implied powers left to the individual states by the Tenth Amendment. Closely related to commerce were Congress's powers to create money and regulate its value, to punish counterfeiting, to set rules for bankruptcy, and to provide a postal service. State governments were forbidden to take actions that would impair private contracts, to issue paper money, or to make anything except gold or silver legal tender.

In the early days of the new republic, state and local governments maintained traditional forms of licensing, inspection, and regulation. These faded away as economic growth and free-enterprise ideology became dominant in the nineteenth century. The federal government undertook no significant regulation of interstate buying and selling of goods until after the Civil War.

As the farm sector experienced economic distress in the postwar deflation, a new sentiment for regulation arose. It focused initially on railroads, spread toward trusts and monopolies in general, and took particular aim at public utilities. In each instance, the problem was perceived to be monopoly, leading to high prices and discriminatory treatment of different customers. Individual state governments tried to regulate railroad rates through the Granger laws of the 1870's. In 1886, the U.S. Supreme Court struck down as unconstitutional state regulation involving interstate shipments. Federal policy moved into this vacuum with the creation of the Interstate Commerce Commission (ICC) in 1887. Initially, the ICC was empowered to require railroads to publish their rates and refrain from unfair discrimination; in 1906, it was given explicit authority to set rates.

Congress confronted the issue of business monopoly directly when it passed the Sherman Antitrust Act in 1890. The act outlawed contracts and conspiracies in restraint of trade or commerce as well as actions to monopolize or attempt to monopolize any part of that trade or commerce. An early case against the sugar trust was dismissed by the courts on grounds that it was directed against manufacturing, rather than commerce. This distinction was soon swept away by the doctrine that monopoly in manufacturing would produce monopoly in commerce as well. The Sherman Act did not prevent a wave of corporate mergers and consolidations, highlighted by the formation of the world's largest corporation of its time, United States Steel, through merger in 1901. Successful prosecutions were brought, however, against Standard Oil and American Tobacco, two notorious trusts, each of which was broken up into several components by court decisions in 1911.

With the spirit of reform associated with the Progressive Movement, federal regulatory programs expanded after 1900. The Pure Food and Drug Administration was created in 1906. In 1914, the Clayton Act attempted to extend the Sherman Antitrust Act by adding restrictions on price discrimination, interlocking directorships, binding and exclusive dealing contracts, and mergers. That same year the Federal Trade Commission (FTC) was created with the authority to enforce the Clayton Act and a prohibition against unfair methods of competition.

World War I led to vast but largely temporary extensions of government regulatory authority. The Lever Food Control Act of 1917 was the principal instrument. Government price controls were put into effect, and direct controls were imposed on businesses vital to national defense and economic strength. The federal government took over direct management of the railroads and telegraph system. These programs were rapidly reversed when the war ended in 1918. Efforts to improve labor standards by direct regulation were also removed. The Supreme Court ruled the Federal Child Labor Law of 1916 unconstitutional, because it went beyond the bounds of interstate commerce.

The Great Depression of the 1930's radically altered the regulatory atmosphere. Franklin D. Roosevelt was inaugurated president in March, 1993, with 25 percent of the labor force unemployed and the nation's banking system in shambles. Many of Roosevelt's advisers, unlike other contemporaneous thinkers, believed that the Depression resulted from excessive competition. As a result, major New Deal policies attempted to promote recovery by encouraging producers to group together to reduce competition. In 1933, Congress adopted the first Agricultural Adjustment Act, which provided incentives for farmers to reduce output in order to receive higher prices. In 1935, the Supreme Court invalidated the program as going beyond the scope of interstate commerce.

This was the last notable example of judicial opposition to an expanded role for federal economic regulation, however. Beginning in 1937, court decisions no longer impeded the regulatory trend. In the National Labor Relations (Wagner) Act of 1935, federal authority was placed squarely behind the promotion and encouragement of labor unions. The law forbade various antiunion activities by employers and created the National Labor Relations Board to conduct elections for workers to decide if they wanted union representation. In 1937, the Supreme Court acquiesced. The Fair Labor Standards Act of 1938 established minimum wage and maximum hours regulations for interstate commerce; the Supreme Court sustained the law in 1941. A new Agricultural Adjustment Act was adopted in 1938. Even though it went so far as to dictate what individual farmers could grow on their own land, it was upheld by the Supreme Court in *Wickard v. Filburn* (1942). This case definitively ended the use of the commerce clause of the Constitution as a restraint on federal government regulation. By 1942, the role of regulating commerce had been extended from the buying and selling of goods to all types of production and employment.

World War II brought vastly extended federal regulation. Price and wage controls were imposed. Products such as gasoline and sugar were rationed. Business firms were told what they could or could not produce. As before, these regulations were quickly removed once the war ended, although some were temporarily restored during the Korean War (1950-1953). The Taft-Hartley Act of 1947 prohibited some unfair labor practices by labor unions. Effective restraint on big-business mergers was enacted in the Celler-Kefauver Anti-Merger Act of 1950.

Commerce in medical goods and services was gradually brought under extensive government regulation after the creation of Medicare and Medicaid in 1965. New domains of regulation came in 1970 with the creation of the federal Environmental Protection Agency (EPA) and Occupational Safety and Health Administration (OSHA). During the presidency of Jimmy Carter (1977-1981), significant deregulation decreased the federal control of prices and entry in such sectors as railroads, natural gas, highway and air transport, and banking.

Context

Government regulation of commerce has always been controversial because conflicts of interest are always involved. There are also profound ideological issues. Critics of government regulation often argue in the tradition of Adam Smith. Smith's classic *The Wealth of Nations* (1776) argued that competition and free entry would protect consumers and workers against being exploited by business more effectively than would government regulations. Government officials are likely to form alliances with powerful business groups to the detriment of the general public.

Poor economic performance in the 1930's strengthened the position that market economies were subject to extensive market failure resulting from monopoly, lack of information, or the existence of significant "externalities"—major costs or benefits that result from decisions, but are experienced by persons not involved in the decision making. For example, pollution is often a negative externality; education is often a positive externality. Decisions that do not internalize all costs and benefits—that is, assign them to those who made the decision—will not be optimal. Government regulation, it was argued, could improve outcomes.

Optimism about the benefits of government regulation was challenged by economists, such Nobel Prize winners Friedrich Hayek and James Buchanan, who developed the theory of public choice. In this view, government officials are seeking to promote their own self-interest just as anyone else does. Officials seeking reelection will try to generate large flows of campaign contributions and perhaps to line up private sector jobs for themselves in the future. This often leads to special-interest programs that give substantial benefits to a small but well-organized clientele group (usually producers), while imposing a cost on the rest of society that is large in the aggregate but small for any individual. Producers then find it necessary to spend money on lobbying to secure such advantages or prevent others. Regulatory programs often have created an organized clientele powerful enough to prevent removal of the benefits. Actions intended to increase a group's share of total income, rather than increasing the total income through higher productivity, are termed "rent-seeking" by economists. Issues of this sort were manifest in the campaign for a comprehensive national medical program advocated by President Bill Clinton after his election in 1992. Prospective beneficiaries sought programs that would shift costs to others. Critics pointed to the danger that a vast new federal bureaucracy would be created. Campaign contributions poured in from many interested parties. In such situations, there may be no simple and obvious public interest, but rather a tug of war between competing private interests, with no assurance that the outcome will be either fair or efficient.

Bibliography

Cowen, Tyler, ed. *Public Goods and Market Failures: A Critical Examination*. New Brunswick, N. J.: Transaction, 1992. Essays by academic authorities present the justifications for government regulation based on the concepts of public goods and market failure, and also criticisms.

Cramer, Gail L., and Clarence W. Jensen. *Agricultural Economics and Agribusiness*. 5th ed. New York: John Wiley & Sons, 1991. University text; chapters dealing with agricultural price and income policies, natural resources, and a comparison of agricultural systems in the United States, the former Soviet Union, and communist China.

Friedman, Milton, and Rose Friedman. *Free to Choose*. New York: Harcourt Brace Jovanovich, 1980. The Nobel-Prize winning economist and his wife collaborated on this tract condemning many forms of government regulation. For the general reader . Readable style and insightful analysis.

Gormley, William T. *The Politics of Public Utility Regulation*. Pittsburgh: University of Pittsburgh Press, 1983. Clear statements of the economic conflicts and complexities in utility regulation. Extensive survey data on the political and administrative dimensions of regulation.

Hughes, Jonathan. *The Governmental Habit Redux: Economic Controls from Colonial Times to the Present*. 2d ed. Princeton, N. J.: Princeton University Press, 1991. Distinguished economic historian looks at the evolution of economic controls in the United States with particular concern for the political and social factors that led to particular programs.

Mason, Alpheus T., and William M. Beaney. *American Constitutional Law*. 6th ed. Englewood Cliffs, N. J.: Prentice-Hall, 1978. Chapter 6 of this university text, "Congressional Power Under the Commerce Clause," gives excerpts from eleven major cases.

Miller, G. Tyler. *Living in the Environment*. 8th ed. Belmont, Calif.: Wadsworth, 1994. Extensive treatment of environmental problems and policies, with a bias toward more regulation rather than less.

Nowotny, Kenneth, David B. Smith, and Harry M. Trebing, eds. *Public Utility Regulation: The Economic and Social Control of Industry*. Boston: Kluwer, 1989.

Good overview essays, followed by more sophisticated case studies of electric power, telecommunications, natural gas, and water supply.

Rockoff, Hugh. *Drastic Measures: A History of Wage and Price Controls in the United States.* New York: Cambridge University Press, 1984. Argues that governments are the source of inflationary pressure, but try to prevent inflation by controls that create problems worse than those they solve.

Stigler, George J. *The Citizen and the State.* Chicago: University of Chicago Press, 1975. Nobel laureate Stigler's witty style is laced with shrewd skepticism about many types of regulation. Brief essays discuss why regulatory programs were adopted and what their consequences are.

Paul B. Trescott

Cross-References

Agriculture Management, p. 41; The Arts and Government, p. 101; Business and Government, p. 177; Communications Management, p. 370; The Constitution of the United States, p. 425; Corporatism, p. 452; Energy Management, p. 604; Industrialization, p. 916; Interest Groups, p. 936; Iron Triangles, p. 981; Labor Relations, p. 1038; Mercantilism, p. 1173; National Economies, p. 1248; Policy Development and Implementation, p. 1414; Political Economy, p. 1455; Public Utilities, p. 1640; Regulatory Agencies in the United States, p. 1678; Transportation Management in the United States, p. 2006.

COMMONWEALTHS

Field of study: Types of government

In its most popular modern usage, the term "commonwealth" signifies a collection of countries (or other entities) that regularly and formally consult each other, coordinate their policies, and otherwise join in association for mutual benefit. Some form of historical, cultural, or ideological ties typically bind the various members together.

Principal terms
COLONIALISM: resettling of persons to a different territory for the purpose of extending the influence of the parent country, which usually makes a claim to the new territory
EMPIRE: group of countries under the control of a single power
FEDERALISM: division of sovereignty between a central government, with authority over the country as a whole, and several regional or provincial governments, with authority over their own parts of the territory
FEDERATION: federalism at a supranational level, as with the European Union
IMPERIALISM: extension of a state's power through conquest and colonialism, with the goal of creating or extending an empire
REPUBLIC: government whose powers derive from the people, rather than a monarch
SELF-DETERMINATION: principle that a distinct people, or "nation," should govern itself
STATE: territory with distinct borders, a population, and a government with supreme authority

Overview

The term "commonwealth" derives from the phrase "common weal" (meaning public good), which the English philosopher Thomas Hobbes used to describe the collective interests of the members of a society. As a description of a political order, commonwealth originally emphasized that the members of the polity were bound together in common cause to protect their shared interests. For Hobbes, the greatest threat to the public good was anarchy—the hypothetical state of nature in which life is "solitary, poor, nasty, brutish, and short." Hobbes applied the term commonwealth to a society which, in order to escape anarchy, confers its "power and strength upon one man, or upon one assembly of men, that may reduce all their wills, by plurality of voices, unto one will."

Over time, commonwealth came variously to mean any sovereign state, a republic (that is, a representative democracy), or a federal state. Thus, in reference to the first meaning, the sixteenth century French philosopher Jean Bodin used the term to describe an entity which had "puissant sovereignty," regardless of governmental form. In fact, Bodin held the absolute monarchy of France to be a model of a "just" commonwealth. The second meaning of commonwealth is more restrictive: a republic, in contrast to a monarchy. Thus, when the forces of Oliver Cromwell overthrew the monarchy in Great Britain in 1649, the resulting republic was called the Commonwealth—until the monarchy was restored in 1660. The third meaning of the term is more restrictive yet: a federal state, as opposed to a unitary one. In its official name, Australia, for example, is described as a commonwealth, reflecting the fact that the country is a federation containing six states. Of the fifteen or so of the world's countries that can be considered true federal states, few are officially called commonwealths. To add to the confusion, a number of nonsovereign entities also have claimed the title of commonwealth. Within the United States, for example, Kentucky, Maryland, Massachusetts, Pennsylvania, and Virginia have officially designated themselves as commonwealths. In the eyes of the United States government, however, they are politically indistinguishable from the rest of the fifty states.

From the above discussion it might seem that "commonwealth" is merely an affected term meant to call attention to the decentralized (or federal) aspects of a government and the interdependent (common weal) aspects of a polity. Yet the term remains important for describing a unique feature of some modern political relationships: namely, a political association among otherwise sovereign states. In this sense, the best example is the Commonwealth of Nations, which comprises the United Kingdom and almost fifty states which were once colonies of the British Empire. The purpose of this organization is to coordinate policies and otherwise consult on issues of common concern. The Commonwealth of Nations was created after World War I as the British colonies were increasingly granted political equality and ultimately independence. The Commonwealth might therefore be seen as a "kinder and gentler" successor to the British Empire. Membership in it is strictly voluntary; several former colonies choose to remain outside of it. The sovereignty of the members is acknowledged, although the entire Commonwealth is ceremonially headed by the British monarch. The formal institutional apparatus is centered on a secretariat based in London. Although it does not have legislative powers over member countries, it does have a bureaucracy for research, analysis, communication, and administration.

Is the Commonwealth of Nations then just another alliance or is it an international organization? Two features distinguish it from security-pact organizations, such as the North Atlantic Treaty Organization (NATO) and trade organizations, such as the North American Free Trade Agreement (NAFTA). The first difference derives from the fact that the members of the Commonwealth have a shared history of existing as a larger political unit—in this case, the British Empire. As the ceremonial leadership of the monarch illustrates, the members of the Commonwealth remain united in some measure by a common political and cultural legacy, which undergirds their governments and societies. Further, the members of the Commonwealth are linked together through institutional, economic, trade, and security relationships which began during the years of the British Empire and which continue to play important roles for many of those countries. The second feature that distinguishes the Commonwealth of Nations relates to its structure and purpose. Typically, states join international organizations like NATO and NAFTA to achieve narrow functional objectives, such as mutual security or increased trade. They also take on treaty obligations to help promote those functional goals. Unlike those organizations, the Commonwealth of Nations places no treaty obligations—indeed, no binding commitments whatever—upon its members. It does, however, define areas of focus, such as economic and technical cooperation, rural development, and youth services. But these are topics that are to be discussed, not issues to be legislated. In short, whereas members of international organizations like NATO, NAFTA, and even the United Nations join to achieve functional objectives, the Commonwealth of Nations is founded on a more organized, preexisting relationship.

These different examples of commonwealths, including the Commonwealth of Virginia, the Commonwealth of Australia, and the Commonwealth of Nations, illustrate the considerable breadth of the term. A common thread is the commitment both to the member's collective interests and interdependence and to their individual uniqueness and autonomy (or even sovereignty). These entities have adopted the term "commonwealth" to emphasize the relationship among their members, whether those members are citizens of the polity, provinces of the federation, or countries of a former empire.

Applications

One of the newer examples of a commonwealth is the Commonwealth of Independent States (CIS), which was created in December, 1991. The CIS was founded by the three Slavic republics of the former Soviet Union (Russia, Belorussia, and Ukraine) with a declaration that the Soviet Union was "ceasing to exist." For several years the Soviet Union had been weakening, with its various constituent republics declaring autonomy and even independence from Moscow. These defections had been prompted by the economic and political crises which resulted from Soviet president Mikhail Gorbachev's foundering attempts to reverse his country's long-term economic decline. After all fifteen of the Soviet Union's republics had declared independence, the CIS was founded and the Soviet state was formally dissolved.

The CIS soon expanded to include most of the former Soviet republics (only the three Baltic republics of Estonia, Latvia, and Lithuania are not members). Membership, which is voluntary, was prompted in large part by fears of regional chaos. In one sense at least, the CIS was created for much the same reason as the Commonwealth of Nations: as a way to structure relations among countries whose interrelationship as members of an empire was coming to an end. Yet the stark differences between the Soviet Union and the British Empire virtually guaranteed that their successor organizations would be equally different. The British Empire had been geographically extended and governmentally dispersed. It was created primarily through colonialism, rather than annexation. The British Empire had been built with a variety of motives, including a desire for favorable trade links and a strong missionary spirit.

By contrast, the Soviet Union was a single country, albeit a multinational one with an enormous landmass. The Marxist-Leninist ideology which was the official doctrine of the Soviet government was used to justify a number of efforts, such as the annexation of territory, the isolation of the population from external—especially Western—influences, governmental ownership of business and industry, central control of economic and trade decisions, and severe restrictions upon speech, assembly, and other civil liberties recognized in the West. Marxist-Leninist ideology also was used to rationalize the purges of government and party officials, and the torture, execution, and starvation of millions of citizens. Throughout all of this, the Soviet government sought to mitigate national differences within the country—and thereby create a Soviet "nationality"—although many of the non-Russian peoples saw this effort as "Russification."

The republics of the Soviet Union defected partly out of a desire to escape the oppressive, malignant ideology of Marxism-Leninism, and partly to fulfill their individual nationalist aspirations of self-determination. Yet achieving the ideal of sovereignty did not negate the reality of mutual interdependence—an interdependence which had been intentionally nurtured and augmented by the Soviet leaders as a way of cementing their empire. As newly independent states, the former Soviet republics had to address financial matters (they had shared a common currency and banking system), create new trade relations, coordinate their transportation and communications networks, apportion their shared assets from the Soviet state (especially weapons and other military materiel), and otherwise ensure stability and security. Thus, the CIS was seen by its members as a way of coordinating security and economic policies while maintaining individual sovereignty. In other words, like the former colonies of the British Empire, the former republics of the Soviet Union perceived that the demise of their empire, however desirable in terms of self-determination, left an unacceptable void in terms of their shared interests.

The founding documents of the CIS declared commitments to human rights, rule of law, and policy coordination, but the institutional framework of the CIS remained vague. A "Council of Heads of State" and a "Council of Heads of Government" were charged with leading the CIS, but these bodies met infrequently. The councils comprised, respectively, the presidents and prime ministers of the member states. Any decisions made by these councils had to be unanimous and then were subject to ratification by the parliaments of the member states. Such high-level summitry typically is unwieldy and inefficient without permanent, lower-level institutions empowered to discuss, negotiate, and compromise on issues of importance to the group. There were some attempts in the mid-1990's to create stronger institutions such as these, but the continuing disputes among the members on a variety of matters severely hampered the significant long-term strengthening of Commonwealth institutions. Meanwhile, the CIS lacked joint military forces and a central bank. There was no joint citizenship, nor were there any governmental leaders elected by the Commonwealth as a whole. As a symbolic statement, the CIS did not even have a capital; however, Minsk, the capital of Belarus, served as its "Coordination Center."

Some outside observers (as well as many member states themselves) feared that the

CIS was little more than an institution to justify Russian meddling in the affairs of the other member states, which the Russians collectively called "the Near Abroad." Russia deployed troops in various parts of the CIS, ostensibly to help stabilize and resolve regional disputes, such as ethnic fighting in Azerbaijan. Georgia, which initially chose not to join the CIS, felt compelled to join in order to receive Russian military assistance in quelling a separatist revolt within its Abkhazia region. Some observers speculated that the Russians helped generate the separatist revolt as a way to prompt Georgian membership. Further, Russia claimed a special interest in the Near Abroad on the basis of the fact that about twenty-five million ethnic Russians lived in those countries. In short, some see the CIS as a way for Russia to reestablish a de facto Russian empire.

Despite these criticisms, the CIS achieved some success in its founding purpose. It established several protocols to coordinate trade relations, rail and air traffic, and visa policies. Further, no one can say how much worse relations among the former Soviet republics might have been had the CIS not existed. One point is clear: The CIS remained a weak, vaguely-defined institution whose members enjoyed full de jure sovereignty, although the de facto power of Russia far outweighed that of the other member states combined. For all of its flaws, however, its members evidently believed that the benefits of membership outweighed the costs.

Context

The term "commonwealth," at all levels of analysis, denotes a system whose purpose is to promote and protect the common "weal" or "good." It suggests a political relationship based on mutual benefit. As logical and unremarkable as that might seem, it contrasts markedly with other political systems and political philosophies. Many governmental structures have been created not for the express purpose of promoting the public interest, but for less idealistic purposes, such as maintaining minority rule over ethnic or racial majorities (as in South Africa until the 1990's) or promoting one class over another (as in Russia in 1917). Some philosophies, such as fascism, place the interests of the state above the interests of the polity. Still others seek to reshape or redefine the polity (totalitarianism). Supranational entities such as empires (including the German and Soviet empires, leaving aside the question of the British Empire) have been built for the benefit of one nation above others.

These categories of political philosophy, government, and political relationships are not mutually exclusive. Intentions, structures, and functions can be combined in a number of ways. Indeed, the mere self-designation as a "commonwealth" does not necessarily indicate which particular governmental structures or principles are in place. A commonwealth can thus be structured as a federal system, as a unitary state, as a nonsovereign part of a larger country, or as a nonsovereign collection of sovereign states. In the latter context, the term's meaning is slippery still. As possible replacements for the British Empire were being debated in the early twentieth century, several different proposals (including true federation) were put forward, all using the term "commonwealth." During the 1990's the various members of the CIS argued over the nature of their association.

Rather than signifying a particular type of government, the term "commonwealth" seems to be selected primarily for symbolic reasons. In the cases of the Commonwealth of Nations and the Commonwealth of Independent States, the term was pointedly expounded for what it did not mean—in particular, federation.

Bibliography

Bodin, Jean. *The Six Books of a Commonweal.* Edited by Kenneth Douglas McRae. Cambridge, Mass.: Harvard University Press, 1962. Bodin describes the concept of a "commonweal" as a "lawful government" and argues for using it as an organizing principle. He further defends sovereignty, which is the commonweal's central feature. This work provides an excellent treatment of the commonwealth in its most general form: as a sovereign state.

Diller, Daniel C., ed. *Russia and the Independent States.* Washington, D. C.: Congressional Quarterly, 1993. Discusses Soviet history and examines the individual CIS states, which had been Soviet republics. Contains some discussion of the Commonwealth of Independent States, but this is not the central feature of the book.

Hobbes, Thomas. *Leviathan.* Edited by C. B. MacPherson. New York: Penguin Books, 1983. Classic treatise explaining the existence of governments and sovereign states. Hobbes is one of the first major thinkers to discuss the "common weal" in this way. The editor's introduction provides a clear summary of Hobbes's arguments.

Underhill, Frank Hawkins. *The British Commonwealth: An Experiment in Co-Operation Among Nations.* Durham, N.C.: Duke University Press, 1956. Collection of lectures on the origins and development of the Commonwealth of Nations as a successor to the British Empire. A short, highly readable book.

Watts, R. L. *New Federations: Experiments in the Commonwealth.* Oxford, England: Oxford University Press, 1966. Examination of the federal governmental systems that have been created within the Commonwealth of Nations since the end of World War II. Provides a useful set of examples which place the "shared sovereignty" aspects of federalism within the context of the Commonwealth.

Steve D. Boilard

Cross-References

Alliances, p. 47; Colonial Government, p. 344; Colonialism and Anticolonialism, p. 351; Empires and Empire Building, p. 597; Federalism in the United States, p. 668; Federations, p. 675; Government Types, p. 785; Hobbes's Political Philosophy, p. 836; Imperialism, p. 889; Independence Movements and Transitions, p. 896; Pacific Islander Governments, p. 1362; Self-Determination, p. 1796; Vico's Political Philosophy, p. 2103.

COMMUNICATIONS MANAGEMENT

Field of study: Functions of government

Communications management is a universal concern of modern governments, often motivated as much by political considerations involving power and influence as by the need to retain order in a world of rapidly changing communication technologies.

Principal terms

FAIRNESS DOCTRINE: U.S. requirement that radio and television stations cover issues of public concern in a manner reflecting divergent relevant viewpoints

MASS MEDIA: organs of mass communication, including newspapers and magazines, radio, and television

NATURAL MONOPOLY: enterprise for which local competition is unlikely to develop and the public's interests can best be served by a regulated monopoly

OFFICIAL SECRETS ACT: British law passed during World War I that has a significant impact on the coverage of political news

PREFERRED STATUS DOCTRINE: belief that the freedoms of speech and press are more important than other Bill of Rights guarantees

Overview

To communicate is to make something known, and a communications system provides a means of imparting or transmitting information. Communications systems linking governments with one another and with their citizens, as well as citizens with one another, are of considerable importance to modern governments. During the twentieth century, a trio of compelling reasons converged to make communications policy and management major concerns of governments: the increasing complexity of the instruments of mass communications, a growing appreciation of the link between communications networks and societal integration, and the apparent relationship between the form and content of communications on one hand and political power and support on the other.

The nineteenth century's principal instrument of mass communication was the press, in the forms of penny newspapers, street handouts, and pamphlets. Even when governments sought to censor it, the medium proved difficult to manage because the printing press was already a decentralized, relatively inexpensive, and widely diffused technology. By contrast, the principal vehicles for twentieth century communications increasingly have involved high technology, electronic modes of mass communication such as telephones, radios, televisions, fax machines, and interfacing computers. Individually and as a set, these technologies both have lent themselves to greater government control and have required it.

The development and mass deployment of telephones was long regarded in the

United States as requiring a natural monopoly arrangement favoring American Telephone and Telegraph (AT&T). Elsewhere in the world, the telephone industry remains essentially a government-owned or tightly controlled monopoly. Likewise, because radio and television broadcasting can function effectively only when airwaves and wave bands are assigned in such a manner as to avoid interfering signals, these media also came under public management, almost from their inception. As the range for broadcasting has increased, first through improved transmitters and later through satellite communications, the regulating arrangements have often moved beyond national agencies to international meetings and agreements. Even the states most reluctant to regulate have been forced by technological change into ever-expanding managerial responsibilities in the field of mass communications.

An expanding appreciation of the role of communication grids in knitting together the members of a society has given governments a second set of reasons for concerning themselves with the evolving industries of mass communications. The widespread utilization of these technologies has come to be viewed as a barometer of social integration, measured in such terms as the number of telephones, radios, and televisions per thousand people. These measurements consistently have placed the United States at the head of the list. By 1980, there were 744 telephones per thousand U.S. residents (versus scarcely any in the developing world and fewer than two hundred in the developed states of Eastern Europe) and nearly 2,000 radios and 600 televisions per thousand U.S. residents (versus fewer than 250 of either in some Eastern European states).

Finally, the desire to exercise political power more effectively has encouraged countries throughout the twentieth century to attempt to control the complex and rapidly expanding instruments of mass communications. Like control over the educational process, management of the modes of communication is a powerful tool of political socialization and a potentially powerful means of manipulating the ideas of a society. Information is often inseparable from opinion formation: Efforts to influence the latter have frequently motivated governments to try to control the former.

Government itself, as an institution exercising control over an extended territory and the people within it, would be impossible without the ability to communicate its rules to the governed. The fostering and management of systems of communications as a means of achieving political control and stability have been concerns of governments and political analysts alike since the days of Plato's *The Republic*. The king's highways in Britain and France were constructed during the Middle Ages as arteries of communication to link the centralizing monarchies with their subjects. By the time the U.S. Constitution was ratified in 1789, the role of government in fostering a system of postal communications was so firmly established that the provisions empowering the new federal government "to establish post-offices and post-roads" were among the least controversial of those enumerating powers given to Congress. Governments' concern with communications policy increased when the age of electronic communications suddenly provided governments with instantaneous, mass access to their citizens.

Applications

Nondemocratic—and especially totalitarian—forms of government have little need to differentiate among these various areas of government interest in communications. The need to manage the technological problems posed by the continuing revolutions in communicative technologies, the use of communication grids for social integration, and the utilization of news management to affect opinion development can all be achieved by the same means. The state can directly exercise a monopoly over all modes of communication, from the post office, telephones, and the telegraph to newspapers, journals, radios, and television. Modern military coups and revolutions usually begin with battles to achieve control over the local radio (and now television) stations, the modern links between people and the government. Once taken, they are usually the last areas over which control is relinquished. In the former Soviet Union, all disseminators of national news, from the organs of the Communist Party in Moscow to the smallest factory newspapers, thus took their cues, and news, from the centralized state and party information machinery (TASS) and from the newspapers of the Soviet state (*Izvestia*) and Communist Party of the Soviet Union (*Pravda*).

The value of control over the mass media to political control was even more vividly illustrated by Adolf Hitler's Third Reich, whose minister of communications was also the National Socialist (Nazi) party's director of propaganda, Joseph Goebbels. The party used its control over the German press and radio, along with annual national rallies, to mobilize the German people first for national reconstruction during the Depression and then for national expansionism and for revenge against those deemed responsible for Germany's defeat in World War I.

In democracies committed to the free exchange and competition of ideas, communications management poses the delicate task of regulating the media to the degree necessitated by its electronic nature without succumbing to the temptation of trying to manipulate or censor it for political gain. The responses to this challenge have varied widely within the democratic world, though perhaps nowhere more so than in post-World War II France and West Germany. Under the latter's constitution, adopted in 1949, both radio and television (which was being programmed in Berlin as early as 1935) were placed under public ownership; however, in order to prevent the new federal government in Bonn from recreating the Third Reich by using these media to mold the minds of postwar Germans, that ownership was given to the states, sometimes with results maddening to nation builders. As late as the 1980's, for example, the Bavarian television station was still signing off the air by playing the Bavarian national anthem, to the considerable discomfort of the federal government.

Meanwhile, the postwar government in France, a country long destabilized by social and political fragmentation, cast an envious eye on interwar Germany's experience with a centrally controlled media and elected to nationalize its electronic media. The government's intent was obvious. In addition to trying to influence the French press, whose wire service historically had been subsidized by the state, France's government anticipated using its influence over the electronic media to enhance support for itself. It soon matched policies to its intent. More than a decade into the Fifth French

Republic, which began in 1958, any government ministry could still censor any television program prior to the airing of a story it deemed prejudicial to its interests. Likewise, the news anchors of the principal state channels have consistently been chosen (and fired) by the president of France. Particularly when the same political bloc has controlled both the French presidency and the French assembly, the tendency has been for the government to use the electronic media to portray its performance favorably while denying its opposition virtually any visibility on the national news programs. President Charles de Gaulle (1958-1969), in particular, so used French television to establish a direct and flattering link between himself and the people that several of his biographers have referred to his presidency as a "teleocracy," or government by television. Moreover, although the most heavy-handed instances of partisan politics impinging on the freedom of the media abated following de Gaulle's retirement, they did not disappear entirely. In early 1995, for example, the French government had no qualms in pulling the plug on a Nice radio station and keeping it closed for twenty-four hours without a hearing as punishment for an impolitic but hardly seditious antipolice remark on one of the most popular programs.

France stands out essentially because of the overt manner by which its government has periodically affected the content of communications. There are, however, numerous examples of less direct shaping of information by democratic governments. Even the British Broadcasting Corporation (BBC), justifiably famous for its accuracy even when giving bad news to Britons during World War II, must operate within the framework of Britain's restrictive Official Secrets Act, a leftover from World War I. The act broadly limits what the media may report in covering official government business and meetings in Great Britain, even when the news has nothing to do with national security matters.

The United States displays minimal governmental intrusiveness into the day-to-day operations of the communications media. The generally followed principle has been to regulate the electronic media to the extent necessary in a nation of thousands of radio and television stations and hundreds of millions of telephones, avoiding hindrances to the free flow of information and the public's ability to communicate. The Federal Communication Act of 1934 gave the Federal Communications Commission (FCC) control over the licensing of radio (and later television) stations throughout the country. The FCC's explicit charge was to seek the "public interest" in its activities. Its approach subsequently has been pragmatic, not doctrinaire. Cross-media ownership among newspapers, radio, and television stations has been permitted, but only within the framework of a fairness doctrine that requires that the coverage of stories by the electronic media fairly acknowledges the diversity of viewpoints involved in the issues, much as the equal time doctrine has been applied to require radio and television stations airing the views of one candidate running for public office to give equal air time to challengers. On the rare occasions when stations have grossly violated the fairness doctrine, their three-year, renewable licenses to broadcast have not been renewed by the FCC, and the FCC's actions have been sustained by the courts.

Federal courts have played an important role in encouraging the free flow of the written word in the United States. The Supreme Court has persistently given a broad, "preferred status" interpretation to the freedoms of speech, press, and assembly guaranteed in the Constitution. It has also explicitly denied the states and the federal government the right to exercise prior restraint against the publication of stories in all except the most obvious instances of national security violations. The federal courts in general have made it so difficult to prove a charge of libel that newspapers rarely have been inhibited by threatened lawsuits from publishing stories. Even in the field of telephone communication, laws consistently have emphasized the public interest. The telephone industry was originally exempted from antitrust regulation as a natural monopoly in order to facilitate the spread of telephones. The courts subsequently ordered the breakup of the AT&T monopoly over interstate and foreign communications in response to changed circumstances of the 1980's. Interstate telephone competition had become possible by that time and could result in lower consumer rates. Competition no longer necessitated costly duplication of facilities, destroying the basis for designating telephone service as a natural monopoly.

U.S. politicians are not above attempting to use the media to manipulate public opinion. Political leaders regularly try to influence presentation of messages. Former president Ronald Reagan's media aides, for example, have been quoted as saying that they spent five hours every day trying to get their "spin" on the ninety seconds of evening television news about the White House. So-called "sunshine laws" permitting public access to government information consistently have been more important than national secrecy acts in defining the relationship between the written and electronic media and the government. Anchors of the networks' news programs continue to be appointed by network executives based on experience and audience appeal, not by the president of the United States for their personal and partisan loyalty.

Context

The factors that have required or tempted government to become actively concerned with communications management throughout the twentieth century continue to be relevant. The still-unfolding revolutions in modes of communication, combined with the interdependency of the countries in today's world, their need to communicate instantaneously and effectively with one another, and the globalization of culture via international communicative grids generate a series of questions involving public administration. Given their importance, should communications industries be public monopolies, regulated private monopolies, or competitive? What are the most efficient means for advancing the new communications technologies and facilitating public access to them? Governments will play roles in the multichannel programming technologies available through cable television, telephones, fax services, and computer-accessed information networks. The question is what those roles will be.

The recognized linkages between communications systems and social integration, and between informational media and public opinion, similarly continue to attract governmental attention to the communications industry in all countries. They pose especially difficult questions to democracies, whether they are nation-building Third

World states, advanced Western democracies experiencing fragmentation or societal disintegration, or the democratizing states in the former Soviet Union or its European empire. Especially for the democratizing polities, progress toward more free and uninhibited communications systems is difficult. Old habits of censorship die hard, especially when the new governments are still the owners of the modes of communication and are staffed by people recruited into public service during the old order. The state-owned television system created on January 1, 1993, in the democratic Republic of Slovakia, for example, had more than a dozen different directors during its first year of operation, largely as a result of the meddlesome nature of the country's political leaders. By contrast, Russian television reported both accurately and critically in covering Russia's assault on the secessionary province of Chechnya in the winter of 1994-1995, perhaps illustrating that free and open communication systems prosper only when governments resist the temptation to mold the journalistic marketplace and journalists and newscasters are willing to question authority. Even in the older democratic countries of the world, those twin traits have taken nearly as long to emerge as have the technologies of modern mass communications.

Bibliography

Alexander, Alison, and Jarice Hanson, eds. *Taking Sides: Clashing Views on Controversial Issues in Mass Media and Society*. Guilford, Conn.: Dushkin, 1995. Periodically revised, this undergraduate reader highlights the principal issues involving the media, government, and American society.

Deutsch, Karl Wolfgang. *Nationalism and Social Communication: An Inquiry into the Foundations of Nationality*. Cambridge, Mass.: MIT Press, 1962. For advanced research. One of the best statements of the role of communications in knitting societies together.

Maltese, John Anthony. *Spin Control: The White House Office of Communications and the Management of Presidential News*. Chapel Hill: University of North Carolina Press, 1992. Excellent account of "informal communications management" and the White House's ongoing effort to shape the president's image.

Paletz, David L., and Robert M. Entman. *Media Power Politics*. New York: Free Press, 1981. Although somewhat dated in its examples, still one of the best analyses of the media's influence on public opinion, and hence politics, in the United States.

Sargent, Lyman Tower. *Contemporary Political Ideologies: A Comparative Analysis*. Homewood, Ill.: Dorsey Press, 1969. Succinct work whose description of fascism, communism, and modernizing nationalism illustrates vividly the importance of communications to all modern states.

Joseph R. Rudolph, Jr.

Cross-References

Accountability in U.S. Government, p. 1; Autocracy and Absolutism, p. 127; Business and Government, p. 177; Civic Education, p. 278; Civil Liberties Protection,

p. 291; Despotism and Tyranny, p. 527; Dictatorships, p. 546; Education Management, p. 565; Government Roles, p. 778; Individual Versus State Rights, p. 910; The Media and the Conduct of Government, p. 1167; One-Party Systems, p. 1350; Postal Service, p. 1563; Propaganda, p. 1615; The Supreme Court: Role in Government and Law, p. 1935; Technology and Citizen-Government Relations, p. 1949.

COMMUNIST PARTIES

Field of study: Politics

Communism is a political, economic, and social theory that advocates collective ownership of all land and capital and the exercise of political power by the masses. In the twentieth century, countries that have been controlled by communist parties have tended to become totalitarian systems.

Principal terms
BOURGEOISIE: property-holding class who own the means of production in capitalist societies
CAPITALISM: economic system in which private individuals can own productive resources and use them as they see fit
DICTATORSHIP OF THE PROLETARIAT: condition of the state after the working class seizes control of the means of production, rules over the bourgeoisie, and determines new social values
PROLETARIAT: industrial working class
SOCIALISM: economic system in which government owns or controls the means of production and distribution of goods; in Marxist theory, the intermediate stage between capitalism and communism

Overview
After analyzing the capitalist economic class relations existing in industrialized Europe in the mid-nineteenth century, Karl Marx and Friedrich Engels developed a theory outlining the working-class revolution they believed would inevitably overturn capitalist economic relations and liberate the working class. Marx, an influential socialist theorist, believed that class-based conflict was the driving force behind historical change. He contended that the working class and the bourgeoisie were each bound, as a group, by a set of economic and material interests. Marx also believed that the working class should be organized to carry out a revolution against the bourgeoisie to seize governing political power by force and that a communist party should be the instrument by which the organized working class seized power. Because Marx never clearly defined the role of the communist party, his twentieth century disciples have had to theorize the relationship between the party and the working class based on historical experience.

In the *Manifesto of the Communist Party* (1848), Marx and Engels, his collaborator and intellectual cohort, distinguished communists from proletarians. They identified communists as the most class-conscious members of the working class, who understood most clearly the source of the workers' oppression, the course of action that was necessary to eliminate that oppression, and the new form of organization that society would take when the workers seized power. They did not specify, however, whether communists could organize within existing political parties that represented workers' interests, such as the popular Social Democratic parties, or whether communists had unique political functions that demanded a political party organization of a new type. The Social Democratic parties in Europe in the late nineteenth century had been organized as mass parties of the working class. They fought to expand political democracy by extending suffrage and instituting the direct vote for electing representative governing posts, with the ultimate goal of extending social democracy—that is, equalizing social and economic opportunities for all members of society—through the electoral system.

V. I. Lenin (1870-1924), the foremost Marxist theorist of the twentieth century, adapted, expanded, and applied Marxist theory in Russia. He emphatically rejected the notion that communists could work within Social Democratic parties, and summarized the defining characteristics of a Marxist political party in his treatise, "What Is to Be Done?" (1902). Lenin argued that since communists were to be organized for the purpose of leading a working class revolution, they could not work within reformist political parties, such as the Social Democratic parties. The communist party was to be composed of a vanguard of professional revolutionaries who acted according to a clear, pure understanding of Marxist theory. The vanguard communist party envisioned by Lenin would be an elite within the working class, acting in the "true" interests of the working class. This vanguard would need to remain vigilant in combating opportunism within the working class, ensuring that no group of workers within the working class sacrificed the interests of the whole working class to obtain immediate material gain for the group. The communist party would be organized to struggle against both the bourgeoisie and bourgeois interests within the working class.

The critical roles that Lenin assigned to the Communist Party—to lead the working class in revolution and afterward, advancing and protecting a true Marxist theoretical perspective, and developing a corresponding plan of political action—exalted the importance of the Communist Party and gave new meaning to party membership. Party members would have to participate actively in leading the revolution; they could not merely support the goals of the political party with their material resources or their vote. Party members were responsible for socializing the population to accept the Marxist perspective and for mobilizing the population to carry out party policies. Since party members had such critical tasks, Lenin argued that they had to adhere to a strict party discipline that would be accomplished through party organization. The party would be organized hierarchically in a pyramid structure, from a wide base of membership to a ruling elite.

Lenin proposed that decision making within the Communist Party be based on the concept of democratic centralism. Democracy was an essential element of democratic centralism, because the party was to be used to liberate the working class. Yet centralism was also essential. The Communist Party had to be highly organized in order to successfully overthrow the highly organized capitalist states. According to the Leninist concept of democratic centralism, all party members would participate in policymaking debate and selection of leaders. After policy decisions were made and leaders were selected, all members were required to carry out policy without question and to demonstrate complete loyalty to the leadership. According to Leninist theory, ideas and raw social and economic data drawn from actual social conditions, along with new leaders, would form the elements of policy input. This input would flow upward through the pyramid structure of the party. Policy decisions based on a rational blending of Marxist theory and practical experience would flow downward through the party's pyramid structure to the local party members and downward through the government bureaucracy set up to administer the party's decisions to the general population.

Applications

In Russia, after the Communist Party of the Soviet Union (CPSU) staged a successful revolution and captured governing power in 1917, it recruited and selected government officials and directed state policy. Up until the assumption of CPSU leadership by Mikhail Gorbachev in 1985, and the subsequent political reforms he introduced, all government offices in the Soviet Union were filled by party appointment. The CPSU also selected candidates for elected offices in collectives, trade unions, and other associations. Party members were recruited at the lowest level of the organization through the party cells organized in the workplaces. Starting at this lowest level of organization, party delegates were elected to fill posts in city, town, or district party conferences, from the district level to the provincial level, and then to the national level. National party policy decisions were discussed at the National Party Congress, which was held at approximately five-year intervals.

During the years of Lenin's rule, from 1917 to 1924, the party leadership believed that efficiency and streamlined decision-making procedures were necessary to consolidate CPSU rule and to begin the socialist reorganization of Russia's preindustrial economy. Therefore, the party created smaller committees of party officials that exercised the real decision-making power. The National Party Congress, made up of approximately five thousand members, was directed by the Party's central committee, approximately three hundred members, directed by the Politburo, consisting of twelve or more members. A party secretariat was also created to disseminate the CPSU's policies to the government officials, keep political peace, and be responsible for the economic successes or failures under their watch. The general secretary of the CPSU became the most powerful party official in the Soviet Union. The secretariat of the party, composed of full-time state-employed party officials, became responsible for the most important areas of governing activity: defense, security, heavy industry, energy, government appointments, and discipline of party members.

Beginning during Lenin's rule as general secretary and continuing during the rule of his successor, Joseph Stalin, the communist parties of the industrialized states in Western Europe and the United States closely followed the Leninist model of party organization, and the policy directives of the Communist International (Comintern). At the Second Congress of the Third Comintern, held in 1920, the CPSU imposed the "21 Conditions" of membership in the Third Communist International on all existing communist parties, which became branches of a global party dominated by Soviet leadership. Under Stalin's leadership, 1926 to 1953, the Soviet Union's foreign policy imperatives determined Comintern directives. In the 1930's, Comintern directives seriously weakened the communist parties in Western Europe and the United States. When the Soviet Union signed a nonaggression pact with Nazi Germany in 1939, the Comintern directed the parties in Western Europe and the United States to advocate the unpopular position of opposition to the war against fascism waged by the Western European states. Even though the communist parties of Western Europe and the United States joined the war against fascism when Nazi Germany attacked the Soviet Union in 1941, and although Stalin dissolved the Comintern in 1943, communist parties operated under a cloud of suspicion in the West. After World War II ended, communist party members were persecuted in the West, especially in the United States, when the Cold War between the West and the Soviet Union began and Stalin revived the international organization of the communist parties, thereafter known as "Cominform," in 1947.

Western European communist parties broke away from Soviet domination and the Leninist party mold during the 1970's, developing an alternative program for the socialist transformation of capitalist society termed "Eurocommunism." Advocates of Eurocommunism emphasized the need to preserve democratic forms during the socialist transformation, to promote socialist policies within the legal and constitutional framework of the capitalist states, and to retain multiparty systems during and after the socialist transformation period.

The Leninist model of communist party organization, apparatus, and rule was imposed on the Eastern European states that the Soviet Army occupied after World War II. Local communist party leaders selected by the CPSU, many of whom had been trained in the Soviet Union, exercised communist party rule through the secretariats, politburos, and party central committees. Following the example set by the Soviet leaders, the Eastern European communist parties eradicated the noncommunist political party opposition and instituted one-party rule, which was supported and maintained by the Soviet military and security police. Popular opposition to communist party rule exploded across Eastern Europe in 1989, when Mikhail Gorbachev relaxed Soviet military control and called for political democratization of the Soviet governing system. After 1989, communist parties in Eastern Europe and the Soviet Union competed for political power with other political parties and factions.

In Asia, Africa, and Latin America, communist parties developed as the revolutionary parties of national liberation from Western colonial rule. Following Leninist party organization, the communist parties in colonial and semicolonial countries adapted the Russian revolutionary strategies to the specific circumstances of their national experience of imperialist exploitation. In China, where the Communist Party led a successful revolution and seized governing power in 1949, the party used a well-trained and politicized guerrilla army to undermine an unpopular and undemocratic noncommunist national government that had been supported by Western capitalist countries. The premier leader of China's Communist Party, Mao Tse-tung, adapted

Lenin's concept of the socialist dictatorship of the proletariat. Mao invented the concept of the dictatorship of the people to emphasize the leading revolutionary roles of the Chinese peasantry and army and the assisting revolutionary role of China's small industrial proletariat.

In Latin America, national communist parties struggled against a national bourgeoisie—as well as an international bourgeoisie dominated by U.S. capital—that claimed ownership of the means of production and all farmland. Drawing inspiration from the Chinese communists, Latin American communist parties have been primarily composed of peasant revolutionaries, employing guerrilla warfare tactics against unpopular, noncommunist regimes backed by the United States.

Context

Although Lenin's communist party formulations have dominated the histories of communist parties worldwide during the twentieth century, they have not gone unchallenged by Marxist theorists and Marxist organizations. Indeed, the ranks of the Russian Social Democratic Labor Party (RSDLP) split in two when Lenin insisted on an activist, revolutionary party membership and program to overthrow Czarist rule in Russia in 1903. At that time, the Bolsheviks, the majority faction within the RSDLP who agreed with Lenin, broke with the Mensheviks, the minority faction who disagreed with Lenin. The Bolsheviks led a Marxist revolution in Russia in October, 1917, which succeeded because the Russian army, weary of fighting Germany in World War I, had mutinied against the democratic parliamentary government that had overthrown the Russian Czar in March, 1917. The Bolsheviks established the socialist state known as the Union of Soviet Socialist Republics and instituted Leninist Communist Party rule.

Rosa Luxemburg, a Polish Marxist, also criticized Lenin's ultracentralist conception of the communist party in the pamphlet "Organizational Questions of Russian Social Democracy" (1904). Luxemburg defined the communist party's role as one of propagandist for the working class, and de-emphasized party discipline, which she feared could lead to blind, unthinking obedience to authority and a subsequent abuse of power by the party leaders. In Luxemburg's view, the party articulated the interests of the working class and led the revolutionary struggle against the bourgeoisie, after the struggle was begun spontaneously by the working class.

Leon Trotsky, a Russian Bolshevik who led the opposition to the leadership of the Communist Party of the Soviet Union during the 1920's and 1930's, criticized the Leninist party structure for creating a dictatorship of the party, rather than a Marxist dictatorship of the proletariat. To consolidate their rule over the Soviet Union in the 1920's, the leaders of the CPSU had outlawed all other political organizations and associated party officials closely with all government agencies and social organizations. This led to virtual party control over all aspects of Soviet society and, according to Trotsky, party alienation from, and dictatorship over, the working class.

Twentieth century Italian Marxist theorist Antonio Gramsci also reformulated Lenin's conception of the revolutionary communist party to better suit the conditions of industrialized European societies. Gramsci asserted that the purpose of the revolutionary communist party was to provide an intellectual challenge and alternative to the political and cultural hegemony, or domination, of the European bourgeoisie. As long as the working class acquiesced to the social structure, ideas, and values of the bourgeoisie, it would never participate in a revolution. In Gramsci's view, the communist party had to provide the intellectual stimuli for the creation of a working-class hegemony developed by working-class "organic" intellectuals, that is, intellectuals whose working-class experience had led them to a Marxist analysis of capitalist economic relations and the need for revolutionary social change.

Eurocommunist theorists also have opposed the Leninist concept of a dictatorship of the proletariat, and the resultant dictatorship of the communist party. They proposed extending direct democracy to expand popular participation in the governing and policymaking process so as to transform existing European industrialized capitalist states into socialist states without revolutionary violence. Eurocommunists understood Lenin's theory of a revolutionary communist party as applicable to a unique time and place, rather than as a universal model that could be applied to diverse societies at various stages of economic development.

Bibliography

Meyer, Alfred G. *The Soviet Political System: An Interpretation*. New York: Random House, 1965. General picture of the entire Soviet Stalinist governing system, its institutions, and practices at the peak of its power. Comparisons to other political systems, in particular to the U.S. system.

Miliband, Ralph. *Marxism and Politics*. Oxford, England: Oxford University Press, 1977. Defines Marxist politics; a chapter on "Class and Party" explains how Lenin theorized the leading role of the party in socialist states.

Molyneux, John. *Marxism and the Party*. London: Pluto Press, 1978. Traces the theory of a communist party's purpose and organization from Marx and Engels, to Lenin, Luxemburg, Trotsky, and Gramsci, demonstrating how theory was grounded in historical context.

Narkiewicz, Olga A. *Marxism and the Reality of Power, 1919-1980*. London: Croom Helm, 1981. Explains how the Communist Party of the Soviet Union has influenced the development of communist parties worldwide, and how those parties have shaped the policy of the Communist International.

Staar, Richard F. "Checklist of Communist Parties in 1989." *Problems of Communism* 39 (March/April, 1990): 75-84. List of communist parties worldwide, including for each party membership statistics, national communist party leader, legal status of party, and percentage of votes won by communist party in the last national election.

Whetten, Lawrence L. *Current Research in Comparative Communism*. New York: Praeger, 1976. Discusses governing changes that have occurred in the Soviet Union and Eastern Europe, including changes in the role of the party.

Yoder, Amos. *Communist Systems and Challenges*. New York: Crane Russak, 1990.

Examines and compares the changes in the major communist party-ruled political systems throughout the world, focusing on the impact and implications of Mikhail Gorbachev's political reforms in the Soviet Union.

Karen Garner

Cross-References

Chinese Communism, p. 223; The Civil Service in the United States, p. 310; Comparative Government, p. 384; Dialecticism, p. 540; Insurgencies and Coups d'État, p. 930; Irrationalism in Politics, p. 987; The Left and the Right, p. 1079; Marxism-Leninism, p. 1155; One-Party Systems, p. 1350; Political Parties, p. 1485; Revolutionary Governments, p. 1725; Revolutionary Parties, p. 1731; Russian Political History, p. 1770; Social Democratic Parties, p. 1846; Socialism, p. 1865.

COMPARATIVE GOVERNMENT

Field of study: Comparative government

Comparative government is the study of the similarities and differences among the forms, processes, and institutions of the governments of the world's politically organized peoples. Various cultural factors shape the forms and functions of governments.

Principal terms
AUTHORITARIANISM: government by arbitrary authority that ignores fundamental rights of individuals and rules through force rather than consent
CONSTITUTIONAL GOVERNMENT: government that is limited in practice by the provisions of a written or unwritten constitution
ECONOMIC DEVELOPMENT: process of economic modernization, usually characterized by movement of the rural population to cities and increases in per capita income, education, and industrial production
LIBERAL DEMOCRACY: form of government characterized by protection for fundamental individual rights, limited government, and free elections coupled with widespread popular participation
POLITICAL DEVELOPMENT: changes in political institutions, generally conceived as moving from simpler to more complex forms, that generally accompany economic development

Overview

In 1989, U.S. Department of State official Francis Fukuyama published an article that became an overnight sensation. In "The End of History," he postulated that at the end of the Cold War, the battle of ideas over the most desirable form of government, was over: Liberal democracy, the form of government of Western Europe, North America, and elsewhere, had won. A few years later, however, observers were not so sure. Political scientists tried to determine the conditions for the success of democracy and evaluate where it was taking hold or likely to take hold.

For the most part, the Middle East has been dominated by regimes that vary from authoritarian or traditionalist to revolutionary extremist or totalitarian. The area has not appeared to be fertile ground for democratic development. The most prominent exception is Israel, whose institutions have been democratic since the nation's birth in 1948. Despite its split between Christian and Muslim populations, Lebanon for some time had democratic institutions and pro-Western governments. The civil war between Muslims and Christians that erupted in 1975 wrecked the country's prosperous economy. A Syrian military force later kept the peace.

Elsewhere in the region, the prospects for constitutional democracy seemed little better. Outnumbered democrats held a conference on civic education in Lebanon in 1994, but few observers were hopeful about the emergence of democratic regimes.

Jordan was dominated by a relatively benign monarchy, and Iran was ruled from 1979 by revolutionary Muslim extremists. By the mid-1990's, the Iranian economy was a shambles, and little progress had been made toward creating the social and economic infrastructure required for democratic development. Neighboring Iraq was dictatorially ruled by secular forces, led after 1979 by Saddam Hussein. By the 1990's, Hussein had created a totalitarian state that had ruined the middle class, impoverished the country, and led to the death of many hundreds of thousands by execution, aggressive warfare, and other policies.

Regimes around the Persian Gulf such as Saudi Arabia, Kuwait, and the Gulf sheikdoms were governed by traditionalist rulers who seemed little inclined to move their countries toward modern democracy. They illustrate the character of states whose economies depend on a single commodity such as oil, rather than on general economic development that creates an independent middle class. Because government receives much of the nation's wealth from royalties from abroad, it retains control of society.

In North Africa, governments have come under increasing pressure from Islamic fundamentalist movements. Notwithstanding the apparent failure of the Islamic revolution in Iran, Muslim militants have been proselytizing for the installation of Islamic governments that strictly follow the letter of Islamic law. In some cases, as in Algeria and Egypt, Islamic extremists have resorted to terrorist campaigns. Nowhere in the area did democracy appear likely to emerge.

In the early 1990's, calls for democratic government could be heard throughout sub-Saharan Africa. Nearly everywhere in this region the end of the Cold War aided the decline of socialist ideology, privatization of state industries, and progress toward democratic governments. In Nigeria, the military government came under increasing pressure to relinquish power to the forces of democracy. In Zambia and Malawi, authoritarian regimes abandoned power without bloodshed after being pressured into free elections. Namibia, Africa's last colony, shed its identity as South-West Africa and embarked upon the road to democracy. Botswana continued its record as a stable democracy. Above all, the continent took heart at the transition from white-minority rule in South Africa to democratic elections.

Nevertheless, as the 1990's took shape, constitutional democracy seemed out of the reach of much of the sub-Saharan region. In some cases, for example Zaïre and Somalia, the state ceased to exist during long periods. Civil war raged for long periods in Angola, Liberia, and the Sudan. In Kenya, strongman Daniel arap Moi clung to power. Uganda was rescued from years of bloody dictatorship under Idi Amin and Milton Obote but remained an authoritarian state. In many parts of the continent, ethnic rivalries undermined democracy, as political parties were seen to be the creatures of tribal politics. Savage genocidal attacks generated primarily by ethnic hatred took the lives of hundreds of thousands in Rwanda.

The future of democracy in Africa appeared especially bleak because of the poor prospects for economic prosperity in much of the area. If it is true, as many students of democratic development believe, that stable democracy is far less likely in poor countries, then many sub-Saharan countries will not soon become democracies. This prognosis, however, does not necessarily doom the entire region to autocracy. Some countries may succeed despite their poverty, and others may be able to develop economically and create a middle class, on whose talents and support democratic institutions may depend.

The character of government and political culture varies considerably in Asia. The prospects for democracy likewise appeared to vary from excellent to bleak. Although demands for democratic or at least constitutional government were heard in much of the continent, optimism must in many cases be muted. India, for example, is usually considered a democracy, but Indian democracy was in poor condition at the local level, where local authorities often ignored democratic norms. Violence and corruption were widespread. Human rights violations were frequent in some areas, such as Kashmir. Even at the national level, where democratic elections have indisputably taken place, a single family, the Gandhis, ruled the nation for most of the period from independence (1947) until the 1980's. Ethnic and religious rivalries between Muslims and Hindus threatened peace. Although the country had a sizable middle class, its burgeoning population foreshadowed permanent impoverishment of hundreds of millions, putting maintenance of democratic institutions into question.

The future of democracy in much of East Asia is, if anything, more difficult to predict. Strong antidemocratic currents feed the Confucian traditionalism of educated elites in China, Singapore, and elsewhere. Confucianism places strong emphasis on social hierarchy and obedience to authority, which run counter to the democratic ethos. By the mid-1990's, neo-Confucian authoritarianism, exemplified by the philosophy of former Singapore prime minister Lee Kuan Yew, was widely influential in the region.

In China, the largest and (with Japan) one of the two most important states in the region, the quashing of the 1989 Tiananmen Square demonstration dashed the hopes of Chinese democrats. Economic reform, especially the opening of free markets and the privatization of state industry by the Chinese Communist Party, China's all-powerful ruling body, resulted in impressive economic growth. Outbreaks of violence in the countryside and strikes in cities, combined with traditional Chinese fear of chaos, diminished chances for democracy, a form of government that many Chinese view as potentially catastrophic for order. Also, poverty on China's scale—in the hundreds of millions—is unlikely to be compatible with democratic development, especially where democratic roots do not exist.

Other Asian countries exhibited a mixture of positive and negative indicators for the future of democracy in the region. In the Philippines, a shaky democracy in a poor economy was harassed by a communist insurgency movement. Populous Indonesia, an authoritarian regime led for decades by General Suharto, was dominated by the army, which seemed little inclined to hand power to a democratic civilian government, as occurred in South America, notably in Brazil and Chile. Indonesia did, however, attract increasing levels of foreign investment. In Taiwan and Korea, however, prodigious economic advancement led to creation of democratic institutions as new, prosperous middle classes demanded a role in governance.

Neighboring Japan is a complex and controversial case of successful post-World War II economic development. The world's second largest economy, Japan loomed large in the future of East Asia. Some analysts see Japan as clearly democratic; others see the nation as a quasi democracy, resting upon a structure of "soft authoritarianism."

After decades of authoritarian regimes, often coupled with political instability, by the 1990's much of Latin America appeared to be on the road to stable democracy. Nations such as Argentina and Brazil that had endured decades of military or civilian dictatorship, sometimes combined with political instability, appeared to have changed course for a democratic future. Chile, once South America's model of democracy, peacefully removed its military strongman and reestablished democracy. Even long-suffering Paraguay ousted one of the region's most durable dictators and attempted to set up a multiparty system. Like many others in Europe and Africa, governments of a number of states in the region accomplished considerable privatization of state industry in the 1990's.

The movement to democracy was not smooth everywhere. The demise of democratic institutions under President Alberto Fujimori clouded the future of democracy in Peru. In Central America, the tide of democracy was hesitant. Civil war in Nicaragua and El Salvador had ended, and constitutional institutions were in place, but whether democracy could succeed in the long term was not known.

In the choice between democratic development and authoritarianism, other countries seemed ambivalent. Guatemala hovered between the traditional power of the often brutal armed forces and reform as demanded by champions of human rights. Mexico's population approached 100 million by the turn of the twenty-first century, and the country struggled to abandon an outmoded authoritarianism and to embrace the mores and institutions of constitutional democracy.

The character of government in the countries of the former Soviet Union and the formerly communist countries of Eastern Europe was among the world's most potentially dangerous problems. Leading the list was the enigma of Russia, laden with nuclear weapons and lacking traditions of both democracy and humane government. Some students of Russia argued that because it lacked the cultural background of democratic mores and because it was unlikely to attain a Western-style market economy for some time, the outlook for democracy was bleak. They looked instead for a continuation of Russia's long authoritarian traditions, with nationalist overtones.

Of the former Soviet nations, the Baltic nations of Estonia, Latvia, and Lithuania seemed most likely to attain democracy, but lack of a strong, independent middle class, rampant organized crime, and poverty presented considerable obstacles. With few exceptions, the Central Asian republics were in the hands of deeply entrenched authoritarian forces. Elsewhere, in Belarus and Ukraine, a tug of war between pro- and anti-Russian forces seemed to place the development of democratic institutions and processes on the back burner. Again, the ingrained habits of authoritarian political culture seemed to place obstacles in the path of democracy.

Outside the former Soviet empire, attempts to consolidate constitutional democracy varied considerably. On the positive end of the scale, the Czech Republic and Poland were most clearly successful in making a transition from a socialist economy to capitalism. Hungary, Slovenia, and Slovakia were also relatively successful.

Although at times nations elected former Communist Party governments, the "recycled" communists were not communists of previous regimes and did not attempt to destroy fledgling democratic institutions. Efforts to foster genuine democracy seemed least successful in former Yugoslavia, where years of savage ethnic hatreds reaped a bitter civil war.

Applications

Democracy in Western Europe and North America might be said to have entered a paradoxical period. On one hand, except for a handful of extremists, democracy had no rivals—it was "the only game in town." On the other hand, many observers believed democracy to be in some form of decline or decomposition.

One symptom of this malaise was the nearly uniform dissatisfaction with their governments of the populations of these areas. In the United States, public confidence in government had been declining since the 1960's. In 1958, 75 percent of the American public said that it trusted government to do what is right all or most of the time. By the beginning of the 1990's, this confidence had sunk, with only 35 percent trusting government. In 1993, confidence had fallen even further, with only 20 percent of respondents expressing belief in the competence of government. In much of the Western world, public cynicism about government and politics had risen. Some 70 percent of Americans in the early 1990's thought that government creates more problems than it solves. In Europe, confidence in government generally declined. In France, for example, polls in 1993 saw a record 82 percent of the public dissatisfied with government. In Canada, 1991 polls showed that 77 percent of the electorate disapproved of the prime minister and his government. In Italy, chronic and general corruption throughout the political system triggered a popular revolt that resulted in an end to the postwar domination of the Christian Democrats and the trial and conviction of numerous politicians.

Dissatisfaction with the performance of the governments of Western democracies did not, however, mean that citizens were moving to the embrace of authoritarianism. Antidemocratic movements were few and weak; liberal democracy was still the clear winner in the century's ideological battles.

What, then, did the public mood portend for Western democracy? In some countries, it seemed to mean that angry electorates would turn on those in power, as occurred in Canada, France, Italy, and the United States. In the United States, it also meant voter attraction to the amateur politician. In the 1992 elections, an astonishing 19 percent of voters opted for presidential candidate H. Ross Perot, a billionaire with no experience in elective office. That was the largest vote for a third-party candidate since 1912 and Theodore Roosevelt. The movement for term limits for members of Congress also expressed citizen distrust of the political status quo.

Context

The extent to which the nations of the world can be expected to become Western-style constitutional democracies is a widely debated issue. Students of comparative government identify distinct "stages" of democratic development and the factors that lead toward or away from a democratic order. One reason to be concerned about future democratization is that major wars may be averted if democracy prevails. Some analysts believe that democracies are unlikely to wage war on other democracies because, for example, democratic governments must justify military action before popular legislatures. Democracies tend to band together for protection and would be deeply reluctant to wage aggressive war against states with which they share an identity.

If democracies are peaceable with one another, the future of democratization is of overwhelming importance. Important new military powers of the future may include such states as Brazil, China, Germany, India, Indonesia, Japan, Nigeria, and Pakistan. Russia, already an important nuclear power, faces an uncertain future as a democracy.

A second motivation for predicting the future of potential democracies is to determine if scarce Western and Japanese aid to developing countries can be effective or if it might be counterproductive or wasted, as it might be if a state has little chance to democratize. Because respect for human rights is unlikely under authoritarianism, the future of fundamental rights is closely tied to democratization.

The character and degree of economic development appears to be highly influential in the creation and maintenance of democracy. This is not to say that a nation's wealth determines whether it becomes or remains democratic. Poor states such as Namibia have been democracies, and rich ones such as Saudi Arabia and Singapore are not. Nevertheless, it is not accidental that nearly all the world's richest countries are democracies, and nearly all the world's poorest countries are authoritarian. As wealth resulting from general development (and not from oil revenues) increases, middle classes grow, and states tend toward democracy.

Cultural factors also affect democratization. Many political scientists believe that cultures dominated by mystical religion or that refuse to accept the separation of church and state cannot become democracies. Many argue that Confucian societies, which emphasize hierarchy and obedience as opposed to democratic equality, are unlikely to democratize; they argue that democracy will remain largely the product of Western and Western-oriented countries. Others, however, believe that countries can democratize in spite of cultural factors adverse to democracy.

Bibliography

Friedrich, Carl J., and Zbigniew K. Brzezinski. *Totalitarian Dictatorship and Autocracy.* New York: Praeger, 1956. Classic work in the field. Defines each form of government and explores major twentieth century examples.

Huntington, Samuel P. *The Third Wave.* Norman: University of Oklahoma Press, 1991. Acclaimed study of the democratization process in the second half of the twentieth century. Qualified optimism.

Journal of Democracy, 1990-. A quarterly journal of the National Endowment for Democracy, published by The Johns Hopkins Press. Contains dozens of well-written and well-researched articles each year that are indispensable in keeping up with expert opinion and relevant events around the world.

Sorensen, Georg. *Democracy and Democratization: Processes and Prospects in a Changing World*. Boulder, Colo.: Westview Press, 1993. Readable and thorough examination of the arguments about the future of democracy around the world. Argues for a pessimistic outlook.

Weiner, Myron, and Samuel P. Huntington, eds. *Understanding Political Development: An Analytic Study*. Boston: Little, Brown, 1987. A comprehensive survey of political development, including numerous references to empirical case studies that illustrate the authors' arguments.

Charles F. Bahmueller

Cross-References

Africa: Politics and Governments, p. 21; Asia: Politics and Governments, p. 108; The British Parliamentary System, p. 146; The Canadian Parliamentary System, p. 190; Chinese Communism, p. 223; Democracy, p. 513; Feudalism, p. 688; Government Types, p. 785; History of Government, p. 829; Islam and Government, p. 994; Legal Systems in Anglo-American Governments, p. 1085; Mexico: Politics and Government, p. 1179; Russian Political History, p. 1770; Totalitarianism, p. 1987.

CONFEDERATIONS

Field of study: Types of government

A confederation is a form of government in which sovereign polities join together to form a limited-purpose general government, often for security reasons or economic advantages. Thus the confederation is a community of constituent units of government rather than a community of individuals.

Principal terms

ARTICLES OF CONFEDERATION: early attempt by the former British colonies to establish a government in which the states were protected from a strong central government; the Articles were soon replaced by the Constitution

CONSTITUTION: legal document upon which a state is based; spells out the rules under which a government can operate

FEDERALISM: system that joins units of government into a permanent but limited relationship of shared sovereignties, in which various units of government impact upon each other and the people; a more comprehensive union than a confederation

POLITY: form of government that exists in a given society; includes the institutions, politics, and organizations that function as the government

SOVEREIGNTY: possession of ultimate power over a given sphere or area

UNITARY GOVERNMENT: government with a central authority; other governmental units in such a system are lesser units and are under the sovereignty of the central government

Overview

The term "confederation" describes a system of government in which sovereign polities join together to create a new common government whose powers and duties are strictly limited. Unlike international treaties in which the political units that enter into them retain complete and total sovereignty, reserving the right to withdraw from these arrangements at any time, confederations involve surrendering some portion of sovereignty and empowering the common government with some degree of authority over the constituent units. Thus the confederation that is formed enjoys some limited, defined power over the political units that have created it; however, the members of the union do not lose their identities as political units. Rather, the confederation is often created to further the continued existence or enhancement of its members' powers.

The traditional reasons for which confederations were formed were for defense and security. Usually this involved smaller states seeking protection from a larger external threat. In recent years, economic concerns have motivated states to join confederations. The factors motivating confederation can be very different from those factors motivating other forms of union. Where there are political motives, confederation can be a viable option. In forming a confederation, there is no necessity for social or cultural ties. Forms other than confederation that lack economic or political ties are often doomed to fail.

The principal historical examples of confederations include the early Swiss Confederation (1291-1789), the reconstituted Swiss Confederation (1815-1849), the United Provinces of The Netherlands (1579-1795), the German Bund (1815-1856), the United States of America (1781-1789), and the European Community (founded in 1957). In each of these instances, the member polities sought to enhance either their overall security or general welfare by relinquishing a limited portion of their sovereignty for this guarantee. The authority of the confederation is usually limited to the constituent units and does not extend to the citizens of these units. Because the laws or rules made by the confederation apply only to the member states, confederations are considered weak compared to unitary or federal states.

In unitary systems of government, the national government has complete authority over both its constituent units and its citizens. Power resides in the central or national government. In a federation, the national or federal government is empowered with some limited authority over the constituent units and their citizens. Power is shared between the federal government and the constituent units. In a confederation, the national or confederal government is granted limited powers by the constituent units. Power is shared, but the preponderance of power resides with the constituent units. A federation is more concerned with the preservation of individual liberty, while a confederation places greater emphasis on preserving the local liberties of its constituent polities.

Although a confederation appears decentralized, it is, in reality, noncentralized. This distinction is important, because it is the difference between a government choosing not to be centralized, as in the case of a decentralized unitary system, and not having the authority to centralize, as in federal and confederal systems. A system with a strong central government may choose to remain administratively decentralized for any number of reasons. A confederation, on the other hand, is made up of constituent parts that retain real and substantial control over internal politics.

Several minimal elements must exist for an international arrangement reached by states to be identified as a confederation. The first element is that the confederation is based on some constituent treaty or constitution. By entering into this treaty or adopting this constitution, the individual constitutions of the members are altered in some manner. The confederation constitution is intended to be permanent, that is, an indissoluble union is created. This agreement must provide some mechanism to serve as an arbiter to settle any disputes that might arise among the constituent members or between the members and the confederation.

All members of the confederation must be represented in some body that serves as the decision-making organ. Representation in this organ may or may not be equal. The confederal government must also have some lawmaking authority. Usually this authority resides with the confederal body in which all the members are represented, although this authority may be delegated to an executive agency.

Finally, the confederation must be recognized externally by other nation-states within the international political system and have the power to act within the realm of international relations. In order for a government to be viewed as legitimate by other governments, it needs to be able to participate with them in international affairs. This is generally a major reason why the confederation was formed to begin with.

Late twentieth century confederations, on the other hand, have been established through limited constitutional agreements among the partners on specific topics. The European Community pioneered this technique, beginning with the various Treaties of Rome, first establishing a coal and steel community, then adding other areas—first of economic and then of political integration—leading to the Single Europe Act and the Maastricht Treaty in the mid-1990's. The constituting states only needed to agree on which functions they wanted to provide in common as they reached consensus, enabling them to maintain more reserved powers than would have been possible in a federation.

Applications

On March 1, 1781, the Articles of Confederation and Perpetual Union creating the United States of America officially came into force. The Articles were written and adopted by the Second Continental Congress, which served as the provisional government for the thirteen colonies for much of the revolutionary war. After a year-and-a-half in the Congress and three-and-a-half years of consideration by the state legislatures, the Articles were finally ratified by all thirteen states in 1781.

The language of this document makes it clear that the union created was to exercise a limited number of powers, which were explicitly stated in Article 9. These powers included the sole authority to declare war and peace, to receive and send ambassadors, and to enter into treaties, including regulating relations with Native American tribes. The union also could build and equip a navy, borrow money, and make requisitions from the states for money and military forces. These powers appear to be quite substantial, but a number of defects existed in this document.

The government under the Articles of Confederation was not altogether different from the government under the later U.S. Constitution: The Articles were designed to create a "Confederation and perpetual union," while the Constitution was designed to "form a more perfect union." The Articles created a real confederation with real sovereignty in intended areas, not just a treaty arrangement. Confederation in the United States can be seen as a form of federalism. The confederation was based on many of the same notions of liberty and authority as the Constitution was. The Constitution, then, was a maturation of the attempts at union by the Articles of Confederation.

The Articles placed a number of restrictions on the states, many of which were then included in the Constitution. The extension of the privileges and immunities of the citizens of the several states was guaranteed to all residents, and "full faith and credit" was given to the official records and documents issued by each state's government. The states were also required to engage in peaceful relations with one another.

Despite these enumerated powers and restrictions, several shortcomings existed in the Articles. The union was empowered to make requisitions from the states for money, but there was no mechanism through which the states could be compelled to fill those requisitions. Additionally, the union could not levy taxes nor raise revenue without the consent of the states. This meant that it could not repay the money it had borrowed to finance the war with Great Britain. Not having this ability made it difficult for the new government to borrow additional funds.

The government of the Articles of Confederation was created by the Second Continental Congress. This congress put into place a document that legitimized the way the government of the United States had been functioning since declaring independence. This new government was described by the Second Continental Congress as a "firm league of friendship." Under the Articles of Confederation, Congress was limited by the states primarily to coining money and establishing post offices, and the government was chronically poor because it had no real power to coerce payments from states.

A final shortcoming of the government under the Articles of Confederation was that the union could not regulate commerce between the states, nor with foreign governments. This adversely affected the national economy as individual states set their own tariffs, and the union was unable to respond to British commercial policies that adversely affected American trade. The result was a national economy in shambles, which was the principal justification for the Annapolis Convention that ultimately led to the call to revise the Articles.

The structure of the confederal government under the Articles was similar to that of the Second Continental Congress. Each state was granted one vote, although it could send between two and seven delegates to Congress. On major issues, such as declaring war, entering into treaties, coining, raising and borrowing money, and various military decisions, a super-majority of nine states was required. On other matters, only a simple majority was necessary. One feature that probably doomed the Articles was the requirement that all amendments be adopted unanimously.

The American confederation did produce a number of positive achievements. Peace with Great Britain was negotiated by the confederal government. A small bureaucracy was developed that became the basis for the civil service. Finally, the confederation was able to establish the principles for the political development of the western and northwest territories, and it called the convention that framed the nation's more enduring Constitution.

Context

Confederations are important supranational forms of government that create relationships between constituent units for the benefit of the whole. The two characteristic features of a confederal framework are that there is no commitment to creating a "nation," and that non-majoritarian instruments are used for decision making. The obvious objection against the non-majoritarian formula is that it relies on consensus, requiring unanimity.

At the beginning of the modern era, there were three confederations in existence: the Holy Roman Empire, finally abolished by Napoleon; the Swiss Confederation, later to become a federation; and the United Provinces of The Netherlands, which became a decentralized unitary monarchy. Confederation proved inadequate for the needs of these three examples. In the nineteenth century, the federation became an increasingly common form of union. Where there is a need for a clear international actor and a desire to identify with one state, federation is often chosen over confederation. In the three examples above, the confederations' powers were clearly limited, and the constituent units reserved and exercised most of the power. If more is desired from a system, a confederation is inadequate. Federations, on the other hand, require more from the constituent parts. The European Community is a good example of a trend toward federalism, because the goals require such a system. The former Soviet Union, however, appears more suited for a form of confederation, because there is a lack of sentiment for one supranational state and there are independent-minded constituent parts.

Confederations are communities of polities. The government created by the formation of a confederation, whether that government is weaker or stronger than other confederal arrangements, represents its constituent units. Emphasis is placed on the liberties of the constituent polities, not those of individual citizens. In a confederation, the constituent units continue to be the governments that impact directly on their citizenry.

Bibliography

Earle, Valerie, ed. *Federalism: Infinite Variety in Theory and Practice.* Itasca, Ill.: F. E. Peacock, 1968. Articles in this collection emphasize the various manifestations of federalism and confederation that serve as unifying forces while maintaining diversity.

Elazar, Daniel J. *Exploring Federalism.* Tuscaloosa: University of Alabama Press, 1987. Examines the various types of governments and power-sharing arrangements that exist in the world today. Excellent study in comparative federalism.

Forsyth, Murray. *Unions of States: The Theory and Practice of Confederation.* New York: Leicester University Press, 1981. Theoretical analysis and historical account of the development of confederation as a form of government.

Hughes, Christopher. *Confederacies.* Leicester, England: Leicester University Press, 1963. Although now somewhat dated, this is the classic work tracing the development of confederations throughout history.

King, Preston. *Federalism and Federation.* Baltimore: The Johns Hopkins University Press, 1982. Addressing the ideas and principles behind federalism, this book gives the reader insight into the various forms of government from confederal to centralized.

Joseph R. Marbach
Paul T. Neal

Cross-References

Alliances, p. 47; Commonwealths, p. 364; Federalism in the United States, p. 668; Federations, p. 675; Government Types, p. 785; History of Government, p. 829; Leagues, p. 1072; Supranational Government Institutions, p. 1922; World Government Movements, p. 2174.

CONFLICT RESOLUTION

Field of study: International Government and Politics

Conflict resolution is a set of practices and procedures available to any government that serves to defuse, reduce, settle, or even to avoid disputes and tensions with other governments.

Principal terms
BARGAINING: actions and discussions in which two or more parties seek to resolve conflicts
CONCESSION: offer of one party to lower its terms of settlement in a conflict
CONFLICT: confrontation in which two or more parties favor alternative types of actions
CONFLICT MANAGEMENT AGENT: party directly involved in seeking resolution of a conflict
CRISIS: acute situation in which catastrophic results may emerge from making the wrong choice in a conflict
ISSUE: subject of a conflict or dispute
PACIFIC SETTLEMENT: peaceful methods of conflict resolution

Overview

Conflict exists when a problem arises but there is no clear or immediate agreement on how the parties involved in the conflict can solve the problem. Conflicts are usually complex, concerned with personal, local, national, or international issues in which there are several interrelated disputes. Conflict resolution strategies work to settle disputes. That is, the strategies overcome objective differences, finding concessions on specific disputes, leading to compromises acceptable to all parties involved so that the conflict may be settled. Since not all conflicts can be settled easily, several types of formal conflict resolution methods have been developed so that war and other violent methods of conflict resolution may be avoided. In general, the term "conflict resolution" refers to international conflicts, whereas "dispute resolution" refers to methods for resolving conflicts inside countries.

Analyses of methods of international conflict resolution tend to focus on how conflicts arise, the methods for handling conflict, and the outcomes produced by efforts to resolve conflicts.

Most conflicts and disputes arise gradually over time, eventually ripening to the point at which the issues in dispute become clear, mutually unacceptable alternatives are discarded, and conflict resolution techniques become appropriate. Some conflicts, however, emerge suddenly in crises, situations in which failure to act might have catastrophic consequences for one or more parties. As a result of time constraints, crises often pose a limited range of possible responses, and violent methods are thus seriously considered.

Methods for handling conflict involve various procedures, which are usually classified by the number of conflict management agents or parties involved.

In unilateral conflict resolution, one party tries to resolve a conflict without negotiating with another party. Coercive violence is a common form of unilateral conflict resolution, as when an army massacres unarmed persons in a village. Genocide—the disarmament and later extermination of an entire people—is the logical extreme of unilateral conflict resolution. Alternatively, one party can facilitate peaceful conflict resolution by conflict avoidance or self-abnegation; that is, one party may decide not to object to an action or a policy of another party. Another method of unilateral conflict resolution is to impose unilateral sanctions, such as a trade embargo, in order to force another government to change policies.

Bilateral conflict resolution can involve mutual coercion, including force or threats of force. Military confrontations and wars can continue until opposing parties negotiate a truce. When the bilateral conflict management technique is direct bargaining, resolution is more likely when both parties to a dispute offer concessions at the bargaining table. If the dispute is about a numerical matter, the parties can split the difference. If the dispute involves several issues, a concession on one issue can be traded for a concession on another issue.

Indirect or tacit bargaining can also be used in bilateral conflict resolution. Deterrence is the threat of violence in order to coerce an opponent into backing down from a hostile move. For social psychologist Charles Osgood, who designed a program of graduated reciprocated initiatives for tension reduction (GRIT) to defuse the Cold War, tacit bargaining can also occur when one side takes unilateral action to undo a hostile posture in an effort to encourage the other side to reciprocate, resulting in a spiral of reciprocated moves, known as confidence-building measures.

Multilateral conflict resolution occurs when third parties intervene into ongoing conflict situations to assist in conflict resolution. The three forms of third-party conflict resolution are pacific settlement, collective security, and peaceful change.

There are several forms of pacific settlement. A third party that extends good offices is one that promises to act as a go-between, that is, to pass messages back and forth between parties to a dispute without any comment of its own. In mediation, the third party not only passes messages but also actively proposes solutions to both sides in an attempt to resolve the dispute through a mutually acceptable compromise. Occasionally, parties to a dispute believe that impartial information is lacking and hence call upon intermediaries to conduct an inquiry. Conciliation combines inquiry and mediation. In domestic disputes, votes in a legislative body are ways of resolving conflicts. At the international level, conferences including disputants may play an equivalent role. Conference diplomacy, accordingly, is a multilateral pacific settlement device, under which third parties meet together, though sometimes without all disputants, in order to determine appropriate action. Collective sanctions, another third-party method used to resolve conflicts, involve punitive but nonviolent measures

METHODS OF CONFLICT RESOLUTION		
Parties Involved	*Alternative Methods*	*Examples*
0 (no-party)	obsolescence	end of four-power rule in Berlin (after reunification), 1994
1 (unilateral)	coercive violence genocide conflict avoidance unilateral sanctions	Iraq's attack on Kuwait, 1991 Nazi extermination of Jews, 1939-1945 Philippines' not pressing claim to Sabah, 1967 U.S. embargo of Cuba, 1958
2 (bilateral)	mutual coercion direct bargaining tacit bargaining	War between Argentina and Great Britain, 1982 U.S. negotiations with Vietnam, 1968-1973 U.S. scrapping of missile bases in Turkey, 1962

3 or more
(multilateral)
	pacific settlement
	  good offices
	
	  mediation
	  inquiry
	
	  conciliation
	
	  conference diplomacy
	  collective sanctions
	
	  adjudication
	  arbitration
		
		Good Offices Commission re Dutch-Indonesian conflict, 1948
		Camp David negotiations, 1979
		U.N. Security Council inquiry re mining of Corfu Channel, 1947
		U.N. Special Commission on Palestine, 1948-1949
		Hague Conferences 1899, 1907
		U.N.-approved embargo of Rhodesia, 1968-1979
		Nicaragua vs. United States (ICJ, 1985)
		Egyptian-Saudi arbitration of Syrian-Lebanese dispute, 1949

	collective security
	  coercive action
	
	  peacekeeping
		
		U.N. Persian Gulf War coalition against Iraq, 1991
		UNTAC, 1992-1993

	peaceful change
	  plebiscite
	  territorial exchange
	
	  decolonization
	
	  development aid
		
		plebiscite of Sabah and Sarawak, 1963
		Israel's return of the Negev to Egypt, 1979
		British decolonization of Sabah and Sarawak, 1965
		World Bank loans

to do damage to a party in a dispute. The measures may include severance of diplomatic relations, trade restrictions, or verbal denunciations, but all fall short of war.

There are two judicial forms of conflict resolution—adjudication and arbitration. In adjudication, which largely awaited the establishment of the Permanent Court of International Justice (PCIJ) under the League of Nations, a fixed number of jurists serve as judges of a world court, which determines which disputant, if any, has violated international law. The International Court of Justice superseded the PCIJ when the United Nations was established.

In arbitration, two parties refer their dispute to an ad hoc tribunal with instructions to apply specific norms or rules. In many cases, the two disputants chose two arbitrators each, and the four select a fifth arbitrator, who chairs the tribunal and controls the outcome in case there is a split vote. The Permanent Court of Arbitration was established at The Hague Conference of 1907 to provide for a permanent panel of jurists from which disputants could select arbitrators. Commercial arbitration tribunals are available in several cities around the world, and provisions for their use are often included in commercial contracts.

United Nations peace agents are increasingly used in multilateral conflict resolution. An observer group can handle fact-finding, such as whether a country is holding free and fair elections. Truce supervision missions make reports on violations of armistice agreements. A noncombatant military force may enter a middle ground between opposing armies, thereby effecting a cease-fire.

Collective security involves third parties using or restraining the use of coercive action. In Europe, nations have often intervened in conflicts on behalf of other nations in order to maintain a balance of power. One country was not allowed to dominate the Continent. The League of Nations and the United Nations were based in part on the premise that all governments should practice collective security by aiding any victim of aggression. International forces have engaged in violent and nonviolent forms of collective security; the latter is known as peacekeeping.

Peaceful change, finally, is the most subtle form of multilateral conflict resolution; the aim is to change the situation. If countries vie for control of a territory, one way to determine which country will rule over the area is to put the matter to a vote of the population. If countries have restive minorities inside their borders, one possible solution is an exchange of minority populations or territories. Decolonization is another form of peaceful change. The League of Nations entrusted territories not considered ready for independence to the rule of certain major powers, which in turn were responsible for preparing former colonies of defeated countries in World War I for eventual independence; the former colonies were called mandates. The United Nations continued the practice as the trusteeship system, and all the countries involved later became independent. The most intensive form of peaceful change is the use of development aid to enable poorer countries to move from conditions of economic desperation to relative prosperity.

There are several possible outcomes produced in conflict management. The most desirable outcome is for the parties to walk away completely satisfied. This is a "win-win" resolution. Zero sum conflicts tend to have a "win-lose" outcome in which one party persuades or imposes a settlement on the other, as in a debate or a war victory. In a "lose-lose" situation, the parties engaged in a conflict inflict damage on each other or on themselves; such a conflict can be resolved when both parties equally agree to cut their losses. In a stalemate, neither party wins, and neither loses. Instead, the conflict is left unresolved.

An ideal goal of conflict resolution is conflict settlement. In such a resolution, the parties completely agree with each other after negotiations about former differences. More modest outcomes from conflict resolution include freezing the conflict (delaying conflict resolution or restraining the parties), encapsulating conflict (containing the conflict to just two parties or to a small geographic area), or reducing conflict (lowering the level of violence or the number of parties or issues involved).

Often, outcomes are not entirely rational, and misperceptions can frustrate conflict resolution. Social psychologists agree that subjective tensions may prevail over more objective considerations; the identity of a group or individual may be maintained by denying facts pertinent to a resolution of the conflict.

Conflict resolution processes occur after problems have arisen. Disintegrative conflicts, such as divorces, tend to resign the parties to the proposition that conflict is inevitable between humans who seek their own self-interest. Conflicts also may often produce integrative outcomes by bringing parties together to solve common problems. Conflict in human affairs is inevitable, but can be mitigated by increasing interdependence between groups, persons, and states.

Applications

The Cuban Missile Crisis of 1962 arose when photographic evidence revealed to John F. Kennedy, president of the United States, that the Soviet Union was preparing to install nuclear missiles at sites in Cuba. These missiles threatened the United States. Among the various responses considered by Kennedy, the effort to use the United Nations (a multilateral decision mode) failed, because members of the Soviet Union's politburo would not allow Party Secretary Nikita Khrushchev to back down in response to mere words. When the United States Navy took unilateral coercive action by boarding Soviet ships bound for Cuba to determine whether they contained nuclear warheads, Khrushchev responded by engaging in an act of self-abnegation by recalling Soviet ships with nuclear warheads bound for Cuba. Kennedy unilaterally announced thereafter that missile bases in Turkey would be scrapped, and Khrushchev declared that the Soviet Union would no longer manufacture strategic bombers. A détente resulted but was shattered in a few years, when the United States invoked collective security considerations among its Asian and Pacific allies to defend South Vietnam, which was involved in a civil war with North Vietnam, which was aided by China and the Soviet Union.

An example of conflict resolution by avoidance and peaceful change occurred during the 1960's elsewhere in Southeast Asia. Indonesia asserted a claim for sovereignty over Sabah and Sarawak, territories of British North Borneo, in 1961, when the

United Kingdom offered the territory to independent Malaya, a country that would be renamed Malaysia in 1963. Although the conflict heated up when Indonesian troops were sent to the borders of Sabah and Sarawak, Indonesia renounced its claim after accepting the results of a U.N.-sponsored plebiscite in 1963. In 1967, when both countries joined the Philippines, Singapore, and Thailand in forming the Association of South East Asian Nations (ASEAN), the Philippines also decided not to press an independent claim to Sabah, believing that there was more to gain as a member of ASEAN than as a recalcitrant claimant to Malaysian territory.

A classic example of mediation occurred in 1979, when President Jimmy Carter effected an agreement between Anwar el-Sadat of Egypt and Prime Minister Menachem Begin of Israel at Camp David. The former lose-lose stalemate between the two countries was replaced with a win-win outcome when Egypt promised to extend diplomatic recognition and a pledge never to attack Israel in exchange for the return of Negev territories to Egypt and the eventual return of sovereignty to the Palestinian people.

There are many examples of U.N. efforts at conflict resolution. In 1950, the Security Council authorized a U.N. force to fight in Korea, allowing the United States to organize the coalition of countries defending South Korea. In 1960, an independent U.N. force in the Republic of the Congo, commanded by a Canadian general, was responsible for defeating and dismantling a mercenary force that was engaging in civil war against a newly independent state. In the Persian Gulf War of 1991, the Security Council authorized military action against Iraq for annexing Kuwait. The United States organized the coalition, as it had in Korea. In 1992, the U.N. Transitional Authority for Cambodia (UNTAC) sought to create a framework for a free and fair election to establish a government. Although 90 percent of the eligible voters dared to vote, despite death threats from the Khmer Rouge (a faction that initially agreed to UNTAC but later refused to demobilize its forces), elections produced a new government that was split between two contending factions, and the Khmer Rouge continued to engage in guerrilla warfare. Whether the nearly two billion dollars spent on UNTAC, the most expensive U.N. peacekeeping group ever, was worth the investment, is still a matter for debate.

Several systematic studies have attempted to ascertain conditions under which conflict resolution will be more likely to be peaceful and third-party intervention will be successful. In an analysis of 310 attempts at conflict management, the only consistent predictor of successful conflict resolution was the perception among parties involved that a third party was unbiased.

In another study, fifty-six cases of peaceful change were analyzed. The principal findings were that attempts at peaceful change are more successful when major powers are uninvolved, vital interests are unaffected, the issue is nontrivial, and the conflict management agent is an organ of the United Nations.

Context

Conflict resolution is an ongoing process. The Hague Conferences of 1899 and 1907 brought many governments together in a common forum to discuss disarmament and methods of conflict resolution. The next scheduled conference was to be held in 1915. The inflexibility of the weapons systems in place by 1914 meant that one effort to deter aggression provoked a response that was seen as provocative, and each resulting countermove ultimately meant that nothing could reverse the outbreak of a war that nobody wanted. After the war, a better system was desired by all, and the League of Nations resulted. Under the League, various forms of multilateral conflict resolution were developed in case bilateral methods failed and violence appeared possible, but the rise of militarism in Germany and Japan proved too intractable. The League failed in its mission, and World War II began.

The United Nations further perfected forms of international conflict resolution, but could not handle disputes linked to the Cold War. Through tacit bargaining, the two superpowers avoided a direct violent conflict, but did not decline to fight proxy wars with allies, shoring up their alliances by resolving intrabloc differences and by negotiating various arms control agreements. With the end of the Cold War, the major powers began to cooperate, much in the manner anticipated by the founders of the United Nations, but demands for multilateral conflict resolution overloaded the capabilities of the United Nations and the world's governments. More United Nations peacekeeping forces were in place throughout the world than ever before, but successes did occur, for the most part, when these forces served as observers.

Bibliography

Bloomfield, Lincoln P. *Evolution or Revolution? The United Nations and the Problem of Peaceful Territorial Change*. Cambridge, Mass.: Harvard University Press, 1957. Analysis of fifty-six cases of peaceful change from the League of Nations era through 1956.

Burton, John, and Frank Dukes. *Conflict: Practices in Management, Settlement, and Resolution*. New York: St. Martin's Press, 1990. Comprehensive analysis of principles of international conflict resolution.

Fisher, Ronald J. *The Social Psychology of Intergroup and International Conflict Resolution*. New York: Springer-Verlag, 1990. Informative about the social nature of conflict resolution.

Haas, Michael. "Dimensions of International Conflict Resolution." In *World Peace Through the United Nations*. Seoul, Korea: Kyung Hee University Press, Kyung Hee University Press, 1984. An analysis of more than two hundred efforts at bilateral and multilateral international conflict resolution.

James, Alan. *Peacekeeping in International Politics*. London: Macmillan, 1990. Analysis of about sixty attempts at international peacekeeping after 1920.

Miall, Hugh. *The Peacemakers: Peaceful Settlement of Disputes Since 1945*. New York: St. Martin's Press, 1992. An analysis of international conflicts from 1945 to 1990.

Osgood, Charles E. *An Alternative to War or Surrender*. Champaign: University of Illinois Press, 1962. Proposes a methodology of conflict resolution.

Schelling, Thomas C. *The Strategy of Conflict.* Cambridge, Mass.: Harvard University Press, 1960. Eloquent statement of the theory of deterrence as a method of tacit negotiation.

Simmel, Georg. *Conflict and the Web of Group-Affiliations.* New York: Free Press, 1955. Presents the argument that conflict is fundamentally integrative.

Zartman, I. William, et al. *International Multilateral Negotiation: Approaches to the Management of Complexity.* San Francisco: Jossey-Bass, 1994. States basic principles of successful negotiation.

Michael Haas

Cross-References

Alliances, p. 47; Ambassadors and Embassies, p. 53; Arms Control, p. 95; Diplomacy and International Negotiation, p. 552; Foreign Relations, p. 718; Geopolitics, p. 759; International Law, p. 956; North Atlantic Treaty Organization, p. 1332; Peace, p. 1390; Supranational Government Institutions, p. 1922; United Nations, p. 2045; The World Court, p. 2161.

CONFUCIANISM AND GOVERNMENT

Field of study: Religion and government

Confucianism is the political and moral philosophy taught by Confucius (551-479 B.C.E.) and his disciples and interpreted by later followers. It became China's official philosophy during the second century B.C.E. and continued as such until the fall of dynastic government in 1912.

Principal terms
HUNDRED SCHOOLS OF PHILOSOPHY: many teachers who tried, c. 600-221 B.C.E., to find solutions to China's political and social ills that accompanied the decline of the Chou dynasty (c. 1122-256 B.C.E.) and the wars between the feudal states
JEN: human kindness, an important virtue emphasized by Confucians and key to the development of the superior person
LI: proper conduct or propriety, a key Confucian virtue
MANDATE OF HEAVEN: political concept endorsed by Confucians that heaven was the universal ruler, giving its mandate to a worthy man to rule; although the mandate can be passed down to the family of the ruler, it can be revoked by heaven for unworthy behavior
TAO: the way. All philosophers of the Hundred Schools sought to restore harmony to society through the teachings of Tao. One school came to be called Taoism, the philosophy of the way

Overview

Confucius is the Latinized name of K'ung Ch'iu, whom the Chinese call K'ung Fu-tzu, meaning Master K'ung. His philosophy has had such a great impact on China during the past two thousand years that he is doubtless the most important individual in Chinese history. Confucius founded a philosophy, not a religion, that interpreted the past, molded the Chinese mind, and guided China's government and society, becoming an inseparable part of the Chinese character.

A member of the *shih* class (originally knights or lower aristocrats), Confucius devoted his early adult life to politics and public service, seeking to find a ruler who would employ him so that he could put into practice his ideas of government. Failing in this quest, he turned to teaching, founding a school with three thousand men as his students. Eighty of these men were disciples; they continued his teachings after his death. Confucius wrote a book called the *Spring and Autumn Annals*, a historical chronicle with moral lessons. Confucius and his students reputedly also compiled and edited ancient documents called the *I-Ching* (book of changes), the *Shu-Ching* (book of history), the *Shi-Ching* (book of poetry), and the *Li-Ching* (book of rituals). Revered as the Five Classics, these works are considered the distillation of ancient wisdom.

After Confucius' death, his disciples compiled his thoughts and dialogues into a small book called *Analects*. Among his followers, Mencius (Meng-tzu, or Master Meng, c. 372-289 B.C.E.) was the most important. His writings were compiled into a volume called the *Mencius*, in which he expounded and enlarged on Confucius' views on government and society. He emphasized the government's duty to provide for the people's economic well-being and endorsed the people's right to overthrow tyrannical rulers. Mencius became the second sage of Confucianism and has been revered as second only to the master himself.

In time a consensus developed regarding Confucianism, embracing the following principal points: An impersonal heaven governs the universe; heaven decrees humans to live in harmony by following the Tao, which means an ethical and virtuous life; an ethical and virtuous life can be achieved by following proper conduct (*li*) and developing humanity and love for fellow humans and creatures (*jen*); Tao, *li*, and *jen* can be cultivated through the study of history; and the study of history can return the world to the Golden Age of the past, when sages ruled. Confucians also taught that humans and society are perfectible, that an ethical education and not birth made people superior, and that it is the duty of superior men to dedicate their lives to public service. Confucians stressed reciprocal and generally hierarchical human relationships, which they divided into five key categories, called the five relationships. These include the relationships between father and son, husband and wife, elder and younger siblings, friends and neighbors, and rulers and subjects. Each individual has responsibilities and duties in each relationship. Three of the relationships are within the family, important because the young learn their first lessons within the family, which is regarded as a microcosm of the state. By extension, the ruler is regarded as the father of the entire country.

A virtuous ruler governs the country as a benevolent father governs his family; likewise, subjects should serve a ruler as children serve their father. Further, Confucians maintain that during the Golden Age of antiquity, rulers did not hand over power to their sons in a dynastic succession, but sought out the most capable men as successors. Although the nationwide search for the best-qualified ruler was no longer possible after the Golden Age, heaven still decrees that rulers be virtuous. It does so by appointing the best-qualified man to rule and bestowing on him the mandate of heaven. Rulers are therefore called sons of heaven. The title does not confer divinity on rulers, but rulers had heavy ritual responsibilities and performed a schedule of sacrifices designed to maintain harmony between the cosmos and humanity. Good weather and bountiful harvests were seen as signs of heaven's satisfaction with the performance of a ruler, and natural disasters were interpreted as a show of its displeasure with his failings, and called for personal penance and better government. Although a ruler can pass his power to his family members in a dynastic succession, his successors still need to heed the mandate of heaven and govern benevolently. Otherwise heaven will repeal its mandate and authorize a worthy man to rule instead. Thus revolutions are sanctioned and dynastic changes are legitimized.

For more than three hundred years after the master's death, Confucianism was one of the many schools of philosophy that contended with others for acceptance. Taoism, a philosophy that taught passivity and a return to a primitive simplicity in which no government existed, was a principal rival and has remained a complementary philosophy to Confucianism through the ages. Other philosophies such as Moism, which taught universal love, and Legalism, which taught the supremacy of the state and a ruthless exercise of power, were once major challengers that later faded. Still other schools taught rhetoric, military strategy, and other skills.

After centuries of wars and chaos and the fall of the Chou dynasty in 256 B.C.E., China was briefly unified under the ruthless Ch'in dynasty (221-216 B.C.E.), which practiced Legalism. Legalism was discredited and discarded after the fall of the hated Ch'in. In 202 B.C.E., a commoner called Liu Pang established the Han dynasty on the ruins of the Ch'in. It lasted until 220 C.E. Early Han rulers abolished Legalism, lifted its harsh laws and restrictions, and called on talented men to serve the state, but instituted no official philosophy. Confucians responded by joining the government and teaching in schools, thereby gaining influence.

Later, Emperor Wu of the Han adopted measures favoring Confucianism, enshrining it as China's official ideology for the next two thousand years. He banned all individuals except professed Confucians from state service and established a state university with a Confucian curriculum to train officials. This university enrolled around thirty thousand students toward the end of the dynasty.

The need for numerous civil servants led to a system of recommendation and examinations during the Han, which developed into an examination system. Coinciding with the three-tiered administration of the empire, exams were held every three years in the county, province, and the national capital, at increasing levels of difficulty. The candidate who passed the county-level exam received a degree equivalent to a modern B.A. He was eligible for the provincial-level exam, passage of which was equivalent to a modern master's degree. Men who passed the provincial exam qualified for the national exam, passing which gained him a degree similar to a modern Ph.D. Possession of a degree became increasingly important for a government or higher teaching position; by the end of the first millennium C.E. a degree became almost mandatory for any civil service position. The examination system, based on a Confucian curriculum, made Confucianism China's governing ideology and realized Confucius' teaching that it was education and not birth that made a man superior and that superior men should dedicate themselves to public service. The universal application of the examination system made China's governmental administration a meritocracy without equivalent in the premodern world.

Han Confucianism was a synthesis that incorporated and classified knowledge into a coherent whole. It taught that heaven, earth, and humans formed an eternal trinity, and that it was the first duty of humans to understand the law of heaven. It was the first duty of the government to concern itself with the welfare of the earth and of the humans on it. Additionally, the government must attend to the moral training of the people through education and moral examples. Since the ruler's position was hereditary, it was the moral duty of superior men (morally educated men) to advise and guide him. If the ruler failed to heed the mandate of heaven, heaven would first send portents to remind and frighten him, failing which it would repeal the mandate and replace him with a worthy man. The implicit lesson is that force cannot rule the world.

Confucianism was challenged by Buddhism, which came from India. Buddhism explains that life is a never-ending cycle of karma or deeds, and teaches that *nirvana* or liberation from the round of karmic rebirths is the ultimate goal. Buddhism achieved great popularity during the first millennium, but its preeminence faded after the beginning of the second millennium, due in part to the resurgence of reinterpreted Confucianism, called Neo-Confucianism. Neo-Confucians condemned the other-worldliness of Buddhism, and insisted that people can have fulfilling lives through self-cultivation and attention to such virtues as benevolence, righteousness, and sincerity. They explained evil as a result of the neglect of virtues. Since many Neo-Confucian leaders were also government officials, they emphasized the need for a benevolent government. Thus Confucianism regained its vitality and remained China's state ideology for centuries.

Applications

The adoption during the Han dynasty of a school curriculum and an examination system based on Confucianism produced an educated class that subscribed to a uniform ideology. Confucianism, the product of a culture that prevailed over a continent-sized nation, was thus also important to sustaining a common culture in a vast land. Confucianism provided the moral foundation for the government, and the Confucian interpretation of history provided the framework for government institutions, laws, and actions. China ruled parts of Korea and Vietnam directly for several hundred years after about 100 B.C.E., and both lands indirectly as overlord until the end of the nineteenth century, so Confucianism became the foundation of the government and society of those two lands also. Although China never exercised political authority over Japan, the latter's voluntary acceptance of the Chinese civilization resulted in Confucianism's overwhelming influence in Japan also. For example, sixteen articles of the Seventeen Article Constitution adopted by Japan's "great Civilizer," Prince Shotoku, in 604, were based on Confucian principles. Later Neo-Confucianism became the ideology of Japan's shogunal government. Confucian Chinese culture played a role in East Asia that was analogous to the Christian Roman culture's in Western Europe.

While the educational and examination system favored young men from rich and educated families, the Confucian ideal of superior men of education and not birth was instrumental in producing a relatively mobile society, unique in the world, in traditional China. Although women were ineligible for participation in the examinations or the civil service, girls of educated families also received an education, though not as rigorously, in the Confucian classics. Mothers were often their sons' first teachers (before the sons began their formal education) and played the major role in their daughters' training. While most ordinary people did not receive a formal classical education, they too understood and accepted the key concepts of Confucianism as taught through popular novels and plays and through contact with the educated.

Meritocracy allowed the poor to hope for upward mobility and increased the general respect for education and its values throughout society.

On the negative side, the continued prestige of Confucianism tended to foster conservatism in the Chinese culture, the exaltation of the past, and the denigration of innovation. Moreover, the great reverence accorded to such subjects as history, philosophy, and literature tended to give short shrift to other fields of study, especially those pertaining to the sciences and technology.

China's humiliating defeats by Western powers in the nineteenth century resulted in reevaluations of its political, economic, and social systems, With the fall of the imperial system and the establishment of the republic in 1912, Confucianism lost its official status. It came under attack by both Marxist and liberal intellectuals as a key reason for China's backwardness in the modern era, for an oppressive patrilineal family system, and for the subjugation of youth to age and of women to men. Sun Yat-sen, father of the Chinese republic, and founder of the Nationalist Party or Kuomintang, sought to reconcile Confucianism with what he believed was admirable in Western civilization. He sought to preserve the civil service examinations and the censorate (watchdog branch) of Confucian imperial China, and added them onto the legislative, executive, and judicial branches of a Western style government. The Nationalist government commemorated Confucius by making his birthday a national holiday, Teachers' Day. This day is still celebrated on Taiwan. Since 1949 the Republic of China (ROC) on Taiwan has regarded itself as the guardian of China's cultural traditions. Although Japan, South Korea, Singapore, Hong Kong, and Taiwan have modern, plural societies, many aspects of Confucian society, such as reverence for education, family obligations, and the work ethic, continue strong and are credited for these societies' successful transformation to modernity.

Since 1949 the Communist government of the People's Republic of China has striven to destroy remaining Confucian societal values and has attempted to replace them with those of Marxism. Its attitude to Confucianism is analogous to European Marxist governments' attitude to Christianity. China's Communist Party leaders also have distrusted intellectuals and students, leaders of Confucian China, and subjected them to repeated purges. Mao Tse-tung's maxim that power stems from the barrel of a gun was diametrically opposite to the Confucian dictum that leaders should be moral and lead by example. The victimization of intellectuals adversely affected China's educational and research institutions. The distrust of intellectuals and students was partly responsible for the harsh repression of the democracy movement and for the Tiananmen massacre in 1989. The destruction of Confucian moral teachings and other traditional values, and the moral bankruptcy of Marxism left a vacuum in the lives of many in China.

Context

Confucius and others of the classical age of Chinese philosophy lived during the Eastern Chou period (770-256 B.C.E.), a time when a decline of royal authority left China leaderless. As the once subordinate feudal states struggled for survival and supremacy, political and social order deteriorated. Thinking men criticized the disorder, reflected on philosophical problems, and offered solutions. The number of solutions they proposed gave the age its name: the era of the Hundred Schools of Philosophy. The three most important schools were Confucianism, Taoism, and Legalism. Taoism advocated rising above the turmoil of the world and seeking comfort in passivity. In government, it taught that less was better. Early Han rulers practiced Taoist style government up to a point. Their governments were characterized by laissez-faire economic policies. In the long run, however, Taoism was not a practical government ideology. Legalism was practiced by the state of Ch'in during the later Chou. This amoral philosophy exalted state power and ruthless means. It measured policies only in terms of practical results; this did, temporarily, succeed in making the Ch'in strong and enable it to overpower all other states and unify China in 221 B.C.E. Ch'in oppression was so intolerable, however, that the dynasty was overthrown within a generation. Legalism was so abhorred that it was abolished by the succeeding Han and never restored to official status again, although some Legalist practices were modified and retained.

Confucianism, on the other hand, is a social and political teaching that is rooted in morality and an optimistic view of the perfectibility of people and society through a moral education and the practice of morality. Dedicated to transmitting the wisdom of the past, Confucius and his disciples nevertheless gave new meaning and interpretation to old terms, making them more egalitarian. The most notable example was Confucius' reinterpretation of the term "superior men." Confucius found superiority not in birth, as in the feudal era, but rather in education and moral worth. The egalitarian trend in Confucianism, as well as its humanitarianism and optimism, suited the Chinese temperament. Adopted as the state ideology during the Han dynasty, it remained the foundation of the Chinese government to modern times. Chinese power and culture dominated East Asia, so Confucianism also became the cornerstone of the cultures of Vietnam, Korea, and Japan.

When Jesuit missionaries arrived in China in the late sixteenth century and studied Chinese culture and philosophy, they became acquainted with the Confucian classics and admirers of Confucian philosophy. Jesuit scholars translated the Confucian classics into Latin, making them available to European scholars. They also wrote books extolling many features of Confucian society in China, in particular the examination system, a society based on merit, and a government based on a moral philosophy rather than on religion. In seeking to reform European societies, eighteenth century philosophers often looked to Confucian China as an example worthy of emulation. Voltaire, the Physiocrats, and Deists especially praised Confucian Chinese society for moral teachings that were separate from revealed religious ones. Thus Confucius came to be called the patron saint of the European Enlightenment. Jesuit accounts of the Chinese civil service recruited through examinations and not through birth inspired European reformers to demand similar systems in their countries. When the government of Great Britain instituted civil service exams in the early nineteenth century, opponents of the reform accused it of copying the Chinese.

Bibliography

Confucius. *The Analects of Confucius.* Translated and annotated by Arthur Waley. New York: Vintage Books, 1989. Good introduction that makes the sayings of the master meaningful.

Creel, H. G. *Confucius: The Man and the Myth.* Westport, Conn.: Greenwood Press, 1972. Explanation of the man, the development of the myth, the triumph of Confucianism, and its universal significance.

De Bary, W. T., et al. *Sources of Chinese Tradition.* New York: Columbia University Press, 1960. Collection of documents providing concise introductions to works by Confucius and important Confucians through the ages, and on Confucianism as applied in government.

Feng, Yu-lan. *A Short History of Chinese Philosophy.* Edited by Derk Bodde. New York: Macmillan, 1948. Overview of Chinese philosophies by an eminent authority. Sets Confucian teachings alongside other philosophical schools.

Hucker, Charles O. *China's Imperial Past: An Introduction to Chinese History and Culture.* Stanford, Calif.: Stanford University Press, 1975. Excellent overview of Chinese history from earliest times. Includes essays on philosophy in every era of Chinese history.

Nivison, David S., and Arthur Wright, eds. *Confucianism in Action.* Stanford, Calif.: Stanford University Press, 1959. Excellent book by many experts on the different facets of Confucianism, in theory and application.

Waley, Arthur. *Three Ways of Thought in Ancient China.* Garden City, N.Y.: Doubleday, 1956. Useful comparison of Taoism, Confucianism, and Legalism, with many quotations from original texts, along with explanations.

Wright, Arthur, ed. *Confucianism and Chinese Civilization.* New York: Atheneum, 1964. Analyzes the important contributions of Confucianism to every aspect of Chinese civilization.

Jiu-Hwa Lo Upshur

Cross-References

Asia: Politics and Governments, p. 108; Buddhism and Government, p. 152; Chinese Communism, p. 223; Education Management, p. 565; Government Roles, p. 778; History of Government, p. 829; Individual Versus State Rights, p. 910; Revolutionary Governments, p. 1725; Succession, p. 1909.

CONGRESS

Field of study: Functions of government

Congress is the legislative branch of the United States government. It passes legislation, represents the interests of the American people in the national government, oversees the operation of the executive branch, conducts public investigations, and through its 535 individual members performs a variety of services for the citizens of the United States.

Principal terms
BICAMERAL LEGISLATURE: legislature with two separate and distinct lawmaking bodies
ENUMERATION OF POWERS: listing of legislative powers assigned to Congress by the U.S. Constitution in Article 1, section 8.
HOUSE OF REPRESENTATIVES: one branch of the U.S. Congress, comprising 435 voting members who serve two-year terms apportioned among the states according to population
LEADERSHIP STRUCTURE IN CONGRESS: system of party leadership in the House and Senate, headed in the House by the Speaker and in the Senate by the Majority Leader
SENATE: one branch of the U.S. Congress, comprising two members from each state of the union who serve six-year terms
VETO POWER: authority of the president of the United States under the Constitution to prevent congressional enactments from becoming law, unless overturned by two-thirds of each branch

Overview

The legislative branch of the United States government, the U.S. Congress, consists of two separate bodies: the Senate and the House of Representatives. The Senate has one hundred members, with two from each of the fifty states, who serve six-year terms. Originally, senators were elected by the individual state legislatures, but since the ratification of the Seventeenth Amendment to the U.S. Constitution in 1913, they have been elected directly by the people. The House of Representatives, whose members serve two-year terms, has 435 voting members apportioned among the states according to population, with each state, no matter how small, guaranteed at least one representative. Under the Constitution of 1787, the House began with sixty-five members, but it was allowed to increase in size after each decennial census. By the beginning of the twentieth century it had grown to 435 members, at which time Congress passed legislation limiting it to that size. Since then, population shifts within and among the states have required reapportioning congressional seats so that, as much as possible, each member of the House represents the same number of constituents.

Although the Constitution places no limit on how long a member of the House and

Senate can serve, the Framers of the Constitution expected that the House of Representatives in particular would experience substantial turnover. In fact, it was not unusual during Congress's first century for up to half the membership of the House to turn over after an election. This began to change at the end of the nineteenth century as serving in Congress became more of a full-time job and as more members of Congress tried to make "careers" out of serving there. By 1990, the average House member had served about twelve years in that body, and the average senator had served eleven years. Reflecting growing levels of public dissatisfaction with Congress, fifteen states passed laws or state constitutional amendments in 1992 and 1993 limiting congressional terms to twelve years in the Senate and either twelve or six years in the House. Opponents of term limits argued that the only legal way to limit congressional terms would be through an amendment to the U.S. Constitution.

The modern Congress carries out five key functions in the American governmental system: lawmaking, representation of the interests and desires of the American people, oversight of the executive branch (the bureaucracy) to ensure that programs are properly administered, investigations to inform the public about serious national problems or issues, and constituency service of various types (such as intervening on behalf of constituents with the bureaucracy). The first two of these functions were explicitly intended by those who wrote the Constitution of 1787; the other three have developed over time.

The Constitution vests seventeen specific legislative powers in Congress. These range from some of the highest powers exercised by government—such as taxation, regulation of commerce, and declarations of war—to others of much less importance—such as establishing post offices. This list is followed by a clause giving Congress the power to "make all Laws which shall be necessary and proper for carrying into Execution the foregoing Powers." This "necessary and proper" clause suggests that the enumeration of legislative powers was not intended to be a strict limitation on Congress. Indeed, in 1791, within only two years of the first assembling of Congress, it established a national bank, although such a power was not explicitly included in the constitutional enumeration. Some, such as Thomas Jefferson, opposed the creation of the bank as too loose a construction of the powers accorded to Congress by the Constitution. The bank's supporters, on the other hand, defended it as "necessary and proper" for carrying into effect other explicit legislative powers, such as control of the currency and the regulation of commerce. Over the years, expansive interpretations of its lawmaking powers by the members of Congress and sympathetic U.S. Supreme Court decisions have effectively transformed Congress's enumeration of powers into a general legislative power. Rarely is it publicly debated whether the constitutional enumeration authorizes the entry of Congress into new policy fields.

The House and Senate possess approximately equal shares of the lawmaking power. For a bill to become a law it must be passed in identical form by both branches, with each branch completely free to amend proposals from the other. Under the Constitution, however, all revenue bills (tax measures) must originate in the House, which was expected to be closer to the people than the Senate. Moreover, the Senate possesses several nonlegislative powers not shared with the House: the confirmation of presidential nominations to high offices and the ratification of treaties.

In one crucial respect, Congress shares the lawmaking power with the president, for any bill passed by the House and Senate must be presented to the president for action. If the president signs it, it becomes law. If the president vetoes it, it is returned with a list of objections to the branch in which it originated and must then be approved by two-thirds of each legislative house. If the president neither signs nor vetoes the bill, it becomes law after ten days unless Congress has adjourned, in which case the bill dies (a so-called "pocket veto"). From 1789 to 1990 presidents formally vetoed 1,431 bills passed by Congress (of which only 103, or 7 percent, were overridden) and pocket-vetoed another 1,054 bills. Seven presidents vetoed no bills at all; five vetoed more than one hundred, led by Franklin Roosevelt with 635. The Constitution also vests the president with the authority to "recommend to [Congress's] Consideration such Measures as he shall judge necessary and expedient." Presidents have varied greatly in how frequently and energetically they have promoted legislation in Congress. Nineteenth century presidents tended to defer to Congress on matters of domestic legislation.

To some extent Congress also shares the lawmaking power with the Supreme Court, for since 1803 the Court has asserted the authority to rule acts of Congress unconstitutional. Although this power of "judicial review" is not mentioned in the Constitution itself, the Court maintained that it was necessarily implied as part of the constitutional order. It took until 1857 before the Court once again ruled an act of Congress unconstitutional. Indeed, judicial review did not prove a serious impediment to the congressional will until the New Deal during the 1930's, when the Court overturned key legislation enthusiastically endorsed by the president and Congress. By the end of the decade, however, the Court shifted its position. In recent decades the Court's judicial review power has been exercised much more often against state legislatures than against Congress.

The most important organizational features of the House and Senate are their leadership structures, which centralize power and influence, and their committee systems, which decentralize decision making. In each of the branches, the two major political parties—Democrats and Republicans—select their own leaders. In the House, the leader of the majority party becomes Speaker of the House. Next in line is the majority leader and then the majority whip. The whip is responsible for communicating leadership decisions to party members, informing members about forthcoming votes, maximizing party representation during floor votes, and generally promoting party voting on the floor. The minority party has essentially the same leadership structure, with the exception that there is no minority party equivalent to the Speaker: The top minority party officer is simply called the minority leader.

The parties in the Senate have a similar leadership structure. The principal exception is that under the Constitution the vice president of the United States is the president of the Senate, having the right to preside over debates (which rarely occurs) and to cast tie-breaking votes. The Senate also chooses a "president pro tempore," which is essentially an honorific position usually given to the most senior member of the majority party. In reality, the top officer of the Senate on a day-to-day basis is the majority leader, whose importance in Senate debates and scheduling of legislation is signified by the tradition that the majority leader is always recognized first during debate or discussion on the floor.

Although party leaders in the House and Senate do possess some real influence in the legislative process, their power pales in comparison to their equivalents in parliamentary systems. For example, congressional leaders have almost no control over the election or reelection of their party colleagues in Congress. Because there is almost nothing they can do to keep unresponsive members from being returned to Congress, their influence comes more from persuasion and bargaining than from command.

Counteracting the centralizing influences of the leadership system is the decentralizing effect of the committee and subcommittee system. Both the House and the Senate divide the legislative workload among committees organized according to subject matter. There are twenty-two such "standing committees" in the House and sixteen in the Senate. (There are also "special committees" and "joint committees" in Congress, but these are generally of less importance than the standing committees.) The standing committees are further subdivided into subcommittees, again based on subject matter; these numbered about 220 in 1994. The subcommittees have become increasingly independent of their parent bodies, thereby spreading power to the large percentage of majority party members who serve as subcommittee chairpersons.

Applications

In September, 1986, the U.S. Congress passed the Tax Reform Act, a major reform of the U.S. tax code that dropped millions of low-income Americans from the income tax rolls, decreased the highest income tax rates from 50 percent to 28 percent, and ended numerous tax deductions or "loopholes." How and why Congress passed this landmark bill illustrates key features of the lawmaking process in Congress.

Although members of the House and Senate had introduced bills embodying the principles of what became the Tax Reform Act as early as 1982, these efforts were of no avail until President Ronald Reagan made tax reform a major public issue in his 1984 State of the Union address. Over the next year and a half, officials in the Department of the Treasury and the White House worked to formulate a detailed plan, which was formally introduced to Congress in May of 1985. Since this was a tax measure, it went first to the House of Representatives, where public hearings were held before the Ways and Means Committee. After the hearings, six weeks of additional meetings and negotiations were necessary before a bill was drafted and reported to the full House. Unlike in the Senate, most important bills in the House are not debated on the floor until a "rule" governing the terms of debate and specifying allowable amendments is issued by the Rules Committee and approved by a majority vote on the floor. After Republicans successfully led a revolt against the rule on tax reform, thereby keeping the committee bill from the floor, President Reagan personally visited House Republicans at the Capitol to keep the reform process moving. The rule then passed and the Tax Reform Act was approved by a voice vote on the floor in December of 1985.

The bill then went to the Senate, where it was referred to the Finance Committee. Ignoring many elements of the House-passed bill, the Finance Committee approved its own measure in May, 1986. In June, the committee bill was approved by the full Senate. Because the House and Senate passed different bills, a conference committee was convened to iron out the differences. Within two months, the conference committee had reached agreement; a month later, the two branches approved the conference report. In October, the president signed the bill into law.

Several features of the passage of the Tax Reform Act characterize lawmaking in Congress more generally. First, it is not unusual for presidential involvement to be decisive to the passage of new policy initiatives. No single member of Congress can compete with the president in getting a novel proposal onto the national agenda. Key members of Congress, who might personally have preferred to let tax reform die, feared the public reaction if Reagan blamed Congress for the defeat of the top domestic initiative of his second term. Although the final bill was not identical to what the president proposed, it did include the essential elements, thus illustrating that many laws passed by Congress begin as proposals from the executive branch.

Second, interest groups were involved throughout the process as they tried either to defeat the elimination of deductions or to affect the details of the legislation. Many such groups are heavy donors to congressional campaigns and may also have a substantial presence in the legislator's home district or state. Although many legislators are genuinely sympathetic to the interests that lobbyists represent, they also have more self-interested reasons to be responsive.

Third, even in the face of powerful interests opposed to new policies, ideas about what constitutes good public policy do play a major role in Congress. The members of the House and Senate are not merely self-interested politicians. To varying degrees they respond to information and arguments about ways to solve social, economic, or political problems.

Finally, each legislative branch is, in effect, a world of its own and makes an independent judgment about legislation. It is rare for either branch to defer to the other, even on tax matters, which, according to the Constitution, must originate in the House.

Context

Congress is one of the three independent branches of American national government. Because it is listed first in the Constitution of 1787 and because it is the principal lawmaking branch, many have concluded that American government is characterized by congressional supremacy. Adherents of this view often cite the words of Roger Sherman, a delegate to the Constitutional Convention of 1787, who maintained that the executive should be "nothing more than an institution for carrying the will of the Legislature into effect." Opponents of congressional supremacy, on the other hand, point out that the Framers rejected Sherman's proposals for reducing the president to a subordinate position (for example, having Congress elect the president and remove him from office at will) and that in the Federalist Papers defending the proposed Constitution, James Madison and Alexander Hamilton decried the tendency of the legislature in a democracy to draw "all power into its impetuous vortex" and thus strongly argued for an independent executive branch not dependent on the legislative will.

Whatever the original intention regarding the role of Congress in the governmental system, for much of the nineteenth century Congress was clearly the dominant branch on matters of domestic legislation, especially in the decades just before and after the Civil War. By the twentieth century, however, political, social, and technological developments had combined to raise the prominence of the presidency in the governmental system. The rise of a more activist national government, the growing importance of foreign affairs, and the development of mass media (especially radio and television) had the effect of making the president, in Woodrow Wilson's words, "the political leader of the nation" and "the vital place of action in the system."

Nevertheless, despite the fact that the modern Congress often operates in the shadow of the presidency, it remains the most independent and powerful legislative body among Western democracies. While the American separation of powers system, as opposed to parliamentary government, creates the possibility of conflict, and even deadlock, between the legislative and executive branches, it has also ensured that the legislature remains free to exercise its independent will, even against the wishes of the executive branch.

Bibliography

Barone, Michael, and Grant Ujifusa. *The Almanac of American Politics*. Washington, D.C.: National Journal, yearly. This annual volume provides detailed portraits of each member of Congress and their districts or states.

Binkley, Wilfred E. *President and Congress*. 3d ed. New York: Random House, 1962. Useful and highly readable history of the presidency and Congress. Contains a subject index as well as a good, if somewhat dated, bibliography.

Congressional Quarterly Weekly Report and *The National Journal*. These two weekly journals cover legislative and other activities within the House and Senate. Each year Congressional Quarterly also publishes an *Almanac* that reviews the accomplishments of each session of Congress and provides detailed information on voting records. Congressional Quarterly also publishes a highly informative *Guide to the Congress of the United States*.

Hamilton, Alexander, James Madison, and John Jay. *The Federalist Papers*, edited by Clinton Rossiter. New York: New American Library, 1961. Essays 47-51 describe the Framers' theory of separation of powers; 52-58 describe the House of Representatives; and 62-66 describe the Senate. There is no better source for the original understanding of the nature and role of the Congress in U.S. government.

Ornstein, Norman J., Thomas E. Mann, and Michael J. Malbin. *Vital Statistics on Congress, 1991-1992*. Washington, D.C.: Congressional Quarterly, 1992. The best single source for up-to-date statistics on the members of Congress, congressional elections, committees and subcommittees, and workload within Congress.

Joseph M. Bessette

Cross-References

The British Parliamentary System, p. 146; The Constitution of the United States, p. 425; Democracy, p. 513; Filibuster, p. 694; Iron Triangles, p. 981; Legislative Body Types, p. 1091; Legislative Functions of Government, p. 1098; Lobbying and Lobbyists, p. 1130; Parliamentary Government, p. 1377; Policy Development and Implementation, p. 1414; Political Representation in the United States, p. 1525; The Presidency in the United States, p. 1590; Separation of Powers: Presidential Government, p. 1815; Term Limits, p. 1956.

CONSERVATISM

Field of study: Political philosophy

Classic conservatism has endured for approximately two hundred years as a major branch of political philosophy. It emphasizes traditions, authority, legitimacy, and the concept that government reflects human nature.

Principal terms
AUTHORITY: right to rule asserted by rulers and recognized by subjects; employing, but not reducible to, power
NATURAL LAW: system of ethics and political philosophy that sees right and wrong as universal and sees human law as based on morality
PERFECTIBILITY: belief that human nature can be perfected and that society can be made utopian
POLITICIZATION: process by which independent spheres of human life (family, religion, education) are drawn into the political arena

Overview

Classic conservatism has roots in Western traditions of political philosophy and morality, but it did not develop into a self-conscious political creed until the time of the French Revolution, in opposition to which it arose. Edmund Burke (1729-1797), a member of Great Britain's Parliament, is the father of classic conservatism. He brilliantly analyzed and condemned the French Revolution in a series of works that had profound influence in their own day and for succeeding generations. *Reflections on the Revolution in France* (1790) and *Letters on a Regicide Peace* (1796) are two examples.

Burke struck many of the themes that would dominate the philosophy of classical conservatism. Reacting against the Enlightenment's worship of reason, he emphasized that people are not exclusively rational creatures, especially regarding society and the state. People are moved by such nonrational things as symbols, habits, and traditions. This, Burke argued, is for the best, because the individual's reason is weak and fallible, but tradition embodies the reason of many, tested over long periods of time.

Since the reconciliation of governance with liberty is so delicate a matter, conservatives (following Burke's example) have been slow to support revolution. Burke looked to the Glorious Revolution of 1688, which expelled James II from the British throne, as the model of a necessary, just, and successful revolution. The nation revolted only after the designs of the king on absolute power had become manifest. As little change as possible was produced in the traditional forms of government, and the traditional rights of the people were better secured by their enactment into law.

In the French Revolution and in the thoughts of the thinkers whose writings presaged it, conservatives have seen the rise of political ideology, which they view as the deadly enemy of all stable government and ultimately of all human happiness. The ideologies unchained by the French Revolution included nationalism, democratism, and egalitarianism, and conservatives have seen these as directly linked to the rise of Nazism, fascism, anarchism, communism, and socialism in the nineteenth and twentieth centuries.

Patriotism has always enjoyed the enthusiastic support of conservatives, but nationalism was viewed as a kind of idolatry, threatening the disruption of all states. Conservatives saw egalitarianism as an essentially false doctrine that would ultimately become suppressive of all liberty. Democratism, on the other hand, was opposed by conservatives not out of any inherent dislike of democracy, but out of their understanding of natural law, which argues that the central ethical question in governance is whether a particular government made just and prudent decisions, not how those decisions were made.

The structure of government is important, however, and conservatives have tended to support the mixed constitution as recommended by ancients such as Aristotle and Polybius and by medieval scholastics such as Thomas Aquinas. According to the concept, the best form of constitution is the mixed constitution embodying elements of the monarchical, the aristocratic, and the democratic. In Europe, this has often made conservatives monarchists—supporting a constitutional monarchy, with a titled aristocracy and a legislature with one of its chambers based on popular suffrage.

In part, the mix is aimed at balancing the interests of the social classes, but more importantly, the mixed constitution aims at avoiding the evils inherent in each pure form of government. Each pure form of government can, by Aristotle's reasoning, degenerate: monarchy into tyranny, aristocracy into oligarchy, and democracy into mob rule.

In many lands outside of Europe, conservative support for the mixed constitution has continued but altered in form to suit the particular society. In America, the Constitution of the United States embodied the ideal of the mixed polity, with the presidency equivalent to an elective monarchy, the Supreme Court and the Senate acting as an aristocracy, and the House of Representatives based on a democratic model. Conservatives also recognize the point made by Aristotle in his *Politics* that different peoples with differing cultures and economies may be best served by government that reflects their diversity.

Ideology is essentially foreign to the conservative mind. An ideology strongly suggests that political philosophy is at the heart of the human experience. Conservatives have tended to view some political questions as clearly metaphysical, or even theological in nature. Some classical conservatives have been agnostic, deistic, or even atheistic. The Scottish philosopher and historian David Hume wrote as a deist (and may well have been an atheist), but he strongly embraced most conservative doctrines.

Most conservatives, however, have had a religious dimension to their political philosophy, and the doctrine of Original Sin has played a major role in conservative rejection of the leftist belief in the perfectibility and rationality of humanity. This firm belief in the fallen nature of humanity has made conservatives immune to the myriad utopianisms of the Left, as well as to the various right-wing utopias offered by some forms of libertarianism, anarcho-libertarianism, and theocracy.

Almost of equal importance to the conservative worldview is the notion of free will and moral responsibility. Rooted in the Judeo-Christian notion of the importance of freely chosen virtue, many conservatives reject schemes of human perfectibility that fail to recognize the importance of the means of its achievement. While recognizing that power is necessary to the maintenance of any system of government, conservatism has emphasized the importance of authority over brute force.

Applications

Modern conservatism has become allied and intermixed with other political movements over the years. Chief among these has been the general controversy of the free market. The alliance between classical conservatism and advocacy of a free market might appear strange, for in its earliest days, conservatism fought against classical liberalism's attempt to reduce political economy to pure laissez-faire. Traditional conservatives have always felt that government has a role to play in providing a safety net for society, but they have become strong in their advocacy of the free market as society has developed private substitutes for governmental intervention and as the opponents of capitalism have shown their opposition to the traditional moral and religious values of society.

A kind of paternalism is often in evidence in conservative thinking, in part as a result of the movement's aristocratic origins and in part because its organic view of society was never completely reconciled to the radical individualism implicit in unrestrained capitalism.

The antireligious bias of modern society has been a major concern for conservatives. In pluralistic societies, conservatives have not tended to push for the formal establishment of state churches, but they have resisted the drive for secularization in general. For conservatives, religion is a vital aspect of humanity and a part of public life, not merely a private advocation. Since moral values are, in the conservatives' view, the basis of law and of societal values, it is natural for religion to be the wellspring of authority for law and for rulers.

With the increasing secularization of society, and with the increasing politicization of society, conservatives have moved away from enthusiastic support for public education. As public schools became value-neutral, conservatives have come to support private education for the passing on of culture and tradition.

Conservatism in general seemed to oppose enlargement of the voting franchise. As time went on, however, conservatives often backed new suffrages, as when Benjamin Disraeli, the Tory prime minister of Great Britain, enfranchised the urban working classes. The conservative rule for granting suffrage seems always to have been prudence, with classes and groups admitted to greater citizenship rights as soon as conditions made their participation a stabilizing rather than a destabilizing factor.

In America, conservatives have been concerned with the system of checks and balances set up by the Constitution and with federalism. In the twentieth century, conservatives became concerned with what was termed the imperial presidency and with the failure of Congress to exercise its constitutional role in decision making, especially in regard to foreign policy and war powers. In regard to federalism, modern conservatives have been concerned with the increase of the power of the federal government at the expense of the states.

Conservative concern over federalism has often been oversimplified as a regard for states' rights, but a more accurate rendering would be that conservatives favor a balance between state and federal power, with each level of government restricted in its powers. In the early days of the American republic, that balance was also absent as a result of the weakness of the federal authority and the excessive power of the states. In this view, federalists such as Alexander Hamilton, John Jay, and John Marshall have more in common with modern conservatives than have early states-righters such as Thomas Jefferson, Patrick Henry, and George Mason.

Regarding the Constitution, conservatives have been most upset by the abandonment of original intent as the chief interpretive guide of the federal courts. Some have mistakenly spoken of strict constructionism versus loose constructionism, but Judge Robert Bork, a conservative legal scholar, has emphasized that loose constructionism has been a dead issue since *McCulloch v. Maryland* (1819)—a Supreme Court decision that justified Congress's chartering of the Bank of the United States by reference to the "necessary and proper" clause of the Constitution.

Conservatives see original intent jurisprudence as vital to preserve the Constitution from unrestrained judicial tampering and to preserve the ideal of the Constitution as a contract of the present society with its past and future citizens. This is only really possible when the Constitution has genuine substantive content, not when it serves as a blank slate ready to receive the imprint of the most recent judicial trend.

Conservatives see the Constitution as a restraint on the political passions of the moment. They point out that its meaning can be comprehended and that judicial decisions, to a degree, may be predicted by citizens who are active and knowledgeable in politics.

The political climate has become corrupted, furthermore, according to conservative commentators, by complex systems of largesse in the modern government-dominated economy. In such an economy, conservatives argue, citizens, classes, and regions court the favor of those in power to obtain governmental money, rather than make money independently.

Context

The conservative movement in America is concentrated in the Republican Party, but the Republican Party can in no way be equated with a purely conservative party. Persons with a general conservative bent in economics and on social issues seem to control that party in general, but many moderate politicians and pragmatists are active in its ranks and as candidates for political office. The Democratic Party, furthermore, though dominated by modern liberalism, has a large contingent of conservative members and officeholders.

In terms of political activism, conservatism is often mixed with libertarianism, isolationism, as well as with elements of nativism and racism. In the intellectual sphere, however, many scholarly and popular magazines have lent a lively intellectual life to the conservative movement.

Numerous think tanks and foundations also play a vital role in the intellectual life of conservatism. These include, among others, Young Americans for Freedom, the Intercollegiate Studies Institute, the Federalist Society, the American Enterprise Institute, the Foundation for Economic Education, and the Heritage Foundation.

Some issues divide the conservative movement, particularly those that have the concept of personal autonomy in conflict with the moral basis of society. Abortion and the legal status of drugs are examples of two such issues. A split over such issues occurs within conservatism over the application of laws that large segments of the population might be expected to disobey. Conservatives disagree on prohibition of an activity that is socially accepted among many.

In the late twentieth century, the Republican Party enjoyed many impressive victories, such as the election of Ronald Reagan as president of the United States in 1980 and the appointment of a number of conservative judges and justices to the federal bench. Until the mid-1990's, however, conservatives had only limited success in setting the national agenda.

What has proven true for the United States has also proven true for conservative movements elsewhere. In the wake of British prime minister Margaret Thatcher's campaign of privatization of state-owned industry, numerous countries jettisoned public ownership of large segments of the means of production, but the demand for the benefits of the welfare state remained undiminished in most industrialized nations. Secularization, along with signs of social decay such as crime, sexual promiscuity, illiteracy, and other ills, seemed to proliferate.

The collapse of the Soviet Union and the end of the Cold War proved a mixed blessing for conservative electoral success. A strong anticommunist foreign policy had often been the factor that most distinguished the conservative parties in the world from their left-wing opponents. With the elimination of the great global challenge to the West, foreign policy seemed to become less urgent, although factors such as nuclear proliferation, international environmental degradation, and mass illegal immigration from the Third World, prevented a return to isolationism in most countries.

Bibliography

Buckley, William F., Jr., and Charles R. Kesler, eds. *Keeping the Tablets: Modern American Conservative Thought*. New York: Perennial Library, 1988. Gives an excellent cross section of thinking within the modern American conservative movement.

Burke, Edmund. *Selected Writings and Speeches*. Edited by Peter J. Stanlis. Washington, D.C.: Regnery Gateway, 1991. Many of Burke's most important writings are in this volume.

Kirk, Russell. *The Conservative Mind: From Burke to Eliot*. 7th rev. ed. Chicago: Regnery Books, 1986. First published in 1953, this book was credited with initiating the modern American conservative movement.

_____. *The Politics of Prudence*. Bryn Mawr, Pa.: Intercollegiate Studies Institute, 1993. Presents the conservative response to recent events.

_____. *The Roots of American Order*. Malibu, Calif.: Pepperdine University Press, 1974. Argues that the American founding was part of a long conservative tradition in political philosophy.

Kuehnelt-Leddihn, Erik von. *Liberty or Equality: The Challenge of Our Time*. Edited by John P. Hughes. Caldwell, Idaho: Caxton Printers, 1952. Investigation of the intellectual currents of modernity in their relationship to political developments.

Oakeshott, Michael. *Rationalism in Politics and Other Essays*. Indianapolis: Liberty Press, 1991. Combines traditional conservative wisdom with modern political insights.

Schuettinger, Robert Lindsay, comp. *The Conservative Tradition in European Thought*. New York: Putnam, 1970. Features the thoughts of major conservative figures of the last two centuries.

Witonski, Peter, comp. *The Wisdom of Conservatism*. 4 vols. New Rochelle, N.Y.: Arlington House, 1971. This treasury of conservative thinkers has the advantage of combining post-Burkean thinkers with their intellectual predecessors from ancient, medieval, and early modern times.

Patrick M. O'Neil

Cross-References

Aristotle's Political Philosophy, p. 83; Augustine's Political Philosophy, p. 121; Autocracy and Absolutism, p. 127; Burke's Political Philosophy, p. 171; Constitutional Law in the United States, p. 439; Federalism in the United States, p. 668; Hobbes's Political Philosophy, p. 836; Hooker's Political Philosophy, p. 842; Individual Versus State Rights, p. 910; Irrationalism in Politics, p. 987; The Left and the Right, p. 1079; Legitimacy, p. 1105; Liberalism, p. 1118; Neo-Conservatism, p. 1281; Neo-Idealism, p. 1287; The New Right, p. 1293; Power Divisions in Governments, p. 1578; Right of Revolution, p. 1744; Succession, p. 1909; Thomas Aquinas' Political Philosophy, p. 1974; Utopianism, p. 2084.

THE CONSTITUTION OF THE UNITED STATES

Field of study: Law and jurisprudence

The United States Constitution codified several unique governmental concepts. It divided power among three branches, with checks and balances to prevent any one branch from seizing control. It assigned specific powers to the federal government, and others to the states. Its "elastic clauses" have enabled it to respond to changing conditions for more than two centuries.

Principal terms

ARTICLES OF CONFEDERATION: agreement ratified by the thirteen states in 1781, forming a government in which the states retained important powers while the national government received only limited power

BICAMERAL LEGISLATURE: legislature with two separate chambers

CHECKS AND BALANCES: a major feature of the U.S. government, by which each of the three branches of government restrains actions of the others

EXECUTIVE POWER OF GOVERNMENT: power to enforce law and administer the government

FEDERAL GOVERNMENT: system in which government power is shared by a national government and constituent units

JUDICIAL POWER OF GOVERNMENT: power to judge disputes arising from the law

LEGISLATIVE POWER OF GOVERNMENT: power to make law

UNICAMERAL LEGISLATURE: legislature with one chamber

WRIT OF MANDAMUS: court order directing a government official to perform a duty of office

Overview

The most fundamental law of the United States, the Constitution is the document that designed the framework of the federal system of government. It establishes the three branches of government, grants them the authority to perform the activities of government, and limits that authority. It stipulates the qualifications individuals must meet in order to serve in Congress or the presidency and the general jurisdiction of the federal courts. It consists of seven articles and twenty-seven amendments. The purpose of the Constitution is defined best in its Preamble:

> We the People of the United States, in Order to form a more perfect Union, establish Justice, insure domestic Tranquillity, provide for the common defense, promote the general Welfare, and secure the Blessings of Liberty to ourselves and our Posterity, do ordain and establish this Constitution for the United States of America.

Article 1 creates Congress, designates its bicameral form, sets forth qualifications for membership, and lists powers of Congress, powers denied to Congress, and powers denied to the states. Article 2 creates the executive branch, defines qualifications for the presidency, and outlines presidential power. Article 3 creates the judicial branch of government and defines the act of treason. Article 4 provides guidelines that state governments must follow in their relationship with citizens and one another, outlines the procedure for admitting a new state to the union, and guarantees to every state a republican form of government. Article 5 sets out the procedure for amending the Constitution. Article 6 ordains that the Constitution, the laws of the United States, and treaties approved by the United States government shall be recognized by the states as superior to their laws or constitutions. Article 7 stipulates ratification requirements for the Constitution.

Amendments to the Constitution fall into several categories. Some provide guarantees of citizen rights by limiting the power of government on either the national or state level; others extend specific rights not included in the original text of the Constitution; still others grant additional authority to government not provided by the original text, or modify a procedure provided for in the Constitution.

In addition to its specific grants of authority to government, the Constitution also grants general authority that has allowed Congress to exercise its legislative power in ways not envisioned by the men who wrote the document. These so-called elastic clauses are found primarily in Article 1, section 8 of the Constitution. The first paragraph of section 8 allows Congress, among other powers, to legislate for the "general Welfare of the United States," while its last paragraph allows Congress "to make all Laws which shall be necessary and proper for carrying into Execution" the powers specifically enumerated. The "general welfare clause" and the "necessary and proper clause" give Congress great latitude in its power to legislate because of the imprecision of their language. Providing for the general welfare can be interpreted to include many acts that the Constitution did not specifically authorize Congress to accomplish, providing funds for public education programs or subsidies for agriculture, for example. Government leaders have debated the precise meaning of the "necessary and proper clause" since President George Washington's administration, when Secretary of State Thomas Jefferson and Secretary of the Treasury Alexander Hamilton argued over the necessity and propriety of creating a national bank to expedite the government's financial affairs.

Disagreement over the proper interpretation of the elastic clauses has led to the development of two competing theories of constitutional interpretation. Loose construction, advocated by Hamilton, stressed the "proper" portion of "necessary and proper," and allowed generous interpretation of Constitutional provisions; strict construction, advocated by Jefferson, stressed the "necessary" portion, and limited government actions to those authorized explicitly in the document or those absolutely necessary for carrying out a designated responsibility. Congressional practice and decisions rendered by the United States Supreme Court have favored Hamilton's loose construction and the general legislative authority that it implies. The necessary and proper clause is generally understood to give Congress great latitude in determining the means by which it will carry out its delegated responsibilities.

Disagreement over constitutional provisions is a long-standing tradition in the United States. The Constitution, in fact, is the product of debate and compromise. Delegates to the Philadelphia Convention that wrote the document during the summer of 1787 came close to being deadlocked on several issues that threatened to end their attempt to create "a more perfect union," but they agreed to a series of key compromises that allowed their work to continue. These issues included the method by which the states were to be represented in Congress, how government power was to be divided within the national government, and how government power was to be divided between the national government and the states.

The first of these issues provoked intense debate over two plans of representation. Delegates from New Jersey introduced a plan favored by small states that would continue to give each state an equal voice in a unicameral Congress, as had been done under the Articles of Confederation. Virginia delegates proposed a plan favored by large states that would have apportioned state representation in proportion to their populations. Connecticut delegates formulated a proposal that assuaged both sides in the discussion. This plan, called the Connecticut Compromise or Great Compromise, divided Congress into two branches, a House of Representatives and a Senate, and provided that representation in the House would be apportioned according to population, while each state would be equally represented in the Senate.

Even that compromise, however, did not address all questions about representation. Southern state delegates contended that slave states should be allowed to count their entire slave populations for apportionment of their shares of House seats, while free-state delegates thought that no slaves should be counted. The result was the adoption of a compromise that allowed Southern states to count three-fifths of their slave population for apportionment. This resulted in approximately equal representation of slave and free states in the House of Representatives when the new government began.

The discussion about the division of power within the national government centered on the question of whether to continue Congress as the sole authority with power to create executive and judicial branches, or to create those two branches separately from Congress. Delegates decided that each branch would be independent, with Congress receiving the legislative power, the presidency the executive power, and the judiciary the judicial power.

Each branch was also limited by interaction with the other two, creating a system of checks and balances that the delegates envisioned as a safeguard to keep one branch from becoming powerful enough to abuse the fundamental rights of the people. Congressional acts, for example, can be vetoed by the president, but Congress can override that veto by a two-thirds majority vote in both chambers. The delegates further developed this safeguard by giving each branch of government a different source of authority. The president is elected by the electoral college, while federal judges are appointed by the president and confirmed by the Senate. Originally, members of the House of Representatives were elected by voters whose eligibility to vote was determined by their state, while senators were elected by state legislatures. The Seventeenth Amendment, in 1913, changed the method of electing senators to election by popular vote.

Discussion about the division of power between national and state governments surfaced because some delegates wanted to consolidate power in the national government, while others favored preserving the preeminence of state power as in the Articles of Confederation. Delegates agreed to create a federal system, in which the two levels shared power. The national government received new, substantial powers, including the power to levy and collect taxes and to regulate foreign and interstate commerce. States retained significant authority, including the power to levy and collect taxes on their own and to regulate their own internal commerce; however, they were denied the power to tax foreign or interstate commerce, to issue paper money, or to pass laws impairing the obligations of private contracts. They were also required to acknowledge the supremacy of national laws, the Constitution, and treaty provisions.

The spirit of compromise exemplified by these agreements enabled the delegates to produce a new plan of government and helped in the ratification process. Some opponents of the Constitution maintained that it should not be ratified because it did not provide enough specific guarantees of personal rights. Supporters of ratification agreed to add those protections in a series of amendments, now known as the Bill of Rights, as soon as practicable after ratification. The Constitution was ratified in 1789, and the Bill of Rights was added in 1791.

Applications

The Constitution has lasted as the basic document of government in the United States for more than two centuries, even though the country has changed dramatically. There are three primary reasons for its longevity: The Constitution is a general framework of government and not a detailed outline which could have become outmoded; it could be amended to address problems as they arose; and it became subject to judicial interpretation, which allowed for expansion of government authority as circumstances required.

The Constitution is a relatively short document (4,543 words) that establishes the government, grants power, and limits power in general terms without providing minute detail. The members of George Washington's first administration, therefore, established many governmental practices consistent with the document, while succeeding administrations filled in more details as circumstances forced consideration of constitutional issues. The elastic clauses, couched in general language, allowed later expansion of authority to encompass activities unimagined in the 1780's.

Constitutional amendments allow the Constitution to change as the country changes. Amendments can be proposed in one of two ways: by a two-thirds vote of both chambers of Congress, or by a special convention called by Congress upon the request of two-thirds of the state legislatures. To date, only the first method has been used to propose an amendment. After an amendment has been proposed, it must be ratified by three-fourths of the states, either in their legislatures or in specially called ratifying conventions, before it is added to the Constitution. These requirements for amendment ensure deliberate, often slow, consideration of changes but also allow needed and popular changes to be accomplished. The earlier Articles of Confederation, by contrast, required unanimous consent of states for amendment. That unrealistically high requirement prevented needed change, such as two amendments proposed for the Articles that would have addressed the pressing need for improved government finance. Both amendments failed to achieve unanimous consent.

Judicial review is the process by which acts of legislatures, including Congress, are subjected to scrutiny by the federal court system. The concept of judicial review of acts of Congress was not explicitly included in the Constitution, but evolved during an opportunity provided by the court case *Marbury vs. Madison* in 1801.

The case arose when President John Adams appointed several political followers to federal office shortly after his defeat for reelection. He signed commissions naming these appointees to office and Secretary of State John Marshall affixed the Great Seal of the United States to them, but they were not delivered before incoming president Thomas Jefferson's inauguration. William Marbury and several other appointees filed suit in the Supreme Court asking for a writ of mandamus ordering Jefferson's Secretary of State, James Madison, to deliver Adams' commissions. John Marshall, the chief justice, devised an ingenious ruling in the case that vastly increased the Court's power. The Court's decision in the *Marbury* case was that Marbury and the other men were entitled to their commissions but that the Court itself had no authority to issue the writ. Congress had seemingly granted that power in the Judiciary Act of 1789 but in doing so, had expanded the authority of the Court beyond that granted by the Constitution. The portion of the Judiciary Act of 1789 granting the authority was, therefore, unconstitutional. The lasting significance of the case was thus not Marbury's own fate, but the Court's assumption of the power to overrule an act passed by Congress.

The major constitutional issue during the pre-Civil War era was the question of who properly could interpret the Constitution. Thomas Jefferson and James Madison maintained in the Kentucky and Virginia resolutions that state courts were competent to interpret the document. Marshall's contention that the Supreme Court possessed the power to declare unconstitutional acts of Congress that violated the Constitution was accepted by later generations and helped to establish the Court as a truly co-equal branch of government.

Context

When the United States declared its independence from Great Britain in 1776, the question of who properly exercised the power of government arose. The Continental Congress assumed governing responsibility simply because there was no other institution capable of supporting the war effort and exercising the authority of government at that time. The process of transforming the Continental Congress into a legitimate government began with the approval of the Articles of Confederation in 1777. The Articles of Confederation became the first governing document of the new nation after it was ratified by all thirteen original states in 1781, and it remained in effect until the adoption of the Constitution in 1789.

The Articles of Confederation stressed limited government and states' rights. Each state received one vote in a unicameral Congress. Congress received authorization to maintain a volunteer army, conduct foreign relations, dispose of western lands ceded to it by the states, regulate trade with Native Americans, borrow money, request funds from the states, issue paper money, create executive offices, and exercise a limited judicial power in admiralty cases and disputes arising among the states. All other powers of importance, including the power to levy and collect taxes and to regulate foreign and interstate commerce, were reserved to the states.

Demands for revision of the Articles of Confederation began soon after its adoption, and increased after 1784 for a variety of reasons. Some people realized that Congress was too weak to alleviate the severe economic depression that began in 1784, caused by interstate trade barriers and British and Spanish limitations on American trade with their empires. Some worried about the potential problems of concentrating too much power in Congress without effective checks on that power. Others worried that the government could not repay its loan obligations without a dependable source of revenue. Still others realized that the Articles' requirement for unanimous consent from all thirteen states for amendment limited its ability to grow with the country. Finally, some people were concerned with an occurrence of civil disobedience in western Massachusetts known as Shays's Rebellion. Farmers in that area stopped foreclosure proceedings on their farms by seizing control of county courthouses, and the national government had no authority under the Articles to halt that breakdown of orderly legal procedures.

Congress called the Philadelphia Convention in 1787 to revise the Articles in order to address the concerns that had developed about that system of government. Delegates to the convention decided, however, that the Articles of Confederation were too flawed and that they should devise a wholly new document of government. The result was the Constitution.

Bibliography

Bernstein, Richard B., with Kym S. Rice. *Are We to Be a Nation?: The Making of the Constitution.* Cambridge, Mass.: Harvard University Press, 1987. Detailed discussion of the debates that surrounded the writing of the Constitution.

Cox, Archibald. *The Court and the Constitution.* Boston: Houghton Mifflin, 1987. The former Watergate special prosecutor, Cox provides a unique insight into the background of the Constitution and how that document grows and changes with the nation. Endnotes provide a valuable guide for additional information on many subjects.

Lockard, Duane, and Walter F. Murphy. *Basic Cases in Constitutional Law.* 2d ed. Washington, D.C.: Congressional Quarterly Press, 1987. Provides essential background information, along with selected Supreme Court rulings and concurring and dissenting opinions. Helps readers to understand the judiciary and its role in interpreting the Constitution, influencing governmental procedures, and developing public policy.

Peltason, J. W. *Corwin and Peltason's Understanding the Constitution.* 13th ed. San Diego, Calif.: Harcourt Brace, 1994. This classic in Constitutional studies features sections on the background of the Constitution and its basic features and detailed discussion of each of its sections and amendments. Includes a section on how the document functions in the contemporary political process.

Wood, Gordon S. *The Creation of the American Republic, 1776-1787.* New York: W. W. Norton, 1969. Analyzes the sources of revolutionary thought in the United States and the manner in which the Founders used that thought to overthrow the British imperial government and design their own system of government after winning their independence.

_____. *The Radicalism of the American Revolution.* New York: Alfred A. Knopf, 199ss2. Additional analysis of the democratization of early America. Emphasis on the Founders' consideration of ordinary citizens' desire for individual fulfillment helps to explain the tremendous changes experienced by the revolutionary generation.

Jerry Purvis Sanson

Cross-References

The Bill of Rights, p. 134; Checks and Balances in U.S. Government, p. 216; Constitutional Law in the United States, p. 439; The Electoral College, p. 584; Judicial Review, p. 1012; Legal Systems in Anglo-American Governments, p. 1085; Separation of Powers: Political Philosophy, p. 1809; The Supreme Court: Role in Government and Law, p. 1935.

CONSTITUTIONAL GOVERNMENTS

Field of study: Types of government

Constitutional government employs regularized procedural and substantive restraints on its powers, usually through written constitutions, popular accountability, and bills of rights.

Principal terms

BILL OF RIGHTS: constitutionally specified restraints on the powers of government, often involving social as well as civil rights

CHECKS AND BALANCES: institutional arrangements enabling different branches of government to protect their independence through specific involvement in each others' activities

JUDICIAL REVIEW: process by which courts rule on the constitutionality of statutory law, executive action, and the decisions of lower courts

POPULAR ACCOUNTABILITY: idea that decision makers should be held accountable to the people, either directly or indirectly, through election processes

RULE OF LAW: concept that all persons are equal before the law and can be equally restrained by the law

SEPARATION OF POWERS: governmental power organized by functionally dividing it among lawmaking, law-enforcing, and law-adjudicating bodies

Overview

It is easier to define constitutional government, or constitutionalism, than it is to ascribe a common form to it. As Carl Friedrich observed in his classic *Constitutional Government and Democracy* (1946), constitutionalism "has, for modern political science, a very distinct meaning as the process by which government action is effectively restrained." The term commonly refers to systems with an emphasis on the rule of law, respect for the fundamental rules of the political process, and regularized procedural and substantive restraints on the powers of government.

There are, however, nearly as many arrangements for restraining the powers of government in the democratic world as there are variations on the theme of democracy itself. The breadth of the limitations on government, the capacity of ordinary citizens to challenge government action, and the bodies charged with interpreting and enforcing constitutional government vary widely from country to country, complicating the task of comparative analysis.

In the English-speaking world, such differences are represented by the political processes of the United States, with the world's oldest, continuously functioning written constitution, and Great Britain, the birthplace of parliamentary democracy. Despite their shared democratic nature, these two nations stand at opposite ends of the spectrum in terms of the methods chosen to limit government power.

The U.S. constitutional system is based on a rather clear and not very flattering view of human nature. As the author of Federalist No. 51:

> If men were angels, no government would be necessary. If angels were to govern men, neither external nor internal controls on government would be necessary. In framing a government which is to be administered by men over men, the great difficulty lies in this: you must first enable the government to control the governed; and in the next place oblige it to control itself.

Toward these ends, the authors of the U.S. Constitution chose to supplement popular accountability with a variety of methods. Governmental power would be distributed between differing levels of government—the U.S. "invention" of federalism. At the center, there would be three branches of government with a separation-of-powers system sustained by a complicated process of checks and balances. Lawmaking authority was to be further divided between two coequal houses of Congress. The judiciary would be independent, endowed with the power to review the constitutionality of laws, and soon was entrusted with guaranteeing a Bill of Rights (1791), further limiting the powers of the central government.

In stark contrast, despite the legal sovereignty of Great Britain's Parliament, the British system has historically relied on an unwritten constitution, enforced by popular sovereignty and what more recent political scientists would call the British political culture, to regulate the behavior of its political authorities. In *Introduction to the Study of the Law of the Constitution* (1908), A. V. Dicey succinctly summarized that system by observing that under this arrangement, Parliament could even outlaw the preservation of blue-eyed babies if it chose to do so. No constitutional law would override the act of Parliament and no court would protect the victims. But, Dicey argued, legislatures would have to be insane to enact such laws and subjects would have to be idiots to submit to them.

To Dicey, the real restraints on the power of government rested with the consent of the people, and within a generation tragic support could be found for his argument. Politics in Britain has generally flowed in moderate and tolerant channels, despite Parliament's legal ability to make or unmake any law by the action of a simple parliamentary majority. In sharp contrast, the constitutional rules of the game did not prevent interwar Germany from rushing into a holocaust policy of slaying Dicey's proverbial blue-eyed babies. Nevertheless, after World War II most democratic countries—including those preferring the parliamentary union of executive and legislative powers to the U.S. model of separation of powers and checks and balances—have generally chosen not to rely on political culture alone to restrain the powers of government. Despite the diverse and creative institutional arrangements now governing the democratic decision-making process on the continent of Europe, most states have moved at least partially in the U.S. direction of adopting a judicial review process for examining the constitutionality of laws in order to protect individual rights and limit the actions of governments.

Postwar steps in this direction have been taken by states as different as Sweden, France, Italy, the Federal Republic of Germany, and India. All employ a body capable of rendering decisions on the constitutionality of parliamentary authority. Most also give specific protection to individual rights. The effectiveness of these provisions, however, has varied widely from state to state.

Sweden has a Law Council charged with reviewing the constitutionality of proposed legislation in the fields of criminal and civil law. Although its decisions are nonbinding, something of an informal checks and balances system prevails. By convention, the government shelves legislation ruled unconstitutional by this body. Meanwhile, the protection of individual rights against government abuse is in the hands of a powerful ombudsman office, which can hear cases at its own instigation or on appeal from persons adversely affected by state action.

France also has a Constitutional Council to rule on the constitutionality of pending legislation, and its decisions are legally binding. By the 1990's, it had come to operate more as a part of an evolving checks and balances system in the Fifth Republic than guarantor of the rule of law, because its members tended to be appointed on the basis of partisanship and they tendered their opinions on that basis. The protection of the individual from government abuse rests with the Council of State, which can hear cases involving enacted laws, not just pending legislation, but whose rulings are nonbinding on the government.

Similar examples can be found elsewhere in Europe. There are central constitutional courts in Germany (the Federal Constitutional Court in Karlsruhe) and Italy (the Constitutional Court), and both exercise judicial review in cases instigated by persons affected by the law—a power more akin to that of U.S. federal courts than the judicial bodies of France, Great Britain, or Sweden. In both Italy and Germany, the rulings in these cases often have had a substantial impact on the policy process; however, an initially inhospitable political climate in Italy erected far more obstacles to its constitutional court's hearing cases on appeal than occurred in Germany. As a result, the German court has probably contributed more to the development of the rule of law than its Italian counterpart, whose legacy has been more mixed. Most mixed of all has been the heritage of India's Supreme Court, whose critics charge that it often has been too lenient in protecting the elaborate Indian Bill of Fundamental Rights from government abridgement, especially when Prime Minister Indira Gandhi used the constitution's emergency rule features to govern the country.

Applications

As the above examples illustrate, diverse pathways have been pursued to achieve the rule of law in the twentieth century. Even the often unwieldy process of leaving the determination of unconstitutional action by local authorities in the hands of the central legislatures of unitary states rather than judicial bodies still finds its practitioners. London may be seen as at least implicitly having exercised this judgment when it dissolved civilian government in Northern Ireland in 1972. Nor have the only relevant experiences in developing constitutional government been those of the older democracies of Western Europe. Many countries have only recently traversed this path—not only Italy, West Germany, and India, whose current constitutions date from the late 1940's, but also post-Franco Spain, Greece after the generals, and postrevolutionary Portugal are worthy of mention as post-1970 experiments in constitutional government.

In some instances, the constitutional systems of democratic states result from an immediate need for a rule-of-law framework in order to conduct the business of government. At the same time, a substantial number reflect an implicit or explicit desire to engineer the political process to deal with a particular view of human nature or persistent problems associated with governing a particular society. The U.S. Constitution offers perhaps the most conspicuous example of a constitutional structure fashioned on the basis of a specific view of human nature and designed to overcome, in the minds of its Framers, a chronic danger of democratic government: a tyrannical majority.

A similar link between broad political and societal inquiry and the devices chosen to achieve constitutional government can be found in Western Europe's constitutional systems. Dicey stresses citizens' commitment to the supremacy of the law in concluding his study of the "substance" of the British constitution. Charles de Gaulle fashioned the constitution of France's Fifth Republic around his belief that France needed a strong executive—preferably drawing his mandate directly and regularly from the people—to offer France the firm leadership necessary to overcome the centrifugal tendencies present in traditionally fragmented French society. The architects of postwar Germany's Basic Law (constitution) pinned their hopes for stable democracy on a combination of limiting parliamentary representation to only those parties winning at least 5 percent of the national vote, public financing of elections, and a strong chancellor system. Collectively, these have enabled West Germany to avoid the paralysis that gripped the Weimar Republic as a result of its social diversity, numerous small parties, and weak coalition governments. The effort to shape constitutions over time to make societies more governable has been a common pattern in post-World War II constitution making. The state-makers in post-Franco Spain relied on federalism as a necessary step in the democratization of that country, given its large, territorialized national minorities in the Basque region and Catalonia. The authors of India's extraordinarily long constitution, containing 395 articles and nine schedules, labored for more than two years to produce a document capable of endowing India with the strong government it needed while still protecting individual rights through a central government armed with emergency rule provisions and an aggressive, independent judiciary charged with protecting the rights of the citizens.

Similar efforts during the 1990's could be found among the constitution makers in the Eastern and Central European states newly liberated from control by the Soviet Union, and within the large number of new countries that once composed the Soviet Union itself. The long but sincere struggle to achieve constitutionalism in the former

Soviet Union testifies eloquently to the degree to which constitutional government had become both a goal and form of government in an increasingly large part of the globe toward the end of the twentieth century.

The struggle to establish constitutional, rule-of-law systems in the former communist states of Europe has been especially difficult given the large agenda of quotidian political problems confronting their governments. The sudden, largely unforeseen, revolutions that ended more than forty years of single-party communist rule there, and the bundle of economic and social problems confronting the successor regimes, often left little time for sweeping philosophical debates on the nature of humankind and government. Taxes needed collecting; local governments needed to be linked to the center; law-and-order systems had to be reshaped to the newer, less repressive nature of politics. Time was often consumed by basic questions, such as the shape of state in Czechoslovakia, and overriding economic and nationality concerns. The task of building constitutional systems frequently has suffered from the embryonic nature of parties and other participatory institutions; the comparative weakness of the civic culture in such areas as participatory tradition or a give-and-take approach to reconciliation politics; citizens' frequent distrust of institutional authority, including that of a judiciary long used to implement communist law; and a shortage of political personnel untainted by prior association with the old structure.

Constitutions are, unfortunately, rarely written under circumstances in which there is time for reflection and choices are open-ended. Normally, constitutions are written during the worst of times: When the American colonies were militarily weak and on the edge of bankruptcy in the 1780's; when France was on the edge of civil war in 1958; when West Germany and India were torn by partition and poverty and faced with accommodating millions of refugees in 1949. In Eastern Europe, the 1990's became a time of opportunity and a time of turmoil. As the euphoria of achieving independence dimmed, the problems of creating constitutional governments embodying respect for the rule of law and vouchsafing individual rights loomed large, as did the temptation to rely on more unfettered systems of government to clear the table of these problems.

Context

Constitutional, rule-of-law changes are almost always hard to engineer, and typically involve setbacks and prolonged problems. The development of a commitment to constitutionalism is, in Friedrich's analysis, a multifaceted process, with philosophical elements—the rejection of totalitarianism; legalistic elements—emphasizing the rule of law, not individuals; structural elements; and procedural elements. Achieving it is, at best, a difficult and lengthy process.

The struggle to achieve and retain constitutional government is, inevitably, a long and enduring one. The United States has been building constitutional government and fitting it to an expanding view of freedom, liberty, and equality for two centuries, largely relying on the Supreme Court to expand these areas by broadening the meaning attached to the general provisions composing the country's Constitution. France's constitution only belatedly acquired legitimacy in its own right, after resting on de Gaulle's prestige for nearly a decade after its adoption in 1958. Unification of East and West Germany confronted the fundamental guarantees of West Germany's Basic Law with new tests, revolving around a resurgence of political intolerance, economic shortages, and social dislocation. Italian politicians in the 1990's were seeking a new beginning in building the rule of law in that previously corruption-riddled democratic state.

On the other hand, as indicated by the successful round of constitution-making in post-World War II Germany and Italy, and the even more recent phenomenon of constitutional change to democratic, rule-of-law government in post-Franco Spain, the obstacles to moving from authoritarian to democratic, law-oriented societies and systems of government, even under inauspicious circumstances, are not insurmountable.

Bibliography

Almond, Gabriel A., and Sidney Verba. *The Civic Culture: Political Attitudes and Democracy in Five Nations.* Princeton, N.J.: Princeton University Press, 1963. Ground-breaking study of the relationship between political culture and constitutional government.

_____. *The Civic Culture Revisited.* Boston: Little, Brown, 1980. Follow-up study to the above volume.

Chilcote, Ronald H., et al. *Transitions from Dictatorship to Democracy: Comparative Studies of Spain, Portugal, and Greece.* New York: Crane, Russak, 1990. One of the better comparative studies of the search for constitutionalism in Mediterranean Europe.

Dicey, A. V. *Introduction to the Study of the Law of the Constitution.* 7th ed. London: Macmillan, 1908. Reprinted as recently as 1959, Dicey's work remains the definitive study of the development of constitutional government without a written constitution in Britain.

Friedrich, Carl J. *Constitutional Government and Democracy: Theory and Practice in Europe and America.* Boston: Ginn, 1946. Classic on the topic and the point-of-departure reading for anyone researching this topic. Particularly interesting because it was written before the effort to remake the political culture in post-World War II West Germany.

Greenberg, Douglas, et al. *Constitutionalism and Democracy: Transitions in the Contemporary World.* New York: Oxford University Press, 1993. Outstanding essays on constitutionalism, institutional arrangements and democracy, human rights, and the quest for constitutional government in new states.

Grew, Raymond, ed. *Crises of Political Development in Europe and the United States.* Princeton, N.J.: Princeton University Press, 1978. Excellent study of the obstacles to achieving constitutionalism even in the developed states of Western Europe and North America.

Hamilton, Alexander, James Madison, and John Jay. *The Federalist Papers*, edited by

Clinton Rossiter. New York: New American Library, 1961. **First and still the best** explanation of the U.S. model for controlling the state **by means of a series of** internal and external restraints on the powers of government.

Joseph R. Rudolph, Jr.

Cross-References

Accountability in U.S. Government, p. 1; Checks and Balances in U.S. Government, p. 216; Civil Liberties Protection, p. 291; The Constitution of the United States, p. 425; Constitutional Law in the United States, p. 439; Human Rights and International Politics, p. 848; Individual Versus State Rights, p. 910; Judicial Review, p. 1012; Locke's Political Philosophy, p. 1142; Modern Monarchy, p. 1209; Separation of Powers: Political Philosophy, p. 1809; The Supreme Court: Role in Government and Law, p. 1935.

CONSTITUTIONAL LAW IN THE UNITED STATES

Field of study: Law and jurisprudence

Constitutional law is the area of jurisprudence in which laws, governmental actions, and judicial decisions are examined to determine whether they have violated principles in the Constitution that were formulated to limit governmental abuse of citizens and protect individual rights.

Principal terms

CHECKS AND BALANCES: principle that the judicial, legislative, and executive branches of government have the power to limit and counteract one another's decisions

CONSTITUTION: basic or fundamental law of a politically organized body, such as a nation

EQUAL PROTECTION BEFORE THE LAW: principle that citizens are to be treated equally by government with regard to laws and their application

LEGISLATIVE VETO: power of legislatures to negate or invalidate decisions by members of the executive branch of government without employing the constitutionally required process of lawmaking

PROCEDURAL DUE PROCESS: constitutional principle that all citizens are to be provided fair procedures, such as timely notice and a hearing

SEPARATION OF POWERS: doctrine that prohibits the judicial, legislative, and executive branches of government from infringing on one another's powers

SUBSTANTIVE DUE PROCESS: constitutional principle that courts may define the meaning of the words in the due process clauses, including what constitutes life, liberty, and property that government may not deny

Overview

Most nations have constitutions that enumerate the powers of government and individual rights. The degree to which constitutional law safeguards individual rights and limits abuse by governmental officials depends on the nation's history and traditions. In the United States, constitutional law centers on the interpretation of the nation's Constitution, which is derived from the people and superior to laws passed by Congress and the states. The primary function of constitutional law is to ensure that governmental officials do not abuse their powers or violate individual rights. Constitutional law limits abusive government only if citizens demand that their public officials be guided by such principles. Courts of different nations vary widely in their power to engage in judicial review to decide questions of constitutional law and, most important, to declare unconstitutional, and thus invalidate, laws that violate constitutional principles.

The U.S. Constitution, including its amendments, is the fundamental law that defines the powers of the executive, legislative, and judicial branches of the national government; offers guidelines to the distribution of powers between the national government and the states; and specifies the rights of its citizens that government may not abridge, such as the rights to freedom of speech, religion, and the press in the First Amendment and rights against unreasonable searches and seizures in the Fourth Amendment.

Most changes to the Constitution have not occurred through the use of the formal amendment process in Article 5 of the Constitution. They have occurred through Supreme Court, lower federal court, and state court decision making. The Supreme Court's interpretation of the Constitution to include fundamental rights that are only implied by its words and its basic principles has been of great importance to the development of constitutional law. Some of the most controversial implied fundamental rights are those derived from the "due process clauses" of the Fifth Amendment, as applied to the national government, and the Fourteenth Amendment with respect to the states. These amendments state that public officials must not deprive any person of life, liberty, or property without due process of law. Judicial interpretation of the due process clauses has gone beyond requiring that government use correct procedures to deprive a person of life, liberty, or property. The clauses have been interpreted substantively to include rights to privacy, to use contraceptives, and to choose abortion, which are among the most controversial of all Supreme Court decisions.

The equal protection clause of the Fourteenth Amendment also has been interpreted to include implied fundamental rights, including the rights of citizens to procreate, vote, travel interstate, and gain access to courts, although the Fourteenth Amendment was drafted to ensure equal protection before the law for African Americans.

Some of the most important and controversial questions of constitutional law are decided when a court uses its power of judicial review to declare a statute to be in violation of the Constitution, that is, unconstitutional, and thus null and void. Individuals or advocacy groups start the process of judicial review in state or lower federal courts by arguing that the government has abused its powers or violated the rights of citizens and thus has violated the Constitution.

A party that loses the case in a lower court can appeal to the Supreme Court, the United States' highest court. The Supreme Court receives thousands of appeals each year to overturn lower court decisions, interpret laws, and invalidate government actions, laws, and regulations. The Supreme Court has unlimited discretion as to whether it will hear a case. Because reading legal briefs, hearing oral arguments, researching and debating constitutional issues, and writing opinions are lengthy processes, the Court considers fewer than 175 cases each year for full argument and written opinions. The Court uses two major constitutional principles to decide questions of constitutional law: those based on the powers of government institutions, which may be termed institutional principles, and principles based on individual rights in the Constitution, which may be termed rights principles.

Institutional principles involve the legality, fairness, and legitimacy of the powers exercised and procedures used by public officials, including national, state, and local legislators, bureaucrats, chief executives, and judges. In deciding constitutional law cases, justices apply deeply held views on institutional principles, particularly with regard to whether constitutional questions should be decided in federal courts by nonelected judges or by institutions that are accountable to citizens through elections. Judicial decisions are least controversial when they are grounded structurally in the powers that are enumerated in the Constitution, such as the powers of Congress and the president, or are directly implied by these principles of governance, such as the principle of separation of powers. In many cases involving the application of institutional principles, however, courts must interpret the language of the Constitution, consider the history of government in operations, and formulate a theory of governance.

Rights principles are the legally enforceable claims by individuals and groups to be free from government constraints on their liberties, including the basic freedoms in the Bill of Rights. Rights principles also may be based on affirmative responsibilities that courts have placed on government to ensure that citizens' rights are protected. For example, the Supreme Court has ruled that when states provide welfare benefits to their citizens, they may not deny these benefits to new arrivals. To do so would deny citizens the right to interstate travel, a right the Court has stated is implicit in various parts of the Constitution.

Most landmark cases require that justices consider both institutional and rights principles, determining what principles are at issue, whether they are in conflict, and, if so, how they are to be resolved.

Justices' backgrounds and experiences prior to joining the Court help to shape their judicial philosophy. Application of judicial philosophies, in turn, shapes constitutional law. The two major approaches to interpreting the Constitution are originalism and nonoriginalism. Originalists advocate that justices and judges must rely on the institutional and individual rights principles of the Founders and ratifiers of the Constitution and values that are directly implied by these principles. Nonoriginalists believe that constitutional law must not be based on the institutional and rights principles that were specifically adopted by the Founders or that can be directly implied from those principles. They argue that the Founders' views on present constitutional questions cannot be known because of the subjectivity of the judges and scholars who are analyzing the Founders' views and because of the lack of adequate records of the Constitutional Convention and the ratifying conventions. Nonoriginalists also argue that what words and doctrines in the Constitution mean in contemporary society can only be determined by reconsidering their meanings in light of Court precedents, theories of constitutional interpretation, and ever-changing moral values, national problems, and expectations of government. The majority of justices have been nonoriginalists.

Topics that are central to the study of constitutional law include the powers of the courts; the distribution of power between the president and Congress and between the federal and state governments; equal protection before the law and discrimination based on such factors as race, gender, and country of origin; implied fundamental rights under the due process and equal protection clauses; freedom of expression, religion, and the press; the rights of citizens against government's arbitrarily taking property; and the rights of criminal defendants.

Applications

Marbury v. Madison (1803) was the landmark case in which the Supreme Court decided that it had the power of judicial review and used that power to invalidate an act of Congress. The Court ruled that Congress could not add to the Court's powers as stated in the Constitution; thus, Congress could not require the Court to decide whether government officials were duly appointed. The Court reasoned that to allow Congress to change its original powers would violate the following constitutional principles: The written Constitution is fundamental law and superior in authority to the laws made by Congress; the powers of branches of government are limited to those granted to them in the Constitution; the principles of separation of powers and checks and balances require that the Supreme Court have the power of judicial review, including the power to declare an act of Congress unconstitutional.

In a more recent case in which institutional principles predominated, *Immigration and Naturalization Service v. Chadha* (1983), the Court decided that Congress' use of the legislative veto to overturn a decision by the Immigration and Naturalization Service to allow Chadha, an alien, to remain in this nation violated the Constitution. It said that allowing Congress to deport Chadha through the use of the legislative veto rather than the full lawmaking process as listed in Article 1 of the Constitution violated the Constitution and would lead to an abuse of government powers. The Court emphasized that for lawmaking to be valid it must be presented to and pass both the House of Representatives and the Senate and be signed by the president, or if vetoed by the president, overridden by a two-thirds vote in both houses of Congress. Legislative vetoes were determined to violate the principles of separation of powers and checks and balances that were designed to limit government abuse of its authority.

In constitutional law cases in which the application of rights principles predominate, Supreme Court discretion is even greater than in cases involving institutional principles, for two reasons: First, the Constitution is more open-ended in its rights language than in its discussion of institutional powers. Second, it is a central premise of constitutional law that not all citizen rights were, or could be, listed in the Constitution; therefore, the Court may define and reinterpret the nature of individual rights.

At times, the Supreme Court's use of or failure to use its power of judicial review has been highly controversial; for example, when the country has been at war, and generally on issues affecting the military, the Court has avoided deciding questions on constitutional grounds, in order not to counter the will of Congress, the president, and the people. On many questions of individual rights, however, the Supreme Court has been a major force for political and social change. On controversial questions, the

Court typically has chosen to protect individual rights rather than follow public opinion that opposed such rights. Examples include the Court's order to desegregate schools, the establishment of the right of a woman to choose to have an abortion, and the right to burn flags as an aspect of the right to political speech.

The justices' commitment to defend individual rights principles, follow legal precedent, and support the rule of law, at times requires them to support previously defined rights, and even create new ones, that are in opposition to popular opinion, the political agenda of the president who nominated them to the Supreme Court, and even their personal views. For example, in *Planned Parenthood of Southeastern Pennsylvania v. Casey*, the 1992 case in which the Court restated a woman's right to choose abortion, three justices who personally opposed abortions supported the continuation of this controversial right.

Context

American constitutional law has its roots in institutional and rights principles formulated in the late eighteenth century, as informed by ancient political theory and the European, British, and Scottish political thought of the day. The relationship between institutional principles and the protection of individual rights was of central concern to both the antifederalists and the federalists, the two major factions of the Founders. The central issue was the distribution of power between state and national political institutions. The Founders perceived questions of governmental power as an issue of how the allocation of governmental power influences the protection of individual rights and securing the public interest.

Of central concern to both Federalists and Antifederalists was whether state or federal government would better protect individual rights and the public interest. The Antifederalists felt that states, being smaller and more homogeneous, would be better forums for the deliberation of public issues, protection of minority rights, and educating citizens and linking them to government. They questioned the Federalist assumption that federal supremacy over the states would protect citizen rights, maintain the confidence of citizens in the Constitution and the new governmental institutions, and protect citizens against tyranny by either the majority or a governmental elite. Federalists and Antifederalists also differed over whether rights could best be protected by securing institutional principles in the Constitution, the Federalist position, or by stating specific individual rights in a Bill of Rights.

The Federalist theory of government won out over Antifederalist arguments, in part because some Antifederalists feared that minority factions in the states would retard economic development and the military security of the nation. Although the Antifederalists lost most of the battles over institutional principles, they secured a listing of individual rights in the Constitution through the passage of the Bill of Rights. Both Federalists and Antifederalists supported the power of judicial review. Since the founding, but especially since the 1950's, the Supreme Court as a decision making body has had to balance increasingly complex institutional and individual rights principles, requiring it to be more innovative in its decision making and raising controversies, in part because of conflicts between the originalist and nonoriginalist philosophies. It is likely that constitutional law will continue to be controversial, but it will also continue to play an important role in the process of change in the United States.

Bibliography

Chandler, Ralph C. *The Constitutional Law Dictionary*. 2 vols. Santa Barbara, Calif.: ABC-Clio, 1985. Overview articles and summaries of major cases. Supplements were published in 1987 and 1991.

Congressional Quarterly's Guide to the U.S. Supreme Court. 2d ed. Washington, D.C.: Congressional Quarterly Press, 1990. Discusses the Supreme Court; congressional, presidential, and state powers; individual rights; and the Court at work, described in the light of constitutional law principles and landmark cases.

Hall, Kermit L., ed. *The Oxford Companion to the Supreme Court of the United States*. New York: Oxford University Press, 1992. Brief entries and short articles covering major Supreme Court cases, justices, and constitutional principles.

Kluger, Richard. *Simple Justice: The History of Brown v. Board of Education and Black America's Struggle for Equality*. New York: Alfred A. Knopf, 1976. Description of the battle for American school integration, covering the legal, political, and sociological events culminating in the landmark *Brown* decision.

Levy, Leonard W., et al., eds. *Encyclopedia of the American Constitution*. 4 vols. New York: Macmillan, 1986. Survey articles on general constitutional topics, major Supreme Court cases, and justices.

Stone, Geoffrey R., et al. *Constitutional Law*. 2d ed. Boston: Little, Brown, 1991. The most-used American law school text, this book includes all major cases in constitutional law, the Constitution, and biographical notes on Supreme Court justices.

Witt, Elder, ed. *The Supreme Court A to Z: A Ready Reference Encyclopedia*. Washington, D.C.: Congressional Quarterly Press, 1993. Condensed version of the *Congressional Quarterly Guide to the U.S. Supreme Court*.

Ronald C. Kahn

Cross-References

The Bill of Rights, p. 134; Checks and Balances in U.S. Government, p. 216; Church and State Relations in the United States, p. 236; Civil Liberties Protection, p. 291; Civil Rights and Liberties, p. 298; Conservatism, p. 419; The Constitution of the United States, p. 425; Constitutional Governments, p. 432; Courts: U.S. Federal, p. 471; Government Powers, p. 772; Intergovernmental Relations, p. 942; Judicial Review, p. 1012; Jurisprudence, p. 1019; Locke's Political Philosophy, p. 1142; Montesquieu's Political Philosophy, p. 1228; Separation of Powers: Political Philosophy, p. 1809; The Supreme Court: Organization and Purpose, p. 1929; The Supreme Court: Role in Government and Law, p. 1935.

SURVEY
OF
SOCIAL
SCIENCE

ALPHABETICAL LIST

CATEGORY LIST

POLITICS

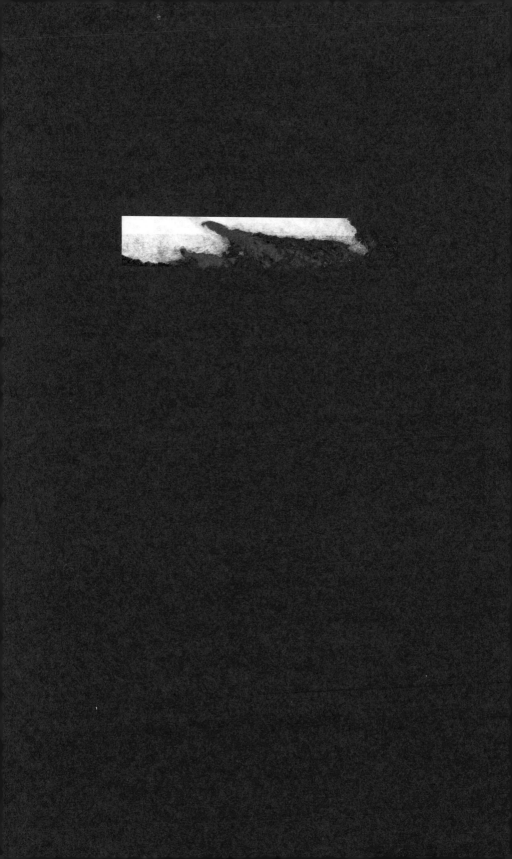